THE GREATER
ANGLO-SAXON CHURCHES

by the same author

*

AN INTRODUCTION TO
ANGLO-SAXON ARCHITECTURE
AND SCULPTURE

THE GREATER
ANGLO-SAXON CHURCHES

An Architectural-Historical Study

by

E. A. FISHER
M.A., D.Sc.

FABER AND FABER LIMITED

24 Russell Square

London

First published in mcmlxii
by Faber and Faber Limited
24 Russell Square London W.C.1
Printed in Great Britain by
R. MacLehose and Company Limited
The University Press Glasgow
All rights reserved

PREFACE

THERE are many books on Anglo-Saxon art and architecture. Some justification therefore seems required for the publication of yet another book in this field. It may be asked, apart from a few new discoveries, is there very much that is new to be said that has not already been discussed by those scholars whose works are familiar to all students in this sphere? My own debt to these writers will be evident from the references to their works in the following pages. Why then has this book been written?

The works of earlier writers tell the fascinating story of Anglo-Saxon art, its history and development, the influences which made it what it eventually became and from where those influences emanated, and the contributions which the Anglo-Saxons themselves made from their own genius towards the final result: that hammering together of sometimes conflicting, sometimes co-operating influences to form that indefinable but entirely recognizable thing—a national style of art. The story is punctuated, for illustrative purposes, with partial descriptions of some monuments. For a complete description of any one monument, or for a general description of all, we must look elsewhere; to the monuments themselves and to many scores of separate publications scattered in archaeological journals, not all of which are readily accessible. Our Saxon heritage of monuments seems worthy of detailed description in a form readily available to all, viz. in a book or books where the scattered information may be gathered together and critically examined. This is the object of the present book: primarily to record, to describe and as far as possible to trace the architectural history of the greater Anglo-Saxon churches, and to collate the published literature concerning them.

Although Anglo-Saxon churches are far less numerous than the later Anglo-Norman there are too many, more than 300, to be dealt with adequately in a single volume. A selection has had to be made, and it is difficult to select on any logical basis. The historical distinction between minsters and lesser churches is unhelpful in this connection for with many, perhaps most, pre-Conquest churches the precise origin is unknown while many others are now mere fragments. The term 'greater churches' is too vague to be useful unless one equates it rather arbitrarily with the possession of a tower. It is assumed here, for no other reason than convenience. It is certainly not entirely true that towered churches are among those which in early days were considered to be major churches. At the same time it cannot be concluded that all major Anglo-Saxon churches had towers, or that all churches which were given towers were large ones. For the practical purpose of keeping this book of reasonable dimensions only those churches, with some exceptions, are dealt with which have or are known to have had towers.

Excluding the round towers, so numerous in and characteristic of East Anglia, there are about 115 towered Anglo-Saxon churches. Not all are of great interest. Twenty-one have been excluded from consideration as they are non-controversial and have few features of interest. They are: Hornby (Yorks, N.R.), Stevington (Beds), Barnetby-le-Wold, Coleby, Corringham, Cuxwold, Hainton, Harmston, Harpswell, Heapham, Holton-le-Clay, Irby-upon-Humber, Laceby, Little Bytham, Worlaby (all in Lincs), Bawsey, Castle Rising Chapel (Norfolk), Debenham (Suffolk), Corringham, Steeple Bumpstead, West Mersea (Essex). In place of these, five churches outside the list of towered churches are included: Hexham, Peterborough, Stanton Lacy, Bywell St. Peter, and St. Martin, Canterbury. The first three are not known to have had towers but they are or were large and important transeptal churches which cannot logically be excluded from any list of 'greater Anglo-Saxon churches'. Bywell St. Peter had neither tower nor transept but was certainly a large and important church. St. Martin, Canterbury, is towerless and small, but of quite exceptional interest; it is certainly the oldest building in England still in use as a church.

More than half the towered churches are to be found in Lincolnshire and East Anglia. The remainder are widely scattered from Northumberland to Hampshire and from Shropshire to Essex. Among the remaining two hundred or so smaller churches are some of very great interest and historic importance, such as those at Escomb (Co. Durham), Bradford on Avon (Wilts), Worth and Clayton (Sussex), Duke Odda's Chapel, Deerhurst (Glos), Wittering (Northants), Wing (Bucks). These will be missed by the interested reader from the present volume. These and others could not be included without making the book uneconomically and perhaps uncomfortably large. They and other 'lesser churches' are reserved for a possible later book.

One or two criticisms of some earlier writers may perhaps be permissible here. The marked differences sometimes met with between measurements of the same building published by different writers is surprising. The tower arch at Corbridge (Northumberland) is given variously as 8 ft. 2 ins. and 8 ft. 6 ins. wide. The internal dimensions of Whittingham tower, in the same county, are given as (*a*) west wall 10 ft. 7 ins., north wall 11 ft., south wall 11 ft. 2 ins., longer axis east-west; and (*b*) west wall 10 ft. 11 ins., north wall 10 ft. 10 ins., almost square but with slightly longer axis north–south. Such differences are not easy to justify or even to excuse and they tend to weaken a reader's confidence in other, less quantitative statements. Many measurements have been checked and corrected or confirmed by the author; in some instances published alternatives are given; others are the author's.

A more serious criticism is of the considerable number of non-quantitative factual and observational errors to be found here and there in the literature: a pair of modern hot water pipes mistaken (from a sketch) for a twelfth-century double moulding; a tympanum of a Christ in Majesty described as a Virgin and Child; an accurate description of one church published under the name of another. Less important perhaps, but misleading, is the inadequate locating of churches. Giving the county is not enough. There are two Thurlbys in Lincolnshire, two Flixtons in Suffolk, two Middletons in Yorkshire—and so on almost indefinitely. It is exasperating to travel many miles only to arrive at the wrong village.

There is much descriptive matter in the book not previously recorded. There are also undoubtedly some errors, which must be attributed to the author. He has at least done his best not to perpetuate the graver mistakes of some earlier writers. And he has indicated the location of each church in relation to some well-known neighbouring town or village so that its position may be identified easily on a map.

Sculptures and carved fragments lying in or attached for safety to the walls of churches or vestries are not dealt with. Those only will be considered which form part of the structure, such as carved capitals or string courses or door jambs.

The cost of publication nowadays makes lavishly-illustrated books impossible to produce at reasonable prices. Illustrations here, though numerous, are reduced to a minimum for reasons of economy. The book would be better with twice the number. As partial compensation many references are given to plates and other illustrations in readily accessible books and archaeological journals. In many cases alternative sources are quoted to give the reader a choice of accessibilities.

The writer's thanks are due to Mr. Bruce Allsopp, B.Arch., F.R.I.B.A., Senior Lecturer in Architecture, King's College, Newcastle upon Tyne (University of Durham), for reading part of the MS., for supplying some photographs taken specially for this book and for help in other ways.

Thanks are also due, and to a very special degree, to Mr. C. E. Coulthard, of West Bridgford, Nottingham, for permitting the writer to draw without restriction on his very large collection of prints of Anglo-Saxon churches and details. Ninety-seven of the plates are from Mr. Coulthard's negatives; some were made for this book. Without his generous help the pictorial part of the book would have been gravely deficient. Thanks are due, too, to Mr. D. Meads of Long Eaton, Nottingham, for the high-quality enlargements he made from Mr. Coulthard's negatives.

The writer must also acknowledge his indebtedness to Mr. Cecil Farthing, Deputy Director, and to Miss M. Gossling, Librarian, of the National Buildings Record for help in collecting photographs, some of which were taken specially for inclusion in this book, and to his publishers' technical staff for re-drawing some of the author's text figures, and to their readers for helpful comments and criticisms.

Akeley, Buckingham   E. A. FISHER
October 1960

GENERAL ACKNOWLEDGMENTS

ACKNOWLEDGMENTS and thanks are due to the following for permission to use copyright material (details are given in the Lists of Plates and Text Figures): The Trustees of the British Museum; The National Buildings Record; The Courtauld Institute of Art, University of London; The University of Edinburgh (for reproductions from Baldwin Brown's *Anglo-Saxon Architecture*); The Clarendon Press, Oxford (for reproductions from A. W. Clapham's *English Romanesque Architecture before the Conquest*); The Controller of H.M. Stationery Office (for reproductions from the publications of the Royal Commission on Historical Monuments (England)); The Editor of the Victoria County Histories; The Hampshire Field Club and Archaeological Society; Mr. Bruce Allsopp; Mr. R. L. S. Bruce-Mitford; Mr. W. A. Call; the late C. J. P. Cave's Exors.; Mr. C. E. Coulthard; Mrs. F. H. Crossley; Mrs. D. Dobson Hinton; Dr. P. Eden; Mr. J. E. Edmunds; Mrs. D. R. Fyson; Dr. E. C. Gilbert; Mr. W. H. Godfrey, C.B.E.; Mr. F. Goldring; Mr. R. de Z. Hall; Rev. D. E. Hood; Mr. L. E. Jones; Prof. A. W. Lawrence; Mr. E. C. Le Grice; Mr. R. H. Linsell; Mr. A. S. B. New; Mr. W. F. Oakeshott; Mr. P. S. Spokes; Mr. W. T. Taylor; Mr. S. Toy; Miss G. M. E. Trail; Dr. G. Zarnecki.

CONTENTS

13

Contents

Contents

III. LINCOLNSHIRE

IV. EAST ANGLIA AND ESSEX

Contents

LIST OF TEXT FIGURES

List of Text Figures

List of Text Figures

MAPS SHOWING THE DISTRIBUTION OF ANGLO-SAXON CHURCHES

LIST OF PLATES

(At the end of the book)

List of Plates

INTRODUCTION

TYPES OF ANGLO-SAXON CHURCHES. There were four types of churches in pre-Conquest days, all built and endowed by kings, bishops and nobles on their estates.

1. *Head minsters*, or cathedrals—the seats of bishops.

2. *Ordinary minsters*, or old minsters, often called in mediaeval MSS. *matrix ecclesia*, a mother church. These churches were in effect the central churches of large areas, areas that later in the Anglo-Saxon period developed into *parrochia*, parishes. Like the head minsters they were served by groups of clergy living together as a community, a practice instituted in this country by St. Augustine at his church at Canterbury and copied at other places. *Mynster* is the Old English equivalent of the Latin *monasterium*, and some of these churches were indeed monasteries, as at Breedon-on-the-Hill (Leics) and SS. Peter and Paul, Canterbury (but not Augustine's cathedral church of Christchurch, Canterbury, which was communal but not monastic). Most however were communal since each minster required a considerable number of priests to preach, baptize, bury and sing mass at many centres—graveyards, cross-roads, villages, manors—in the large *parrochia*. These spots became *loci sancti* and on them would be erected from the late seventh century onwards standing crosses, at first no doubt of wood, later of stone, many beautifully carved. Throughout the earlier centuries of Christianity in this country some thousands of these crosses must have been built and they must have been as familiar characteristics of the countryside as church towers and spires are today.

As Christianity spread and Christian communities increased in number permanent churches, each served usually by a single priest, became desirable in place of the occasional open-air meetings and services. Such churches were built first on, or attached to, graveyards, the most obvious and permanent of the *loci sancti*, and were endowed by the local thegns. These churches were the:

3. *Lesser churches with graveyards*. They were the absolute property of the local lords who built them, who could, if they wished, move or destroy them. It is interesting that Archbishop Theodore (668–90) decreed that if a church was pulled down the timbers should be used for some other religious purpose. Such churches were therefore presumably smaller than the ordinary minsters and were often, perhaps usually, of timber though often later replaced by stone buildings. They became the central churches of parishes, smaller than and carved out of the larger *parrochia* of the ordinary minsters.

Even up to the end of the eighth century there were still Christian communities, some of long standing, without churches, as there had been in the late seventh when Archbishop Theodore had allowed priests to say Mass 'in the field'. In course of time still smaller and more modest churches were erected on these *loci sancti*, and were known as:

4. *Field churches.* These also would be in many if not in most cases originally of wood, though also many were replaced later by more permanent stone structures. Many doubtless disappeared altogether, burnt by the Danes or removed or destroyed by the local thegns who, or whose forbears, had built them.

It is impossible now to attribute individual existing churches, except in relatively few cases, to any one of these four classes. Certainly no head minsters, or cathedrals, of the pre-Conquest period remain above ground.[1] Only the complete crypt and some excavated foundations of Wilfrid's seventh-century cathedral remain at Hexham, and little more than the foundations of the later, early eleventh-century, cathedral at North Elmham, Norfolk.

Of the ordinary minsters, or old minsters, of the communal type, the foundations exist of the tenth-century one at South Elmham (Suffolk). Corbridge (Northumberland) was probably one of this group. Of the genuinely monastic minsters a few remain: Deerhurst (Glos), Brixworth (Northants), Jarrow and Monkwearmouth (Co. Durham), all still in use as churches; the crypt of Ripon; the foundations of Medeshampstede (below Peterborough Cathedral), of SS. Peter and Paul, Canterbury, and a few fragments of walling of the nunnery of Shaftesbury (Dorset) founded by King Alfred in 888. Minster in Thanet was founded as a monastery for women, and dedicated to the Virgin Mary, on the site of the present St. Mary's Church, *c.* 670, by Domneva, also called Eormenbeorg and Eabba, a daughter of the Royal House of Kent. Eadburga, or Bugga, a later Abbess and great friend and correspondent of Boniface, the Apostle of Germany, founded another nunnery close by *c.* 748 dedicated to SS. Peter and Paul. Some remains still exist of the latter. The stair turret in St. Mary's Church *may* be a fragment of the first monastery of St. Mary's, though it is more likely to be of the twelfth century. Both monasteries were burnt by the Danes in 839 and again in 980 and in 1011. They were still standing when Canute in 1027 transferred the land and remaining buildings to St. Augustine's monastery, Canterbury.

BUILDING PERIODS. There were two periods of Anglo-Saxon church architecture which should be clearly distinguished for there are many differences between the two ways of building. The two periods were separated by the prolonged Danish invasions of the late ninth century. The Danes began raiding the north-east coast in 797 when

---

[1] Sherborne Abbey (Dorset), though mainly of later periods, contains pre-Conquest fragments here and there in its structure. It was founded as a head minster, the cathedral of a new diocese of Sherborne, by Ine, King of Wessex, in 705 and remained a cathedral until the see was transferred to Salisbury in 1075.

they burnt Lindisfarne Priory and in 798 when they burnt Jarrow. They first wintered in England, in the Isle of Thanet, in 850, but their great invasion of East Anglia in 865 followed by the occupation of York in 866–7 was the real beginning of their long-sustained and partly successful effort to conquer and settle in the country. The invasions continued until Alfred's peace with the Danish leader, Guthrum, of 886, as a result of which England was divided into two parts: a Danish part—the Danelaw—roughly east and north of Watling Street, the great Roman road running from London to Chester, and an English part south and west of Watling Street. There was, there could have been, little or no church building during this period of more than twenty years of almost continuous fighting. When Alfred had reconstructed his devastated country the churches which arose in this Late Saxon period—*c.* 870–1066 with a Saxo-Norman Overlap from 1066 to *c.* 1100–10—showed marked differences in many respects from those of the earlier, pre-Danish,[1] Early Saxon period.

The characteristic differences and similarities of the two ways of building have been described and discussed elsewhere.[2] Here it may be useful to indicate briefly a few details which are more or less typical of the churches in each of the two periods. The Late Saxon period of building developed into a national style, affected in its development by Carolingian and Ottonian influences from north-east France and the Rhineland. Towers, with their characteristic double belfry openings and bulging mid-wall baluster shafts, occur only in this period; also 'long and short' and 'upright and flat' quoins, plinths, decorative and structural pilaster strip-work, circular windows (in addition to other types common to both periods), double splaying of window openings, doorways generally unrebated (the doors shutting flat against the interior wall) and, late in the period, capitals and bases to shafts. Apses were rare; only four are known. The churches of the Early Saxon period were of two types which arose in Kent and in Northumbria respectively. Churches in other areas show details from both types. The Kentish churches had small, rectangular naves with a length–breadth ratio of $1\frac{1}{2}$ or $1\frac{3}{4}$ to 1, and apsidal chancels almost as wide as the nave entered by single or triple arches almost as wide as the apse. The Northern churches had very long, narrow, very high naves with length–breadth ratio of 3 or more to 1. The chancels were small and square with tall narrow chancel arches, sometimes hardly more than doorways. The Kentish churches had north and south porticus or wings overlapping nave and apse; in some cases these porticus were multiplied to extend all round the north, west and south nave walls, as at Reculver. Porticus were less numerous and typical in the North. Quoins and jambs were monolithic, or mega-lithic, or of irregular big slab work; window openings were single-splayed (but not so widely as the later Norman openings); doorways were commonly rebated for

[1] The year *c.* 870 is often taken as a rough median date dividing these two building periods. The expressions pre- and post- *c.* 870 are useful in this connection.
[2] See G. Baldwin Brown; A. W. Clapham, (*a*); E. A. Fisher.

doors. Baluster shafts were common, especially in Northumbria, but differed from those of the later period in purpose and design: they did not bulge, they were ornamented with many half-round bands and hollows, and were better finished than the roughly wrought later ones. Many window openings were cut through walling without stone dressings to heads, jambs or sills; flat lintels, arched lintels, gable heads and round arches of real voussoirs or of slabs only, occur in both periods.

WALLING. In examining and appraising pre-Conquest churches no characteristics have greater diagnostic value than the types of walling and quoining employed. These characteristics are so revealing that some detailed consideration of them seems desirable.

Walls of Anglo-Saxon stone buildings are either of rubble, ragstone, flint or ashlar. The commonest by far is *rubble*. This may be described as stones, sometimes roughly dressed, of irregular shape and size set in mortar. The irregularity however varies within fairly narrow limits. Thus however irregular the shape and size, the three dimensions—length, breadth, thickness—if not similar are comparable in magnitude. The stone of course varies in geological character and consequently in hardness and permanence in different areas. A rubble wall is of rubble throughout; it has no core of some different or inferior material. Rubble was sometimes laid in regular courses but was often uncoursed, i.e. just piled up in the wall, especially when very small or of marked irregularity of size and shape.

Rag or ragstone, like rubble, is of variable geological type and hardness, being sometimes very hard. Unlike rubble it breaks up into thin flattish slabs of about the dimensions of an ordinary brick, though thinner. It is laid normally horizontally. One exception to this rule is when it is used for *herring-boning*.

Ashlar, i.e. walling faced on both sides with well-dressed carefully squared stones with fine joints, was rarely used. A few examples only are known, as at Bradford-on-Avon (Wilts), Escomb (Co. Durham) and Wareham (Dorset). Some walls, though not of true ashlar, are of fairly well squared rubble throughout, carefully coursed and having an appearance approximating to ashlar.

Under ashlar should be included some churches built partly or entirely of re-used dressed stones from local Roman remains. Wilfrid's churches at Hexham and Ripon were built of this material.

In some areas, such as East Anglia and parts of Kent, where local building stone is not available but flints from local chalk deposits are, walls may be built of or faced with *flints*. In Kent the local Kentish ragstone is also used.

Another building material occasionally used is *Roman bricks*, also pillaged from local ruins. These bricks may be up to 16 inches by 11 inches in area and $1\frac{1}{2}$ to 2 inches thick. The tower of Holy Trinity, Colchester, is wholly and that of St. Mary in Castro, Dover, partly built of this material. Such bricks may be seen in fact in a surprising number of pre-Conquest churches, sometimes to a considerable extent as in the arch heads and quoins of Brixworth; sometimes just here and there in the fabric may be single bricks or single courses. They appear occasionally in unexpected places, as in the shaft of a column in Repton crypt.

Anglo-Saxon mortar was very good, greatly superior to the much later Norman mortar which was so often of poor quality. It set very hard, almost like cement, and was used for flooring as well as in walls. Two Saxon floors exist today at Barnack tower and at the ruined Saxon abbey church of Medeshampstede, modern Peterborough, below the present Norman cathedral.[1] The excellence of the mortar was probably a factor in enabling the Saxons to employ very thin walls in spite of their relatively great height. Many Saxon walls exist today no more than two feet two inches thick; they were rarely more than three feet thick.[2] Norman walls were rarely less than three feet. Saxon rubble walls have a rough unfinished appearance, but when built they were normally plastered both inside and out.

QUOINING. Quoining is the strengthening of corners of buildings by special treatment with relatively large stones. In areas where suitable stone was not available locally, such as East Anglia and some other districts, quoining was not employed. The corners were made of the same rubble as the walls. Often, to avoid quoining, the towers in these areas were made circular in plan.

Megalithic quoins of very large stones were commonly employed in and confined to the Early Saxon period, i.e. up to *c.* 870. In the Late Saxon period Slab Work and 'Long and Short' and allied forms of quoining were alike popular.

The term 'long and short' was introduced in 1835 by Thomas Rickman who seems to have been the first to notice this characteristic of Anglo-Saxon building—'a peculiar sort of quoining . . . of a long stone set at the corner, and a short one lying on it and bonding one way or both into the wall; and when plaster is used, these quoins are raised to allow for the thickness of the plaster.' Sir Gardner Wilkinson published an interesting study of it in 1863. He pointed out that such work is not confined to quoins but occurs also in pilaster strips and similar decorative wall strengthening and that similar work is to be found in Germany, e.g. at Lorsch (probably eighth century) and Gernrode (*c.* 950–1000). He saw and illustrated Roman buildings in Tunisia built in a similar way in which the longs and shorts were definitely structural, the intervals between being filled in with rubble or small stones. He claimed that both the German and English forms were derived directly from such Roman buildings. Baldwin Brown, whilst agreeing that the German long and short, the so-called *lisenen*, was derived ultimately from Roman sources, made out a very strong case for the direct derivation of the English form from the German lisenen.[3]

[1] See below, under Peterborough.

[2] Brixworth (Northants) is an exception; its walls are 3 ft. 8 ins. thick. Monkwearmouth (Co. Durham) tower walls are only 1 ft. 9 ins. thick.

[3] See below, p. 216.

Introduction

More recent and detailed studies have been made by E. C. Gilbert in 1946 and by E. G. M. Fletcher and E. D. C. Jackson in 1944 and by Jackson and Fletcher in 1949. Gilbert maintained that the diagnostic value of quoining was very great and that some simple system of describing quoins was desirable. He divided quoin *stones* into various types: long, thin, slender ones, or pillar stones (P); thin, flat, square or squarish, which he called clasping stones (C); fairly large, brick-shaped stone slabs with faces (F), sides (S) and rectangular (E) or square (X) ends. When the ends are square, faces and sides are of course of identical dimensions and are simply sides (S). On this basis he was able to describe a quoin from base to top by a combination of the above letters. To take the two simplest examples: a quoin made of a number of pillar stones, one above the other, a rare and unsatisfactory form of quoin, would be denoted by PPP: the same kind strengthened by the insertion of a flat clasping stone between each pair of pillar stones would be PCPC. This system is elaborated further in later paragraphs.

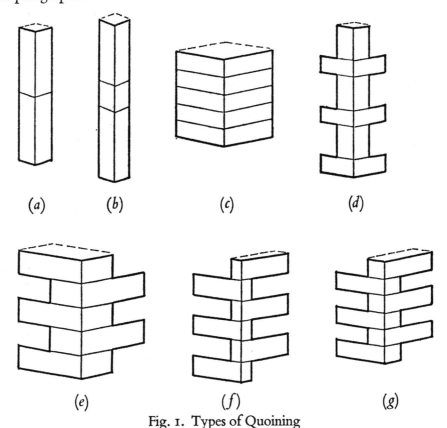

(a)   (b)   (c)   (d)

(e)   (f)   (g)

Fig. 1. Types of Quoining

(a) Pillar quoins. (b) True long and short work. (c) Clasping quoins.
(d) Regular upright and flat. (e) Face alternate. (f) Side alternate.
(g) Dovetail quoins.

Introduction

Jackson and Fletcher from a rather different point of view divided quoins into three groups or classes. The classification adopted below is a slight elaboration of the views of Gilbert and of Jackson and Fletcher.

1. *Megalithic Quoins.* These were made of large stones up to four feet high by, say, $2\frac{1}{2}$ and $1\frac{1}{2}$ feet in other dimensions. One stone is placed on end, one or several others laid flat on top of this, then another large one on end, and so on. Examples are at St. Mildred's, Canterbury (I), Brigstock (Northants) and the Saxon porch at Bishopstone (Sussex).

2. *Pillar Quoins.* In this rare type tall stones of relatively thin cross section were employed on end, one above the other, possibly in imitation of the corner posts of a timber building (Fig. 1*a*). From the point of view of strength these were the least satisfactory of the various types. In Gilbert's notation they would be denoted by PPP.

3. *Clasping Quoins.* These consist of comparatively large square, or squarish, thin slabs laid flat (Fig. 1*c*). They may be denoted by CCC. They are so-called on account of their resemblance to Norman clasping tower buttresses.

4. So-called *Long and Short Quoins.*

(*a*) *True Long and Short Work.* This consists of rectangular or square-sectioned stone strips, two to four feet long and often six to eight inches in lateral dimensions, bedded on edge and often with a projection from the wall similar to the intended depth of plaster; then between each pair of longs would be a short piece of similar cross section to the longs. They may be denoted as L.Sh.L. (Fig. 1*b*). This type is more usual with pilaster strip wall decoration than in quoins.

(*b*) *Regular Upright and Flat.* In this type, between each pair of longs or uprights is a clasping slab laid flat and built into the wall, as it were to tie-in the angle. It may be denoted LCLC (Fig. 1*d*). Though in some books it is called loosely 'long and short' it is really a different and stronger type of quoin. It corresponds to Jackson and Fletcher's Type I. The longs may be, say, $2\frac{1}{2}$ feet high by 8 inches and the flats 5 inches high by 1 ft. 9 ins. by 1 ft. 9 ins. There is much variation in the individual sizes. Thus, while the ratio of the heights of uprights to flats may average about 5 to 1, it may vary between 7 to 1 and 2 to 1. In this type the uprights and flats rarely project from the wall face. It is often employed in walls of rubble or faced with coursed flints, and most frequently in chalk counties where walls are often of chalk rubble and flint.

(*c*) *Slab Quoins.* These include Baldwin Brown's Big Stone work. They are made of fairly large irregularly shaped stone slabs, just chosen and not cut but well dressed and squared on the two external faces. They are laid flat with their long faces on alternate faces of the wall corners: thus, in a tower south-west quoin one long face would lie north and south, the one above east–west and so on. Examples are at

---

(I) *Plate* 1.

Escomb (Co. Durham), and at Brigstock and at Stow-Nine-Churches (Northants). These are Jackson and Fletcher's Type II. The flats are of variable heights and often not much wider than the longs. The longs may be of the order of 2 ft. 9 ins. high by 10 inches by 10 inches; the flats 9 inches high by 15 inches by 18 inches. This type is not used in flint walls, but usually with coursed or uncoursed rubble and is hence popular in the oolitic limestone belt.

In this type there can be three regular forms of arrangement of the stones:

(i) *Side-Alternate*, with the slabs lying on their sides with faces and ends exposed to view: SSS (Fig. 1*f*).

(ii) *Face-Alternate*, with the slabs lying on their faces with sides and ends exposed: FFF (Fig. 1*e*).

(iii) *Dovetail Quoins*.[1] These are of square-ended slabs, i.e. with sides, not faces. In denoting (i) and (ii) as SSS and FFF respectively there is no ambiguity owing to the similar, though not identical, appearance of the two faces of the quoin. (It is assumed that the quoin is being viewed from the corner, so that both faces are to some extent visible.) The same denotation would be ambiguous with dovetail quoins as it would give SSS, identical with side-alternate. It is better, in this case—and is essential with irregular slab quoins (type (iv))—to denote the slabs from bottom upwards on one face only instead of on alternate faces as with (i) and (ii). Dovetail quoins (Fig. 1*g*) may then be denoted by SXSX (each face being similar, the other face would be simply XSXS).[2]

(iv) *Irregular Slab Quoins*. In these the slabs may lie on their sides or faces alternately or in any order, and clasping slabs may be included among them. As examples may be given: SFSF or FSFS; SSSSSSSXS; XSSXSFFFFFFCFSSS; SSSSSSS-XXXXXX; SSXSSSSCS. The other face of SSXSSSSCS might be XXSXXXXCX or EESEEEECE, but whether E or X would make little or no difference.

(*d*) *Hidden Upright and Flat*, or *Apparent or Pseudo Long and Short*. This is structurally identical with 4(*b*) (Regular Upright and Flat) but the exposed edges of the flats (and sometimes of the uprights too, so as to make them appear of uniform width throughout) are cut back to the level of the wall surface so that when the walls are plastered the quoins would look like 4(*a*) (True Long and Short) though they are in fact upright and flat, LCLC. These are Jackson and Fletcher's Type III, similar to Type II but cut back. Today with the old plaster stripped from the walls, as is so often the case, they look like Type II with a raised vertical band worked on both exposed faces. The stones are of similar dimensions to those of Type II.

---

[1] Not a very happy or accurate term (Gilbert's), but the writer cannot think of a better one.

[2] These three sub-divisions are probably of little importance for diagnostic, as distinct from descriptive, purposes. If, for example, one finds side alternate quoins at the base of a tower with face alternate above or elsewhere in the church, it would not be safe to infer two building periods, in the absence of other evidence. It might mean no more than that two masons were employed, possibly even drawing on the same heap of quoin stones, one of whom preferred one arrangement, the other another.

Introduction

In studying Anglo-Saxon churches it is convenient to divide the country into five zones or areas, divisions which are not entirely arbitrary for there are good geographical and historical reasons for them.

The areas are:

1. England north of the Humber, corresponding roughly to that part of the old Anglian kingdom of Northumbria which lay south of the Tweed.

2. England between Humber and Thames, excluding Lincolnshire, East Anglia and Essex. This corresponds broadly to the old Anglian kingdom of Mercia.

3. Lincolnshire, which was for centuries a bone of contention between Northumbria and Mercia. Of all counties it has the greatest concentration of Anglo-Saxon churches, especially of towered churches.

4. East Anglia and Essex. East Anglia, i.e. Norfolk and Suffolk, was the kingdom of the East Angles; Essex was that of the East Saxons. East Anglia has a large number of pre-Conquest towered churches, being second only to Lincolnshire in this respect. Essex has very few; for that reason it is included, as a matter of convenience only, with its east coast neighbours, Norfolk and Suffolk.

5. England south of the Thames, excluding Cornwall which was never under close Anglo-Saxon control and has few Anglo-Saxon remains. This area corresponds to the old Saxon kingdoms of Kent, Sussex and Wessex.

Part I

ENGLAND NORTH OF THE HUMBER: THE SIX NORTHERN COUNTIES

HISTORICAL INTRODUCTION

The three eastern counties of this area—Yorkshire, Durham and Northumberland—formed the core of the old Anglian kingdom of Northumbria. This arose from a partial unification of two earlier kingdoms: Deira, which covered most of Yorkshire between Humber and Tees, and Bernicia, originally between Tees and Tweed. Deira was founded, or rather grew up, in the second half of the fifth century. Bernicia arose out of Anglian settlements at Bamborough in 547. Little is known of their early history. The earliest known great leader to arise in this region was Æthelfrith, King of Bernicia, 593–616. He extended his frontiers northwards to the Forth and westwards to the Irish Sea. He married the daughter of Ælle, King of Deira, and ruled Deira as well from c. 600 onwards. He was the real founder of the historic Northumbrian kingdom. He was killed in battle against Rædwald of East Anglia at the River Idle near Doncaster.

Northumbria was fortunate in that five of its first six kings were men of outstanding ability and personality, and all but the first were Christians. Under the second ruler, the great Edwin, 616–32, brother-in-law of Æthelfrith and son of Ælle, Northumbria reached the height of its political power. Edwin's overlordship was accepted throughout the whole country, Kent being the only one of the Anglo-Saxon kingdoms which did not formally acknowledge it. In 625 Edwin married Æthelberg, a daughter of the Christian Æthelberht of Kent and Bertha of Paris. Æthelberg was accompanied north by the priest Paulinus and his companions who preached the Gospel in Northumbria, eventually converting Edwin to the Faith in 627. Paulinus became the first bishop of York, and Bede records that four churches were built during his ministry: one of wood at York for Edwin's baptism; a square stone one on the same site (enclosing the earlier wooden oratory), which was completed by Edwin's successor Oswald; one at Campodunum, possibly Doncaster, probably of wood as it was burnt soon afterwards, and a stone one at Lincoln which, roofless, was standing in Bede's day, c. 731. It seems likely that Paulinus had with him masons from Kent, for at this early date the northern Anglians could hardly have built stone churches, their whole building tradition being in timber.

Paulinus's ministry lasted only seven years. He and Queen Æthelberg fled the kingdom to Kent after Edwin's death in 632 and did not return. Edwin was defeated and killed at the battle of Hatfield, near Doncaster, fighting against the British Cadwallon, Prince of Gwynedd, and his ally the pagan Penda of Mercia.

41

The next king was Oswald, St. Oswald, son of Æthelfrith, who reigned from 633 to 641. He had lived for some years in exile at Iona and it was he who invited Aidan from Iona to form his monastery at Lindisfarne in 634. Oswald defeated and killed Cadwallon at the battle of Hefenfelth, or Heavenfield, near Hexham in 633. It was before this battle that Oswald erected a large wooden cross near by, which was a prototype of the carved stone standing crosses which became the characteristic expression of the plastic art of the early Anglo-Saxon period. According to Bede this was the first Christian symbol to be erected in Bernicia. He writes definitely as though it was still in existence in his time, some hundred years after its erection. Oswald was himself defeated and killed by Penda of Mercia at Maserfelth, probably near Oswestry, in 641.

Oswald was succeeded by his brother Oswiu in Bernicia only (as Deira was occupied by Penda) until he defeated and killed Penda and his ally Æthelhere of the East Angles[1] at the Winwaed, a stream near Leeds, in 654. After this he ruled a re-united Northumbria until his death in 670. From this time on Northumbria lost its supremacy of all England to Mercia under Wulfhere, the Christian son of Penda, 657–74. Henceforth Northumbrian military and political activities were confined to north of the Humber, much to the benefit of the kingdom, for it allowed that internal consolidation which paved the way for the magnificent Anglo-Irish[2] art of Northumbria which began to develop about this time.

It was in Oswiu's reign that the Synod of Whitby was held in 664 at which, due largely to the efforts of Wilfrid of Ripon and the King himself, the Roman method of calculating the date of Easter and the Roman tonsure were accepted as official. As a result of this many of the Celtic clerics returned to Iona or Ireland and the Roman Church eventually replaced the Scoto-Celtic teaching of Lindisfarne.

Oswiu's son and successor Ecgfrith, 670–85, was killed fighting the Picts at Nechtanesmere, near Forfar, in 685, a disaster from which recovery was slow and perhaps never complete.

Aldfrith, brother of Ecgfrith, who reigned from 685 to 704, gave stability to his almost ruined country. Bede wrote that Aldfrith 'ably restored the shattered fortunes of the kingdom, though within smaller boundaries', and Stenton that the learning of the age of Bede was possible only through the work of Aldfrith in 'the critical years following the battle of Nechtansmere'. Aldfrith, like his greater successor Alfred the Great, was a considerable scholar and patron of the arts, and under him the Church established its position securely in Northumbria. He was educated in the Celtic part of Wessex under the Celtic Aldhelm, Abbot of Malmesbury, who had been a pupil

[1] It seems likely that the famous Sutton Hoo ship and its treasures dug up near Woodbridge in Suffolk in 1939 was the memorial of Æthelhere. Much of the treasure was undoubtedly family or tribal heirlooms and may have belonged to Rædwald who was Bretwalda, i.e. supreme overlord of England, from c. 616 to his death in 624 or 625. (See Bruce-Mitford, op. cit.)

[2] Usually called Hiberno-Saxon.

of Theodore and Hadrian at Canterbury and was not therefore entirely Celtic in outlook. Before Aldfrith became king he had spent some years studying Celtic culture in Ireland and Iona. He was indeed a Celtic scholar of distinction and originality. It was in his reign that learning and art reached their peak of distinction in the Northumbrian monasteries. The Lindisfarne Gospels were produced under Bishop Eadfrith *c.* 700, and the *Codex Amiatinus* was one of the three complete bibles ordered to be written by Ceolfrith, Abbot of Jarrow, 690–716. The earliest and finest of the great carved standing crosses, those at Ruthwell in Dumfries and Bewcastle in Cumberland, are dated to *c.* 690[1] and so would belong to the reign of Aldfrith; and the construction of this great series of carved monuments went on undiminished in Aldfrith's and later reigns, as well as much church building. Stenton writes of Aldfrith: 'He was undoubtedly one of the most learned men in his own kingdom, and it is probable that his influence on the development of Northumbrian learning was much greater than appears on the surface of history. He is the most interesting member of the remarkable dynasty to which he belonged, and he stands beside Alfred of Wessex among the few Old English Kings who combined skill in warfare with desire for knowledge.'

The kings who came after Aldfrith were all politically obscure, but a few were of great piety and probably exerted a greater influence on the development of culture than their political obscurity would indicate. Thus, Ceolworth, 729–37, otherwise almost unknown, was 'the Most Glorious King' to whom Bede dedicated his famous book *A History of the English Church and People* in 731. Ceolworth abdicated in 737 and 'entered the monastery of Lindisfarne; he gave to [the monks of] St. Cuthbert his royal treasures and lands, that is to say Bregesne[2] and Werceworde,[3] with their appurtinances, together with the church he had built there, and four other vills also, Wudecestre,[4] Hwitingham,[5] Eadulfingham,[6] Eagwulfingham[7]'.[8]

Ceolworth's successor Eadberht, 737–58, also abdicated to live as a monk in the

---

[1] This approximation is widely accepted but is not unquestionably acceptable. The date has been subject to much debate. J. Brøndsted, G. Baldwin Brown, A. W. Clapham, T. D. Kendrick, H. Leclercq, A. Kingsley Porter, F. Saxl and L. Stone accept a seventh- or late seventh-century date; O. E. Saunders thought they might date from 700 or even earlier; W. G. Collingwood and, later, R. G. Collingwood supported a fairly late eighth-century date. From linguistic evidence C. L. Wrenn suggested the early eighth century for the Ruthwell cross. R. I. Page (op. cit.; he gives earlier references) argued that Wrenn's conclusion cannot be upheld or disproved, but thought a date between 700 and 750 would agree with the linguistic evidence; a date before 700 seemed to him to be too early. He qualified this by adding: 'On the evidence available a date any time in the eighth century seems to be possible, so that even if Collingwood's [late] date for the cross is accepted there need be no conflict between linguistic and artistic dating.' He concludes wisely that, 'In the present state of our knowledge . . . the dating of inscribed stones by either art historians or linguists is seldom more than tentative'.

[2] Perhaps Brainshaugh, near Warkworth.

[3] Probably Warkworth.

[4] Not the obvious Woodchester for there is no village of that name in Northumbria; probably Woodhorn.

[5] Whittingham.   [6] Edlingham.

[7] Eglingham.   [8] Simeon of Durham, (*b*), I, Bk. II, Chapter I.

monastery of his brother Ecgberht or Egbert, Archbishop of York. This Ecgberht, who had been a pupil of Bede and was later the teacher of Alcuin, founded the school at York which was later built up and developed by his kinsman Æthelberht, also later Archbishop of York. Through Ecgberht the substance of Bede's teaching was transmitted to a group of scholars, including Alcuin, who rapidly made York a prime centre of English scholarship. Through Alcuin the work of Bede, via York, was a contributory factor, and an important one, in the revival of Western learning under Charlemagne. Charlemagne invited Alcuin in 782 to become head of his Palace School at Aachen, and later made him Abbot of St. Martin's at Tours, 796–804, a monastery which Alcuin converted into a great centre of learning.

This export of religion and culture to western and north-western Europe is an essential part of the story. Northumbria was not a small outlying kingdom which developed a brilliant art and culture and architecture and sculpture in isolation. It could not of course have developed very far, if at all, in isolation. It influenced and was influenced by, it grew up in cultural association with, the Celtic learning of Ireland and south-west Scotland. Later its scholars and missionaries went abroad to Europe and founded monasteries which also became centres of learning, and which in turn influenced the art and architecture of these Islands. Thus, Willibrord from Northumbria spent more than forty years, from *c.* 690, among the Frisians and founded the famous Abbey of Echternach, near Trier, *c.* 710. Later, from the other end of England Boniface of Devon did similar and even more effective work among the west Germans between 719 and 754, and founded the great Abbey of Fulda *c.* 744. His work has been stated to be the most important single influence on the history of Europe that any Englishman has ever exercised (Christopher Dawson).

The great achievements of Northumbrian culture, though rendered possible, or at least facilitated, by the outstanding personalities and patronage of the Northumbrian kings, were brought about by four great churchmen whose work resulted in what has been called the Heroic Age of the Anglo-Saxon Church in the eighth century. These men were Benedict Biscop, 628–90, Wilfrid of Ripon, 634–709, Bede of Jarrow, *c.* 673–735, and that great organizer and ecclesiastical statesman Theodore of Tarsus, Archbishop of Canterbury, 668–90. Theodore indeed has been described as 'the first man in English history to whom we can fittingly give the name of statesman'.[1] He, not Augustine, was the true founder of the organized Anglo-Saxon Church. He made his authority effective throughout the whole country. He cut several dioceses out of the single unwieldy one of Northumbria and brought them all under the authority of Canterbury.

Bede has been sufficiently referred to above. His genius was in letters, theology and above all in history. He was not only the first British historian and the greatest of his age; his equal did not appear again for five hundred years. But apart from his very

[1] Sayles, op. cit.

great general influence on culture he had no direct influence on architecture or on church building and so does not directly concern us here.

Benedict Biscop and Wilfrid, both members of royal houses, were great builders. They must be regarded as the initiators of church building in stone in Northumbria. Benedict Biscop made six journeys to Rome, bringing back pictures, books, treasures for the churches he intended to build. He also brought masons, glaziers and other craftsmen from Gaul to help him build *more Romanorum*, i.e. in the manner of the Romans, in stone.[1]

Wilfrid was also a great traveller and builder. Though he, too, was trained in the Scoto-Celtic Church, he studied for five years in Gaul and Italy and, like Biscop, became a strong supporter of the Roman Church and of the Benedictine Order. Later he built monasteries in various parts of England, for his personality was continually getting him into trouble with royal or ecclesiastical authorities and he spent many years in two long periods (677–86 and 691–702) of exile from Northumbria. Eddius[2] reports that Wilfrid, on his return from consecration in Gaul in 665, took north with him masons 'and artisans of almost every kind' from Rome[3] and that his churches were magnificent—as indeed they may well have been for two of them at least had crypts which remain today, the only two in Northumbria, two out of only five or perhaps six built, so far as is known, in the entire period of Anglo-Saxon history. According to Eddius all Wilfrid's churches were built before his first period of exile which began in 677.

Wilfrid was made Abbot of Ripon *c.* 660 by King Oswald, who had founded the monastery, and Bishop of York in 664. He stayed so long in Gaul after his consecration there that when he returned home in 665 Chad had been appointed bishop in his place and he returned to Ripon until 669 when he was made Bishop of York and of all Northumbria by Theodore. He then began his building operations. He rebuilt Paulinus' stone cathedral at York in 669–71. It had been neglected for nearly forty years and was roofless. In the words of Eddius[4] he 'renewed the ruined roof ridges, skilfully covering them with pure lead; by putting glass in the windows he prevented the birds or the rain from getting in, although it did not keep out the rays of light. He also [white] washed the walls'. According to Simeon of Durham[5] this 'monasterium' was burnt in 741.

At Ripon, between 671 and 678, 'he built and completed from the foundations in

---

[1] See below, p. 85, for a fuller account of Biscop's career.

[2] Eddius accompanied Wilfrid in 669 from Canterbury to Northumbria to take charge of the music in Wilfrid's churches. As usual with early chroniclers he wrote in extravagantly eulogistic terms of his master's works and activities. Not all he writes about the churches need, or should, be accepted as literally correct, but it does show that according to the ideas of his time Wilfrid's churches were impressive and even magnificent. This was demonstrated during excavations of Wilfrid's churches at Hexham in 1908–10 (see below, pp. 66).

[3] Richard of Hexham wrote 'from Rome'; Eddius did not mention Rome.

[4] Op. cit., Chapter XVI.

[5] Op. cit., (*b*), II, *sub anno* 741.

the earth up to the roof, a church of dressed stone,[1] supported by various columns[2] and side aisles[3].[4]

His great church of St. Andrew at Hexham was built 672–8. It is described below.[5]

Wilfrid is reputed to have built three other churches at Hexham: St. Mary's a little to the south-east of St. Andrew's; St. Peter's and, according to Richard of Hexham, St. Michael's, of which no traces remain and their sites are unknown. St. Mary's is described below.[6]

Wilfrid's churches were contemporary with or slightly earlier than Biscop's and were likewise built by foreign masons. They differed however in some respects from Biscop's. In their great length and height, a Northumbrian characteristic, they resembled Biscop's. In their possession of apses they resembled Augustine's Kentish churches built under Italo-Byzantine influence; Wilfrid's apses, aisles (or porticus), columns, crypts, staircases and, at Hexham at least, transepts were evidently inspired by Roman models which would be familiar both to Wilfrid and to his Roman masons.

Although Wilfrid's and Biscop's churches began the tradition of church building in stone in Northumbria, it is Biscop's which must be regarded as the prototypes on the pattern of which the other Northumbrian churches, to be discussed below, were based.

The spread of Christianity throughout Northumbria, in fact throughout all England, was surprisingly rapid and extensive, and the conversion of kings and nobles apparently genuine and sincere. The kings became great patrons of the arts. They supplied lands and endowments for church building and were fortunate in that great ecclesiastics—like Benedict Biscop and Wilfrid—were available, able and willing to take full advantage of the royal patronage. As will be seen later, similar considerations apply to the other regions of the country. But it must be emphasized that in this early period England was not a single unified country but comprised seven politically separate kingdoms—those of the so-called Heptarchy—developing culturally along their own lines, although of course deeply influenced by the not very dissimilar cultures of their neighbours. Church building in stone began in the two extreme ends of the country, Kent and Northumbria: in Kent after St. Augustine's arrival in 597, in Northumbria rather later, *c.* 670. The cultural influences at work in the two areas were different: Italo-Byzantine in Kent, and Italian via Gaul mingled with Scoto-Celtic and perhaps some Anglian originality in the north. Church build-

---

[1] There are mediaeval additions to the crypt easy to recognize as they are of rougher work than Wilfrid's.

[2] Probably taken from Roman remains nearby; Aldborough, the Roman Isurium, was only seven miles distant.

[3] The Latin word *porticus* was more reasonably translated by Baldwin Brown as 'side chapels' or 'porticus'. At Hexham there really were aisles. The same word '*porticus*' was used in mediaeval Latin for both aisles and side chapels; sometimes for emphasis both words would be used for the same thing, e.g. *alas vel porticus*.

[4] Eddius, Chapter XVII.   [5] pp. 64–73.   [6] p. 73.

ing spread with Christianity from these two regions to the rest of the country, with intermingling of ideas where the two streams met. Thus in Mercia both Kentish and Northumbrian motifs are evident in the churches; St. Cedd, a Northumbrian, built St. Peter's at Bradwell juxta Mare, Essex, a church partly Kentish and partly Northumbrian in design; while Wilfrid, another Northumbrian, evangelized Sussex and started church building there.

It is not surprising that a considerable variety of architectural motifs is to be found in early Anglo-Saxon churches, for there was not in this period any national manner of building, but a number of local, even personal, styles. And all the churches were towerless. Later, after the first great series of Danish invasions was over, and Alfred had reorganized his devastated part of the country, and after his son and grandson had reconquered the Danelaw and created one country—England—a new great wave of church building developed, again under royal patronage, the patronage of Edgar, and Canute, and Edward the Confessor. And again great ecclesiastics—this time St. Dunstan, St. Æthelwold of Winchester, St. Oswald of Worcester and York, and one may add St. Edward the Confessor himself—were available to build monasteries and churches, in this time in a truly national style, that of the *Late Saxon* period. It was in this period that the towers were built. Many new churches were built, many churches partially destroyed by the Danes were rebuilt, and these often retained Early Saxon characteristics in the form of early quoins, windows and archways and other details. Among these churches, as among the towers, there is less variation in architectural design and detail than in the churches of the Early period: they are no longer Northumbrian or Kentish or Mercian, but Anglo-Saxon, i.e. English. Even so, as will be seen, there is variety enough in these later churches and towers: no two towers are exactly alike, each one is an individual and needs individual description. Even among the simple round towers of East Anglia it is fascinating to see how the builders managed to make a simple stone or flint tube—for that is what a round tower really is—look different from every other simple stone tube.

NORTHUMBERLAND AND DURHAM

GENERAL CONSIDERATIONS

The churches of Northumbria form a group with many similar characteristics. Those of Yorkshire (Deira) in some respects show differences from those of Durham and Northumberland (Bernicia). The churches of Durham and Northumberland are so similar that no useful purpose would be served—it would in fact be misleading—to separate these two counties for separate study. They form a single unit. The rivers Tyne and Wear were areas of settlement, not boundaries (as the Tees was originally a boundary between Bernicia and Deira). The churches of Northumberland and Durham will therefore be considered together.

Three general considerations must first be dealt with. Many churches, originally towerless, belong to the Early Saxon period of architecture, i.e. prior to c. 870. The towers were added later, in the Late Saxon period, for towers were not introduced into England until the first half of the tenth century. In some cases, as at Monkwearmouth and Corbridge (and possibly Bywell St. Andrew's and Whittingham), the churches originally had one- or two-storeyed porches, these being raised later into so-called 'porch towers' by the addition of two or three more stages in the Late Saxon period. In other cases the towers were built *de novo* from the ground. There are therefore two groups of towers which differ in some respects. Porch towers have thin walls, usually less than 2 ft. 7 ins. thick, as the walls were intended to support porches only. They are rectangular in cross-section with their longer axes lying east–west, and their external width is generally less than the interior width of the nave.

The *de novo* towers have walls thicker than 2 ft. 6 ins. and may be wider than the interior width of nave. They approximate to square in cross-section, but where there is a slightly longer axis it lies normally though not always[1] north–south.[2]

One peculiarity of these northern towers should be noted. All the window openings are single-splayed. Single-splaying of openings was characteristic of the Early Saxon period; double splaying, though not universal, was typical of the Late Saxon period during which all Saxon towers were built. Why single-splaying was so general in this area throughout the entire Anglo-Saxon period is an interesting question to which a satisfactory answer cannot as yet be given.

[1] Cf. Bosham (Sussex), below p. 371.
[2] All Anglo-Saxon towers were built without buttresses. Their remarkable stability over the centuries must be attributed to good foundations, strong quoins and excellent mortar.

In orientation these northern churches were stated by Honeyman to fall into three groups: early Norman churches with a nave length–breadth ratio of about two to one have an east–west orientation; pre-Conquest churches in the Tyne valley and Co. Durham built by Wilfrid and Benedict Biscop or in their building tradition have a length–breadth ratio of about three to one and are orientated in an east–west direction; other northern churches, though having a length–breadth ratio of three to one, are orientated more nearly in an east-north-east direction. Honeyman raised the question: is this a British or Celtic tradition? This unusual east-north-east orientation however is not confined to Northumbrian pre-Conquest churches or indeed to English churches at all. In Syrian churches orientation was not strictly east–west but frequently varied in the direction of east-by-south up to as much as 12°. It has been suggested that these deviations had no significance and may have been due to inaccuracies in the instruments used and to lack of competence by the builders. The English deviations may be as great as twice the Syrian ones and in Northumbria are usually on the north of east. The Anglo-Saxons were notoriously bad in their setting-out methods;[1] there were few strict right angles in their stone churches, and the walls of a tower were often of different lengths.[2] But up to 20°+ deviation from the east seems unlikely to be due merely to incompetence or carelessness.

C. J. P. Cave made a statistical study of the orientation of 647 English churches of all periods and found that only 1·6% were orientated exactly due east, although if due east is taken to mean $90° \pm 2\frac{1}{2}°$ east of north (i.e. the range $87\frac{1}{2}°$ to $92\frac{1}{2}°$ to cover accidental variations) the percentage was $16\frac{1}{4}$. Against this, 48% fell between $67\frac{1}{2}°$ and $87\frac{1}{2}°$ and a total of 55% fell north of $87\frac{1}{2}°$, and 29% fell south of $92\frac{1}{2}°$. Such deviations cannot be accidental, but intentional. Cave considered that the large percentage lying within the range $67\frac{1}{2}°$ to $87\frac{1}{2}°$ (i.e. approximately within 20° to the north of east) could be explained by assuming that at the time when the foundations were laid out the orientation adopted was either (*a*) towards the rising sun, or (*b*) towards the point of sunrise at the Equinox. He claimed his figures definitely disproved the suggestion first made by William Wordsworth in a poem of 1823 that orientation of churches was determined by the direction of sunrise on the feast day of the saint to whom the church is dedicated. Figures by the earlier workers F. C. Eeles, T. W. Shore, and W. Airy seemed to support the same negative conclusion. H. Benson on the other hand claimed that his figures for churches dedicated to St. Peter certainly showed a marked correlation between their orientation and the direction of sunrise on St. Peter's festival day.

There are twenty-four sites on which it is known, believed or presumed there were pre-Conquest churches and of which tangible evidence remains. Of these only

---

[1] This is not strictly true of timber buildings, and is not true at all of MS. illuminations, the high quality of which would not have been possible without accurate setting out. So the Saxons were not incapable of good setting out. Why they were so careless over their stone buildings is not evident.

[2] Cf. Corbridge.

eleven have towers. These and two towerless ones are described below. They are:

Ingram, 10 miles W. by N. of Alnwick; Whittingham, about 7 miles W. by S. of Alnwick and about 8 miles SE. by S. of Ingram (these are the two most northerly of the pre-Conquest churches of England); Bolam, 7 miles W. by S. of Morpeth and about 19 miles S. by E. of Whittingham; then come six sites in the Tyne valley, all very close to the river: Hexham, Warden-on-the-Tyne, about 2 miles NW. of Hexham; Corbridge, about 4 miles E. by N. of Hexham; Bywell (two churches, St. Andrew's and St. Peter's) about 4 miles SE. of Corbridge; Ovingham, about 6 miles E. of Corbridge and 3 miles NE. of Bywell; Jarrow (in Co. Durham) about 6 miles E. by N. of Gateshead and about 3 miles above the mouth of the Tyne. In Co. Durham are: Monkwearmouth, just N. of the mouth of the Wear and now part of Sunderland which is on both banks of the river; and in Teesdale, Norton, less than 2 miles N. and now part of Stockton-on-Tees; and Billingham, about 1 mile NE. of Norton.

BILLINGHAM

ST. CUTHBERT's CHURCH.[1] The first mention of Billingham is in Simeon's *Historia Regum* (*sub anno* 866). He wrote of Ecgred, who was Bishop of Lindisfarne 830–45, that 'He built also Billingham in Heart-ernysse', i.e. Billingham in Hartness. Simeon also mentioned that Ælla, a king of some part of Northumbria despoiled the church at Billingham, but gives no date. There was an Ælla, a usurper not of royal birth, who was king for a short period and who was killed in 867 fighting against the Danes who had captured York. This may be the Ælla referred to by Simeon.

Built into the south wall of the tower are stated to be at least six pieces of carved cross fragments. From this Hodges inferred that there was an earlier church on the site, though not necessarily of stone. Such an inference is a *non sequitur*. The cross or crosses probably marked the site where services were held. They would be replaced by Ecgred's towerless church of nave and chancel belonging to the Early Saxon period. When the tower was built in the Late Saxon period the crosses, probably broken up during the Danish invasions, may have been used, as in so many other cases, as building material. Most of these stones if present are now so badly worn as to be unrecognizable as ornament, except two pieces to east and west of the third stage south opening at impost level, one long piece on each side.

The tower is built of rectangular and square rubble blocks. The quoin slabs are side alternate (I). Baldwin Brown dates the tower to post-1040; V.C.H. *Durham* to mid-eleventh century though possibly earlier; Gilbert to perhaps 1000. It is 17 ft. 6 ins.

[1] E. C. Gilbert, (c); C. C. Hodges, (a), viii; N. Pevsner, (c); J. R. Surtees, III; V.C.H. *Durham*, III.

(I) *Plate* 2.

square externally and about 70 feet high. There are two string courses of plain projecting bands of stone. The lower string is at about two-thirds the tower height above the ground and the part of the tower below this, comprising three internal stages, is more than twice the height of the portion above between the two string courses which comprises one stage. The second string course, the walling above and the cornice and embattled parapet are probably fifteenth century.

The lowest stage, which is *c.* 20 feet high, is open to the church by a tall narrow round-headed doorway.

The east wall of the tower was built *on* the nave gable; that is, the earlier nave west wall was raised to form the tower east wall. The tower opening to the church is therefore not a tower arch but a western doorway to the earlier aisleless nave. It was in fact a doorway, being too narrow for a tower arch. It is tall, 8 ft. 3 ins. to the crown of the arched lintel, and only 2 ft. 9 ins. wide. The arched lintel is double arched (i.e. arched above and below; a form that may be called a double arched lintel); the lintel block is *c.* 4 ft. 2 ins. by 1 ft. 10 ins. The jambs are roughly upright and flat but not through-stones. The north impost is plain chamfered, the south hollow chamfered. The imposts are returned on both wall faces but are flush with the wall. It had no real door, only a very slight one hung across the opening on the tower side. A rebate for a door, about half-way through, was cut in modern times. There is no hood mould. It may be the original doorway of the early church, or perhaps rebuilt in Norman times from the old materials.

There is no external entrance to this stage of the tower. The rectangular window in the south wall is modern. This stage was vaulted in the thirteenth century with a groined vault on chamfered ribs. It has a not quite centrally placed hole to allow access to the upper floors.

The second stage *c.* 15 feet high has a narrow window on the west with arched lintel, Norman type of sill and primitive looking jambs of three stones each, a lower upright with two flats above—the flat in the south jamb is quite inordinately long. Formerly there was an opening on the east wall opening to the nave, now either blocked or hidden, as at Ovingham and some other places.

The third stage, *c.* 12 feet high, has a large opening with arched lintel on the south wall *c.* 35 feet above ground with strip-work round the arch head and jambs. The jambs are of through-stones. The strip-work shares the same thin imposts, hollow chamfered below, as the arched lintel but rests on cubical blocks above the imposts and on similar blocks on the plinths below the jambs. Immediately above this window is the first string course, above which is a lofty fourth stage or belfry, *c.* 20 feet high.

The belfry stage has one large two-light double-headed window with arched lintel in each face with strip-work round its head and jambs, as in the window below. The openings have monolithic straight mid-wall shafts, one of which on the north looks like a modern renewal. They consist really of long rectangular slabs with their outer edges rounded to look like circular shafts. They have no capitals but have bases of simple cubical form, except the north one which appears to be a genuine circular shaft with no base. The central imposts are hollow-chamfered below. The jambs are of four through-stones almost square sectioned. As at Ovingham there is a hole in each tympanum between the double arch head and the strip-work above: two, those on the east and west walls, are circular; the other two are in the form of eight-pointed stars or octofoils with pointed terminations.

The belfry stage may possibly be later, though not much later, than the stages below: it is of rather lighter coloured smaller stones and quoins and has no carved fragments built into it. On the other hand the window structure and especially the hood moulds are closely similar to those in the stage below.

The nave is *c.* 48 feet long and of singularly long and narrow proportions,[1] the length being about four times the width; at Monkwearmouth the ratio of nave length to width is three to one. It is very high. There are two fine Norman Transitional arcades of four piers each leading to aisles. The west wall is original; its early megalithic quoins are visible below the tower. A good deal of the original north wall remains and may be part of Ecgred's church. The north arcade was apparently cut through the Anglo-Saxon wall for the piers are pieces of walling slightly double chamfered into piers. The eastern and western edges of these piers have thinner inner orders similarly chamfered and forming continuations of the inner orders of the arch heads. The fourth pier retains a wider piece of wall than the others. The piers of the south arcade are rather later and of different form. The east and south walls are modern rebuildings.

There are four early rectangular windows single-splayed high up in the north wall. A similar one is in the west end of the south wall.

BOLAM

ST. ANDREW'S CHURCH.[2] The tower and probably the western quoins and a fragment in the north wall of the nave are pre-Conquest. Baldwin Brown dates the tower to post-1040, other writers to probably *c.* 1000.

The tower (I) is about 54 feet high and measures externally 17 ft. 5 ins. north-south, with a projection on its north side of 15 ft. 1 in. from the nave. Its internal dimensions are 12 ft. 5 ins. along the west wall and 12 ft. 4 ins. along the south. The walls are of squared rubble 2 ft. 7 ins. thick, about 3 inches thicker than the nave

---

[1] See view looking west in V.C.H. *Durham*, III, Pl. facing p. 202.
[2] C. C. Hodges, (*a*), vii; N. Pevsner, (*e*); F. R. Wilson.

wall. In some respects it differs somewhat from the Tynedale towers. The quoins are of slab work, side-alternate (1). A few of the lower stones are very large, measuring up to 2 ft. 9 ins. by 2 ft. 4 ins. by 9 ins.; those higher up are smaller. There is no indication of re-used Roman worked stones. There is no plinth. A string course divides the tower externally into two about equal stages, but internally there are four stages, two below and two above the string course.

The ground floor is open to the nave through a wide Norman Transitional arch, round headed, plain and unmoulded, with short columns recessed in each pier; the capitals have rude foliage and abaci: all unmistakable Norman of the twelfth century. There were two original windows, one on the west and one on the south wall. The lower parts were destroyed and the upper parts built up when the present large modern windows were inserted. The original heads are visible on the exterior and the very wide splay, a late feature, on the interior walls. The light openings were only 4 inches wide and the interior opening splayed to 2 ft. 6 ins.

In the second stage there is a tall arrow-slit window on each of the north, south and west walls. These are taller than those in any Tynedale tower and have chamfered megalithic arched lintels. The jambs have two stones each in their upper parts; the lower parts and sills are indistinguishable from walling. The light apertures are 4 inches wide and the jambs are inclined slightly towards the top.

The third stage, immediately above the string course, is the belfry (2); in Tynedale towers the belfry is the fourth stage. There is a double-headed two-light window with arched lintel in each wall with tall monolithic circular-sectioned mid-wall straight shafts. The shafts have worn bulbous bases on square plinths. The capitals (3) except on the north, are corbelled out by a kind of hollow chamfering to the thickness of the wall, supporting the double arch head. This is not the same construction as the well-known and more general mid-wall shaft with or without capital supporting a separate through stone impost which may or may not be chamfered below. There are similar constructions at Jarrow, Scartho and Sompting. The northern shaft is of different construction (4). This has a straight-sided capital supporting a through-stone central impost in the usual Saxon manner; the lower face of the impost is widely chamfered along the east and west lower edges giving an inverted gable shape to the cross-section. There are plain neckings above the bases and below the capitals, which are cut from separate stones from the shafts. The sills are very thin and rest on the string courses. The jambs are of large slabs, side-alternate, but not through-stones. These windows are loftier and narrower than other belfry openings in the area. Hodges suggested that the bells were actually hung in the openings and were supported on one side by the mid-wall shaft.[1]

[1] As at Glentworth (Lincs), which see below, p. 276 and Fig. 24.

(1) *Plate* 4; (2) *Plates* 3, 5, 6; (3) *Plate* 5; (4) *Plate* 6.

The fourth and top stage has a single-light window in each wall. The one on the south (I) has an arched lintel; the other three are gable-headed. These minor differences are interesting; similar small differences are frequent in mediaeval architecture. It is likely that they are due to several masons being employed on the work, all working to a general scheme sketched out by the master mason but each being free to add his own finishing touches. The jambs are of slabs not easily distinguishable from the walling. Above is one course of masonry, then a plain cornice and above that a plain parapet of three courses, all later than the tower and probably of the twelfth or thirteenth century. Below the single masonry course and in line with the window heads, on the south and west only, is a single course of herring-boning.

The nave is 39 ft. 6 ins. long by 15 feet wide. Some of the lower courses of the north wall are of very large stones and look pre-Conquest. The rest of the nave is mainly Norman. The north-west and south-west quoins however look more Saxon than the tower quoins, being of larger and thinner slabs, side-alternate. The north-east quoins are of small stone work characteristic of the Norman period. The window openings are modern.

BYWELL

There are two ancient churches in this Tyneside village: St. Andrew's and St. Peter's, within 200 yards of each other.

Bywell was first mentioned under the name Biguell by Simeon of Durham who stated that Ecgberht was consecrated 12th Bishop of Lindisfarne here on June 11th, 803. Some writers think this consecration took place at St. Andrew's; Gilbert makes out a strong, though perhaps not entirely convincing, case for St. Peter's.

St. Andrew's has been largely reconstructed in modern times but the ground plan is preserved, i.e. the side walls of the modern nave have been built on the old foundations. Only the tower and the west wall of the nave with its quoins are of pre-Conquest date. Some other parts are early thirteenth century.

St. Peter's is the larger church. Much of the nave and chancel are ancient: Hodges and Pevsner say Norman, Gilbert equally definitely pre-Conquest. The History of Northumberland says more cautiously that there is nothing in the church to indicate that it is earlier than the end of the eleventh century, i.e. presumably (though it doesn't say so) early Norman and that its Anglian origin 'is only presumptive'. There is in fact no documentary evidence concerning the Anglian origin of either church, except the above quoted statement of Simeon. The architectural evidence for a pre-Conquest date for St. Peter's is however strong.[1]

[1] See below, pp. 57–60.

(I) *Plate* 3.

St. Andrew's at one time belonged to the Norbertian monastery of 'White Canons' at Blanchland, a few miles distant, and St. Peter's to the Benedictine monastery of Durham; the churches were known accordingly as the White and Black churches respectively. In 1093 William Rufus granted Bywell to Guy de Baliol. One of Guy's successors, Eustace, stated in 1194–5 that the church was given by his ancestors to the monks of St. Albans. As Guy is known to have given lands in Hertfordshire to St. Albans he may well have given Bywell St. Peter's too. According to the History of Northumberland it is likely that the earlier, pre-Conquest, church was replaced by the present one by the St. Albans monks. The tower is dated to *c.* 1310.

ST. ANDREW'S CHURCH.[1] The tower (I) is one of the best in the county. Unlike nearby Corbridge it is all of one date according to Hodges; Gilbert however provides structural evidence for two dates. The tower is certainly later than the earliest work at Corbridge and appears to be about contemporary with Ovingham, Warden, Bolam and the upper parts of Corbridge, probably not long before the Conquest. Baldwin Brown dates it to post-1040. It is 55 feet high. Its external dimensions are 16 ft. 3 ins. on the west with projections from the nave wall of 14 ft. 11 ins. on the north and 14 ft. 9 ins. on the south. Its internal dimensions are: west wall 11 ft. 1 in., east wall 11 ft. 4 ins., north wall 9 ft. 8 ins., south wall 9 ft. 11½ ins. The walls are 2 ft. 7 ins. thick, except the east wall (which is the west wall of the nave), which is 2 ft. 3 ins.

The first nine quoins are of poor sandstone, well cut and large, some very large; one is 3 ft. 7 ins. by 18 inches by 9 inches. They are arranged, using Gilbert's notation, in side-alternate manner. These correspond approximately to the first internal stage. The next seventeen quoins are irregular in size, some being quite small and badly cut; some are on end, others face-alternate with some side-alternate stones. This change in quoin character suggests that the upper stages are later and may have been erected on a one-storeyed porch. This is also supported by examination of the masonry: the first stage, like the quoins, is of weathered coursed, large, square or rectangular, coarsely dressed, well preserved grey stone; above, the fabric is of softer more weathered brown or red sandstone. There is no visible plinth.

The first stage has no western doorway. It opens to the nave by a low reconstructed arch of the thirteenth century, pointed (unusual for that period), made of old through-stones reset, on probably ancient jambs which look ancient but are not through-stones. It is of one order, with chamfered hood mould above on the east face but not on the west. Its imposts are not returned but are chamfered on the soffits

---

[1] C. C. Hodges, (*a*), vii; E. C. Gilbert, (*a*); N. Pevsner, (*e*); *History of Northumberland*, VI.

(I) *Plate* 7.

and ends. There is an early, not very narrow, splayed window in the south wall of the same date as that part of the tower. It has a roughly triangular arched lintel. The jambs are of three rough stones each, arranged flat-upright-flat on the west and up-right-flat-flat on the east, the two top flats being suggestive of imposts. The sill is of a large wall slab on the exterior and of two deep steps on the interior. The window in the west wall is modern.

In the second stage there is a window in the west wall of similar type to the one below on the south, except that it is taller and the jambs are of four stones each. Built into the south jamb on the inside is part of a carved cross shaft. According to the *History of Northumberland* this once stood in the cemetery attached to an earlier church on the site, perhaps of wood. More probably it may have marked the spot or a graveyard where services were held before a church was built. There is a doorway in the east wall with the dressings gone.

In the third stage is a large opening, called a doorway by Gilbert, in the south wall. It has an arched lintel with a strip-work hood mould above supported on vertical flat pilaster strips with bases and imposts similar to those in the belfry stage above. This opening is curious internally: there are three-stepped imposts, rounded on the lower edges, and covered with a lintel; between the impost and the jamb on the west is a black pebble, similar to one in the Hexham crypt. If this is a door the tower had separate entrances to the three lowest stages, as at Deerhurst (Glos).

A string course of square projection badly worn is high up on the exterior dividing the top or belfry stage from the stages below. This tends to emphasize the importance of the belfry and gives it prominence. The belfry stage has a double-headed two-light opening in each wall. The individual heads are arched lintels and rest on circular mid-wall monolithic columns, without bases or capitals, with long through-stone square-cut central imposts which project slightly beyond the wall face. The jambs are of long and short through-stones and have projecting imposts. There are strip-work round-headed hood moulds, springing from blocks above the imposts, and vertical pilaster strips with flat bases and thin imposts as in the opening below but larger, i.e. wider and of greater projection which gives them a more imposing appearance. In the tympanum between arch head and hood mould is a circular hole, cut from a single rectangular stone, of the same diameter as the openings in the arched lintels. There are similar circular openings also, on a level with the crown of the hood mould, in the spandrels flanking the hoods, two in each face. The object of these holes (they are blocked on the interior) is unknown but the effect is good. Such openings in spandrels are rare and these are the only ones in Northumberland.

Above the belfry stage is another plain string course, then a plain parapet two courses high of later date, perhaps thirteenth century, and a modern flat roof.

The nave was higher originally by 2 ft. 6 ins. as indicated by marks on the tower exterior wall.

ST. PETER'S CHURCH.[1] The church is close to the river; the churchyard in fact is bounded on its south side by the river.

As already stated, the pre-Conquest date of the church is much disputed. Gilbert after a thorough examination of the building maintained definitely that the date is pre-Conquest. The evidence for such a date is certainly strong. However, the late eleventh-century church, whether pre-Conquest or not, appears to have had no tower; it consisted of an aisleless nave and chancel. It is a large church, larger than St. Andrew's, and on account of its controversial character, its nearness to and close historical association with St. Andrew's, and its many similarities to Monkwearmouth, it seems desirable to include it here.

The north wall of the nave with its four original windows is *not* later than the end of the eleventh century. Whether this eleventh-century church was the earliest here or replaced an earlier one is not known. There is a perhaps thirteenth-century south arcade and aisle, a thirteenth-century chancel, a western tower dated to *c.* 1310,[2] a low chapel formerly a schoolroom opened out by two large bays into the north-east end of the nave in the nineteenth century and a nineteenth-century vestry on the north side of the chancel.

The Nave. The north and south walls have original quoins at the east ends. The south-east quoins are hidden by whitewash. The north face of the east end of the north wall is hidden by the chapel, but assuming that both northern and eastern faces of the north-east quoin are similar, the quoin is arranged in side-alternate manner for about 12 feet; above this the material is similar but degraded. The lower quoins are very large big stone work. Above, the walling appears to be later, although ancient, as it is made very largely of red sandstone, while the lower part is almost devoid of it, being of brown and green sandstone. The walling is good, of fairly well-cut and squared stones, and might almost be called rough ashlar. The wall is only 2 ft. 2 ins. thick.

As at the west end of Monkwearmouth the nave windows (four) are high up, the sills being about 20 feet from the floor. The openings are 4 ft. 6 ins. high. They are closely similar to the Corbridge windows in type and dimensions: the heads are massive arched lintels, one lintel being 50 inches across by 22 inches high, others 36 inches across. The apertures are 17 to 21 inches across, slightly splayed to about 3 feet. The jambs are almost monolithic, of one long stone with two shorts below. In one window the two big jamb stones are different, one being of red sandstone, the other of green, while one jamb has one small stone and the other two small stones below the tall one. Monolithic jambs are not Norman: Norman jambs have either two or three stones of similar height and not through-stones (there may be two or

---

[1] C. C. Hodges, (a), vii; E. C. Gilbert (a) and (b); N. Pevsner, (e); *History of Northumberland*, VI.
[2] There is a large blocked rectangular opening in the east wall of the tower, i.e. the present fourteenth-century western wall of the earlier nave, a most unusual feature of a fourteenth-century tower.

three stones per course) or they may be just walling. These almost monolithic jambs at Bywell are similar to those at Jarrow north doorway (now blocked) and to those of Monkwearmouth doorways and windows. The sills are of thin fairly short slabs.

Arched lintels too are quite un-Norman. They occur at Jarrow, Escomb and also at Brigstock (Northants). Brigstock was dated by Baldwin Brown to *c.* 950, but there is much in the church to suggest two dates, one much earlier than 950, even as early as one in the Early Saxon period (i.e. prior to *c.* 870).[1] The sills are thin and narrow, only slightly longer than the width of the aperture.

In the lower part of the north wall near the west end and about 5 feet above the ground are four small square voussoirs, part of the eastern end of an arch of about 5 feet original width. They are similar to the very small voussoirs of Corbridge west doorway. Jambs, if any, are hidden by the later brick facing of the wall.

The present nave is 54 feet long by 19 ft. 2 ins. wide but was originally longer on the west, possibly to as much as 80 feet. The early fourteenth-century tower is built partly on and partly in the old nave: it rests *on* the south and west walls but falls short of the north wall, which here has been destroyed. On the line of the nave north wall are footings 8 inches wide, which run the full length of the tower and return on the west to meet it. There is also a cross-footing 11 ft. 4 ins. from the west wall of the tower. It is not unreasonable to assume that these cross-footings represent the original west walls, we would have an original nave about 66 ft. 8 ins. long (the tower being 12 ft. 8 ins. east–west), with a compartment at the west end which from its shape—11 ft. 4 ins. east–west by 19 ft. 2 ins. north–south—may have been a narthex. This nave would be closely similar both in length and width to Monkwearmouth.

The eastern pillar of the thirteenth-century south arcade has a crude semi-bulbous or hemispherical base.[2] It consists of a roughly cut hemispherical outer half of a rectangular base to the pillar, resting on a relatively low plinth of square plan with perhaps a chamfer at the corners giving it a somewhat circular outline. The profile of the base appears hollow above, changing to slightly convex, almost vertical, below. There are no neckings. The whole is badly worn and it is not easy to obtain a clear idea of its original design. It seems typologically earlier than the bulbous bases of the chancel arch pillars at Monkwearmouth, usually dated to *c.* 1075: these are bulbous, not semi-bulbous, and have neckings which are a late, post-Conquest, feature. The bulbous type of capitals and bases is an Anglo-Saxon feature. It began *c.* 800, the capitals continuing until the mid-eleventh century and the bases until after the Conquest. They were not common in Anglo-Saxon architectural settings, for columns were themselves unusual. They occur not infrequently in sculptures and in MS. illuminations. There are hemispherical bases to the collonettes in the figural slab on the south chancel wall of Castor (Northants),[3] dated to the earliest years of the

---

[1] See below, under Brigstock. [2] E. C. Gilbert, (*a*), Pl. II, 2. [3] See E. A. Fisher, Pl. 47B.

ninth century. Though perhaps not entirely convincing, this base strengthens the other evidence for an early date for this church well before the Conquest.

The Chancel. The first 16 feet length of the north chancel wall is identical in fabric with the old walling of the nave. Also it is of the same height, about 26 feet, as the nave, a most unusual feature in a chancel. The wall may be a relic of an earlier church. The chancel is 17 feet long and was probably square. It is really spacious, unlike northern chancels and more like those of southern England. In the north wall is a blocked doorway, probably rebuilt at some time of re-used stones. The jambs are long-flat-long, with additional flats to support the rather short lintel. The stones appear to have been renewed, except one which looks ancient. The big lintel has also been renewed.

Above the blocked doorway are the remains of a gable with its apex about 18 feet from the east wall of the nave. It may be inferred that it marks the remains of a porticus overlapping nave and chancel. The door was the door to the chancel. As the south aisle overlaps the chancel by about 11 feet, this suggests that there may have been a porticus on the south, opening to the aisle. There are in fact faint but distinct signs of the western part of the gable head and jambs visible through the whitewash on the south side of the chancel wall within the organ recess. North and south porticus are early features, more common in the south than in the north.

The indications, emphasized by Gilbert, of an early, or at least a pre-Conquest, date, may be summarized as follows:

1. Bishop Ecgberht's consecration in 803 must have been in a church. St. Andrew's is the smaller and hence originally the less important of the two. At the same time there may have been earlier churches on both sites.

2. The plain, aisleless nave and chancel with north and south porticus and possible western narthex, is of early type and has affinities with Monkwearmouth. Both narthex and porticus are very early features.

3. The very thin nave walls. It is difficult to accept such walls as Norman; even if post-Conquest in date they must surely have been built by Anglo-Saxon masons.

4. The windows are of early type, like those at Corbridge, and are high up in the walls, another early feature.

5. The church was shortened in the thirteenth or early fourteenth century when the tower was built. Such shortening rarely happened, if ever, to a tenth- or eleventh-century church.

6. The evidence for two not widely separated dates for the nave north wall. The lower part may be the remains of an earlier church. But the early windows high up and the similarity in walling and quoins in the two parts suggest no great difference in date between the two parts.

Further, Mr. Bruce Allsopp gives another indication:

7. St. Peter's stands on a mound which forms a promontary round which the river bends. There are records of this mound having been used as a refuge when the rest of the village was flooded and it is altogether a much more prominent site than that of St. Andrew's. Unless, as is possible, St. Peter's site was already occupied by a fortification or important house it seems likely that the first church would have been built on this site.

Gilbert suggests, as a pure hypothesis but one consistent with the facts, that the first church may have been burnt by the Danes in their raids of 793 and 794 and rebuilt for Ecgberht's consecration in 803.

CORBRIDGE

ST. ANDREW's CHURCH.[1] The core of the present nave and porch supporting the tower are very early, probably of the seventh century: Baldwin Brown, Clapham, Hodges, Gilbert, the *History of Northumberland* all agree. Baldwin Brown suggests 650–700, Gilbert *c.* 669, the *History of Northumberland* late seventh or early eighth century. It is known that the church was in existence in 786 when Adulf was consecrated Bishop of Mayo by Eanbald, Archbishop of York, 'in the monastery which is called Et Corabrige.'[2] This is essentially the same church standing today. It was an ordinary minster, part of a monastery but not only monastic; it was the centre of a large ecclesiastical area of the type which later developed into a *parrochia*. There are no monastic remains, it being more than likely that the monastic buildings were of wood. It may have been built on royal land or on land granted by the king. It is known that at least one Northumberland king, Æthelred in 796, was murdered at 'Corribrigge' so there may have been a royal villa here. Its nearness to Hexham and its dedication to St. Andrew suggest that Wilfrid may have been the real founder. His churches at Hexham and at Oundle (Northants) were dedicated to St. Andrew; as also were the churches at Bywell, Hedden-on-the-Wall and Newcastle.

The church was built of Roman dressed stone plundered from Corstopitum, the neighbouring ruined Roman town, as were other churches and many houses in Corbridge, Hexham and elsewhere. It consisted of aisleless nave and chancel and western porch.

The Nave. The nave is 47 ft. 3 ins. long by 17 feet wide and was originally 34 feet high to the roof eaves. It was later lowered to 29 feet, by 5 feet at the eaves and rather more at the ridge to produce a flatter roof. It was originally 50 feet to the roof ridge.

There were three windows on each side wall. The part heads of two are still visible in the spandrels on the north wall between the nave arches at 19 feet above the floor. They have arched lintels; each head is cut from two through-stones; the open-

[1] C. C. Hodges, (*a*), vii; H. L. Honeyman; E. C. Gilbert, (*a*); *History of Northumberland*, X; N. Pevsner, (*e*).
[2] Simeon of Durham, (*b*), I.

ings are about 6 inches wide and widely splayed on the interior where they measure 7 ft. 6 ins. across by 2 ft. 3 ins. high. They are similar to the short window in the west wall of the porch. Another window, much altered, is in the high-pitched west gable and above the present roof; it opened above the level of the former porch roof and is splayed towards the nave, indicating that it was intended to light the nave. It is now in the east wall of the tower. At some time after the erection of the tower, perhaps in modern times, the outer, i.e. western, edge was hacked away to admit more light to the ringing chamber. At first sight it looks like a double splay—unlikely at the date of this wall—but was originally single splayed.

On the exterior the quoins are megalithic, another indication of early date, some of the stones being as much as 4 feet long. All lie on their faces in face-alternate arrangement, comparable with those at Jarrow, Monkwearmouth and Escomb.

The ancient gable, before the lowering, is stated to have had no water-tabling but to have had sloping quoins on the outer face which stood up above the rest of the wall and against which the thatch was brought. When the nave roof was lowered by 5 feet or so the north and south portions of the old gable above the modern roof, and on either side of the tower, were left flanking the tower like thin buttresses.

Foundations of the original east wall exist below ground for about 6 feet from the north and south angles of the east end of the nave, indicating a chancel arch of perhaps 9 feet wide. This is wider than usual in such early churches, so it may have been a Roman arch, transferred from elsewhere, like the tower arch.

To judge from some loose foundations of clay and cobbles the width of the chancel was probably about 12 feet.

The Saxon floor of the nave was discovered some years ago beneath the early mediaeval pavement contemporary with the pointed arches cut through the Saxon nave walls when the north and south aisles were built. This floor is visible in more than one place near the piers of the north arcade by lifting up small floor boards round the bases of the pillars.

The Tower (I). The tower quoins look early. They are upright and flat arrangement with the flats lying on their sides (side-alternate). The lower stones—of the earlier porch—are larger than those higher up—in the later tower. The west porch is about 16 feet square on the exterior. The interior dimensions are: west wall 10 ft. 11½ ins., east wall 10 ft. 7 ins., north wall 11 ft. 1½ ins., south wall 11 ft. 5 ins.; as with most porch towers the longer axis lies east–west. The walls are 2 ft. 7 ins. thick, the same as the responds of the tower arch but about 4 inches *less* than the nave west wall to the north and south of the tower. The height of the original porch and pitch of the roof are visible on the interior walls.[1] The height was 26 feet to the eaves and

[1] *History of Northumberland*, X, p. 186, fig. 3.

---

37 feet to the roof ridge, an unusually great height for a one-storeyed porch, if it was of one storey. The external west doorway (1), now built up with an inserted modern three-light lancet window under the old arch head, was 4 ft. 10 ins. wide and about 9 feet high. It has a round head of small stones of which three appear to be renewals with a similar, relieving, arch in the masonry above, the voussoirs of which have rude ornaments resembling saltires in form, one in each voussoir. These are now very faint and not distinguishable in detail. The arch has no imposts and has jambs of crude upright and flat work. The two lowest stones are massive uprights, about 2 ft. 9 ins. by 1 ft. 6 ins., above which are two not very wide flats, then two large cubical blocks with two smaller ones above. It is deeply rebated to *c.* 1 ft. 9 ins. on the interior for a door to open inwards to the nave, and there is an iron crook, one of two which supported the two valves of a door. The supposed relieving arch does not go far into the wall; it does not correspond with the interior arch head.

Above the west doorway (1) is a window, 19 inches wide externally, with widely splayed jambs, each of which is of three roughly cut stones, the top one being laterally longer and serving as impost. The arched lintel is of two rings of stones, one outer and one inner; the outer one is 3 ft. 9 ins. wide by 1 ft. 9 ins. high and the inner one 6 ft. 2 ins. by 2 ft. 10 ins. The sill of the window was lowered later and cut into the relieving arch of the doorway below; later still it was raised to approximately its possible original position. There is no evidence of any other window in the porch. This window presents difficulties of dating. All early windows in Northumbria have monolithic jambs. Bradwell-on-sea (Essex), a church belonging architecturally to the early Kentish group (but, being built *c.* 663 by Bishop Cedd, a Northumbrian, shows some northern features), does not have monolithic jambs. Gilbert suggested that the Corbridge window might represent a phase of building earlier than the earliest work at Monkwearmouth (674) and Jarrow (682). More likely however it may be merely indicative of differences in ideas and building techniques between Wilfrid's and Biscop's masons.

There is a window in a similar position in the west wall of the porch at Monkwearmouth, but in the second stage. There is no other known example in Northumberland of a window lighting the first stage of a porch. Perhaps the porch was originally of two storeys, the window lighting the second stage. If this were so, the tower arch cannot be of the same age as the porch; it is too tall. As all other early porches in the area have doorways or *small* arches to the nave it may have been the same at Corbridge: a two-storeyed porch with western portal and small opening to nave, and a window in the stage above. The relatively great height of the porch, 26 feet compared with about 13 feet at Monkwearmouth, supports this view.

The tower arch (2) opening to the nave is a Roman arch transferred from else-

---

(1) *Plate* 9; (2) *Plate* 10.

where. It has jambs and voussoirs of through-stones. There are thirteen voussoirs above the springing, each 2 ft. 4 ins. long, i.e. 3 inches shorter than the wall thickness. The arch is stilted by about one foot by an introduced flat stone, thicker than the voussoirs and slightly less in width, set above the moulded imposts. The projecting imposts—10 inches thick—are classical and of different sections; and are 10 ft. 6 ins. above the floor. They are moulded on the soffits and western ends, but are too badly worn on the eastern ends to show whether the moulding was on these ends too. The imposts are not returned along the east and west wall faces but the ends are wide or deep, *c.* 2 feet. The arch is 8 ft. 2 ins. wide[1] and about 16 feet high; very wide and chosen, according to Honeyman, in order to suit the Roman arch head. About eight feet is a not uncommon width for Roman arches in the north of Britain.

The porch was raised into a tower in the eleventh century. The east wall of the tower rested on the western gable of the nave. It was carried up past the ridge of the nave west gable, i.e. to more than 50 feet, at which point there is a plain string course. In the north face of the tower is a small rectangular opening about 5 feet below the string course; its lintel and sill are of single slabs and the jambs just walling. In the east wall, high up under the nave roof, is a small square opening. Above the string is the belfry stage with an opening on each face. Originally these openings may have been similar to those at Bywell St. Andrew's and at Ovingham of similar date, that is double-headed openings with arched lintels supported on imposts and mid-wall shafts. Externally, and visible on the east and north walls only, parts of the old jambs remain, one upright stone and one flat. Internally, too, parts of the old jambs remain; on the south jamb of the east window was a moulded impost the moulding of which was hacked off in 1887 when new bells were hung. The outer faces of the windows were altered in 1715 and replaced by the present large and ugly single openings. The jambs, however, of five small stones each, look ancient and are certainly earlier than the modern imposts and arch heads.

Above the belfry stage is a plain string course. The tower east and west walls probably terminated in gables which are stated to have been covered with water-tabling and surmounted by gable crosses. (An early gable cross apparently of this period is preserved in the church.[2]) The roof was stated to be a high-pitched saddle-back. In these east and west gable walls above the upper string course were windows, comparatively tall and narrow, with their sills on the string course. They were not centrally placed, being a little to the south of centre. When the nave roof was lowered these windows were partly destroyed and partly built up. The bottom jamb stones are large slabs running north and south; the remainder is indistinguishable from walling except that straight joints are visible between walling and blockings. The seven courses of masonry now above the upper string course (quite different from

[1] The author's measurement; C. L. Woolley, op. cit., says 8 ft. 6 ins.
[2] Drawing in C. C. Hodges, (*a*), vii.

that below), the battlemented parapet and flat roof were probably added at the same time, perhaps not earlier than the eighteenth century.

There are no indications on the north and south walls of the porch of any communication with lateral adjuncts as there are at Brixworth (Northants), of probably similar date. The later aisles are built westwards to enclose the lower part of the tower, the western walls of the aisles being flush with the tower west wall. The western end of the south aisle is used as a vestry. The corresponding part of the north aisle has no entrance. In the north wall of the ground floor of the tower is a large blocked rectangular opening; nothing appears to be known about this; was it the former entrance to the western compartment of the north aisle and therefore not Saxon? It seems too near the east end of the wall to have been an original north entrance to the tower. However, running west from the north and south walls and in line with them are traces of foundations[1] of what might have been an atrium or, perhaps more likely, a passageway.

A step 5 inches wide runs along the west face of the porch. It is now level with the ground, but is not a plinth as might be supposed. There is no plinth.

HEXHAM

ST. ANDREW'S CHURCH.[2] This church was built by Wilfrid, 672–8, as a monastic and parochial church. It was made a cathedral in 681 by Archbishop Theodore when he divided the unwieldly diocese of York, of which Wilfrid was bishop, into three separate dioceses of which Hexham was one. Wilfrid himself became the third bishop of Hexham for two periods, 686–91 and 702–9. The bishopric came to an end for unknown reasons, *c.* 821.

The church was adorned by Wilfrid's friend and successor, Acca, who according to Bede, 'enriched the structure of the church with manifold adornments and marvellous workmanship'. To quote Eddius: 'in Hexham he [Wilfrid] founded and built a house of the Lord in honour of St. Andrew the Apostle. My feeble tongue will not permit me to enlarge here upon the depths of the foundations in the earth, and its crypts of wonderfully dressed stones,[3] and the manifold building above the ground, supported by various columns and many side aisles[4] and adorned with walls of notable length and height, surrounded by various winding passages and spiral

[1] The massive bottom stones of the north-west and south-west tower quoins project westwards as roughly cubical blocks partly below and partly above ground.
[2] G. Baldwin Brown; A. W. Clapham, (*a*); C. C. Hodges and J. Gibson; W. H. D. Longstaffe; E. S. Savage and C. C. Hodges; *History of Northumberland*, III; also the old historians and chroniclers: Bede, Eddius Stephanus, Simeon of Durham, Ælred of Rievaulx, Richard of Hexham, William of Malmesbury; also above, pp. 45–6.
[3] Roman worked stones from nearby Corstopitum (Corbridge) were used in its construction.
[4] 'Porticibus' again, see above p. 46, *n.* 3.

stairs leading up and down. . . . Nor have we heard of any other house on this side of the Alps built on such a scale.' A slightly fuller account was given by Richard of Hexham, prior 1142–74, when Wilfrid's nave may have been still standing. He stated that the nave was of three storeys, i.e. that there were tribunes or galleries around it, and that there were *cochleae* or small round towers or turrets containing newel staircases for access to the galleries: these *cochleae* would normally be placed in the angles between transept and nave.

Excavations carried out in 1908–10, before the erection of the present nave, showed that the praises and eulogies the early writers lavished on the church were not excessive or undeserved. The apse and ground plan were revealed. The church was built on a grand scale and must indeed have been impressive, even magnificent. It had three or five aisles, transept with central crossing probably towerless, apse, nave of three storeys and a crypt. Its greatest length was 165 feet. The extreme width across the transept was 126 feet (Hodges). Baldwin Brown suggested about 100 feet for the transeptal length and 24 feet for the east–west transeptal width, with an apse span of *c.* 24 feet. The exterior width of the nave, including the aisles, was *c.* 70 feet. The design was evidently inspired by the basilican churches Wilfrid had seen in Gaul and Italy, and especially by Old St. Peter's at Rome. The twelfth-century historian William of Malmesbury wrote: 'those who have visited Italy allege that at Hexham they see the glories of Rome over again.' It exceeded Brixworth[1] in size and magnificence, Brixworth being 150 feet long by 64 feet wide, with no transept. A cruciform, truly transeptal church in England at so early a date was indeed a phenomenon, perhaps unique.[2] Such another was not built here for perhaps 400 years. It was sufficient in itself to justify the description of Wilfrid, given on other grounds, as an Anglo-Saxon Wolsey.

The church was burnt in 875 during the raiding of the whole of Tyneside by Halfdene the Dane.[3] History is vague after this for nearly two centuries, though it is known that secular priests were administering the establishment until one Eilaf (sometimes called Larwa, or Lareow=Doctor), who had been provost or priest at Hexham since *c.* 1050 and who at the time was treasurer of Durham, obtained a grant of the church *only c.* 1083 from Archbishop Thomas I of York for the purpose of rebuilding it. It is recorded by Ælred of Rievaulx[4] that the church was at this date in ruins. Eilaf died *c.* 1100 but the work of rebuilding, presumably in the Norman manner, was carried on by his son Eilaf II (who was the father of Ælred of Rievaulx) starting as was usual at the east end. He is stated, *inter alia*, to have laid a pavement of squared stones in the east part. Eilaf II died in 1138. Before this, in 1113, Archbishop Thomas II of York had given the monastery to some secular Canons who rebuilt the

---

[1] See below under Brixworth.   [2] See however below under Stow (Lincs).
[3] As recorded by Simeon of Durham, (*b*), I, Bk. II. Chapter VI.
[4] *On the Saints of Hexham.*

monastic buildings in stone. Later Eilaf, just before his death, transferred to the Canons the church also. A little later Archbishop Thurstan of York replaced the secular Canons by Austin Canons, a regular Order then but recently established in England. These Canons continued the rebuilding or perhaps built a new and enlarged Norman choir in order to provide a finer housing for the many relics. Ælred of Rievaulx records a great translation of relics which took place at Hexham in 1154. Probably the Norman apse unearthed by Hodges in 1908 dates from this time.

As the concourse of pilgrims increased the extended accommodation proved inadequate and a further enlargement was begun *c.* 1180. A new and larger chancel was built in the transitional Early English style. Building continued up to 1296 as far as the western walls of the transept, so it is probable that an entirely new church was contemplated. But all was burnt in the dreadful devastation wrought by the Scots in that year. The later history does not concern us here. The monastery was dissolved in 1536 and the church became entirely parochial. But it was greatly neglected and in 1907 the part west of the transept was a grassy yard with odd bits of walling of various ages here and there. This was excavated in 1908–10 under the direction of C. C. Hodges. Unfortunately the excavations were not carried out at all satisfactorily. They were incomplete and far from thorough. The results, such as they were, were inadequately documented and no detailed account of them was published. The accounts given in the books of Hodges and of Baldwin Brown are meagre and the two writers differ seriously in their interpretation of the remains. Nevertheless a great deal was learnt about the early church.

The central nave, according to Hodges, had two aisles on each side, like Old St. Peter's at Rome. The main or inner arcade on the north side of the nave was of four bays, the piers being at a distance apart of *c.* 23 ft. 6 ins. from centre to centre. The outer arcade, dividing the outer from the inner aisle, was stated to be of circular sectioned monolithic columns with coloured capitals. The outer walls were 2 ft. 8 ins. thick. A long stretch of about 70 feet of north walling, extending eastwards to about 25 feet west of the west wall of the mediaeval transept, remains above ground about three courses high and now forms the base of the north wall of the modern nave. The foundations of the south wall were also exposed and some stones of the lowest course appeared to be *in situ*.

At the west end, partly embedded in some mediaeval walling at a height of about 5 or 6 feet with later stonework below, was a strip of walling, *c.* 2 ft. 6 ins. thick, which both Hodges and Baldwin Brown accept as a bit of Wilfrid's church. It is plainly visible in the exterior of the modern nave west wall built around it. This bit of wall enabled the overall length of the church to be determined, and also showed that the west end was square and not apsidal.

The foundations of the south arcade were not exposed (Hodges does not say whether they were looked for).

At the west end too were found foundation courses of huge Roman stones. The foundations were up to about 18 feet square and Hodges inferred they originally supported two western towers. Baldwin Brown surprisingly makes no mention of these massive foundations, from which it may be inferred that he did not accept the idea of western towers in England at so early a date. This is understandable: the earliest towers in England of which we have certain knowledge were of the tenth century and were single western towers. Hodges's foundations must be accepted: he is explicit about them and writes that they were made of large Roman worked stones and that in one of them, in the south-west foundation, was a piece of the inscribed imperial stone of which two larger parts are in the roof of the north passage of the crypt. But they must have been foundations of something other than twin western towers, perhaps of the north and south ends of a long western narthex. Their massiveness may have been due, not to any extra burden they were intended to support but simply to the fact that massive stones were readily available from Corstopitum and were easier and more economical to use than smaller ones. Similar massive stones were used as foundation courses in the crypt.

It may be pointed out that two of our best authorities—A. W. Clapham in this country and C. Ricci in Italy—are of opinion that bell towers were not introduced into Italy till the ninth century and that no surviving example in France can be dated before the tenth century. The basilican churches of Italy were towerless. Stair turrets were earlier and were popular in Carolingian times, but they were small and served a different purpose. On the other hand K. J. Conant states definitely that in the first Church of St. Martin at Tours, built 466–70, all three types of early tower were represented: a fortified or defensive western tower, and central lantern tower with belfry above.[1] He regards this church as the prototype from which St. Riquier (790–800) and other Carolingian towered churches developed. It is not unlikely that Wilfrid may have seen St. Martin's, as rebuilt in the sixth century, during his travels in Gaul; so one cannot say that towers at Hexham were impossible. But the evidence is too slender for positive acceptance; and in any case *twin* western towers would certainly have been an innovation.

Baldwin Brown's view that the church had three and not five aisles is reasonably based and probably correct. He points out that Hodges's foundations of piers were on the line of the present north arcade and were too far apart (23½ feet) to be Wilfrid's row of columns. No other arcade foundations were found (even the southern one is conjectural). A row of columns to the north of the piers would make the aisles less than 10 feet wide. On the other hand Hodges is definite about the piers, but perhaps less definite about the columns: he refers to the discovery of 'two significant pieces, including a half-round pilaster and the drum of a circular column of limestone, which may have been used in the lesser arcade of St. Wilfrid's church, forming

[1] K. J. Conant, Pl. Ib.

when complete, one of the "polished" columns mentioned by Eddius and Prior Richard'. (Elsewhere however he says the columns were monolithic.) The size of the piers is not recorded. The piers may have been pieces of walling between which narrow arches may have been cut. Or, if they were genuine piers, the openings would have been unusually wide, perhaps too wide for stability no matter whether the arcade carried arches or flat lintels. It may be significant that the distance between the pier centres—23½ feet—is almost exactly the same as the stated width of nave— 24 feet. Is it possible that there was a single arcade on each side, with columns between the piers forming intermediate arches of reasonable width?—an instance, as

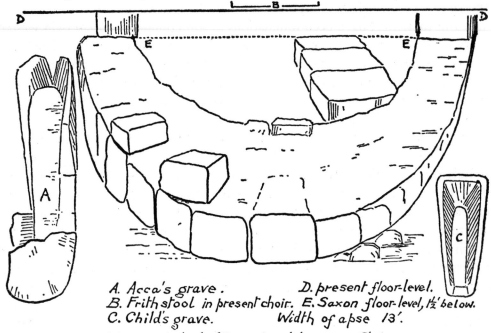

A. Acca's grave.
B. Frithstool in present choir.
C. Child's grave.
D. present floor-level.
E. Saxon floor-level, 1½' below.
Width of apse 13'.

Diagrammatic sketch of Saxon Apse, below present Choir
Fig. 2. Hexham Saxon Apse, drawing

it were, of an Ottonian Anticipation. Such a plan of dividing a nave into squares by piers and sub-dividing the squares into rectangles by columns between the piers was later to be the basis of that Ottonian articulation of nave into bays which later still developed into the Romanesque.

The foundation or base courses of two apses were discovered, a presumed Saxon one below the first bay of the chancel just to the east of the present transept and a later Norman one further to the east below the third bay of the chancel. The Norman apse, 14 to 15 feet wide, is not now viewable as it is beneath the chancel floor. The Saxon apse (Fig. 2), about 13 feet wide internally, can be examined by lifting a trap door and descending a short ladder. This apse is semi-circular, made of wedge-shaped Roman stones and there is a straight piece of walling, a little thicker than the apse wall, lying east–west between the apse wall and the east wall of the transept. Within the apse a small piece of the floor was found undisturbed. It is presumed that in the semicircle of the apse there were the usual stone seats, possibly more than one row, with the bishop's stone seat, or frith stool, in the centre of the row. This seat still exists and has been placed in the church immediately above its presumed former position.

Curiously, Baldwin Brown makes no reference to Hodges's Saxon apse. He appears to think Hodges unearthed only one apse, the Norman one, although Hodges stated explicitly that both apses were exposed in the same week in May 1908. Baldwin Brown rejects the Norman apse as Wilfrid's on the ground that it is too small to accord with the lordly dimensions of the church, and that it is too far to the east—57 feet between the centre of the apse curve and the eastern limit of the crypt—for the crypt to be under the high altar, where it should be if the altar was in its normal place, in the apse. He agrees that in some great churches the high altar was elsewhere, as in the early ninth-century monastic church of St. Gall, in Switzerland, where it was in a presbyterial space to the west of the actual apse, corresponding at Hexham to the raised sanctuary in the central part, or crossing, of the transept. He therefore preferred what he called a conjectural apse of a conjectural width of about 24 feet projecting directly from a conjectural transept in a conjectural position so far to the west that the sanctuary with its high altar would be above the crypt.[1] Clapham considers Baldwin Brown's conjectures to be unnecessary: 'The apparent evidence of the remains may . . . be accepted—that here the crypt was designed to lie below the east end of the nave.' The high altar was usually placed above a crypt to indicate the spot where the body of the dedicatory saint lay below. There were exceptions, however. Moreover at Hexham the crypt contained no saint's body, but many relics, many from overseas. The normal reason for the crypt being under the high altar did not apply to Hexham.

Foundations were also discovered which Hodges thought were those of the western walls of the transepts. Baldwin Brown accepts these only grudgingly as a slender basis for accepting the transeptal character of the church. But other foundations had been discovered in the 1880's under the present south transept. So there is substantial evidence for the existence of transepts further to the east than Baldwin Brown's conjectural ones and the suggested plan of the early church given by Clapham (Fig. 3) shows the western walls of the transept immediately to the east and clear of the eastern limit of the crypt.

At the east end of the nave was a large raised central area or sanctuary, presumably the central portion or crossing of the transepts. The two lower steps of this at the west end remained, and to the west of them, at the east end of the nave and above the crypt, an area of original flooring was found *in situ*. A raised platform at the east

[1] See his conjectural plan, his fig. 71.

end of the sanctuary is presumably where the high altar stood. The west part of this altar platform was reported to be *in situ*, the great blocks being jointed with typical hard Anglo-Saxon mortar.

It was inferred that the sanctuary was separated from adjoining parts by stone screens, or cancelli, with carved panels. Among the loose details identified, now to be

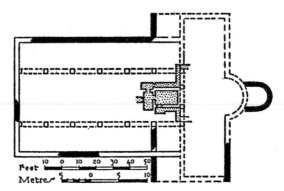

Fig. 3. Hexham, St. Andrew's Saxon Church, suggested plan

seen in the niches in the nave north wall, was a panel found built into the floor of the triforium of the mediaeval south transept. It is a beautiful piece of work.[1] It is a square with a triple border within which is a circular half-round double border, in the centre of which is a rosette. The circular space between the central rosette and the circular border is filled with thirteen carved hollow features similar to, and perhaps the artistic ancestors of, the later so-called 'Jew's harp' ornament of Lincolnshire.[2] The general effect is of one rosette forming the centre of another.

Other structural details discovered, also now reposing in the nave niches, were two pieces of string course decorated one with interlacement the other with a coiled serpent with open mouth attacking a larger beast of which only the snout is left; an impost stone; two pieces of abaci of a capital of one of the columns decorated with small baluster shafts; and a head grave stone with incised plain cross.[3]

Some of the early chroniclers wrote that chapels, oratories or porticus were built out from the main structure. This may well be true; porticus were common, even usual, in these early churches although mainly in the southern part of the country. That no foundations were found does not disprove the chroniclers' statements. The entire site was not excavated; there may have been chapels or porticus or even apses built out on the eastern sides of the transepts where no excavations were carried out. On the other hand, in the interior of the church there were probably many separate chapels or compartments, with altars, divided off by cancelli, as at St. Gall.[4] Some of the fragments found may have belonged to such cancelli; not all may have come

---

[1] See below, p. 301, fig. 33, b.   [2] See below, pp. 300–2.
[3] See H. E. Savage and C. C. Hodges, Pl. XL.   [4] See K. J. Conant, p. 21, fig. 3.

from the screens round the sanctuary. It is significant that Bede wrote that Acca 'set up altars in separate chapels (*distinctis porticibus*) made for the purpose within the walls of the church'.

There is one very puzzling feature. In 1907 Hodges found—hidden by later masonry—and uncovered the base of a Norman respond at the west end of the nave north arcade. Both John Bilson and St. John Hope considered it to be of late Norman date. This might have belonged to a Norman nave built by the Austin Canons in their rebuilding of the early twelfth century preparatory to the great translation of relics of 1154 referred to above. There is no other evidence for the existence of a Norman nave. If it existed Richard of Hexham must have written about Wilfrid's church with this Norman nave in front of him, which would lend support to Allcroft's view that Prior Richard may have attributed to Wilfrid some later work of the monks of Hexham. Alternatively the respond might represent the beginning of a projected Norman nave, not completed, by the Eilafs or by the earlier secular Canons of the early twelfth century. But the Eilafs began their work at the east end; the Norman apse may be theirs, which makes it difficult to explain the respond. As a result it is doubtful, as Baldwin Brown pointed out, whether the nave written about by Prior Richard and which was destroyed by the Scots in 1296 was Wilfrid's or an early Norman one.

The Crypt. The crypt needed no excavation. It has been open and accessible throughout the centuries. It consists of four chambers, two side passages and three

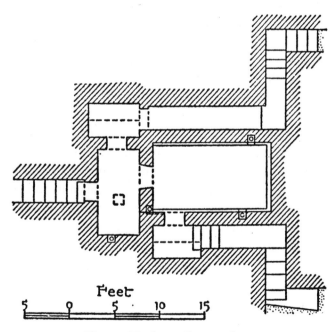

Fig. 4. Hexham Crypt, plan

stairways (Fig. 4). The main chamber, which would house the relics, is rectangular in an east–west direction, 13 ft. 4 ins. long by 8 feet. A smaller chamber, rectangular north–south, lies to the west of the main chamber; this was used probably for preliminary examination and assembling of relics prior to their permanent housing in the main chamber.

Two smaller square chambers at the west ends of the north and south passages were ante-rooms for the assembly of pilgrims to avoid congestion at the door of the main chamber. The north passage was for the use of pilgrims and led to a right-angled bend to the north at its east end leading to a staircase exit to the church above. This point of exit was to the north of and outside the screen surrounding the sanctuary. At the east end of the south passage was a staircase entrance and exit for the use of priests. This entrance, being for priests and monks only, was within the sanctuary above, i.e. on the sanctuary side of the screen. As a result the eastern arm of the north passage is longer than that of the south and probably extended beyond, i.e. to the north of, the north arcade before turning east, while the eastern arm of the southern passage turned east before it reached the south arcade (See Fig. 3). The extremities of these two passages were built up in 1908 as it was necessary to underpin the tower piers which were immediately above them. The floor of the main chamber was cemented at the same time. A staircase at the west end leading from the nave to the western chamber was the entrance for pilgrims. It has 13 steps, the top three being modern renewals.

The entrance to the main chamber is 6 ft. 3 ins. high and has a double-arched lintel. It is slightly splayed towards the exterior giving a width of 2 ft. 3 ins. to 2 ft. 10 ins. The main and western chambers are vaulted with barrel vaults running respectively east–west and north–south. The two small vestibules are roofed with stone slabs laid at acute angles and meeting at an axis or ridge running east–west, i.e. they are gable headed. The passages, which rise somewhat towards the east, have flat, not gabled, coverings of large stone slabs, some 8 inches thick and about 3 ft. 7 ins. long by 2 ft. 10 ins. The walls are built of great blocks chosen as nearly as possible of one thickness, 1 ft. 5 ins., which is the thickness of the wall. (At Ripon the crypt walls are 3 feet thick.) The blocks are worked Roman stones, some of which have inscriptions. Foundation stones of the walls, unhewn stones of varying sizes, are visible in the main chamber. Some of the original plaster on the roofs remains. It is of sand and lime, with too much sand and no hair or other binding material. In consequence, during the years before the modern rebuilding of the church, when the crypt was to some extent open to the elements and became damp through over-ventilation, much plaster disappeared. Since then the crypt has dried out and the remaining plaster has dried and hardened.

In the western chamber in the centre of the crown of the vault is a rectangular opening, widening upwards to the nave floor above: this was a ventilator. It had been blocked with stones; when these were removed soot was seen to be present, from the lamps in the niches of the crypt. There are four lamp niches: one in the south wall of the western ante-chamber, and three in the main chamber, of which two are at the east ends of the north and south walls and one in the extreme south of the west wall.

A stone image bracket of half-octagonal section at the north end of the east wall of the main chamber is probably fifteenth century.

St. Mary's Church. This church was built by Wilfrid after his return from his second period of exile, i.e. in 705–9; it was completed by Acca. It is mentioned very briefly by Eddius and by Richard of Hexham. Unlike St. Andrew's, which was basilican in style, St. Mary's showed marked Byzantine influence. It was in the form of a Greek cross. It had a central space or rotunda, circular or octagonal,[1] probably towered in stone or timber, though this is not certainly known. Four arms or wings projected from the four sides—east, west, north and south. It is the earliest instance in this country of a centrally planned church.

St. Mary's, like St. Andrew's, was burnt by the Danes in 875. Being the smaller church it was restored before St. Andrew's. It continued in use as a church at least up to the time of the renovation of the priory church by the Eilafs.

According to Hodges there are some remains of this church, including two bulbous shaped capitals. Bulbous capitals however appeared late in Anglo-Saxon architectural history and it is unlikely that these came from Wilfrid's church. Probably they were part of a later rebuilding, of which we know little or nothing, or from the thirteenth-century church which succeeded it.

In 1854 during repairs to the house of a Mr. Bell, a local pharmacist, a gable-headed window 6 feet high by 7 inches wide was opened out; this may have come from St. Mary's.

Richard of Hexham wrote of both St. Mary's and St. Peter's in the past tense. Presumably they had disappeared by his time.

INGRAM

St. Michael's Church.[2] The first church here was of early date. All that remains of it if anything is perhaps the lower part of the nave west wall on either side of the tower arch. The church was rebuilt in the earldom of either Siward, 1041–55, or Tostig, 1055–65, perhaps after the destructive raid of Malcolm of Scotland in 1060, although it is just possible that it may be as late as Earl Waltheof, 1072–6, or Walcher, who was also Bishop of Durham, 1076–80. As thus reconstructed the nave was

---

[1] Almost round, *fere rotunda*—in the words of Richard of Hexham.
[2] H. L. Honeyman; N. Pevsner, (e); *History of Northumberland*, XII; F. R. Wilson.

probably of the same dimensions as the present one, 47 ft. 6 ins. long by 15 feet wide. It is orientated east-north-east. The west wall is 2 ft. 9 ins. thick. There may have been north and south chapels (porticus or wings) near the east end, and presumably a chancel. There was also a western adjunct, either a tower or a two-storeyed porch, for the upper part was built or rebuilt in the thirteenth century in the reign of Edward I. It is stated that this adjunct was not bonded into the earlier nave wall, the face of which had been re-pointed before the adjunct was built.

The Tower. The tower is almost square, 12 feet by 11 ft. 6 ins. internally, and heavy looking like early Norman; Pevsner considers the lower part to be early Norman. It has thick walls, 3 ft. 6 ins., built of regular courses of well squared stones, i.e. ashlar, not rubble. It was unbuttressed. A set-back of chamfered stones but no string course, about two-thirds of the way up, divides the tower externally into two stages. The ground floor stage is lighted by narrow windows with arched lintels, *wide* inner splays (typically Norman and unusual in late Anglo-Saxon buildings) but no external chamfers, as Norman windows would be expected to have. Above the set-off are small rectangular windows chamfered all round and above them are bell openings of two small blunt lancet windows side-by-side with the thirteenth-century rebuilding. Each double opening has a single arched lintel, chamfered edges all round and jambs of walling. There are similar openings of the same date at Eglingham in the same county. A wide stepped buttress of about one-third the height of the tower was built against the north end of the tower west wall in the eighteenth century to prevent further subsidence.

Wilson stated that by digging out some of the turf which had accumulated round the tower base he discovered the plinth to have double chamfer of a twelfth- or thirteenth-century type. This is shown in his sketch of the church as it appeared in 1870. Other writers including the author state definitely that this is not so. The plinth has a plain single chamfer above.

The tower was rebuilt stone by stone in 1895–1900. It was under-pinned with a new concrete foundation and then, beginning at or near the base, taken down in small sections and rebuilt piece-meal in cement mortar. All the facing stones were numbered and replaced as nearly as possible in their original positions. Even the dipping courses at the north end of the west wall were imitated in the new stone facing where the buttress stood. The buttress was not retained. The new stone was darkened to match the old but many old stones, especially in the interior, were re-tooled to match the new.

On the tower east wall, *c.* 18 inches above the present nave roof, are what look like the marks of the earlier higher roof. They may however be imitations of the original marks for they appear to be parts of the actual wall stones; i.e. they look like lower projecting edges to the stones immediately above them.

The tower has no external entrances; the only entrance is from the nave by a very wide arch which Wilson thought might have belonged to the earliest church. This seems unlikely in view of its width. The arch is too wide for stability. When built there were no aisle walls to serve as abutments and the tower was not bonded in. The arch began to collapse probably soon after erection; its responds are much out of plumb. The opening had been built up and reduced to a small doorway, probably in the eighteenth century, but was opened out again in the late nineteenth-century rebuilding.

The tower arch may have been pierced when the tower was built, or it is possible the tower may have been built on or within the walls of an earlier and larger western adjunct, perhaps a narthex, to which the arch may have belonged. The arch consists of two flush arches of voussoirs, the upper one probably acting as a relieving arch. This is rare but is no indication of date. Nearly all the arches at Brixworth (Northants), usually dated to the late seventh century, are of this type, though of Roman bricks; and there are relieving arches, though in the masonry above the arch heads, at the western entrance at Corbridge of *c.* late seventh century and in the late twelfth-century chancel arch at Longframlington (Northumberland). The voussoirs are not through-stones; there are two to three per course, a late feature. The imposts are chamfered on the soffit sides only and not returned.

The Nave. The plain square western responds of the north and south nave arcades with clumsy ill-fitting imposts may be pre-Conquest, i.e. of the second church. They rest badly on very thin moulded Early English bases of semi-octagonal plan. This might imply an unfulfilled intention to rebuild the responds when the arcades were erected in the thirteenth century.

At the east end of the nave arcades are stretches of plain walling as far as the fourteenth-century arches of the very short transepts. Each piece of walling has a cornice or impost similar to those of the western responds. It is plain that these imposts originally turned into the transepts, indicating the existence of earlier transepts or porticus. This suggests, but does not prove, that the eleventh-century church was cruciform with wings or porticus, later heightened to transepts in the fourteenth century.

Why these stretches of walling were left intact instead of forming parts of the nave arcade is an interesting question. At the east end they have sunk by about three and a half inches. This might suggest the former existence of a central tower.

Below the return of the impost in the south transept is a Norman scratch dial, an unusual position for a sundial. Probably it was re-used as building material when the transept was built or enlarged.

The church shows some peculiarities remarkably similar to Lavendon Church in north Buckinghamshire, dated by the Royal Commission on Historical Monuments[1] to the mid-eleventh century. Thus, the two towers have almost identical superficial

[1] See below, p. 158.

dimensions, 12 feet by 11 ft. 6 ins. The two chancels and towers are not in line with the naves, the chancels sloping slightly to the south of east and the towers slightly to the north of west. In each case the south wall of the tower is parallel to, but not exactly in line with, the south wall of the chancel, instead of with the axis of the nave which is out of line with both. Ingram nave is of the same length as Lavendon but was rebuilt about 10 inches narrower.

JARROW

ST. PAUL'S CHURCH.[1] It is difficult to write about Jarrow. There are so few remains, hardly more than bits and pieces of the pre-Conquest buildings, that a discussion of it can be little more than an attempted unravelling of its probable or possible history from few and insufficient clues. The present nave is modern, built in 1866 by Sir Gilbert Scott to replace an earlier modern nave which replaced an earlier and apparently the original nave in 1783. The north porch is also modern though it contains a collection of twenty-one baluster shafts and other carved stones from Anglo-Saxon times. These had been taken from the original church and re-used as building material in the nave built in 1783. They were removed to the vestry during the rebuilding of 1866. The central tower is of early post-Conquest date, as also are the monastic remains flanking the south side of the church. Incidentally, in these remains is a gable-headed doorway of characteristic Anglo-Saxon type and rare in Norman times, indicating that such building forms did not end abruptly at the Conquest.

The only certainly early pre-Conquest work is the greater part of the chancel walls, though parts of the tower may include some earlier work.

The church and monastery were founded by Benedict Biscop in 682 on land granted to him by King Ecgfrith of Northumbria and were intended to be part of a joint monastery of St. Peter and St. Paul situated at Monkwearmouth and Jarrow, only seven miles apart. Biscop, while remaining abbot of the joint monastery, appointed his friend Ceolfrith to be sub-Abbot or Prior of Jarrow in 684. According to a dedication stone still in the church the church was dedicated in the fifteenth year of King Ecgfrith, which would be 685. This stone (I), a through-stone, was formerly built into the north wall, at its east end, of the old nave which was destroyed in 1783, an unusual position suggesting that it had been moved from elsewhere. It was then transferred to its present position in the west wall of the tower within the church, i.e. it is visible from the present nave.

[1] Bede; J. R. Boyle, (a), (b) and (c); G. Baldwin Brown; B. Colgrave and T. Romans; J. Gibson; E. C. Gilbert, (d); C. C. Hodges, (a), vii; J. F. Hodgson; W. Hutchinson; N. Pevsner, (c); C. A. R. Radford, (d); H. E. Savage; Simeon of Durham; J. R. Surtees, II.

(I) *Plate* 16.

Some earlier writers doubted whether the stone is of the age of Ceolfrith, but it was admitted by all to be undoubtedly pre-Conquest. Modern writers agree that it is of Ceolfrith's time. The letters are bold Roman capitals except six—one C out of nine, one E out of ten and four O's out of eight—which are in Anglo-Saxon script. It has been inferred from the Anglo-Saxon letters that the stone was carved by an English mason and not by one of Biscop's Gaulish ones. This appears to be a *non sequitur*. Only 6 of 105 letters (including numerals) are Saxon. If Biscop and Wilfrid had to send abroad for building masons, presumably because there were none in Northumbria where the building tradition was in timber, is it probable that there were local masons capable of carving an inscription, and doing it with evident experience? It might seem at least as likely that, as 99 letters out of 105 were Roman, the stone was inscribed by a Gallic mason who, perhaps, was assisted by a Saxon mason or learner who carved a Saxon letter here and there when his master was engaged elsewhere.[1] This suggestion is consistent with the unfinished attempt to carve a Q at the end of the fourth line where there was insufficient space; the attempt was abandoned and the Q repeated in the next line.

It is of great interest that this is the earliest 'written' inscription in Northumbria of known date.

The inscription begins with the Chi-Rho monogram which is so close to the edge of the stone that the left side of the X may have become knocked off. The inscription reads:

> DEDICATIO BASILICAE
> SCI[2] PAVLI VIII KL[3] MAI
> ANNO XV EGFRIDI REG[4]
> CEOLFRID ABB[5] EIVSDEMQ[6]
> Q ECCLES[7] DO[8] AVCTORE
> CONDITORIS ANNO IIII

It may be translated:

> The dedication of the Church of St. Paul, on the 24th of April, in the fifteenth year of King Ecgfrith, and in the fourth year of the Abbot Ceolfrith, who under God founded the same church.

Apparently therefore the church was built in about three years.
Biscop made his sixth journey[9] to Rome in 685–6 and returned with fresh treasures

---

[1] See also above, p. 54.
[3] KL = Kal = Kalend.
[5] ABB = Abbas.
[7] ECCLES = Ecclesiae.
[9] See below under Monkwearmouth.

[2] SCI = Sancti.
[4] REG = Regis.
[6] EIVSDEMQ = Ejusdemque.
[8] DO = Deo.

of books, ornaments and relics for his new churches at Jarrow and Monkwearmouth. It was his desire to make his joint foundation of St. Peter and St. Paul not only a great religious centre but a great centre of learning as well. This in fact it became. Bede spent the whole of his life after 684 at Jarrow and all his books were written there. His influence as writer and teacher has been referred to above.[1]

Ceolfrith the first abbot, 684–716, who became Abbot of Monkwearmouth as well, i.e. of the joint monastery, in 689, arranged for three copies of St. Jerome's version of the Bible, the Vulgate, to be made, one for Jarrow, one for Monkwearmouth and the third as a present to the Pope. These books were made and illuminated at the joint monasteries. He set out in 716[2] to deliver his present to the Pope but died on the journey at Langres in Gaul. Later, in the ninth century, the book was presented to the monastery of Monte Amiata, near Siena, hence its modern name of *Codex Amiatinus*. It eventually passed to the Biblioteca Laurentiana at Florence, where it now is, but was not recognized as being one of Ceolfrith's three books till 1887.[3]

It may indeed be said that the joint monastery of Jarrow and Monkwearmouth, with its later offshoot the scriptorium at York, and Lindisfarne, where the beautiful Lindisfarne Gospels were produced *c.* 700, were the three great centres of learning and of art which made Northumbria famous and its art supreme in the Europe of its time. The influence of this art persisted for centuries and even today its study can be a source of pure delight.

The monastery was sacked and burnt by the Danes in 794. In 866, at the beginning of the great Danish invasions of 865–86, Jarrow, together with Monkwearmouth and other churches in the area, was again burnt. After this, for 200 years, it fades from history. Some repair work however must have been carried out at some time for in 1069 Bishop Æthelwine of Durham and his monks, carrying St. Cuthbert's remains from Durham to Lindisfarne, spent the first night of the journey at Jarrow, so presumably the monastery must have been to some extent habitable. It was burned again in 1069–70 by William the Conqueror and remained derelict until *c.* 1075. In 1074 some Benedictine monks under Abbot Aldwine from Winchcombe in southwest Mercia migrated northwards and after a temporary sojourn at a place called Muncaster, near the modern Newcastle, were established at Jarrow (and later at Monkwearmouth also) in the following year by Bishop Walcher of Durham. The church is described as roofless at this time so presumably the walls were standing. Aldwine rebuilt the monastic buildings and the church, and built at least a part of the present tower. There are no references anywhere to an earlier tower at Jarrow.

In 1083 William of St. Carilef, Bishop of Durham, translated the monks from Jarrow and Monkwearmouth to Durham and replaced them by secular canons from

---

[1] See above, p. 44.
[2] His setting-out is depicted in a panel on the standing cross at Roker, near Sunderland.
[3] See Sir H. Howorth, op. cit.

Durham as he wished to convert his monastic cathedral into a Benedictine Abbey. From this date Jarrow and Monkwearmouth became mere subordinate cells of the great Abbey of Durham.

The Nave. No information about the original nave can be obtained by examination of the present one. A drawing by Buck of 1728 has been reproduced by Savage and by Gilbert; a plan of the old church prior to 1783 in the British Museum is reproduced in Plate 12. A short account of the church before the 1783 rebuilding is given by Hutchinson. From these it appears that the church was 78 feet[1] long by 18 feet wide on the interior and more than 30 and perhaps as much as 40 feet high. It had a low western porch of two stages with a round-headed arch to the nave, on the north jamb of which was a figure of what appeared to be a bishop's crozier's staff and which Hutchinson thought was possibly a re-used part of some ancient tombstone. The porch had a western doorway in the ground stage and a western window in the upper stage, both Anglo-Saxon features. There were three steps down from the porch to the nave. The nave had four chapels, or porticus, on each side entered by round-headed arches of one square order supported by plain rectangular piers. These arches formed the nave arcades; they were *c.* 14 feet wide and sprang from piers 5 feet wide. The chapels were separated by solid walls and were vaulted with plain quadripartite vaults supported on corbels at the four corners.

The eastern part, 16 feet or so, of the nave appeared newer than the rest as though the nave had been extended eastwards to join up with the tower. This part was of solid walling with no openings. There is nothing to suggest a date for the side chapels; they may possibly have been due to Ceolfrith or were perhaps eighth-century insertions. The vaulting certainly was later than the seventh century; it may have been added by Aldwine, or even later, to pre-existing chapels.

The Chancel. The chancel today is 41 ft. 6 ins. long by 15 ft. 9 ins. wide (Hodges); Savage gives 41 ft. 11 ins. long (including the space originally occupied by the west wall) and 15 ft. 8 ins. wide at the west end and 16 ft. 1 in. at the east. Radford's measurements are 39 feet by 15 feet.

It is built of well squared stones (1) which some writers state were taken from Roman buildings. Bede however records that Biscop obtained masons from Gaul, and Conant regards the walling as Gallic and the work of Gallic masons. He writes that Gallic masonry was very characteristic, 'normally a rough core of rubble enclosed by neatly cut facing blocks of stubby rectangular form, set with wide mortar joints,' a description which agrees with the appearance of Jarrow. The quoins are of very large slabs in side alternate arrangement.

The side walls were heightened by *c.* 3 feet at some time, probably *c.* 1300 when

---

[1] G. Baldwin Brown wrote 74 feet, E. C. Gilbert about 65 feet.

(1) *Plate* 11.

the first of the lofty mediaeval windows, the east one in the north wall, was inserted. This however affords no indication of the height of the original walls.

It has two, perhaps three, types of early, pre-Conquest openings:[1]

(1) In the south wall high up near the west end and just east of the large fourteenth-century window are small remains of round heads and jambs, a few stones only but enough to show their similarity to those at the west end of Monkwearmouth nave. They may be of the same period and if so they are of the earliest work at Jarrow. Taylor has shown that this opening was not splayed, as Saxon windows would be, but cut straight through the wall. It was therefore presumably a doorway and may have led to a western gallery (probably of wood), as at the much later churches of Deerhurst, Tredington (Worcs) and Wing (Bucks). Incidentally, a western gallery across a chancel is, to say the least, unusual; the gallery may have been across Ceolfrith's nave, which the present chancel originally was,[2] and the opening contemporary with it. Access would presumably have been by ladder from the exterior since on the interior the gallery would have been a hindrance.

(2) In the south wall *c.* 11 feet above ground are three small windows of pre-Conquest date which have arched lintels, jambs of single upright slabs and thin plain imposts. The single-splayed apertures of two are nearly filled with stone light slabs, cut from single stones, in which small irregularly shaped apertures have been pierced. Two interpretations of this curious feature have been put forward. One, that they were made to fit peculiarly shaped pieces of glass which were available, glass being scarce and not, perhaps, at this time an Anglo-Saxon manufacture. The other, that they were made during a rebuilding after Danish raids as a fire precaution; it would not be easy to throw lighted torches through such small apertures.

(3) In the interior north wall, at about the same height as the small south windows, are two straight joints which may represent the remains of a blocked early window; it may have been one of a range of three, remains of two of which have disappeared.

In the north wall too, at about the middle, is a built-up doorway of early date.[3] It has a round head of five voussoirs. The west jamb consists of one small and one long upright slab with a large cubical block above; the east jamb has two small slabs below and one long slab above. There is some evidence of an early doorway in the south wall near the west end, below the fourteenth-century window: a western exterior jamb and part of an interior arched lintel. In view of the arched lintel it may be contemporary with the range of south windows. Other features are later and of various dates; the narrow, round-headed window above the blocked north doorway is of the late eleventh century.

In the east wall of the chancel are two straight joints equidistant, 2 ft. 7 ins., from

---

[1] Good drawings are given by J. R. Boyle, (*b*), Pls. 7–10.
[2] See below, p. 83.
[3] E. C. Gilbert, (*a*), Pl. IV, 2.

the north and south angles, and from which foundations were traced eastwards. Across the west end of the chancel is the foundation of a wall, just to the east of the tower. There are straight joints, too, where the tower and chancel join and large angle quoins at the same places. These remains indicate that the chancel was once an independent building terminating west just a little east of the present tower (to which of course it is now joined) but extending further to the east than the existing chancel does.

The Tower. The tower (1) has remained substantially unchanged since its erection in *c*. 1075. It is of rectangular section, 21 ft. 3 ins. north–south by 13 feet east–west (Savage). Its narrowness east–west has suggested to some writers that the builders may have found the site encumbered on the west as well as on the east. This seems very unlikely. The chancel of the old church to the west of the tower may have been in ruins, which would explain why the nave was extended eastwards to meet the later tower. There should have been ample room on the west for the erection of a normally square tower. Gilbert suggested that the eastern church (now the chancel) may have had a narthex which normally would be wider north–south than east–west, and that Aldwine built his tower on and to the shape of the narthex foundations. He goes further and considers that the two lower stages of the tower contain a good deal of the earlier narthex fabric; that they were in fact a rebuilding, and that the ground stage may be largely the original ground stage of the Anglian narthex, only slightly modified by Aldwine, who cut the east and west arches. That this may well be so is supported by Savage's observation that in the second stage there are straight joints down the inner corners whereas on the exterior there is normal quoining. It looks as though an inner skin, as Savage called it, was inserted to strengthen the walls in view of the heavier load they had to carry when a tower was erected, as the walls were intended originally for a two-storeyed narthex. Its masonry is rough and irregular. Built into its north wall is a cross fragment ornamented with interlacement.

The tower has four stages.

The first stage, *c*. 15 ft. 6 ins. high, opens to the church, east and west, with low wide arches of plain square-cut type (2). They do not look as old as the narrower north and south arches, though roughly built: their heads are set back behind the jamb faces, a late feature. They are of one order with arched heads of slabs, not true voussoirs, and with plain chamfered imposts. There were narrow arches of Saxon type on the north and south. One has a jamb of one tall pillar stone, the other jamb has two uprights and a middle flat. The heads are of rough voussoirs, similar to those of the blocked original north doorway. The central span was vaulted with a quadripartite vault.

---

(1) *Plate* 13; (2) *Plate* 14.

The second stage had originally five arched openings,[1] two on the east, one on the west and one on the north and south. The western one is wide and round-headed, of Norman type, with square-cut voussoirs, plain-chamfered imposts and chamfered jambs. It may have opened to an eastern upper chamber in the nave. Of the two cut straight through in the east wall the central one is of Norman type, like the one in the west wall but smaller. The one to the south is close to the south wall and is of Saxon type; it has no imposts and the jambs are of long upright stones. On the exterior face of the wall is a blocked opening centrally placed; it may be earlier than the other two.

The openings in the north and south walls are double-splayed and are therefore windows. The south one has a head of four long irregular square-cut rough voussoirs, no imposts, and jambs of three stones each, of similar heights but arranged upright-flat-upright. It is now used as a doorway,[2] the only entrance to the stage by ladder from outside, its sill being level with the floor. The floor presumably must have been raised at some time, perhaps when the stage below was vaulted. Here is another suggestion that the stage is ancient, like the one below, and perhaps part of a pre-existing narthex. The window on the north looks late Norman because at a later date a half round moulding was put round the opening and complex billet ornament added to the head and hood mould. The opening is not Norman; no Norman opening would be double splayed.

The third stage, Aldwine's original belfry, begins at c. 34 feet up. It has three openings. In the west wall a few feet above the floor is an unsplayed gable-headed opening, now blocked, c. 7 feet by 2 feet. The present roof line cuts across it, but originally it would have been below the roof ridge communicating probably with an inter-roof chamber. The openings in the north and south walls are of the typical Anglo-Saxon belfry type: two-light openings with heads of voussoirs, mid-wall shafts of c. 7 inches in diameter and projecting chamfered imposts above supporting the arch head. The shafts have necked bulbous bases and capitals which are corbelled out to the thickness of the wall with square-cut abaci to support the imposts, as at Bolam and Sompting. The jambs are of four similar sized slabs each, not through-stones, with thin imposts. There is no belfry or other opening in the east wall, perhaps because the chancel roof may have been above this level. There is a string course between stages three and four; just below this the rectangular tower is made more square by three-stepped off-sets on the north and south walls.

The fourth stage begins at c. 46 feet up. It is a belfry, and probably a later though not much later addition to Aldwine's belfry, for the openings of the usual double type, two in each east and west wall and one in each of the north and south, are of definitely Norman type. They have double arched lintels set in a wide voussoired relieving arch above, the whole set back in rectangular panels. The circular shafts

[1] See plan in E. C. Gilbert, (d), fig. 15.   [2] See E. C. Gilbert, fig. 14.

82

have moulded bulbous bases, of more advanced type than those of the belfry openings in the third stage, and voluted capitals of very definite Norman type.

The south cloister too may probably be the work of Aldwine. The inner walls of the south and west range remain in part. They are, like the tower, of much weathered ashlar. Two doorways remain, one round-headed, of two plain orders, very thin imposts, angle shafts with bulbous bases and cushion capitals with plain neckings, jambs of similar stones to the walling. The tympanum is of three stones, the lower one acting as a massive lintel filling almost the entire tympanum space. There is also a gable-headed doorway (1) with thin chamfered imposts and jambs of fairly well-dressed stones similar to but larger than the walling stones, and arranged in approximately face-alternate manner.

The interpretation of these somewhat scanty details which may be accepted as reasonable—even probable, for it fits the known facts—is due to Hodges, based on a suggestion of Boyle that at Jarrow we have the remains of two churches later combined into one. This is not improbable. There were three churches at Monkwearmouth, and three, perhaps four, at Hexham, two very close together, and clusters of small churches were common, even usual, in Irish monasteries. At Canterbury and at Glastonbury there was more than one church, in each case close together and in axial relationship.

The old, pre-1783, nave was the original nave of Benedict Biscop and on the site of the east part of it, later rebuilt, was a short square chancel which did not extend as far as the site of the present tower. The lost crozier ornament in the porch may have been a serpentine animal similar to those in Monkwearmouth porch, a suggestion which supports the view that the nave may have been Biscop's work. The chapels north and south of the nave may have been oratories added by Ceolfrith, though vaulted much later in the eleventh century, perhaps when the nave was extended eastwards by walls added to its side walls to meet the present tower; the eastern part was clearly later than the western.

The smaller eastern church was probably of a date not much later than the western one, though possibly later than Bede's time for he does not mention it. Its nave is the present chancel. Its chancel, now destroyed, was also short and square and is represented by the two straight joints in the east wall and the foundations to the east of these.

The present chancel is of two periods. The remains of the larger opening high up at the west end of the south wall may be part of the original church—Biscop's church. This earlier church, being the smaller of the two, was the one most likely to be repaired, with the limited means available, after the Danish raids and to this rebuilding the smaller windows with the arched lintels to the east of and lower than the older openings probably belonged. This church would have remained in use till

---

(1) *Plate* 15.

William the Conqueror destroyed it in 1069 after which it remained abandoned until Aldwine and his monks arrived and settled here in 1075. He found both churches roofless and he combined them by removing the two chancels, carrying the nave walls of the western church up to his intended tower, and joining the nave of the eastern church to the tower to form a chancel. Hodges added that the result was a not uncommon Norman plan: a long aisleless nave and chancel with intervening tower, as at Iffley (Oxon) and in a more or less altered form at other places. This last conclusion of Hodges, implying that Aldwine's work was consciously Norman, seems difficult to justify either historically or architecturally. It is certainly not true that a building erected after 1066 must necessarily be Norman. It should be remembered that Aldwine and his monks were Saxons. Walcher, Bishop of Durham, who settled them at Jarrow was a Lotharingian from Liége well known for his saintly life and not for any building activities. Northumbria was a wild and turbulent area only nominally subdued by William who had devastated the district and burnt Jarrow only a few years before. Moreover, it was William's policy at first to leave Northumbria to be ruled by native earls acting for him: Copsi, 1067; Cospatric, 1067–72; Waltheof, 1072–6. It seems most unlikely that there were Norman masons and builders available in the north to help Aldwine erect a Norman church, even if he had wanted one. The probability appears to be that the work was done by a Saxon, Aldwine, with Saxon ideas, assisted by Saxon, or Anglian, masons available in the north, or whom he had brought with him from the south, for the double-splaying of some of his windows was a southern, not a northern, feature. The first genuinely Norman building to be erected in this area was the great monastic cathedral at Durham, begun in 1093 by the Norman bishop, William of St. Carilef, who was in a position to import Norman masons and craftsmen to convert his Norman ideas of building into stone.

Architecturally, too, Hodges's inference seems weak. The rough-looking masonry, the gable-headed windows, the two-light lower belfry windows with arched lintels and mid-wall shafts, and corbelled-out capitals are essentially Anglo-Saxon ideas. Even the tower arches are of very late Anglo-Saxon type. Only the vaulting is non-Saxon. But we do not really know the date of this; with the vaulting of the side chapels it may be later. The only unquestionably Norman work is the fourth stage of the tower and that bears much evidence of being later than Aldwine, though perhaps not much later. The Norman Durham Cathedral was begun *c.* 1092; from then on Norman ideas would percolate outwards, for masons were essentially travellers, not tied to the soil like the peasants, and the exchanging of ideas and methods would be easy.

MONKWEARMOUTH

ST. PETER'S CHURCH. This church and St. Paul's at Jarrow are perhaps the most interesting and puzzling of all Anglo-Saxon churches. They have been very extensively studied. Each fresh examination by a fresh mind while answering some old questions raises new ones for further study.

The main early authorities are Bede of Jarrow (d. 735) and Simeon of Durham (d. *c.* 1130). Historical accounts are given by J. R. Surtees, W. Hutchinson, and J. R. Boyle, (*d*). The most important modern writers on Monkwearmouth are the Greenwell Committee, just before the extensive excavations, restoration and rebuilding of 1866, C. C. Hodges in 1894, J. Hall during the later rebuilding of 1924–5, Baldwin Brown in 1925, E. C. Gilbert in 1947, B. Colgrave in 1948 and C. A. R. Radford in 1954. Of these the most important and certainly the most rewarding are the studies of Hall and of Gilbert. The following description of the church is based on all the authorities mentioned, including the present writer's observations; the dating and interpretative remarks are based largely on Hall and Gilbert, though differing in some respects from these two writers.

The church and monastery of Monkwearmouth were founded by Benedict Biscop in 674 on land granted to him by King Ecgfrith of Northumbria. Perhaps no founder of a church ever stamped it with his own personality as Biscop did Monkwearmouth. Some account, however short, of Biscop's career seems necessary to a proper understanding and appreciation of its architecture and ornamentation. He was born in 628 of a noble family related to the Royal House. He early decided to adopt a religious calling and, like all other Northumbrian clerics, was trained in the Scoto-Celtic church. He first visited Rome in 653, accompanied part of the way by Wilfrid of Ripon. His second and most important visit was in 665 after which he spent two years in the monastery of Lérins in southern France and here he became strongly attached to the Benedictine Rule. From Lérins he went again to Rome and returned to England in 669 as guide to Theodore. He remained at Canterbury for two years as Abbot of SS. Peter and Paul, and then made his fourth visit to Rome in 671. It was after this visit that he founded his monastery at Monkwearmouth in 674. According to Bede the church was built in one year. 'When the work was drawing to completion, he sent messengers to Gaul to fetch makers of glass [more properly artificers], who were at this time unknown in Britain, that they might glaze the windows of his church, with the cloisters and refectories. This was done, and they came, and not only finished the work required, but taught the English nation their handicraft. . . .'

In 678–9 Biscop made a fifth visit to Rome, accompanied by his friend Ceolfrith, whom he later made Abbot of Jarrow, and brought back pictures, books, relics for the adornment of his church. He also brought with him John, the arch-chanter of the church of St. Peter in Rome and Abbot of the monastery of St. Martin, to develop the music at his new church and to teach it. After a sixth visit to Rome in 685–6 he died in 689.

Besides the church of St. Peter there were two other early churches in the monastery dedicated respectively to St. Mary and St. Lawrence. St. Mary's was certainly, and St. Lawrence probably, built by Biscop. There are no remains of these and nothing apart from their actual existence is known about them.

In 866, at the very beginning of the great Danish invasions of 865–86, Monkwearmouth was burnt, together with Jarrow, Whitby, Tynemouth and Lindisfarne priories. After this the church fades from history for two hundred years, though presumably some restoration was undertaken at some unknown time for it was again burned by Malcolm of Scotland or by William the Conqueror in 1069–70. Abbot Aldwine and his monks, from Winchcombe in south-west Mercia, after settling and building at Jarrow in 1075, were transferred to Monkwearmouth a year or two later by Bishop Walcher of Durham. According to Simeon, 'They made little dwellings of boughs, and took pains to clear out the church of St. Peter, of which only the half-ruined walls were then standing; they felled the trees and uprooted the briars and thorns, which had filled the whole structure; and when the roof was laid as it is seen at this day, they had done their best to restore the place to a fit state. . . .' Simeon makes no reference to the tower.

In 1083 William of St. Carilef, Bishop of Durham, translated the monks of Jarrow and Monkwearmouth to Durham and replaced them by secular canons as he wished to convert Durham into a Benedictine Abbey. From this date Monkwearmouth and Jarrow became mere subordinate cells of the great Abbey of Durham.

There were alterations and additions in the fourteenth century. But by the nineteenth it had again become almost derelict. The greater part of the western porch was hidden by many years' accumulation of ballast and cinders from collier ships of the local ship owners. Then in 1866 a general restoration was begun under the auspices of the Architectural and Archaeological Society of Durham and Northumberland. The accumulated waste round the lower parts of the tower was cleared away and the three arches in the ground floor of the tower opened out. All the remaining original features of the church were brought to light. Foundations were discovered to the west of the tower, though how far to the west they ran was not determined, and, according to Greenwell, also on the north and south, all belonging presumably to early western outbuildings. Later excavation in 1924 revealed no foundations to north and south but confirmed those to the west. These, as at Jarrow, may have led to or been part of another church—one of the two which have disappeared without trace. Colgrave thinks this doubtful as it would have hidden the rich ornamentation of the porch. But there was undoubtedly something in front of the porch so the ornamentation would be hidden to some extent. Another possibility is that the porch may have formed part of a western narthex, as at Brixworth (Northants) of much the same date.

The only parts of the present church undoubtedly Anglo-Saxon are the tower, the west wall of the nave, some eastern nave quoins like those at Bywell St. Peter's. In some respects there is close similarity between these two churches and a close comparative study of the two made by Gilbert proved most revealing: they both have similar high walls and high-up windows, remaining east nave quoins and similar general measurements.[1] At Monkwearmouth the present nave is built on the original Anglo-Saxon foundations, as indicated by the Anglo-Saxon west wall and eastern quoins. It is 65 feet long by 19 feet wide (Baldwin Brown), or according to Hodges 63 ft. 6 ins. by 18 ft. 6 ins. internally. Patterson gives external measurements as 68 feet by 22 ft. 8 ins. It had probably a square chancel (again like Bywell) as wide as the present one, which would explain why no original chancel foundations were discovered in the excavations of 1866. Bede called it a porticus—a chapel with an altar, perhaps with a very narrow chancel arch as at Escomb. It must be conceded however that there is no positive evidence as to the type of east end, whether square or apsidal. In either case, behind the high altar would probably be the usual stone seating arrangements for the presbyters with the Abbot's seat in the centre against the east wall. In the vestry are two stone lions dated by Clapham (op. cit., (*h*)) to between 674 and 890 and which he showed convincingly to be bench supports, one of the Abbot's seat and the other of the presbyters' bench on the north side.

The porch was apparently a little later, for it is built up against but not bonded into the west wall; but not much later, for Eosterwine, the first abbot appointed by Biscop, was buried in it in 685. Was it an afterthought, an original touch of Biscop's original mind? For it and the very high walls appear to have been innovations in England at this time. It may well be that this is the first western porch to be erected in England. There is no evidence that the early Kentish churches of St. Augustine originally had western porches; the latest of these, Reculver, dated to 669, had no porch unless it was of wood; the existing foundations are of later date. Bradwell-on-Sea (Essex) had a porch but there is no evidence that it is contemporary with the church; it may have been added later. Moreover, Bradwell was built by Bishop Cedd, a Northumbrian, *c.* 660–3; it has the Northumbrian features of relatively great length and height and its porch if it had one may have been due to Northumbrian influence.[2]

The long narrow nave and high walls were also innovations in England. Baldwin Brown thought a long nave an Anglo-Saxon peculiarity. If it were, why was it confined to the Anglian north? In any case, where did the idea come from? Clapham suggested it might be of Gallic origin, as Biscop obtained masons from Gaul. This might be so but unfortunately there are singularly few remains of the Merovingian era in France and none that throw any light on this question. It is not of Italian or of Italo-Byzantine or of Scoto-Celtic origin. It might be, as Gilbert suggested, an original Anglian contribution to church architecture and design or, perhaps more likely, an original contribution by Biscop himself.

[1] See above, under Bywell, St. Peter's, p. 57.

[2] Bishop Cedd returned to Northumbria in 663 or 664 to die. Bradwell, therefore, must be at least ten years earlier than Monkwearmouth. The Northumbrian influence supposedly seen at Bradwell is consequently puzzling.

Similarly with the high walls and high-up windows, Baldwin Brown regarded them as a safety measure against firing by Danes: it is not easy to throw lighted torches through such windows. But those high walls are pre-Danish. Whether the earlier Pictish raids were sufficiently frequent and serious in the Anglo-Saxon period to result in such protective measures is not known. Here again perhaps we have an original Anglian or Biscopian innovation.

Gilbert makes the intriguing point that such high walls and windows suggest that the church may have been of two storeys, the high-up windows lighting the upper storey, in which case there may have been a lower range of windows to light the lower storey. Some Irish churches of the ninth century had two storeys but there is no evidence of such churches prior to Monkwearmouth unless Biscop had seen some in Gaul of which we now know nothing. There is of course no evidence in the church either of two storeys or of two ranges of windows for the existing side walls are not original. The idea is pure suggestion: Gilbert himself wrote, 'We cannot, of course, assume that it occurred at Monkwearmouth unless further evidence appears, but it must be borne in mind.' If this were so the upper floor would have been about 21 feet up; below this the sills of the lower ranges of windows might have been, say, about 14 feet above the floor.

There are other features in the church characteristically Northumbrian, or Anglian, or Saxon. Porticus flanking the nave derive immediately from Kent and ultimately from Italy–Byzantium. Many of the window and door openings are closed above with round arched heads of real, often finely worked, voussoirs. These would be familiar to the Northumbrians in the many Roman remains in the area. At least two genuine Roman arches are almost certainly to be found transported from elsewhere and re-erected in Corbridge[1] and Escomb churches. And Biscop would have seen others during his travels. It is interesting and significant that in the church are also openings closed with arched lintels, i.e. a round arch cut from a single stone. Such arched lintels are characteristic of and widespread throughout the entire Anglo-Saxon period and are found even in early post-Conquest work. Was this, too, asked Gilbert, an original Anglian contribution to church building?—a contribution made, after the departure of Biscop's foreign masons, by a people more familiar with timber building in attempts to copy these round-headed openings. In this connection there is one doorway[2] in the second stage of the tower which is rectangular, made of long thin stones, with sill and flat lintel exactly the width of the opening plus jambs, a mere copy in stone, as it were, of an ordinary timber-framed doorway. This is an early feature; there are similar doorways at St. Martin's (Canterbury) and at Bradwell-on-Sea (Essex).

Against this background of history, inference, suggestion and speculation a detailed description of the church, necessary in any case for a real understanding of it, may

---

[1] See above, under Corbridge, p. 62.   [2] See below, p. 94.

seem less indigestable: the description will strengthen the story and the story will illuminate the detailed account.

The Nave. The West Wall: Interior (1). On the interior there is evidence of three building periods. The lower part up to the sill of the upper central opening, about 14 feet, is of rough uncut rubble with wide mortar joints. There is a little herring-boning, also in rubble, which goes right through the wall on the south side of the interior western doorway. It consists of a single course of seven or eight stones only. It is in the blocking of the old doorway which suggests that it may be seventh century. There are clear indications in the wall to the south of the central western doorway of a built-up portion of a round-headed opening. It is not centrally placed being close to the south end of the wall suggesting a space for an altar to the north, either in the nave or, perhaps, in the porch. The opening was about 12 feet by 4 feet, very unusual proportions. It may have been built up when it was decided to build a porch, which would require a more central opening.

Above 14 feet and up to the south gable mark the rubble is fairly well squared, suggesting a later rebuilding probably after the damage suffered during the earlier Danish raids of the late eighth century. Here and there are some roughly carved stones which may be cross fragments broken by the Danes and later re-used as building material. Above the upper central opening is built-in a half-round stone—which has a slight central half-round depression—placed centrally about 20 feet from the floor which Hall considered to be a saddle stone of a porch. If so, it must have belonged to a one-storeyed porch of about 12 feet high to its eaves, and not to a second storey with apex at about 28 feet. Above this is a blocked-up square-headed opening 2 ft. 3 ins. wide with sill 27 feet above floor level.[1]

Above the gable mark the walling is again slightly different; it probably belongs to Aldwine's rebuilding of *c.* 1075.

The central arched opening leading to the tower[2] is a doorway, not a tower arch. Though not universal, doorways rather than arches were the customary entrances to porches from naves especially in the North in the Early Saxon period. This one is 3 ft. 7 ins. wide between the rebates. It has jambs each of one large upright slab 4 ft. 4 ins. high with flat imposts flush with the jamb face and running far into the walls on north and south. Its round head is of eight large voussoirs of through-stones and of the usual one order.

Above the west doorway, at 14 ft. 2 ins., is a doorway to the upper stage of the original porch. This is now the only means of access to the interior of the tower. It was originally a window. Its east face is modern to half the wall thickness; its western face has its original arched lintel. The aperture is 4 ft. 2 ins. by 1 ft. 6 ins. The head is

[1] See below, p. 96. [2] E. C. Gilbert, (b), Pl. IV, 2.

deeply and its jambs slightly splayed inwards towards the tower, i.e. it was intended to light the porch from the nave.

Further above, at 23 feet, are two windows[1] 11 feet apart. They are single-splayed internally to the nave and the apertures measure 4 ft. 3 ins. by 1 ft. 6 ins. externally, and 5 ft. 5 ins. by 2 ft. 9 ins. internally. Each head is of three long curved voussoirs, with short thin imposts to north and south jambs.[2] These windows are of unique design in that in the lower part of the jambs, below the single upright stones which form the jambs, are baluster shafts similar to those in the porch[3] but less elaborate. The shafts are of the same height as the long upward-sloping sills so that their tops are on a level with the bottom of the window apertures. They show signs of being partly lathe turned and partly not, being not strictly circular throughout their length. These windows had been plastered up and were opened out in 1866. It was found that the fronts, i.e. the east faces, of the shafts had been hacked off flush with the wall face, which suggests that they may have been transferred here from elsewhere, the defacing being necessary to make them fit their new position snugly. Hall agrees that they were re-used but says the hacking was to enable a smooth plaster surface to be obtained as the balusters protruded beyond the wall face. They were turned round in 1866 so that their sound faces now face east.

The West Wall: Exterior. The wall is only 2 ft. 0½ in. thick. It is 23 ft. 6 ins. wide and extends 6 ft. 2½ ins. north and 6 ft. 6 ins. south of the tower. It is 31 feet to the springing of the gable. Within the tower is a horizontal band of cut stone work from about 27 feet to 35 feet up. Above this the rubble wall continues to about 42 feet and then comes the walling of the superimposed tower. The gable is steep, about 50° to the horizontal, and the apex of the original nave was at about 52 feet above floor level. On either side of the tower the exterior of the nave wall has been refaced from about 26 feet up on the north and from rather lower on the south; in between the old wall appears unbroken.

In the middle of the band of cut stones surviving within the tower is a hollow-moulded string course, about 12 inches deep; this therefore looks like an insertion. To the north and south of the tower this string course has been cut away but is still visible and it does not reach the quoins, which also suggests it is an insertion.

The south-west quoins are replacements, probably of the rebuilding of 1866. The lower north-west quoins show signs of fire damage, which suggests they are original. The first ten from the ground are well cut big stones, measuring about 18 inches thick, lying on their sides in good side-alternate[4] arrangement. Baldwin Brown wrote that they are not big stone work, but they are; one at least measures 3 ft. 5 ins. by 16 inches by 8 inches. Their megalithic character may not be immediately recog-

---

[1] E. C. Gilbert, (b), p. 146, fig. 2; also Canon W. Greenwell, Pl. V; and Boyle, Pl. IV.
[2] E. C. Gilbert wrote that imposts were on the south jambs only and not on the north; this is not so.
[3] See below, p. 92.   [4] E. C. Gilbert, (b), Pl. II, 2.

nized on account of their good dressing. The quoins above these ten, including some re-used material, are poor, irregular and formless, rather similar to some eleventh-century work. They may be part of Aldwine's rebuilding. He may also have hacked away the string course.

The Nave: East End. At the east end of the nave are some old quoins which enable the original nave measurements to be ascertained.

The south respond of the chancel arch has three engaged half-columns, one on the east and west face and one on the face of the soffit. These are later and the capitals are modern, but the three half bases are of the slightly squashed bulbous type sometimes seen in very late Anglo-Saxon work as at Bosham (Sussex) and Corhampton (Hants). They are not quite circular in plan, they rest on square blocks and have half round neckings above. They are probably part of Aldwine's work of *c.* 1075 and should be compared with the somewhat similar bases at Bywell St. Peter[1] and Jarrow.

The Tower: Exterior.[2] The tower (I) is of five stages, separated by string courses, of a total height of 60 feet. There are no offsets between the stages. The individual stages measure 13 feet, 8 feet, 10 feet, 17 feet and 12 feet respectively. The first or lowest stage is, or corresponds to, the original one-storeyed porch to the church. Its walls are very slightly later than the lower, oldest, part of the nave west wall. The fabric is of similar material, uncut rubble of similar size, though much patched on the exterior with small square stones, especially on the south and west. Built into the north wall about one foot from the ground on the exterior is a stone 12 inches by 6 inches with crudely carved interlacement. A similar one is in the interior north wall which Hall stated was proved to be of the same date as the porch, though he gives no evidence. Another similar stone is in the vestry show case. These may be cross frag-ments used in early repair or restoration work after the Danish raids, though Hall thought they proved a late, post-Danish, date for the original building.

The quoins are not very similar to those of the nave wall; they are smaller and include more square-ended stones. Some, though old, are renewals. They show the signifi-cant peculiarity that those on the north and south correspond in their irregularities.

The external measurements are:[3] west wall 11 ft. 4½ ins. with projections from the nave wall of 11 ft. 1½ ins. on the north and 11 ft. 2¾ ins. on the south. Baldwin Brown states that the weight of the tower has caused the western arch to spread slightly so that here the tower is 'an inch or two' wider than at the summit. As the walls are only 1 ft. 9 ins. thick, intended only for a one-storeyed porch, this spreading is not sur-prising. It was discovered during the repairs of 1924–5 that the tower had become inclined westward out of vertical leaving a gap of some inches between it and the

[1] E. C. Gilbert, (*a*), Pl. II, 2.
[2] J. R. Boyle, Pl. III, shows west end before restoration; also A. W. Clapham, (*a*), Pl. 7.
[3] See plan in E. C. Gilbert, (*b*), p. 155, fig. 3.

(I) *Plates* 17, 18.

upper part of the nave wall. This again is not surprising as the porch and subsequent tower were not bonded into the nave wall. In view of this, the fact that the tower has remained in being for nearly a thousand years is a great compliment to the excellence of Saxon mortar.

The First Stage (1). The internal dimensions are 8 ft. 2½ ins. north–south and 9 ft. 5 ins. east–west. It is covered with a barrel vault, 15 ins. thick, of rectangular rubble blocks quite different from the walling and much later than the walls, running east–west. The crown of the vault is 12 ft. 6 ins. above the floor. The vault springing is cut into the porch walls, an indication that the vault is a later insertion not, as Baldwin Brown seemed to think, contemporary with the walls; nevertheless it is the earliest vault above ground in the country.[1]

There are arched openings on all four sides, as at Brixworth (Northants) of similar early date. Those on the north, east (opening to the nave) and south are doorways rebated deeply to about half-way through the jambs externally for doors to open outwards from the porch. The western opening is not rebated; it was never a door-way, just an open entrance to the porch. It is 7 feet high and 4 ft. 8½ ins. wide between jambs. The jambs are of monolithic slabs of through-stones, 4 ft. 3 ins. high, with flat slabs lying above. Above these, forming the upper parts of the jambs are two baluster shafts on each side (1), each about 1 ft. 9 ins. high and 10 inches in diameter. The shafts do not bulge and are covered with many half-round projections and hollows as though turned on a lathe, as indeed they probably were. Above these twin collon-nettes are slab imposts, 11 inches high, plain-chamfered below on the soffit sides only and with small roll mouldings all round on the arrises, i.e. three on each impost. The arch head is of nine carefully cut voussoirs of various sizes, all through-stones. The arrises between the west and east faces and soffit have small roll mouldings like the imposts. All these roll mouldings are very badly worn. Baldwin Brown and Gilbert state that the arch head is recessed on both faces. This is true but misleading, as it might suggest a recessed two-ordered arch. The arch head is a plain, square-edged arch of one order the outer faces of which have their lower halves recessed by dressing, 'planing', by about a millimetre; the slight shadow cast makes it look like a semicircular quirk round the arch head.

The monolithic jambs have similar ornamentation on both faces: two intertwined long animals of no recognizable species, with snake-like heads with much elongated snouts (2), and fish-like tails. Their bodies are twisted together from the tails down-wards along the centre of the slab face. They then diverge at right angles along the

---

[1] Two underground vaults in Wilfrid's crypts at Hexham and Ripon are earlier by, perhaps, more than a century. G. Baldwin Brown wrote that the Monkwearmouth vault agrees in character with Wilfrid's crypt vaults. This is not so: it agrees only in shape, its material is quite different.

---

(1) *Plate* 18; (2) *Plate* 21.

base and then upwards along the corners of the jambs, forming roll mouldings, till they reach the upper part of the top slab where they converge and develop into heads with their snouts crossed as though biting each other.[1] A modern copy in stone mosaic is in the centre of the chancel floor. This ornamentation has a bearing on the dating of the church and will be considered further below.[2]

The doorways on the north, south[3] and east have jambs of large upright single slabs, slab imposts running far into the wall, very large sill stones, and round heads of seven large voussoirs each, with unmoulded square edges. The imposts are flush with the wall face and with the soffit. The crowns of both arch heads are single-splayed outwards. If the entire arch head were splayed it would have fitted awkwardly on the unsplayed imposts and jambs. To avoid this the splay decreases downwards towards the springing stones which are not splayed. This simple but ingenious device is rare. The writer can recall no other example of it. The north and south openings are 2 ft. 6 ins. wide, compared with 3 ft. 7 ins. for the eastern opening and 4 ft. 8 ins. on the western.

Radford considers that the three arches are original, with the porch (which may have been the central feature of a series of western adjuncts, possibly a narthex, extending along the whole width of the west front, as at Brixworth). The patched south wall and renewed lower quoins are consistent with this view. He also thinks it likely that the sculptured frieze separating the first and second stages and which, unlike string courses, is on the west face only instead of extending all round the tower, may have continued along the whole length of this western narthex.

The Second Stage. The gable lines of the second stage, still visible on the interior wall of the tower (the west face of the nave wall), fouled the two western windows of the nave,[4] which proves that the windows are original. Moreover, the saddle stone noticed by Hall[5] on the east side of the nave wall must have belonged to a one-storeyed porch. Between the two storeys is a carved string course or frieze (I), referred to above, on the exterior west wall face only, 12 inches wide and 13 ft. 3 ins. above ground level, badly decayed. It was divided into panels with cable borders (as on the Easby cross), carved in low relief with animals and at least one human figure, one in each panel.[6] The upper edge originally corresponded to the floor of the second stage before it was raised.[7] There are in some other churches bits of decorated string course of pre-Conquest date; this is the only decorated one now *in situ*, except the

---

[1] See C. C. Hodges, (*a*), vii, good drawing, p. 145; also G. Baldwin Brown, p. 125, fig. 58.
[2] Below, pp. 99–100.   [3] Canon W. Greenwell, Pl. 3.
[4] See E. C. Gilbert, (*b*), p. 159, fig. 7: a sectional drawing of the first three stages.
[5] See above, p. 89.
[6] See C. C. Hodges, (*a*), vii, p. 145, drawing: also J. R. Boyle, (*d*), Pl. IV.
[7] See below, p. 98.

(I) *Plate* 18.

geometrically decorated one at Deerhurst. This stage is now only 6 ft. 10 ins. high internally. The floor is of clinker bricks laid flat-wise on the vault below. Since its gable was removed for the construction of the tower it now has no ceiling and is open to the tower. It had openings on all four faces, those on the south (now blocked) and west being windows and those on the north (now blocked) and east doorways.

Internally the second stage throws much light on the history of the church, as brought out by both Hall and Gilbert.[1] It can be entered only by the doorway, originally a window, referred to above, from the nave. The single splay of this opening is towards the tower; the aperture on the nave side (modern) is 4 ft. 6 ins. by 1 ft. 6 ins., and on the tower side 5 feet by 2 ft. 6 ins. No door would be splayed as much as this. There are similar windows in similar positions at Brixworth and at Deerhurst. It is an early feature. This one may be the earliest of its kind in England. The interior has an arched lintel cut from one large stone 3 ft. 6 ins. by 2 ft. 7 ins. Each jamb consists of one long stone with two small stones below. Its sill is on a level with the floor which suggests that the floor was raised at some time, no doubt when the vault of the ground floor was inserted.

On the extreme east end of the north wall is a blocked doorway. The sill is 11 ft. 3 ins. above ground level and 3 feet below the present floor, the head being 2 feet above the floor. This suggests the floor was once lower by about 3 feet, about the distance the east window would require. This blocked doorway is of rough workmanship. It is rectangular with jambs of three about equal stones each, the sill and lintel being of single stones equal to the width of the opening plus jambs.[2] The inferences seem plain: this doorway and the east window are earlier than the floor, as is also the vault below; and the vault below is later than the doorway and must have been inserted, i.e. it is not original with the one-storeyed porch. Colgrave agrees that the date of the doorway is uncertain but thinks it is modern and that it gave access to or from a modern outbuilding which in Blore's engraving[3] was attached to the north side of the tower and which may have had a covered staircase leading up to this chamber. Some modern, e.g. eighteenth-century, work is very rough. An eighteenth-century doorway at Nassington Church (Northants) might easily be mistaken for one of pre-Conquest date. Colgrave's suggestion however seems unlikely. The sloping lean-to roof of the outhouse was certainly above the doorway but from the look of Blore's engraving there would have been room in the adjunct, which was perhaps four feet wide, for little else than a staircase. In that case why enclose the stairs in a stone outhouse with tiled roof?—especially as adjoining this outhouse on its north side was an unenclosed stone stairway leading up to a modern doorway in the upper part of the north aisle.

In the south wall between the centre and the west end is a blocked window, flat headed with narrow plain stone jambs. On the interior it is 2 ft. 6 ins. wide and

---

[1] See plan in E. C. Gilbert, (*b*), fig. 6.   [2] See also above, p. 88.   [3] In J. R. Surtees, II, p. 10.

2 ft. 1 in. high. On the exterior the lintel and sill have gone but the jambs remain and these show that the aperture was about 1 ft. 5 ins. wide and 2 ft. 1 in. high; that is, it had lateral splay but no upward or downward splay. It is about 1 ft. 8 ins. from the floor, nearer to it than to the ceiling.[1]

On the west wall is another window (1), centrally placed, 3 ft. 7 ins. high and 2 ft. 6 ins. across on the modernized exterior; on the interior it is original and is 5 feet high by 2 ft. 9 ins. wide. It has cable moulding (as on the late seventh-century Ruthwell cross) round the edge of its round head and carried down the jambs.

The eastern position of the north doorway may have been to make room for an altar on its west, a peculiar position for an altar, which would be lighted by the also peculiarly placed window in the west end of the south wall as is suggested by the unusual splay of this window—lateral, and no vertical, to throw the light straight ahead.[2]

Radford however thinks that the second stage originally had a pent roof reaching from about 20 feet, its height above ground on the west, to about 35 feet against the nave wall, and that the low south window was made low to avoid the lower, western, part of the pent roof. This is not very convincing and does not conflict with Gilbert's view because although the pent roof, if there, might explain the window's shape, it does not appear to explain its position.

The Third Stage. Above the second string course, which is hollow moulded,[3] the original gable of the second stage began. Its outline is visible on the tower west wall exterior as the stones in the newer part are larger than those in the earlier gable-end. The total height from ground level to apex was 28 ft. 2 ins. The third stage (2), with a plain string course above, was built around the gable-end (after removal of the roof) and the top two stages, separated by a fourth string course, completing the tower, at the same time.[4] The quoins are different from those below; they are thinner and laid flat. The walls of the third stage rise in front of the two nave west windows. This would have blocked out the light. To avoid this the north and south walls at this point are splayed along their eastern edges where they abut on the nave wall leaving vertical slits which admit light to the windows.

Within the gable end of the third stage, on the exterior of the west wall, are five large stones let into the wall (2), with one smaller bracket-like stone on either side of the lowest stone. The top thin stone projects like a semicircular disc placed

---

[1] Colgrave writes that above this window are indications of another opening of uncertain date.

[2] This second stage may have been inhabited by a sacristan or other church official, as many other such storeys were. But here it seems unlikely if Gilbert's suggestion of an altar is correct.

[3] The third and fourth string courses are square sectioned. Evidently hollow-chamfered string courses were earlier than plain sectioned though the latter are also pre-Conquest for they occur at Bywell, St. Andrew's.

[4] But see below, p. 96.

(1) *Plate* 18; (2) *Plate* 17.

horizontally. On the second stone is the outline of a human head about $10\frac{1}{2}$ inches by 7 inches, the right ear being plainly visible, while on the left side of the face are marks of a moustache. The two very large intermediate stones have been hacked away level with the wall face. The lowest stone is a modern insertion. There was clearly a statue here in high relief, about 6 feet high. The two bracket-stones, right and left, probably supported figures. The group may have been a crucifixion. Its date is not known but there is evidence to suggest the fourteenth century. Radford however suggests the ninth or tenth century. On the interior there appears to have been an opening here. Evidently the statue had been inserted and the wall made good behind it.

The third stage now has no external openings, as there are at Billingham, Bywell, and Ovingham. There was however at one time a window cut in the south wall at about 31 feet above ground level.

The Fourth Stage (I). This also is dark except for one small rectangular round-headed window in the west wall. This is cut from a single stone externally; internally it has a flat head and ordinary Romanesque, i.e. dressed and chamfered, jambs. At 42 feet the old wall of the nave gable ends and above is the later tower east walling. Centrally placed in this tower walling is a Maltese cross, 18 inches by 15 inches. It has a central round or boss and slightly hollow curved expanding arms. It is in clear relief on a square bed. There is a similar one in the vestry show case. It may be a piece of a grave slab built in; there is such a grave slab at Corsenside (Northumberland).

On the east wall at about 26 feet (i.e. in the old nave wall) are signs of an early flat-headed doorway, now blocked, and not centrally placed. This is visible also from the nave.[1] Beside this are faint signs of an opening or recess of which a narrow stone on end, probably part of the dressing, survives. It may mark the site of an altar, perhaps as at Skipwith (Yorks), or of a squint as at Deerhurst (Glos) or Bosham (Sussex). Above these, on a level with the string course at 31 feet, are faint signs of a round-headed doorway, not visible on the nave side of the wall. It has no dressings and is built hard up against the south wall. The indications are faint but both Hall and Gilbert noticed them. The present floor, at 35 feet, is obviously not original. The original floor must have been at 26 feet or at 31 feet if the evidence of the blocked doorways is to be accepted. If at 26 feet the floor would not correspond to the string course at 31 feet as a floor at 31 feet would. It might be inferred that the present tower succeeded something else. There is no evidence, architectural or historical, to assume an earlier tower. Perhaps a third stage was added at some time to the porch making a three-storeyed porch of, say, 38 feet high, the top storey beginning at 26 feet. Later, when the tower was built the floor might have been raised to 31 feet and a new doorway cut at this height. This of course is pure speculation; but some

[1] See above, p. 89.

(I) *Plate* 17.

explanation is required if the evidence of the upper blocked doorway is accepted. Gilbert writes: 'We may say, therefore, that there are faint traces which may suggest that there may have been something which might have been a three-storied porch, anterior to the present tower.'

Radford considers that the second stage with its supposed pent roof was later demolished and a small square chamber (the existing second stage) with gabled roof carried up above the porch. The hollow moulded second string course, at 21 feet up and, unlike the carved one below, returning along the north and south walls, marked the springing line of the gable. The band of cut stone in the nave west wall at 27 to 35 feet up and the string at 31 feet would mark the springing of the nave gable.

The Fifth, or *Belfry Stage* (I). This starts at 46 feet. It is built of roughly cut stone. It appears to have been extensively renewed, at least on the exterior. The quoins are of normal size, i.e. not big stone work, and are largely modern; they are quite different from those of the porch.

The belfry double window openings on each face are rather similar to those at Bywell and Ovingham, but different from those at Jarrow. They are 4 ft. 9 ins. by 2 ft. 4 ins., with arched lintels, both heads cut from a single stone, 3 ft. 2 ins. by 1 ft. 1 in. The jambs are of four stones each, with hollow-moulded thin imposts. The arched lintels are supported by mid-wall plain shafts, cylinders without capitals. The north one is original, slightly bulbous and has a square base cut from one piece of stone with the shaft, as at Brixworth (Northants). Between shaft and arched lintel is a through-stone impost longer than the wall thickness. There is surrounding strip work of Mercian type, i.e. carried round the head and down the jambs. The eastern jamb of the strip work is monolithic with a half-round front edge; the west jamb is very worn. The strip work rests on cubical corbels placed just above sill and impost levels. The head part is a renewal. The western opening has a thin widely projecting sill and the straight shaft has no base. The other two shafts, on east and south, are modern replacements. Above and centrally placed in each wall is a single circular hole, single splayed, in its own stone. These also are renewals.

At some time a circular opening about three feet or so in diameter was cut in the west face of the top stage, below the existing small circular opening and cutting into the strip work arch of the belfry opening below. It is shown in some pre-restoration photographs.[1] It was built up during the restoration of 1924. Its outline and the renewed strip work below are plainly visible. The opening does not appear in Grimm's drawing in the British Museum of the tower as it was in 1704, nor in Blore's engraving in Surtees, Vol. II, 1820, nor in Baldwin Brown's drawing nor Greenwell's engraving of the tower prior to the 1866 restoration. It may have been

[1] E.g. Pl. 27 in A. W. Clapham, (*a*).

(I) *Plate* 17.

cut by the Greenwell Committee in 1866. Its purpose is unknown; but there was a clock here at one time.

Interpretations. From his observations and the earlier work of Hall, Gilbert inferred five building periods at Monkwearmouth, and suggested dates for them.

1. The original nave with chancel (Bede's eastern porticus with altar) and one-storeyed porch (Bede's western porticus ingressus): this work is attributed to Benedict Biscop, of date 674.

2. The erection of a second storey to the porch. For this there is a good case for a date between 710 and 735. By 710 both Benedict Biscop and Wilfrid were dead and

(*a*) Crundel Down sword pommel
(*b*) Sutton Hoo belt buckle
(*c*) Book of Durrow

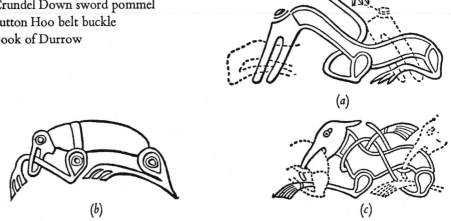

(*a*)

(*b*)   (*c*)

Fig. 5. Sutton Hoo animal and some relations

their foreign masons may have returned home; by 735 Ecgberht, Archbishop of York, was importing new ideas from overseas. Between these dates seems a likely one for the second stage.

3. The making in their present form of the three arched exterior openings to the ground floor of the porch, including the ornamentation of the western arch jambs and the decorated string course, the raising of the floor of the second stage to admit of the vaulting of the ground floor, and the insertion of the western window in the upper stage. Gilbert dates all this to round about 800. Few writers accept this dating for the three arched openings and the ornamentation, all of which are now generally accepted as being of Biscop's time.[1] Gilbert's dating of the other items seems reasonable.

4. The removal of the gabled roof of the second stage and the erection of three more storeys above to complete the five-staged tower. This he attributed to Aldhune, Bishop of Chester-le-Street, *c.* 990–5. This date seems reasonable. As pointed out,

---

[1] See also below, p. 100.

above the nave west wall to the north and south of the tower, but not within the tower, was extensively repaired twice after the tower was built. The second time would be by Aldwine *c.* 1075 after the burning by William the Conqueror in 1068–70. The earlier repair would be either after the Danish raids of 867 or after those of *c.* 995 which compelled Aldhune to remove his see from Chester-le-Street to the safer Ripon. The latter date is the more likely as there was no tower in 867. If the earlier date is accepted the tower must have been standing then, and there is no evidence that the tower pre-dates Aldhune. Moreover he is stated to be the first to build in stone in the North after the first Danish invasion. Radford, without giving any evidence, attributes the tower to Aldwine, *c.* 1075.

The early Norman type of small window in the fourth stage and the mid-wall long slender columns in the belfry windows are common features in the period immediately following the Norman Conquest which Baldwin Brown called the Saxo-Norman Overlap, but may well have occurred earlier. It is known that there was a renewed wave of building activity in the period 950–1000. There were many cultural contacts with the Continent at this time as a result of which many motifs may have been adopted earlier than Baldwin Brown thought.

5. The considerable restoration and repair work of Abbot Aldwine, *c.* 1075 or a little later. This included raising and steepening the nave gable and re-roofing, and also a new chancel arch of which the bulbous bases of the existing, much later, columns remain.

The date of *c.* 800 for the third building stage mentioned above seems reasonable. Thus the vault of the porch was erected presumably as a protection against fire sometime after the Danish raid of 794. But it seems impossible to accept this date for the zoomorphic ornamentation of the western jambs of the porch. Gilbert stated that the animals are of similar type to those on the cross at Colerne (Wilts), which was dated by T. D. Kendrick to *c.* 875 though more purely serpentine. Actually, apart from their great length, the animals could hardly be more different. The Colerne animals have deeply hatched bodies and extremely lively, fierce looking, savagely biting open jaws. The Monkwearmouth animals have smooth bodies and their heads are entirely devoid of liveliness, and indeed have no jaws at all. The heads indeed are most interesting. Similar heads occur in early Anglo-Saxon metal work and MS. illumination. It is known that the book illuminator got many of his motifs from earlier and contemporary metalwork and both provided motifs for the later sculptor. Heads with excessively prolonged snouts closely similar to those at Monkwearmouth occur on the Crundel Down sword pommel of *c.* mid-seventh century, on the Sutton Hoo belt buckle, dated to the first quarter of the seventh century, and in the Book of Durrow *c.* 670. Three points should be noted (Figs. 5 and 6):

(1) In the Crundel sword pommel and the Book of Durrow the heads have jaws which are biting or holding something, such as the animal's own tail. (2) In the

Sutton Hoo buckle the animal has not two jaws but a single long snout with a long lateral slit in it through which the animal has passed its own left fore-leg. The Monkwearmouth animals have the same long snouts as the Durrow animals and the lateral slits of the Sutton Hoo ones; the snout of one however does not pass through that of the other, the two snouts being linked together like two adjacent links in a chain. (3) In later MSS., such as the St. Chad Gospels of *c.* 710 and the Lindisfarne Gospels

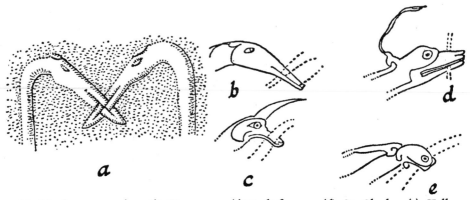

(*a*) Monkwearmouth. (*b*) Durrow. (*c*) Lindisfarne. (*d*) St. Chad. (*e*) Kells.

Fig. 6. Monkwearmouth animals and some of their relations

of *c.* 700, the long snake-like head of the Durrow animal has become shorter and definitely birds' beaks or animal heads; the long snouts of Sutton Hoo and even longer ones of Durrow having apparently disappeared.

All this seems to the present writer very strong evidence for dating the ornamentation, and indeed all three western openings, to Biscop's time. It might be suggested that the jamb stones are re-used material from elsewhere. Against this is the fact that each jamb is composed of one large upright slab and one large slab lying flat above, and the ornamentation covers both stones. It is relevant to point out, too, that the sculptor may have borrowed his motif direct from metalwork, or even from East Saxon metalwork. The Sutton Hoo treasure may have belonged to Rædwald of East Anglia, who was Bretwalda, that is supreme overlord of England, from 615 until his death *c.* 625. He invaded Northumbria in 616 and helped Edwin to gain his throne; and Æthelhere, of East Anglia, whose cenotaph the Sutton Hoo ship is supposed to be, also invaded Northumbria where he was killed in 654 fighting against Oswiu. Some East Saxon metalwork may have been left behind in the North.

With regard to the decorated string course, the animals here show little resemblance to the typical Anglian Beast found on many standing crosses and other monuments of the Early Saxon period. They are less lively and gazelle-like, have little animation and are reminiscent of the animals on the bases only of Irish crosses of the Ahenny group[1] dated to the eighth century and similar and earlier crosses at Iona and

[1] See M. and L. de Paor, Pl. 27.

district. Iona influenced both Ireland and Northumbria so the string course animals may show Scoto–Celtic influence; which would also suggest a date earlier than 800.

NORTON

ST. MARY THE VIRGIN'S CHURCH.[1] This was made a collegiate church in 1083 for some of the secular canons expelled from Durham by Bishop William of St. Carilef to make room for Benedictine monks. It is the only Anglo-Saxon church in Northumbria built on the cross plan complete with central tower and transepts (I). Baldwin Brown dated it to post-1040; Pevsner and V.C.H. think it probably early eleventh century. This is a late and unusual form of pre-Conquest church. Others are Stow (Lincs), Repton (Derby), and St. Mary in Castro, Dover; and perhaps Stanton Lacy (Salop) and Wootton Wawen (War).

The present church at Norton consists of nave with Norman Transitional aisles and clerestory, aisleless transepts and chancel, south porch and a modern vestry.[2] The remains of the early church comprise almost the whole of the transepts, with the arches opening to them, the whole of the central tower, except the top stage and battlemented parapet, and portions of the nave walls. The nave was practically rebuilt in the Norman Transitional period, i.e. late twelfth century, and the chancel in the Early English or thirteenth century. Both have later additions and alterations such as arches cut through the transept west walls. The nave is of the same internal dimensions as the original, 43 ft. 6 ins. long by 14 ft. 10 ins. wide; the chancel was rebuilt rather wider than its original. The original tower western and eastern arches leading to nave and chancel were replaced during the twelfth-century rebuilding. The arch heads are supported on corbels built into the original walls. The original arches to the transepts (2) were retained but were widened by removal of the inner order of voussoirs and those parts of the jambs supporting them. The original outer orders remaining are of thin stones, not voussoirs, some very long, cut to the curved shape of the arch, seven in the northern arch head and ten in the south. There are massive double square-sectioned imposts; the upper ones project north and south from the lower and east and west from the arch head, and the lower imposts in turn project beyond the jamb faces. The jambs are not of through-stones, but of two or three stones per course of fairly uniform thickness. The arch heads are of two rings with rubble filling between, and they project about four inches beyond the wall

[1] G. Baldwin Brown; C. C. Hodges, (a), viii; W. H. D. Longstaffe, (b); J. R. Surtees, III; V.C.H. *Durham* III; N. Pevsner, (c).
[2] V.C.H. *Durham*, III, plan on p. 310.

(I) *Plate* 20; (2) *Plate* 22.

faces on both sides. The jambs are chamfered on the north and south edges and have no internal plinth. It looks as though the jambs were refaced when widened, for the soffit stones are much better dressed than the imposts and the original walling to east and west, some of which is very roughly and irregularly dressed. Perhaps the chamfer, a late feature, is of the same date. The later lead-covered roof is of very flat pitch, as are those of the south transept and chancel.

The north transept (I) except the roof is substantially as it was with its original walls and large quoins, but with no original openings (the north three-light window is modern). Like the rest of the early building it is of large irregular rubble blocks with wide joints. It was originally plastered on the exterior and some plaster remains here and there. The quoins are not rudely cut, as stated by some writers, but finely dressed on the exposed faces. They do however look earlier than those at Stow. The quoin stones are large, almost megalithic (one is 3 ft. 4 ins. by 2 ft. 2 ins. by 9 inches) though some are smaller and lie in face-alternate position.

The south transept was altered considerably in the 1870's, the south wall being entirely rebuilt and angle buttresses added. No original openings or architectural features remain, except a cross fragment with interlacement built into the south-east interior wall where it abuts on the chancel south wall. Its former appearance is shown in Blore's engraving.[1]

The total width of the church across the transepts is 51 ft. 8 ins.

The tower (I) built of rubble is the largest in Northumbria. It is 20 ft. 9 ins. square on the exterior and 15 feet square inside. (Ovingham is 18 ft. 6 ins., Billingham 17 ft. 6 ins., and Monkwearmouth only 11 ft. 9 ins.) It was wider than the nave or transepts, a real central tower. The walls are 3 feet thick. The transepts, nave and chancel were built up against it, with what look like straight joints. Short pieces, about 3 or 4 feet, of the tower north-west and south-west quoins, appear above the later aisles like triangular buttresses, in the re-entrant angles between the tower and the four limbs of the church. The whole scheme is almost, but not quite fully, Romanesque: the tower arches are not built on piers, in true Romanesque fashion; they were cut through the walls and given the usual dressings.

Above the crossing and within the gable marks of the earlier roofs visible on the exterior walls are four openings (I), one in each wall. These openings are 7 feet high and 2 feet wide, with gable heads and chamfered imposts of through-stones which are flush with the walls on the exterior but project somewhat on the interior. The jambs are splayed slightly inwards. The openings on the east and west differ in some interesting respects from those on the north and south. The former have jambs of walling cut straight through the walls, i.e. without splay, and the imposts are chamfered.

---

[1] In J. R. Surtees, III, p. 199.

Those on north and south have unchamfered imposts and slightly splayed jambs, also of walling; as a result the unsplayed imposts, viewed from the crossing (1), appear to increase in lateral internal projection as the splay increases.

Above these was a floor and a little above this are two openings on each face above the original nave roof lines (2). These, one on each side of the old roof gable, have arched lintels, are chamfered all round and are only 6 inches wide on the exterior but are splayed internally. The two windows in the west, and the south one on the east, are roughly rectangular and are each cut from a single stone; the south-east one looks inverted for the lintel is straight and the sill an inverted half-round. The other five openings have long and short jambs: one lower short and one upper long, with stilted arched lintels. Sills are of walling. The very wide roof grooves show plainly on the tower wall, having been filled in with small stones flush with the wall face. The roof pitch was very sharp, quite 60° to the horizontal.

Higher still internally are indications of a second floor, i.e. of the third stage. It is possible that the tower originally may not have been higher, or much higher, than roof ridge level, a common height for early Norman towers. The first floor (second stage) was entered by a very large rectangular doorway high up in the south wall (3) near the south-west angle above the south arch and reached now by a ladder from the south transept. The floor was immediately above the crowns of the crossing arches; it has been removed but the doorway remains and is in use. There is now a permanent ladder of access from this doorway to the third stage of the tower.

The portion above, including the double belfry windows and plain embattled parapet are fifteenth century; the masonry is quite different from that below.

OVINGHAM

ST. MARY THE VIRGIN'S CHURCH.[1] Only the tower is pre-Conquest, the greater part of the church being thirteenth century. The tower is closely similar to that of nearby Bywell, St. Andrew's, and is the tallest and biggest in Northumberland. It is 105 feet high. Its external lateral dimensions are: west wall 18 ft. 6 ins. and projection from the nave wall of 14 ft. 10½ ins.; internal measurements are 13 feet north–south, 12 ft. 4½ ins. east–west. The longer axis lies north–south. The walls are 2 ft. 9 ins. thick. It has no plinth and is built of well coursed fairly well dressed ragstone. Some stones in the lower part of the tower and some quoin stones are Roman. The quoins are of very regular large slabs, up to 2½ feet by 1½ feet by 1 foot, in side-alternate arrangement.

[1] C. C. Hodges, (a), vii, and (b); *History of Northumberland*, XII.

---

(1) *Plate* 23; (2) *Plate* 20; (3) *Plate* 22.

On the exterior it is of one stage for three-quarters of its height (I). Then comes a string course and slight offset which separate the belfry from the part below. Internally there are five stages, four below the external string course and one, the belfry, above.

The interior of the ground floor was deprived of most of its interest about the end of the eighteenth century. There are no remains of the ancient tower arch leading to the nave; the present arch is eighteenth century. The only original feature in this stage is a window in the south wall, about 12 feet from the ground. Its light opening is 11 inches wide and is splayed internally to 2 ft. 1 in. Internally and externally it has an arched lintel and a 3-inch chamfer round the opening. It has no imposts. There is one large slab to each jamb immediately below the lintel; the lower parts of the jambs and the sill are plain walling. There is no western doorway or other external entrance to this floor.

In the second stage there are window openings on the east and west walls. The western one is taller than and otherwise different from that in the ground floor south wall. It has arched lintel, long slab imposts and sill, monolithic jambs and no chamfer. The eastern window, visible only from the nave, is large, 5 ft. 6 ins. high by 2 ft. 2 ins. wide, has an arched lintel and a stepped sill in three steps. It is cut straight through the wall and shows no indication of having been closed with light shutters or door. It is 27 ft. 4 ins. above the floor. Such openings on east tower walls (or west walls of nave) and above the tower arch may indicate that such towers were inhabited (on this floor), probably by some church official. Or the opening may have been an ingress to the second stage, though it is rather high above the floor for such a purpose.

The third stage has no openings in the walls.

In the fourth stage there is a window in the south wall larger than the one below. It has an arched lintel, jambs which are not of through-stones and has no chamfer. The exterior string course is just above this window.

There are no openings in the north wall below the belfry.

The belfry stage has a double-headed two-light window, with arched lintel, in each face, all four exactly alike and closely similar in all details, except for slight differences in dimensions, to those at Bywell, St. Andrew's. The double heads are supported on thin impost stones, rather more carefully dressed than those at Bywell. The jambs are of four almost square-ended stones each, not through-stones. The mid-wall baluster shafts are slightly barrel shaped and 10 inches in diameter. The shaft to the south window only has an angular flattish band between two quirks near the foot. Below the band the shaft assumes a conical shape giving the appearance of a rude base: the bottom is square, no wider than the shaft, with roughly rounded corners and the upper part slightly curved inwards into the lower quirk of the band.

(I) *Plate 24.*

Each double opening is framed in a narrow band of square-sectioned strip-work with arched head, some of the stones of which are long and cut to the appropriate curved shape, resting on small cubical corbels above the imposts. The vertical side strips are thin, monolithic and rest on cubical corbels above the slab sill.

In the tympanum between the strip-work head and the lights is a small circular opening about the same diameter as the light openings and cut from one square stone. Above the belfry windows is a slightly overhanging cornice. The line of this is broken on the north and south walls by projecting stone spouts, two on each north and south face. These are of later date than the tower. Above the cornice the walls are continued up, on the line of its outer edge, to the extent of two courses of original masonry. Above this is a modern plain parapet two courses high. The roof is flat and modern.

The date of the tower is not precisely known. There appears to be no reference to Ovingham in early writers to serve as an indication of date or of whether there has been more than one pre-Conquest church on the site. The tower however is similar to some others on Tyneside[1] which belonged to a period of revival in church building which some writers think occurred not long before the Conquest, probably about the middle of the eleventh century, and others at any time between 950 and 1000. All have or had similar belfry openings and show a similar blending of early and late characteristics. It has been suggested as evidence of definite pre-Conquest date that the tower shows no Norman influence and that the large lower quoin stones are characteristically Anglo-Saxon. But some of these stones are re-used Roman stones, readily available in the area, and are no evidence at all of date. Baldwin Brown dates the tower to *c.* 1040.

WARDEN

ST. MICHAEL'S CHURCH.[2] The village and church stand on meadow land in a fork between the North and South Tyne Rivers and not far from the foot of High Warden Hill, the summit of which is 593 feet above sea level. The name is probably derived from Waredun—watch or ward hill. There is a British fort on the hill, probably used as a watch tower by the Romans for there is a fine view from here of Corstopitum (Corbridge) and the surrounding country. A spur of High Warden, called Little Warden Hill, runs for a mile south-west towards Warden Village and overlooks the church. At its summit, 244 feet up, is another camp. There were two fords across the North and South Tynes and much Roman building material available at nearby Corstopitum. It was an almost ideal site for an Anglian settlement in alien country.

[1] E.g. Warden and Bywell, St. Andrew's.
[2] J. Gibson; C. C. Hodges, (*a*), vii; E. C. Gilbert, (*a*); N. Pevsner, (*e*).

The head of an Anglo-Saxon cross about five feet high (1), formerly in the garden of Low Warden House is now in the churchyard to the south of the tower. It may originally have stood on or near the site of the church.

Wilfrid is traditionally supposed to be the founder of the church though the evidence is scanty. The existing pre-Conquest parts are much later. The west wall and the north-west angle of the nave are stated to be pre-Conquest. They look however like the rest of the nave; perhaps they were refaced at some time. The remainder was rebuilt in the eighteenth century. The pre-Conquest remains are of one period. The nave was probably aisleless, of exterior dimensions 30 feet by 23 feet, with walls 2 ft. 10 ins. thick. There are no remains or even indications of an earlier church. On the western face of the south part of the nave west wall and on the north of the north-west corner of the nave are footings of large stones projecting about three inches beyond the wall line.

The tower (2) is the smallest in Northumberland. Its external dimensions are 16 ft. 5 ins. north–south with projection from the nave wall of 12 ft. 10 ins. The internal measurements are west wall 10 ft. 8½ ins., north wall 9 ft. 11 ins. Like Ovingham and other rectangular non-porch towers its longer axis lies north–south. The walls are 2 ft. 10 ins. thick, approaching the usual Norman dimensions of 3 feet or more. A few Norman walls are indeed less than 3 feet as at Great Waltham (Essex) where the nave wall is 2 ft. 6 ins.

The quoins are of large Roman worked stones. Some of them retain the sinkings for iron or lead clamps used for lifting the stones by the Roman masons (lewis holes). A few are placed upright, others of similar length lie along the wall surfaces in irregular mixed face and side alternate manner.

The tower had four stages internally, three of which have windows which are of Saxon type on the exterior: thin slits with wide internal splays and arched lintels; on the interior they are of Norman type with rubble vaulting and angle dressings.

In the first stage there is a window (1) in the south wall, 8 feet from the ground a little to the east of centre. The jambs are of three large flat slabs each and the aperture 7 inches wide at the sill and 6 inches at the top. This narrowing upwards is an early characteristic and suggests Scoto-Celtic influence.

The interior of the tower is stated to have been plastered in 1936. If so most of it has peeled off and what is left looks old. No joist holes of the former floor of the second stage are visible; this stage is now open to the ground. The second stage has a window in the west wall closely similar to that below on the south but wider; and another opening in the east wall about 20 feet above the floor and opening originally to the nave. It is now built up and is visible only from the tower side. Baldwin Brown states there is no opening here, which would be unusual as such

---

(1) *Plate 26*; (2) *Plate 25.*

openings generally provided access, by ladder or staircase, to the tower from the nave. It is possible that he did not write from personal observation.

The tower has only three sides up to the height of the nave west gable; the east wall of the tower above this rests on the earlier nave west wall. Below, the north and south walls of the tower merely meet the nave wall in straight joints; they are not bonded in. The tower is evidently later than the original nave and is of one date only. Hodges thought it was built between the last quarter of the seventh century and the first Danish invasions, say, 675–870, mainly on account of the single belfry window openings which he considered to be ancient and of that period. This however is an impossible date, for towers were not introduced into England for another 200 years or more. Baldwin Brown suggested *c.* 950 or later. Gilbert after careful examination concluded that the interior of the belfry windows, though roughly built, were not Anglo-Saxon,[1] but he accepts an eleventh-century date for the church. The date is really uncertain; whether pre- or post-Conquest it is impossible to say. The evidence seems equally strong for or against either date.

The low tower arch (I) to the nave has a plain soffit of two rings of long, very rough stones with a wide irregular joint along the centre of the crown covering perhaps half the arch head; the north and south ends of the soffit are rubble filled. The plain jambs of large slabs are splayed[2] towards the nave. The imposts, only 5 ft. 1½ ins. from the floor, are Roman base mouldings reversed, 10 inches thick. They are ornamented with a square fillet, two quarter rolls on the north and three on the south, and a chamfer; they return for a short distance on both sides but both returns are modern replacements. The arch is 8 ft. 6 ins. high, 5 ft. 2½ ins. wide on the western face and 5 ft. 5½ ins. on the eastern.

There is a modern wooden floor to the third stage. This stage has a window in the south wall similar to but rather taller and narrower than those on the west and south below. It is slightly to the west of centre. It has a large arched lintel, monolithic jambs and no separate sill.

There is no opening in the north wall of the tower.

The fourth, or belfry, stage was greatly altered *c.* 1765. The wall faces were renewed with fresh plain ashlar set back 3 inches from the older wall face below. There may have been a string course as at Corbridge, Bywell and Ovingham, but if so it was removed. Wide, modern single windows were inserted in the exterior walls: plain slightly pointed openings, 3 feet wide, with square jambs. On the interior the windows look old and both Hodges and Baldwin Brown thought they were ancient. Gilbert considers that though rough and poor work they are not ancient, certainly

---

[1] E. C. Gilbert, (*a*), Pl. II, I.
[2] As at Hexham crypt. Anglo-Saxon doorways were rarely splayed though Norman and Early English doorways sometimes were. There is a plain splayed thirteenth-century doorway at Bywell, St. Peter's.

(I) *Plate* 27.

not pre-Conquest.[1] H. M. Taylor suggests they may possibly represent an early type of single belfry openings, like those at Bardsey.[2]

The battlement, with flat stones laid on merlons and crenelles, is also eighteenth century.

WHITTINGHAM

ST. BARTHOLOMEW'S CHURCH.[3] Bede records that Cuthbert was elected Bishop of Lindisfarne in 684 at 'a place called Twyford, or the Two Fords, near the river Alne'. It is considered by some writers that Twyford was Whittingham. Though 'a great Synod was held [here] under the presidency of Archbishop Theodore of blessed memory, and in the presence of King Egfrid' Bede does not mention a church. The synod may have been held here as Whittingham was a royal vill and the King was present. There may have been no church here at this time. Indeed, later in 737, as recorded above, King Ceolworth abdicated to retire to Lindisfarne and gave six royal vills to the monks of St. Cuthbert among them being 'Werceworde . . . together with the church he had built there and Hwitingham', with no mention of a church. So at this date there may have been no church, or possibly only one of timber. Bishop Esred consecrated a church here. Nothing more is known of Esred, but his name is Anglo-Saxon.

The only pre-Conquest parts of the church are the lower part of the tower (I), the western wall and north-west corner and some south-east quoins of the nave.[4] These may date from the eighth century.

The twelfth-century north aisle and the thirteenth-century south aisle were built with straight joints against, and not integrated with, the nave; the nave quoins (I) are plainly visible. There is a chamfered plinth and for about 10 feet above the plinth at the north-west corner of the nave and 6 feet at the south-west corner the quoins are different from those above and from those at the south-east corner. These lower quoin stones are 14 to 16 inches high, 11 to 12 inches deep and 26 to 33 inches long; they are arranged in side-alternate manner. The upper quoins are upright and flat and more regular. The south-east quoins are large and less regular, a mixture of face and side-alternate. At the north-east corner of the nave the early quoins have been removed but there is a straight joint representing the wall face. The nave was about

---

[1] E. C. Gilbert, (a), Pl. II, I.   [2] See below, p. 133.

[3] Bede; T. Rickman, (a) and (b); C. C. Hodges, (a) vii and (c); H. L. Honeyman; G. Baldwin Brown; *History of Northumberland*, XII; N. Pevsner, (e); F. R. Wilson.

[4] See plan in Honeyman, or Hodges (c).

(I) *Plate* 31.

51 ft. 8 ins. long by 17 ft. 6 ins. wide at the west end and about 18 ft. 3 ins. at the east. The walls were about 2 ft. 6 ins. thick.

About 3 ft. 8 ins. of the nave north wall, forming the western respond of the north-west arch, is probably pre-Conquest; in it are visible parts of the round head and western jamb of an old arch. It is not known whether this arch (1) stood alone as the entrance to a side chapel or porticus or northern porch, as at Bradford on Avon (Wilts), or (2) was one of a series of arches leading to side chapels or porticus, as at Jarrow, or (3) to aisles as at Brixworth (Northants). The workmanship is poor and it is possible that the arch may be a later insertion.

The tower has three stages (1), originally four according to Wilson and Hodges, later reduced to three. Only the lowest stage, up to about 30 feet (2), is of Anglo-Saxon workmanship. The change in masonry between old and new is plainly evident. The tower stands on a chamfered plinth, like the nave. This is denied by some writers, but it does exist and is indeed very evident. It is chamfered on the upper edge[1] and there are two grooves round the vertical faces producing a flattish half-round moulding between them. The tower base does not fit squarely on the plinth, one side of the tower being about 2 inches shorter than the other.

The quoins of the Anglo-Saxon part are large irregular side-alternate slab work below and regular upright and flat above, like the western quoins of the nave. The masonry throughout is of fairly regularly coursed rubble, well but not finely dressed, with no Roman-worked stones in it. Honeyman stated that at about 12 feet up a course of ashlar runs like a string course right round the tower and across the west wall of the nave. This is not visible in the photograph; in fact the writer, and a companion, could see no significant differences anywhere in the old masonry of the tower.

The tower now has no original window. Hodges writes that even in Rickman's time only the top windows in the upper part, removed in 1840, were original.

The lower part of the tower measures externally 15 ft. 3 ins. north–south. It projects from the nave wall 13 ft. 8 ins. on the north and 13 ft. 10 ins. on the south. Internally it measures 10 ft. 7 ins. at the west end, the north and south walls being 11 feet and 11 ft. 2 ins. respectively;[2] i.e. its longer axis lies east–west as at Corbridge. It has therefore been suggested that it may originally have been a porch, raised later into a tower. This is mere conjecture. Elsewhere are towers built as such with longer axes east–west, as at Bosham (Sussex). In such cases the different axial dimensions differ only slightly, as here by a few inches. In porch towers the east–west axis may

---

[1] The chamfer is shown on the lower edge in Honeyman's drawing (his fig. 9, p. 168); this is incorrect.
[2] These measurements are Honeyman's. Hodges gives 10 ft. 11 ins. for the west wall and 10 ft. 10 ins. for the north, i.e. like Ovingham practically square with its slightly longer axis lying north–south.

---

(1) *Plate* 29; (2) *Plate* 31.

be up to two feet or more longer than the north–south. Also, in view of the very high tower arch at Whittingham it seems very unlikely that this is a porch tower.

Baldwin Brown suggested post-1040 as a likely date.

It is like Corbridge too in dimensions which are similarly variable, though slightly less so. The walls are 2 ft. 7 ins. thick, about the same as the responds of the tower arch but about three inches more than the nave wall to north and south of the tower.

The first stage was lighted on its west face by a rectangular opening (I), 2 feet by 16 inches wide. The head, sill and jambs were of one stone each. About four feet above this was the sill of a large round-headed window of through-stones, the head being of two stones or possibly of one that became broken. The north jamb was of one upright slab, the south of one stone with a small one below. Both were destroyed in the 1840 rebuilding.

The sills of the belfry windows were at 40 feet above the ground. Originally they were single plain arched openings in the north and south walls; on the west and east they were two-light openings with double arched lintels and mid-wall baluster shafts which had capitals and bases, square plinths and square impost blocks. If Rickman's drawing is correct[1] the shape of the baluster shaft was rather Roman, like some at Housesteads on the Roman wall, than typically Anglo-Saxon.

Above the belfry windows there were three courses of probably thirteenth- to fifteenth-century ashlar and then a plain parapet between two string courses. The present battlements with pinnacles belong to the 1840 rebuilding. The total height above the plinth was 51 feet.

The tower arch leading to the nave was built up in the fifteenth century. In 1816 the central part of the arch head was destroyed to make a doorway from a modern west gallery to the tower. This part was replaced by voussoirs in two rings when the arch was opened again in 1909. The original voussoirs were not through-stones; they were in two rings, those on the east face being about 16 inches deep, i.e. east–west, and about 24 inches high, those of the west rather thinner. There are fairly large springers cut to shape on each side; the voussoirs immediately above were inserted apparently after a fire, the reddish marks of which are still visible on some of the stonework. The arch is 17 ft. 10 ins. high by 7 ft. 4½ ins. wide. The jambs are two inches thicker than the arch above them, and rest on plain chamfered plinths. The arch head is set back a little behind the jamb faces. The jambs are of large through-stone slabs, upright and flat, lying on their sides, but not of the strict Escomb type.[2]

[1] A necessary proviso. The beauty of early nineteenth-century engravings tends to produce a confidence in their accuracy not always justified. Even John Britton was sometimes at fault. His engraving of the Brixworth baluster shafts is misleading and that of the Barnack sundial simply wrong.

[2] C. C. Hodges, (c), Pl. XXVIII. G. Baldwin Brown gives a drawing by J. T. Dixon (his fig. 189) and writes: 'the moulded foot of the jamb will be noticed.' There is no moulded foot; the apparent moulding in the drawing is really a pair of modern hot-water pipes.

(I) *Plate* 30.

The imposts are very thin, chamfered below on the soffit side, and on the soffit edges have an enrichment of egg-shaped or oval pellets.[1]

The tower arch is not quite in the centre of the west wall; it was apparently opposite the centre of the nave east gable, which was displaced a little to the north owing to the inclination of the nave wall towards the north of east.

Above the arch but concealed by modern plaster it has been supposed that there are traces of the arched opening often found in the east walls of the second stage of Anglo-Saxon towers giving access to the tower from the nave, but nothing of this is now visible in the unplastered tower interior.

[1] C. C. Hodges, (*c*), p. 83, fig. 2.

WESTMORLAND

MORLAND

THE CHURCH OF ST. LAWRENCE. This is the only towered Anglo-Saxon church in the three counties of Cumberland, Westmorland and Lancashire. It lies about five miles north-east of Appleby.

It is certain that it existed before *c.* 1100 for Ranulf Meschin, the first Norman lord of Cumberland, transferred his churches of St. Michael and St. Lawrence in his castellum or fortified town of Appleby to his newly founded Benedictine priory of Wetheral, near Carlisle.[1] This was founded not later than 1112 and perhaps as early as 1106. Morland tower is considered[2] to be mainly of the late eleventh or early twelfth century; Baldwin Brown dated it to the Saxo-Norman Overlap. The nave was rebuilt in the late twelfth century, the choir and transeptal chapels are thirteenth century, the nave south arcade of the time of Edward I, and the chancel debased Tudor. It was restored in 1759 and again in 1896.

The tower (I) is built of local sandstone rubble with some ashlar. It is of three internal stages. On the exterior there is a tall lower stage of about two-thirds the total height, and a short upper or belfry stage which is recessed, without a string course, behind the one below. The upper stage is of two dates, the lower half, the old belfry, being Anglo-Saxon; the upper half, the present belfry, with its corbelled parapet and lead-covered short spire is of ashlar and of the sixteenth century. The tower is 11 feet square and the east wall is 4 ft. 9 ins. thick, a Norman thickness. The east wall has a bold plinth of two members which does not appear on the exterior of the tower.

There are narrow, slightly splayed windows fairly low down in the north, south and west walls of the ground stage; the west one has been enlarged externally. In the lower part of the upper stage are two-light round-headed double openings of the usual Anglo-Saxon belfry type in all four walls with mid-wall shafts with plain chamfered bases and square-cut through-stone central imposts. The top, later, half of the upper stage has in each wall two square-headed two-light windows with modern mullions.

There is no tower arch. Instead there is a tall narrow doorway with a round head of voussoirs, of one square-cut order, with the springing set back behind the jamb faces. The jambs have draw bar holes. There is no external entrance to the tower.

[1] Quoted in V.C.H. *Cumb.* II, from J. E. Prescott's edition of the *Register of Wetheral.*
[2] By V.C.H., and R.C.H.M.

(I) *Plate 28.*

YORKSHIRE

In this very large county there are only thirteen Anglo-Saxon churches of the towered type. These are: one in York city; in the North Riding, Hornby,[1] 7 miles N. of Northallerton; Appleton-le-Street, 4 miles NW. by W. of Malton; Hovingham, *c.* 8 miles NW. by W. of Malton and on the same road as Appleton; Middleton-by-Pickering, *c.* 1 mile NW. of Pickering; in the East Riding, Skipwith, 9 miles SSE. of York; Wharram-le-Street, 6 miles SE. of Malton; Weaverthorpe, 11 miles E. by S. of Malton and 7 miles NE. by S. of Wharram; in the West Riding, Bardsey, 4 miles SW. of Wetherby and *c.* 7 miles from Leeds; Burghwallis, 7 miles NNW. of Doncaster; Kirk Hammerton, 9 miles NW. of York; Ledsham, 10 miles and Monk Fryston, 7 miles W. by S. of Selby.

[1] Not considered here. Only the tower is Saxon, in part only, and is post-Conquest.

YORKSHIRE: NORTH RIDING

Appleton-le-Street

ALL SAINTS' CHURCH.[1] The tower, the west wall and the north-west and south-west quoins of the nave are Anglo-Saxon. V.C.H. dates it to probably the first half of the eleventh century, Baldwin Brown to post-1040.

The tower (I) is badly set out: the west wall is not at right angles to the north and south walls and these are not at right angles to the nave. It has no plinth. The walls, of large rectangular rubble blocks with wide joints, are 3 feet thick except the east wall which is 2 ft. 7 ins. The quoins are large in face-alternate arrangement; one stone measures 3 ft. 6 ins. by 15 inches by 12 inches high.

There are three external stages, separated by plain projecting string courses. A third string, hollow chamfered and deeply projecting, is at the top below the later very low pyramidal roof. The top stage shows some Norman details; the two lower ones are entirely Anglo-Saxon. The bottom stage occupies about half the total height; the second stage is taller than the third.

In the tall first stage are now no original openings. The round-headed window in the lower part of the west wall is a modern insertion; the walling below looks as though it had been filled in with well-dressed stones, so possibly there may have been a western entrance. A north doorway was inserted in the early twelfth century; this is now the only entrance to the church. Two former large rectangular openings high up in the west and south walls are now blocked. They had flat lintels of long selected (i.e. not dressed) wall slabs and no separate sills. The west one had no jambs, only walling; the south one had jambs of one tall lower upright stone with two irregular squarish slabs above.

In both second and third stages there are double light windows in each wall. All are similar except that those in the top stage are rather shorter and much narrower than those in the second. They all have mid-wall shafts with moulded square bases but no capitals, and projecting chamfered imposts to jambs and shafts. The mid-wall shafts of the upper windows in the north and south are ornamented all over with zig-zag or chevron ornament; that on the west has a spiral depression round the shaft. The east shaft, central impost and heads are modern renewals; the shaft is plain. The

---

[1] G. Baldwin Brown; C. C. Hodges, (a), viii; V.C.H., *Yorks, N.R.,* I. (Plan on p. 469.)

central shafts of the upper windows are circular in plan, except the one on the north which is of roughly rounded rectangular section. This one rests not on a moulded base, like the others, but on a long stone which projects beyond the outer face of the wall, its outer end being carved into the head of a (now much worn) beast resembling a gargoyle. The heads of all are arched lintels, the lower ones square cut, the upper ones chamfered all round. The upper shafts are more mid-wall than the lower ones, the latter being nearer the exterior with their bases almost flush with the wall face.

The tower arch opening to the nave was widened or reconstructed in the twelfth century; it is now 14 feet high and 10 feet 6 ins. wide.

Internally the tower has been divided by wooden floors into four stages. There is no staircase; ascent to the upper floors is by ladders.

The nave is 26 ft. by 14 ft. 6 ins. internally and was formerly very high. The marks of the high pitched earlier gable are visible on the exterior east wall of the tower. The western quoins of the formerly aisleless nave are similar to those of the tower. The nave west wall extends 13 inches to the north and 11 inches to the south of the tower, indicating an external width of nave of 18 ft. 10 ins., the tower being 16 ft. 10 ins. wide. The nave west wall is *c.* 2 ft. 2 ins. thick.

The north aisle is early thirteenth century; the chancel and chancel arch were re-built about the same time. The south aisle is fourteenth century.

HOVINGHAM

ALL SAINTS' CHURCH. Only the tower is Anglo-Saxon. It is dated by V.C.H. to the mid-eleventh century and by Baldwin Brown to the Saxo-Norman Overlap, post-1066. Baldwin Brown suggested that the tower may have been reconstructed at an early date on account of the considerable number of carved or moulded stones re-used in the walling.

The rest of the church was rebuilt in 1860 in thirteenth-century style, perhaps in imitation of the previous church. Two windows of the earlier church were re-set in the south wall of the chancel. One of them is small with an arched lintel, jambs of three upright stones, i.e. pillar jambs, and flat imposts; the opening is chamfered all round. The other window is a lancet. Some quoins of the early nave are visible on the north side of the tower, but not on the south.

The tower (l) is built of large rectangular rubble slabs, some very large; above the ground stage the rubble is smaller and flatter. The east wall has a very Saxon appearance: the stones are of very irregular size and shape; it has recently been re-pointed. The quoins are of large thin slabs, arranged side-alternately. The tower is of

(l) *Plate* 33.

three stages separated by rather thick plain string courses; each upper stage is very slightly recessed behind the stage below. The walls of the ground stage are 3 feet thick. There is a modern tall pyramidal roof of stone slates carried on a modern corbel table.

The Ground Stage. On the west wall below the string course and above the west doorway is a single course of herring-boning of large rubble slabs on edge. Below this, built into the wall, is a square stone on which is carved an equal-armed cross. The arms are straight and square-ended, separated by semicircles; there is no central boss. The background is deeply cut away, leaving the cross in high relief.

The west doorway is round-headed and of two orders, with square-edged projecting hood mould. The main feature of the outer order is a heavy roll-moulding on the west face, carried by attached shafts of similar diameter which have capitals of two quarter-rounds under square imposts. On the outer sides of the roll is a quarter hollow between which and the hood mould the wall face is plain with a vertical quirk. The bases are badly worn but appear to be similar to the capitals. The inner order is plain, square edged, with long voussoirs and imposts. The imposts are chamfered on the soffits and are deep enough to support the whole head, including the hood mould. The jamb stones are side-alternate but are not through-stones. The opening is 6 feet high to the top of the imposts, which are $7\frac{1}{2}$ inches thick, and 3 ft. 4 ins. wide. This doorway is of very advanced design. It could hardly belong to a mid-eleventh-century tower but might have been inserted in the Overlap, perhaps during the supposed reconstruction of the tower suggested as likely by Baldwin Brown.

In the south wall, immediately below the string course, which acts as the lintel, is a small rectangular window; it has no sill and the jambs are of single stones.

Second Stage. Here there are small rectangular windows in the north and west walls, one in each, immediately below the string course and similar to the one below in the south wall, except that the jambs are of one long and two small stones each. In the south wall, high up also, is a large double-splayed round-headed window; it has no impost and the head and jambs are not of through-stones. In the east wall is a small opening, just below the apex of the nave roof and now overlooking the nave. Originally it may have opened to a roof chamber. It is not centrally placed, being above the north jamb of the tower arch.

The third or belfry stage has the usual Anglo-Saxon double lights with central shafts, which are of rectangular cross section. The jambs are splayed. The jamb and central imposts are similar and hollow chamfered all round. The sills are of thin slabs. The details are different on the four faces. On the south the shaft is square edged and the jambs of three rectangular stones on end. In the west the shaft is a very deep rectangular slab, also square edged; the top and bottom are of separate stones but are not real bases or capitals; the jambs are of four upright-and-flat stones. On the north the shaft is of three stones, as on the west, but the jambs are of five flat slabs of mixed face and side-alternate arrangement. On the east the shaft has a separate massive irregular base, a great blob of stone not even roughly cut to shape; the jambs are of four upright and flat rough slabs as on the west. The heads of the belfry windows are not arched lintels but primitively constructed arches. The eastern one has rough voussoirs sloping improperly so that the cutting of the inner ends to fit the arch curve is not normal to the sides. The heads of the north, south and west openings are of two to four long stones cut to appropriate arch shape.

Above the south belfry opening built into the wall is a Saxon cross (1) of similar design to that lower down on the west wall, but it is a latin cross with a central boss and is cut in lower relief. It is worn badly, but there were undoubtedly figures—human or animal or grotesque—carved on the long shaft.

The tower arch (2) has a Saxon appearance, being tall and narrow, nearly 7 feet to the base of the imposts, which are 9 inches thick, and 5 ft. 5 ins. wide. The arch head has two rings of voussoirs, an eastern and a western, rubble filled in between and plastered. It is of one square order, chamfered on the east face. The ten voussoirs are rather large. The imposts are chamfered on the soffit sides, but the ends are flush with the wall east face. The jambs are of large thin slabs arranged side-alternate, like the tower quoins, and are not of through-stones. The west face of the arch is plastered smooth; it appears as a plain round-headed opening with no details visible; presumably it is similar to the east face. The jambs, that is the nave west wall, are 3 ft. 3 ins. thick. The tower is 12 ft. 9 ins. square on the interior, and therefore *c.* 19 feet on the exterior. Internally the high ground stage is divided into two storeys, the upper being the ringing chamber. Above the tower arch is a single course of herring-boning.

The well-known frieze, which Baldwin Brown classified with the Breedon-on-the-Hill–Castor–Fletton–Peterborough Group of late eighth- early ninth-century carvings, and which was formerly built into the south exterior wall of the tower, has been removed. It is now attached to the east wall of the south aisle, as a small reredos to the altar there. It has eight panels of much worn figures: the two on the left (facing) are of the Annunciation, the next two the Salutation, the next four the Flight into Egypt. A narrow frieze forming a border below is an inhabited vine scroll.

MIDDLETON-BY-PICKERING

St. Andrew's Church.[1] The tower is of three stages. The two lower stages are pre-Conquest, dated by Baldwin Brown to post-1040, as are also parts of the nave

[1] G. Baldwin Brown; V.C.H., *Yorks, N.R.,* II.

---

(1) *Plate* 33; (2) *Plate* 34.

walls and the nave north-west and south-west quoins. The rest of the nave was rebuilt *c.* 1130, the north and south aisle and chancel arch *c.* 1200 and a clerestory added in the fifteenth century. The nave and aisles were again rebuilt *c.* 1700. Junctions of Anglo-Saxon, Norman and thirteenth-century work are visible on the exterior of the nave west wall on both sides of the tower.

The tower (1) is of coursed long rubble slabs with wide joints. The lower quoins are massive, almost megalithic though thin, some stones being up to 2 ft. 5 ins. by 1 ft. 7 ins. by 6 inches. Above about 12 feet they are smaller though still large. They lie side alternate. The north-west nave quoins are similar. The tower is 11 feet east–west and 9 ft. 6 ins. north–south internally. Though the longer axis lies east–west it is not a porch tower.

The blocked western doorway (2) was Anglo-Saxon and proves the tower to be also, as it is not a porch tower. The doorway was 9 feet high by 2 ft. 10 ins. wide between jambs, with Saxon strip-work, 6 inches wide, all round it. It was originally round-headed but a later (*c.* 1200) vesica-shaped window was inserted above which cut into the crown of the arch head leaving only five of the original voussoirs on the north and three on the south; these voussoirs are not well shaped. The jambs are of pillar type, each of four stones on end. The imposts are hollow chamfered. The strip-work is square sectioned, three long strips to each jamb, and the head of short appropriately shaped strips. There are double square-cut imposts to the strip-work, the lower members above the vertical strips extending north and south *c.* 10 inches, the upper shorter ones supporting the head and projecting from the wall *c.* 3 inches.

A few feet above the blocked doorway is an equal-armed cross carved on a square stone (2). The arms are square-ended and there are semicircular angles between them. It is badly weathered but knotwork patterns are visible on the arms. There is a large central boss with a smaller one at the centre; in the annular space between is stylized leaf decoration, not unlike Jew's harp ornament.

There was no other opening in the west and north walls below the belfry.

In the south wall are two rectangular windows (3), one above the other. The lower one has no lintel, sill or separate jambs; the upper one has flat lintel, jambs of one tall and two thin flats lying above, and no sill.

In the east wall above the tower arch and within the nave is an almost square window. It has flat lintel and sill of large long slabs, and jambs of three upright-flat-upright stones. It looks renewed but may be part of the twelfth-century rebuilding.

The tower arch is of two orders of the same date, *c.* 1200, and character as the chancel arch.

The belfry stage, above the single square cut string course, was added *c.* 1200. It

---

(1) *Plates* 35, 36; (2) *Plate* 36; (3) *Plate* 35.

is not known whether it replaced an earlier one. It has two-light windows in each wall which have been modernized.

The embattled parapet rests on a corbel table with badly worn grotesques.

The nave walls may be pre-Conquest.

This church is particularly rich in large and small fragments of particularly interesting pre-Conquest sculptured stones, now collected mainly at the east end of the north aisle. They cannot be considered here. One however may be referred to briefly as it has been discussed by a number of writers.[1] It was built into the exterior of the tower but has now been removed to the interior of the church.

[1] T. D. Kendrick, Pl. LXIV (*a*); E. A. Fisher, Pl. 33 B.

YORKSHIRE: EAST RIDING

SKIPWITH

ST. HELEN'S CHURCH.[1] This is an attractive church with a very fine tower. The tower, except the belfry, and the western part of the originally aisleless nave are Anglo-Saxon. Baldwin Brown dates it to post-1040 but perhaps early in that period.

The present belfry stage of the tower and battlemented parapet with corner pinnacles are fifteenth century. According to Baldwin Brown it probably replaced an earlier Saxon belfry; this however is surmise. The ground stage (1) occupies more than half the total height of the tower and is divided on the interior into two by a wooden floor. The second exterior stage is very short. String courses separate the stages. The lower string is mainly a renewal; its condition is too good for it to be original.

The Saxon part of the tower is built of coursed, large, rectangular, roughly dressed rubble blocks, the bottom course being of very large stones up to 2 ft. 6 ins. by 1 ft. 9 ins. The lower half of the second internal stage is of similar but smaller blocks; its upper half and the top Saxon stage are of very thin, ragstone type of slabs. There is a two-membered plinth, the upper member being chamfered. The quoins are very large, almost megalithic below where they measure up to 3 ft. 6 ins. by 14 inches, by 18 inches; about half way up they become smaller. All are arranged in side-alternate manner.

In the south wall below the later belfry stage are four window openings (1). Three lie in the centre line of the wall and three are in the tall bottom stage. The lowest window, about 10 to 12 feet up, is rather large and double splayed with the greater part of the splay on the interior (i.e. the glass line is near the outer wall face). On the exterior as far as the glass line it has arched lintel, slab jambs with jamb stones lying on their faces but in no particular arrangement, no imposts and no separate sill. On the interior the jamb stones lie on their sides and are mostly through-stones as far as the glass line. The interior head is of voussoirs which have their narrow ends outwards leaving a large V-shaped space at the crown filled with a very large keystone.

The window above in the second internal stage is rather smaller. It has a round head of thin selected (not dressed) stones with their thinner ends inwards, no imposts or

[1] G. Baldwin Brown.

---

(1) *Plate* 37.

sill, and jambs of selected flattish stones. To the east of this window and on a level with its crown is a smaller one with arched lintel, slab jambs, no imposts or sill; it is double-splayed. It lights the curious recess on the interior east wall discussed below.

The fourth window is in the centre of the south wall of the second external stage. It is a small rectangular loop window made of four large, well dressed stones and chamfered all round. It looks later than those below.

In the west wall are three openings (I), all windows; there is no west doorway. The lowest, about 4 feet from the ground, has an arched lintel, well dressed stone jambs and sill, all very obviously renewals (was there an original?). It has a single not very wide splay towards the interior. Higher and about half way up is a window very similar to the one in a corresponding position in the south wall (the second from the ground referred to above). In the second external stage is a rectangular loop window similar to that on the south; the lintel and sill look original, the jambs may be renewals.

In the north wall are two double-splayed windows. The lower is in a corresponding position to the one on the south wall. It is tall, relatively narrow, with arched lintel on the exterior, jambs of big slabs and no separate sill; on the interior it is similar to the one on the south. In the second internal stage is a loop window similar to the other two loops. It is original but may have renewed jambs.

In the east wall is another loop window, on the exterior above the nave roof. The jambs of all the loop windows look like renewals but may not be. They are made of different, darker, harder-looking stone from the walling and may have worn better than those lintels which are of similar stone to the walling. Around the four loop windows in the low external stage are the remains of earlier and wider blocked windows which appear to have been round-headed single openings. They may have been built-up, and narrower windows inserted in the blockings, to strengthen the fabric, when the fifteenth-century belfry was added. H. M. Taylor is of opinion that these earlier windows were the original Saxon belfry openings, of an earlier type than the more usual double-light variety. If this were so it might suggest an earlier date for the tower than Baldwin Brown's post-1040. The shortness of this stage is consistent with the view that this was the original belfry and that the later belfry was an addition and not a substitution for an earlier top stage as Baldwin Brown thought.

Lower down, in the east wall, above the tower arch and below the roof of the nave, is a large rectangular opening now blocked. The jambs are of small slabs of mixed face and side-alternate arrangement. The top and bottom stones, both shorts, of the jambs have their inner corners chamfered off to produce lintel and sill with

(I) *Plate* 37.

sloping ends; that is, the outline of the opening is a rectangle with the corners cut off. There is no separate sill between the two inwardly projecting bottom jamb stones.

The tower arch (1) is very fine, large and round-headed. Of the voussoirs a few are renewals, a few are through-stones but most are two or three per course with no rubble filling. The jambs have some through-stones but are mostly two stones per course. They are 2 ft. 10 ins. thick. The plain imposts, *c.* 7 inches thick, project 4 inches from wall and soffit, and are returned on each face to *c.* 3 ft. 8 ins. The arch is 8 feet high to the bottom of the imposts and 8 ft. 3 ins. wide. The total height is very nearly 13 feet. The plinth is 12 inches high and projects 3 inches. A double strip-work hood mould runs round the head and down the jambs on both east and west faces. It is reminiscent of the magnificent arch at Stow (Lincs). The outer strip-work is square edged, 5 inches by 5 inches, and forms the extreme border of the nave west wall. The inner strip-work, 6 inches within the outer band and 2 feet from the soffits, is 9 inches wide with a projection of 5 inches; it is segmental in plan.

In the interior east wall of the second internal stage of the tower, now the ringing chamber, is a shallow recess[1] 3 feet high by 3 ft. 5 ins. wide and 6 inches deep; the sill is *c.* 2 feet above the present floor. It has a flat lintel chamfered below and below the chamfer is a half-round moulding which forms the lower edge of the lintel, a late feature. There is no separate sill. The jambs are of round monolithic columns under rectangular, square-edged block imposts of pre-Conquest type. The bases appear to be slightly bulbous. It is lighted by the small window in the south wall described above; the window sill is a little below the level of the lintel of the recess. The original object of the recess is not known. It is not recognizably an altar and there is no evidence that there was an altar here. It is later than the tower for it is behind the blocked opening in the east wall above the tower arch. Baldwin Brown suggested that it may have held reliefs, like those now at Chichester Cathedral, but this is a mere surmise. It has no close parallel elsewhere in England, though there is a smaller and simpler recess in the tower at Glentworth (Lincs).[2]

WEAVERTHORPE

ST. ANDREW'S CHURCH.[3] This church, with its rather earlier neighbour Wharram-le-Street, was studied in some detail by John Bilson who established the facts that both churches are definitely twelfth century, i.e. well within the Norman period, but equally definitely Anglo-Saxon in design and technique of building. This very

[1] See G. Baldwin Brown, p. 333, fig. 149.   [2] See below, p. 274, fig. 22.
[3] J. Bayly; John Bilson; G. Baldwin Brown.

(1) *Plate* 38.

protracted survival of pre-Conquest building methods for forty or fifty years after the Conquest was due to the thoroughness of and consequent slow recovery from William the Conqueror's devastation of this part of Yorkshire in 1069. Bilson states that in an area of 20 miles by 12 to 16 miles, including this village, no ploughing oxen and no population were recorded in Domesday Book—and this nearly twenty years after the great devastation. The area was not necessarily depopulated but there was no systematic agriculture which would or could bear taxation: peasants here and there doubtless managed to scrape a subsistance from the soil in wretched conditions, but nothing more.

The church is a fine one and full of interest. It stands on an eminence and is visible from several miles away; from it a fine view of the surrounding country is obtainable.

The nave, chancel and western tower are of the early twelfth century—1110–1120—the south porch of the early fourteenth century. The whole[1] was restored by G. E. Street in 1871–2.

The Tower. The tower (I) rises for more than three-quarters of its height with no string courses, set-off, batter or buttresses from a chamfered plinth. There is a half-round stair turret built out from the south-east corner which has three narrow single-splayed loop windows, all facing south-west. A chamfered string course separates the belfry stage from the tall exterior stage below and is continued round the stair turret which finishes just below. The belfry stage is slightly set back above the string. Above the belfry is another string course, then two courses of masonry which form a plain top to the tower. Street added a pyramidal lead-covered roof which was removed in 1898. It now has a flat roof, not visible from the ground.

The walls are 3 ft. 5 ins. to 3 ft. 7 ins. thick.

The tower is of three stages, the tall exterior lower stage being divided into two internally. It is built of ashlar, in courses 9 to 12 inches high, of squared stones of calcareous grit obtained from an outcrop of the Yorkshire Wolds among which the church is situated. The stones have axed tooling, and the joints are wide—$\frac{5}{8}$ to $\frac{3}{4}$ of an inch.

In the ground stage there is no west doorway. Higher up is a rather narrow rectangular window with no separate lintel or sill but with dressed jambs single-splayed internally; this is the only opening in this stage. In the second stage, the ringing chamber, there is a rectangular window with slight internal splay in each of the north, west and south walls.

The belfry has in each wall the normal Anglo-Saxon type of double-light window with central shafts under a single round-headed arch of one plain order. Those on the north, west and east have square-cut jambs of walling resting on the string

[1] Plan in J. Bilson, p. 53; also J. Bayly, Pl. 4.

(I) *Plate* 39.

course, heads of voussoirs, chamfered imposts which are returned along the wall faces and support the double arch heads and the outer relieving arch as well. Below the imposts are columns with cushion capitals, round chamfered bases and plain neckings below and above. In the tympana above the double arch heads project curious plain corbels, one in each tympanum. The south belfry opening is similar to the others in general design but differs in some details. The jambs and heads as well as the relieving arch above are recessed behind the wall face, the relieving arch being of two plain orders. The capitals are not strictly cushion; they are rather flat, the four faces are convexly chamfered and the corners rounded by means of convex chamfers to bring the square to a circle below. This window is a little to the west of central on account of the stair turret which is to the east of it. The turret was therefore part of the original tower, not added later.

The tower arch (1) is very tall and narrow. 7 ft. 2 ins. wide and 14 ft. 9½ ins. high to the springing. The round head is of one plain square-cut order but of two rings of voussoirs, an eastern and a western, with rubble and plaster filling between the rings. There are no imposts. The square-cut jambs are of ashlar, three or four stones per course, and indistinguishable from the walling. Above the tower arch is a doorway 3 ft. 2 ins. wide by 5 ft. 11 ins. high with square unrebated jambs and flat lintel. Its sill is about two feet above the slight set-back remaining from the earlier ceiling. This doorway provided access from the ringing chamber to an inter-roof space.

The Nave. The nave, like the chancel and tower, is built of ashlar on both exterior and interior faces. The north and south walls of both nave and chancel are 2 ft. 4 ins. thick, the nave east wall 2 ft. 7 ins. The nave is 42 ft. 11 ins. long by 23 ft. 1½ ins. wide on the interior, and *c.* 21 feet high. Almost horizontal marks (1) on the east and west walls, at the height of the side walls, probably indicate the original flat ceiling; the walling in the gable above looks newer. The original roof of nave and chancel had been lowered; the present open roof was put up by G. E. Street.

There are two original unaltered round-headed windows in each of the north and south walls; they are not very high up, the glass line being only 9 feet from the floor. They are 1 ft. 5½ ins. wide by less than 6 feet high. The jambs and heads, but not the sills, are widely single-splayed on the interior.

There are two—north and south—doorways[1] near the west end. Externally they have square-cut jambs only 6 inches thick of face-alternate arrangement with flat lintels and semicircular relieving arches in the walling above. Internally the jambs have no lintels but support a round-headed arch; these inner jambs are 1 ft. 10 ins. thick as far as the inner face of the outer jambs, with two or three stones per course; there are no imposts and the round head is of voussoirs of one or two per course.

[1] J. Bilson, p. 55, fig. 2.

---

(1) *Plate* 40.

The construction is peculiar: the thin outer jambs project 3 inches inwards—i.e. towards east and west—beyond the face of the inner jambs so that the exterior opening is narrower than the interior by 6 inches. In fact the inner jambs form a deep rebate in the nave wall for the door which shuts against the inner face of the outer jambs. In the south doorway the lintel is of a large thin rectangular stone on edge which forms the greater part of the tympanum (1) between it and the relieving arch above. The rest of the tympanum, slightly recessed, is filled with ashlar on one stone of which, larger than the others, is a Saxon sundial. The lower part of the stone is occupied by the dial, the upper part by an inscription. The stone now rectangular, 14 inches by $12\frac{1}{2}$ inches, was originally square, as indicated by the fact that part of the top line of the inscription has been cut away; possibly the sundial has been removed from some other position. The inscription[1] reads:

+ IN · HONORE · SCI · ANDREAE
APOSTOLI · HEREBERTUS
WINTONIE · HOC · MONASTERI
VM · FECIT · IN · TEMPORE · RE[2]

The Chancel. This is 22 ft. 10 ins. long by 16 ft. 11 ins. wide internally, really spacious for an Anglo-Saxon chancel. It has no original windows, the existing windows are fourteenth century. Two aumbries near the east ends of the north and south walls appear to be original. The south one is square with jambs and lintel of three well-dressed thinnish slabs and no separate sill. The north one is rectangular; the lintel and short upper portion of the jambs are cut from a single stone; the lower parts of the jambs and the sill are walling.

The chancel arch (2) is very fine but wide and low, in marked contrast to the much taller and narrower tower arch. It is 11 ft. 7 ins. wide by 8 feet high to the springing. The arch head and jambs are plain, square-edged, and are recessed, i.e. of two orders, on the west face only. The imposts have large quirked rolls on their lower edges, and are not returned on the east and west wall faces—an early feature. The arch head is of small voussoirs, very regular in size and length in both orders: 38 in the outer or upper order, 24 in the inner. They are not through-stones; in the outer order there are three voussoir stones per course.

Bilson made out a strong case for believing that the Herebertus Wintonie of the sundial, who built the church, was Herbert the Royal Chamberlain and father of St. William, Archbishop of York, 1142–47 and again in 1154. The church was given

---

[1] J. Bilson, p. 58, fig. 3.
[2] The E is incomplete; W. G. Collingwood suggested that RF stood for REGIS.

---

(1) *Plate* 42; (2) *Plate* 41.

by Robert, son of Herbert, to Nostell Priory probably between 1114 and 1121 and certainly before 1129. It was on this basis that Bilson dated the church to 1110–20. He writes: 'It [the church] follows in the main the new manner of building introduced by the Norman conquerors, but it shows some indication of overlap in style in its retention of some pre-Conquest characteristics, including the dial which particularly enables us to identify its builder and its date.'

There is in fact nothing specifically Norman about the church except the fine ashlar and the recessing of the chancel arch, and perhaps the cushion capitals of the belfry windows. The capitals however are not characteristically Norman. Cushion capitals were not introduced into England until a very few years before, or possibly after, the Conquest, probably from Germany via Flanders, and were adopted by the Anglo-Norman builders. They are usually regarded as an English contribution to Norman architecture. More interesting perhaps is the absence of any chevron ornament which was the earliest of Norman ornaments to be introduced into England.

On the other hand there is nothing specifically Anglo-Saxon in the church, except the double-light type of belfry window and the thinness of the nave and chancel walls. There are no pilaster strips, or long and short work, or strip-work round openings, or arched lintels or early quoining or high-up nave windows. The tower is of generally Saxon proportions: plain, unbuttressed, relatively tall and slender.

WHARRAM-LE-STREET

ST. MARY'S CHURCH.[1] This church lies on the Roman road or street which runs south-east from Malton, in continuation of the street which runs from the west to Malton on which are two other towered Anglo-Saxon churches: Appleton-le-Street and Hovingham.

Wharram-le-Street is earlier than its neighbour Weaverthorpe, though probably not much earlier. Baldwin Brown dated it to the Saxo-Norman Overlap, Bilson as post-Conquest. It is probably either very late eleventh or very early twelfth century, i.e. before 1110–20, the date of Weaverthorpe. Originally it consisted of chancel, aisleless nave and western tower. A Norman north arcade was cut and a north aisle built in 1300–50. The south wall of the nave is a modern rebuilding. The chancel was rebuilt and a south porch added in 1862.[2] The tower, the west wall of the nave and the east wall on both sides of the chancel arch, with a short return on the nave north wall, are original.

The tower[3] (I) is built of calcareous grit from the neighbouring Yorkshire Wolds,

---

[1] J. Bilson; G. Baldwin Brown. [2] J. Bilson, plan on p. 52, fig. 1.
[3] J. Bilson, Pl. V, 1 (view from SW.) and Pl. V, 2 (upper part of S. face).

of squared stones in rough ashlar with wide and irregular joints on both interior and exterior faces. The quoins are of similar but larger stones arranged in side-alternate manner. The ashlar courses are *c.* 10–11 inches high, the quoin stones *c.* 2 feet by 10 inches by 15 inches high. The tower measures 11 ft. 5 ins. east–west by 10 ft. 7 ins. north–south on the interior; the exterior width of the west wall is 15 ft. 8 ins., the walls therefore being *c.* 2 ft. 6 ins. thick. The present height is 51 feet. It is of similar dimensions to those of the Tyneside church of Corbridge. Externally the tower has no buttresses and no plinth, though there is a foundation set-off 5 to 7 inches wide at ground level. It is of four stages, though there is now no floor between the second and third stages. The first three stages are plain with no string courses or set-back. A chamfered string course separates the belfry stage, which is slightly set back, from the stage below.

The west wall. The western doorway (l) was very tall and narrow: 8 ft. 2 ins. to the springing and 2 ft. 6 ins. wide. The upper half is now filled with glass and the lower half blocked. The round head is of two orders. The inner order is square-edged with a deep quirk round the soffit about 2 inches from the face. The jambs are not rebated and are inclined 2 inches inwards towards the top. The square imposts are hollow chamfered on the soffit sides. The outer order has a moulded head; it has a roll round its outer edge, outside of which is a shallow hollow moulding between two quirks; outside the hollow moulding is a plain square hood mould flush with the wall face. The head is stilted and of properly shaped voussoirs, each of which, like each of the stones of the outer and inner jambs, is cut to the appropriate profile or plan. The head rests on imposts similar to those of the inner order, hollow chamfered on the soffit sides only. Below the imposts are circular angle shafts in the recesses between inner and outer orders. The shafts have tall bases, badly worn but which appear to have hollow chamfers, east and west, with wide rather bulbous bands above instead of neckings. The capitals are of primitive design (Fig. 7): the faces and edges are chamfered downwards, and the chamfered edges are rounded off to fit the circular shaft below. The jambs are of large slabs in mainly side-alternate arrangement. Apart from the head, the opening is very similar, even in details, to the tower arch.

Above, in the second stage, are two loop windows with apertures 6 inches wide, arched lintels, monolithic jambs slightly inclined and flat sills; the openings are chamfered all round.

In the south wall are two loop windows, one in the second and one, just below the string course, in the third stage. They are similar to those in the west except that the upper one has jambs of fairly large walling stones. About 15 feet above the ground is a dial stone which may be in its original position.

(l) *Plate* 44.

The north wall has no opening below the belfry.

In the east wall, above the tower arch, is a blocked doorway, 4 ft. 6 ins. high to the springing of the stilted round head. The jambs are slightly inclined, being 2 ft. 0½ ins. wide at the sill and 1 ft. 11 ins. at the top. The sill is *c.* 3 feet above the undersides of the wall plates of the modern nave roof. The opening presumably gave access to an inter-roof space. It is not now visible from the nave owing to its covering of cream wash.

The belfry openings[1] are of pure pre-Conquest type: narrow double openings with central mid-wall shafts with tall cubic capitals rounded down to circular shape and no neckings (I). The shafts support through-stone central imposts, hollow chamfered on front and sides as are also the jamb imposts. The double lights have arched lintels. Narrow square-edged pilaster strips flank the jambs; the jamb imposts abut against the strips. The strips are finished above the level of the jamb imposts with similar small hollow chamfered imposts and they rest below on similar reversed imposts, acting as corbels, above the level of the string course. It looks as though these upper strip imposts were to support a half-round strip-work head, as at St. Mary the Younger, Bishop Hill Junior, York, a church with no Norman features. There is however no evidence for this as the three-course plain parapet and hollow-chamfered corbel table under it are a much later replacement of the top courses of the tower.

The tower arch (2) is tall and rather narrow, 6 ft. 1 in. wide by 10 ft. 9 ins. high to the springing of the arch head. The square jambs are recessed on the nave side only, with an 8-inch detached angle shaft in each recess. The bases of the shafts are of unusual design[2] and certainly not Norman. They rest on chamfered plinths. The

Fig. 7. Wharram-le-Street, Capital

bottom face of 3 inches of each base is vertical and above that is a 12½-inch single shallow only slightly curved hollow chamfer to bring the base to the same diameter as the shaft. The capitals (Fig. 7) are also unusual, and not Norman, of tall cubical or

[1] J. Bilson, Pl. V, 2.   [2] J. Bilson, p. 59, fig. 3.

(I) *Plate* 43; (2) *Plate* 45.

cylindrical type: the faces and corners are converted to triangles by chamfering and then the chamfered corners rounded off to circular form below. The abaci above have flat thin upper faces, with long hollow chamfers below. The north abacus is chamfered on both soffit and east faces; the latter projects from the wall face. It seems likely that the south abacus was once similar but has been cut back flush with the wall face. The thick imposts, separate from the abaci, of the inner order are similar to the abaci of the columns. They are hollow chamfered on their soffits only, and are roughly flush with the walls and not chamfered on their east and west faces. The jambs are inclined, the opening being $2\frac{1}{2}$ inches narrower near the imposts; such inclination is unusual in a large opening. The arch head is slightly horse-shoe at the springing. The arch is of one order on the west, the narrow inner order being flush with the wall face: there are no angle columns as there are no recesses. The voussoirs of the inner order are through-stones. The cream-washed plaster hides most small details but Bilson states that the joints of some voussoirs do not radiate correctly but slope towards points below the centre of the arch curve.[1]

The constructional relation of the two orders is curious. The thinner inner order is not built against or bonded in a normal manner into the outer. The two orders are flush on the west face but on the recessed east the face of the outer order is carried along in front of part of the front face of the inner order; in other words, the inner order is bonded in on the east, where the outer overlaps it, but not on the west where they are flush; the outer order is L-shaped in plan.

Unlike those of the tower walls the joints of the tower arch and jambs are fine and accurately worked to about $\frac{1}{4}$ to $\frac{3}{8}$ of an inch in thickness. The inner order is 1 ft. $8\frac{1}{2}$ ins. thick (east–west), the outer order projecting to the east 10 inches (the depth of the recessing) beyond the inner; total wall thickness is therefore 2 ft. $6\frac{1}{2}$ ins.

The Nave. The nave overlaps the tower on the east and projects from it 2 ft. 9 ins. on the north and 2 ft. 7 ins. on the south. It is plastered inside and out but probably its walling is similar to that of the tower, both being of the same date. The south-western corner looks original but most of it is behind a later buttress which reaches just above the eaves of the nave roof. The north-east, north-west and south-west quoins are original; the south-east quoin has been renewed at some time. Unlike the tower the nave has a plinth of two members; the upper one, 13 inches high, is chamfered. The south wall was rebuilt in 1862 and its thickness reduced on the exterior by *c.* 6 inches from *c.* 1 foot above the plinth.

The nave is *c.* 29 feet long by 15 ft. 10 ins. wide; the walls are 2 ft. 7 ins. thick (the north wall at the east and west responds of the arcade is 2 ft. 9 ins. including the plaster on both faces) and 17 ft. 2 ins. high from the present floor to the underside of the wall plates of the modern nave.

It has no original windows; all are modern.

---

[1] See for example, G. Baldwin Brown, p. 67, fig. 37.

The south doorway, near the west end, is 3 ft. 1½ ins. wide. It is similar in plan to the west doorway of the tower but the jambs are rebated and splayed on the interior. This rebate and splay may or may not be original; the doorway was badly mutilated when it was reset in the rebuilt south wall and it has lost its shafts and shaft bases. The capitals remain. The capital of the lost west shaft has an angle volute similar to that of the north capital of the chancel arch (1); the capital of the east shaft has a row of stiff vertical stylized leaves turned over at the tips similar to the corners of the chancel arch south capital (2) but without the volute. Both capitals have neckings. The outer order has a wide hood of small projection with chevron ornament incised (hardly more) on it, with billet ornament below.[1]

The Chancel. The chancel is 16 feet long and was originally 12 feet wide, with walls of the same thickness as the nave. It was rebuilt in 1862 with walls thinner on the interior by 6 inches, so the width now is 1 foot greater. The east wall was rebuilt to about its original thickness. It is plastered inside and out. It has no original windows; all are modern. However, in a drawing made in 1862 by Messrs. T. B. and William Atkinson, the architects, an original window is shown in about the middle of the chancel north wall. It was a single narrow light *c.* 6 inches wide and 2 ft. 10 ins. high, including its round head, with jambs chamfered on the exterior and wide single internal splay to jambs, head and sill.

The chancel arch has a later pointed head of two orders. The jambs are original. The plan is closely similar to that of the tower arch—square and recessed on the nave side only, with a 7-inch detached angle shaft in each nook. The bases of the columns have Norman profiles of a hollow top member with three successive flattish rolls below. The capitals too are of Norman inspiration. The north one (1) has a large spiral angle volute flanked on each side by two upright stylized leaves turned over at the top. The south capital (2) has an angle volute with a smaller volute on each side of it. The abaci have a common Norman profile of a quirked chamfer below and a flat vertical face, the whole returned as an impost to the square jambs. The height to the top of the abaci is 7 ft. 10 ins. and the width of the opening is 7 ft. 1 in. The thickness of the inner jamb order is 2 ft. 9½ ins. and the projection of the outer arch beyond the inner on the west face is 9½ inches; the total thickness of the wall is therefore 3 ft. 7 ins.

The date of this church must be based on consideration of its most advanced details, not on its archaisms. There is only one specifically Norman detail in the tower—that of the west doorway—and two in the nave—the chevron and billet ornament of the south doorway. Both nave and tower—and original chancel—are of

[1] J. Bilson, p. 62, fig. 5 (drawing).

(1) *Plate* 46; (2) *Plate* 47.

one date, built at the same time. The chevron and billet ornament indicates the early years of the twelfth century. The arch mouldings of the western doorway—as pointed out by Bilson—are closely similar to those at St. Etienne at Caen of *c.* 1080 and at St. Nicholas at Caen of a few years later. At Lincoln Cathedral, derived from Caen, they occur in the arches of the recesses of the west front of probably *c.* 1090; in the intersecting wall arcade inside the choir aisles at Durham, a cathedral begun in 1093; and in the ground storey of Norwich apse begun in 1096. Bilson writes: 'It is therefore impossible that it could have made its appearance in a Yorkshire church which is otherwise so backward before the last decade of the eleventh century, and its date here is much more likely to be in the early part of the twelfth century.'

Bilson makes out a strong case for the building of the church by Nigel Fossard, mentioned in Domesday Book as sub-feudatory of Robert, Count of Mortain, the Conqueror's half-brother. Later when Robert's lands were forfeited Nigel became a direct tenant of the Crown. His son Robert gave the church to the Austin Canons of Nostell Priory, a grant not later than 1129. This gift is historically important because King Alexander I of Scotland established at Scone some regular canons whom he had brought from Nostell *c.* 1120. Alexander died in 1124. His successor David I made one of the canons, Robert, Bishop of St. Andrews *c.* 1126 or 7. Bishop Robert built the church of St. Rule or St. Regulus at St. Andrews and established regular canons there, one of them being brought direct from Robert's own former monastery, Nostell, to be prior. There is a very close similarity between St. Rule's church and Wharram-le-Street: as Bilson writes 'some forty years after the Conquest an English mason employed by a Norman lord built a church [Wharram-le-Street] which followed to a great extent the building tradition of pre-Conquest times, with a tower in which only a single detail can be pronounced to be of distinctively Norman inspiration; and . . . this Englishman, or one of his colleagues, took a leading part in the building of one of Scotland's most important surviving monuments of the earlier years of King David's reign'.[1]

[1] For a detailed account of St. Rule's Church see J. Bilson, (*b*). Scottish Anglo-Saxon churches are outside the scope of this book.

YORKSHIRE: WEST RIDING

BARDSEY

ALL HALLOWS CHURCH. The tower is slender (I), of rectangular cross section and built probably over an earlier porch. The battlemented parapet and corbel table of grotesques are later, as are all the nave and chancel windows. The rest of the tower, and the nave and chancel walls are pre-Conquest. Baldwin Brown dates them to between the late eighth and the early tenth centuries; the lower part of the tower, nave and perhaps chancel are probably of one date, possibly pre-870, the upper tower later and post-870.

The tower has no exterior stages or string courses. The interior was later divided into four stages by wooden floors, the beams of which rest on projecting stone corbels of mediaeval date.

The walls of the tower and nave are 2 ft. $0\frac{1}{2}$ in. thick; those of the third stage of the tower are two feet and the top stage only 1 ft. 8 ins. thick. The height is 50 feet. The tower is 10 ft. $2\frac{1}{2}$ ins. deep (east–west) and 8 feet wide (north–south) internally; externally the west wall is 12 feet wide. It is built of well coursed rectangular rubble blocks which is unusual for a very early church, although Escomb (Co. Durham), probably eighth century, has similar wall work. The top stage is of more rubble-like appearance, though still fairly regular and well coursed. The western quoins up to c. 12 feet, i.e. of the presumed earlier porch, are of large blocks or slabs, some about 3 ft. 6 ins. by 2 feet, apparently side-alternate; above, the slabs are smaller and arranged face-alternately.

The later, probably originally Norman, aisles have their west walls flush with the west wall of the tower, as at Stevington (Beds) and Deerhurst (Glos), so the north and south lower parts of the tower are visible only from inside the church.

There is no western entrance, which fact is rather against the porch tower theory. The original main entrance was on the north. This is an unusual position for a tower entrance except when required for access to side adjuncts or in turriform churches. It is especially unusual for a main entrance. About 5 feet above ground level in the west wall is a late Gothic two-light window. Above this is a small rectangular window with no separate lintel, sill or jambs. Higher still, in the third stage, is a single pointed thirteenth-century lancet; and in the fourth or belfry stage is a Gothic two-light cusped window.

(I) *Plate* 48.

In the north wall is a round-headed doorway, the original main entrance, only 2 ft. 6 ins. wide and not rebated. The head is of two rings, an inner and an outer, each of which is an arched lintel half-round both above and below. The jambs are of through-stones, except the top one on the east which is of two stones per course. A window, c. 8 feet above ground level, is similar to that on the south with slight single internal splay and slightly sloping jambs. Higher up still is a small rectangular opening similar to that on the west. In the fourth or belfry stage is a cusped Gothic two-light window like that on the west.

In the south wall at ground level is a round-headed doorway which looks renewed. Its head is of voussoirs, jambs of slabs, no imposts, and a slab sill. It is 2 ft. 8 ins. wide and 5 feet to the crown of the arch—rather taller than the north doorway. Above, c. 8 feet above ground, is a small round-headed opening, with slight internal splay and sloping jambs; the head is of five real voussoirs, jambs of four selected walling slabs each, the top and bottom slabs being longer than the others and the top ones serving as imposts; there is no separate sill. Higher still, in the third stage and in the fourth or belfry stage, are double-light windows (1) of typical Anglo-Saxon pattern. Two such windows one above the other in two stages of the same wall are also an Anglo-Saxon feature, though not common. The double heads are of small voussoirs with central baluster shafts, c. 2 ft. 11 ins. high,[1] only slightly bulging and supporting central through-stone imposts with chamfered ends below the arch heads. The shafts are not mid-wall; they are nearer the exterior, their bases being almost flush with the outer wall face. The bases of the shafts are rough cubical blocks hollow chamfered above to meet the shafts. They have no capitals (though Baldwin Brown wrote that they have, and gave a drawing). The jamb imposts are small and almost indistinguishable from the jamb stones which are just walling stones.

In the east wall the belfry opening is a single narrow window with an arched lintel and which appears to be contemporary with the double openings on the south. Below, in the third stage, is a similar narrow but slightly smaller opening. H. M. Taylor considers these two windows to represent a type of belfry window earlier in design than the more familiar and complicated double belfry openings. The latter are too complex to have arisen suddenly; they almost presuppose a preliminary period of development. Here at Bardsey we may have on adjacent walls the familiar double opening and a precursor, both of contemporary date.

The tower arch (2) is of Anglo-Saxon type but has much renewed work. The round head of through-stone voussoirs is of one square-cut order. The jambs are 1 ft. 11½ ins. thick (east–west). The large bottom stones of the south jamb look

---

[1] H. M. Taylor's measurement. Baldwin Brown gave 3 ft. 8 ins. but this included his supposed capital, really the separate impost.

original; they are 4 ft. 6 ins. high by 1 ft. 11½ ins. by 7 inches (north–south). The imposts are quirked and chamfered and are returned a long way to north and south; the north one dies into the similar abacus of the north arcade respond. There is a round-headed quirked and chamfered hood mould round and in contact with the arch head. The label stops are human heads, not Saxon. The arch is 6 ft. 11 ins. wide and 8 ft. 4 ins. high to the lower face of the imposts. The quirked chamfer suggests an Overlap date, at the earliest. It seems likely that the arch head is later than the fabric of the tower. It may have been reconstructed when the early Norman north aisle was built.

The nave is *c.* 31 feet long by 15 ft. 3 ins. wide internally, with walls 2 feet thick. It extends 3 ft. 10 ins. to the south and 3 ft. 6 ins. to the north of the tower. The nave north-west and south-west quoins are visible within the church; they are massive stones up to 3 ft. 6 ins. by 16 inches by 15 inches up to about 10 or 12 feet, but smaller above. Arrangement is side-alternate. The south-east quoins appear to be of short pillar stones. There are straight joints between nave and aisles. The upper parts of the nave walls on the exterior look later, like the later part of the chancel, but the lower parts are hidden by the aisles so any difference in walling, suggestive of a later heightening, would not be visible (the interior is plastered).

The chancel is the same width as the nave; it is built against the nave and may be later. Certainly it was heightened at some time; the top nine courses, those above *c.* 20 feet, are different from those below; the stones are more nearly square and are better dressed; they are probably Norman like the aisles. The quoins, too, at the higher level are different, being smaller and not very different from the walling and arranged in no particular way. The lower quoins are larger but most are hidden by the later buttresses jutting from the east end.

On the east side of the east wall of the nave, above the chancel arch, are marks of the earlier lower steeply gabled chancel roof.

The chancel arch is rather similar to and later than the tower arch, and also larger. It has no through stones and is chamfered on the west face. Its round head is of two voussoirs per course. The jambs, 2 ft. 3 ins. thick, have two or more stones per course, but some on the east side of the north jamb are smaller, of similar size to the walling stones and look older; a few have holes (lewis holes?) and may be re-used. Many have irregular tooling. The imposts are similar to those of the tower arch. There is no strip-work hood mould on the east face. The opening is 9 ft. 10 ins. wide and at least 3 or 4 feet higher than the tower arch.

BURGHWALLIS

ST. HELEN'S CHURCH. This church has western tower, nave, chancel and north chapel, all apparently Norman in fabric as suggested by the large amount of herring-boning. Pevsner regards it as Norman. There are however many Anglo-Saxon features, both early and late, and Baldwin Brown is probably justified in dating it to the Saxo-Norman Overlap.

The tower (I) is of thin flat well-coursed rubble with many large blocks, largely of reddish stone, here and there. It has a chamfered plinth rising 18 inches above the present ground level. The quoins are of large slabs in side-alternate arrangement. There are three stages, recessed and separated by under-chamfered string courses.

In the south wall, just below the first string, is a large tall and narrow window with arched lintel, jambs of four slabs each, a slab sill, and single internal splay; it is chamfered all round and looks renewed. There is a similar window, which looks older, on the west but there is no opening in the north wall.

In the second stage there is no opening in the south or west wall; there is a circular opening in the north wall cut straight through a single square slab of reddish stone similar to a majority of the large blocks here and there in the walling.

The belfry openings in all four walls are of 'mid-wall work in its last stage of decline'. The curious double openings have pointed heads, each pair being cut from five long stones cut to appropriate curved shape; the middle stone is common to the pair, and each pointed apex with a portion on each side is cut from one stone. The jambs are of four stones each, not through-stones, arranged side-alternately and have no imposts. The central impost is long, thin and square cut. The central columns are tall and slender, not mid-wall but near the outer wall face. The east and west columns have behind them lengths of rubble walling which with the shafts support the imposts. The north and south columns have columns behind them, one of which is of circular and the other of square section. These rear columns are of a different (grey) stone from the others and appear to be modern replacements; the under surfaces of the imposts are rough and badly worn and suggest that here too was formerly rubble walling.

The tower arch is later, probably thirteenth century. It is very pointed and of two orders. The outer and thicker order is chamfered. The imposts are very small and also chamfered. The jambs of the inner order are half-round; that is, the apparent half-columns form the soffits of the inner order. The arch stands on a two-membered plinth, *c.* 16 ins. high, the lower member being chamfered. The upper member is 3 feet thick (east–west), which is the thickness of the wall—hardly a Norman thickness. The arch is 7 ft. 6 ins. wide and *c.* 9 ft. 9 ins. to the imposts.

Above the tower arch and rather to the south of the pointed crown is a round-headed opening, tall and wide—a common feature of Anglo-Saxon towers.

The nave is of large rubble of various shapes and sizes. Three courses in the north wall and almost the whole of the south wall are of herring-boning (I), with no

---

(I) *Plate* 51.

spines. As there is no herring-boning in the tower the nave may be later. No plinth is visible. The quoins are of very large, though not megalithic, slabs below but smaller above. The north-west quoins are of mixed face and side-alternate; the north-east are roughly upright and flat; the south-east and south-west are side-alternate.

In the middle of the north wall is a blocked rectangular former opening, *c.* 5 feet high. It has a flat lintel much worn and a western jamb of eight large slabs, chamfered. The south jamb is hidden by a later buttress.

The chancel is narrower than the nave. It is similar in fabric to the nave with much herring-boning and many very large slabs among the rubble in the north wall. The east wall is later and of ashlar. The south-east and north-east quoins are of very large slabs in side-alternate arrangement.

There is a north but no indication of a south wing or chapel to the chancel. From marks on the wall the wing appears to have been originally open to the chancel by almost its whole width. This opening has been built up and a door inserted. The chapel is now a vestry.

KIRK HAMMERTON

ST. JOHN'S CHURCH. The tower, nave and chancel are Anglo-Saxon. The Saxon nave and chancel (1) now form the south aisle and south chapel of a new church built in 1891. Baldwin Brown dates the old church to post-1040 but very near the Conquest.

The tower is tall but not particularly slender. It is built of large stone blocks. The quoins are of large slabs, up to 2 ft. 6 ins. by 1 ft. 10 ins. by 18 inches; they are smaller above a height of *c.* 6 feet and of side-alternate arrangement. The exterior is of two stages, separated by a square-edged string course. The lower stage occupies about five-sixths of the total height; the upper or belfry stage is very short. There is a low pyramidal roof, not original.

In the south wall, high up and level with the nave roof, is a rectangular window with lintel, sill and jambs of one large slab each. There is a similar window higher up immediately below the string course. Similar windows in similar places are in the west and north walls. There is no opening in the east wall between the belfry and the tower arch. No window has a double splay.

There is a curious narrow western doorway (2), 3 ft. 3 ins. wide and 7 ft. 2 ins. high to the imposts. The arch is of two similar square-cut orders. The outer one has a head of nine voussoirs and projects hardly more than an inch east and west from

(1) *Plate* 53; (2) *Plate* 56.

the inner order of six voussoirs. The head is parabolic with its longer axis vertical. Both orders rest on short imposts badly worn but formerly chamfered on the outer narrow faces. Below the imposts are attached columns in front of the jamb west faces. The capitals are badly worn but originally had some simple geometrical carving on their faces; there are no bases. The inner order has badly worn jambs which appear to be of pillar stones. The columns and jambs rest on badly worn two-membered plinths, apparently not chamfered.

The belfry double openings of the usual Anglo-Saxon type are tall, with arched lintels and mid-wall almost straight circular shafts which have no capitals but rest on square chamfered bases. The imposts are chamfered, the jambs are of large slabs which appear to be through-stones at least as far as the present lattice.

The tower arch (1) is of one order, tall and narrow with no mouldings or imposts. Instead of imposts the top jamb stones are hollowed on their soffits giving a recessed and horse-shoe appearance to the arch head which is vertically parabolic, like that of the west doorway. It has two—one outer and an inner—rings of eleven voussoirs each; the voussoirs are of irregular width but of similar length. There is plaster filling, with presumably rubble behind, between the rings.

The nave is high. The exterior of the walls (2) is a medley of large rubble stones with admixture of small stones in rose, amber and grey colours. The nave projects from the tower 2 feet on the south and 2 ft. 9 ins. on the north. The south-west, south-east and north-west (the latter visible only inside the church) quoins are similar to those of the tower. The north-east quoin no longer exists; the wall here has been incorporated into the wall of the modern church.

There is a south doorway (3), 6 feet high to the imposts and 3 ft. 6 ins. wide. The round head is of nine through-stone voussoirs, some renewed. The west jamb is of three slabs, two very massive with one short between; the east jamb and imposts are renewals. The west jamb, 2 feet thick, has one thick square-edged impost of two stones side by side. On the lower part of the impost soffit face and on the projecting underface are two quirks—four altogether. The outer impost face is too worn to show any original quirk here but as the renewed east impost has similar quirks but none on the outer face it seems likely that the originals had none. The outer imposts act as such to vertical strip-work below, the strip-work passing also round the arch head; it is 3 inches from the crown of the arch and 9 inches away at impost level. The vertical strips are short-long-long-short; the head is of 14 short strips, the east six being renewals.

Very near the east end of the south wall, to be seen only on the interior, is a blocked doorway. The east part of what appears to have been a round head (it is not very clear) is visible, but the east jamb and part of the west are plainly to be seen. There is

---

(1) *Plate* 58; (2) *Plate* 53; (3) *Plate* 57.

vertical strip-work alongside the jamb, 6 inches wide and of one inch projection; the width between the strip-work is 4 ft. 2 ins., so the doorway was narrow.

The chancel is high. In the south wall are two windows, one tall with an arched lintel, the other further east is a crudely built narrow lancet; both are Norman and they partially hide the remains of a blocked Anglo-Saxon former opening which is not visible on the exterior but plainly so inside.

The original chancel arch (I) is of two plain square-cut orders only slightly recessed. There is heavy strip-work round the head and down the jambs, flush with the wall and on the west face only. The arch has been rebuilt on the north, but the south half is original. The plain impost of two superimposed 9-inch slabs is stepped; the upper member, supporting both orders, projects beyond the lower which in turn projects beyond the abacus below. Below is an angle shaft engaged on the west face of the inner jamb; it has a cubical capital with chamfered faces and corners to bring it roughly to fit the shaft. On the east face the double impost and chamfered capital are duplicated to support the two orders; the two edges of the plain jambs are chamfered increasingly from the top downwards so that at the base the two edges have been cut off completely and converted to one wide face.

On the west the bottom voussoir of the inner order is a long stone cut to appropriate curved shape (as at Wootton Wawen and elsewhere); the corresponding stone in the outer order is L-shaped, the left arm being cut to shape while the other lies along the top of the impost. The arch is 6 ft. 2 ins. wide and 6 ft. 10 ins. high to the imposts.

LEDSHAM

ALL SAINTS' CHURCH. The lower part of the west tower up to where ashlar changes to rubble, the chancel arch and parts of the nave are Anglo-Saxon. The belfry stage and tower arch are Norman, the parapet and stone spire fifteenth century and the chancel thirteenth century.

The tower is of well coursed ashlar, changing to fairly large rectangular rubble higher up in the upper half of the tall first stage. The quoins (2) are of large slabs, a few at the base very massive, arranged side-alternately for about half the height, above which they are a mixture of face and side alternate. There is no plinth.

Internally the tower is 12 ft. 3 ins. deep (east–west) by 9 ft. 8 ins. wide. The longer axis being east–west does not imply a porch tower; some *de novo* towers, such as those at Wharram-le-Street and Bosham, show this peculiarity, and Baldwin Brown denied that it is a porch tower. But the walls are thin, only 2 ft. 2 ins., a common thickness for Saxon porches, and H. M. Taylor has produced convincing evidence

---

(I) *Plate* 59; (2) *Plate* 52.

that Ledsham tower was raised above an earlier, perhaps eighth-century, porch of two storeys. He saw the marks of the gabled roof line of the porch on the interior of the east wall of the tower. The change in quoining and walling about half way up the tall first stage and the two south tower windows at different levels are consistent with this view. The lower part of the tower is not bonded into the nave wall, which suggests that the original porch was later than the nave; but not much later for the two are similar in fabric and type of openings.

In the west wall is a round-headed window *c.* 8 feet above the ground which looks like a modern insertion. Above is an almost square window with square lintel and jambs and sill of one pillar stone each. It is chamfered all round.

There is no opening in the north wall.

In the south wall is a doorway (1) unusually near the west quoin with quite remarkable decoration. It has a plain round head of through-stone voussoirs and jambs of well-squared stones, one long one on end in each with those above flat and in no particular arrangement. The renewed short imposts project and their outer and soffit faces are convexly chamfered from the top edges, the convex faces being covered with thin interlacement, possibly copied from originals. Round the arch head and down the sides of the jambs, and in contact with them, is a continuous flat band of unusually wide strip-work, unbroken by imposts. It is 7 inches wide and projects 3 to 5 inches. It is ornamented with not very good conventional vine scroll-work, continued all round except at the crown where it is interrupted by three rosettes. Most of it is a modern renewal of 1871 and not necessarily a copy of earlier decorations; that there was earlier decoration however seems indicated by the bottom stone on each side; both are badly worn and apparently original. The doorway is 2 ft. 4 ins. wide and 4 ft. 1 in. high to the imposts which are 5 inches thick. On the interior it has a flat lintel and is rebated all round for a door. At some time it was built up but was opened out and renewed in the restoration of 1871.

To the east of this doorway, near the east quoin of the tower, with its head about on a level with that of the doorway, is a window with arched lintel and jambs of ashlar, like the walling, sloping slightly upward—an early feature. Above is a similar but slightly shorter window. Both are slightly splayed towards the interior, including the sills; the arched lintels are backed by round heads of voussoirs.

The belfry stage of ashlar is Norman. The double openings have heads of small voussoirs and are enclosed in a large single round-headed arch of voussoirs. The jambs have thin square imposts. The central shafts are not mid-wall; they support square quirked imposts and have two-scalloped capitals and plain neckings.

The tower arch is wide but not tall: 7 ft. 2 ins. wide by 7 ft. 9 ins. high to the imposts. It has Norman features and Taylor has demonstrated clearly that it is in

---

(1) *Plate 52.*

fact Norman, inserted when the belfry was built. The head is not of through-stones, but of three or four stones per course with no rubble filling. The jambs, 2 ft. 5 ins. thick, are also of three or four stones per course. The imposts are chamfered and quirked. There is no plinth.

Above the tower arch there is what appears at first sight to be—and which Baldwin Brown stated was—the usual Saxon opening in the tower east wall. Taylor has shown that it is not the usual doorway but a window splayed internally towards the nave: it was therefore intended to light the nave and originally must have been above the two-storeyed porch. Taylor compares it with the similar window at Monkwearmouth above the nave western doorway.[1] It has an arched lintel on the east backed by narrow flat slabs running east–west which are, so far as they go, through-stones. The jamb slabs are face-alternate, three stones to each jamb. The sill cut from one stone is upturned at the ends, the upturnings forming the two bottom jamb stones. This is a Norman feature, though the rest of the window is Saxon; it was put in apparently when, according to Taylor, the sill had to be built up by one course to make sufficient room for the Norman arch below. Taylor thinks that the Norman tower arch replaced a Saxon doorway similar to the existing one at Monkwearmouth, and that at Ledsham we have a Norman tower raised on an early Saxon porch.

The nave is 45 ft. 8 ins. long by 17 ft. 3 ins. internally. The walls, of ashlar like the tower, are *c.* 2 ft. 4 or 5 ins. thick. The quoins, plainly visible at the north-west, south-west and south-east corners are similar to those of the tower. There are no original windows but remains of three blocked early openings in the south wall and of one in the north (above the thirteenth-century arcade leading to the north aisle) are plainly visible both inside and out. One is near the west end of the south wall of the nave; on the exterior it has arched lintel, no jambs or sill except of walling and is generally similar to but larger than those in the south wall of the tower; internally it has a round head of voussoirs and separate jambs. Its external aperture was 1 ft.10 ins. wide, single splayed internally to 3 ft. 3 ins. and was *c.* 6 feet high. These dimensions are rather great for Late Saxon or Early Norman windows which are more often of the slit or loop type. A little to the east is the eastern bit of an arched lintel of another window. A large early Perpendicular window has been inserted between these. There is a similar Perpendicular window further east beyond the south porch similarly obscuring the remains of another early window.

The remains of a fifth opening are visible internally and externally above the south-west doorway, opening to the south porch. It is round-headed on the interior with a flat lintel outside. The jambs are wider apart by 4 inches on the exterior due to a 2-inch rebate for a door to open, originally, outwards. Taylor is of opinion that

[1] At Monkwearmouth however the window was splayed outwards, i.e. it was intended to light the upper storey of the porch from the nave.

the south porch represents a former single-storeyed porticus (with perhaps formerly a similar one on the north). It is not bonded into the nave wall and in fabric, wall thickness and quoins is similar to the nave. Like the west porch it may have been slightly later than the nave. Later it was converted to a porch by the insertion of a doorway in its south wall. The remains of the early doorway in the nave wall indicate an opening to this porticus 14 feet high by 2 feet wide, unusual dimensions. There is no other evidence of a two-storeyed porticus. But, assuming a porticus, it would seem possible, perhaps likely, that it was of two storeys (as at Deerhurst and elsewhere) and that the remains are of upper and lower narrow entrances to the two storeys. In this case Taylor thinks there should be at least some sign or indication of an upper window or windows; and there is none. Some upper courses may have been renewed so there is a possibility that an early window may have been blocked. However Taylor writes that 'it seems more reasonable to regard the doorway as an extreme example of the Saxon love of tall narrow openings', and he may well be right.

The south-west doorway, the main entrance to the church through the porch, is mediaeval. Its chamfered jambs are badly worn but appear to be of the pillar type, three long stones per jamb. Its chamfered flat lintel is modern.

At least two rather debased Saxon stones with interlacement, a cross and an inhabited vine scroll have been built into the north aisle north wall.

The chancel arch is early but the details have been renewed. It is larger than the tower arch: 7 ft. 10 ins. wide by 9 ft. 9 ins. high above the nave floor to the imposts. Its round head is of through-stone voussoirs; these may be renewals—they certainly look newer than those of the tower arch. The jambs, 2 ft. 4 ins. thick, are of a mixture of through-stones with smaller ones up to three per course. The imposts are renewals and are similar to those of the tower south doorway but the decoration is different, not vine scrolls but of an essentially modern type.

MONK FRYSTON

ST. WILFRID'S CHURCH. The three lowest stages of the square western tower (l) are Anglo-Saxon, dated by Baldwin Brown to post-1040. The top storey, battlemented parapet and corner pinnacles, also the corner buttresses and tower west window, are all *c.* 1400. There is some eleventh-century walling at the ends of the thirteenth-century nave arcades, the clerestory is fifteenth century, the chancel early fourteenth.

The tower is built of coursed large rubble blocks, all very white with modern

(l) *Plate* 54.

plaster or wash. The quoins are largely hidden by the corner buttresses but short stretches above appear to be face-alternate. The walls are 3 feet thick. There is no plinth.

The first stage is very tall. Below the string course on the south wall is a pointed, fairly wide window. The head is cut from two thin shaped stones, the jambs are of two pillar stones each, the sill of one stone. On the interior the window has a round head of very thin strips which appear to be through-stones; the jambs are of similar flat strips and have no imposts and no splay. This interior opening is wider than the outer one. The thin outer pointed face is presumably a later insertion. There is no other opening in the south wall and none in the north wall in this stage. The west wall has no original openings; the large pointed window is later. There are signs of repair work in the wall below the window; one of the stones has on it a Norman scratch dial, an impossible position for a sundial. It seems likely there was a western opening here, later built up.

Above the string course is a very low second stage, the original belfry; it is only a little higher than the belfry openings which rest on the string course. The openings are of the usual Anglo-Saxon type: double-light windows with mid-wall columns which have cubical capitals, roughly chamfered to bring them to approximate column size below (rather like those of Wharram-le-Street),[1] but no neckings. The jambs are not of through-stones but of ashlar, face-alternate. The double heads appear to be arched lintels. The east belfry opening is below the very high nave roof and is visible only from the nave.

Above the belfry is a widely projecting string course supported by plain block corbels, and a few feet above is a similar corbelled string. Two corbel tables so close together are most unusual, perhaps unique.

Above the second corbel table is the top stage, the later belfry put up *c.* 1400. It has a two-light Gothic window in each wall, another hollow chamfered string course, not corbelled, above and then the battlemented parapet and corner pinnacles.

The tower arch is dated *c.* 1400. It is flush with the wall east and west faces and is 3 ft. 2 ins. thick, which is probably the original wall thickness.

No nave quoins are visible; the later aisle walls are bonded into and are integral with the nave east and west walls.

[1] See above, p. 128, fig. 7.

YORK CITY

CHURCH OF ST. MARY THE YOUNGER, in Bishop Hill Junior. The somewhat complex title of this church is to distinguish it from an older church, no longer existing, of St. Mary the Elder in nearby Bishop Hill Senior. The church is near the centre of the city, not far from the railway station.

The tower (1), like that of Appleton-le-Street, shows a considerable family resemblance to those of Northumberland and Durham. It has no plinth, no buttresses, only one string course, similar belfry openings with similar adornments, and similar set back. Baldwin Brown dated it to post-1040; Hodges described it as Anglo-Saxon but suggested no date. The cornice above the belfry and a plain battlemented parapet of three ashlar courses are later.

The walling is of limestone rubble of variable size, reasonably well coursed though less well coursed above than below. There is a considerable admixture of whole courses of small white limestone rubble, especially in the north wall, and larger long slabs of darker stone, like that of the quoins. There are some courses and part-courses of herring-boning, some double and some single and some in which the rubble stones are laid on edge. The quoins are of dark coloured sandstone slabs with rather long bonding stones of the same material at intervals. Some of the lower slabs are very large, those above are smaller and flatter and all arranged side-alternately.

The tower is of three stages with only one string course, which separates the recessed top or belfry stage from those below. The string is square-cut on the east, very badly worn away elsewhere. The gable marks of the former higher nave roof are visible on the east wall, about 2 or 3 feet above the present roof. The two lower stages appear on the exterior as one very tall stage.

In the south wall there is a large rectangular window about half way up, at the height of the aisle roof. It has jambs of pillar stones, three in each jamb, and a thin sill. The lintel is too badly worn to be recognizable as such. Higher up, near the string course, is a smaller and narrower rectangular opening cut straight through the wall; the jambs are of selected flattish rubble slabs and the lintel is one slab. The sill is deeply worn and not recognizable as a separate sill. A similar opening is in the north wall. Both these are in the second stage.

In the top or belfry stage there are the usual double-headed two-light openings,

(1) *Plate* 55.

143

treated very similarly to those at Billingham in Co. Durham and at Bywell, St. Andrew's (Northumberland). Originally these were very tall but have been shortened by being built up for some feet above the sills. The arch heads are of very thin limestone slabs which give a brick-like appearance. The mid-wall shafts are of circular section and support long central imposts chamfered below. The jambs appear to be of through-stones. Large thin strips projecting from the wall face form a frame up the sides of the jambs and round the arch heads. The strips end below the openings, at the bottom of the built-up but formerly sloping sills, on cubical corbels just above the string course. The strips round the head have their own small cubical imposts projecting from above the long jamb imposts. The upper part of the western opening has been renewed as two lancets under a single round-headed arch; the lower parts of the original jambs and strip-work remain.

The tower arch[1] is a fine one of two plain square-cut orders. The arch head (I) is of well-cut voussoirs, not through-stones but of two stones per course. There is a projecting hood mould of square section round the arch head; it does not go down the jamb sides. The hood appears to extend through the wall to the west face where it ends flush with the wall. The west face of the hood is wider than the east, is indeed almost as wide as the outer arch order. It follows that the hood is not of through-stones, but consists of at least two rings, a western and an eastern of different widths; or more probably there are simply two hood moulds, an eastern and a western. The jambs are 3 ft. $1\frac{1}{2}$ ins. thick. The inner order is 18 inches thick (east–west) and projects $8\frac{1}{4}$ inches from the soffit of the outer order. The jamb stones are through-stones in which the recessing is cut. The plain imposts are of two layers, the upper larger ones project slightly beyond the lower, which project beyond the jamb soffit. The upper layers are double right-angled at the outer—north and south—ends, these T-shaped ends forming continuations upwards and downwards of the hood mould. The arch is 9 ft. 9 ins. wide and nearly 16 feet high. It has chamfered plinths; the south one has its north-east corner chamfered vertically. The whole arch is of red sandstone.

[1] Plan in Hodges, (*a*), viii, p. 203.

(I) *Plate* 60.

Part II

ENGLAND BETWEEN HUMBER
AND THAMES
Excluding Lincolnshire, East Anglia and Essex

THE MIDLAND COUNTIES

K

HISTORICAL INTRODUCTION

This area, excluding Lincolnshire, East Anglia and Essex, comprised roughly the old Anglian kingdom of Mercia at the height of its optimum expansion. Mercia arose from late fifth-century settlements of Anglian tribes. There were three groups. One worked its way from the Wash up the River Welland, across country through what is now Rutland and Leicestershire, then down the rivers Wreak and Soar to the Trent to settle south of the middle Trent. There they mingled with a second group which penetrated later from the Humber and up the Trent. This area of settlement became North Mercia, the heart and centre of the later Mercia. A third group moved from the Wash up the Rivers Welland, Nene and Ouse to settle in the district now represented by Bedfordshire, Cambridgeshire, Northamptonshire and parts of Nottinghamshire and Leicestershire. These were the Middle Angles. They were incorporated into greater Mercia by Penda in the mid-seventh century, but for long retained a loose kind of local semi-independence, both politically and culturally. Thus, the pagan Penda made his Christian son Peada sub-king of the Middle Angles. Later, the area had its own bishopric, split off from the greater Mercian see of Lichfield and later fixed at Leicester from 737 on until it ended during the Danish invasions. This distinction between North Mercia and Middle Anglia should be borne in mind as both groups of people developed a characteristic Christian culture and art along somewhat different lines.

Little or nothing is known about the early history of Mercia, perhaps because the Mercians' struggle against the forces of Nature in clearing the forests and draining the swamps of this, at that time, inhospitable part of the country in order to establish their settlements left them little time to make history, which in those days meant making war against other tribes and leaders. They first came into the full light of history with their tough, fighting, pagan King Penda, 632–54. He, in alliance with Cadwallon, British prince of Gwynedd, defeated and killed the great Edwin of Northumbria in 632, and was later himself killed fighting against Oswiu of Northumbria in 654.[1] In between these years he incorporated the Middle Angles and other settlements of the south and west and south-west midlands into his kingdom and made Mercia comparable in power with Northumbria. Though pagan he was apparently a tolerant man for he permitted his eldest son Peada to marry the Christian daughter of Oswiu of Northumbria and to become Christian. Peada

[1] See above, p. 41.

during his short reign as sub-king of the Middle Angles under his father and his even shorter reign as King of Mercia, 654–6, introduced Christianity among the Middle Angles and, later, among the North Mercians and endowed the great monastery at Medeshampstede, now Peterborough. Under Peada's brother Wulfhere, 657–74, Mercia became supreme overlord of all England south of the Humber. This supremacy was not however permanent owing to a temporary rise to strength and independence of southern England under the two successive kings of Wessex, Cædwalla, 685–9, and Ine, 689–726.

Wulfhere was succeeded by his brother Æthelred, 674–704, a man of great piety. He continued the development of Christianity in his country with the help of Wilfrid of Ripon who spent the eleven years of his second exile from Northumbria, 691–702, in Mercia as a personal friend of the king and for part of that time as acting bishop of the Mercians. Æthelred and Wilfrid founded several monasteries, among them that at Oundle in which Wilfrid was reputed subsequently to be buried. Some time during the reign of Wulfhere or Æthelred the magnificent, aisled, basilican church at Brixworth was founded. Æthelred abdicated in 704 and retired to a monastery. He was succeeded by Cenred, a son of Wulfhere, who likewise abdicated in 708 and died later at a monastery in Rome. Æthelred's son Ceolred, a worthless youth, ruled 708–16 and after him came two kings whose reigns covered eighty years and who were the founders of that Greater Mercia which exercised supremacy over all England. These kings were Æthelbald, 716–57, a descendent of Penda's brother Eowa, and Offa, 757–96, another descendant of Penda's brother and a distant cousin of Æthelbald. After quietly consolidating his country, and after the abdication of Ine of Wessex in 726, Æthelbald made himself supreme overlord, i.e. Bretwalda, of all England south of the Humber. His successor Offa brought Northumbria, too, under his suzerainty and Offa's reign indeed was the great age of the Mercian kingdom. This rise to power is indicated by the successive titles adopted by these two kings, as seen in their various charters. Æthelbald from 'king of the Mercians' became 'king of the South English', 'king not only of the Mercians but of those neighbouring peoples over whom God has set me', and 'rex Britanniae'. Offa went further and spoke of his kingdom as 'kingdom of the whole land of the English' (regnum totius Anglorum patriae) and his contemporaries addressed him as 'king of the English', the first ruler to get that title.[1] Offa has been called 'the Great' and was not undeserving of that description. He was the first English king to realize the importance of close intercourse with other nations and to have a definite foreign policy. He corresponded and negotiated, on commercial as well as political matters, with Charlemagne on terms of equality. In his reign, too, a papal legatine mission visited England from Rome in 786, the first such mission in Anglo-Saxon history and the last until the reign of Edward the Confessor more than 250 years later. Towards the

[1] See F. M. Stenton, op. cit.

end of his reign he built the well-known Offa's dyke, more than 70 miles of earth-works put up not as a defence but more probably as a frontier demarcating his boundary with Wales.

The power of Mercia declined under Cenwulf, 796–821, Offa's distant cousin and successor and the last king of the House of Penda, and the supremacy of Mercia disappeared for ever in the great and decisive victory of Egbert of Wessex at Ellandun in 825.

It was long thought that Mercia was a culturally backward country, a mainly militaristic state, a kind of Anglo-Saxon Sparta. This was due probably to the fact that she produced no early chroniclers. Early literary references to the region are mainly in Northumbrian and South English annals written by chroniclers who would have regarded Mercia as an enemy. Historical and archaeological research in the present century has revealed a different picture. Study of existing illuminated MSS. and monuments proves that though in quality and output Mercian art may not have equalled the best of the earlier Northumbrian or the later South English it was far from being inconsiderable or insignificant; it was in fact fine. It is indeed true that the great centre of Anglo-Saxon art travelled south following the political ascendancy. It arose and reached its first peak in Northumbria in the last third of the seventh and the first half of the eighth century. After the Northumbrian political decline it flourished in Mercia in the last quarter of the eighth and the first half of the ninth century, after which it passed to Wessex.

Mercia had two ecclesiastical centres from an early date: Lichfield, which was the seat of a bishopric from 669 and for a short period, 788–803, was an arch-bishopric set up by Offa in opposition to that of Canterbury; and Repton, where a double monastery for men and women was founded by Diuma, first bishop of the Mercians and Middle Angles, appointed by Peada in 652. Both were in North Mercia. The political capital, that is the main residence of the king, had been moved from Tam-worth to Repton by Penda.

The Book of Cerne, an illuminated book which provided many motifs to con-temporary and later artists and sculptors, has been described by T. D. Kendrick as 'the first indubitable Mercian book', made probably at Lichfield between 818 and 830, that is at the very end of the period of Mercian military supremacy.

In sculpture she produced three distinct schools. The Mercian standing crosses[1] were of characteristic type and design, clearly distinguishable from those of other regions. The East Mercian or Fenland School of figural and ornamental sculpture,[1] developed among the Middle Angles, produced very beautiful carvings, many of which remain today, though some in much weathered condition, at Breedon-on-the-Hill, Peterborough, Fletton and Castor. These are dated to the late eighth and early ninth centuries. In south and south-west Mercia the sculpture was influenced

[1] See E. A. Fisher, pp. 83, 90–2, 75.

partly by East Mercia but more significantly from Wessex and the Continent. A good example of this is the Lechmere stone at Hanley Castle (Worcs) which, showing a Crucifixion scene, has a plant growing from each side of the base of the cross. Very similar motifs are found on a cross at Whitchurch and also on the Crucifixion panel at Romsey, both in Hampshire.

In architecture, too, Mercia was not behind the other great areas of the country. Three of the greatest and finest Anglo-Saxon churches are to be found there: the late seventh-century aisled and apsed basilican church at Brixworth (Northants), the church with its famous crypt at Repton (Derby)—perhaps 750–800 originally, which was burnt by the Danes in 875 and not rebuilt till 974—and the early eighth to tenth-century apsed church at Deerhurst (Glos). All three were monastic.

Most of the churches discussed below, and of course all the towers, are post-870, many being of the tenth and eleventh centuries. That is, they were built long after the ascendancy and even the independence of Mercia had passed away, when Mercia had become merely a region of England after the re-conquest from the Danes and unification of the country by Edward the Elder, 900–24, and Æthelstan, 924–39. But many of these churches are rebuildings of earlier churches founded in the Early Saxon period before the first Danish invasions and destroyed, partially or completely, during those invasions. In the existing churches are many remains of the earlier ones, as is plainly evident at Brigstock, Deerhurst and elsewhere.

Of the nineteen counties in this area eight have no towered Anglo-Saxon churches: Cheshire, Herefordshire, Staffordshire, Worcestershire, Leicestershire, Huntingdon-shire, Hertfordshire, Middlesex. Eight others have or had one towered church each: Derbyshire, Nottinghamshire, Rutland, Cambridgeshire, Buckinghamshire, War-wickshire, Gloucestershire, Shropshire. Bedfordshire has three churches, Oxford-shire four and Northamptonshire six. These twenty-one churches are located as follows: Bedford; Clapham, 1½ miles NNW. of Bedford; Stevington,[1] 4½ miles NW. of Bedford; Lavendon (Bucks), 7½ miles WNW. of Bedford; Cambridge; Repton, 6 miles SSW. of Derby; Deerhurst, 2 miles SSW. of Tewkesbury (Glos); Barnack (Northants), 3 miles SE. of Stamford (Lincs); Brigstock, 6 miles WSW. of Oundle and 7 miles NE. of Kettering (Northants); Brixworth, 6 miles N. of Northampton; Earls Barton, 6 miles NE. of Northampton; Peterborough; Stowe-Nine-Churches, 5 miles SE. of Daventry; Carlton-in-Lindrick, 3 miles N. of Worksop (Notts); Langford, 8 miles SW. of Witney and 3 miles NE. of Lechlade (Oxon); North Leigh, 3 miles NE. of Witney; Caversfield, 1 mile N. of Bicester (Oxon); Oxford; Market Overton, 5 miles NNE. of Oakham (Rutland); Stanton Lacy, 2 miles NNW. of Ludlow (Salop); Wootton Wawen, 7 miles NW. by N. of Stratford-on-Avon.

---

[1] So little of the tower is Saxon it is not included among those churches described below.

BEDFORDSHIRE

BEDFORD

ST. PETER DE MERTON'S CHURCH.[1] The original dedication is not known; if pre-Conquest it could not have been the present one.

The tower, now central, was originally a western one with a small aisleless nave, and chancel to the east. Baldwin Brown thought from signs on the western face that there was some building joined to it on that side too. The old nave is now the chancel. The old chancel has been destroyed; it may have been apsidal for the foundations of an apse some feet to the east of the present chancel (old nave) were exposed during the exploration and restoration of the 1860's. This indicates that the present east wall is not original; its date is not known. There is evidence that the chancel (old nave) was probably shortened at some time by about 10 feet; the east wall is not properly bonded into the side walls. The tower and chancel are tenth or eleventh century; Baldwin Brown suggested 1000–50. The tower is built of small uncoursed limestone rubble interspersed here and there with some very large stone slabs of irregular size and shape. Two are specially large and noteworthy; in the west wall of the tower behind the pulpit and lectern respectively are two very large irregularly shaped monoliths, which might almost be called megaliths, *c.* 6 feet high and up to 12 inches wide. The chancel is of larger stones than the tower and roughly coursed with numerous large stones here and there. There is no specific quoining, except in three places. In the west wall of the tower, seen from the nave, from just above the pulpit to where the rest, if any, is hidden by the modern roof timbering, is a very fine specimen of genuine upright and flat quoining, consisting of three uprights and three flats belonging to the north-west corner; none is visible at the south-west corner. Similar specimens are visible in the north-west corner of the chancel (seen only from the interior of the modern vestry) and the south-west corner (seen only from outside the church). These are parts of the chancel (old nave) quoins. The south-west corner projects *c.* 9 inches from the south of the tower wall and extends *c.* 3 feet to the west of the tower south-east corner, showing plainly that the western tower was narrower than the old nave and extended *c.* 3 feet into the nave. Such an extension was unusual in Saxon churches: the normal position for a western tower is flush with the nave, that is, the east wall of the tower was normally part of the west wall of the nave. The tower quoining here, as elsewhere except the lower north-west portion referred to

[1] Beds Nat. Hist. and Arch. Soc., 1941; G. Baldwin Brown; V.C.H., *Beds*, III.

above, is of selected flat stones, similar to those of the walling but more uniformly flat, laid above one another.

The tower is 50 feet high and 16 ft. 9 ins. square. No plinth is visible. There is a modern stair turret attached to the west end of the south wall, with a spiral staircase leading to the second stage.

When the plaster was stripped from the tower and chancel walls in 1890 bad cracks and marks of calcination were found, indicative of former fire damage perhaps by the Danes in the early eleventh-century invasions under Sweyn and Canute. The damage is especially noticeable on the east side of the tower east wall, seen from the chancel.

In the exterior south wall of the tower are six or more courses or part-courses of herring-boning, but none in the chancel walls. In the south wall too, close to and just above the clock, in the second stage of the tower are the round heads of two blocked Saxon windows. A similar pair is in the north wall, one of which is not blocked.

In the east wall of the same stage is a large gable-headed opening with plain square jambs, an ingress to a former chamber between roof and ceiling of the old nave. It was discovered walled-up when the old roof was removed in 1890. The lower part is visible from the interior of the chancel (old nave). For some reason it is now closed and spoiled by a wooden door and the jambs and sill enclosed with cheap painted modern timbering. One of the stones in the south jamb is part of a Saxon cross shaft carved with interlacement.

In the north wall of the ground floor is an arch, now occupied by the organ console, about 8 feet high and 5 ft. 6 ins. wide. The head is elliptical rather than segmental and is well made of similar rubble to the wall. The head is of two rings of roughly dressed rubble stones, thin (1 to 4 inches), with rubble filling and plaster in the soffit between the rings. There are no imposts. The jambs are of walling, are *c.* 2 ft. 8 ins. thick and are plastered. The date of this opening is doubtful; it may well be of the Saxo-Norman Overlap cut through the existing earlier wall. There is no evidence of its purpose or into what it opened. The corresponding position in the opposite wall, the south, is occupied by a modern stained glass window; it is not known whether a similar arched opening preceded the window.

The west pointed tower arch is modern, as are the nave, wide western porch, south porch and north vestry. The east arch of the tower is plainly fourteenth-century work of three chamfered orders with moulded half-octagonal capitals and responds. The top part of the tower with its battlemented parapet and double billet ornament in place of a string course, and shallow arcading of round heads only, is modern. Modern also are the imitation Norman double belfry windows in the west, south and east walls of the top stage. In the north wall is a single modern large rectangular window, closed with a wooden lattice.

In the north-east corner of the Sanctuary, to the north of the altar, is the greater part of a round-headed window. It is of similar rubble construction to the north tower (organ) arch, except that head and jambs but not sill have wide single splays, suggestive of Norman work. The north-east and south-east Sanctuary windows and the north lancet window are of the thirteenth century, when the church was restored.

CLAPHAM

CHURCH OF ST. THOMAS OF CANTERBURY.[1] This is a large parish of 1995 acres close to Bedford. It was rich and prosperous in Saxon times for it is referred to in Domesday Book as worth '24 pounds', a large sum in those days.

An early reference is that Æthelstan Mannesunu in 986 gave the manor of Clapham to his wife as dowry with reversion to Ramsey Abbey (Hunts). Domesday records it as belonging to one Nula Crispin under grant from Ramsey Abbey, but mentions no church. The latter point has little significance for Domesday Book was an economic survey; it is stated that only four Bedfordshire churches are mentioned in the Book—those at Houghton (Regis), Leighton, Luton and St. Paul's, Bedford—in marked contrast to the neighbouring county of Suffolk where more than four hundred are mentioned. What is surprising is that a parochial chapel at Clapham is mentioned for the first time in a record by Bishop St. Hugh of Lincoln (1186–1200). Parochial chapels, small and perhaps normally of timber, were built in large numbers in the twelfth century, more especially in the reign of Henry I and Stephen, to serve small villages and hamlets remote from parish churches. Why was one built at Clapham if there was a church there? The architectural evidence shows that much of the existing tower is pre-Conquest. Baldwin Brown suggests 1000–40 as a likely date.

As St. Thomas of Canterbury was murdered in 1171 there must have been an earlier dedication. It is not often that a dedication has been changed, though cases are known as at Brixworth, at Bedford (St. Peter de Merton) and at Stevington. Is there another suggestion here that there may not have been an early church even though the tower is early? If so, why was the tower built? The idea put forward by one writer that it may have been a watch tower to which a church was attached later is not satisfying.

The church, except the tower, western bays of the nave arcade, the chancel arch and parts of the chancel walls, was rebuilt and enlarged in 1861 by Sir G. G. Scott, using as much of the old material as possible. The nave arcades were originally thirteenth century. Only the lower three stages of the tower are pre-Conquest. The fourth or belfry stage is Norman; above this is an embattled parapet. There is no evidence to indicate the form of the original roof.

[1] G. Baldwin Brown; V.C.H., *Beds*, III.

The tower (1) is 15 ft. 8 ins. long by 16 ft. 2 ins. wide (north-south) on the interior; on the exterior it is 24 feet square. It is wider than the nave, like those at Barton-on-Humber and Broughton-by-Brigg (Lincs), but there is no other evidence to suggest it may have been turriform. It is 81 feet high. It is built of small stones without special quoining, the quoins being of selected rubble slabs laid flat on one another. It is plastered all over on the exterior. The walls are *c.* 4 feet thick at the base and a few inches less at the top. There are no string courses. The later belfry stage is recessed or set back.

The Ground Floor. The large western doorway with rounded segmental head of large dressed stones has either been altered or is a later insertion. Its jambs are of five squarish blocks each, with two longer and thinner slabs acting as imposts. It is 3 ft. 10½ ins. wide and 8 ft. 3 ins. to the base of the imposts above the step which is 6 inches above ground level. There are no windows in the ground stage and no indication in the fabric of there having been any.

The Second Stage. There are single double-splayed round-headed windows, all plastered, in the north, south and west walls. In the east wall is a gable-headed doorway, presumably an ingress to this stage from the old nave. This opening is not visible outside as it is below the level of the other openings in this stage, and is below the present nave roof. It is not visible either from the nave as the modern wooden ceiling slopes downwards at the west end and hides it. It is visible only from the interior of the second stage of the tower.

The Third Stage. Here there are single double-splayed windows, plastered, in all four walls.

The belfry is post-Conquest. There is a two-light arched opening under an enclosing arch in each wall. The enclosing arch of dressed stones is set back considerably at the springings where there are short chamfered imposts. The faces of the double lights are also set back behind the wall faces, their walls being in consequence thinner than the tower walls. The double openings have shafts which are not mid-wall, being nearer the outer wall face. The shafts support square flat chamfered central imposts. The north and south shafts, half-round neckings and cubical capitals are of octagonal plan. The south capital has spirally ornamented volutes, and projecting from its outer face between the volutes are two parallel ornamental tongues or flanges; the north capital has no volutes. The east and west shafts and neckings are of circular plan and the capitals are rounded below with spirally ornamented volutes above. All the shafts have bases of cubical blocks the upper parts of which are hemispherical—a type of bulbous base. Neckings are above the bases.

The jambs of the openings are of flat slabs arranged in face-alternate manner.

On the tower south wall are the marks of a gabled roof of some former, not

---

(1) *Plate* 61.

necessarily ancient, adjunct. They are not centrally placed: the apex is just below and a foot or two to the west of the sill of the second stage centrally placed window.

The tower arch is plain and of one order. The head is of two rings (an eastern and a western) of small voussoirs with no specific keystone. It is plastered between the rings so it is not possible to see whether there is rubble filling between the rings as in so many towers of the Lincolnshire type. The arch head is set back slightly behind the jambs and is chamfered on the east face only. The jambs are of small slab work, thin and mainly face-alternate. There are thin dressed imposts, 8 inches thick, chamfered below on the soffit side only and not returned along the wall face. The arch is 7 ft. 6 ins. wide and 8 ft. 2 ins. high to the underside of the imposts. The jambs, that is the tower wall at this point, are 3 ft. 10½ ins. thick.

The chancel arch is very similar to the tower arch but rather smaller and has no chamfer. It is old work rebuilt stone for stone. In its original form it may have been contemporary with the tower arch. It is 6 ft. 11 ins. high to the imposts above the chancel floor which is six inches above the nave floor; its wall is only 1 ft. 10 ins. thick.

BUCKINGHAMSHIRE

LAVENDON

St. Michael's Church.[1] This church consists of aisled nave, chancel and western tower (Fig. 8). The tower, nave and the western part of the chancel south wall are pre-Conquest (R.C.H.M.), early eleventh century (V.C.H.). Baldwin Brown dates

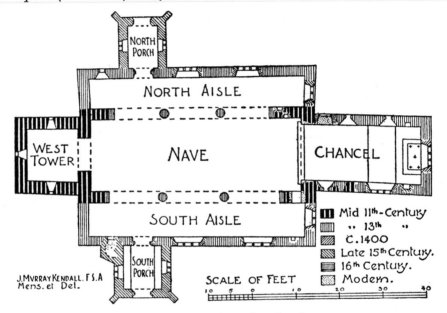

Fig. 8. Lavendon Church, plan

it to the Saxo-Norman Overlap, i.e. post-1066, but the primitive character of the remaining early windows suggests an earlier date. Considerable restoration work was carried out in 1859.

The tower (1) is a well preserved example of pre-Conquest work, originally of three stages, all still intact. It has no string courses. The fourth stage is a fifteenth-century belfry with slight set-off and string course below. The tower is built of limestone rubble in thin flakes with wide joints. There are two courses of rough herring-boning in each wall below the windows of the third stage. The quoins are of

[1] G. Baldwin Brown; R.C.H.M., *Bucks*, II; V.C.H., *Bucks*, IV.

(1) *Plate* 62.

large flat uncut stones, similar to but larger than the walling stones, laid flat. The dimensions are 11 ft. 6 ins. north–south by 12 feet on the interior. The exterior of the west wall is 17 ft. 3 ins. making the walls *c.* 2 ft. 10 ins. thick. It is not quite centrally placed; the nave wall projects 1 ft. 7 ins. to the north and 2 ft. 2 ins. to the south. There are straight joints between nave and aisles. The tower projects 14 ft. 6 ins. from the nave. It has no plinth.

There are three original window openings, vertically disposed, one in each stage, in each of the north, south and west walls. They are round-headed of uncut stones like the quoins, with plain jambs of rubble walling without dressings. In the heads of some, especially on the north, the arch stones are placed at wrong angles, i.e. the joints converge roughly to a point or area well above the centre from which the arch head is supposedly struck. Consequently a wedge or V-shaped space was left at the top of the crown which was filled with odd stones. Such poor workmanship was not uncommon in Saxon openings and suggests an early date.[1] The windows in the lower two stages are of similar size, tall and narrow. Of the top ones those on the north and west are taller and wider than those below, and the south one and the blocked one on the east (behind the clock) are wider than those on north and south. These were the original belfry windows and may belong to an earlier tradition of belfry openings than the more usual double openings;[2] this again suggests an early date for the tower. The windows, including the sills, have slight single splay towards the interior; on the ground floor they are plastered inside, as is the entire church, so the poor workmanship is visible only on the exterior.

In the east wall of the second stage, above the tower arch, is a tall round-headed doorway, opening to the nave.

The tower arch is round-headed of one plain square-cut order; the springing is not set back behind the jamb faces. The rough imposts are thin, 4 inches, and are not returned on east or west face. The structure of head and jambs is hidden by thick plaster. The arch is 6 ft. 6 ins. high to the imposts, and the jambs are 2 ft. 10 ins. thick.

The nave is 48 feet long by 16 feet. The north wall near the blocked Saxon window is 2 ft. 8½ ins. thick without the plaster. The original windows were removed when the aisles and high nave arcade were built in the thirteenth century, but half the round-head of one is plainly visible near the apex of the east arch of the north arcade, which is rather lower than the late thirteenth-century south arcade. This Saxon window is of rough workmanship similar to that of the tower windows. It is about on a level with the sill of the tower east doorway.

The nave was lofty with a fairly steep gabled roof. In the fifteenth century the side walls were raised to accommodate a clerestory, and a flatter roof was added; the apex of the gable does not appear to have been raised. This alteration is visible on

[1] Cf. Caversfield, below, p. 227.   [2] See above, p. 121.

the exterior of the west end where the original nave north-west and south-west quoins, of similar rubble slabs to those of the tower quoins, can be seen with the later small well-dressed fifteenth-century upper quoin stones above and a little behind the early ones. At the east end later quoin stones only are visible above the chancel.

The chancel, 27 ft. 6 ins. long by 12 ft. 8 ins. wide, was rebuilt and lengthened in the thirteenth century, but a portion of the south wall was retained and still remains. In it are visible on the exterior only (on the interior they are hidden by plaster) the round head and parts of the jambs of an original window, high up and above the thirteenth century priest's doorway near the west end of the chancel. Like the rest of the Saxon work here it is made of thin uncut stones set with wide joints.

The close similarity in plan and dimensions between this church and that at Ingram (Northumberland) is discussed above.[1]

[1] p. 75.

CAMBRIDGESHIRE

CAMBRIDGE

ST. BENET'S CHURCH.[1] The western tower and parts of the nave and chancel are Anglo-Saxon. The parts which are Saxon are the foundations and parts of the base courses of the south and east walls of the chancel, the east wall of the south aisle and the north-east corner of the nave where it joins the old chancel. It was dated by Baldwin Brown to post-1040.

The tower (I) is one of a group of five decorated with flat pilaster strips and with clearly defined upright and flat quoins. The other four similar, and even more highly decorated, towers are those at Barnack and Earls Barton (Northants), Barton-upon-Humber (Lincs) and Sompting (Sussex). The flats are cut back to the wall surface so that when the walls were plastered or rough cast the quoins appeared as long and short. The plaster was removed in 1840 by Thomas Rickman. The tower is 20 feet square and the walls 3 feet thick. It is of three stages; the ground stage is about half the total height. The stages are separated by square-edged projecting string courses. The upper two stages are slightly recessed. The doorways and windows in the ground stage exterior are not original. The north and south doorways are fourteenth and fifteenth century; the lower part of the tower at that time was used probably as a passage way.

In the top stage are the usual Anglo-Saxon double-light belfry openings with central bulging baluster shafts supporting square-edged central imposts. Round the middle of each baluster is a central band of several rings. The shafts are not mid-wall but are, most unusually, nearer the inner wall face. The double heads on the exterior are arched lintels, each double lintel being cut from a single stone. The lintels do not go through the walls; the inner arch heads are of rough selected rubble stones. The jambs, like the tower quoins, are of upright and flat stones and rest on the string course. There are two circular holes in each wall cut on the exterior from single stones; the north one on the east face has been built up on the interior. They are widely splayed on the interior with walls of rubble, the upper parts being strengthened by rough selected rubble slabs arranged in arch-like manner round the tops. These openings are above and slightly outwards from the double openings.

[1] G. Baldwin Brown; L. Cobbet; R.C.H.M., *City of Cambridge, Pt. II*; R. Willis and J. W. Clark.

(I) *Plate 63.*

There is also a large single slightly splayed opening on each side of the old double belfry openings, two in each face. All but one have on their exteriors thin double-arched lintels; that is, the upper and lower sides of the lintel are cut to round arch shape. The jambs and sills, and the head of one, are of rubble. The heads and sills are above the levels of the corresponding members of the double openings. In each of the two windows on the north, and the south one on the east, at the highest under point of the lintel, is a small circular projection the outer face of which is carved with incised circles filled in with some black material, probably pitch. Similar knobs may originally have been on the other lintels. The lintels penetrate only a few inches into the walls. On the interior the arch heads are of rubble indistinguishable from walling and not, as are those of the inner double and circular openings, of selected rubble slabs. One of these windows, the north one on the east face, fouled the nearby circular opening which was built up in consequence. This proves that the single windows were later insertions. Carved on the lintel of the south opening in the west wall are a date with a cross—15 + 86—and the initials R P on the lower ends of the lintel. On the northern lintel in the same wall the date is repeated, with no cross, and the letters below are T E. The numbers are filled in with a black pitch-like material, like that in the incised knobs. The stone of the lintels is not Barnack, as are the tower quoins, but an oolite similar to that of the upper, later, parts of King's College Chapel, which came from Weldon. These windows are undoubtedly later insertions. Willis and Clark, following some earlier writers, thought the date 1586 did not refer to these openings but to some repair work of that time. L. Cobbet however from his close examination of the interior concluded that the date given is that of the insertion of the windows. Apart from the monumental evidence given above it would appear unlikely that ordinary repair work would be commemorated by putting the date of it on the lintels of two pre-existing windows. Cobbet pointed out too that the old bells had been lost or destroyed, possibly at the Reformation, and that new bells began to be made and hung in Elizabeth's reign; the earliest existing bell is dated 1588. These new and larger windows were probably inserted in connection with the hanging of new bells.

The tower has no staircase. The internal floors were added later.

The present flat top, finished with a square-edged string course, is unusual and probably not original. In the centre of each face of the top stage only is a thin pilaster strip resting on a square corbel just above the arched lintel of the double belfry light and ending at the string course. Similar pilaster strips are on the tower at Sompting (Sussex) which go up to the point of the curious roof gable. It may be that the original roof at St. Benet's was a Rhenish helm like that at Sompting.

The tower arch (1) is large and fine. The square-cut arch head is of thin voussoirs

(1) *Plates* 64, 65.

of different thicknesses, all through-stones. The jambs are of through-stones of the Escomb type of upright and flat—six uprights and six flats. Around the head and down the jamb faces is double strip-work of two separate members: an inner one of half-round plan *c.* 5 inches wide, and an outer one square-edged *c.* 5 inches wide with a projection from the wall of 2 inches. The two members are about four inches apart and both rest on square plain block corbels which rest on the plinths. The inner member round the head is in contact with the voussoirs. This double strip-work is rather similar to that at Skipwith (Yorkshire, East Riding) and at Stow (Lincs). Stow is dated to *c.* 1040 so perhaps St. Benet is of similar date. The strips round the head rest on their own corbels in the form of couchant lions (which Rivoira derived from Lombardy), which rest on the arch main imposts. These imposts are moulded and of complex, rather classical, profile not unlike, though larger than, the capitals in the chapel in the White Tower of London. They go round, not through, both members of the strip-work, acting as imposts to them and pass along the nave west wall as far as the aisle walls.

Above the tower arch is a large round-headed opening with jambs of upright and flat, two of each; above the upper flats are square block imposts.

The nave and chancel.[1] In 1853 the north aisle was pulled down by R. Brandon and it was discovered that the east and west aisle walls had been built without bonding against the north wall of the nave and were on earlier foundations. At two points, the north-east corners of the nave and tower, there were quoins of the same kind as those of the tower and fragments of walling with rough-cast still adhering. From these remains it was concluded that the original church was probably aisleless and that the nave length was twice the width.

The chancel was removed in 1872 during the rebuilding by R. Blomfield who built a new south aisle. During this work the walls of the original chancel were discovered. The east wall was original and contemporary with the tower; its nature had been hidden by an interior facing of later coarse plaster. The south end of this wall had apparently never been disturbed. The foundations and part of the base were of very big stones, larger than those of the tower. The walls of Corpus Christi College had been built against the south-east angle of the original chancel. This east wall was 3 feet thick. The south wall of the present chancel, built by Blomfield, stands on original walling of large blocks of Barnack stone; one block tied into the east wall was $3\frac{1}{2}$ feet by 1 ft. 10 ins.

The east wall of the south aisle, projecting to the south from the south wall of the chancel, or at least the lower part of it, is original. The north end of this wall, where it meets the south wall of the chancel and against which the south pier of the chancel arch abuts, is also of rough large blocks of Barnack stone.

When the north-east pier of the nave was opened up by the destruction of the

---

[1] See plan in R.C.H.M., *City of Cambridge, Pt. II.*

north wall of the chancel its east face (that is, the north-east corner of the nave, or north end of the chancel arch) was found to be part of the first church with original rough-cast undisturbed, and the quoins were of blocks laid rather irregularly but roughly upright and flat, contrasting with the extreme regularity of the tower quoins. This east wall of the nave was joined at right angles to the north wall of the chancel.

The bases of the original chancel arch were found in their original position. Immediately above these were remains of a much later pattern, perhaps of the thirteenth or fourteenth century. The chancel was *c.* 20 feet by 15 feet and the nave *c.* 37 feet by *c.* 15 feet. The aisles according to Willis and Clark were 55 feet long by 10 feet wide.

The floor of the nave was taken up in 1872 and faint traces of a foundation of a supposed south aisle—or perhaps porticus—were found of *c.* 10 feet width, corresponding to that on the north taken down in 1853. The evidence for early aisles seems weak. The possibility that the supposed aisles were porticus cannot be ruled out.

The church was transferred to Corpus Christi College in 1353 and was used as the College Chapel until a new chapel was built in the sixteenth century.

DERBYSHIRE

REPTON

ST. WYSTAN'S CHURCH.[1] This is the only pre-Conquest church in Derbyshire. Although it was at an early date a place of great importance, the ecclesiastical and political centre of North Mercia and the residence and burial place of Mercian kings, there are no sculptural remains here. This is in marked contrast to the richness of the county in carved crosses and fragments, nearby Bakewell being outstandingly rich in such remains.

A monastery was founded here c. 654 by Diuma, the first bishop of the Mercians. It is mentioned three times in the Anglo-Saxon Chronicle, under the years 755, 874 and 875, the last two being the years the Danes wintered there. The name means Hreopa's tun or hill fort. According to W. Skeat Hreopa was the name of an Anglian warrior about whom nothing else is known. In Domesday Book the place was called Rapendun. It became the burial place of the Mercian kings in the eighth century. Æthelbald (716–57) and some of his successors, including Wiglaf c. 830, were buried here. Wigstan, or Wystan, a grandson of Wiglaf, was murdered here by his uncle Bertulph or Britfardus and was buried at Repton in 850.

The place was devastated by the Danes in 874–5 and it apparently remained desolate until a church was built here in Edgar's reign, 959–74, and dedicated to St. Wystan. This church was stated by some early writers, as recorded by Hipkins, to have been of oak beams or planks on a foundation of stone. The side walls were filled between the beams with wattle composed of twigs interlaced and daubed inside and out with clay or mud. The chancel floor was at a higher level than the present one and was supported on wood beams: it was presumably of two floors, the lower being the early crypt—of stone, like the foundations. It seems likely that this description applies to an earlier church, probably pre-Danish; Clapham wrote that the early crypt 'may go back to before the Danish invasion'. The church built in Edgar's time was probably of stone. It is unlikely that a church rebuilt at so important a centre as Repton, during the great monastic revival brought about by such a trio of ardent reformers and builders as Dunstan of Canterbury, Æthelwold of Winchester and Oswald of Worcester and York, would have been of wattle and daub. The date 950–1000 is accepted by most writers as the probable date of the earliest part of the

[1] A. Ashpitel; H. Brakspear, (a); G. Baldwin Brown; A. W. Clapham, (a); J. C. Cox, (b) and (c); F. C. Hipkins; W. H. St. J. Hope, (a) and (b); J. T. Irvine, (a), (b) and (c); A. Hamilton Thompson, (g).

church standing today. The early crypt was retained; the stone vault and supporting columns are later, perhaps early eleventh century.

The saint's relics were transferred to Evesham in Canute's reign (1017–35). The mediaeval priory at Repton was founded in 1172 by transference from Calke where it had been founded in 1161. Later the relics were returned to Repton from Evesham and were laid 'not as beforetime in the mausoleum of Wigstan's grandfather, Wiglaf, but in a shrine' in the priory chapel. This reference to an early mausoleum suggests a crypt. The early Mercian kings may have been buried in the crypt or, perhaps more likely, in sepulchral side chambers which have not been excavated or discovered.

The pre-Conquest parts of the existing church are the lofty square-ended chancel, the greater part of the foundations and part of the walls of the north transept, small portions of the south transept, the former crossing or presbyterial space (Fig. 9) and

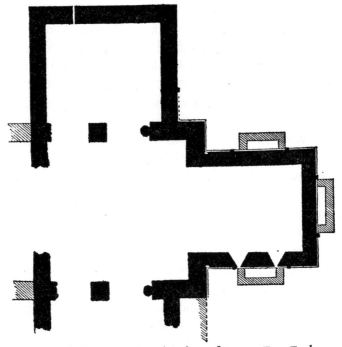

Fig. 9. Repton Church, plan of Saxon East End

the crypt (Fig. 11). The square presbyterial space, now the eastern part of the nave, is similar to those at Brixworth and Deerhurst, all three churches early Mercian foundations. It is thought by some writers that these presbyterial spaces were intended to support towers, possibly of timber. In no one of these three churches is there any thickening of the walls to provide the strengthening required for a tower support (as there is at Dunham Magna, Norfolk, where there is a stone tower, and at South Elmham, Suffolk, where it seems likely there was a tower). At Breamore (Hants) there is no thickening of walls, but here the crossing is surmounted by a mainly timber superstructure. There is no actual monumental evidence at Brixworth or Deerhurst to prove a central tower, but at Repton above the later chancel arch is a large rectangular opening of the type commonly seen in the east walls of Anglo-Saxon towers. It has renewed flat lintel and sill. The north jamb is of upright and flat slabs, the top flat having its lower inner corners hollow chamfered so as to produce an opening with rounded corners. The opening is not centrally placed, its south jamb being a little to the north of the keystone of the much later chancel arch below it. To the south of this opening is much renewed walling. It would appear therefore likely that Repton had a central tower, the lower part of which at least was of stone.

North and south transeptal chapels—really wings or porticus—open from the crossing. The lower courses of reddish Anglo-Saxon walling can be followed from the chancel round the north-east quoin of the nave (crossing), along the present east wall of the transept and returning west—here of three courses only—for two-thirds of the length of the transept north wall. In the west wall of the south transept is a bit of Saxon walling stated to be on the line of the old Saxon west arch, which perhaps indicates the width of the original openings (it is presumed that the two porticus were similar) for the north transept begins *c.* 5 feet to the west of the nave north-east quoin.

The low remains of the eastern responds of the two transepts have large, square, thin, flat bases of their original soffit columns and about two feet of the lower parts of the columns still standing. The upper parts of the columns, *c.* 7 feet high with their capitals (1), and unlike those of the crypt not monolithic, are now in the south porch. The capitals are closely similar to those of the crypt columns (2) which suggests that the vaulting of the crypt and the building of the transepts or, more likely, a widening of the entrances, were contemporary. An old water colour, reproduced by Hipkins, shows an arcade of two openings of unequal size across the transept; but all that is known monumentally are these eastern responds. Clapham thought that the transepts were widened to the west at some time perhaps in the Saxon period, and that originally there was one opening, not two, to each transept.

The old north and south walls of the presbyterial space—now merely the eastern part of the nave with no separation between them—join the walls of the later nave at a point between the second and third eastern arches of the nave arcade. The junction is plain: the string course along the presbyterial wall is at a higher level than the nave string and has a different profile. The nave string is square-cut with a plain chamfer

---

(1) *Plate* 68; (2) *Plate* 69.

below; the eastern string is plain square-cut above and below, with a shallow convex segmental moulding between.

On the exterior, from the north door of the crypt (at about the middle of the chancel north wall) eastwards as far as the later north-west buttress, is a massive four-membered plinth; a similar plinth is at the north-east corner of the nave. At the north-east corner of the nave, also, at the level of the aisle roof is a piece of string course, plain chamfered above. About a foot below this, and on the east wall only, is a piece of another string course of similar section to that of the interior string; on the south-east is a similar piece without the upper square-cut member.

The chancel south-east quoin (1) is of very large slab work, especially below the string course, of face-alternate arrangement, not characteristically megalithic, like St. Mildred's, Canterbury, but of large stones laid flat and evenly on one another. The lower part of the walls below ground level and for some distance above—as far

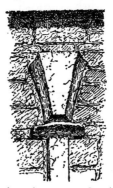

Fig. 10. Repton Church, upper finish of Pilaster Strips

as the bases of the pilaster strips—is of red sandstone; the stones are more massive than the whiter stones above. The red stonework is almost continuous from the south-east nave quoin to the break in the north wall of the north transept. There are no pilaster strips in this work.

About eleven feet above ground is a horizontal string course, chamfered above, running from the south-east wall of the nave round the chancel to the north-east corner of the nave. Above this, but not below, are thin vertical pilaster strips, all fairly short 'longs' with no 'shorts', evenly spaced and terminated above by small imposts—cross pieces—surmounted by stones cut into the form of 'springers' of an arch (Fig. 10). These suggest wall arcading, as at Wing (Bucks); but the strips are too widely spaced for arcading, and the imposts, *c.* 28 feet above ground and close under the present roof, could not support strip-work arch heads unless the original wall was very much higher than the existing one, itself high, which seems unlikely.

(1) *Plate 66.*

Probably the shaped stones above the strip imposts were intended merely as ornamental finishes to the vertical strip-work. These differences in walling and in pilaster work suggest at least two different building periods in the Saxon part of the existing church, the earlier, of red sandstone, perhaps of the age of Edgar *c.*, say, 975, and the later of whiter stone of probably the eleventh century. There are two dates also to the crypt; Clapham was of the opinion that the later part of the crypt was probably contemporary with the later rebuilding of the church in the eleventh century when, in his view, the transepts were widened. The older interior part of the crypt is not however necessarily contemporary with the tenth-century church; its walls are structurally different and more primitive and it may well belong to the pre-Danish church burnt in 874. A viking axe of curious but contemporary form, with a tiny splinter of wood still adhering in its rust, was dug up in 1923 about five feet below

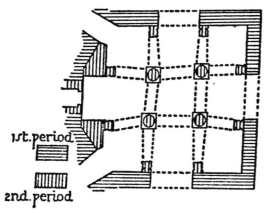

Fig. 11. Repton Crypt, plan

the ground near the south-east quoin. Conceivably the crypt may have been the original burial place of the eighth-century Mercian kings to which the partially wooden church referred to above may have been attached. Of the original church built by Bishop Diuma nothing is known.

The Crypt. When the adjacent Augustinian priory was founded in 1172 the church became the priory church. Additions were made and much rebuilding carried out in the succeeding centuries: a new aisled and clerestoried nave, the existing western tower and spire, and alterations to the chancel. The crypt was lost to history and was not rediscovered till 1779. A grave was being dug in the chancel for Dr. Prior, the late headmaster of the school, when the grave digger disappeared from view: he had dug through the vaulted roof below and had fallen into the crypt. During later restoration work in 1792 the crypt was used as a rubbish dump. Later, in 1802, the northern steps leading from the chancel to the crypt, and the door below, were discovered. The crypt was then cleared and restored to its present form (Fig. 11).

It is small, *c.* 15 feet square and *c.* 9 feet high (1). The walls are of the earliest period; the four columns, eight wall shafts, the vaulting, the western opening and the western wall masses against which the two western piers abut are later, probably eleventh century. The lower parts of the interior walls are of well-dressed ashlar of very large slabs; some are 12 to 18 inches high and at least one is 5 feet long. Such large slab ashlar suggests an early date. The masonry above is not quite so good. At 6 feet from the floor is a triple cornice of stepped pattern rather like that on Barnack tower but, unlike Barnack, the top member projects further than the lower one (Fig. 12). As at Barnack the lower member is chamfered but, again unlike Barnack,

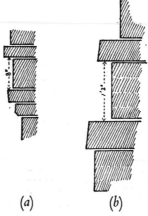

(a)   (b)

Fig. 12. (a) Repton Crypt, String Course
(b) Barnack Tower, String Course

the upper member, 2 inches thick, is square-edged while the lower member has a small under-chamfer (at Barnack both members have wide upper chamfers). The middle stone is 8 inches wide and has only slight projection from the wall; Barnack's middle stone is 14 inches wide. Baldwin Brown suggested a date of 950–1000 for Barnack and, on account of the cornice, 'perhaps' a similar date for Repton crypt. This evidence however is not conclusive. The differences in walling above and below are consistent with different building periods or with much repair and restoration of the upper part. There have certainly been alterations here and there in the interior. It is not possible to say from the present structure whether the cornice originally passed round the three north, east and south recesses (Irvine said they did); the two lower members of the cornice, but not the upper one, as it would have fouled the opening, are carried round the western recess. There is now no cornice on the east wall nor in the north doorway. This doorway however is not original.

In the north-west and south-west corners are stone staircases of access from the

---

(1) *Plate* 67.

chancel. In the centres of the north, east and south walls are tall rectangular recesses, *c.* 17 to 24 inches deep and 6 ft. 2 ins. wide, which may possibly have led to chambers, perhaps sepulchral, of which, however, nothing definite is known. During Hipkins's excavations of 1898 a skeleton was discovered under two ancient slabs several feet below ground and some feet to the south of the south recess. The south recess below the opening is now built-up; there is no cornice here in the recess, it runs only along the flat south wall. The eastern recess is blocked to a height of *c.* 4 feet flush with the wall; this blocking is surmounted by a single flat slab, much worn, which may be part of an ancient grave slab. Above the blocking the recess is *c.* 13 to 14 inches deep. In the upper parts of the eastern and southern recesses the thinner walls have been pierced with rectangular openings, now glazed, *c.* 2 feet high, which presumably lighted the upper part of the crypt. On the exterior these slits (1) are *c.* 2 feet above the present ground level. The lintels and sills look ancient but the jambs are chamfered and may be later. On the exterior walls too are marks of the former gabled roofs of possibly protective porch-like adjuncts.

Hipkins excavated the ground to the south of the south recess in 1898 and discovered 2 ft. 3 ins. below the surface two large slabs side by side, 1 ft. 10 ins. long by 1 ft. 5 ins. by 1 ft. 5 ins. and 2 ft. by 1 ft. 4 ins. by 1 ft. 9 ins. respectively, and *c.* 2 ft. 2 ins. apart, obviously foundations of the shallow porch-like adjunct. They rested on a large flat slab below. It was at the depth of this slab and to the south that the skeleton was found beneath another slab which had been broken across. Nothing was found with the skeleton to indicate its age or period; perhaps the grave had been robbed at some time, the stone being broken during the robbery.

The exterior of the eastern recess (1) was much altered at some time, but prior to the blocking, by the insertion of steps leading to the interior. The existing steps outside are roughly made and rest on earth only without mortar. Six more would be required to reach the crypt floor but these were evidently removed when the blocking was inserted. J. C. Cox was of opinion that these steps may have been put in by the Augustinian Canons who took over Repton in 1172.

The north recess is now a doorway approached from the interior by two crudely built high steps, possibly original. In the western jamb however is a holy water stoup perhaps put in by the twelfth-century Canons.

In the west wall of the crypt is an arched recess within which is a roughly made triangular opening *c.* 18 inches high. The object of this is not known; it has been suggested that it may have been (*a*) a 'holy hole' for relics, (*b*) a lamp niche to hold a lamp perhaps let down from the chancel above; or (*c*) a hagioscope.

The vaulting and the monolithic columns are of the second building period. The columns (2) are the only detached columns of the pre-Conquest period now remain-

---

(1) *Plate 66*; (2) *Plate 69*.

ing *in situ*. The capitals are morphologically early and, though quite well finished, may be regarded as primitive in design; each has a square abacus with two parallel horizontal quirks (a late feature), and the faces are hollow chamfered below to a smaller square, showing no attempt to fit the circular shaft below. The columns have half-round narrow banding running spirally down from capital to base, the spirals of adjacent columns being in opposite directions. The shafts between the banding bulge slightly. They have plain hemispherical or half-bulbous bases. The north-east column has eleven courses of flat Roman bricks, $\frac{1}{2}$ inch thick, just above the base on the south-east part of the face, presumably later repair work. Reddish paint is visible in places on the chamfer of the capitals. The columns are 5 feet apart and are 5 ft. 9 ins. high. The vaulting is primitive: mostly segmental and sometimes described as crude groining. This supposed groining is probably accidental, or at least not intentional. Thus, if intentional one would expect to find it in the square central bay, but here it is in fact of segmental barrel type running north–south. In the other bays the vaulting appears to be quite haphazard. It is inferior to such crude early Norman groining as that in Westminster undercroft. Baldwin Brown considered that the Repton vaulting owed nothing to Norman influence. Nor would Norman influence be necessary; a more likely source of inspiration would be the Rhineland, where such vaulting was well known at this time. It would seem likely however that at Repton we have an Anglo-Saxon mason trying to do an unaccustomed job, as with the Brixworth supposed cushion capitals.[1] The vaulting is supported at the walls by eight square pilaster-like responds, which are not bonded into the walls. All have square quirked abaci and capitals chamfered below like those of the columns, except that the chamfering is on the soffit sides only. There are no bases. The three exposed faces are panelled; the panels are shallow, round-headed and have their faces cambered from the sides to a central vertical ridge.

[1] See below, pp. 212–13.

GLOUCESTERSHIRE

DEERHURST

ST. MARY'S PRIORY CHURCH.[1] Deerhurst is an ancient place. It is not mentioned in any existing book by Bede though the sixteenth- and seventeenth-century chroniclers Leland and Camden wrote that it was. Dugdale and other writers refer to a monastery here before 804. In that year large estates were conferred on the monastery by Æthelric, son of Æthelmund, earl or ealdorman of the Hwiccian district of Mercia. This is the earliest recorded gift to Deerhurst, but a gift of such magnitude implies that the monastery was already one of some importance and it may have taken many years to develop from small beginnings.

Deerhurst was in the country of the Hwicce, the area which is now Gloucestershire, Worcestershire and the western part of Warwickshire. It formed one of the twelve so-called kingdoms into which Saxon England was divided in the sixth century. Later, in the seventh century, five of the smaller kingdoms were absorbed by more powerful neighbours, the famous Heptarchy of seven kingdoms resulting. The Hwicce were conquered by Penda in 628 and attached to Mercia when he became king c. 632. Before then the southern part, modern Gloucestershire, had belonged to Wessex since 577 and had been settled by Saxons from Wessex. The Hwicce had been Christianized early probably, as their more powerful neighbour to north and east, Mercia, was pagan, from either Celtic Glastonbury (very likely in view of the connection of the southern part of the area with Wessex), or by the British Church in Wales (unlikely, in view of the hatred of the British Church for the Saxons), or directly from Ireland. It is known that Æthelwalh, a king of the South Saxons, married Ebba, a daughter of king Eanfrith of the Hwicce, and was baptized c. 675.[2] Many monasteries grew up in the area in the late seventh and eighth centuries, among them Deerhurst, Tewkesbury, Gloucester, Evesham, Pershore, Ripple, Bredon (Worcs), Winchcombe. One of the earliest appears to have been Deerhurst, founded probably c. 700 (the traditional date is 715); Winchcombe was later, c. 800.

When Peada and Wulfhere began to evangelize Mercia after Penda's death[3] Diuma, an Irishman from Lindisfarne, was made bishop 'of the Mercians' c. 652

---

[1] G. Baldwin Brown; Canon Bazeley; J. C. Buckler; G. Butterworth; A. W. Clapham, (a); E. C. Gilbert, (e), (f) and (g); D. H. Haigh; W. H. Knowles; C. R. Peers, (b); A. Hamilton Thompson, (f).

[2] See below, p. 369. [3] See above, p. 42.

but with little or no authority, though perhaps with some influence, over the Hwicce. The first independent bishop of the area with his seat at Worcester was appointed by Archbishop Theodore *c.* 679. This lack of an early bishop and the numerous monasteries suggest strong Celtic influence in the early Hwiccian church. The Celtic Church was essentially a Monastic Church; the important prelates were the abbots; bishops were less important and often subordinate to abbots. Certainly Northumbrian influence might be expected in the church architecture in the earlier period, though after Theodore's creation of an independent see for the area Kentish influence might also be expected. Both are observable at Deerhurst: the long, narrow, very high nave is quite evidently of Northumbrian inspiration; the apse may derive

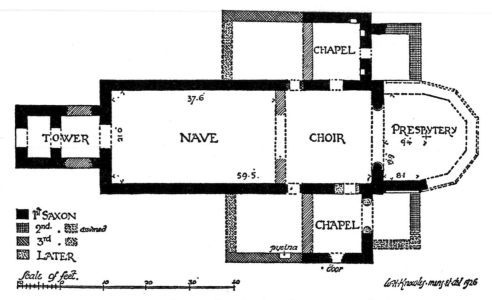

Fig 13. Deerhurst Church, plan. (W. H. Knowles.)

from Kent. At the same time there may be details of local origin, such as the string course and the peculiar shape of the apse; others are Scandinavian, the numerous animal headed corbels and ornaments. Others again look of Norman inspiration and have been regarded by some writers as Norman. They may be Norman; but, as Gilbert argues, not without considerable evidence, they may be better attributed to influences from Western Europe which began to show themselves in England long before the Conquest, even in the Early Saxon period.

The date of the church has been subject to much discussion and has been given by different writers variously from the seventh to the eleventh century. The first writer to hazard a guess was Haigh in 1845; he suggested the early eighth century. Butterworth in 1887 more cautiously thought it might be any period between the eighth and the tenth centuries. The church, or more strictly a church, at Deerhurst is stated to have been burnt by the Danes during the great invasions of 865 on. In 970, during the monastic revival under King Edgar, Oswald, Bishop of Worcester, installed Benedictine monks at the place, so presumably the church had been or was then rebuilt. Some early nineteenth-century writers stated that it was rebuilt by Edward the Confessor. There is no evidence for this and it seems unlikely for Edward gave the Abbey and most of its lands to the Abbey of St. Denis, near Paris, *c.* 1059, a gift confirmed by William the Conqueror in a still existing charter of 1069. From that date Deerhurst became a subordinate priory to St. Denis. It is hardly likely that Edward would rebuild the church in order to give it away.

As W. H. Knowles pointed out 'unlike the recognized development of Gothic

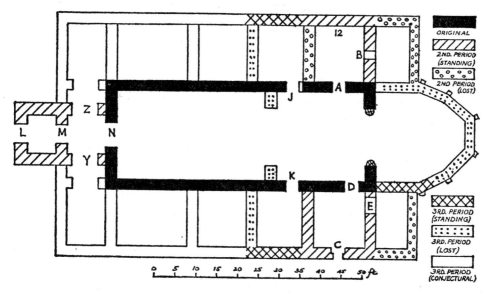

Fig. 14. Deerhurst Church, plan. (E. C. Gilbert.)

work, Saxon buildings do not exhibit pronounced details of definite progression', so it is not possible to assign accurate dates from architectural evidence alone. From the literary evidence Knowles's suggested date of *c.* 970 or earlier might seem reasonable. Later however, according to Gilbert, he abandoned the idea of a single date for the church. Baldwin Brown without specific evidence suggested the first half of the tenth century; Clapham regarded the church as 'mainly a monument of the tenth century'. A. Hamilton Thompson thought the date uncertain but suggested that the apse and the eastern pair of porticus were probably mid-eleventh century and that the upper half of the tower 'was altered at a later period'. E. C. Gilbert in 1939 and again in 1954 from a thorough examination of the building has revived the older idea of a very early date, or rather dates, for the church. His evidence suggested three building periods for those parts of the original church still above ground, the first two periods not widely separated, the third perhaps a century later. The upper half of the tower is undoubtedly of the Late Saxon period, probably of the tenth century. He also conjectured, though the conjectures have some evidential basis, that a fourth pair of porticus to the west of the others and a western narthex on either side of the tower may have been put up at some time, making the church like Reculver surrounded with porticus on north, west and south (Figs. 13 and 14). As will be seen, his case for four building periods, three early and a late one, when the upper half of the tower was erected, is very strong if not entirely convincing; it certainly necessitates some modification to earlier views of a single-dated or two-dated church, and his story is remarkably well and closely reasoned from the evidence.

He concludes that the Saxon church we have today, except the upper half of the tower, is essentially pre-Danish; the church, if burnt in 867, was not destroyed: there are signs of fire in the south porticus, which may however be due to the great fire of the early fifteenth century, and not that of the ninth. He claims that the first period 'could be about 715' and the church built then, the original church of the monastery, consisted of a long nave only, divided into two unequal parts to provide a square chancel at the east end. Here the influence is Northumbrian: long, narrow, high church. The second period he places prior to the reign of Offa of Mercia which began in 756; in this he places the two pairs of eastern porticus and a two-storeyed porch. The third period is put between Offa's accession in 756 and the Danish invasions which began in 865; i.e. mid-eighth to mid-ninth century. To this period he attributes the apse (Kentish influence perhaps), the western pair of porticus and a third stage to the porch, including the famous and elaborate double gable-headed opening in that stage. Jackson and Fletcher[1] also accept an early eighth-century date for the church.

Gilbert's case for very early dates for the church may seem less acceptable than that for several building periods. Two features might be considered to militate against it: the herring-boning and the primitive animal heads on the exterior walls.

The considerable patches of herring-boning (l) are in the earlier parts of the building, though in the opinion of most writers it is a very late feature. J. F. Curwen denied that it was ever used by the Saxons. Baldwin Brown and Clapham more cautiously regarded it as a late feature found in the Saxon period in buildings put up within a few years of the Conquest. The former wrote 'where it is found in a Saxon wall we should be inclined as a rule to suspect reparation by a Norman or Norman-trained mason', Clapham that 'it is practically always an indication of early [Norman] date, and though it was used occasionally in the Saxon period it is commonly distinctive of late eleventh-century building'. It was however used by the Romans,

---

[1] Op. cit.

(l) *Plates* 70, 76.

from whom via the Merovingians and Carolingians the Normans obtained it. It was used to some extent in Romano-British buildings: e.g. in the core, though not in the block facings, of the town walls at Caerwent (Mon). It is not unlikely that some Saxon masons may have adopted the technique in areas where there were Roman remains showing it. Baldwin Brown indeed regarded its use at Deerhurst as 'most likely' Saxon. It also occurs at Brixworth; and there is a very small strip at Monkwearmouth of unquestionably early date.

The animal head ornamentation is discussed below.[1] It is generally regarded as of Scandinavian origin and would hardly be expected in England before *c.* 870–900. The three primitive heads in the exterior walls (1) are certainly earlier than the others at Deerhurst; they look contemporary with the walls, but whether they can reasonably be dated to the eighth century appears doubtful. The rather similar heads at Barnack, where they are corbels and not as at Deerhurst merely ornamental, are probably tenth century.

Of the many publications about Deerhurst three are of outstanding interest and importance and are necessary reading for a proper understanding and appreciation of the church, its architecture and its history. These are the works of G. Butterworth, who was vicar of the parish for many years and who authorized and studied closely the excavations and rebuilding of 1861; of W. H. Knowles, the architect who superintended the restoration of 1926; and of E. C. Gilbert, whose observations and conclusions are given in his 1954 paper.

The walls (2) of the earlier parts are of oolitic limestone rubble roughly built on both faces mainly in courses about four inches high with wide joints. The upper half of the tower is of rougher workmanship than elsewhere; it is of very thin ragstone with a few courses of rough ashlar. On the whole it is inferior work to that below, but it has quoins while the lower part and the nave have none. Throughout is much herring-bone work except in the upper part of the tower and the north-south dividing wall within the tower where there is none. Also there are no fewer than fourteen openings, twelve of them perhaps original, in the lower half of the tower, and only one in the upper part below the belfry. Knowles wrote that the walls are from 2 ft. 3 ins. to 2 ft. 6 ins. thick; Haigh that the north and south tower walls, including the dividing wall, were 2 ft. 6 ins. thick and the east and west tower walls 2 ft. 9 ins.; Butterworth gave the thickness of the tower walls generally as 2 ft. 8 ins.

The Nave. The walls of the nave and choir are largely original apart from patches of restoration and repair in the north wall and clerestory. The walls are 39 feet high to the eaves and *c.* 60 feet to the apex of the roof ridge marks on the tower east wall. This is an exceptional height for a Saxon nave (Monkwearmouth was only *c.* 31 feet

---

[1] pp. 183–4.

(1) *Plate* 79; (2) *Plate* 70.

to the eaves and *c.* 52 feet to the roof ridge). In the east wall, *c.* 22 feet above the floor, are two brackets decorated (1) with double-hollow chamfer and two quirks below. Above these, visible on the exterior, are the remains of two widely splayed narrow slit windows, one on each side of the existing fourteenth-century light. From these three facts—the great height, the high-up windows, the brackets—Gilbert inferred that the nave may have been of two floors, the brackets being parts of the support to the floor. He further suggested that the lower floor may have been used as a sleeping apartment for the monks as early Celtic monasteries had no cloisters or dormitories; this however is surmise.

The nave is 21 feet wide on the interior and 37 ft. 6 ins. long to the destroyed west wall and chancel arch of the choir, and 59 ft. 5 ins. to the existing east wall of the church. This gives a length-breadth ratio of three to one which, like the great height, is a Northumbrian characteristic.

The nave walls were pierced with north and south arcades of three bays each when the aisles were built, probably in the thirteenth century. The wall between nave and choir with its wide and lofty arch comparable with that in the east wall was removed at some unknown time. Its foundations, projecting about 4 feet north and south from the nave walls, were uncovered during the 1861 restorations. The position of the wall was marked on the north and south faces of the nave walls. The only original openings in the walls are two small triangular ones about 18 feet above the floor in the middle of the north and south walls. They are closely similar to the one in the east wall of the tower. Their sides have no stone dressings but are of oversailing wall stones, i.e. of stepped pattern, now hidden by plaster. Being so roughly made and so small and high-up as to admit little light, it is possible that they may not have been intended as permanent openings. On the other hand the corresponding tower opening was undoubtedly intentional and there seems little justification for thinking the nave ones were not. Gilbert suggested they were squints through which the nave interior could be seen from former central porticus.

Nothing is really known about any other original nave side windows. On the exterior of the nave south wall *c.* 25 feet above ground is a much weathered string course *c.* 11 inches wide which passes also along the west wall and behind the tower. The porch must therefore be later than the nave. The string course ended at the west wall of the central porticus, about 6 feet to the east of the west wall of the choir. Butterworth concluded after careful examination after removal of plaster in the 1861 restoration that it was below and probably acted as a sill to a range of old Saxon windows presumably in the position now occupied by the larger fourteenth-century clerestory windows. Knowles in 1926 agreed with this view.

The original choir, now part of the nave, was *c.* 20 feet long (east–west). Although

---

(1) *Plate* 75.

its walls are continuous with those of the nave, with no thickening, Clapham and Peers thought it was probably intended to support a central tower, as at Repton, though perhaps of timber. The east wall had a very large round-headed arch, now built up (1), but which led originally to the apsed sanctuary. The arch was 12 ft. 3 ins. wide and 13 ft. 2 ins. high to the tops of the capitals, or *c.* 20 feet to the crown of the arch. The round head, of a single ring of large rectangular stones, has a plain strip-work hood mould resting on corbels in the form of beasts' heads (2) of similar type but cruder than those in the tower. They are less dynamic in appearance, more bovine and stolid and altogether of poorer workmanship than the really magnificent creatures in the tower. They are not of Norman type (though label stops are a Norman feature) but look as though they were attempts by less experienced craftsmen to provide something similar to the, to them, unfamiliar animals of the tower and so provided bull-like heads, a type of animal with which they were familiar. The jambs are in the form of half-round attached columns with capitals of unique design (3). They have square-cut abaci, hollow chamfered below. Below the chamfer is a square-cut depression which turns up and tapers at the abacus corners almost to the top of the hollow chamfer. Below, instead of necking, are two square-edged fillets; the upper one is hollow chamfered below and the lower one, immediately above the shaft, has its outer ends turned up into the empty corners of the upper depression. Although skilfully carved, as though by an experienced craftsman, these capitals are of primitive design. They show a rather crude and unsuccessful attempt to pass from the square of the abacus to the usual circular shape below. They might be better described as elaborately carved imposts showing some feeling towards the idea of a capital. They are derived from flat impost slabs, not cubical blocks. The columns have plain slightly moulded bases *c.* 2 feet high.

The window high up above the blocked arch is probably fifteenth century. On each side of this window on the interior is a rectangular slab with gabled top, *c.* 4 feet by *c.* 3 feet. They have puzzled some writers. Butterworth suggested, reasonably and almost certainly correctly, that they are interior blockings of the two ancient narrow windows, traces of which are visible on the exterior and which were widely splayed towards the interior. Just below the fifteenth-century window, nearly 30 feet above the floor, is a large slab (4) which suggests the blocking of an original opening to the apse roof or roof chamber, corresponding to a similar one in the tower east wall. Objection has been made to this that such a chamber would have blocked the two lateral windows. It would, and probably did. The apse roof fouled these windows, which would be of little or no use when the apse was built as the choir would receive better lighting from the windows which the apse must have had.

There are six blocked openings in the choir, three in the north (5) and three in the

---

(1) *Plates 75, 76*; (2) *Plate 77*; (3) *Plate 78*; (4) *Plate 76*; (5) *Plate 75.*

south walls, which led formerly to the upper and lower floors of the central north and south porticus and to the lower floors of the western porticus. The openings are blocked thinly on their centres leaving the openings as recesses *c.* 2 feet deep in the north and south faces of the choir walls.

The Porticus. The central north and south porticus are considered by most writers to have been originally the only ones. Gilbert however thinks that the two pairs of eastern porticus were contemporary, built at the same time but slightly later than the nave and choir, in the second building period. The remaining fragments of the eastern porticus are bonded into the walls of their western neighbours. This is strong evidence, for the Saxons seem to have disliked bonding in additions, and avoided it whenever possible.

The central porticus, both north and south, were of two storeys. It is not known whether the others were. No other two-storeyed porticus are known in England. Gilbert stated that Saxon Hexham had two-storeyed porticus, but this is by no means certain: there is no monumental evidence and the literary evidence is ambiguous.

The north central porticus is 13 feet long (north–south) and 11 feet east–west. The west wall and the floor between the two stages have been destroyed as this porticus with its western, later, neighbour was opened out to form part of the later north aisle; the north wall is now part of the aisle wall. The door to the ground floor (1) from the chancel, centrally placed (Fig. 14, A), was gable-headed and 3 ft. 2 ins. wide. The head is supported on chamfered imposts and the jambs beneath the modern plaster are of through-stones. The upper floor was entered from the choir, 10 to 12 feet above floor level, by a large round-headed doorway (1) 5 feet wide and 8 ft. 10 ins. high from sill to crown of arch. The square-cut head is of voussoirs and is set back a little behind the plastered jambs. The imposts are chamfered. There was a square-edged strip-work hood mould. This doorway is the main evidence for the existence of an upper floor, though there are indications of a straight joint on the exterior of the aisle wall. There were a doorway and a window in the west wall of the upper storey. In the east wall of the ground floor, now the east wall of the north aisle, is a blocked square-headed opening (Fig. 14, B), 5 ft. 10 ins. high and 2 ft. 2 ins. wide. This led formerly to the north-east porticus. On each side of this opening in the wall is a small square aumbry-like recess. A similar recess is near the east end of the north wall (Fig. 13). Some writers have suggested that before the eastern porticus was built there may have been an altar between the two eastern aumbries replaced later by the doorway. In this connection it is interesting that the porticus is longer north–south than east–west, which is unusual. It is possible that this was to accommodate two altars, one between the two northern aumbries and one between the two eastern aumbries. This would be consistent with the doorway being a later

---

(1) *Plate* 75

insertion replacing the altar and leading into the later eastern porticus. If the porticus are contemporary the puzzle remains. It is however possible that there may have been an entrance to the east porticus from the apse, as at Reculver.

The north-east porticus, now destroyed except its foundation, was *c.* 10 ft. 6 ins. long (north–south) and *c.* 8 feet east–west. It flanked the apse but its sole entrance is supposed to have been from the central porticus.

The north–west porticus was *c.* 15 feet long (east–west) by 13 feet north–south, the same width but longer than the earlier central porticus. It has disappeared but its position is indicated by straight joints in the aisle wall with no herring-boning to the west and on the interior wall by a lesser thickness and slight cant or bend in the wall. The entrance to this chapel was by a small but heavily built rectangular doorway in the extreme south-east end of the south wall of the porticus (Fig. 14, J). This door-way, now plastered like the others, had rebated jambs of through-stones. It is visible though blocked in the chancel.

The south porticus are, or were, in general very similar to the north ones. The central one was very slightly smaller than the corresponding northern porticus, perhaps unintentionally so; the difference, 6 inches shorter (north–south) and 3 inches longer (east–west), is no more than is consistent with the well-known bad setting-out of Saxon masons. The west wall was replaced later by a Norman wall and arch. The door from the choir (Fig. 13 and Fig. 14, D), is probably not original and may not be in its original position: it is not opposite the corresponding doorway of the north chapel but further to the east, almost at the extreme east end of the porticus north wall; and it is wider, with properly quoined jambs of greenstone similar to that used in the thirteenth century nave arcade, and it has a flat lintel. Also unlike the north one this porticus has an outer doorway centrally placed in its south wall (Fig. 14, C). It is almost certainly a later insertion for early porticus rarely had exterior entrances. It is known as the Prior's Doorway.[1] It has a square-cut round head of voussoirs with fine joints and a square-sectioned strip-work hood mould on the exterior resting on animal heads as label stops. Above is another primitive animal head projecting from the wall. The jambs are inclined, being 2 ft. 6 ins. apart below and 2 ft. 4½ ins. above; they are splayed (unusual in a doorway) and rebated on the interior. In the east wall is a blocked round-headed archway (Figs. 13 and 14, E) with a half-round roll up the jamb faces and round the soffit of the head, resembling that of the blocked sanctuary arch. This is a later insertion of unknown but perhaps of post-Conquest date. It probably replaced a narrower earlier entrance to the eastern porticus, which like the corresponding one on the north flanked the apse. It is fire-stained, especially on its eastern face.

Like the north porticus the south central porticus was of two stages. The entrance to the upper floor from the choir was similar to the corresponding opening to the

---

[1] See Knowles, fig. 13.

north chapel. The west wall of this upper stage still exists (1), above the Norman arch and wall of the stage below. In it is a built-up rectangular doorway very close to the choir wall, that is at the north end of the porticus west wall; and to the south of centre is a rectangular window with wide single splay towards the east, i.e. it was intended to light the chamber. The two-light window in the south wall is fourteenth century.

The south-west porticus has disappeared except the south wall which is now part of the south aisle. Like the corresponding north-west chapel it had an entrance from the choir at the extreme east end of the porticus north wall (Fig. 14, K). In the south wall, near the east end, is a recessed piscina (Fig. 13) which has inclined jambs of evident Saxon design. The roof of this chapel would have blocked the door and window in the west wall of the upper stage of the central chapel unless the western chapel was itself two-staged, in which case the doorway above would have been a communication between the two upper stages.

In the south choir wall above but to the east of the blocked entrance to the south-west porticus is a tall rectangular opening, rebated for a door, with thin lintel and jambs. There is no corresponding opening in the choir north wall. It is not Saxon, but probably an entrance to a later rood-loft not now existing. In apparent connection with this there are three steps visible in the south side of the wall, in the aisle, the bottom one *c.* 6 feet from the floor.

The straight joint in the aisle south wall *c.* 31 feet from the east quoin of the chancel marks the west end of the western porticus. Twelve feet further west is another straight joint so far unexplained. Gilbert suggested that it marks the west end of a fourth south porticus, which he called the mid-west porticus, later than the other western one and obliterated when the aisle was built. There may have been a corresponding one on the north. The two small triangular openings in the nave walls are above this position and may have served as squints.

Butterworth refers to a foundation, uncovered in 1861, of an early cross-wall between nave and south aisle, continuous with the west wall of the nave (Fig. 14); also that later, he thought in the twelfth century, a wall was built in line with the internal mid-wall of the tower running southwards to meet and perhaps cross the south aisle; and that the nave south wall was extended westwards to meet this new wall; and further that an arch was cut in this nave wall extension, similar to those (Fig. 14, Y and Z) already in the tower north and south walls, making a line of three arches in what was in effect a western aisle. Gilbert points out that the Normans rarely if ever extended nave walls westwards although they often extended aisle walls, returning the walls to north and south to end flush with the tower west wall. He considers it likely that at some time a fifth porticus was built at the south-west end of the nave and that Butterworth's western aisle was also really a porticus of true

---

Kentish type and of pre-Conquest, perhaps of eighth-century, date. This would make Deerhurst, like Reculver (dated *c.* 669), to be surrounded by porticus on the north, west and south. This is largely conjecture though not without some evidential basis and is at least consistent with what little evidence there is.

The Apse. This is of great interest.[1] Only the foundations and a portion of the south-west stilt and angle exist (Fig. 13). The foundations are semi-circular on both outer and inner faces and consist of very thin square slabs, *c.* $\frac{1}{2}$ to 1 inch thick. The foundation wall is 3 ft. 9 ins. thick and *c.* 7 feet deep through the sandy earth to the marl below. This depth was necessary mainly on account of a fall in ground level from west to east of the church site. Although the apse area was well trenched no evidence of a crypt was found.

The apse stilts are 8 ft. 1 in. long (east–west), i.e. slightly longer than the other faces of the apse. The width of the foundations is 18 ft. 3 ins. north–south and they are 18 ft. 6 ins. east–west, on the interior. On the exterior they are 25 ft. 9 ins. by 22 feet. The apse itself, above the foundations, was 19 ft. 9 ins. wide and 18 ft. 9 ins. long (east–west) on the interior.

The apse was polygonal and Knowles showed conclusively that the semi-circular foundations were intended to support a polygonal apse, as at Wing and Brixworth (though Brixworth is polygonal only on the exterior). It is stilted and of the full width of the choir, as at Wing. The stilts are in line with the choir walls; at Wing they incline somewhat towards the east, and at Brixworth the apse is narrower than the presbytery though the stilts do not incline. Deerhurst apse is five-sided, or seven-sided if the stilts are included; that is, it is part of a dodecagon, equilateral but not equiangular. A regular dodecagon has interior angles of 150°; here the western angles are 166°, the middle angles 144° and the eastern angles 140°. At Wing the western angles are greater owing to the inward inclination of the stilts, and at Brixworth they are greater, too. The origin of the form is obscure. Clapham wrote that 'the semi-polygonal apse at Reculver and Brixworth are an obvious copy of those of the sixth-century churches at Ravenna or their prototypes'. This is probably true of Reculver. Brixworth however has proportions which make its Ravennate derivation at least not obvious; it shows closer resemblance to the Deerhurst–Wing group of apses polygonal on both faces. These appear to derive neither from Ravenna nor North Africa nor Syria. Polygonal Carolingian apses are rare, but Knowles points out that there is one at Civaux (Vienne)[2] which is seven-sided with its widest angle of 165° at the west, as at Deerhurst. Knowles writes, 'Clearly the three English apses, whatever their respective dates may be, belong to the same tradition.'

The south-west stilt and angle remains to a considerable height (I). A flat pilaster

---

[1] For detailed drawings, see Knowles, fig. 16.   [2] See Knowles, fig. 16.

(I) *Plate 76.*

strip 6 inches wide with a projection of 6 inches on the extreme west of the stilt and against the chancel wall rises to the eaves. A fragment of another angular pilaster strip is at the south-west angle. It is narrower than the corresponding one at Brixworth; it is *c.* 8 inches wide with a projection of 5 inches (the Brixworth one is 22 inches by *c.* 6 inches). At 16 feet above the two-membered plinth is a horizontal string course along the stilt acting as a base to gable-headed arcading similar to that at Wing and Brixworth. At Brixworth however there is no string course and at Wing (1) there is round-headed arcading below the gable-heads, in lieu of a string course. In this respect Wing may be considered an advance on Deerhurst and perhaps later. Within the remaining gable is a carved angel (2). It is not known whether the arcading or angels were carried all round the apse, as is the arcading at Wing and Brixworth. At the last two churches there is no carved ornament, but there are windows in alternate bays. Deerhurst apse must have had windows, though nothing is known of their distribution. There would however have been room for windows in every or in alternate panels between the arcading and the eaves, room enough, that is, for windows above the arcading and angels below, or for windows and angels in alternate panels. The edges of the pilasters, string course and arcading are cut back to wall level to show a regular outline through the plaster. Bits of plaster an inch or so deep can still be seen here and there.

The apse was very high, only a little lower than the choir, for the marks of its roof are visible on the exterior of the choir east wall. Knowles was of opinion that the presence of herring-boning in the apse walls (3) though there is none in the west porticus nor in the upper half of the tower, though all are Saxon, suggests that the apse was part of the original plan and structure of the church. The walls too are of the same thickness, 2 ft. 6 ins. C. R. Peers suggested that the arcading and angle pilaster strips suggested a different and perhaps later building tradition from the rest of the church. Gilbert produced strong evidence to prove that the apse was not part of the early church but later. Thus it blocked the east windows of the choir which were only about two feet above the top of the surviving bit of apse south wall and below the roof line of the apse. The pilaster strip-work and arcading also suggest a later date, for there is no similar work elsewhere in the church, though earlier than the Brixworth re-constructed apse with its much wider pilasters.

Gilbert is also of opinion that the apse is later than the eastern two pairs of porticus; i.e. that the porticus belong to a second building period and the apse to a third. This is consistent with the architectural evidence: the porticus look earlier and the apse shows late features. But there are difficulties in accepting an earlier date for the porticus. If there was no apse the porticus would have projected beyond the east wall, a position in the highest degree unlikely: porticus normally abutted flatly

---

(1) *Plate* 103; (2) *Plate* 81; (3) *Plate* 76.

against a flat wall. To avoid such projection a projecting chancel of equal width with the nave must be postulated, an unlikely adjunct. There is strong northern influence at Deerhurst and in northern churches, and in some southern ones of early date such as Bradford-on-Avon, the projecting eastern chancel was small and narrower than the nave. No porticus would overlap nave and narrower chancel. Moreover no chancel foundations were exposed during a thorough trenching of the whole apse area. The extreme eastern porticus have disappeared, except their foundations. The only monumental evidence that they were contemporary with the existing east porticus is a bit of bonding noted by Gilbert. Knowles and Clapham thought the lost porticus later than the existing eastern pair, but the bonding is certainly strong evidence of contemporaneity of the two pairs of eastern porticus and it is difficult to accept them as other than earlier than the apse. There must surely have been something earlier than the present apse and almost as wide as the nave between the two eastern porticus. Gilbert has suggested in a private communication to the writer that there may have been an earlier apse as wide as the existing one and perhaps on the same foundations, but lower. In that case the present apse would be a rebuilding and heightening of an earlier one and not an entirely new construction. There is no evidence for this, but the suggestion is consistent with the known facts, one might almost say is an inference from them, and would explain an otherwise puzzling feature.

The Tower. This has been less altered than the rest of the church. The outside measurements are 21 ft. 6 ins. east–west by 14 ft. 6 ins. north–south; at the top it is 20 ft. 6 ins. east–west, the upper part being slightly battered in an east–west direction only. It is 70 feet high. It has no string courses or offsets. The upper half is of later date than the lower though still of the Saxon period. The early Saxon walling includes the lower three stages, to a height of about 36 feet, but on the east it goes a bit higher and can be seen to end in an irregular line in the fourth stage *c.* 3 feet above the inter-roof opening. The belfry window openings and the western parapet are fourteenth century.

In the western wall are three openings (1). The main western opening on the ground floor has a pointed fourteenth-century arch built within a larger blocked Saxon opening. The Saxon arch head is of voussoirs with a square-sectioned semicircular hood mould, above the crown of which is a much worn beast's head projecting *c.* 18 ins. This animal head (2) is one of many in the church. They may be divided into three groups: the early ones on the exterior, the magnificently finished creatures (3) in the interior of the tower,[1] and the less fine ones acting as label stops in the choir east wall (4).[2] Such animal head ornamentation is considered by

[1] See below, p. 188.   [2] See above, p. 176.

(1) *Plate 70*; (2) *Plate 79*; (3) *Plate 80*; (4) *Plate 77*.

Baldwin Brown and Clapham to be of Scandinavian origin and it does not normally appear in England until after the Danish invasions. The presence of such heads at Deerhurst, those on the exterior appearing to be original with the fabric, would seem to militate against Gilbert's very early dating of the church; they would be more consistent with the more usual tenth-century dating. This western head is an amazing piece of work. It is extremely primitive without being crude. But it has no features and is not recognizably an animal head. The mason by a few bold strokes, producing a few simple curves in a projecting stone, has made two jaws, suggestive to a re-markable degree of an animal head of great vitality, vicious, angry, biting—or preparing to bite. It looks like a first attempt by a sculptor of originality to copy, perhaps from memory, an unfamiliar model—a Scandinavian animal head. He, or a successor, later mastered the technique and the beautiful creatures now in the interior of the tower were the result.

Above, in the second stage, is a smaller square-headed window (I) with head, jambs and sill of one stone each, probably a later though Saxon insertion.

In the third stage, nearly 30 feet above ground level, is a large round-headed door-like opening (I) with arched lintel of two stones apparently renewed, 2 ft. 3 ins. wide and 6 feet high to the crown of the lintel. It has a flat lintel at the rear, its east face. The arched lintel in front is cut square on top and above is a square hood mould terminating in small beasts' heads. The jambs, of two pillar stones each, are inclined upwards and rebated. The sill is of one stone. This doorway must have led some-where, possibly to the upper part of some western annexe; Micklethwaite suggested a chamber over a baptistry. It is too high up to be reached by a ladder from the ground and so could not serve as an access to the tower as a refuge in times of trouble.[1] Above this doorway is a large grotesque animal head similar to the one below.

There is no opening in the tall fourth stage on the west, north or south.

In the north and south walls in the second stage of the tower are two small square-headed windows, one in each wall. They have slight single internal splay and are 3 ft. 6 ins. high by 2 feet wide. In the third stage is a small rectangular, almost square, window centrally placed in each wall. The stone jambs are inclined upwards, rebated and splayed. Each window is *c.* 3 feet high and *c.* 2 feet wide; one is slightly wider than the other. On the interior walls[2] close to each window, is a small aumbry-like recess each sharing a jamb with the window. They are 1 ft. 7 ins. high by 1 ft. 11 ins. wide and have arched lintels. They are not unlike the recesses in the corresponding walls of the ground floor of Barnack tower.[3] It may be that this stage was once used as a chapel.

[1] Cf. St. Michael's, Oxford, below, p. 234.   [2] See Knowles, fig. 9.   [3] See below, p. 195.

Gloucestershire

In the east wall, i.e. the west wall of the nave, above the tower arch and in the second stage of the tower is a small round-headed doorway (1). It is *c.* 16 feet above the nave floor and is placed to the north of central. It has an arched lintel on the east and a flat one on the west; its jambs of two stones each are inclined. It is 2 ft. 1 in. wide at the base, tapering to 1 ft. 9 ins. above, and 5 feet high to the crown of the arched lintel. This was probably an entrance to a gallery at the west end of the nave, possibly of wood, resting on stone brackets, remains of which are visible at the north and south ends of the wall about 13 feet up and a little below the opening. Originally these brackets, or short lengths of string course, may have been continued along the north and south walls to support the gallery; these parts may have been removed or hidden when the nave arcades were cut. These brackets are similar though not identical in design, at a height of about 22 feet, to those at the east end of the nave which also must have supported something.[1] Gilbert suggested that these western brackets may have been moved, for their new purpose, from an original position higher up, at the same level as the eastern ones. Near this opening and a little to the south of it, and very slightly south of central, is a small three-sided, i.e. triangular, opening (1) plastered on its inner sides, 16 inches wide at the base and 22 inches high to its apex. This was probably a window or squint.

In the third stage is the well-known massive, gable-headed double-opening (2), its sill *c.* 28 feet above floor level.[2] It has a broad sill supporting a short almost square-sectioned central pier irregularly and rather roughly fluted and reeded. There are five and seven flutes on the two wider, north and south sides and six on the east and west. The flutes are reeded rather irregularly, some reeds being in the upper and some in the lower flutings. The jambs are narrow and treated similarly but with only three flutings on their east faces, one on their returns and none on their western faces. The base of the central pier is rectangular, 1 ft. 9 ins. wide (north–south) with upper hollow chamfer reducing the width to 1 ft. 4 ins., the width of the central pier. The imposts of the pier and jambs are rectangular and square-cut, and with what Knowles described as a 'series of small oversailing fillets', in other words cut below with the common Saxon step pattern, five steps to each. The apertures are 13 inches wide between the bases and 18 inches between central pier and jambs. The bases are $13\frac{1}{2}$ inches high, the stepped imposts $8\frac{3}{4}$ inches and the pier shaft 20 inches high. The total height from sill to the top of the impost is *c.* 3 ft. 6 ins. and to the inner apex of the gable 5 feet. The gable heads are of two through-stones 3 ft. 6 ins. long on their outer edges, each enclosed within a gable-shaped square-edged projecting hood mould. A massive sill originally underlay the whole but the south opening was at some time cut down to the floor level of the stage, presumably to afford access to the

---

[1] See above, p. 175. [2] See also drawings in Knowles, fig. 9.

(1) *Plate* 71; (2) *Plates* 72, 73.

gallery below by means of a ladder. Gilbert thinks this stage is of later date than the two below and was built definitely as a chapel. The cutting down was obviously subsequent to the making of the opening and might suggest that the gallery was later than the opening. This however would leave the doorway in the second stage unexplained, unless it was originally an ingress to the stage from the nave. The cutting down of the opening may however have been merely an afterthought—a convenience to a church official who may have lived in the chapel. Many corresponding stages in Anglo-Saxon towers were inhabited.

Strictly speaking the central pier is not a mid-wall shaft comparable with those occurring in the more usual Saxon belfry double openings: the base is a throughstone equal in depth to the thickness of the wall; that is, the base faces are flush with the east and west wall faces; the pier has a depth 10 inches less than the wall thickness, so its faces are 5 inches from either wall face: it is symmetrically placed between the wall faces. One has only to imagine the pier replaced by a slender shaft, not a big change, and, decoration apart, the normal Saxon double opening would appear. In spite of its elaboration it may well be of early date and a precursor of the normal double opening. Baldwin Brown considered it to be vaguely early, between the early ninth and mid-tenth centuries. He also referred to 'somewhat close parallels' in Carolingian art and mentioned specifically some resemblances between this opening and features in Charlemagne's palace at Aachen and in the much discussed Thorhalle at Lorsch, near Worms, both of the late eighth or very early ninth century. These comparisons appear to be fruitless. A casual glance at pictures of the Deerhurst opening and the Thorhalle reveals the general similarity of gable heads and flutings. On a closer examination the similarities fade and the striking differences emerge. At Lorsch the pilasters are fluted but not reeded and they have debased Ionic capitals, not stepped imposts. The bases are thin and convexly moulded, not tall and hollow chamfered. At Lorsch too the gable faces are grooved, too finely to be called fluted, and have no projecting hoods. There is a classical, Roman, air about Lorsch which is absent, or at least only very superficially evident, at Deerhurst. The Deerhurst opening has been called unique, and so it may be. But its uniqueness consists in the unique association of a larger number of Saxon characteristics than is normally found together in a single monument: the plain gable heads with projecting hood moulds, the stepped patterns, the hollow chamfers, the imposts instead of capitals, the double opening, the through-stones, the square-edged features, the mid-wall pier, the imposts and bases flush with the wall faces—all Saxon motifs. Its sheer massiveness is Saxon, reminiscent as it is of the massive megalithic quoins of the Early Saxon period. The only foreign motif, which alone gives the opening its somewhat spurious classical air, is the reeded fluting. And there is no need to go to Rome, or to Lorsch or to the Rhineland for this. It was a common Romano-British ornament which must have been familiar to the Saxon masons of the area. It is to be seen on a

Romano-British grave slab in Gloucester Museum, and on two stones lying against the tower at Market Overton (Rutland) (1). One may safely echo Butterworth's words of more than seventy years ago: 'Our English window is Saxon.'

Immediately above the double opening is a rectangular slab (2), a through-stone *c.* 3 feet by 2 ft. 6 ins. built into the wall. It is plain and shows no sign of paint. Its object is unknown; but Gilbert suggested that it may have had carving on one face, perhaps the west, similar to the group in the tower west wall at Monkwearmouth, and later defaced. This suggestion seems reasonable in view of the defaced carving in the stage below, on the west face of the mid-wall.

Higher up, in the fourth stage and partly above the existing modern nave ceiling, is a massively built opening, *c.* 5 ft. 6 ins. high and 2 ft. 7 ins. wide; the sill, *c.* 40 feet above the nave floor, is of a single massive stone, invisible beneath the plaster, which almost rests on the built-in slab. Its jambs are massive, one stone being about $2\frac{1}{2}$ feet long by $2\frac{1}{2}$ feet deep (into the wall) by 6 or 7 inches wide. It has an arched lintel on its western, tower side and a flat lintel on the nave side. It, like openings in similar positions elsewhere, almost certainly led to a space or chamber between original nave roof and ceiling. Similar openings were common lower down serving sometimes as ingresses to the second stages of towers from the nave, or perhaps more usually as at Deerhurst opening to a western gallery from the tower. Bosham (Sussex) (3) is another well-known church with both types of opening. Deerhurst is unusual in having three such openings, due to the great height of the nave, the third being the elaborate double opening in the third or middle stage of the tower.

The fifth stage is the belfry. The windows in all four faces are two-light fourteenth-century openings on the exterior. They were inserted into earlier plain round-headed openings, *c.* 3 ft. 2 ins. wide, which have rather crude jambs of two slabs each and thin sills turned up at the ends in Norman manner. On the interior the openings are chamfered all round.

The tower is capped on the western portion by a low probably fourteenth-century parapet between two string courses with very low plain upward projections, of similar design to the parapet, at the corners. These are the remains of squinches belonging to a probably mediaeval spire, very likely of timber, which fell in 1660. The eastern portion is barrel-roofed, and gabled east–west on the exterior.

The bottom two stages of the tower are, or were, divided internally by a mid-wall into two unequal sections (Figs. 13 and 14), the eastern one in each stage being approximately 8 ft. 9 ins. square and the western one 8 ft. 9 ins. by 5 ft. 3 ins. As there is no straight joint in the mid-wall positions in the north and south tower wall it seems likely that the tower's pronounced oblong shape—east–west—is original, but not the mid-wall. In the second stage the mid-wall covers the splayed western

---

(1) *Plate* 120; (2) *Plates* 72, 73; (3) *Plate* 213.

jambs of the two north and south windows; moreover it has no herring-boning, unlike the exterior walls of these two stages. The wall was a later insertion in the Saxon period. The small square window in the west wall (1), referred to above,[1] was inserted to light the western portion of the stage. A rectangular doorway, with lintel and sill of single stones and jambs of walling, was cut in the mid-wall to allow access to the eastern chamber from the west. Access to the west was probably by ladder from below. The reason for this mid-wall is not known, though the exceptionally great oblong shape of the tower would seem to suggest that the builders may have had some kind of division in mind. If this were so the mid-wall may not be very much later than the main fabric. The third and upper stages were not divided in this way.

In the ground stage the north and south walls of the eastern portion were pierced with arches, Butterworth thought in the twelfth century, to lead to a western aisle or porticus.[2] Later these portions of the wall were removed to provide unimpeded aisles (Fig. 14, Y and Z), from the tower to the north and south aisles which were extended westwards so that the west walls of the aisles are now flush with the west wall of the tower. At some time the mid-wall was pierced with a round-headed opening (M in Fig. 14) similar to the western (L) and eastern (N) (tower arch) openings. There are in consequence three monumental western portals, of different heights.

The western opening (1) has been discussed above.[3]

The eastern opening (2), in the normal position of a tower arch to nave, has a round head of square-cut voussoirs not all of which are through-stones. There is a square-cut strip-work hood mould largely hidden by the plaster. The 9 inch projecting imposts are square-cut above, with a quirk and hollow chamfer below and are returned c. 13 inches along each wall face. The jambs, i.e. the wall, are 2 ft. 9 ins. thick. The opening is 5 ft. 6 ins. wide between jambs and 7 feet to the top of the imposts and c. 10 feet to the crown of the arch.

The mid-wall opening is a modern reconstruction of 1861. It has beautiful beast head (3) terminations[3] to the boldly projecting square-cut strip-work hood. These ornaments are not in their original position. Butterworth, the vicar who authorized the rebuilding, had them transferred from elsewhere but does not say from where. This arch is about two feet lower than the eastern one and rather higher than the blocked western one appears to have been.

The ground stage was originally c. 16 feet high; the floor between this stage and the one above was removed at some time. Above the mid-wall arch, in the wall

---

[1] p. 184.   [2] See above, p. 187.   [3] See above, p. 183.

itself on its western face, is a tall narrow panel, 3 ft. 7 ins. high and 1 ft. 4 ins. wide, which was once ornamented with a nimbed figure, probably a Virgin and Child (1) but now cut back almost flat with the panel. Some geometrical ornament below the figure's feet is of typical Saxon step pattern. The panel is probably in its original position.

The original mid-wall did not extend above the second stage. The third stage is also divided into two but by a wall of later, post-Saxon, date.

---

(1) *Plate* 82.

NORTHAMPTONSHIRE

BARNACK

St. John the Baptist Church. *The Tower: Exterior.* The tower only is Saxon, except the belfry stage which is Norman and the spire which is thirteenth century. Syers thought Wilfrid was the builder of the present tower, partly because Irvine[1] considered the sundial to be original with the tower, and, as A. R. Green later pointed out, the foliage on the sundial is closely similar to that on the sundial at Warnford Church, in the Meon Valley, Hants; the original church at Warnford on this site is attributed to Wilfrid *c.* 681 and Romilly Allen[2] considered that the sundial at least was a relic of Wilfrid's church built into the later twelfth-century church. An elaborate structure of the late style of Barnack could not however have been built at so early a date as the seventh century and Irvine[3] disposed effectively of this tradition. Irvine dated the tower with that of Earls Barton and attributed both to Earl Waltheof, the husband of Judith, the Conqueror's niece, at *c.* 1070–5. Baldwin Brown dates the tower to A.D. 950–1000; another writer[4] suggests 1000–50, probably in the time of Canute when building activities could be resumed after the second series of Danish invasions.

Barnack tower (1) is aesthetically the most attractive of the decorated Saxon towers. In its details it is better finished and, one might say, better thought out than Earls Barton. This may perhaps be due to the peculiar, unusual, possibly unique and not now really understood use to which the tower was put. Moreover the later belfry and even later spire, with the shapely corner pinnacles, seem to fit into the picture, producing altogether a most attractive ensemble.

It is built in uncoursed rubble of Barnack stone from the local quarries as were many other buildings of the area including Peterborough Cathedral.[5] The tower is 26 feet 6 ins. wide, from north to south and 21 feet deep from west to east as far as the nave wall. Interior measurements are *c.* 19 feet by *c.* 14 feet. It is 65 feet high to the top of the upper string course. The walls are 3 feet 8 ins. thick at ground level on the north, west and south sides, and 3 ft. 1 in. on the east side; they are about one foot less at the second stage. It is of two stages of diminishing height and slightly

---

[1] Quoted by H. S. Syers.   [2] Quoted by A. R. Green.   [3] Op. cit., (*f*).
[4] V.C.H., *Northants*, II.   [5] For the history of these quarries see V.C.H., *Northants*, II.

---

(1) *Plate* 83.

diminishing width. String courses, wide enough (*c.* 2 feet) and of sufficiently complex design to be regarded as cornices, separate the two stages, and the upper stage from the Norman belfry. As a string course is an unusual finish to a top stage of a tower, the Norman belfry presumably replaced a Saxon finish of some kind. The profile of the string course is unusual (Fig. 12*b*). It consists of three superimposed layers of stones, the middle one being the thickest (14 inches). The lowest stone projects slightly from the wall face below; the top projects rather more from the wall face above, being on a level with the wall face below and therefore behind the lowest stone. This is a reversal, possibly unintentional, of the classical cornice design in which the top stone is the one which protrudes most. The face of the middle stone is recessed behind the faces of the other two and lies between the faces of the upper and lower walls. The faces of the top and bottom stones are slightly bevelled upwards. This cornice design is an example of the popular Saxon step pattern; it should be compared with that at Repton (Derby).

Between and below the string courses are vertical pilaster strips as at Earls Barton, but without the semi-circular and triangular headings, three on each face dividing each face into four panels. The strips are 10 to 11 inches wide below, tapering to 5 inches above and have a projection of 6 inches. The strips on the lower stage start from square corbel stones resting on the plinth; one indeed rests on a corbel stone just above the keystone of the arch head of the south doorway (as no buttress would). The strips of the upper stage start from corbel stones with semi-circular ends. E. G. M. Fletcher and E. D. C. Jackson point out that the lowest rubble courses on the west tower face from the south-west corner as far as the first pilaster strip (but no further) slope downwards towards the south, showing that at some time soil subsidence occurred. The quoins were repaired but not apparently the damaged courses. The fact that the sloping stopped at the first pilaster strip suggests that the strips are deep seated (i.e. are probably slabs with one dimension bonded deeply into the walls) and were strong enough to prevent the wall damage from spreading. If this is so, it follows that pilaster strips were not purely decorative but might in some circumstances exert a strengthening effect on thin Saxon walls. Fletcher and Jackson have indeed made out a strong case for the strengthening effect of pilaster strip-work generally though it may sometimes be merely decorative. They maintain that the pilasters in the lower half of Barnack, as at Sompting, are structural while those in the upper halves of these two churches are decorative.[1] There is upright and flat work at the quoins, of less projection than the pilaster strips, the flats being cut back to the wall face in the upper stage only; it is very regular in the upper storey but curiously irregular in the lower.

Foundations were discovered of a western adjunct and the irregular lower quoins **might** be due to repairs after removal of the adjunct, but nothing is known of the

---

[1] See also below, under Earls Barton and Sompting.

date of the foundation. Moreover, some of the lower quoin stones have been cut back suggesting a later building put up against the tower; the foundations might belong to this.

There is no west door, the original main entrance being a door in the south wall of the tower—an unusual position for a Saxon main western entrance (1). The door jambs are not rebated in the way usual with doorways of the earlier period: the door shut flat across the inside, a common Saxon method in the later period. The doorway has jambs of the Escomb type, a round head of rather long voussoirs and plain slab imposts. There are vertical strips on both sides of the doorway resting, like all the others, on square corbels near the ground; strips also go round the head but these rest on their own independent square corbels projecting just above the imposts.

Above the south doorway and to the east of it is a round-headed window (1) with square hood mould the ends of which rest on the imposts. In each spandrel is a sculptured bird. Above this, *c.* 25 feet from the ground, is a circular Saxon sundial (2), the only one in Northants. The lower half is so worn that the hour lines are not visible though the small central style hole is plainly to be seen. The upper half has foliage decoration: two side stems with three leaves attached to each, and a central vertical stiff stylized leaf. The background is cut away leaving the foliage and border in strong relief.[1] In the south-east corner of the same south wall just below the string course is a small round headed built up window.

A little above the level of the south window (with hood mould) but on the west face of the tower is a triangular-headed window (3) with single inner splay, rather crudely built; it has pillar jambs of through-stones with rectangular block imposts. Just above this is a projecting, but very much worn, animal head resting on a wide flat stone corbel; this head acts as a corbel to the pilaster strip above. Such animal heads are not uncommon on late Saxon monuments.[2] They are probably of Viking origin as they are common in early wooden Norwegian architecture and do not appear in England before the early tenth century. They are also interesting as the later well-known Anglo-Norman beak head ornament, a definitely English contribution to late Norman ornament, was according to some writers[3] developed out of these animal heads.

In the north wall is a roughly constructed round-headed window with jambs of a single stone each, square block imposts and a very wide single stone flat sill. The head appears cut from a single stone with a decorative groove round the front.

The upper stage of the tower was divided originally horizontally into two (or

[1] This sundial is sometimes described as a circle containing foliage. This error probably originated with J. Britton (op. cit., p. 195) who gives an engraving of the circle with foliage in both halves.

[2] See also above, under Deerhurst, p. 183.

[3] G. Zarnecki, op. cit., (*b*).

---

(1) *Plate* 85; (2) *Plates* 84, 85; (3) *Plate* 83.

possibly three) stages, the floors of which have disappeared. Like many other Saxon towers the upper storeys were probably inhabited, possibly by church officials. The lower of these two floors was lighted by five round-headed windows (1), two on each of the south and north sides and a smaller one on the west. The east one on the south face is a modern (1936) replacement; the others have single stone jambs, heads made from two stones and hollow chamfers all round; heads, jambs and sills are splayed. The stone frames are rebated to take wooden shutters. On the west wall in lieu of the second round-headed window is a large triangular-headed doorway (1), in the second panel from the south quoin. This has no jamb, being cut as it were on the outside straight through the walling. The triangular head is of two large flat stones, one for each sloping side. This outer gable is of very slight depth into the wall and is separate from the inner soffit which is made of large but not through-stones. It has slight internal splay.

The floor above (no longer a separate floor) was lighted by four triangular-headed windows (1), one on each of the four faces, high up and just below the upper string course. They are roughly built on the outside, with no jambs, only walling, and heads of two slabs each. Those on the west and east are closed with stone light slabs in each of which are four rectangular openings to admit light. The stone closures of the north and south windows are more elaborately carved. They are of identical pattern and contain flat interlacings like continuous figures of eight with circles or flat rings cutting the middle intersecting parts of the '8's' (2). Baldwin Brown writes that though the *pattern* is of Norse origin and came to the north of England after the great Danish invasions of the late ninth century, the *idea* of such carved light slabs was more probably of Italian origin as they were well known decorative features in that area, where they are called *transennae*. T. G. Jackson points out the close resemblance of the Barnack pattern (except that the Italian had the usual Italian three-strand interlacement) to one he saw and sketched at S. Lorenzo in Pasenatico in Istria. So we may have Byzantine or at least Italo-Byzantine influence here. H. M. Taylor considers these windows to be the original Saxon belfry windows and that the Saxon tower did not extend above the upper string course which now separates the Early English belfry from the Saxon work below.

On the east wall the pilaster strips extend down to just below the sill of the tri-angular-headed window where they rest on slab corbels; below these are the marks on the wall face of the original gabled roof of the Saxon nave. Below these marks is a square-headed doorway, the south jamb of which is just below the north jamb of the triangular-headed window. This doorway has long and short work in the jambs. It is about 35 feet above the present nave floor, is above the present nave flat roof and some 12 feet below the marks on the tower east wall of the former gabled nave

---

(1) *Plate* 83; (2) *Plate* 84.

roof. As at Earls Barton, Deerhurst, Bosham and many other churches, it may have given access to a chamber or space between an exterior and interior roof of the early nave.

There are three elaborately carved slabs in the centres of the north, west and south tower faces just above the lower string courses (1). They are carved in high relief with vine scrolls; each one has a central stem with foliage scrolls on each side containing bunches of grapes, and with the scrolls terminating in four-lobed leaves of Carolingian acanthus. Each slab has a plain stone border which in two of the slabs seems complete at top and bottom. In two of the slabs the side scrolls appear as though they are attached to the border by stone hooks; i.e., they look like stone copies of a metal grill. All three have birds above, two carved on separate stones. The bird on the north slab is bending down to peck at the leaves; that on the west one, rather resembling an eagle, has outstretched wings; the third, on the south slab, resembling a cock, appears to be part of the slab itself and is closely similar to the birds in the spandrels of the window below. This window is original with the tower and this suggests the possibility that the slabs are also part of the tower as built. Apart from this Baldwin Brown makes out a strong case for contemporaneity of slabs and tower. He may be correct in this; indeed there is no valid reason for rejecting his view which was based on close visual examination of the south slab during repairs to the roof. On the other hand the carving itself may be earlier than the tower. Foliage scrolls of this type were not a common form of ornament in the tenth century in England, and it is quite arguable that the birds in the window spandrels were copied from the one in the carved slab above it. D. Talbot Rice suggests that the slabs may be broken cross shafts of earlier date, e.g. broken in the Danish invasions, incorporated as decoration in the tower when built. He adds: 'It has usually been dated to the tenth century (i.e. contemporaneously with the tower), but might be earlier, and if a cross and not a slab, it almost certainly would be.' Against this however is the acanthus ornament; this did not appear in Saxon sculpture till well into the tenth century.

The Interior. About A.D. 1220 a stone vice or stone circular staircase was built in the south-west angle of the tower as communication with the upper storeys. At the same time the ground storey was vaulted and the octagonal belfry stage added. The other three corners of the tower were strengthened by angle piers fitting into each corner.

The interior of the tower is extremely interesting and in fact unique in more than one respect. There is a magnificent tower arch (2) opening into the nave. It is 20 feet high, 15 feet to the top of the imposts, and of the exceptional width of 13 feet. It is 3 feet deep. The jambs are not of the Escomb type, but made of numerous long

---

(1) *Plates* 83, 84; (2) *Plate* 86.

and short through-stones. The arch head is turned with genuine voussoirs which are also through-stones. There are flanking vertical pilaster strips on each side, made of real long and short work, supported by plain rectangular corbels resting on the tower plinth. The strips end without capitals or enlargement at the under faces of the imposts. Above, strip-work, consisting of square-sectioned stones similar in width to the voussoirs, is continued round the arch head. The effect is good, making the arch look like a recessed Norman arch of two orders. The imposts are most unusual and probably the most striking and complicated example of the popular Saxon step pattern. Each looks at first sight like a dozen flat stone slabs imitating Roman bricks and arranged stepwise. It is in fact composed of *three* stones only, the profiles being carved to produce the particular effect. Slabs arranged stepwise are common enough decoration in Saxon buildings; here is one of the very rare cases, possibly unique, where the step pattern is produced by carving. Moreover, the apparent slabs are not square-sectioned or chamfered but are carved to comprise a profile of complicated curves.

In the centre of the interior west wall of the tower, below the triangular-headed window, is a triangular-headed recess obviously intended as a seat. It is 3 ft. 6 ins. wide, 1 ft. 4 ins. deep and the seat is 1 ft. 8 ins. above the present floor. The jambs are of the Escomb type with rectangular-sectioned imposts. Head and jambs are of narrow stone slabs 4 inches thick. During restoration work in 1854–5 traces of wooden seats sufficient for 40 people were discovered on either side of the central stone seat. These seats had no canopies and consisted of rude stone risers with oak slabs for seats. During this restoration work much debris was found in the tower from a fire supposed to be that from the burning of the church by the Danes under Sweyn in 1013. Beneath the debris was a Saxon hard plaster floor. On the north and south walls, near the tower arch and 4 feet above the floor, are recesses resembling aumbries. Baldwin Brown puts forward his considered opinion that the tower was not only used but was designed for judicial purposes, the central seat being the judge's seat. In support of it he points out that parts of other churches were often so used even when, as in the porch tower of Canterbury Cathedral, there were altars. This explanation of what is admittedly a puzzling problem is far from convincing. Village churches in early times, especially of the non-monastic type, were used for many purposes other than religious ones. They were the social centres of the villages: fairs, markets, social gatherings, even dances were held in them, i.e. in the naves. Certainly judicial business was often transacted somewhere in them and it was quite unnecessary for them to be designed specially for such a special purpose. It seems in the highest degree unlikely that any such idea should be in the minds of the builders of Barnack tower.

Clapham, wisely perhaps, is silent on the problem. Talbot Rice makes the more likely suggestion that the aumbry-like recesses were really aumbries, that there was an altar in front of the central seat, and that the tower was in effect a western apse though square instead of round. Western apses, in addition to eastern ones, were characteristic of Carolingian churches but though there are references in contemporary literature to double-apsed churches in Saxon England, they were even less popular than the more usual single eastern apse. In some cases the English preference for a fine west portal made them replace the western apse by a gallery with altar raised on the west wall of the nave (as at Deerhurst, Glos and Tredington, Worcs), or go without a western apse altogether, or as at Barnack, as Talbot Rice suggests, to have the altar in the tower ground floor with a south instead of a west portal.

The tower is bonded into the west wall of the nave which extends a little north and south beyond the tower quoins. There are no signs of upright and flat work on the lower part of the east wall of the tower but they are visible a little to the north and south of the tower on the western wall of the nave. The indications are therefore that Barnack was never a turriform church.

The Nave. As indicated by the marks on the east wall of the tower and the upright and flat work on the west wall of the nave, the original Saxon nave was 32 feet high and 33 feet wide, i.e. about $6\frac{1}{2}$ feet wider than the tower. A Norman arcade was cut through the north wall *c.* 1180 when the north aisle was built, and the south arcade was made *c.* 1200. The wall above the north arcade is stated to be only 2 ft. 2 ins. thick. It may therefore be the original Saxon wall or, much less likely, a later rebuilding to the same thickness. That it may be original is suggested by the presence in the east end of the wall, just beyond the north-east arch, of the remains of what appears to be a Saxon arch, plainly visible from the north aisle. It is roughly made of blocks of stones, not voussoirs, the east springer being a slab just tilted on edge and supported below by a large block about two feet long standing on end. This also suggests that the Saxon nave was of similar length to the existing one, i.e. 60 ft. 6 ins.

Nothing is known of the Saxon chancel.

BRIGSTOCK

ST. ANDREW'S CHURCH. R. H. Carpenter in a detailed account of the church and its history thought the existing Saxon portion to be a rebuilding in post-Danish times, using much old material, of an earlier church burnt by the Danes. He based this conclusion on the presence in the tower walls of stones stained red by fire. In addition, the interior walls in each angle of the tower are also discoloured by fire, the very old door to the stair turret is charred on its face, and at the west end of the nave near the tower under the paving a thick deposit of charcoal ashes was found during repair work in the 1870's. There is no sign of fire in the Norman part of the church and Carpenter inferred that there was a second fire damaging the fabric of the second church, and that the Normans restored it either before or during their own reconstruction, when they built the north aisle. Carpenter suggests that the first church may have been built before 825 when the power of Mercia finally fell before Egbert of Wessex at the Battle of Ellandun. A likely date would be in the reign of Offa, 757–96, whose supremacy over England resulted in a development of Mercian art and architecture. It is also possible that the first church may have been due to Wilfrid who lived in Mercia for eleven years, 691–702, and founded some monasteries there including, it is thought, one at nearby Oundle; this however is little more than conjecture. The second church, according to Carpenter, may have been built in the period of Alfred's church-building activities. This however seems unlikely as Brigstock, being east of Watling Street, was in the Danelaw. On the whole Baldwin Brown's suggested date for the second church, 950–1000 seems the most likely. Parts of the earlier church may have been incorporated in it, for the present church has some early features.

The Saxon parts of the existing church are the tower (I), up to the belfry stage (which is thirteenth century, rebuilt in the fourteenth when the spire was added), the stair turret, the greater part of the west quoins, west wall and west ends of the north and south nave walls, and part of the south-east angle of the old chancel (now the south-west corner of the present chancel) incorporated in the south pier of the present chancel arch. The height of the Saxon roof eaves is indicated on the outside south-west angle of the nave, above the aisle roof and just above the level of the springing lines of the fourteenth-century clerestory windows, by the smaller angle quoins and smaller rubble of the walling.[1] The nave was lofty, like most Saxon naves, but is now three or four feet higher.

Carpenter states that very probably the Saxon church consisted of a western tower and stair turret, a nave, a narrower rectangular presbytery or sanctuary, and an eastern apse (similar in fact to Brixworth but with no aisles). He considers the Saxon corner now incorporated with the south pier of the present chancel arch, with a strip of foundation running four feet north, as indicating the south end of the arch leading into the apse.[2]

The nave was 40 ft. 4 ins. long by 15 feet wide inside; the presbytery *c.* 22 feet by *c.* 13 feet. The walls are 2 ft. 10 ins. thick. The walls are built rather roughly of fairly large rubble, with wide irregular mortar joints. The turret stonework is also of local rubble except for four courses about five feet above the ground which are of large roughly squared stones from Little Oakley. The mortar on the interior was as hard as the stone itself, very different from the soft[3] Norman mortar used in the north arch of the tower.

[1] See Carpenter, op. cit., drawing facing p. 237.   [2] See Carpenter, op. cit., Plan I.
[3] Almost like dried mud (Carpenter's words). Norman mortar was often very poor. It was the poor mortar, even more than the frequently shoddy wall and pier fillings, which caused so many Norman towers to collapse.

(I) *Plate* 87.

The tower is narrower than the nave. The quoins (1) are of big upright and flat stonework, roughly dressed, with projecting stones at the base of each quoin. The north-west and south-west nave quoins, almost megalithic in size and of upright and flat type, are plainly visible *inside* the church (2). (The north aisle was extended westwards by the Normans and the south aisle in the late twelfth or early thirteenth century to enclose the lower north and south sides of the tower.) The tower walls are 2 ft. 6 ins. thick.

The tower arch (3), leading to the nave, is sturdily built and of typical Saxon form. The opening is 7 ft. 6 ins. wide and 11 ft. 6 ins. high to the springing of the arch. It is round headed with voussoirs. The jambs (4) are of the Escomb type with three upright slabs, each over 3 feet high, and two flats separating them in each jamb. There are plain square-sectioned impost blocks, 7 to 8 inches thick, protruding 4 inches beyond the east face of the wall and the jamb face, but flush with the wall on the west face. On the east face only are vertical pilaster strips of square section on both sides of the arch resting on square corbels at the base which themselves rest on the tower plinth (a Saxon peculiarity). These strips share the main imposts above which they pass round the arch head.

There is another tower arch leading into the north aisle, but not one on the south. This north arch (4) is 4 ft. 8 ins. wide and 5 ft. 8 ins. high to the springing. The jambs on the south face *look* Saxon: the lower part of the east jamb is of one large flat stone 3 ft. 6 ins. high by 2 ft. 4 ins. wide and 9 inches thick. In spite of its appearance this arch is Norman and was cut when the north aisle was built and extended westward to enclose the lower part of the tower. The north face was made of carefully worked masonry fitted to the older work by very small stones and pebbles and very poor soft mortar. It has obviously been reconstructed in modern times.

In the interior west wall of the tower is a triangular-headed doorway (5) leading into the stair turret. It still has a door of great age which Carpenter thought was Saxon. The gable head is of two massive slabs and the jambs are of megalithic upright and flat type, the stones being $1\frac{1}{2}$ to $2\frac{1}{2}$ feet long by 6 to 12 inches thick; all are through-stones over 2 feet deep. There are no imposts. The base is a flat sill *between* the jambs; this is now the lower of two steps leading to the turret.

Higher up in the south wall of the tower and now within the church is a crudely built round-headed single-splayed window (2). On the south or narrow side each jamb is composed of two rectangular slabs on end slightly inclined from the vertical so that the opening is narrower at the top than at the bottom. The head is of massive voussoirs, with keystone, so large that the outer edge of the head extends beyond the outer sides of the jambs. The sill is of one slab, only a few inches wider than the window opening and much narrower than the distance between the exterior edges

---

(1) *Plate* 88; (2) *Plate* 91; (3) *Plate* 89; (4) *Plate* 90; (5) *Plate* 92.

of the jambs. On the north wide face of this window the head is composed of eight through stones of irregular shape; the sill, which does not appear to be splayed, is of four thin flat slabs superimposed. There is a similar window in the north wall (1). In both there are rebates all round, 3 inches wide and 3 inches deep, to hold the wooden frames for window shutters. Higher up still, in the north wall of the second stage of the tower, is a roughly built round-headed window with jambs and arch head of rough rubble. There was formerly a similar one in the south wall, below the present clock, now roughly blocked with stones. These also were recessed for shutters.

The Saxon tower is of two floors but this is not indicated on the exterior by set-offs or string courses, the tower being of the plain Lincolnshire type. The string course visible just above the level of the top of the stair turret marks the top of the Saxon tower separating it from the thirteenth-century third stage.

The $\frac{3}{4}$-round stair turret contained a circular wooden stairway long since destroyed and replaced with ladders to provide access to the upper stage of the tower. Though Saxon it looks later than the tower. It has two rectangular windows in its west face, both double-splayed. The lower window has jambs of single stones; in the upper one each jamb is of two stones; the flat heads are cut from single stones.

On the east wall of the tower is a blocked opening which probably led originally to a space or chamber between an inner and outer nave roof as at Barnack, Deerhurst and elsewhere. The head was a solid oak lintel so much decayed by the 1870's that the stability of the wall above was endangered. It has been replaced by stone. It is not known whether the old lintel was the original one.

BRIXWORTH

ALL SAINTS' CHURCH.[1] Baldwin Brown writes of this church: 'Brixworth is beyond all comparison the most remarkable extant monument of the period,' and A. W. Clapham[2] refers to it as 'perhaps the most imposing architectural memorial of the seventh century yet surviving north of the Alps'. It was not recognized as a Saxon monument until well into the nineteenth century. T. Rickman[3] who first

[1] J. Romilly Allen; G. Hadrian Allcroft; John Britton; G. Baldwin Brown; A. W. Clapham, (a) and (b); Sir Henry Dryden, (a) and (b); A. Hartshorne; W. T. Mellows; A. K. Pavey; G. A. Poole, (a); C. A. R. Radford, (a) and (c); T. Rickman, (a) and (b); E. Roberts; A. Hamilton Thompson, (a) and (d); V.C.H., *Northants*, II and IV; C. F. Watkins.

[2] Op. cit., (a).

[3] Op. cit., (a); this appears to be the first published discussion of the church.

(1) *Plate* 90.

saw it in 1823 thought it Norman but later changed his mind and included it among the Saxon churches he listed in the later editions of his famous book[1] between 1835 and 1848. Confusion at that time was perhaps understandable: the church contained samples of all the mediaeval architectural styles.[2] In particular the chancel was much larger than its original and present size due to alterations and extensions in the Gothic periods; no trace of an apse was visible.

Excavations were begun by C. F. Watkins (vicar from 1832 to 1873) in 1841 and he later, 1863–6, carried out extensive restorations, restoring the church so far as was practicable to its original form. G. A. Poole wrote about the church in 1850 and E. Roberts in 1863, but the first really authoritative publication was Watkins's book of 1867.

The origin of the church remains in some doubt. An early view held by Watkins that the church was originally the secular basilica of a Roman settlement afterwards converted to Christian usage is accepted by no modern writer. F. Haverfield[3] denies it on the ground that the 'evidence seems adequate to prove the existence of some dwelling', but not a settlement on the spot. A. Hamilton Thompson[4] regards the view as ill-founded and adds, 'The Roman bricks have been re-used in obvious ignorance of Roman methods.' Baldwin Brown brings convincing technical evidence to refute the view.

A twelfth-century writer, Hugo Candidus (Hugh White),[5] a monk of Peterborough, asserted that Saxulf, who was Bishop of Mercia, 675–91, and had been the first Abbot of the monastery at Medeshamstede (the later Peterborough) founded *c.* 655, founded a monastery at Brixworth (Bricklesworthe), and that by 690 the church at this place was attached to Saxulf's greater foundation at Medeshamstede. On the strength of this it is generally believed that the church was built before 690 and that parts of it still exist in the fabric of the present church. Baldwin Brown accepts this. Clapham more cautiously says: 'There is every reason to associate this building with the church erected by the monks at Peterborough about 670,' though the precise significance to be attached to the word 'associate' in this connection is not clear. A. H. Allcroft states that Saxulf, like all the northern bishops up to the time of Wilfrid (d. 709), was trained in the Celtic church and would have built *more Scottorum*, i.e. in wood, and that it is indeed doubtful if he could have built in any other fashion. There is substance in Allcroft's view, for all the earlier stone Kentish churches and the northern churches of Benedict Biscop and of Wilfrid were in foreign styles and built by foreign masons. At this time the Saxons were still building in wood and though, to judge from the crudeness of the arch heads, some Saxons may have been employed in the building of Brixworth church, it seems in the highest degree unlikely

[1] Op. cit., (*b*).
[2] Plates of this church as it then was are given by J. Britton, by E. Roberts and by A. Hartshorne.
[3] V.C.H., II.   [4] Op. cit., (*a*).   [5] W. T. Mellows, op. cit., p. 15.

that Saxon masons alone built this elaborate church at so early a date. Allcroft thinks it more likely that there was a *ciric*, i.e., a Christian burial ground, on the spot where Saxulf founded his little Scotic cell in dependence on his greater foundation. The *ciric*[1] may have been associated with an early Christian movement in East Mercia and it may have become neglected or even forgotten during the reign of the pagan King Penda, 632–54. In this case Saxulf was merely recovering a *locus sanctus* to Christianity.

Even though Allcroft may be right,[2] the 'little Scotic cell' (of wood, or possibly wattle and daub if built at all), did not long endure and was soon replaced by a stone church built of Roman material lying about the spot. Who built it is uncertain. Baldwin Brown makes the intriguing suggestion that Wilfrid may have been the brain behind it. He was a great builder and is stated to have built five stone churches at Hexham, Ripon and York, the vaulted crypts of two (at Hexham and Ripon) being still in existence. Also he had the opportunity for, during one of his exiles from Northumbria, he spent eleven years, 691–702, as acting bishop of Mercia, in succession to Saxulf, and as friend of King Ethelred of Mercia. He founded some monasteries there.

On the other hand it seems more likely that the church was at least inspired by Theodore of Tarsus, Archbishop of Canterbury, 668–90. In pushing his influence and authority northwards he might well have seen the desirability of a large and important monastic church in a strategically important area like Northants, near the great Roman Watling Street connecting London with the north-west, and a sort of link between Augustine's group of stone churches in Kent and the rather later stone churches of Benedict Biscop and Wilfrid in the north. Moreover, though on a grander scale than others of the group, Brixworth is architecturally a member of the Kentish group of churches.[3]

General Description. The church (Fig. 15) is, or rather was (for the aisles have been destroyed), an aisled basilica with a triple arcade (like the aisles, long since destroyed) at the east end of the nave dividing it from a square presbyterial space, beyond which was an apse prefaced by an arch considerably narrower than itself. There was a

---

[1] Allcroft maintains that in Celtic areas the burial ground always preceded the church; i.e. burial grounds were not attached to churches, but churches were attached to, i.e. built on, pre-existing burial grounds. *Ciric*, from which the word 'church' is derived, originally meant burial ground and was not applied exclusively to structural churches until the tenth century (op. cit., pp. 239, 243).

[2] Allcroft argues the case for the persistence of Saxon wooden architecture at great length and with much learning. He points out that the Anglo-Saxon Chronicle (*anno* 1020) stated that Canute built 'a minster of stone and lime' to celebrate his victory at Ashingdon in 1016, and adds that at even so late a date the building of a church in stone was sufficiently remarkable to be mentioned. He concludes: 'There can be no doubt that by far the greater number of structural churches existing in England even in the twelfth century were still built of wood only, and this explains the remarkable activity of the church architects of that and the next century: they were replacing in stone the earlier wooden churches, and rebuilding on a larger scale, some of the few mason built churches already in existence' (p. 254). The silence of writers on architectural history over Allcroft's views is curious.

[3] Its resemblance to Wilfrid's great church at Hexham must not however be overlooked.

western porch of two storeys which formed the central part of a range of out-buildings probably a narthex covering the whole length of the west front (including the aisles). This narthex may have been used by catechumens not yet admitted to full membership of the Church as the district had only recently been Christianized when the church was built. During the excavations foundations were discovered of a small building to the west and at right angles to the tower, probably a small outer porch. There was also a north porticus entered by doorways from the north-west corner of the presbytery and from the east end of the north aisle. If the usual custom

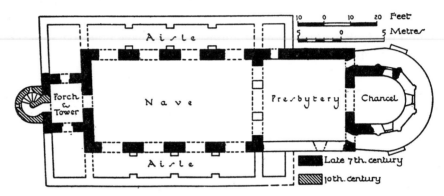

Fig. 15. Brixworth Church, plan

was followed (as it very likely was in view of the magnitude, complexity and obvious importance of the building) there would be a corresponding porticus on the south side.[1] It is however not possible to say definitely whether this was so as all traces would be hidden by the existing large thirteenth-century south-east chapel.

There was a barrel-vaulted ambulatory or covered passage round the *outside* of the apse.

This in outline is the scheme of the original church. The church was presumably partially destroyed during the late ninth-century Danish invasions. The fabric was restored later, according to Baldwin Brown probably during the monastic revival of the mid-tenth century which reached its peak in the peaceful reign of King Edgar (959–74), but certainly in Saxon times. In this restoration Baldwin Brown considers the porticus, aisles and western adjuncts (other than the porch) were removed, and the nave arches filled with windows. The two-storeyed western porch was restored and extended upwards into a tower. To provide access to the uppermost chamber or chambers of the tower the circular staircase tower, attached to the west side of the main tower, was built, almost certainly at the same time.

[1] Such north and south porticus, overlapping nave and chancel, forming prolongations of north and south aisles and entered respectively from chancel and north aisle and from nave and south aisle, were common in the aisled churches of Syria and North Africa: cf. Kalb Lauzeh, A. W. Clapham, (*a*), p. 27, fig. 9.

Hamilton Thompson on the other hand saw what he considered to be clear evidence of repair and/or rebuilding at two different dates, one certainly in Saxon times, the other probably some time before or after the Norman Conquest. He thinks that while the triple opening in the east wall of the tower within the church was part of the first rebuilding, the tower itself (i.e. the portion above the two-storeyed porch) and the stair turret were in fact built in the mid-eleventh century 'or even rather later'. If this were so, the stair turret and the third stage of the tower (but not the triple opening in the second stage) may belong to the Saxo-Norman Overlap period.

Early in the fourteenth century the top, i.e. the fourth or belfry stage, of the tower was taken down and replaced by the present stage, and the attractive broach spire with corner pinnacles was added. Also the stage below the belfry was rebuilt so the existing walls of this stage are not those of the original tower. The Saxon work in the tower itself extends to 38 feet above the ground. The stair turret was retained at its full height of 48 feet. It is not known whether the top part of the turret stair and its vault was removed at this time or later.

The Exterior

The walls (1) are built rather roughly of rubble with some intermixture of Roman bricks, the latter especially at the corners where they are used for strengthening purposes. The total length is 150 feet, excluding the ambulatory. The original breadth was 64 feet; removal of the aisles (which were about nine feet internal width) reduced this to its present width of 38 feet. The walls are 3 ft. 8 ins. thick, an unusual thickness for a Saxon building.

The Nave. The nave consists of two storeys (2), a ground storey and a clerestory separated by set-offs which are where the lean-to roofs of the aisles joined the nave walls. The four large lower round-headed recesses in each wall, each containing a window, represent the original nave arcades of open arches between nave and aisles. The fillings are modern (1863–6). These recesses are separated not by piers but by pieces of walling each approximately 8 ft. 2 ins. long, except the north-east pier which is 8 ft. 10½ ins. The heads are turned in two rows of Roman thin flat bricks, one row above or outside the other; in some, though not in all, the rows are separated by flat courses of bricks concentric with the curve of the arch; in all, similar flat concentric courses of bricks separate the arch heads from the walling above: they look like arches of two orders but the faces are in the same plane. The outer and inner rows of the arch heads are flush with each other and with the wall face; the imposts project 4 inches.

In each clerestory wall are three round-headed windows, with heads similarly

---

(1) *Plates* 93, 95; (2) *Plate* 93.

turned in Roman bricks. Each clerestory window is above the walling separating the ground storey windows; i.e. above the piers, not above the windows below.

The north aisle ended beyond the fourth ground storey window to the east where the exterior set-off of the aisle roof goes vertically upward before becoming horizontal again towards the east. Just beyond this point is a smaller and lower placed built-up aperture, with round-head turned in Roman bricks: this was the former entrance to the north porticus from the presbytery. This porticus, as indicated by the higher set-off on the exterior of the nave wall, was apparently higher than the aisle; it is not known whether it was two-storeyed as at Deerhurst (Glos).

Foundations were found, on the north side of the church, of transverse sleeper walls dividing the aisle foundations into four rectangular chambers. Whether these sleeper walls carried transverse arches of an aisle, or screen walls of four separate porticus is not known. The very large nave arches make continuous aisles highly probable, if not almost certain: porticus always had small doorways to the nave, as at SS. Peter and Paul at Canterbury and the north porticus at Brixworth itself. Moreover, porticus with narrow openings occur as prolongations of continuous aisles with large openings to the nave in some fifth- and sixth-century churches of Syria and North Africa.[1] Recently H. M. Taylor has revived and supported the theory that the aisles were really separate porticus but without providing any new evidence apart from stressing what he considers to be remains of dividing walls projecting from the north wall of the nave. The writer has been less successful in finding any such significant remains.[2]

The north wall of the nave is slightly longer than the south, 60 ft. 5 ins. and 59 ft. 4 ins. respectively, the west wall in consequence being set obliquely to the nave.

The Tower and Stair Turret. The western stair turret (1) is 14 feet in north–south diameter and protrudes from the tower some 10 feet. It is lighted by three vertical tiers of small square-headed openings some of which are now blocked: one tier on the west, one on the north and one on the south. Each opening is single-splayed inwards, but the outer edge in each was fitted with a stone framework which almost closed the opening, leaving only a narrow open loop for aperture. Only two of these

---

[1] A. W. Clapham, (*a*); a comparison of the three plans given by Clapham of Kalb Lauzeh (fig. 9, p. 27), SS. Peter and Paul, Canterbury (fig. 6, p. 18) and Brixworth (fig. 11, p. 34) is interesting.

[2] Since writing the above the author's attention has been drawn to recent excavations by Mr. E. D. C. Jackson and Dr. E. G. M. Fletcher (op. cit., (*d*)). These reveal that Brixworth was originally an aisled basilican church but that later, perhaps not much later, the E. half of the N. aisle (and presumably the S. aisle too) was divided into two porticus by thin screen walls. The reason for this change is not evident: possibly space for additional altars was required. In view of this new knowledge the plan given in Fig. 15 is to some slight extent incorrect. The four E. pairs of pilasters shown in the aisles were not pilasters and did not support arches; they represent the junctions of the screen walls with the main walls. There were no W. pilasters or wall junctions, as shown, as in these areas there was unobstructed aisle.

(1) *Plate 95.*

remain and Hamilton Thompson[1] considered that one (if not both) is 'a comparatively late insertion', so it cannot be said whether these frameworks were part of the original design. The reason for the peculiar fitment is not known.

The tower (I), 21 ft. 6 ins. north–south by 20 feet east–west, had round–headed doorways 3 ft. 6 ins. wide on the north and south sides. The north one is now blocked and a larger western one is hidden by the stair turret. The door heads, like the nave windows, are turned in Roman bricks. There is also a roughly built rectangular window in the lower part of the tower south wall; and a round headed one higher up below the string course, but not one on the north wall. The south tower wall is 3 ft. 3 ins. thick, the others 3 ft. 9 ins. Protruding from the north-west and south-west corners of the tower, near the ground and pointing north and south respectively, are two bits of walling, thinner than the tower wall but in bond with it; these are remnants of the western outbuildings. Originally the north and south doorways of the tower led to the lower floors of these two-storeyed western adjuncts. That they were two-storeyed seems indicated by the holes for the joists, now filled in, in the tower walls. But there are no indications of communication between the upper floor of the porch and those of the side adjuncts.

Some herring-bone courses occur in the turret wall and in the lower south wall of the tower. Some of this ornamentation goes right through the wall and may therefore be Saxon work. It is not inconsistent with a late eleventh-century date for the building of the tower and turret. The herring-boning in the lower south wall of the tower (the original porch) and signs of repairs on the adjoining west wall of the nave may indicate repairs when the upper part of the tower was built. It was at this time possibly—Hamilton Thompson says probably—that the western adjuncts were pulled down.

The tower and turret were repaired in 1900–5. The roof and battlemented parapet are mediaeval.

The Apse. The apse at the east end is polygonal (five sided) outside and semi-circular inside (Fig. 15). At the angles are small buttresses, 20 inches wide, projecting 6 inches at the top and about 16 inches at the bases. The outer surfaces of the buttresses are also angular, being so cut that the two surfaces are parallel to the corresponding walls of the polygon of the apse. The polygon faces between the buttresses are about 6 ft. 6 ins. wide and the walls were originally 2 ft. 7 ins. thick. The heads of the pilaster-buttresses were originally connected by round heads forming continuous blind-arcading round the exterior of the apse, somewhat similar to that at Wing (Bucks). Traces of this are to be seen in the north-west corner. Only a portion of the north-west wall of the apse up to 5 feet above the window impost (above this

[1] Op. cit., (d).

(I) *Plate* 95.

it is conjectural—Watkins) with its bit of pilaster-buttress is original (1), the rest being Watkins's restoration of 1863–6, though to the old design so far as this could be ascertained from existing remains.

The substructure of the apse is semicircular both inside and outside. The upper polygonal outer surface overhangs the semicircular foundation by about 13 inches. Hamilton Thompson believed the original apse was semicircular outside too and that the old polygonal apse was part of the *first* rebuilding[1] 'at an uncertain date'. His reasons were: (1) No Roman bricks occur in the apse wall above the sub-structure, and tufa[2] is used although none occurs in parts of the church known to be original. (2) The use of wide pilaster strips of advanced type clasping the corners of the polygon. Pilaster strips do not occur at all in England before about the middle of the tenth century and are therefore not found in the earlier parts of the church. They normally varied from 4 to about 13 inches in width; only in the late (supposed latter half of the eleventh century) chancel of Tichborne in Hants do they reach two feet. These Brixworth ones are very advanced in size and shape and suggest, as Hamilton Thompson himself appears to think, a late eleventh-century date of possibly the Saxo-Norman Overlap. (3) The north wall of the apse encroaches on that of the presbytery and on the exterior nearly blocks out the north round-headed window there.

The Ambulatory. The exterior ambulatory (1) is 7 ft. 6 ins. wide. The springing of the vaulting was 6 ft. 6 ins. above the floor, which was 6 ft. 7 ins. below that of the nave. The crown of the vault must have been about 3 ft. 9 ins. above the springing. There was probably a lean-to roof over the vault with outer eaves close to the ground.

An ambulatory round an apse but *inside* the church is a common feature in Romanesque churches of the larger kind. In such churches too there was sometimes a small crypt below the chancel of the kind known as a *confessio* used, as the name (derived from confessor, a holy man) suggests, as a place where the tomb or relics of a saint were kept. These relics were made accessible, i.e. viewable, to pilgrims by means of a surrounding passage or ambulatory below nave floor level with stair entrances from within the church; e.g. as at the late seventh-century crypt at Hexham (Northumberland), and the late tenth-century crypt at Wing (Bucks). An ambulatory *outside* the church walls, as at Brixworth, is unusual if not unique. According to Clapham it 'was undoubtedly planned in connexion with a central chamber under the apse itself. Whether the chamber was ever constructed is doubt-ful as excavation has revealed no traces of its existence': the soil was stated by Watkins

---

[1] Poole was also of this opinion, partly on account of the absence of Roman bricks.

[2] Tufa is found at various places in England as calcareous deposits from lime-impregnated underground waters. It is light and easy to work and was used extensively in this country as a building material from Roman times till about the twelfth century. The tufa used at Brixworth was obtained from local glacial gravel beds.

---

(1) *Plate* 94.

to be undisturbed. Radford however considers that Watkins was probably looking for a large crypt underlying the whole area of the apse[1] and that as the excavation apparently was only carried, as a ditch, round the interior wall of the apse foundation, he missed finding the smaller crypt which would be immediately below the altar.

A rough breach in the east end of the apse foundation wall at Brixworth was at first considered by Watkins to be the entrance to the crypt from the ambulatory; later Dryden attributed it to a later burial. Subsequently when Watkins found that the original apse floor was level with that of the nave and that his excavations so far as they went had shown the soil beneath was 'unbroken' he concluded there could be no crypt. Radford considers that the breach really was an entrance to the crypt. He attributes the ambulatory to the late eighth or early ninth century and thinks it was probably attached to a pre-existing small confessio beneath the altar designed to hold relics brought from overseas rather than the complete body of a local saint. In this connection it may be noted that the church, originally dedicated to All Saints, was rededicated at some time in the Saxon period to St. Boniface. A relic supposed to be of this saint, a throat bone, still preserved in the church, may have been one of the relics housed in the crypt.

However, until further excavation is carried out under the apse itself the problem of the Brixworth crypt must remain unsolved.

In the exterior wall of the ambulatory are two arched recesses, one on the north-east and one on the south-east, which might have been used as tomb chambers.[2] They are 6 ft. 4 ins. and 6 ft. 9 ins. long respectively, about 19 inches deep and about 12 inches above the floor. It is not known when they were made.

According to Hamilton Thompson the ambulatory was part of the original church; most of the inner wall is original (it contains some herring-boning) though the outer wall and the tomb recesses have been rebuilt.

The entrance to the church is through a round-headed Norman doorway cut into the built-up western opening of the south nave arcade.

The Interior

The Nave. This is spacious. It is 30 feet wide and 60 feet[3] long to the single-span pointed arch supported on piers which are really inward projections of the north and south nave walls. The jambs of this arch are 3 ft. 10 ins. thick and 2 ft. 3 ins. and 2 ft. 5 ins. respectively in projection. This arch was erected in the fourteenth century to replace the original Saxon triple arcade which separated the nave and presbytery. Remains of the triple arch are to be seen in the north jamb of the present arch. The

---

[1] Like those below the chancels of Canterbury, Winchester and Worcester Cathedrals. Such large crypts in England are all of post-Conquest date.

[2] Similar tomb chambers may have existed, indeed may be inferred from existing remains, in the crypt at Wing (Bucks).

[3] Most measurements given for this church are from Dryden, (*a*).

bases of the two intermediate piers of the former triple arch were discovered beneath the floor during Watkins's excavation of 1841. The centre arch was about 9 feet wide and the side arches 5 feet wide.

The presbyterial space, now forming part of the nave (for the single-span arch is in no sense a separation or obstruction) is 30 feet long by 31 feet wide at the east end, so the entire nave is now some 90 feet long. The entire internal length of the church from the west wall of the nave to the east wall of the apse is 116 feet.

The lower nave window arches (1) vary in width from 7 ft. 4 ins. to 7 ft. 9½ ins.[1] These, like the clerestory windows and the east tower arch, have round heads, each turned in double rows of Roman bricks. In some of the nave windows some of the red Roman bricks have been replaced by (yellowish) bricks of similar size of local oolite, possibly in the tenth century rebuilding. The bricks are 10 to 16 inches long, about 11 inches wide and about 1½ inches thick. As on the exterior, the arch heads are flush with the wall surface though the imposts, also of Roman bricks, protrude. The imposts are of three courses of single bricks, stepped in characteristic Saxon manner. The lowest course projects about 1½ inches, the middle one about 2½ inches and the top one about 4 inches inwards from the foot or springing of the arch. On the wall side they are flush with each other but project from the wall about 4 inches. The arch *heads* vary from 3 ft. 11 ins. to 4 ft. 5 ins. in width and are set back 2 to 3 inches behind the vertical line of the jambs. The window arches rise slightly in height from west to east: thus the height of the imposts above the floor varies from 10 ft. 4 ins. at the west end to 11 ft. 5 ins. at the east, the total rise being different on the two walls—about 7 inches on the south side and about 10 inches on the north.

The arch heads are crudely built, obviously by masons unfamiliar with the principles of arch construction. The flat bricks comprising the head should of course all point towards the centre of the circle from which the head of the arch is struck, and in consequence (flat bricks, not wedge-shaped voussoirs, being used) the mortar joints would be wedge-shaped. The Saxon masons, more familiar at this time with wood construction, did not understand this: they tilted the first brick at some 60° to the horizontal, filling in the gap between brick and impost with a great blob of mortar mixed with bits of broken bricks. This crudeness is seen in the tower arch (2) but is most evident in the nave windows and is perhaps the best proof that this church was not originally a secular basilica of a Roman settlement, for whoever built these arches, they were not Romans or Romanized Britons, who would be quite at home with work of this sort.[2]

[1] Except the east window on the south side which is narrower (6 ft. 8½ ins.), a consequence of the different lengths of the north and south walls.

[2] Clapham (quoted in V.C.H., IV) suggests that this may after all be intentional. Instances are known in Italian and late Roman work of tilting the springer in a similar manner. At Brixworth it may be an indication

(1) *Plate* 97; (2) *Plate* 96.

The upper, i.e. clerestory, windows (I) are of a type uncommon in Saxon England. They are round-headed, splayed and large—about 6 feet high and about 3 feet wide at the outer edge of the splay, much wider than is usual with Saxon windows. They are *single*-splayed and the splay is very slight, so slight indeed that from the nave they look unsplayed—as though they were cut straight through the walls, quite unlike the wide single-splays of early Saxon or Norman window openings. They resemble more the windows of early Christian churches in Rome and Ravenna.

In the south wall above the entrance to the south-east chapel are the remains of another arch head of Roman bricks.

The clerestory walls are thinner than the lower nave portions by the amount of the set-offs. Partly on this account Poole thought the clerestory belonged to a second Saxon rebuilding. If this was so however the aisles must have been almost as high as the eaves of the nave roof, which seems most unlikely. Watkins, a careful observer over many years, considered the nave and clerestory walls contemporary.

Low down in the north wall, just east of the mediaeval arch, is the blocked doorway (referred to above), three feet wide, which formerly led from the presbytery to the north porticus.

Built into the inner western, Saxon, jamb of the south-west Norman doorway is a stone on which is carved in low relief a bird, supposed eagle. The stone lies on its side, obviously a fragment re-used as building material. This bird has been a puzzle to writers; it has been described as Roman and as Assyrian. It has been discussed by J. Romilly Allen and by Sir Henry Dryden. It cannot be considered here, though it may be pointed out that the bird has two pairs of wings, one pointing upwards and one downwards, and no legs. Dryden stated that he had never before seen an eagle without legs except in heraldry.

The Chancel. Further east is the arch leading through the east wall into the apsidal chancel.[1] The arch is 9 ft. 9 ins. wide between the jambs and nearly 22 feet high, the stepped imposts, $6\frac{1}{2}$ inches high or thick, being 16 ft. $4\frac{1}{2}$ ins. above the present choir floor. The arch head, like the others, is turned in Roman bricks but is of one course only and, again like all the other arches, with a thin outside flat course concentric with the arch head; the arch head course is 3 ft. 1 in. wide. The springing of the head is a few inches behind the jamb face. The chancel beyond is 17 ft. 8 ins. wide and 19 ft. 3 ins. long (from east to west). The apse is stilted, the stilts (straight pieces

---

that the masons were closely imitating Roman methods. This seems unlikely. Because it occurs sometimes, i.e. exceptionally, in late Roman work it does not follow that it would occur at all in a remote Roman province like Britain, except through ignorance which is what is claimed at Brixworth. And if it did occur in Britain it would still be exceptional. Why should the Brixworth masons copy what was exceptional rather than build *more Romanorum?* The suggestion seems an exception to Clapham's usually cautious statements.

[1] See A. W. Clapham, (*a*), Pl. 5.

(I) *Plate* 93.

of walling running east and west and dying into the curve of the apse) being nine feet long. The arch head and the bases of the piers are original. The arch opening above the bases was widened in mediaeval times to allow of a screen separating apse from nave. This screen was removed and the archway returned to its original form by Watkins.

There is an original round-headed north-east window 5 ft. 9 ins. by 3 ft. 8½ ins. wide in the apse. The head is not turned in Roman bricks but in stone. It is assumed that there were similar windows in the east and south-east bays; the present windows in these positions are modern insertions. There is no evidence that the apse was ever vaulted; the present roof is flat and plastered. The present floor of the chancel is three steps above the nave floor; the original floor according to Watkins was level with that of the nave.

In the east wall of the nave, on either side of the chancel arch, is a round-headed single-splayed window of 2 feet exterior width with imposts 18 feet above the floor. Below each of these, low down, half below and half above the nave floor, is a built-up round-headed doorway of 2 ft. 7½ ins. clear width. These doors (1) led originally to the ambulatory, as can be seen plainly from the exterior, down flights of steps which began in the church.

On the south side of the chancel arch, and to the north of a later recess with pointed arch, are traces of the upper part of the north jamb and the north half of the round head of an arch. It is placed too high for a squint; it may have been a recess for an image, replaced in later times by the pointed-arched recess. It looks no older than the pointed arch, being made of similar squared, smooth faced stones with fine joints. It is almost certainly not Saxon.

In many early western Romanesque churches the entrance to the apse was by an imposing so-called 'arch of triumph', the whole width and height of the apsidal opening. In East Christian churches, e.g. those of North Africa, Syria and the north-west litoral of the Adriatic Sea from Ravenna to Parenzo, this single arch was replaced by a triple arcade, the apse often being stilted to provide additional accommodation for the clergy. These two characteristics, together with the polygonal exterior to an internally semi-circular apse, were usual in the Kentish group of churches, to which Brixworth belongs, and supply indeed clear proof of the cultural influence of the Early Christian Near East brought to this country by Augustine in 597 and by Theodore of Tarsus in 669. In south-east England however the triple arcade was placed a few feet to the west of the apse entrance in order to provide some extra accommodation for the clergy. Brixworth, being a monastic church with a considerable number of clergy, required still more space and the triple arcade was placed 30 feet to the west of the apse opening, so cutting off a portion of the nave as

---

(1) *Plate* 94.

extra presbyterial space. For this reason too the aisles did not extend east beyond the ends of the triple arcade.

The Tower. In the east wall of the tower, i.e., the west wall of the nave, at ground level is a round headed doorway (1), 4 ft. 10 ins. wide and about 10 feet high. Above are the marks of a similar opening, now blocked, and arch head of similar size, the crown of which is 19 ft. 2 ins. above the floor. It is conceivable, though unlikely, that there was originally a single arch here of approximately 19 feet by 5 feet, the lower arch being a later Saxon insertion. This was Poole's view. Against this are various objections: (1) The ungainly and quite unusual proportions of an arch of height four times the width (19 feet × 5 feet). The only comparable case is similar markings on the west wall at St. Martin's Church, Canterbury (2), which some writers regard as belonging to an originally single arch of *c.* $17\frac{1}{2}$ feet by *c.* $7\frac{1}{2}$ feet (ratio of H : W $= 2\frac{1}{2}$). Clapham thought it probable that there were originally two arches here also, one above the other 'the same as at Brixworth'. (2) The lower arch does not look like a later insertion. It is indeed one of the most primitively constructed arches in the interior of the church. (3) The dimensions of such an arch would bear no relation to those of the external western portal of the tower which originally were 12 ft. 5 ins. high by 6 ft. 8 ins. wide (ratio H : W $= 2\frac{1}{2}$). The inner western portal into a church may be of similar size to or smaller than, the usually monumental outer western portal; in no instance known to the writer is it strikingly higher and narrower than the western entrance.

Clapham thought that the two arches are the original openings into the two lowest stages of the west porch, the upper chamber being entered probably from the nave by means of a ladder or wooden stair. This seems unlikely. The opening is centrally placed: to have a ladder or wooden staircase for access from the nave would obstruct the inner portal below. It would appear to be more likely that there was a western gallery across the nave and that the upper opening was an access to the gallery from the upper storey of the porch. Such western galleries were not uncommon and have left recognizable stone remains at Deerhurst, Tredington (Worcs) and elsewhere. If the (presumed) gallery at Brixworth was of timber remains would hardly be expected—other than the entrance from the porch. (There was of course no stair turret then.) The imposts of the lower arch consist of three Roman slabs arranged stepwise in characteristic Saxon manner.

Above the blocked archway is a triple window opening,[1] the three round heads of which, turned in Roman bricks, are separated by mid-wall baluster shafts, supporting through-stones which hold up the arch heads above (1). The baluster shafts are

---

[1] A similar opening at Earls Barton is five-fold; all others, and they are numerous, are double. At Brixworth the opening is *not* into a belfry which was a still higher chamber, removed later. All other such openings are in belfries.

(1) *Plate* 96; (2) *Plate* 198.

4 ft. 10 ins. long with bases and capitals of crude cubical or cushion form cut in one piece with the shafts. According to both Baldwin Brown and Hamilton Thompson this opening belongs to the first mid- or late tenth-century rebuilding: it not only cuts into the head of the earlier arch below, but baluster shafts *of this type* were not developed in England until the late ninth or early tenth century, while this method of supporting arch heads with through-stones and mid-wall shafts did not reach this country (from Germany) until perhaps the late tenth century. They are characteristic of late Saxon architecture. Unlike the early and rather differently designed seventh-century baluster shafts of Northumbria which were not used in belfry openings as towers were not at that time known in England, and which were carefully finished by being turned in a lathe, these later cruder, bulging shafts at Brixworth and elsewhere were roughly cut to shape with axe or chisel. Whether of early or late types the baluster shaft is a characteristic Saxon feature: it may be regarded as a Saxon invention, particularly in its constructive use as a support to an arch (Roman usage was decorative), suggested by Roman forms.

Capitals on baluster shafts were unusual prior to the Saxo-Norman Overlap while *cushion* capitals are said by Clapham to have reached England from Germany a few years before the Conquest. They had not become firmly established even in Germany until after *c.* 1025. It is therefore surprising that capitals of apparently cushion type should appear at Brixworth nearly a century before the Conquest. But are they really cushion capitals? Baldwin Brown describes them as such and gives a drawing; Britton gives an engraving. Clapham, a cautious scholar, seems uncertain: he writes, 'The cubical capital . . . appears, not as a separate capital but as the finish, both at the top and bottom of a baluster shaft in Brixworth tower, probably of the tenth century.' He correctly describes it as cubical and is non-committal as regards the cushion, though he adds, 'its (the cubical capital's) most usual form is the cushion capital.' G. Zarnecki[1] is of the opinion that these Brixworth capitals are definitely not cushion. Close examination of the capitals seems to confirm Zarnecki's opinion. Britton's engraving and Baldwin Brown's drawing are of idealized, well-developed and well-finished cushion capitals and are quite unlike the actual crude originals.

A cushion capital is derived from a cube by converting the lower half into a hemisphere, the diameter of which is equal to the diagonal of the cube. The hemisphere begins near the top of the vertical edges of the cube so that the lower boundary of each vertical face is a semicircle. This description does not apply to the Brixworth capitals. They are extremely crudely made. The cut-away begins an inch or two from the top and the lower boundary of each face is roughly linear; the top portion in fact looks just like a square abacus. From this the four faces have been chiselled away so that they look like wide hollow chamfers; the vertical edges have been treated similarly, and roughly rounded. As a result the profile is concave, and not

---

[1] Private communication to the writer.

convex as a cushion capital should be, and a horizontal cross section through the lower portion would be not circular but roughly a square with rounded corners.

The bases, though similar to the capitals, are slightly less crudely made. They look as though the mason, having experimented with the capitals, had used his experience to make a rather better job of the bases. The cut-away part begins in one rather above, in the other rather below, the middle of the vertical edges and the lower[1] boundaries of the faces are roughly curved, though rather pointed, not semi-circular. The profiles are only very slightly concave. The horizontal cross-sections might be described as square with rounded corners and with their sides also some-what curved. Also the vertical diameters are considerably longer than the other; i.e. the bases, unlike the capitals, are cut not from cubes but from square sectioned cylinders.

It is difficult to avoid the conclusion that the mason was not trying to make cushion capitals, examples of which it is unlikely he could have seen at this early date, but was merely doing his best to give a decent finish to the two ends of his rather long baluster shafts. What would be more natural, in order to change from the square to the circular, than to slice off the faces and edges, something like sharpening a lead pencil?

Later examples of cubiform capitals are to be found in nearby Lincolnshire. At Broughton-by-Brigg the square has been changed to an octagon by plane chamfer-ing the vertical faces and edges;[2] at Boothby Pagnall, of post-Conquest date, faces and edges are hollow chamfered.

Within the ground floor of the tower (dimensions 15 feet north–south by 12 ft. 5 ins. east–west) the openings on the four sides are visible,[3] those on the north and south sides of similar size; on the west the original monumental centrally placed western entrance can be seen, from the marks left on the wall, to have been 12 ft. 5 ins. high and 6 ft. 8 ins. wide. This is largely blocked, the existing doorway placed to the south of the middle of the wall is only 3 ft. 6 ins. wide and leads into the stair turret. On the in-terior of the stair turret the central column or newel is of rubble and there is a con-tinuous barrel vault of tufa between the newel and the wall, spiralling upwards to near the top. The stone steps are set in mortar upon the back or upper surface of the vault. This is a very different construction from the Lincolnshire turrets. The stair-case within the turret leads up to the first floor chamber in which is the triple opening. The doorway which leads into this chamber from the staircase, only about 3 feet wide, is placed to the north of the middle of the chamber wall; it is part of an original window opening, the other, southern, half having been blocked. The entrance from the turret to the second floor, i.e. the third stage chamber, is through a rough open-ing in the tufa walling.

[1] Really upper, as the base is an inverted capital.
[2] Similar capitals are at Kirkdale (Yorks) of about the same date, post-*c.* 1040.
[3] Except the north one which is behind some modern seats.

There are references in the literature to a supposed original saddle-back or gabled roof above the two-storeyed porch. When this roof, of whatever type, was taken off and the porch converted into a tower by heightening the walls into a four-storeyed tower, tufa was largely used in tower and turret as it was in the apse.

It seems clear that the tower above the two-storeyed early porch, the stair turret and the asymmetrically placed narrow doors into and out of the stair turret are all of a piece and were built at the same time. Roberts thought the tower was later than the nave because he could see in places freed from plaster only straight joints, i.e. no bonding, between tower wall and nave wall. When the plaster was removed later during the restoration intermittent bonding, quite usual with the Saxons, became evident; that is, portions of straight joint alternate with portions bonded in. This, together with similarity of the mixed building materials, indicates contemporaneity of tower (or at least the bottom two stages) and the nave.

The floor of the first floor chamber (the one with the triple opening), i.e. the upper floor of the old porch, was originally lower than it is now. The off-sets can be seen on the walls of the ground floor chamber below the present ceiling. It had a south window, round-headed, still visible (as well as the west one, later converted to a doorway into the turret), which was placed high presumably to be above the roof of the south-western adjunct. The arch head of this window is of tufa so it was probably rebuilt when the tower was raised above the porch.

EARLS BARTON

ALL SAINTS' CHURCH. Only the tower is Saxon, dated by Baldwin Brown to A.D. 950–1000. It is one of five highly decorated Saxon towers, the other four being Barnack, St. Benet's, Cambridge, Barton-on-Humber (Lincs) and Sompting (Sussex). Earls Barton is without question the biggest and most magnificent of all Saxon towers, though aesthetically it is inferior to Barnack. It is 68 ft. 8 ins. high to the top of the modern battlements. The west face is just over 24 feet wide. The south face is one foot shorter than the north ($23\frac{1}{2}$ and $24\frac{1}{2}$ feet respectively), the south-west angle being less than a right angle while the north-west angle is obtuse. This is an example of the bad setting out of much Anglo-Saxon building, though in this case it is not noticeable to the eye.

The tower (1) stands on a square-sectioned plinth. The walls are of rubble covered with modern plaster. It is in four stages of diminishing height and width. The walls are about 4 feet thick at the base, decreasing by the amount of the set-offs to 2 ft. 6 ins. at the top of the belfry (fourth) stage under the battlements.

---

(1) *Plate* 99.

The stages are separated by string courses; the lowest has a hollow chamfer, the upper two have square sections.

There is upright and flat work at all quoins. The flats are not cut back to be in line with the uprights so they would show through the original plaster. The upright and flat work on the lower part of the east wall is visible also inside the church from the nave on the north side; that on the south side is hidden except for a little high up, near the nave roof. The slabs are about 20 inches long by 7 or 8 inches thick.

There are decorative vertical pilaster strips, 4 inches wide, on all four walls arranged somewhat erratically. On the ground floor there are five on the south wall and four on each of the west and north. In the second stage there are five on the south and west wall (on the south wall one is hidden by the clock) and four on the north; in the third stage there are six on the south wall, five on the west and four on the north. The top or belfry stage has two on each wall, each strip resting on a triangular base. All strips have cubical corbels at their bases; the corbels of the ground-floor strips are just above the plinths, those of the upper stages immediately above the corresponding string courses. On the south and west sides (but not on the north) above the lowest string courses are single rows of semicircular strips (1) acting, as it were, as round heads for the pairs of pilaster strips below, suggesting a kind of primitive attempt at blind arcading. Above the second string course on all four sides is a double row of triangular or gable-headed strips, again acting as heads to the pilaster strips below. Small stone cubes separate these triangles at their points of contact. J. Strzygowski maintains that such decorative pilaster work here and on some other Saxon towers is a deliberate copy in stone of the half-timbering construction with which the Saxons were familiar in their wooden houses, just as Greek temples of the classical period show in many of their details a reflection of the wood temple architecture of the earlier Archaic period. He writes: 'Many of the towers so characteristic of Early English architecture show us the wooden prototype translated into stone. The best example is Earls Barton; . . . it remains the most perfect and typical example illustrating the origin of indigenous church architecture in England.' That is to say, Saxon stone architecture developed out of early timber forms which were characteristic of Teutonic races in England and in their original homelands beyond the North Sea. Few other writers agree with this; the evidence to the contrary is too strong. The architecture of the Kentish group of churches was a direct importation from Italo-Byzantine countries; that of the early Northumbrian group from Roman or Merovingian France. English Carolingian, to which Earls Barton belongs, is a thoroughly English national development of the Carolingian forms of north-eastern France (late eighth and early ninth centuries) and of the later Ottonian forms of west Germany and the Rhineland (tenth century). When one remembers

---

(1) *Plates* 99, 100.

the great debt which Carolingian architecture, and to an even greater extent the later Ottonian, owed to the Byzantines (Constantinople) one must agree with Strzygowski when he writes later that in considering 'the remains of Anglo-Saxon churches, . . . crosses, or . . . MSS. . . . Any one who is familiar with the distant East —distant, that is, as seen from Rome—feels himself here in the far West in a closely related province'. In examining churches of the Late Saxon period one must look for prototypes to the Carolingians and the Ottonians, even in the first instance for Byzantine motifs which may have come to us via Germany as well as by more direct trade, pilgrimage and diplomatic routes.

Baldwin Brown shows convincingly that Saxon pilaster strip work was derived directly from similar work in Germany called *lisenen*. The work at Earls Barton shows close resemblances (even in such details as the hollow chamfers at the slightly expanding heads of the strips—like primitive capitals) to that at the Abbey church of Gernrode, of about the same date (Fig. 16). Clapham agrees with this derivation

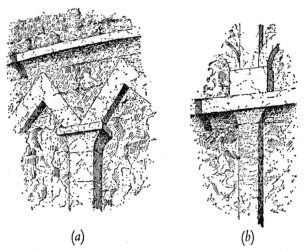

(a) (b)

Fig. 16. (a) Gernrode, Germany. Details of Pilaster Strip Work
(b) Earls Barton. Details of Pilaster Strip Work

and regards it as fully established. Fletcher and Jackson however on the basis of extensive studies of pilaster-work regard it as structural, like quoining used for strengthening purposes. They do not accept its direct derivation from German *lisenen* but think that long and short quoining and long and short pilasters are both native products and arise from the same idea of strengthening walls. They agree that pilasters were used for decorative purposes where strengthening was not required. Thus it is structural in the lower parts of the towers of Barnack and Sompting but decorative only in the upper parts. It is decorative also at Repton and in the arcading at Wing and Geddington.

The suggestion made above that here, at Earls Barton, we may have an attempt at blind arcading is perhaps not entirely without substance. The appearance of arcading is hidden by the general fussiness and complexity (or multiplicity) of the decorative elements, and by the string courses which seem to cut off the heads of the arcades. A comparison of these decorated towers and similar decoration in other parts of some Saxon churches is instructive. At Barnack (1) of about the same date, a more dignified and logical design, there are pilaster strips without any arcade headings. At Barton-on-Humber (Lincs, about A.D. 950–1000) (2), the arcading is plain and unconfused by string courses: a range of gable-headed arcading above a range of round-headed arcading. At Wing (Bucks, 1000–40) (3) are two rows of fully developed blind arcading of pilaster strips, gable-headed above and round-headed below, encircling the apse—one wide arch covering each face of the seven-sided apse—similar to the round-headed arcading formerly round the apse at Brixworth. At Geddington (4) is more primitively constructed gable-headed blind arcading uncomplicated by pilaster strips.

From where did the Saxons obtain this idea of external blind arcading? Immediately and directly from Ottonian Germany, though the idea is of very ancient lineage. It is found in buildings of Sassanian Persia (early third–early seventh century), from whence it spread via Armenia to the Byzantine world. It is found on the exterior of the church of S. Apollinare in Classe at Ravenna (*c.* 550) and was later developed by the Lombards of north Italy and became the most characteristic decorative feature of their architecture; hence the name Lombard bands by which it is sometimes called. From Lombardy it passed across the Alps to west Germany, where it is found on the church at Gernrode (Fig. 16)—on the towers, along the upper part of the aisle wall and under the eaves of the apse—along with the lisenen or pilaster strips already mentioned. There is no doubt of the immediate sources of the Saxon ornament; nor is there any doubt as to its ultimate source: there are striking similarities between the Saxon and German decoration on the one hand and the Italian on the other—*cf.* e.g. S. Pietro at Toscanella, *c.* 50 miles north-west of Rome,[1] which Clapham dates to probably late eleventh century.

Saxon arcading however differs in one respect from typical Lombard and later arcading: it is applied *to* the wall, not recessed *into* it. The arcade arches support nothing; they are probably purely decorative.[2]

It is interesting to see these Saxon experiments in developing in this country a type of exterior decoration which 200 to 300 years later became the most popular and certainly most beautiful of all external decoration. Good examples in this country are the Romanesque eastern apse at Norwich Cathedral, the Norman towers at Canterbury, the west front at Rochester, and the early Gothic at Lincoln Cathedral.

[1] T. G. Jackson, Pl. LVI and Fig. 48.   [2] See however above, p. 191.

(1) *Plate* 83; (2) *Plate* 130; (3) *Plate* 103; (4) *Plate* 108.

These later developments were however due to fresh impulses from overseas and were not direct descendants of Saxon decorative forms.

The west doorway of the tower (1) is 8 ft. 7 ins. high to the inner crown of the arch, and 3 ft. 3 ins. wide between the jambs. The exterior arch head is cut from two stones, the interior from one. Each jamb consists of a large flat slab on end with long narrow ones lying above, two on the right and one on the left jamb; the north slab, the larger, is 4 ft. 6 ins. high by 3 ft. 7 ins. deep and 6 inches thick. The exterior ornament consists of an outer ring of vertical pilaster strips of square section which passes outside the imposts and round the head of the arch. Within this is a strip-work hood mould resting on the imposts and then two inner mouldings above the imposts on the face of the arch head, half-round in section. The outer pilaster strips and jambs stand on independent square-sectioned plinths resting on the tower plinth. The interior, east, face of the arch is undecorated, being flush with the wall except for the remains of a few inches on each side just above the springing of square-sectioned pilaster strips which presumably at one time encircled the arch head. All plinths and imposts are square-sectioned blocks or slabs. On the soffits and faces of the imposts is plain incised round-headed arcading only $\frac{3}{16}$ of an inch deep with faint traces of incised carving in the arched spaces. It may be Saxon though some writers think it Norman.

Above the west doorway is a round-headed internally single-splayed window (2) which must have been a Norman insertion as its head cuts into the space, now blocked on the exterior only, originally occupied by the lower half of a Saxon double window similar to that on the south wall. These two original openings are double-splayed with stone mid-wall slabs in which the lighting apertures are cut, in the form of crosses in the south window and of circles in the west one.[1] The south window heads are segmental (3), cut from single stones, each with two thin roll mouldings surmounted by a cross carved in low relief. Such crosses over windows are very unusual, though they occur frequently above doorways either in the lintel or wall or, later, on tympana. In Palestine the Chi-Rho monogram is often found in similar positions, a practice probably descended from the pagan custom of hanging charms, etc. above entrances to houses to frighten off bad spirits or the evil eye or even lightning. These Earls Barton crosses may be another instance of Near-Eastern influence. On the face of the south wall supported between two square-sectioned upper and lower corbels, between and on either side of the openings, are three baluster shafts, each with three rings. These are purely decorative; they support nothing. The support for the arch head is a thin piece of independent walling immediately behind the centre shaft. To the west of this window is a carved circle containing a

[1] Cf. The window-slab apertures at Barnack, above, p. 193.

(1) *Plate* 98; (2) *Plate* 100; (3) *Plates* 99, 102.

cross of four equal arms (1). This has been stated to be a fragment of a cross-shaft built into the wall. As with the crosses above the windows, the background is cut away leaving the circle and cross in low relief. It resembles in design the consecration crosses of churches.

In the second stage of the tower, just above the first string course, are tall round-headed doorways (2) cut straight through the walls, one in each face. The jambs are of single stones; the heads are of several large irregular sized stones, not properly cut voussoirs. They appear to lead to nowhere and to have no apparent purpose. In some cases, e.g. at Deerhurst, Glos, the east doorway led into a gallery with an altar used as a chapel on the east (nave) side of the tower wall; and at Deerhurst there are indications (protruding brackets) on the wall which support this idea. Such western galleries are not uncommon and Clapham suggested that they were used in England as substitutes for the western apse of Carolingian churches since an actual apse would have interfered with the characteristic English west portal. This explanation could not apply to Earls Barton which was in all probability a turriform church and therefore not Carolingian in ground plan. Here the eastern doorway, about 25 feet above the nave floor, is above the roof of the present nave but below that of the original chancel, the marks of which can be seen on the east face of the tower. Baldwin Brown suggests that the door might have given access to a space or chamber between an outer and inner roof of the original chancel.[1] Such hollow roofs were not uncommon in native Irish chapels and oratories.

The problem of the similar doorways, 7 feet by 2 ft. 6 ins., on the south and west faces remains; the latter is partially built up (there is not one on the north). These are placed rather lower than the one on the east wall. In some cases such doorways may have given access to the roof or upper chambers of north and south western adjuncts. With the highly decorated tower of Earls Barton however it is unlikely that there were western adjuncts and even more unlikely that if there were no traces should be left.

Another suggestion, that they were used as access to the tower when this was used as a refuge against raiders, is not applicable here. The doors are too high above the ground to be reached with ladders; and a tower was only useful as a refuge when the ground storey was stone-vaulted. Earls Barton is timber ceiled so refugees could easily be smoked out. The intention behind these doorways is still unknown.

In the third stage just above the string course is a narrow triangular-headed opening in each face (3). Here too, as in the stage below, the east window is above the level of the north, west and south ones. These look like windows but, unlike windows, are not splayed, but cut straight through the walls.

[1] See also Barnack and Brigstock.

---

(1) *Plate* 102; (2) *Plates* 99, 102; (3) *Plates* 99, 101.

In the top or belfry stage are striking five-fold round-headed openings (I), each head cut from a single stone, one on each face, each with six baluster shafts. The shafts, unlike the Brixworth ones, have no capitals or bases; like those in the double openings below they are not mid-wall shafts, but are in front of and separate from the thin dividing walls supporting the heads of the openings. They are held between upper and lower corbels, supporting nothing: they are purely decorative. They are roughly finished, of oval cross-section, and the banding is on the front faces only, where alone it could be seen.

The church originally was almost certainly of the turriform type. The lowest floor of the tower was the nave, with a chancel, probably short, to the east as indicated by the marks of the roof on the east face of the tower. That this was so is shown by the fact that the upright and flat quoins on the east side of the tower are complete to the ground showing that the eastern adjunct, the chancel, was narrower than the tower. Unlike some turriform churches there was no western adjunct; otherwise there would have been no monumental western doorway; or if there had been the decoration would have been on the east, not on the west face, as it is at Barton-on-Humber, where there was and still is a western adjunct built at the same time as the tower. In 1086 the church passed to Countess Judith, niece of William the Conqueror and widow of the Saxon Earl Waltheof. She may have been responsible for the first Norman nave and small chancel of *c.* 1100.

The tower arch leading into the present nave is not in its original state. It was altered in Norman times and rebuilt in the late thirteenth century re-using the twelfth-century material. It is 12 ft. 6 ins. wide. There is nothing to be learnt from it concerning Saxon forms.

PETERBOROUGH (Medeshamstede)

Description of Remains. The first monastery at Medeshamstede was founded about A.D. 655 by Peada, the first Christian King of Mercia, and his brother to commemorate the revival of Christianity in his kingdom after the death of his father, the pagan King Penda (632–54).[1] The builder and first Abbot was Saxulf, later Bishop of Mercia 675–91. It is not certain whether this building was of stone or wood. Allcroft thought it was of wood. Hugh White[2] (Hugo Candidus), a monk of Peterborough in the twelfth century, wrote a history of the monastery from its foundation until the

[1] For a detailed history of the Saxon monastry see Poole, op. cit., (*b*).
[2] W. T. Mellows, op. cit., p. 8.

time of his death. White refers to *immanissimos lapides*, and says the foundation stones were so large that eight yoke of oxen could scarcely draw one of them! He makes no reference to an early timber building. However, a stone church was evidently erected here at an early date, probably in the seventh century. It was destroyed by the Danes in 870 and Abbot Hedda and all his monks slain. The monastery lay in ruins for nearly a century. It was re-established by Æthelwold, Bishop of Winchester, and the church rebuilt *c.* 966–72 as part of his campaign to re-establish monasticism in the Danelaw.

Abbot Kenwulf, 992–1005, protected the monastery by building a wall round it. As the old chronicler put it: the monastery had become like a city, a strong place, a burgh, and Kenwulf changed its name to Burgh (Burgus), later Petri Burgus or Peterborough.

This church was pillaged by Hereward the Wake in 1070, by French robbers in 1102 and finally burned in 1116. The present Norman cathedral begun in 1117 was built over it.

Parts of the foundations and a few courses of wall of the transepts and choir of the second Saxon church were discovered in 1884[1] under the south transept and nave of the present cathedral. They have been vaulted over and are accessible to visitors. The Saxon nave has not been excavated and it is not known whether it was aisled or not. No traces were found of transeptal arches leading into a crossing and Irvine thought there was no possibility of a central tower. The Anglo-Saxon Chronicle states that the tower was 'gehalgod', i.e. consecrated, in 1059. This tower however may have been at the west end; most of the larger churches of the tenth and eleventh centuries had western towers.

Traces of two walls running south from the south transept must have belonged to the eastern range of the Saxon cloister.

The west wall of the present Norman south transept runs along and above the middle of the Saxon south transept. The south wall of the Saxon transept is just south of the south wall of the present transept; so close indeed are these two walls that the vertical face of the external Norman ashlar is in the same plane as the internal plastering of the Saxon wall below.

The north wall of the Saxon north transept is a few feet to the north of the present south-west crossing pier. This 'crossing pillar and the sleeper walls were merely begun *on the surface of the Saxon plaster-flooring*, which though sunk down and crushed by the enormous weight, yet so remained that its crushed surface could be washed to find whether painting or incising had existed, neither of which appeared'.[2] Saxon foundations were indeed good if, as here, they were good enough for the enormously greater load of the later Norman church.

According to Saxon custom the floor of the church was below the level of the

---

[1] J. T. Irvine, (*d*) and (*e*); plan given.   [2] J. T. Irvine, (*e*); the italics are his.

ground outside. The floor is plastered and the existing interior walling is about three courses high, with some plaster on it.

Some stones from an earlier building were used in the walls of both transepts as indicated by the fact that they still retain pieces of hard grey plaster from the earlier building. From this it seems reasonable to infer that the existing remains are from the tenth-century church and that the church immediately preceding it, whether Saxulf's or not, was also of stone. Later, T. Butterick was of the same opinion.

From the evidence given by Irvine the choir was short and almost certainly square ended. It was 23 ft. 3 ins. wide between the walls which were 2 ft. 8 ins. thick. The floor was two or three steps above that of the nave. The north transept had interior length of 31 ft. 8 ins. and a width of 34 ft. 8 ins. The south transept had the same . dimensions, and the walls were 2 ft. 8½ ins. thick. The total interior length across the transepts was 91 ft. 11 ins. T. Butterick later noted that the first length of the north wall of the choir was deflected inwards, i.e. towards the south, by *c.* 3 feet. He thought this stretch of walling might be the springing of an apse, earlier than the square choir, and that the early church may have been apsidal, of the tau form like North Elmham and Wilfrid's church at Hexham.

Near the centre of the east wall of the south transept is a mass of masonry which supported the reredos of its altar. This was an addition to the Saxon church for the old plaster remained along the wall behind the masonry. The few courses of the south-east quoins are of large stones. Irvine suggests these were brought probably from Roman buildings at the Roman town which belonged to the monastery, now known as The Castles, lying between Alwalton and Water Newton. No trace was found below ground of the great stones referred to by Hugh White.

The outside space to the north and east of the walls was the early monastic cemetery. Stone coffins of Norman date only and Saxon flat monumental tomb slabs were found, the latter practically paving the ancient level of the monks' cemetery. No stone coffins were found below the Saxon tomb slabs; bodies were buried in earth only.

A number of carved and ornamented fragments were found of architectural interest as throwing some light on the nature and decoration of the original church. There were some wrought stones built into the protruding bottom courses of the Norman foundations which showed that 'groping after mouldings, and, at times, slight traces of approach to Norman feeling, which frequently is found just prior to the Conquest'. Elsewhere were two fragments of rudely pillared jamb stones or responds of an arch,[1] slightly reminiscent of the chancel arch at Wittering, a daughter house. There were several fragments of double shafts, roughly shaped and coated with a very thin coat of the finest and hardest Saxon plaster to a smooth round surface, perhaps from the Cloister; no capitals or bases corresponding to these shafts

[1] Drawings are given by J. T. Irvine, (*d*).

were found. There were fragments of moulded string courses and one fragment of string ornamented with interlacement, its top and bottom being plain. There are suggestions of alterations or additions at a late date, before or perhaps during the Saxo-Norman Overlap. A tympanum from over a square-headed door certainly suggests a late date as tympana were only quite exceptionally used as decorative forms by the Saxons—a Saxon doorway was normally either square or round-headed, but if the latter the door was round-headed too. The plane of this tympanum was in advance of the plane of the wall, hence the hood mould was probably a continuation of vertical pilaster strips at the sides of the doorway. Of similar late date were the remains of an arch,[1] impost and two jambs.

There was one fine specimen of 'long' stone[1] from a 'long and short' vertical pilaster strip, indicating the probability of the church being of the typical English Carolingian style.

Other fragments of interest were: a holy water basin of stone, one side straight, the other $\frac{3}{4}$-round; two fragments of an ordinary mid-wall slab having round the outside of the opening a half-round roll, one piece of which retained the holes for the metal fastenings of its window shutter;[1] part of the end of an ornamented perforated mid-wall light slab, similar to those remaining in the upper lights at Barnack and the only other specimen (1894) known in England. Some of the string courses showed traces of the fire of 1116, and one tile badly burnt was found *in situ* in the south transept floor. Some fragments of tiles with ornament in relief were found below the south-east angle of the south transept.

STOWE-NINE-CHURCHES

ST. MICHAEL'S CHURCH.[2] The Mercian Kings had a residence at Weedon, two miles from Stowe, and St. Werburg founded a nunnery here *c.* A.D. 680. St. Alnot, bailiff to St. Werburg, lived later as a hermit in a cell near Stowe church until he was killed by robbers. His remains (relics) were at one time in the church. Saxon remains would therefore be expected at Stowe, but only the tower is of the Saxon period. Baldwin Brown dates it to 950–1000 or perhaps to the time of Canute, 1017–35. The rest of the church is thirteenth century and later.

The tower (I) is approximately 16 feet square, rough cast on the exterior and plastered on the inside. J. Romilly Allen writes that there is long and short work at the quoins. Brereton states that there is no long and short work at the quoins. If there

---

[1] Drawings are given by J. T. Irvine, (d).
[2] J. Romilly Allen; R. P. Brereton, (a) and (b); C. A. R. Radford, (a).

(I) *Plate* 104.

is it is hidden by the plastering. The tower is in two stages separated by a string course of square section. The later belfry windows cut through the string course. The two intermediate bands, one of which passes across the western middle window, are modern iron strengthening bands. The lower stage takes up about four-fifths of the total height. The short upper stage, perhaps of later date, has narrow pilaster strips of considerable projection on its east and west faces. There is a blocked-up western opening in the lower stage with plain jambs and square head, curiously narrow—2 feet—and about 6 feet high.

Built into the exterior north-west corner is a carved stone about 2 feet long, one side 15 inches the other tapering from 15 to 13 inches, probably part of a cross-shaft. One face is panelled, with (probably cabled) half round border, the panel being filled with interlacing-pattern. The other side is too worn to show whether panelled or not; the carving contains circles and what might be a vine scroll. Radford considers this stone to be hardly later than the eighth century.

There are two windows on the west face of the tower, the upper one round headed and double splayed, the lower single splayed with flat lintel (renewed).

The tower arch (I) opening into the nave is characteristically Saxon but rather small: 7 ft. 3 ins. by 3 ft. 7 ins. The wall is 2 ft. 8 ins. to 2 ft. 11 ins. thick. The jambs and voussoirs appear to be through-stones, so far as the whitewash permits them to be seen. The imposts are flat square slabs, cut away on the soffit sides flush with the jambs and the stones of the springing, which is *not* set back from the jamb faces. The imposts, about 5 inches thick, are returned on the east face so as to serve as imposts also for the flanking vertical pilaster strips. These strips are of square section, 4½ inches wide, and are now cut away flush with the wall except for a few inches at base and top. Above the returned imposts is a square-sectioned hood mould round the head of the arch, 4½ inches wide and 14 to 18 inches from the soffit edge of the arch. As is usual the west face of the arch has neither hood mould nor pilaster strips.

(I) *Plate* 105.

NOTTINGHAMSHIRE

CARLTON-IN-LINDRICK

CHURCH OF ST. JOHN THE EVANGELIST AND ALL SAINTS.[1] Parts of the fine western tower and perhaps of the nave and chancel are eleventh century; Baldwin Brown dated them to the Overlap. The north and south aisles, the top (belfry) stage of the tower, and the north-west and south-west tower buttresses and south-west stair turret are fifteenth century.

The two lower stages of the tower (1), separated by a string course, are built of large variably sized rubble arranged above the string course in irregular herring-bone manner. There are no original openings in the tall lower stage on the exterior. In the second stage, also tall, the original belfry, were double openings of the usual type. They were formerly built up, perhaps when the fifteenth-century top belfry stage was added. They were later opened out to their original state. They have double-arched lintels; that is the upper and lower sides of the lintel have been cut to appropriate half-round shape. There are tall mid-wall columns, with simple bases but no capitals, which support long central imposts chamfered on the outer ends. The jambs are of slabs mainly on end with no long and short or upright and flat work. The jamb imposts are plain and chamfered on the soffit sides.

The tower quoins are largely hidden by the later corner buttresses. On the south-west what look like quoins, with small window openings in them, are visible to both north and east of the buttress. These are of similar material and workmanship to the buttress, of the fifteenth century, and form part of the stair turret of the same date; the openings light the turret.

Behind the north-east corner of the tower the old north-west nave quoins protrude at a lower level than those of the later nave quoins above; they are large, almost megalithic, arranged side-alternately. Similar quoins are visible at the north-east and south-east corners.

The tower arch (2) is a fine one. It is round-headed and has a soffit roll and a roll on the eastern but not on the western face. The eastern roll lies in a hollow round the face. Both rolls are continued down the face of the jambs as columns with bases and capitals. The capitals have square-edged abaci above, of one piece with the capital,

[1] G. Baldwin Brown; N. Pevsner (*f*); J. Stacye.

---

(1) *Plate* 106; (2) *Plate* 107.

and below may be said to have their faces chamfered to fit roughly the cabled necking. There is Jews' harp ornamentation[1] on the north capitals and on the south soffit roll capital; the south outer capital has been cut, later, to plain chamfered faces. There is a plain chamfered hood mould round the arch head supported on small cubical block corbels; it does not pass down the jambs. The west face of the tower arch is quite separate from the east face; the two have a straight joint between them. The western face is round-headed, of smaller through-stone voussoirs, jambs of plain stones on end supporting square imposts 8 inches thick, chamfered below. Both arches stand on one large square thin plinth or base. The arch is 6 ft. 8 ins. high to the tops of the capitals, which are tall—12 inches high with the necking. It is 6 ft. 9 ins. wide. The western, older, part of the arch is 1 foot thick, the eastern part 1 ft. 8 ins. The total thickness is that of the east–west dimension of the plinth, 2 ft. 8 ins.

[1] See below, pp. 300–2.

OXFORDSHIRE

Caversfield

St. Lawrence's Church.[1] Caversfield was formerly in a detached part of Buckinghamshire but was incorporated in Oxfordshire by Acts of Parliament of 1832 and 1844. Detached parts of counties or hundreds usually originated by reason of 'the connection between property and jurisdiction'. A powerful lord having an outlying estate or manor would transfer the attendance which the tenant owed to his local county or hundred court and attach it to his own court elsewhere. There is no village; the buildings in the parish are mainly farms.

In Late Saxon times the manor was held by Edward, a man of Earl Tostig, brother of King Harold, but in 1086 it belonged to William de Warenne.

Only the ground stage of the tower is certainly pre-Conquest, probably post-950. The second stage may be later though still perhaps Saxon. The belfry was rebuilt or added in the early thirteenth century. It is surmounted by a saddleback roof gabled east–west. The nave is largely thirteenth century, the rest of the church is thirteenth century or later, including modern aisles.

The tower (I) is built of small limestone rubble. The quoins are upright and flat slabs, side-alternate. A slight set-off marks the work of the two upper stages. The tower is 11 ft. 2 ins. deep (east–west) by 10 ft. 6 ins. wide (north–south).

The ground stage has two original windows (2) in the north and south walls. They are roughly round-headed, centrally placed and have wide double-splays. The aperture in each is c. 6 inches wide by 14 inches high. The actual apertures are cut from single slabs of tufa-like stone. The internal splay is 2 ft. 4 ins. wide by 3 ft. 10 ins. high; heads, jambs and sills are splayed. The external dimensions are similar. The radiations of the stones of the heads interrupt the coursing of the rubble for some distance around. These are good examples of primitive Saxon windows with no special stone dressings. The jambs, of selected thin slabs, are laid in mortar up to the springing of the arch. Then they converge in voussoir fashion with their bedding planes perpendicular to the thrust line of the arch. This leaves a V-shaped gap at the crown which is filled with one vertical slab, in the position of a keystone, on either

[1] G. Baldwin Brown; E. D. C. Jackson and E. G. M. Fletcher (b); V.C.H, *Bucks*, IV.

(I) *Plate* 109; (2) *Plate* 110.

side of which are two shorter slabs sloping in herring-bone fashion. The south window is plastered.

The west window of the tower in the second stage, now the ringing chamber, is entirely modern externally but one or two original stones remain in the internal jambs of perhaps the thirteenth century. The thirteenth-century belfry is lighted on the east and west only by tall lancet windows having modern external stone work.

The tower arch is a modern restoration but probably represents a late twelfth-century enlargement of the original opening. It has square jambs, chamfered imposts, arch head plain and slightly pointed and a chamfered hood mould.

The nave arcades are early thirteenth century but the walls above are only 2 ft. 1 in. thick and may be the original pre-Conquest walls or perhaps, less probably, built on original foundations to the original thickness.

LANGFORD

ST. MATTHEW'S CHURCH.[1] Baldwin Brown dated this church to post-1040.

The tower is central (1), between nave and chancel. As there are no transepts or wings, it is axial. It is rectangular in plan with its longer axis east–west. Its internal dimensions are *c.* 13 ft. 8 ins. by 12 ft. 3½ ins. Externally, as measured from the east face of the east arch plinth to the west face of the west arch plinth, it is *c.* 21 feet giving an average wall thickness of 3 ft. 8 ins.

The tower is built of flattish rubble and was plastered. It has two string courses separating the three stages, and a three-membered plinth standing *c.* 18 inches above the present ground level with the two lower members chamfered. The top, or belfry, stage is recessed. The lower quoins are of selected flat rubble slabs. The upper ones are of dressed small stone work not unlike Norman work and suggesting a later date than those below. Paintin wrote that they were renewed in the fourteenth or fifteenth century. There are pilaster strips (2) in the centre of the north and south faces of the two lower stages, 12½ inches wide and of 2 inches projection. They stand on one-stepped bases on the plinth and meet the first string course with a three-stepped impost. They continue above from one-stepped bases on the first string to end with two-stepped imposts beneath the much worn second string course. These pilasters are of genuine long and short work (not upright and flat), very regular below but higher up the longs are of variable length; in places two or three shorts are used in place of one long. There are other pilaster strips embracing the corners of the walls of the two upper stages like narrow early Norman clasping buttresses. They are not

[1] G. Baldwin Brown; H. Paintin.

---

(1) *Plate* 112; (2) *Plate* 113.

of long and short but of small-stone ashlar work. They are too thin to have much buttressing effect. They might suggest a possible post-Conquest date. Paintin however said they were rebuilt in the late eighteenth century. At the same time a considerable part of the work above the upper string course was renewed, though some of the figures in the corbel table were retained. The present unattractive roof was put on then and may not have been intended to be permanent. It may have been the intention to increase the height of the tower or perhaps to add a spire.

In the south wall, about on a level with the sundial and on either side of it, are two very narrow windows (1) with very wide double-splaying. The key-hole apertures are cut from thin slabs fitted into the central, narrowest part of the openings. There were two similar ones in the north wall; the east one of this pair has been blocked by the later square stair turret built against the north-east angle of the tower. The west splay of the jamb and head are plainly visible within the turret.

In the south wall, too, just above the first string course, is a panel, wider than the pilaster but part of it, carved in low flat relief. It has two human figures with legs and feet in profile but with bodies and legs shown frontally; the knees are bent and heels raised in characteristic Saxon manner giving the figures a dancing attitude suggesting rapid forward motion. Their arms are raised above their heads and support what was once a sundial but is now so badly worn that it is almost unrecognizable as such.

The belfry stage windows (2) are not typically Saxon and are suggestive of a late date. They are almost Romanesque in appearance. In each wall is a pair of large round-headed openings. There are half-round soffit rolls running up the jambs and round the heads, and similar ones up the outer faces of the jambs and arch heads, the one down the centre face being common to both openings. There are no imposts or capitals but in place of capitals are two small half-round mouldings at 'capital' distance apart which extend across the jamb faces and soffits as far as the soffit rolls where they end. There appears to be palmette ornament in low relief between these bands, and above the centre one is a larger palmette. These openings are set back some inches behind the outer wall face so that the outer faces of the half-round pilasters are flush with the outer wall surface.

The belfry stage, like that below, has clasping corner pilaster strips ending above, below the third string course, in a two-stepped pattern. Above this string are two or three feet of ashlar walling capped by a corbel table with corbels of human and animal heads, and an excessively flat low-gabled roof with ridge running east–west.

Both nave and chancel are very high and steeply gabled, the chancel being higher than the nave. The chancel walls look original, being of similar fabric to the tower. Two string courses encircle the chancel. It was restored in 1864. The present choir roof is the successor of two earlier and lower ones, the marks of which Paintin stated

(1) *Plate* 113; (2) *Plate* 112.

were visible on the east wall of the tower; if so they are now hidden by plaster. The nave is later. Both nave and chancel are wider than the tower. The relative narrowness of the tower and its central position make it something of an obstruction between nave and chancel. Under present conditions the nave has its own altar immediately to the west of the tower west arch.

The tower has eastern and western arches (1), the east arch being the larger and finer. The east arch is 5 ft. 9½ ins. wide between the lower plinths and nearly 12 feet high to the lower face of the imposts. The plinths, representing the thickness of the east wall, are 4 ft. 0½ in. wide east–west and the lower members project from the walls 3 ft. 3½ ins. on the south and 3 ft. 2½ ins. from the north. The arch faces project from the walls 10 inches on the north and 9 inches on the south, so the arch behind the inner order and roll moulding (i.e. the outer order) would be 10 ft. 8½ ins. wide. The plinths are of two members, the lower being 18 inches high and the upper one 10 inches. On the soffits and recessed west face of the inner order, but not on the east face, which is not recessed (the arch being of two orders on the west and of one order on the east), are large half-round shafts running up to meet the impost-capitals and continuing above round the arch head. Such face and soffit rolls or half-columns are a late development found in some Late Saxon and Saxo-Norman Overlap churches. A still later development with shafts on both east and west faces with soffit rolls in between is to be seen at Wittering (Northants) and Clayton (Sussex). The capitals are of curious and complex design (2). The upper part is a quirked abacus the lower face of which below the quirk is slightly rounded; below is the capital proper the face of which is of two almost straight-profiled halves meeting at an arris round the capital about a third of the height below the top of the capital. Below is a plain thin necking. The capital is similar to one at St. Peter-at-Gowts, Lincoln (Fig. 28). The bases (3) are also of unusual design, like two truncated cones placed one above the other, similar to those at Broughton-by-Brigg (Lincs), (Fig. 21).

The west arch is slightly smaller and plainer. It is square-cut and of one single order with no face shafts or soffit rolls. It stands on a two-membered plinth, the lower, chamfered, member being 16 inches high, the upper one, unchamfered, 9 inches high. Round the west, but not the east, face of the arch is square-edged flat strip-work which passes down on both sides to north and south of the jambs. It is 8 inches wide and of about 1 inch projection from the wall face below the imposts but rather more, 3 or 4 inches, above the imposts. The plinths project slightly less from the walls than the east arch plinths and are 9 inches thinner east–west. Between the plinths the arch is 5 ft. 11½ ins. wide and *c.* 10 ft. 6 ins. high to the under sides of the plain imposts.

In the west wall of the second stage of the tower, above the western arch and

---

(1) *Plates* 115, 116; (2) *Plate* 117; (3) *Plate* 118.

visible from the interior, is a large rectangular opening, 2 ft. 10 ins. wide and *c*. 6 feet high. The jambs are of upright and flat slabs (from below: flat-short upright-flat-long upright-lintel). The interior ends of the bottom flats show the same step pattern as the outside pilasters. This floor is reached by spiral stairs within a later, probably thirteenth century, north-east stair turret. In the turret are three rectangular windows two of which have widely single-splayed jambs; the sills and lintels are not splayed. The turret has a saddle-back roof and, rather unusually, two entrances, one from the inner north-east corner of the choir and the other from outside the church. Access to the belfry is by ladder from the second stage.

The north wall of the nave began to bulge outwards owing to bad surface drainage. Two very fine flying buttresses were erected against it in 1574 to prevent further spreading.

Built into the east and south walls of the later south porch are two very fine roods (1), moved from elsewhere. They have been discussed by T. D. Kendrick and by D. Talbot Rice.

North Leigh

St. Mary's Church. The tower (2) only is Saxon, probably early eleventh century. Baldwin Brown dated it to post-1040. It has no string course, except a later one deeply hollow-chamfered below the later embattled parapet. It is built of coursed rubble. The lower quoins are of selected rubble slabs; the upper ones, above aisle roof level, are of small stone work. There is no long and short or upright and flat work anywhere. The wall thickness at the south arch, now within the church, is *c*. 3 feet.

On the west and east walls are marks of the steep gable-heads of the old higher nave on the west, not now existing, and chancel on the east, now replaced by the much lower Norman Transitional nave. Just below the apex of these marks on the west face are parts of the jambs of dressed stones of a blocked window; no head or sill is visible.

In the second stage of the tower there are two round-headed windows, one in each of the north and south walls. They have plain-dressed jambs and double-arched lintels above which are relieving arches in the masonry of selected flat wall slabs.

On the ground stage in the west wall is a two-light pointed fourteenth-century window. Around this are the stones of a built-up very wide arch, the former western tower arch leading to the former nave. The head is of thinnish rubble slabs and the jambs are of rubble interspersed with some dressed stones. There are the remains of long, *c*. 2 feet by 5 inches, plain imposts with plain chamfered lower edges; the

---

(1) *Plate* 114; (2) *Plate* 111.

south one is now cut back to the wall surface. There were small pent houses, one on the north end of the west wall remaining, below the marks of the old roofs. These were to protect the ends of two large tie-beams from the weather, and are presumably later.

At about the middle of the south wall is a large circular chamfered stone frame with its centre filled in and plastered. It is not known whether this is a blocked circular window or a later inserted plaque.

There are very large pointed north, south and east tower arches, all now within the church. The north and south ones are thirteenth century and the east one later and larger. In the tower wall above the south arch are the remains of a round-headed arch, probably part of an original window; the plaster has been cut away to show it.

In the top stage of the tower are the usual two-light belfry openings in all four walls. The double heads are slightly chamfered and are enclosed under a single relieving arch in the masonry made of selected rubble slabs. The mid-wall shafts support long projecting central imposts which hold up the arch heads above. The shafts have flat cushion capitals and moulded neckings. The jambs are of dressed stones with square thin slab imposts and thin sills.

The present short nave with north and south arcades of only two arches each are Transitional Norman of about the end of the twelfth century. The aisles are later and extend westwards as far as the west wall of the tower which their returning west walls meet with straight joints.

There are no indications or historical records of transepts or wings. The tower between the old chancel (now replaced by the Transitional nave) and old nave, long since pulled down, was presumably axial.

OXFORD

THE CHURCH OF ST. MICHAEL at the North Gate.[1] The tower only is pre-Conquest. It is certainly the oldest building now standing in the city. The somewhat similar castle tower on a mound near the station is post-Conquest and is reputed to have been built by Robert D'Oyli, the Conqueror's Lord of Oxford, *c.* 1071. The ancient city wall, or what is left of it, is thirteenth century. It was 9 feet thick and a section of it ran south of St. Michael's tower along the site of the present south aisle. The north gateway, called Bocardo, was built laterally against the tower blocking the west doorway. At a later date a section of the city wall only 2 feet thick was built a few feet to the north of the tower and joined the Bocardo gate as a northern extension to it. The Bocardo gate of the city was therefore very deep, the outer gateway being

[1] G. Baldwin Brown; R. R. Martin; R.C.H.M., *City of Oxford.*

well to the north and the inner gateway to the south of St. Michael's tower. There is no evidence that the tower played any part in the defence of the city after the city wall was built, though it is obviously well placed to do so. But there were earlier defences which it is believed were an earthen rampart and ditch and palisade partly bridging the northern gap between the various rivers and streams which almost surrounded Oxford on the east, west and south in early times. The main entrances to it were by ford on the south and by road from the north, and St. Michael's was well placed to play a defensive part. Foundations were discovered in 1904 on the other side of the road, to the west, when the old Northgate tavern was rebuilt. It has been suggested that these were of another early tower which, with St. Michael's, may have been part of a defensive system. This however is largely conjecture.

Why the short stretch of wall to the south of the tower was taken down and re-built in so flimsy a manner to the north is not known. It has been suggested that the original church was not attached to the tower but was on a nearby site (which is understandable if the tower was built originally as a watch or defensive tower), and that in more peaceful times it was moved and rebuilt against the tower on the site previously occupied by a stretch of city wall.

The church is mentioned in Domesday Book, one of five Oxford churches mentioned there. The tower (1) was dated by Baldwin Brown and by R.C.H.M. to the first half of the eleventh century. It is an attractive well-proportioned tower, well built but rather primitive in appearance on account of an almost complete lack of ornament: no string courses, no ornamental finish to the top, no visible roof. An embattled parapet of *c.* 1500 was replaced in 1873 by the present plain parapet, presumably to restore it to its original form, although what this was is not really known. The tower is relatively tall and slender; it is built of rubble. The south-west and south-east quoins are of selected rubble slabs; those on the south-west lower third have been renewed with well dressed stones. The north-west and north-east quoins are of large upright and flat slabs, some up to 3 ft. 6 ins. long. They do not project from the wall surface to allow for plastering and there is no evidence of the walls having been plastered. There is no plinth. What appears at first sight to be a plinth along the base of the west wall and returned a foot or two along the north wall, but not along the south, is a modern 2-to-3 inch thick wall facing put up presumably as the bottom courses of rubble showed signs of wear, as those on the north wall do. This facing cuts across the lower part of the blocked western doorway, which a plinth would not do.

The tower is almost square, 12 feet by 12 ft. 9 ins. on the interior. The walls are *c.* 4 feet thick at ground level and taper internally to 3 feet at the top. It is of four

---

(1) *Plate* 123.

stages internally and as indicated on the exterior by the distribution of the openings, but with no exterior string courses or set-offs. There is no exterior batter.

The Ground Stage. In the west wall is a former doorway, placed a little to the north of central, built up with rubble in 1718. Unlike the other openings it had jambs of large stone blocks arranged in roughly flat-upright-flat manner, the two flats consisting of very large cubical blocks. The round head was of rubble. It was *c.* 2 ft. 10 ins. wide and *c.* 6 feet high to the 'crown' of the arch. This doorway indicates that the tower was older than the city wall as the Bocardo gate of the wall was built against it. In the north wall is a round-headed window similar to those above. It is double-splayed, with rubble jambs and a thin stone sill.

The Second Stage. In the north wall is a window similar to the one below but taller. The round head is of flat rubble slabs which slope towards a point above that from which the head would normally be struck; this left a V-shaped gap at the crown which was filled with three slabs shorter than the others. There is a similar window in the west wall. There are no openings in the south wall in either of the two lower stages.

The Third Stage. In each wall is an original double-light opening with mid-wall bulging baluster shafts supporting long central imposts. The shafts have central half-round bands between two deep depressions. They have crudely cut semi-bulbous bases but no capitals. The heads and jambs are of rubble. The central and jamb imposts have quirks with hollow chamfers below. These openings were walled up in early times and were opened out in 1875. In the north wall of this stage, just below the double opening, is an original large round-headed doorway. Its head and jambs are of rubble, but it has imposts which are quirked and hollow chamfered. This doorway is of great interest. It could not have led to an inter-roof space or chamber, being in a north wall. Conceivably it could have led to a northern adjunct, as similar openings may have done at Deerhurst, Warblington and Netheravon, though nothing is known of any such adjunct at Oxford. Or, it may have been an access to the tower as a refuge in time of stress. Against this is its height above ground, too great to be bridged by a ladder. Also, towers were of little use as refuges against fire except when the ground stage was vaulted. It has been suggested that this doorway may have opened to a wooden platform across the narrow gap between the tower and the later piece of city wall to the north, so that the wall could be manned from the tower. This however could not have been the original intention for the doorway is older than the city wall; there is no indication that it is not contemporary with the tower.

In the fourth or belfry stage, in the north, west and south walls, are exactly similar double openings to those in the third stage. In all the imposts are modern renewals. In the east wall of the belfry is a modern rectangular opening and there is no indication in the exterior walling of any earlier opening in this position. Two such ranges of double belfry-like openings, one above the other, while uncommon are found elsewhere, as at Bardsey (Yorkshire, West Riding).

The tower arch is fifteenth century. This arch is presumably much wider than the original opening, which may have been either a tall narrow arch or a mere doorway, for it caused weaknesses in the tower which had to be remedied by north-east and south-east buttresses put up in 1908.

RUTLAND

Market Overton

ST. PETER AND ST. PAUL'S CHURCH.[1] This church stands in the south-west corner of the rectangular site of a Roman camp. All that remains of a pre-Conquest church is a fine tower arch with adjacent walling. The tower was rebuilt, probably in the thirteenth century and remodelled in the fourteenth, on foundations of an earlier structure—either porch or tower, though the fine arch suggests a tower. Three pre-Conquest carved stones are built into the tower wall near the base. One, in the north wall near the north-west corner, is 3 feet by 8 inches, is panelled and has plaitwork ornament; a second, in the south wall, is *c.* 4 feet by 10 inches wide tapering to 8 inches, has scroll work and is presumably a portion of a cross shaft; a third stone, in the west wall, is *c.* 1 ft. 8 ins. long by 6 inches and has scroll work on it. There are also three loose stones decorated with reed and hollow work (1), the reedings and hollows being *c.* $\frac{1}{2}$ an inch wide, similar to that on the double gable-headed opening in Deerhurst tower.[2] Two long stones, resembling baluster shafts (2), reputed to have come from the early belfry, are now placed upright at the ends of the church-yard stile. These also suggest the likelihood of an early tower.

Baldwin Brown dated the tower arch vaguely as post-950; V.C.H. as late tenth or early eleventh century. It has not the relatively very tall and narrow proportions of so many early Anglo-Saxon tower arches, which is consistent with the later dating. It is 9 ft. 6 ins. high to the underside of the imposts and 6 ft. 8 ins. wide. The jambs are 2 ft. 8 ins. thick which is the thickness of the adjacent walling. It stands on a boldly projecting square-cut plinth, 9 inches high and projecting 6 inches on the soffits and 4 to 9 inches on the east. The jambs are of the Escomb type, upright and flat with three uprights and three flats to each jamb, all through-stones. Rather unusually the uprights are of varying lengths, diminishing upwards. Thus, on the south the uprights are 3 ft. 7 ins. and 2 ft. 5 ins. and on the north they are 4 ft. 5$\frac{1}{2}$ ins. and 1 ft. 4 ins. respectively. In each jamb the top upright is very short being merely a square-ended through-stone. The flats do not run very far into the walls, like those at Wittering (Northants). The imposts are of two flat superimposed stones, with their soffit faces sloping downwards as in the well-known chancel arch at Wittering. They are also very slightly chamfered on the east and west faces. They run into the walls only a little further than the jamb flats. The arch head is of small well-cut and very regular voussoirs, all through-stones.

[1] G. Baldwin Brown; V.C.H., *Rutland*, II. [2] See above, p. 185.

(1) *Plate* 120; (2) *Plate* 119.

SHROPSHIRE

STANTON LACY

ST. PETER'S CHURCH.[1] This is a well proportioned cruciform church though, unlike Stow (Lincs), Norton (Co. Durham) and St. Mary in Castro, Dover, it is not strictly transeptal. The north transept is relatively lofty but narrow, much narrower than the nave. The arch to it, like the other three crossing arches, is later—probably early fourteenth century—so it is not known whether the original entrance to the transept was a narrow arch or doorway. The south transept and the central tower are fourteenth century and it is not known whether the Saxon church had either a tower or south transept; there are no monumental indications of either. If there was originally a tower it may have been either wholly or, as at Breamore (Hants), partly of timber. There may have been no south transept, just as at Wootton Wawen (Warwickshire) there was no north transept. It seems reasonable to regard this church not as transeptal but as a winged church like Breamore, the north so-called transept being a porticus.

Only the north wing and the nave walls are Anglo-Saxon, dated by Baldwin Brown to the first half of the eleventh century (1000–40); Pevsner, more cautiously, writes that it 'is no doubt the C 11'. The rest is mainly fourteenth century. The Saxon walls (1) are of well-fitted polygonal stones with quoins of fairly large slabs, mainly side-alternate. The south wall of the nave is 2 ft. 11 ins. thick.

In the north wall of the north transept are the remains of a blocked narrow doorway; above are the marks of a round-headed single-splayed window. Single splaying was not common south of the Humber in the eleventh century, so the window may be Norman. The window higher up in the gable is not Anglo-Saxon. The other windows are either later insertions or have been altered.

In the nave there is no indication of a western doorway. There is however a blocked but otherwise well-preserved doorway (2) near the west end of the north wall. It has a round head of real, well-cut, very regular voussoirs, almost Norman-looking, jambs of about equal-sized blocks, some of which are through-stones, and rather square thin imposts chamfered below. It has a very low plain-chamfered plinth. There is typical Anglo-Saxon strip-work on the outer sides of the jambs passing outside but in contact with the imposts and round the head in contact with the voussoirs. The head part, but not the verticals, is quirked and chamfered above.

[1] Anon. J. L. P.; G. Baldwin Brown; N. Pevsner, (g).

---

(1) *Plate* 121; (2) *Plate* 122.

Above and round the head the relatively long walling blocks are arranged radially, like imitation voussoirs, as though intended to act as a relieving arch. There are genuine long and short pilaster strips up the walls of the nave and transept resting on small cubical block corbels just above ground level; there is no plinth to nave or transept. The strips are 5 inches wide and of similar projection. None of them on the nave extends further than half-way up the walls. One pilaster however on the nave north wall starts well above the nave north doorway. It rests on a flat wide corbel decorated below with a row of pellets. Between this and the arch head of the door below is a flat equal-armed cross cut in relief from a single stone. On the transept the pilasters extend higher, as far as the roof; one has a very short cross piece, at about three-quarters of the height, which might be part of a former string course.

WARWICKSHIRE

Wootton Wawen

St. Peter's Church.[1] The lower three stages of the central tower are Anglo-Saxon, dated by Baldwin Brown and by V.C.H. to the first half of the eleventh century. The nave was rebuilt and widened in the twelfth century. The eastern nave wall was returned and met the north and south ends of the tower west wall with straight joints. The present eastern Lady Chapel is later, perhaps mid- or late thirteenth century, and its walls too form straight joints at the north and south ends of the tower east wall. The tower (I) is rather isolated, wedged in as it were between the wider nave and Lady Chapel and with a later large south-eastern chapel overlapping its south face. Originally it was undoubtedly a central tower between narrow nave and chancel, with a southern wing or porticus, and a northern doorway leading to something or somewhere other than a porticus.

There is much plaster on the interior and exterior walls but sufficient was removed during repairs in 1906 to expose the nature of the masonry. It is of very rough small rubble with a few larger but undressed stones here and there. The quoins are of upright and flat work, plainly visible in the nave on the interior east wall (2) (i.e. the former exterior west wall of the tower) to the south of the tower arch where some plaster has been removed to show the tower quoins and straight joint between tower and nave. Parts of the north-east and south-east quoins are also visible.

The fourth or belfry stage is fifteenth century.

The tower is 14 ft. 6 ins. square on the interior and the walls are 2 ft. 3 ins. thick. The nave walls are 2 ft. 10 ins. thick which confirms the later date of the nave: in no Saxon church would the nave walls be thicker than those of the tower.

The ground storey is now used as the chancel, the altar being in front of the tower eastern opening; its floor has been raised by two steps, about one foot, above that of the nave. The eastern part of the church, which replaced the original chancel, is used as a separate Lady Chapel with its own altar.

In the ground storey there are round-headed openings in all four walls. The north one (3) has a flat lintel with a thin (c. 4 to 5 inches) round head of voussoirs above, as in arches at Miserdon, Ampney Crucis and Winston (all in Glos) where however

[1] G. Baldwin Brown; V.C.H., *Warwickshire*, III.

(I) *Plate* 124; (2) *Plate* 127; (3) *Plate* 125.

the tympana are filled with rubble. At Wootton the tympanum has, probably modern, glass. The upper edge of the lintel between the arch head springings is plain chamfered (Fig. 17), also as at Winston and Ampney Crucis, but not Miserdon which is of more primitive construction. These details are common to a number of Cotswold churches, but a peculiarity of Wootton not shared by the churches mentioned (though it occurs elsewhere) is that the two bottom arch stones at the springing are not voussoirs, as are those above, but are about two feet long and cut on both lower and upper sides to arch shape (Fig. 17). All are through-stones as far as the blocking. The springing is set back about an inch behind the jamb face; the arch head face is flush with and rests on the imposts. The jambs are of the Escomb type: upright-flat-upright-flat-upright through-stones as far as the blocking. Above the

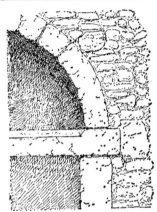

Fig. 17. Wootton Wawen Church, Arch detail

top uprights are rough slab imposts running a considerable distance into the walls and projecting two to three inches, east–west, from the jamb soffits and wall face. This arch is blocked on the exterior, where the jambs are rather different from those within: each consists of three large rough stones.

The south arch (1) is similar to the north except that the jambs are of two uprights and two flats, the upper flat being immediately below the imposts.

The eastern or chancel arch (2) has jambs of three uprights and two flats, the top uprights being under the imposts. The head is of voussoirs, mostly through-stones, and, very unusual in Saxon churches, a genuine keystone is on the eastern face, though not on the west; it projects $1\frac{1}{2}$ inches from the wall face. There is no strip-work on the east face. On the west face there is strip-work round the head only ending at the imposts.

The western arch is the biggest (3). The voussoirs are not through-stones and are of varying and irregular lengths. The imposts, of large blocks, are similar to those of

(1) *Plate* 126; (2) *Plate* 128; (3) *Plate* 127.

the other three arches. The jambs below differ somewhat from each other. The south jamb has two uprights and two flats, one flat being immediately below the impost; the north jamb has one upright with one flat above, and above that two uprights. On the east face of the south jamb is a shallow rebate, perhaps not original, for a door.

The arches are of different sizes. The dimensions are:

	width	height to imposts	height to crown of arch
North arch	4 ft. 1 in.	6 feet.	8 ft. 9 ins.
South arch	4 ft. 2½ ins.	6 feet	8 ft. 10 ins.
East arch	4 ft. 8 ins.	7 ft. 3 ins.	11 ft. 3 ins.
West arch	6 ft. 9½ ins.	9 ft. 4 ins.	14 ft. 3 ins.

Access to the upper storey of the tower is provided by ladders of solid balks from an opening in the west end of the tower north wall, covered by a modern outbuilding.

The second stage has a small narrow opening (1) in the north wall with plastered internal splay and an elliptical arch head on the interior; the exterior is modern brick, probably only crude repair work. The other openings, a window and a doorway, are later.

The third stage has a window (1) in each wall with round or segmental heads and rough jambs. Three are built up flush with the walls though their outlines are visible on the exterior. The eastern window is blocked with a thin filling of bricks flush with the exterior wall face; on the interior the recess shows the rough rubble splayings. These windows may be pre-Conquest.

On the exterior east face of the tower are marks of the gabled roof of the former higher chancel.

---

(1) *Plate* 124.

Part III

LINCOLNSHIRE

HISTORICAL INTRODUCTION

Lincolnshire, though now a well-defined county, was less well defined in Anglo-Saxon times. The northern part between the Humber and the river Witham (on which stands Lincoln city) was known as Lindsey, as indeed for administrative purposes this part of the county is still called. It was colonized by Anglian tribes working south from the Humber, peoples belonging to the same groups as those who had penetrated northwards to Deira and Bernicia, and the later ones who worked south-west and joined up with others from the Wash to form North Mercia. The date of the Lindsey settlements is not known, but might be as early as the second half of the fifth century. The early history of Lindsey is obscure and its kings no more than names. It was a bone of contention, being too small to stand permanently alone, between Northumbria and Mercia, but eventually became a permanent appendage to Mercia.

Christianity was introduced into Lindsey by Paulinus (c. 627) who built a stone church at Lincoln. Little or nothing is known about its ecclesiastical history during the next half-century until in 677 Archbishop Theodore detached Lindsey from the huge diocese of Lichfield and made it a separate diocese of Lindsey with its cathedral at Sidnacester. The site of Sidnacester is not known.[1] The see apparently ended at the Danish invasions and was not revived until the formation of the Norman diocese and cathedral at Lincoln.

The southern part of Lincolnshire, now known as Kesteven and Holland, belonged then as it does today to the Fenland country. It was colonized from the Wash by Anglian tribes allied to those who penetrated west to form North Mercia and to those who moved south-west to form Middle Anglia. It originally formed part of the Middle Anglian Kingdom and was later absorbed into Greater Mercia with the rest of Middle Anglia, after which its association with Mercia was always close, especially ecclesiastically. Thus Guthlac, the founder of Crowland Abbey, was a member of the Mercian royal house and his church was consecrated by Headda, Bishop of Lichfield, between 700 and 706. Ecclesiastically it formed part of the Middle Anglian province. When Theodore in 677 split up the unwieldy see of Lichfield he made a separate see of Middle Anglia (including south Lincolnshire), which became permanently seated at Leicester in 737. This see also ceased to exist at the Danish invasions.

In the late ninth century Lindsey was colonized further by the soldiers of a Danish

[1] See E. M. Sympson.

245

army, and after Alfred's peace with Guthrun of 886 the whole county became part of the Danelaw. Culturally the area became more unified and to some degree separatist, at least until the re-conquest by Edward the Elder *c.* 918. The culture of Lindsey, as expressed in its sculpture and architecture developed along somewhat independent lines owing to its relative geographical isolation from its nearest English neighbours: Lindsey, the heart of the area, occupying about two-thirds of it, might almost have been an island. It was bounded on the north by the Humber, its main access from the sea, and on the east nominally by the sea with no navigable rivers but more effectively by a band of swamp and marsh widening southwards until it merged with the Fens. On the west there were extensive marshes, heaths and forests through part of which the river Trent, flowed forming a western boundary. The only easy access from the land side was the Roman road, Ermine Street, from Chichester via London to the North, which in Lincolnshire ran from Stamford through Lincoln to Scunthorpe and the Humber. This part of the road passed along the eastern lower side of the long strip of oolite, narrowing northwards, which runs from south to north through the county, still called 'The Cliff' locally. A chalky outcrop to the north-east forms the Lincolnshire Wolds.

Much Danish and Scandinavian influence can be seen in the great number of carved stones and fragments scattered throughout the county. Little is known about Lincolnshire churches prior to the eleventh century for, apart from Barton-on-Humber, Broughton-by-Brigg and Stow, where there are significant remains, no early churches remain. All have been rebuilt, some more than once throughout the centuries, leaving only bits and pieces here and there which indicate the existence of earlier buildings. There are thirty-eight towers built in the very last years of the pre-Conquest era or in some cases perhaps a little later.

GENERAL CHARACTERISTICS OF LINCOLNSHIRE TOWERS. Geographically, though not architecturally, the Lincolnshire towered churches may be divided into three groups. (1) A group of twenty-two strung out from south to north of the county on either side of the Cliff, some on the lower ground of the Cliff itself, others further east and west of it on flat land below the 100-foot level which in early days was marsh, fen or heath. Of these, nine are south of Lincoln, in Kesteven, that is in what was formerly part of the Middle Anglian part of the county, three are in Lincoln city, and ten north of Lincoln. (2) A group of eleven situated in or on the immediate outskirts of the Lincolnshire Wolds. (3) A small group of five rather close together on the low land to the west and south of Great Grimsby.

These thirty-eight churches are situated more specifically as follows:

Group 1, from south to north:

Thurlby, 2 miles S. of Bourne in the Fenland area, 5 miles NNW. of Market Deeping, and 7 miles NE. of Stamford.

Little Bytham, 5 miles W. by S. of Bourne.

Great Hale, rather far to the east, 1 mile S. of Heckington and 6 miles E. by S. of Sleaford.

Syston, 3 miles N. of Grantham.

Hough-on-the-Hill, *c.* 7 miles N. of Grantham and 9 miles W. of Sleaford.

Coleby, 7 miles S. of Lincoln.

Harmston, 6 miles S. of Lincoln.

Branston, 4 miles SE. of Lincoln.

Bracebridge, 2 miles S. of Lincoln.

Lincoln, three churches.

Stow, 6 miles SE. of Gainsborough and 9 miles NW. of Lincoln.

Marton, 5 miles S. by E. of Gainsborough and 3 miles W. of Stow.

Glentworth, 8 miles E. of Gainsborough and 4 miles E. of Heapham.

Heapham, 4 miles ESE. of Gainsborough.

Springthorpe, 4 miles E. of Gainsborough.

Corringham, 4 miles E. of Gainsborough and 1 mile N. of Springthorpe.

Harpswell, 7 miles E. of Gainsborough.

Broughton-by-Brigg, 3 miles NW. of Brigg and 5 miles SE. of Scunthorpe.

Winterton, 6 miles SW. of Barton-on-Humber.

Alkborough, 9 miles W. of Barton-on-Humber and 6 miles N. of Scunthorpe.

Group 2, the Wolds group:

Barton-on-Humber, *c.* 6 miles SW. of Hull.

Worlaby, 4 miles NNE. of Brigg.

Barnetby-le-Wold, 4 miles NE. of Brigg.

Irby-upon-Humber, *c.* 6 miles ENE. of Caistor and 7 miles SW. of Grimsby.

Swallow, 4 miles ENE. of Caistor and 8 miles SW. of Grimsby.

Cabourn, *c.* 2 miles ENE. of Caistor.

Caistor, 12 miles SW. of Grimsby.

Nettleton, 1 mile SW. of Caistor.

Cuxwold, 7 miles SE. of Caistor.

Rothwell, 2 miles SE. of Caistor.

Hainton, 5 miles SE. of Market Rasen and 9 miles WSW. of Louth.

Group 3, the Grimsby group:

Old Clee, 1 mile W. of Cleethorpes.

Laceby, 5 miles SW. of Grimsby.

Scartho, *c.* 3 miles SW. of Cleethorpes.

Holton-le-Clay, 4 miles SW. of Cleethorpes.

Waithe, 6 miles S. of Grimsby.

Lincolnshire

Of these thirty-eight towered churches thirteen have few features of particular interest or of controversial character and so, for reasons of space, are not discussed in detail. They are: Little Bytham, Coleby, Harmston, Heapham, Corringham, Harpswell, Worlaby, Barnetby-le-Wold, Irby-upon-Humber, Cuxwold, Hainton, Laceby, Holton-le-Clay.

Five Lincolnshire churches differ so markedly from the others that, though they may be regarded as allied in so far as they possess some characteristics common to the whole group, they are better considered as outside the group. These five are: Barton-on-Humber, a turriform church with a tower elaborately decorated with pilaster strips and blind arcading; Broughton-by-Brigg, which also may have been turriform and which differs architecturally from the others; Stow, a magnificent cruciform, genuinely transeptal church with central tower; Waithe, which has an axial tower in a central position; and Hough-on-the-Hill, which also has some peculiarities.

The main group of thirty-three churches—or church towers, for in most the tower is the only part remaining of pre-Conquest date—are so closely alike in type that a general description may usefully precede a detailed account of the individual buildings. The towers differ mainly in size and in dimensions and decoration of details, these differences however being important as throwing light on the difficult problem of dating the churches. There are many similar towers in other parts of the country so they are not peculiar to Lincolnshire. But they are so characteristic of the county and there are so few towers here not of the type that they are usually called 'Lincolnshire bell towers'. It is not known definitely whether they originated here and spread to other areas; on account of their late date this seems unlikely. They are all western bell towers. The walls are of rubble throughout, usually with no batter though occasionally a very slight narrowing upwards is found as at St. Peter-at-Gowts, Lincoln. The walls approach the Norman in thickness, varying between 2 ft. 6 ins. and 3 ft. 9 ins.; the east wall of Caistor tower is 5 ft. 9 ins., quite exceptional. There is usually a plain string course about three-quarters of the total height from the ground which serves as a set-off for the short, upper, often very slightly narrower belfry stage. The quoins of both towers and naves are normally of smallish oblong blocks laid with their broad faces arranged on alternate wall faces, i.e. in side-alternate arrangement, suggesting the common Anglo-Saxon 'upright and flat' work though the heights of the blocks are comparable. Only occasionally is true long and short or upright and flat work found in quoins; it occurs at the western angles of the nave of St. Peter-at-Gowts, Lincoln, at all four angles at Bracebridge nave, and in the north jamb of the western doorway and south-west nave quoin at Rothwell. At Alkborough and Winterton, neighbouring churches, small cubical blocks of limestone are used, reinforced in places by two blocks of equal size in juxtaposition which serve to bind the quoins into the two wall faces, like clasping quoins. In the

Caistor group large irregular roughly square stones are common in quoins; at Caistor itself very large blocks indeed, almost megalithic, are used in the nave north-west quoin.

The towers are almost square in plan; some measure no more than about ten or eleven feet along each axis. The very slightly longer axis lies usually east–west; in a few cases, as at Caistor and Nettleton, the breadth, i.e. the north–south axis, exceeds the length.

Window openings in the lower stages of towers are few, small and narrow, but tall compared with their width: loop windows of about $2\frac{1}{2}$ feet by 9 inches. The apertures often narrow upwards, though not always symmetrically; one jamb may slope more than the other. Nearly all have single internal splay; in Lindsey the only exception is the lower stage of Barton-on-Humber. Their heads are of arched lintels cut from large single blocks, not from thin slabs. The 'arch' heads are usually stilted; sometimes the stilting is exaggerated to the horseshoe type making the opening like a large keyhole, as at Clee. Window jambs are usually of two large blocks each; a similar block forms the sill, where there is a sill. They have no imposts. A Lincolnshire peculiarity is that behind the arched lintel block the inner splays are in some towers roofed with flat lintels, as in the window above the west doorway at Nettleton and the window of the ground stage at Rothwell. Gable-headed openings are rare; the only ones are in the earlier, lower part of Barton-on-Humber tower and a rather poor example in the rebuilt tower of Springthorpe.

The belfry windows are round-headed double openings with mid-wall straight shafts or columns which may have capitals, plain or decorated, and sometimes bases, and which support through-stone imposts to the double arch head above. The bulging baluster shaft is unknown in Lincolnshire except at Barton-on-Humber. The imposts may be plain or chamfered; they are never moulded. The jambs are roughly dressed and are flush with the wall face.

The tower ground stages have narrow round-headed western doorways with slightly projecting strip-work hood moulds, and imposts to jambs; and eastern arch-openings to the nave which are also round-headed, with plain jambs and heavy projecting imposts. Both eastern and western openings have genuine arch-heads of voussoirs.

Tower arches vary much in height and width, and particularly in ratio of height (to imposts) to width (between jambs). Thus Clee tower arch is 13 ft. 6 ins. high by 5 ft. 7 ins., while Winterton is 7 ft. 11 ins. high by 8 ft. 3 ins. wide. On the whole a low wide arch corresponds to a large tower area; thus at Clee the tower is 11 ft. 6 ins. square and at Winterton it is 15 ft. 6 ins. north–south by 14 feet east–west. In this connection it is interesting that the more Norman technique and details there are in the tower the greater the ratio of area to arch height and of arch width to height; the wider and lower the arch the thicker the tower walls. The most striking instance of this is at Caistor where the arch width exceeds the height by 8 inches and the east wall is 5 ft. 9 ins. thick, 2 feet thicker than any other tower wall in the area.

Typical Saxon dressings for arches and jambs are through-stones, for jambs large slabs equal in width to the thickness of the wall. In these Lincolnshire towers neither arch heads nor jambs show this through-stone technique. Thus the great tower arch jambs at Stow are lined with ashlar, two or three large slabs per course. This is common: of twenty-one tower arches of this period remaining today from twenty-five such towers (excluding Barton) in Lincoln and Lindsey, jamb faces are in courses of at least two stones each (as at St. Mary-le-Wigford, Lincoln, Swallow and Cabourn). In some cases there is rubble filling between jamb facing stones, as at Scartho, and in arch heads between outer and inner rings of voussoirs, as at Clee, Nettleton and Swallow. The only through-stone technique invariably used in these towers is in belfry window openings: the imposts of the mid-wall shafts and of the jambs of the openings they divide. Through-stone imposts occur sometimes in tower arches, but not commonly.

Slight recessing of arch heads, a proto-Norman feature, occurs often. At Brixworth (Northants), a very early church, the arch heads are of two concentric rings, one above or outside the other, with their faces flush with each other and with the wall face; i.e. there is no recessing. In the tower arches at Clee and Scartho, and on the west doorway at Clee there are two rings of voussoirs, the lower one being slightly recessed; the imposts however are not cut to shape. In the tower arch at Broughton is a further development: as at Clee and Scartho the imposts and jambs do not accord with the recessing of the arch head, but there are definite capitals below the imposts with neckings and bases; the details are rudely cut.

Capitals were introduced very late in Anglo-Saxon church architecture; some writers say a few years before the Conquest, others a few years after. Capitals therefore imply a very late date for any apparently pre-Conquest church where they occur. They were used first in mid-wall shafts as small oblong under-blocks to the through-stone imposts above. At Alkborough and Winterton these under-blocks have their narrower ends cut into rough elementary cushion shape. Real cushion capitals in this area were always used in any replacement or rebuilding, as at Cabourn, Springthorpe and Swallow; at Swallow the upper storey of the tower was entirely rebuilt in true Norman manner. At Scartho east belfry window the capital is corbelled out from the shaft below to the impost above, capital and impost block being a single piece, a real impost-capital. There are similar corbelled-out capitals elsewhere than in Lincolnshire: at Sompting (Sussex), Jarrow (Co. Durham), Bolam, (Northumberland). Crude foliage, sometimes in two rows, a Norman motif, is found on some mid-wall shaft capitals at St. Mary-le-Wigford and St. Peter-at-Gowts, Lincoln, and at Harpswell, Bracebridge, and Glentworth. Voluted corners to capitals, with the volutes sometimes incised or carved with spiral patterns, occur occasionally as at Glentworth and Great Hale. This is especially significant for the voluted capital is a very definite Norman form and basically unlike the comparatively rare Anglo-Saxon form of capital.

A very frequently occurring detail of Anglo-Saxon towers, rare in Lincolnshire, is an opening in the tower east wall, above the tower arch and well below the nave roof, and normally in the second stage of a three- or four-staged tower. It provided a good view of the nave interior from the tower and enabled a sacristan or other church official to keep watch on the church. In some cases it gave a means of access to the upper stage from the nave. Only three such openings are known certainly to occur in Lincolnshire, at Scartho, Thurlby and at Winterton.[1]

Most of the original dressed stones of jambs and arches show the typical Norman diagonal tooling, as at Alkborough and Nettleton. Anglo-Saxon tooling was a rather nondescript irregular scratching; none is known for certain to occur in Lindsey.

In Lincoln city and Lindsey there are 26 towers of the type discussed above, partial or entire, 13 with original belfry stages with mid-wall shafts, 4 rebuilt on the old lines, 22 with tower arches which are original or only slightly altered, and 14 with western doorways or traces of such still remaining.

There is no documentary evidence of the dates of these towers. Dates can only be inferred from close examination of architectural details, particularly the Norman details. On this basis it is not difficult to place some of the towers in chronological order. It is reasonable to accept a tower with carved voluted capitals as later than one with plain cushion capitals, and the latter as later than one with no capitals or with capitals of crude cushion shape. But an absolute dating of any particular church is not possible with certainty; and opinion is even divided as to whether they are pre- or post-Conquest. E. A. Freeman, in rhetorical rather than historical language, and with little evidence to offer, maintained that the two churches in Lincoln High Street—St. Peter-at-Gowts and St. Mary-le-Wigford—were being built by Saxon masons while Norman masons were building the great Cathedral a few hundred yards away up the hill. The Norman cathedral of Remigius was begun in 1072–3 and consecrated in 1092. Baldwin Brown, on rather better evidence, agreed with Freeman that these towers were post-Conquest and erected in the Saxo-Norman Overlap. He was perhaps the more inclined to this opinion as he thought the normanizing activities of Edward the Confessor, 1042–66, did not extend far from London. Hamilton Thompson, after a close study of this group of towers,[2] concluded that they were all built a few years before the Conquest and within comparatively few years of one another. Apart from the detailed evidence, the conclusion is inherently reasonable. Norman architectural influence did not begin in 1066. There

---

[1] See also below, p. 286.

[2] Op. cit., (c). His paper is the most closely reasoned and certainly the most rewarding of all studies of this group of churches. The above general account of these is based largely on this paper.

had always been close cultural ties between England and the Continent throughout the entire Anglo-Saxon period, and foreign architectural and artistic motifs were continually being adopted and adapted to Anglo-Saxon tastes. Romanesque architectural influence was indeed a continuous and continuing activity though the tempo of change might alter from time to time. Thus, prior to the cataclysmic changeover to Norman methods from 1066 on, Edward the Confessor had built the essentially Norman Westminster Abbey, begun 1045–50 and consecrated in 1065. Hamilton Thompson concluded that the age of transition towards Norman methods was earlier than this, about the second quarter of the eleventh century, say, 1025–50. Even earlier than this, *c.* 950–1000, there was an era of renewed building activity in some parts of the country, during which there were many cultural contacts with the Continent.

It is perhaps not important to know whether these towers are pre- or post-Conquest by a few years. What is important is to realize that they are essentially Anglo-Saxon towers with Norman details, and were built by Saxon masons with some considerable knowledge of Norman methods; they are not Norman towers in which are retained some Anglo-Saxon motifs. In view of the great number of masons required to build the eleventh and twelfth-century Norman cathedrals it is unlikely that any could be spared to build a group of fifty or sixty Lincolnshire bell towers (including those outside the county). That they were built by Saxon masons seems a conclusion difficult to avoid. The Norman cathedrals of the eleventh century and the grander ones of the twelfth, gripping the imagination as they do, should not blind us to the fact that Saxon masons did not cease to exist in 1066. They went on with their work, sometimes helping Norman master masons to build their churches, sometimes building or rebuilding their own, and acquiring increasing skill in adopting and adapting Norman methods and motifs. It is idle to speculate about what might have happened had there been no Conquest, though Clapham at least thought it was aesthetically a tragedy. But it is possible that as the Early Saxon methods of building developed into Late Saxon, so the Late Saxon might have continued to progress until it had developed into a definite Anglo-Saxon Romanesque. That something like this might have happened is suggested by the marked revival of Anglo-Saxon sculptural ideas and motifs which occurred in the early to middle twelfth century, as discussed by G. Zarnecki and by Lawrence Stone, a revival which was a main factor in the change from Early Norman to Late Norman or, as it might be better to call it, Late English Romanesque ornament.[1] It may be emphasized that though the history of Anglo-Norman architecture began in 1066, or perhaps in 1045–50 with the building of Westminster Abbey, Saxon architecture continued for some time after the Conquest, and that the Saxo-Norman Overlap belongs primarily to Anglo-Saxon architecture and not to Norman.

[1] See E. A. Fisher, op. cit.

Lincolnshire

Alkborough

St. John the Baptist Church. Only the tower (I) is pre-Conquest; Baldwin Brown dates it vaguely as post-1040. It is a very fine tower of massive proportions, looking less massive than it really is owing to the good workmanship and the slender proportions of its quoins and openings. It is of four stages separated by string courses; the top stage is very slightly recessed. The embattled parapet and corner pinnacles are later, probably fourteenth century. It has been stated that the top stage is also a later addition. Although the fabric of this stage appears a little lighter (different) in the plate, to the eye the walling appears to be closely similar to that of the lower stages, the only difference being that the quoin stones are longer. There has been a good deal of restoration work. It is significant that the original belfry was the second stage. The present belfry is the third stage, which has very tall apparently thirteenth-century double lights. The fourth stage has no openings, an unusual feature. Why was it built? It might be inferred that the third stage was added as a new belfry in the thirteenth century to the pattern of the stages below (except the windows) and that the fourth stage was added, perhaps later, to make a tower of very fine and imposing proportions. Without the top stage the tower would look rather squat, with the tall upper belfry windows reaching almost to the top string course.

The tower is built of flat rubble slabs. The quoins are of small cubical blocks of limestone reinforced in places by pairs of large blocks of equal size side by side which serve to bind the quoins into the walls, like clasping quoins. The lowest stage is nearly half the total height. The upper stages are low and increase slightly in height from the second to the fourth.

In the ground floor there are no openings in the north and south walls. In the west wall near the first string course is a narrow single-splayed window with roughly arched lintel; the jambs are of three flat slabs each with a small stone below. There is a western doorway, not now in use, almost hidden on the exterior by weeds and small bushes. It is unduly low on the exterior owing to rising ground-level. It has a round head of voussoirs with a wide strip-work hood mould chamfered below. The jambs are badly worn and of mixed face and side alternate arrangement. On the interior the opening is 6 ft. 6 ins. high to the imposts and *c.* 3 ft. 6 ins. wide between jambs.

The second stage, the original belfry, has the usual type of double openings, with mid-wall shafts, in north, south and west walls. The shafts have primitive capitals which are really no more than oblong underblocks to the central imposts and cut on

---

(I) *Plate* 129.

the outer faces only to rude cushion shape. The jambs are of slabs not unlike the quoins and rest on the string course. The heads are of voussoirs, and the chamfered jamb imposts project. The window in the south wall is partly blocked, and the clock covers the upper half. In the east wall is a wide rectangular window, higher up than those on the other walls and close to the upper string course. The projecting lintel is badly worn, and chamfered below. The lintel, sill and jambs are of four very large stones.

The third stage also has double-light windows, tall and slender and of late thirteenth-century type. The jambs are of six dressed slabs each, of equal heights, arranged face alternately. The central shafts are tall, thin and octagonal, with simple hollow-chamfered capitals below square abaci. The heads are of lancet type. The openings are not at identical levels: the sill of the south opening rests on the string course, that of the west one is a foot or so above.

The tower arch is tall with ashlar head of two rings of voussoirs with slight rubble filling between the rings. The jambs have two or three stones per course. The plinths are 9 inches high and project $3\frac{1}{2}$ inches. The imposts are returned for 18 inches along the walls. Plinths and imposts are of Roman moulded stones and have distinct classical profiles. The western face of the arch has been renewed. The jambs are 2 ft. $5\frac{1}{2}$ ins. thick, the arch 5 ft. $10\frac{1}{2}$ ins. wide between jambs and 5 ft. $3\frac{1}{2}$ ins. between plinths.

BARTON-ON-HUMBER

St. Peter's Church.[1] Whether this is the first or the third church on this site is not known. Ceadda, better known as St. Chad, founded a monastery and church *c.* 670, very soon after the introduction of Christianity into Lindsey, at 'Ad Baruae' which has been identified with Barrow-on-Humber about two miles from Barton. Barton was a more important place than Barrow, being one of the points of access to Lindsey from the sea. It seems unlikely that, after Barrow, it would remain long outside Christian influence and without a church. If one was erected about this time or later it would undoubtedly have been burned by the Danes when they ravaged both shores of the Humber during 867–70 as recorded in the Anglo-Saxon Chronicle. Barrow monastery was burnt at this time and was never rebuilt.

The present church is eleventh century. It seems unlikely that Barton would remain without a church for 150 years or so after its first church, if there was one, was burnt. Of the second church, if there was one, nothing is known.[2] If it existed it would probably have been burned during the Danish invasion of Lindsey by Olaf

---

[1] J. Bilson; G. Baldwin Brown; R. Brown; A. W. Clapham, (*a*) and (*g*); Bishop of Nottingham, (*b*); W. E. Varah.

[2] See, however, below, p. 255.

Tryggvason of Norway and Sweyn of Denmark in 994. If this happened it would afford some support for the date given by R. Brown to the present church of the time of Canute, 1017–35, son of Sweyn, who became Christian after his conquest of England and was a great church builder and patron of the arts. Baldwin Brown dates the church to the mid-eleventh century; A. W. Clapham, without giving any evidence, dates it to the tenth century. The belfry certainly is post-Conquest, though R. Brown suggested 1050–60. During repairs in 1913 the tower floor was lowered by 21 inches and some walling was exposed to view which showed the redness usually produced by fire. The stones above had been so frequently white-washed that their redness, if they too had suffered, had disappeared; or, they may be part of the eleventh-century church. This suggests, but does not prove, that there may indeed have been an earlier church and that the present tower was built on earlier foundations. During some earlier excavations of 1898 massive foundations were discovered below the tower floor (Fig. 18). These have no bearing on the present tower and

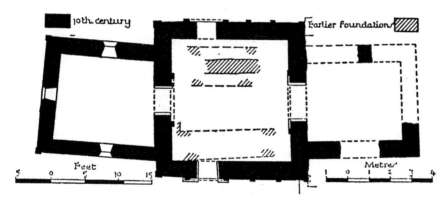

Fig. 18. Barton-on-Humber Church, plan

must ante-date it. Nothing is known about their age and purpose. They might perhaps be the remains of the otherwise hypothetical, seventh- or ninth-century church referred to above.

Barton church is not a typical member of the Lincolnshire class, the tower (¹) is decorated with pilaster shafts similar to Barnack and Earls Barton (Northants). The late eleventh-century belfry is the only feature of the church which is typically Lincolnshire. Originally the church was turriform (Fig. 18) with an eastern chancel which excavated foundations indicate to have been about 15 feet by 11 ft. 6 ins. on the interior, with walls about 2 ft. 6 ins. thick and so not quite square on the exterior like the normal plan. To the west was a small fore-building, or west nave, still standing, also not quite square. This western adjunct was wider than the chancel by

---

(¹) *Plate* 130.

about 9 inches, which Clapham considered was evidence, surely slender, that the fore-building may be of earlier date than the tower. Varah, too, thought it earlier; but the double splaying of the windows and the quoin type resemble that of the tower and suggest contemporaneity.

Unlike the tower, the western adjunct (1) is quite plain with no ornamentation. Its western angles have upright and flat quoins like those of the tower. It has no plinth. In the west wall are two small very crudely built double-splayed circular windows, one above the other, and a small crude round-headed window opening, single-splayed, in each, north and south, wall. The heads of the latter are closely similar to the upper halves of the circular windows. It has been suggested that possibly these windows were circular originally, the lower parts being later insertions. Against this is the different splayings of the two pairs of windows. The circular windows have only slightly external but deep internal splay. They retain remnants of the original mid-wall window slabs pierced with $\frac{3}{4}$-inch holes for admission of light. These light slabs, being mid-wall, are not at the narrowest parts of the apertures, which are nearer the outer wall-face. There is a large plain doorway between annexe and tower similar to and of the same height though narrower than that between tower and nave (2). Its head is of fifteen voussoirs of through-stones. The jambs also are of through-stones, lying on their sides but hardly side-alternate as they are all of similar width. The western face is plain, flush with the wall and has no strip-work hood mould. It is rebated for a door all round including the head; the rebates are $3\frac{1}{2}$ inches deep and 2 inches wide. On the east face there is heavy strip-work of smallish slabs of various lengths round the head making it look like an arch of two orders. The strip-work passes down the sides of the jambs as real long and short pilaster strips. The arch is 4 ft. $1\frac{1}{2}$ ins. wide between jambs which stand on plinths only $4\frac{1}{2}$ inches wide. The jambs are 2 ft. 2 ins. thick, which is the thickness of the wall here. The single imposts are chamfered below; they are returned along the east wall but encircle, instead of cutting through, the vertical pilaster strips.

Traces of a large, tall and wide blocked doorway are visible on the west wall (3). Baldwin Brown thought this doorway was original with the rest of the building. The jambs and arch head have been removed and the gap filled with soft chalk stone. It appears to have been rather narrower than the entrance from the adjunct to the tower-nave. The external blocking is *c.* 9 feet high by *c.* 6 ft. 9 ins. wide; on the interior it is *c.* 3 feet wide which is probably nearer the original arch width including the jambs. There would seem to be no need for a large western entrance to the annexe, especially as the main entrance is and probably always was in the south wall of the tower, unless indeed the annexe was used as a narthex for catechumens not yet admitted to the full rites of the church.

---

(1) *Plate* 131; (2) *Plates* 134, 135; (3) *Plates* 130, 131.

The tower had originally three stages with a string course separating the upper low plain stage from the tall decorated stages below. The post-Conquest top or belfry slightly recessed stage above the second string course is now capped by a low plain lead covered parapet hiding a flat roof, also lead covered, not visible from below. The tower is built of rough rubble including some local chalk. It is 57 feet high and *c.* 22 ft. 6 ins. square. It has no plinth. The tower projects from the western annexe *c.* 3 ft. 3 ins. on the north and *c.* 2 ft. 5 ins. on the south. The total length of the original church from the west wall of the western annexe to the east wall of the original chancel was 57 feet. The quoins of the three lower stages are of characteristic Anglo-Saxon upright and flat work; the belfry has simple Norman small stone quoins.

The square-edged pilaster strips decorating the tower north and south walls (1) are of 4-inch projection, possibly to plaster depth, and 9 inches wide. They are of real long and short work, the longs being up to 3 ft. 6 ins. long. Some of the longs have flat groovings with half-round vertical reedings; they may be Roman decorated stones re-used. The walls were probably originally plastered but are now, since 1898, covered with so-called 'pebble-dash' coating as is much of the present wall surface of the church. The pilaster decoration is similar on the north and south walls. It is in two rows. The lower consists of four tall pilaster strips, those of the second pair from the west being wider apart to allow for a doorway between, dividing the wall face into five panels. The tops are connected by five semi-circular heads, the two end ones (east and west) being against the quoins and supported on small corbels. There are small rectangular imposts between each strip and its arch head, corresponding to the end corbels. Above the crown of each round head is a large projecting block corbel which supports a long pilaster strip similar to those below, five strips in all dividing this part of the wall face into four panels and two of half-width at east and west ends. The pilasters have cubical imposts supporting the four gable heads, with two half-gables above the east and west half-panels. The gable heads touch the lower string course. The wall surfaces of the third and fourth stages, i.e. above the lower string course, are plain.

The north and south doorways are not placed centrally but are exactly opposite each other as is usual in Anglo-Saxon naves. The south doorway, now the only access to the tower from outside, is in the fourth panel from the east, as is also the north doorway. The south doorway (2) is round-headed with a heavy strip-work hood mould which dies into the adjacent pilaster strips (more strictly, the pilaster strips die into it). The arch head is of twelve through-stone roughly cut voussoirs, the hood of six long curved stones. Arch head and hood rest on their own separate through-stone moulded imposts, 9 to 10 inches thick, below which the tower pilasters

---

(1) *Plates* 130, 131, 133; (2) *Plate* 133.

act as vertical continuations of the hood. The jambs are of four massive through-stones each, two tall and two short. The opening is 5 ft. 11 ins. high to the imposts, and 3 ft. 2½ ins. wide, rather taller and wider than the northern doorway. The plinth extends five inches above ground.

The north doorway (1), now blocked, is similar except that its head is gabled, one flat stone 8½ inches wide forming each side of the gable, and it has a similar gabled hood mould of slabs 6½ inches wide. The hood has two stones to each face, the lower ones being large rectangular slabs resting on the imposts below which serve as supports both to the hood mould and to the wall pilaster strips above. The gable head is flush with the wall face, the hood mould projects about 2 inches. The jambs are 12 to 13 inches wide and each is of one massive central pillar stone with a short cubical or rectangular stone above and below. The jambs and the closely adjacent wall pilasters have their own separate imposts at the same level. The imposts, 9 to 10 inches thick, are, like those on the south, moulded below and are probably Roman stones re-used, upside down in each; there is a quirk near the base, and below two very small shallow double-hollow mouldings and chamfers on the front and soffit sides. The opening is *c.* 4 ft. 6 ins. high to the underside of the imposts and 2 ft. 10 ins. wide between jambs. The door was not rebated. On the interior wall face are remains of iron hooks on which the early door was hung to shut flat against the wall face.

In the second stage, in north and south walls only, are double round-headed openings (2) with genuine mid-wall bulging baluster shafts. The shafts are decorated with four central half-round bands of different sizes, and with one near the top and base. Above the top band and below the bottom one the ends of the shaft expand, like truncated cones of convex profile, to appear like primitive capitals and bases. Each half of the double arch head is cut from a single stone, the double head being a pair of double-arched lintels (i.e. arched above and below) with strip-work hood moulds, of two curved stones each, above and in contact with the lintel, giving an appearance of two orders to the openings. The hood moulds rest on their own block imposts which rest on the more massive jamb imposts below. There is no vertical strip-work at the sides of the jambs. The jambs and sill are of through-stones. The openings in the east and west walls (3), almost on a level with the north and south windows, are large doorways of egress from this stage leading into a chamber or space between inner and outer gabled roof of the old chancel, and into the western annexe (R. Brown, Varah, Baldwin Brown and Clapham all agree on this). These doorways are very tall and wide single round-headed arched openings with thin imposts; the eastern one has jambs of several irregular long and short stones each. The eastern doorway is blocked but is visible from within the present nave. In the

---

(1) *Plate* 132; (2) *Plate* 133; (3) *Plate* 136.

west wall of the tower within the annexe at a level of about one-third up the doorway is a single course of large limestone blocks. Above this level the jambs of the opening are of upright and flat through-stones (three flats and two uprights); below this level the jambs of the lower third of the opening are mere rubble walling. Above the eastern tower arch on the west wall face is a rectangular stone resting on the hood mould of the arch and with its base slightly curved to fit the hood. On this stone near the top a head is carved in very low relief (1). The stone below is plain. It has been surmised that the remainder of the figure, or group, was completed below in paint or, as probably at Bradford-on-Avon (Wilts), in stucco.

The whole of the decorated part of the tower, about four-fifths of the original height, was probably a single stage internally, open as far as the lower string course with high-placed openings. Had there been a floor at or about the level of the round heads of the pilaster wall decoration and below the windows the ground floor would have had no lighting, an impossible situation for a turriform church. The present floor is probably a later insertion, perhaps when the thirteenth-century large nave, exterior to the tower, was built. Baldwin Brown on the contrary thought that the floor is original or that it replaced an earlier one contemporary with the tower. He considered the western opening above this floor to be an access to an upper stage of the annexe, the floor of which would be at a level between the two circular windows. He does not consider how, in this case, the tower-nave was lighted.

In the third stage, the original belfry, between the two string courses, are in all four walls double-light windows (2) similar to those in the stage below, except that they are gable-headed with gable-headed hood moulds. The hoods project slightly and have their own separate, thin, imposts outside the jamb imposts. Below the imposts is projecting vertical strip-work resting on cubical corbels, which rest on the string course. The string acts as a sill. The arch heads and jambs are recessed slightly behind the wall face. The baluster shafts do not bulge as much as those below and have only three central bands each.

The fourth stage is of the late eleventh century, of the Saxo-Norman Overlap. It is built of Lincolnshire limestone ashlar; the quoins are of Norman small stone work of hard Yorkshire gritstone. Three of the original belfry windows in this stage, those on the north, east and south, remain. They are of characteristic Overlap type: double openings with heads of true but few, three or four, voussoirs, projecting chamfered hood moulds, jambs of dressed stones with chamfered imposts, straight octagonal mid-wall shafts with capitals supporting long through-stone central plain imposts, and sloping sills of dressed slabs. These windows are about twice the height of those below and they are flush with the wall face, not recessed as are those below. The capitals are curious (Fig. 19). The abaci are 11 inches square and the capitals

---

(1) *Plate* 135; (2) *Plates* 130, 136.

10 inches high. They have the simplest possible curled volutes. They are of square section above but below the vertical edges are chamfered to meet and correspond with the narrow faces of the octagonal shafts. There are no neckings.

The eastern tower arch (1), now opening to the later nave, is of about the same height as the western opening to the annexe, but wider—5 ft. 7 ins. It is plain and flush with the wall on the east side (as the western opening is on its west side), though slightly chamfered on both faces. The head is of twenty-one small through-stone voussoirs of various sizes. On the west face are square-edged double-block imposts, the upper ones projecting from wall and soffit faces. There is square-cut pilaster strip-

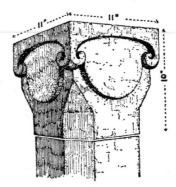

Fig. 19. Barton-on-Humber, Capital

work, 8 inches wide, down the western face of the jambs, 13 inches from the jamb soffit faces, which is continued above the imposts as a strip-work hood mould. The jambs are 2 ft. 6 ins. thick. It should be noted that the two arches are very similar in construction and that the decorative pilaster strip-work is on the western side of the eastern arch and on the eastern side of the western arch; i.e. on the tower side of each arch where it could be seen by the congregation assembled in the nave, which was the ground floor of the tower. The eastern arch is not rebated; unlike the western opening, it is a tower arch (or, rather, originally a chancel arch) and not a doorway like the western one. Originally apparently both arches were higher than they are now, for the eastern arch plinth is now level with the floor and the western one only 3 inches above it.

On the east wall of the tower seen from the nave, the north-east and south-east quoins are visible (2) cut back to the wall surface as at the other quoins. There are vertical roughnesses on the wall which indicate where the north and south walls of the early narrow chancel were torn away when the later nave was built. These marks also indicate the approximate height of the relatively low early chancel. The apex of the outer roof would have been above the large middle opening and the flatter inner

---

(1) *Plates* 135, 136; (2) *Plate* 136.

roof or ceiling rather below. Originally the whole of the wall above the middle opening and outside, i.e. to north and south of, the roughnesses was exterior to the early chancel. The gabled weather courses of a former high pitched roof, lower than the present one, probably belonged to the thirteenth-century nave. These marks cut across to some extent the gabled double opening which the Saxon roof would not have done.

BRACEBRIDGE

ALL SAINTS' CHURCH. The tower and main fabric of the nave are pre-Conquest. The tower (1) has no special features except in the belfry above the only string course which is more than four-fifths of the total height from the ground. The tower is large, 19 ft. 9 ins. wide on the west exterior, projecting 16 ft. 10½ ins. from the nave. The quoins are side-alternate slabs for about one-third of the height; above this they are thinner, about half the thickness of those lower down, but still side-alternate. No plinth is visible. It is built of coursed rubble. Most of the original plaster has peeled off. The low pyramidal red-tiled roof is modern.

There is no original opening in the north or south wall. The two-light window low down in the south wall is modern. In the west wall there is a round-headed window about half way up. Its arched lintel is of two halves, or broken and cemented. It has jambs of several slabs and a sloping sill. The western doorway has jambs of about equal-sized slabs some of which are modern renewals in a different stone. The rather thin imposts are chamfered on soffit and west faces; they project on the west and soffit sides but extend inwards only about 8 inches, as far as the door face; there are no imposts on the interior. The head is of twenty thin voussoirs flush with the wall surface and has a half-round strip-work hood mould projecting as far as the imposts. The opening is *c.* 5 ft. 8 ins. high to the imposts and 3 ft. 6 ins. wide. The wall here is 3 ft. 10½ ins. thick.

The belfry stage is very short; the openings fill nearly its entire height. The four openings have the usual double lights. The heads are of voussoirs and the long mid-wall columns have capitals supporting long projecting chamfered central imposts. The capitals on the east and north are scalloped (Fig. 20, (*a*)) with plain neckings below to the circular shafts. The capital on the west has curious carving in place of one of the scallops: it looks like two vertical rows of cockle shells with no striations (Fig. 20, (*b*)); the column is circular and the necking plain. The capital on the south is rounded off below on square abacus to a semi-bulbous shape; the lower corners where volutes might be expected are also rounded off to fit on to the bulbous part below (Fig. 20, (*c*)). The faces of the square abacus are decorated near the corners

---

(1) *Plate* 137.

with incised spirals or circles, rather similar to but more elaborate than those at Glentworth.[1] The necking is cabled and the shaft octagonal in plan. The scalloped capitals in this Saxo-Norman setting are interesting. Baldwin Brown, quoting John Bilson, states that the scallop was developed in England and became very popular later in Normandy: a definite English contribution to early Norman ornament. Here, at Bracebridge, we see apparently a Saxon mason combining genuine Saxon and Norman motifs.

The tower arch (I) is tall and fine, about as tall as the chancel arch but wider. The head is of two rings of voussoirs, with plastered rubble filling in the soffit

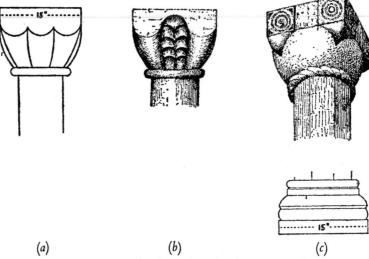

(a)   (b)   (c)

Fig. 20. Bracebridge Church, three Capitals

between the rings. The jambs have three or four stones per course. The imposts are chamfered on the soffit and eastern faces and are not returned along the wall, which here is 2 ft. 9½ ins. thick.

The chancel arch (I) is tall and narrow. The head is of two rings of seventeen small voussoirs with plastered rubble filling between the rings. The jambs are of slabs, face-alternate, three or four stones per course. The imposts are chamfered on soffit sides only and are not returned. The jambs are 2 ft. 9 ins. thick. On either side of the chancel arch is a fairly large rectangular opening of probably the same eleventh-century date as the arch. They may be survivals, or rather derivations, of the screen walls with triple openings traces of which may be found in some very early Saxon churches. Altars probably stood beneath these and the openings may have contained relics or perhaps something of the nature of a reredos or may have

[1] See below, p. 276, fig. 25.

(I) *Plate* 138.

been left open to provide a good view of the main altar at the east end. There are similar openings at Scawton (Yorkshire, North Riding), Avening (Glos) and Castle Rising (Norfolk).

Near the west end of the north aisle is a very tall, though lower and narrower than the chancel arch, blocked opening. It has a typical Saxon round head of six long stones cut to shape, thick imposts chamfered on the soffit sides and jambs of real upright and flat stones. It is 3 feet wide. Perhaps it is the original north doorway transferred to the aisle.

The nave north-east quoins are of upright and flat stones in good condition. The upper south-east quoins, visible from the later south-east chapel, are similar. The north-west and south-west quoins are of very large upright and flat slabs; they project from the tower on the north and south sides like buttresses.

The whole church was restored extremely well by J. L. Pearson in 1875.

BRANSTON

ALL SAINTS' CHURCH. The tower and parts of the nave are Anglo-Saxon. It is built of well-coursed limestone rectangular blocks. The tower extends some feet into the nave; that is, the nave west wall overlaps the tower so that the eastern tower quoins are plainly to be seen in the interior of the nave. The tower (1) is 18 ft. 6 ins. square on the exterior, projecting from the nave walls 15 ft. 4 ins. The quoins on the west above the arcading are a mixture of face- and side-alternate slabs, with some renewals. There is one string course only, square-cut and high up below the belfry stage, which is recessed.

There are no openings in the north and south walls below the belfry. In the west wall high up is a rectangular window with single stone flat lintel and sill, and slab jambs with two uprights on the south and one upright and two flats on the north. Lower down, above the west doorway, is a thirteenth-century cusped two-light window. The west doorway (2) is relatively very tall and narrow, *c.* 2 ft. 10 ins. wide. It forms the central feature of Norman arcading which extends across the entire west front of the tower. The doorway has tall recessed angle columns with voluted capitals; there are plain neckings below and thin chamfered imposts above the capitals. The angle columns have no bases but stand on large tall rectangular blocks. The arch head is of very definite, in fact quite advanced, Romanesque profile, consisting of two half-round rolls, with one hollow between, separated by narrow flats, and a half-round hood mould above, all resting on the rather long imposts. The doorway has a flat lintel below the stilted arch head, and the tall tympanum between

---

(1) *Plate* 140; (2) *Plates* 139, 140.

is filled with geometrically decorated stone work of Norman type. The arcading consists of two narrow arches on each side of the doorway with central and side columns; that is, they are real arches with columns, three to each pair of arches, and not jambs. The capitals are rather badly worn but are of cushion type, some scalloped with two or three scallops each; they have plain neckings and plain chamfered abaci. The bases are inverted cushion capitals. J. T. Micklethwaite considered the arcading to be a later, Norman, insertion. He is probably correct, though dating is made difficult by the renewals in the ashlar walling and corner work. Baldwin Brown prefers to regard it as original and in consequence gave the tower a post-Conquest date. He points out the resemblance between the arcading and that on the Norman part of the west front of Lincoln Cathedral and adds that the Branston arcading 'is influenced by the W front of Lincoln' which was completed *c.* 1092–3. It is difficult to accept Baldwin Brown's conclusions. He adds further 'there are signs of it (arcading) on' the south wall. This is not so. The signs on the south wall are not of arcading but of two Saxon openings of different dates (1). The main one, centrally placed, has a round head of sixteen voussoirs of similar lengths but various widths. The west jamb is of four small side-alternate slabs above with two large slabs below, one of the latter being very large and L-shaped, probably a corner or angle stone re-used. There is a thin flat impost to the west jamb, only a fragment on the east. There are no remains of the east jamb. The opening was *c.* 6 ft. 10 ins. high to impost level and *c.* 2 ft. 5 ins. wide. To the east and very slightly higher are remains of three voussoirs and an impost of another blocked opening quite evidently narrower than the western one. This is curiously far to the east; the impost is in contact with the west wall of the nave, a curious position for a doorway. It may perhaps have been a window to light the ground floor of the tower. No jamb stones are left so it cannot be inferred that the opening extended to the ground. These remains are very dissimilar to the western arcading and suggest an earlier date for the tower; comparing the two it is difficult to avoid the conclusion that the western arcading is later and was applied to an earlier tower. The fact that the actual western doorway is much narrower and lower than the central arch with wide slab jambs and narrow lintel is also consistent with the arcading being built round an existing doorway. The lower part of the wall face below the arcading is of fine ashlar with very fine joints, probably renewals. This ashlar extends a foot or two round the corners and along the north and south walls. Five or six courses of south-west quoining just above the arcading have been renewed with similar ashlar. Below the ashlar west walling is a chamfered plinth *c.* 15 inches high, different and later in type from that on the north side of the nave.

The belfry (1) has the usual double-light openings in each wall. The south opening

---

(1) *Plate* 140.

has double heads of four voussoirs each, renewed, seven altogether as the central one is common to both heads. The central column is of circular section and has a capital of cushion type with two scallops to each face. The north and west openings have arched lintels, badly worn. The imposts and some jamb stones have been renewed; the older stones are of mixed face and side-alternate arrangement. The eastern opening is similar to the south one but has been much restored. It is possible that the east and south arch heads originally had arched lintels, like the north and west one, but later were renewed in voussoirs.

The tower arch is fourteenth century as are also the nave arcades and aisles. The clerestory is fifteenth century. The battlemented tower parapet with corner pinnacles and spire are all later. The whole church was restored by Sir Giles Scott in 1876.

The nave projects from the tower 3 ft. 8 ins. on the south and *c.* 2 feet on the north. There is a low plinth on the north only 2 or 3 inches above ground at the east end and level with the ground at the west. No plinth is visible on the south. There are massive quoins, as far as the aisle roof level, at the south-west corner of genuine long and short work, some longs being as much as 3 ft. 6 ins. Above aisle roof the quoins are of later small stone work put in when the clerestory was built. No original quoins are visible at the north-west.

BROUGHTON-BY-BRIGG

ST. MARY'S CHURCH. This is not a typical member of the Lincolnshire group, but is allied and shows some resemblance to Barton-on-Humber in that it was a turriform church: the ground floor of the tower was the original nave. During the installation of a heating apparatus the foundations of the small square chancel to the east of the tower were discovered.

The tower (1) is square and large, projecting from the present nave 21 ft. 2 ins. There is a later, though Saxon, circular stair turret attached to the west wall. The tower is built of rubble in three different masonry stages. It is not known whether these stages correspond to different building periods. The ground stage is of roughly coursed flattish rubble. Above is much herring-boning in all four walls, six or seven double courses, some with and some without spines, separated into two groups by intervening two courses of ordinary masonry. In the third section as far as the string course the walling is roughly coursed and of larger, more nearly rectangular, blocks than those of the bottom stage. The quoins are of large slabs, side-alternate, some badly worn and repaired with cement. The stair turret is of large square and rectangular blocks of brown sandstone; some blocks are about $2\frac{1}{2}$ feet by 18 inches.

---

(1) *Plate* 141.

The top, present belfry, stage above the string course is later though perhaps not much later. The few courses above the windows may however be much later, perhaps contemporary with the windows, which are fifteenth century. The battlemented parapet and corner pinnacles are modern.

The small early chancel was later replaced by a Norman nave and chancel. The present chancel is later, possibly thirteenth century, retaining some Norman details. The aisle and nave clerestory are probably eighteenth century.

In the tower south wall is a doorway unusually close to the south-west corner (1), a reasonable position as it was really a nave south doorway. It has a round head of two orders. The inner order of voussoirs of two stones per course is recessed behind the wall face. The outer order has a large roll moulding on its face. There is also a hood mould of fifteen voussoirs of square blocks the ends of which rest on walling, not on imposts, i.e. the hood is really a relieving arch. The jambs are badly worn but appear to be side-alternate and of one or two stones per course. The imposts, chamfered on soffit sides only, are long enough to support both arch orders, but not the hood. The total thickness of the wall is 2 ft. 8 ins. but the jambs are recessed to a depth of 13 inches to accommodate angle shafts. These shafts have octagonal capitals similar to those on the tower arch. No bases are visible; the columns appear to go below ground level, which may have risen. The doorway is 6 ft. 11 ins. high to the imposts and 2 ft. 9½ ins. wide.

Above the south doorway and a little to the east of centre is a narrow window with arched lintel, jambs of two upright blocks each and a sill of one block between the jambs. Higher still and in line with the lower window is another similar window with no sill.

In the north wall there is no doorway (as there is at Barton). There is a window with no sill but otherwise similar and in a corresponding position to the lower window in the south wall. Higher up, just below the string course, there has been a considerable replacement of rubble masonry by fairly large rectangular blocks of limestone. In the centre of this near the top is a rectangular filling of rubble. Possibly there was an opening here similar to but higher up than the upper window in the south wall.

The stair turret (1) has three rectangular windows all rather similar with flat lintels, jambs of two stones each and no sills. One rather wider than the others, is high up in the south wall. The other two are in the west, the upper one rather to the north and the other rather to the south of centre. In the interior is a spiral staircase with central newel, built up of drums, separate from the stairs which are fitted in between newel and turret wall.

The tower arch (2), formerly of course the chancel arch, is extremely interesting.

---

(1) *Plate* 141; (2) *Plate* 142.

The west face is of two recessed orders. The arch heads are of fourteen and thirteen short voussoirs respectively and rest on large slab imposts 10½ inches thick and chamfered on the western and soffit faces. The imposts support both orders but do not go through the wall as far as the east face. The jambs are recessed and have angle shafts or columns. The shaft capitals are cubical with square abaci and faces and vertical edges plain chamfered; i.e. the faces comprise eight triangles, four slightly truncated pointing downwards and four not truncated pointing upwards to bring the bottom face of the capital to fit roughly the shaft (Fig. 21). There are plain neck-

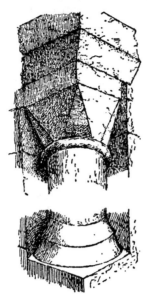

Fig. 21. Broughton-by-Brigg Church, Capital and Base

ings below. The bases are curious and may be described as of two members cut from one stone; the upper member has two slight hollow chamfers, or is bi-concave,[1] the lower acts as a small plinth standing on the main plinth below. The lower half of the north column is badly worn away to nearly half its diameter, due perhaps to its being used as a whetstone for sharpening the tools of gardeners or grave diggers. The east face of the arch is not recessed; it is flush with the wall and is of one order. The head has thirteen voussoirs and no imposts. The jambs are of six slabs each of roughly similar heights arranged in upright and flat manner; the flats are not much longer, north–south, than the uprights. The top slabs of each jamb project north and south to form the capitals (i.e. each capital and jamb stone are cut from a single slab) of two columns standing independently against the jamb soffits within the arch, and with their faces about level with the wall east face. The capitals are similar to those on the western face and there are plain neckings. The columns look as though they

[1] Cf. Langford, Pl. 118.

were intended to support soffit rolls; actually there is nothing above them (I), they support nothing.[1] The lowest stones of the jambs also project north and south into the arch, the inner ends being cut to bi-concave truncated cone shape, as with those on the west, to act as bases to the columns; i.e. each bottom jamb stone and adjacent column base is cut from a single stone.

The columns on both faces rest on massive through-stone plinths, a single plinth serving for both east and west columns on each soffit. As at Barton-on-Humber, the more ornate side of the arch is the western one, which would be seen by the congregation in the tower-nave. In non-turriform churches the more elaborate side of a tower arch is the eastern one, that one viewed from the nave.

The eastern arch face is 2 ft. 7½ ins. wide between plinths and 4 ft. 5 ins. between jambs. The width of the western arch face between plinths is also 2 ft. 7½ ins. but the total width of the outer order, i.e. between the jamb faces behind (north and south of) the angle shafts is *c.* 6 ft. 7 ins. The height to the imposts, which are 10½ inches thick, is 7 ft. 7 ins.

In the west wall of the tower is a doorway, narrower than that at Barton as it leads to the stair turret, not to a large western annexe. The round head, very slightly pointed, is of ten voussoirs, two or three per course with no rubble filling. It is set back 2 inches behind the jamb soffits. The jambs are of massive stones (one 22 inches by 19 inches by 15 inches) and are only 4 feet high to the springing of the arch head which rises a further 22 inches to its apex giving a total height of 5 ft. 10 ins. The jamb, i.e. the wall here, is 2 ft. 10 ins. thick.

CABOURN

St. Nicholas' Church. This tower is a typical Lincolnshire bell tower; it was dated by Baldwin Brown to the Overlap. It has a single string course, renewed, about three-quarters of the tower height above ground, and below the belfry. The belfry was rebuilt in the nineteenth century with a low pyramidal roof. The church itself has been rebuilt but some of the old western quoins, of mixed face- and side-alternate arrangement, were retained in the new masonry.

The tower is built of large blocks of yellowish rubble, roughly coursed. There is a double plinth on the three exposed sides, the two members of which are plain chamfered on their upper edges. The lower member projects beyond the upper one. The quoins are of large stones, a mixture of face and side-alternate.

The lower stage of the tower has no openings in the north and south walls. In the

---

[1] See G. Baldwin Brown, p. 293, fig. 131.

(I) *Plate* 142.

west wall at ground level is a doorway (1) with a plain round-headed arch of nine voussoirs enclosing a plain undecorated tympanum; above the arch head is a typical Saxon strip-work-chamfered hood mould. The square-cut jambs are of large blocks, of side-alternate arrangement, three above the plinth on the south and four on the north. The long plain-chamfered imposts extend some distance along the walls to north and south. The opening is 2 ft. 7½ ins. wide between jambs and 6 ft. 4 ins. high to the imposts. The jambs are 3 ft. 9 ins. thick, east–west. Above the door, about half-way to the string, is a tall narrow arrow-slit window with the usual arched lintel, jambs of two very large flat stones each and sill of two rough flat stones.

The fine tower arch (2) to nave is 5 ft. 11 ins. wide between jambs and 10 ft. 10 ins. high to the imposts. The arch head rises above the imposts by about 4 ft. 6 ins. so the total height of the opening is over 15 feet. The arch head is of two rings, eastern and western, of voussoirs with plastered rubble filling between. The north and south voussoirs at the springing are about twice the length of the others, a not infrequent Saxon practice. The jambs are faced with stones of grey limestone, not yellow like the fabric, two or three stones per course and in side-alternate arrangement. There is diagonal tooling on these dressing stones which appears to be original, i.e. Norman tooling used presumably by Saxon masons. The jambs are 3 ft. 8 ins. thick. The internal dimensions of the tower are 10 ft. 1 in. by *c.* 10 ft. 2 ins. The ground stage is plastered internally.

The rebuilt belfry has window openings of the usual double light type with through-stone central imposts and mid-wall shafts with (as is usual in rebuilt belfries) plain cushion capitals and neckings; the moulded bases of the shafts are on thin square plinths. It is not known whether the original shafts had capitals, cushioned or otherwise.

In the north wall of the nave, towards but not very near the west end, is a blocked round-headed doorway, not visible through the plaster in the nave. It has a plain stone tympanum, not original, and above is a much worn strip-work hood mould. The short imposts are no wider than the jamb stones; the jambs are side-alternate. Jambs and north impost only are chamfered.

Caistor

St. Peter and St. Paul's Church.[1] The tower is built of local ironstone, a friable material which has necessitated much repair work in rectangular limestone slabs, especially on the south face. The fabric was originally of rather large blocks of irregular shapes. The quoins are of large, irregular, roughly dressed stones, a form not

[1] A. Sutton; A. Hamilton Thompson; E. Trollope, (a).

(1) *Plates* 143, 144; (2) *Plate* 145.

unusual in the Caistor district, in mixed face and side-alternate arrangement. In the west wall of the nave, north and south of the tower, are the very large and irregular quoins of the original aisleless nave; they are mainly of large uprights with smaller ones higher up, a type of pillar quoin. The church was enlarged at various dates in the Middle Ages. There are straight joints between the nave quoins and the aisles. The nave projects *c.* 15 inches to the south of the tower and *c.* 18 inches to the north. On the north of the nave a short piece of chamfered plinth is visible; the rest is below ground. In the tower west wall the top of a chamfered plinth is just visible below the west doorway. The top stage of the tower with the string course below was rebuilt in the fourteenth century and has belfry openings of that period. At the same time diagonal buttresses were built at the north-west and south-west corners, and a tall flat buttress against the centre of the south wall to as far up as the first string course. The diagonal buttresses appear to have been built round earlier taller and shallower and narrower clasping buttresses, the tops of which extend above the later ones almost as far as the top string course. In addition, two relatively short flat buttresses are against the west wall, one on either side of the west doorway. The tower has three chamfered string courses in the south, west and north walls, including the later, or renewed, one below the later belfry, an exceptional number for a Lincolnshire tower. The second string on the north is carried round the east wall for 2 or 3 feet only.

The tower is 17 ft. 6 ins. wide (north–south) and 15 ft. 6 ins. long. As at Nettleton, this is an exception to the Lincolnshire rule that the east–west axis is longer than the north–south. The width, too, is exceptional for the county. The original tower is eleventh century, perhaps as early as *c.* 1050. It is possible that the ground floor may have been a porch, raised later in the Saxon period into a tower.

The Ground Stage. In the west wall is a low round-headed square-edged doorway, the arch head having plain zig-zag ornament on its west face. Above the arch head is a chamfered strip-work hood mould. The jambs are plain and square cut of side-alternate arrangement but are not of through-stones. The imposts have chamfered edges and a roll between two quirks on each face. The opening is 4 ft. 8 ins. high to the imposts and 3 ft. 9 ins. wide. The west wall has been stated to be 4 ft. $10\frac{1}{4}$ ins. thick; actually it is 3 ft. 10 ins. The south wall is 3 ft. 8 ins., the north wall 4 ft. 11 ins. and the east wall 5 ft. 9 ins. to 5 ft. 11 ins. thick;[1] the east wall is about 2 feet thicker than any other in the area.

To the south of the west doorway, which impinges on it, is a blocked arch head of long, thin voussoirs. The small south-west buttress is in front of part of the filling, and the north part, just above its interruption by the west doorway, has been crushed and is in consequence lower than the south half of the head. It is in a curious position for a doorway, being very near the south end of the tower west wall. There is a

[1] The writer is indebted to Mr. and Mrs. R. H. Linsell of Caistor for checking these measurements.

similar but narrower blocked round-headed doorway in the centre of the north wall *c*. 7 ft. 6 ins. high and *c*. 3 ft. 7 ins. wide. Above is a relatively wide very roughly built window with a rude ancient gable-headed arched lintel. The jambs are of two rough stones each; there is no separate sill. There are no other openings in the north wall.

On the south there is no trace on the exterior of an early centrally placed window behind the later buttress (as there is at Nettleton), but west of the buttress are the remains of a blocked opening, rather wide for a window, as on the north and west walls but taller. Eleven arch stones remain; they are not true voussoirs but rectangular slabs of the same material as the walls and appear to have belonged to a segmentally shaped arch head. A small portion of the western part is hidden by the buttress, so the opening was very near the south-west corner. Above this blocked opening and about half way up the first stage and just west of the buttress is a small lancet window with wide single internal splay, probably Norman; its head is a lancet-shaped arched lintel of two stones roughly carved to shape.

The two blocked doorways in the north and south walls are plainly visible on the interior. The one in the north wall corresponds to that on the exterior. The south one, being centrally placed, does *not* correspond to the blocked opening on the exterior which is to the west of central.

In the second stage, above the first string course, is a modern window in the west wall. The masonry around and above this window has been much repaired, hiding any original remains. There are no openings in the north and south walls of this stage.

Above the second string course, in the west wall of the third stage, is a thirteenth-century two-light window; the dividing shaft is much decayed. In the east wall there appears to be a small blocked opening just above the present roof line. There are no openings in the north and south walls.

The tower arch (1) is of one plain order. Its eastern face is decorated with V-shaped, not really chevron, ornament: the background has been cut away leaving a V-shaped edging projecting from the surrounding arch head; it may be modern. The square unchamfered imposts are returned along the western face of the wall. The arch is 8 ft. 11 ins. high to the imposts and 9 ft. 7 ins. wide.

CLEE, or OLD CLEE

HOLY TRINITY CHURCH.[1] Only the tower is Anglo-Saxon. The original roof, perhaps a low pyramidal one with no parapet, was replaced in the fifteenth century by

---

[1] G. Baldwin Brown; A. Sutton; A. Hamilton Thompson.

(1) *Plate* 146.

the present parapet and pinnacles. The nave is twelfth century, the transepts thirteenth century; the rest of the church has been restored and largely rebuilt in modern times. The tower was dated by Baldwin Brown to *c.* 1040; perhaps 1040–60 would be more likely. It is a fine lofty tower of typical Lincolnshire character. There is a single chamfered string course separating the recessed belfry stage from the tower below. Curiously there is part of a string course about half way up on the north wall. (There are traces of similar strings at Nettleton on both north and south walls, and at Rothwell on the south wall.)[1] This is the only relief on this wall below the belfry; there are no openings. The tower (1) is built of rubble with irregular quoins of mainly side-alternate but with some face-alternate arrangement. The lower part of the west face has been much repaired but the quoins appear to be original. There are original quoins too at the north-west corner of the nave; those at the south-west are difficult to see as they are largely hidden by the aisle which encroaches on the tower south wall. There is a square-edged plinth to the tower the top of which is level with the ground.

In the south wall almost the only relief below the belfry is a window with arched lintel, jambs of one pillar stone each and no sill; it has slight internal splay. There is also a projecting corbel at about aisle-roof height.

In the west wall is a small round-headed doorway (1). The head is of two rings, an upper and lower, of voussoirs, the lower ring being very slightly recessed. There are six voussoirs in the lower and nine in the upper ring, some of them being rather long stones cut to appropriate shape. Immediately above is a square-cut projecting strip-work hood mould of eleven strips, some long and cut to appropriate curved shape. All three rings rest on the same chamfered imposts which are long and *c.* 8 inches thick. The jambs are square-cut and of five slabs each, and rest on the plinth, the ends of which are flush with the jamb soffits. The opening is 5 feet high to the imposts and 2 ft. 11 ins. wide. The jambs, i.e. the wall here, are 4 ft. 2 ins. thick.

Above the west doorway, more than half-way to the belfry stage, is a key-hole window of sandstone, 2 ft. 8 ins. high. The arched lintel is cut from a large wide block, the jambs are of one wide upright slab each cut with a slight batter, more noticeable on the north jamb, so that the opening narrows upwards towards the key-hole head. It has single splay and no separate sill.

The tower arch (2) has a somewhat segmental head of two rings, an upper and lower, of voussoirs on each face; the lower ring on the east is recessed slightly. On the west both rings are flush with the wall face; there is no recessing. There is rubble filling in the soffit between the east and west rings. The jambs are mainly ashlar, two or three stones per course, and have some rubble filling here and there. The imposts

[1] See below, pp. 291, 293.

---

(1) *Plate* 147; (2) *Plate* 148.

are very short and are chamfered on the soffit sides only. There is a plinth of three members with chamfered upper edges which extends *c.* 3 ft. 4 ins. north and south along the wall. The opening is 6 ft. 8 ins. wide and 13 ft. 5½ ins. high to the imposts. Its total height to the crown of the arch is 17 ft. 6 ins. The jambs, i.e. the wall here, are 3 ft. 8 ins. thick.

In the belfry are double openings of the usual type in all four walls. They have mid-wall shafts supporting central through-stone imposts which have slight chamfers below. The shafts have cubical capitals, *c.* 15 inches across, and bases. The heads are arched lintels, two to each double head. The jambs are of irregular slab work, not of through-stones, mainly face-alternate.

GLENTWORTH

THE CHURCH OF ST. MICHAEL AND ALL ANGELS.[1] This church consists of western tower, nave and chancel. The original nave was destroyed and rebuilt in 1782; nothing ancient remains in it except an incised fragment of probably a grave slab built into the wall near the south door. The steeper pitch of the earlier nave roof is visible on the exterior of the tower east wall.

The tower (1) is mainly original. It is built of flattish rubble reasonably well coursed, with quoins of rather small slabs of mixed face and side-alternate arrangement. It is of two stages of very different heights, separated by a thin, square-cut string course. The upper stage is recessed. The lower stage is 31 ft. 9 ins. high, the upper one 13 ft. 9 ins. from the top of the string course to the bottom of the parapet. Above is another string course and low plain parapet and flat roof, all later. The tower is 15 ft. 10 ins. wide (north–south) and 15 feet deep on the exterior; on the interior it is 9 ft. 9 ins. by 9 ft. 6 ins. The corresponding walls are about 3 feet and 2 ft. 9 ins. thick, respectively.

In the west wall there was originally a western doorway. This was reconstructed in the late eighteenth century. The early jambs of six irregular blocks each arranged in roughly long and short manner were retained. A lintel with queer flattish pointed arch above and tympanum between, all of poor brick, were inserted and a cheap-looking door. All this has now been removed and the wall built up so well that it is not detectable by the eye, though the filling shows up rather lighter in the photograph. Immediately above, only 5 ft. 4 ins. from the ground, is a fourteenth-century three-light window and higher still, rather more than half-way up the first stage, is a narrow window with arched block lintel and no separate sill. Its south jamb is of one

[1] C. H. Fowler; A. Hamilton Thompson, (*c*); E. Trollope, (*b*).

---

(1) *Plate* 149.

monolith, very wide, which looks like an insertion as it is of whiter stone than the rest. The north jamb for more than half its height is of one rectangular block on its side, and has an incised cross on it, probably a grave slab fragment, and a small square block above. The thin imposts project considerably. At about the same level inside in the east wall is a tall narrow rectangular recess (Fig. 22) with a plain flat lintel and a sill of four rectangular-ended, almost square-ended, through-stones. The north jamb is of three tall thin through-stones with one short flat one (second from the bottom); the south jamb has four massive through-stones, one of which (also second from the bottom) is a large flat one, almost a crude approach to upright and flat work. The south jamb also has a thin double impost, chamfered below on its face but not on its soffit side.[1]

Fig. 22. Glentworth, Recess in Tower Interior

In the south wall, high up and immediately below the string course, is a remarkable window of key-hole type. The aperture is 6 inches wide and 3 ft. 9 ins. high to the 'springing' line of the deeply stilted double-arched lintel (the massive lintel block is arched above and below). The jambs are of one massive monolith each. There is no separate sill. There is a strip-work hood mould of three long and one short 'voussoirs' supported by long thin imposts which give it a winged appearance. The strip-work is decorated with Jews' harp ornament.[2]

There is no opening in the north wall of this stage.

The upper stage is the belfry. It is very tall for a belfry and the openings are also unusually tall. The windows in all four walls are of the usual double-headed type with mid-wall columns supporting long central plain through-stone imposts. All

---

[1] Cf. the recess at Skipwith, p. 122.   [2] See below, pp. 300–2.

heads are of voussoirs with, as is usual, the central one in each double head common to both halves. The columns rest on large flat square bases chamfered above. The north and west shafts are of roughly octagonal section; the east one is nearly square; the south one is circular with a strip of crude cable ornament down the flattened face (Fig. 23). The capitals, with plain neckings below, are different and interesting. The north one (Fig. 25, (a)) has deeply cut definite spiral volutes at the front corners of the abaci. Below the volutes the capital is not cushion but semi-bulbous in form,

Fig. 23. Glentworth, South Belfry Opening

as at Marton, and derived not from a cube but from a cylinder. Its abacus is continued backwards, towards the interior, thickened below by a kind of semicircular tongue. It is 11 inches wide at the face and 16 inches deep. This capital might be regarded as a rather hesitating approach to a corbelled-out capital, though it is insufficiently corbelled-out to render a central impost unnecessary.

The south capital (Fig. 25, (b)) is rather similar to the north except that its abacus is square, with no prolongation backwards. Its front corners have spiral volutes rather less pronounced than those on the north capital. It is semi-bulbous below derived

SHAFT OF WESTERN BELFRY
WINDOW SHOWING ORIGINAL
MODE OF HANGING BELLS

Fig. 24. Glentworth, West Belfry Opening Shaft

from a cylinder, not a cube, and in the rear the curvature extends to the top so that here there is no abacus. The jambs of the south opening are of upright blocks, squared and dressed on their outer faces, with a thin slab between them and the impost. In the western opening the south jamb is like that of the south opening, but the north jamb has two blocks below and above those a large number of very thin slabs, giving it a brick-like appearance. About half way up the octagonal shaft on its south face is a right-angled groove with a deep hole at the inner end, surrounded by a shallow circular depression (Fig. 24). In the opposite jamb—the south—on the second slab from the bottom, is part of a larger circle. At some time a small bell

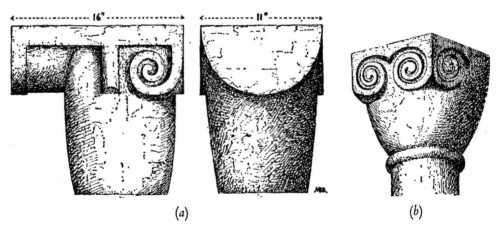

(a)   (b)

Fig. 25. Glentworth, two Capitals

must have been hung here, a practice not uncommon in Italian campanili of the same period. The jambs of the north opening are similar to those of the south.

The tower arch (I) is original and is in good condition. Its head is of 21 voussoirs in two rings—an eastern and a western—with plastered rubble filling between the rings. The jambs are of slabs, three per course. They stand on shallow plinths chamfered on their soffit sides. The imposts, 9 inches thick on the south and 10½ inches thick on the north, are not returned along the walls and are chamfered on soffit sides only. The arch is 6 ft. 3 ins. wide and 6 ft. 11 ins. high to the imposts. The jambs (wall) are 3 ft. 2 ins. thick.

GREAT HALE, or HALE MAGNA

CHURCH OF ST. JOHN THE BAPTIST. The tower is Anglo-Saxon, except the string course, parapet and corner pinnacles which are fifteenth century. The nave and chancel are thirteenth century. The tower is plain, with no original string course or set-off, which makes it look rather primitive, like St. Michael's at Oxford. Baldwin Brown considered it to be post-Conquest. It is built of coursed long, thin, narrow slabs of rubble. There is an internal spiral staircase, not a stair turret, built into the north-east corner of the tower. It is of crude construction though of a rather late type. Its central newel is only 16 inches in diameter and the stairs 18 inches wide. Even so, the wall was not thick enough to contain it: the lower east face of the wall was built out in a somewhat bulging manner to accommodate it.[1] The interior of the north-east corner of the tower is built across with a wall, which forms the south-west wall of the staircase. This staircase differs also from the attached stair turrets at Broughton-by-Brigg and Hough-on-the-Hill in that the steps are not separate from the newel, that is, not wedged in between newel and outer wall. Each drum of which the newel is built and its associated step are cut from one stone. This is a late feature, common after the Conquest and in mediaeval times. The well-known chancel arch at Wittering (Northants)[2] with its complicated profile of inner and outer orders and soffit and face rolls is built up of drums in a similar way, each drum cut to complete profile shape. On this account H. M. Taylor considers that Great Hale staircase implies certainly a post-Conquest and perhaps a genuinely Norman date for the tower. This evidence is the stronger in that the staircase is not an attached turret but an integral part of the tower and contemporary with it.

The tower is 20 ft. 9 ins. wide on the exterior and projects 19 ft. 7 ins. from the nave. It is approximately square and is a little narrower than the later nave.

[1] Plan in Baldwin Brown, fig. 153.   [2] See E. A. Fisher, Pl. 18, A.

(I) *Plate* 150.

In the north wall close to the north-east corner are four short narrow rectangular windows and a circular one below, all vertically disposed. These light the staircase. The circular window is double-splayed with very short outer and a deep and wide inner splay. The rectangular windows have lintels and jambs of one big slab each.

In the south face is a tall rectangular window in the ground stage, and a similar but slightly smaller one in the second internal stage. The jambs of both are of three wide slabs each; sills are of long, thin, single projecting slabs. The heads are large moulded arched lintels, projecting like the sills from the walls, but much decayed.

In the west wall in the ground stage is a narrow window with arched lintel, jambs of two big slabs each and no separate sill. These windows in the south and west walls have single wide internal splays, very Norman-looking.

The belfry stage has in all four walls the usual double-light openings, very tall, with mid-wall circular shafts supporting projecting central imposts. The jambs are of dressed stones, with imposts chamfered on their soffit and outer faces. The sills slope, a late feature. The capitals are most interesting and varied (Fig. 26, (a–d)). They are ornamented on the outer face only. They are not cubical, one being $11\frac{1}{2}$ inches wide at the abacus by 14 inches high, but are a combination of the cushion and volute types. Their abaci are rather longer in the direction of the wall thickness; this gives them a suggestion of long corbelled-out capitals though, as at Glentworth, they are not sufficiently corbelled-out to render central imposts unnecessary. Two are semi-cushion in the upper halves; that is the curved profile is segmental, not circular. Two have spiral volutes at the corners similar to those at Glentworth; two others have none. All have round, almost semi-bulbous lower portions which are carved with what Baldwin Brown called 'cigar-shaped objects'; one has two layers or rows of these objects which Baldwin Brown not unreasonably regarded as debased floral designs elaborated or simplified from the not dissimilar ones at Scartho (Fig. 31). They have been classed with the Jews' harp ornament[1] but the two types are only very faintly similar. It is more likely that they are derived from comparable Roman forms which may have been familiar to the Lincolnshire masons. There is closely similar ornament on a carved Saxon stone found on the site of Wilfrid's church at Hexham (Fig. 26, (e)) which may have been derived from a Roman carved stone (Fig. 26, (f)) found on the same site. All the capitals have plain neckings below.

The tower arch has a round head of twenty-five voussoirs, three or four per course. The jambs are of ashlar, also of three or four slabs per course, arranged side alternately. The imposts are chamfered below on the soffit and east faces, and are returned along the east face only about 6 or 8 inches. The arch is 8 ft. 3 ins. wide and the jambs (i.e. the east wall) 4 ft. 2 ins. thick.

Above the tower arch, on the east wall of the tower within the nave, are marks of

[1] See below, pp. 300–2.

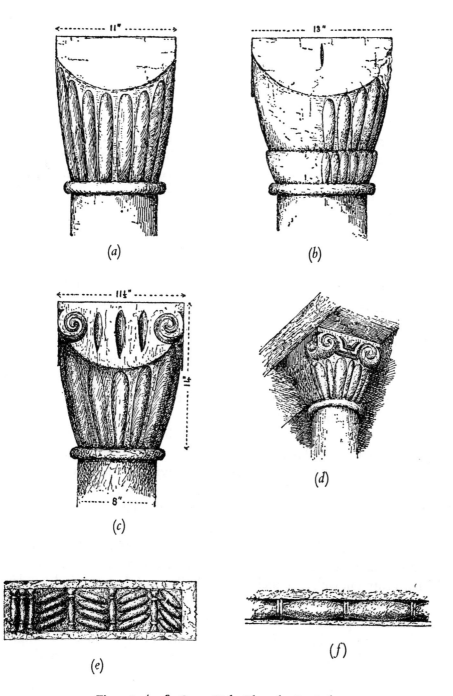

Fig. 26. (*a–d*) Great Hale Church, Capitals
(*e*) Hexham, carved Saxon Stone
(*f*) Hexham, carved Roman Stone

the very steep gabled roof of the old lower nave, and above the apex is a rectangular opening similar to those in corresponding positions in the west and south walls.

HOUGH-ON-THE-HILL

ALL SAINTS' CHURCH.[1] This tower is not a typical member of the Lincolnshire group. It is large, projecting 20 ft. 6 ins. from the nave. For this reason Hamilton Thompson suggested that the tower may have been part of a turriform church. There is no other evidence to support this suggestion. Thompson suggested alternatively that the large superficial area may indicate that the tower is a later development from such towers as Barnack (Northants)[2] which were used for and may possibly have been built for certain special ritual purposes.

The tower (I) has four stages. The lower three, separated by boldly projecting string courses, are Anglo-Saxon. The fourth stage, the belfry, with eight pinnacles and intermediate ornamental features rising from the ornamented parapet, is fifteenth century. The belfry is built of fine ashlar with elaborate double two-light windows characteristic of the period.

The three lower stages are built of rectangular rubble blocks, fairly well coursed, with a good deal of repair work or re-facing in ashlar at the top of the third stage. The quoins are of large slabs, some up to 3 ft. 6 ins. long, arranged in mixed face and side-alternate manner. The ground stage is quite singularly short, only about two-elevenths of the total height of the tower; the top stage is the tallest being six-elevenths, or more than half of the total height of the lower three stages.

Attached to the west wall is a large circular stair turret extending, with its cap, the whole height of the three Saxon stages. It has a heavily moulded cornice near the top from which rises a flat, tiled, sloping roof extending to the third string course. This roof is later than the turret. The turret is of similar fabric to the tower and has window-openings of similar type to the tower windows. It is bonded into the tower wall. For these reasons it is generally considered to be contemporary with the tower. The spiral staircase within is of an earlier type than those at Great Hale and Brixworth. The central newel, *c.* 16 inches thick, built up of drums, is independent of the stairs, which are of large slabs *c.* 30 inches wide, fitted between newel and wall surface. There is no plinth to either tower or stair turret.

For so large a tower the openings are unusually few and small; one might almost call them entirely inadequate. There are no openings on the exterior in the very short ground stage. In the second stage, low down and resting on the first string course, is

[1] A. Hamilton Thompson, (*c*); E. Trollope, (*c*).   [2] See above, p. 195.

(I) *Plate* 151.

one tall, very narrow rectangular window in the north wall; the jambs are of four slabs each, the lintel of one large block, and the sill of one block; it is chamfered all round. It looks old but later than the other openings. In the third stage, also low down and resting on the string course, are two tall narrow original openings with arched lintels, and jambs of one long and two small blocks each, one window in each north and south wall. In the west wall are two lights only, both almost half-way up the third stage, one to the north and one to the south of the stair turret. The north opening is a crude rectangular window with flat lintel and sill, both much broken, and jambs of one long pillar stone each with a short slab above and one below the long. The south window is similar except that it has a segmentally arched lintel, a north jamb of three stones and a south jamb of two.

The stair turret (1) has three tiers of windows vertically disposed, one facing west, one north and one south. On the west are three windows each cut from a single stone, the upper two having mouldings. The apertures are round-headed and are slightly wider at the sills. On the south there are four openings. The two middle ones are circular, double-splayed and have half-round mouldings round them. The top window is of diagonal shape and the bottom one square. In the north wall there are three windows, two circular and one rectangular, the latter cut from one moulded stone.

There is no tower arch in the interior. The only access to the tower is a small thirteenth-century doorway; whether this replaced an earlier opening is not known. The entrance to the stair turret is a gable-headed doorway, similar to that at Brigstock (2) (Northants). High up in the east wall of the tower, in the third stage and below the nave roof, is a large round-headed blocked doorway similar in type and position to many others found in Anglo-Saxon towers. Others in this county are at Barton-on-Humber, Lincoln, Marton and Nettleton.

The nave and chancel are thirteenth to fifteenth century, but high up, above the chancel roof, visible from the exterior, is what appears to be a bit of original nave north-east quoin.

LINCOLN CITY

There are three Anglo-Saxon towered churches in Lincoln, all close together in the High Street across the river to the south of the city: St. Benedict, St. Mary-le-Wigford, and St. Peter-at-Gowts or at the Watercourses. Their origin and precise dating are not known. As stated above[1] E. A. Freeman and Baldwin Brown thought

[1] p. 251.

---

(1) Plate 151; *(2) Plate* 92.

St. Mary's and St. Peter's post-Conquest, though Anglo-Saxon, while Hamilton Thompson thought them pre-Conquest.

Stenton[1] points out that a certain Colswein of Lincoln was one of only two Englishmen south of the Tees who held lands of baronial dimensions direct from the King, as recorded in Domesday Book. Elsewhere[1] he writes that this Colswein bought land, swampy and marshy, south of the river on which to build houses for a considerable number of people. He is also stated to have 'possessed' two churches, which suggests, in view of the context, that he built them. Stenton thought these churches were St. Mary's and St. Peter's as these two are closely similar, even in many details, while St. Benedict's differs from the other two in some respects. The inference seems reasonable that Colswein built the two similar rather than the two dissimilar churches of the three. But a dedication stone in St. Mary's states that this church was built by one Eirtig, which leaves the two dissimilar churches to Colswein. J. W. F. Hall produced some literary evidence to suggest that Colswein's St. Peter's church may have been built on another site: on higher ground to the east of the city, not to the south where St. Peter-at-Gowts is. This would leave the other of Colswein's churches unidentified. So perhaps the origin of these churches has not yet been cleared up satisfactorily. However, both Baldwin Brown and Hamilton Thompson regarded St. Mary-le-Wigford and St. Peter-at-Gowts as the two classical expressions of the Lincolnshire type.

ST. BENEDICT'S CHURCH.[2] The church is stated to have been originally rather similar to that of nearby St. Mary-le-Wigford, but the whole church has been entirely rebuilt. The nave and chancel were destroyed or became derelict in the Civil War. About 1672 the old chancel was rebuilt in its present form of nave-chancel and north chapel and the tower was pulled down and rebuilt further east against the rebuilt church and across the old chancel arch, but not necessarily in its old form. The rebuilding reinserted the original belfry double openings, but 'the absence of other Saxon features proves nothing about its predecessor'. The rebuilders had the tall towers of St. Mary-le-Wigford and St. Peter-at-Gowts and also the rather squat tower of St. Margaret's close at hand, and may have chosen to copy the latter for economy.

The tower (1) is built of coursed rubble with many large square or rectangular blocks of limestone. There is a plain square-edged plinth and above it, one slab high, is a large square and rectangular slab facing to the lower part of the tower; the facing looks and probably is modern. The south-west tower quoins are of regular slabs

[1] Op. cit., (*a*) and (*b*).
[2] G. Baldwin Brown; A. Hamilton Thompson, (*h*).

(1) *Plate* 152.

mainly side-alternate but with some face-alternate slabs which are almost square in section like clasping quoins. The north-west quoins are similar but less well-defined; some are replacements. The north-east and south-east quoins are hidden by the north chapel except in the belfry stage where they are similar to those below on the west.

The tower has two stages, a tall lower one and a shorter upper or belfry stage. The lower stage is divided into two internally by a wooden ceiling, not original. There is a string course separating the two stages and another one above the belfry and below the plain parapet. The tower is 15 ft. 6 ins. wide at the west on the exterior.

There are no openings in the north and south walls below the belfry. In the west wall, low down, is a crude rectangular window with lintel, jambs and sill of one slab each. In the interior it is widely splayed, in Norman fashion, laterally only. The front stone lintel is thin; on the interior it consists of three oak beams. The aperture is 1 ft. 10 ins. high by 7½ inches.

An exactly similar window is higher up in the second interior stage.

The belfry has the usual double openings with mid-wall shafts, without capitals or bases. On the west the heads are of roughly shaped voussoirs with proper V-shaped keystones. The central impost is double, of a thin rectangular slab lying on a thin square one; both have wide chamfers on all four lower sides giving them the appearance of very much flattened cubic capitals with sharp edges. The south jamb is of four large rectangular blocks, the top and bottom ones on their sides, the other two on their faces; the north jamb is of four definite uprights and flats. The sill is badly worn but may originally have sloped like the others. The north, east and south openings are similar.

St. Mary-le-Wigford's Church.[1] The district was known formerly as Wigford, Wickford or Wickerford. The origin of the name is uncertain. It may be derived from Wig or Wik or Vik which was the Danish word for a creek, or from Wick or Wicken which meant an osier. Hence the name may signify the 'ford over the creek' or the 'ford by the osiers'. Either would agree with the early state of the area: marshy, low-lying land through which the early High Street passed as an embankment raised above flood level.

The date of the tower is uncertain; it has been given by different writers from 940 to 1080. It may have been built on the foundations of an earlier Roman building, possibly a temple as suggested by the dedication stone. Also a huge block of stone, evidently Roman work, was dug up near the foundations of the tower when it was underpinned. The stone is in the churchyard.

The tower is very similar to that of St. Peter-at-Gowts. It is tall and massive, with no buttresses or internal stairway. It has the usual double belfry lights in all four

[1] G. Baldwin Brown; J. W. F. Hall; A. Hamilton Thompson, (*h*).

walls, with mid-wall shafts. It has a western doorway and a tall and wide tower arch. It is 20 ft. 4 ins. wide.

The nave, chancel and chancel arch are thirteenth century.

The tower (1) is built of well-coursed rectangular rubble blocks. The quoins are of medium sized rectangular dressed slabs, side-alternate, with some renewals. There is no plinth. The very tall lower part is separated from the recessed belfry by a square-edged string course. The low embattled geometrically ornamented parapet with its own hollow-chamfered ornamented string course below is later. In the west wall is a tall and relatively narrow western doorway. The jambs show considerable repair and replacements but the slabs approximate to upright and flat. The imposts are plain chamfered on the soffit sides only and the chamfered faces have similar geo-metrical ornament to that on the tower arch. The round head of voussoirs is of two orders and has a hood mould with hollow chamfer below with chevron decoration resting on small corbels carved with human heads. As at St. Peter-at-Gowts this western doorway and the window above are probably not original. Immediately above is a later simple two-light pointed window with a square hood mould. The jambs and sill are renewals but are of early type: jambs of three slabs each of equal height but arranged upright-flat-upright, and thin sill. Above this is a window with round head of five voussoirs, jambs of two pillar stones each with a flat above acting as impost, and a short thin sill. Opposite this in the east wall is an exactly similar window.

On the south face high up, just below the string course, is a tall rather narrow window (2) with arched lintel, no separate sill and jambs of five irregular slabs each: arranged flat-upright-flat-upright-flat, the top flats looking like imposts, though of course arched lintels do not need imposts; the flats are of the long and thin clasping variety.

There is no opening in the north wall below the belfry.

The double belfry openings (2) are tall and wide, with heads of voussoirs, jambs of slabs mainly upright and flat but with some clasping slabs. The jamb imposts are thin and chamfered on their projecting soffit sides; the thin central imposts are square with wide chamfers on all four sides. The columns are circular except the north one which is octagonal. The capitals, with neckings below, are badly worn but appear to have crude volutes at the corners except the one on the north which has its faces and vertical edges chamfered below to bring it to conformity with the octagonal shaft below (Fig. 27).

A large dedication stone (3) is built into the exterior west face of the tower on the sinister side of the doorway. It is a Roman memorial stone re-used. Below in the rectangular part is an epitaph to one Sacer, the Sennonian son of Briscus, his wife

---

Carsouna and son, Quintus. Above, in the steep pediment, is the dedication inscription in vernacular Old English.[1] The letters are Roman capitals except three: an Anglo-Saxon W and two 'and's'. The inscription is in five lines to be read from the bottom line upwards. It reads:

MARIE

OFE 7 SCE

NCRISTE TO L

AN 7 FIOS GODIA

EIRTIG ME LET WIRCE

or rearranged for direct reading: EIRTIG ME LET WIRCEAN 7 FIOS GODIAN CRISTE TO LOFE 7 S[AN]C[T]E MARIE. It has been translated 'Eirtig had me built to the Glory

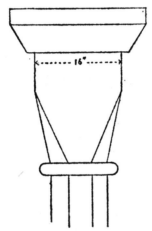

Fig. 27. Lincoln, St. Mary-le-Wigford Church, Capital

of Christ and St. Mary'. Eirtig the founder is otherwise unknown and Professor Bruce Dickens knew of no other example of the name either in England or Scandinavia. The termination -ig is presumably Danish and was a common ending of the names of men of pure or mixed Danish stock active in England in the eleventh century; Tostig, the brother of King Harold II, is an example.

The tower arch (I) is very tall, nearly as high as the pointed nave arcade which is also very high as there is no clerestory. The arch head has twenty-three voussoirs, and is stilted by 2 voussoirs on each side. The jambs are of ashlar, 2 to 4 stones per course. A carved stone with interlacement pattern has been built into the south jamb.[2] (A similar stone is in the nave wall above the south doorway.) The thick imposts are half-chamfered on the soffit sides only and these faces are decorated with

---

[1] Bruce Dickens; J. Wordsworth.　　　　[2] See J. W. F. Hall, Pl. 7.

(I) *Plate* 155.

raised and sunk square patterns, five rows on each face of the chamfer. The arch head is of two rings of voussoirs, but if there is rubble filling between the rings it is hidden by the plaster. The jambs are 3 ft. 5 ins. thick and *c.* 14 to 15 feet high to the imposts. The opening is 10 feet wide.

About 26 feet up, above the tower arch, is a large round-headed opening, a very common feature in Anglo-Saxon towers. There are openings in similar positions at St. Peter-at-Gowts, at Deerhurst 16 feet up and at Bosham at 18 feet, and elsewhere. In the two last-named towers there are similar openings at still higher levels, at 27 feet at Deerhurst and 30 feet at Bosham. Such lower openings are usually regarded as openings of ingress to the upper stages of a tower, probably by ladder from the nave. The upper ones, where there are upper ones, were probably openings of egress from the tower to chambers between inner and outer nave roofs. The opening at St. Mary-le-Wigford corresponds presumably to the upper opening elsewhere; it seems too high above the floor to be reached by a ladder. These openings of ingress and egress were not popular in Lincolnshire. No tower in the county has both types. Three—Scartho, Thurlby and Winterton—have the lower openings. Six have the upper ones leading to roof chambers; these are Barton-on-Humber, Hough-on-the-Hill, Lincoln (St. Mary-le-Wigford and St. Peter-at-Gowts), Marton and Nettleton.

ST. PETER-AT-GOWTS' CHURCH.[1] The tower and nave are of the eleventh century; the present chancel dates from 1888.[2] The tower (1) is tall and massive though rather more slender than that of St. Mary-le-Wigford. It is 18 ft. 4 ins. wide at the base. There is a double plinth, each member of which has a small upper chamfer; the lower member is 21 inches high, the upper member 14 inches. The plinth belongs to the tower only; it is not returned along the nave west wall. The lower member ends a little short, by *c.* 15 inches, of the western door-opening. The tower has no appreciable batter except, curiously, a slight narrowing beneath the first, square-edged, string course. It is built of well-coursed fairly large rubble. The lower stage of the tower occupies about four-fifths of the total height. The top, or belfry, stage is quite deeply recessed behind the stage below. Above there is a narrow plain later parapet of ashlar between two string courses.

The tower quoins (2) are of medium-sized slabs, all of much the same height, in side-alternate arrangement. The nave quoins, as at nearby Bracebridge, are of real upright and flat work. The uprights are up to 2 ft. 6 ins. long and the flats *c.* 2 ft. 6 ins. by 8 inches. The nave projects 2 ft. 6 ins. to the north and 2 ft. 2 ins. to the south of the tower.

[1] G. Baldwin Brown; J. W. F. Hall; A. Hamilton Thompson, (*h*).
[2] A plan as it was *c.* 1840–50 is given by A. Hamilton Thompson, (*h*).

(1) *Plate* 157; (2) *Plates* 158, 159.

In the west wall of the tower is a tall narrow doorway (1), rather similar to that at St. Mary's. It has jambs of long and short through-stones, large slab imposts with wide chamfer below on the projecting soffit sides only. Above is a plain thin lintel supporting a plain arch head of voussoirs enclosing a rather small tympanum decorated with Norman-looking geometrical ornament. A rather elaborate semicircular hood, decorated on the underside with two rows of billet ornament, surrounds the arch head. Its two ends rest on corbels with billet ornament underneath. This doorway was considered formerly to be Norman, and because of it some writers gave a late post-Conquest date to the tower. However, Hall pointed out that an early nineteenth-century water colour by de Windt shows no western doorway or round-headed window above it; both are mid-nineteenth-century insertions. De Windt's painting and an earlier eighteenth-century drawing by Buck show a doorway and porch in the south wall of the tower, where there is now no opening. It seems likely that there was an original western doorway which at some time was blocked when a south doorway and porch were made. The latter was removed and the south doorway built up when the western doorway was re-opened and the existing structure inserted.

High up in the west wall is a tall narrow window not unlike the modern window below in general appearance. However, it has an arched lintel with a half-round hood mould resting on its own flat imposts. Its short slab sill is of Norman type: it is of one stone with ends turned upwards to form the beginning of the jambs, and chamfered above between the turned-up ends. The jambs are of four stones each, of about the same widths, and arranged short-long-long-short. Immediately above is an original carved stone. It is badly worn and few details are visible but the carving is certainly of a human figure.[1]

There is no opening in the north wall below the belfry. In the south wall about half way up is a window similar to that higher up in the west but with no hood mould. It has a double-arched lintel and jambs of three slabs each, upright-upright-flat.

The belfry openings (2) are the usual Anglo-Saxon double-light type with certain peculiarities. The double arch heads are of voussoirs. The jamb stones are finely dressed, in upright-flat-upright-flat-upright arrangement; most, not all, are through-stones. The jamb imposts are thin, chamfered on the projecting soffit sides only, and do not project from the wall face. The central imposts do project and are deeply hollow-chamfered below on all edges. The mid-wall shafts are circular, except the south one which is octagonal. The capitals form two pairs: those on the east and north are alike, and those on the south and west. The eastern one is quite similar to

---

[1] J. W. F. Hall, Pl. 9a.

(1) *Plate* 158; (2) *Plates* 157, 159.

those on the tower arch at Langford (Oxon) (1). It resembles two truncated cones joined at the wider ends forming a sharp arris round the middle of the capital. There is plain necking below and a square square-edged impost above between the capital and the hollow-chamfered impost proper. The capital on the south is of more complex design. The hollow-chamfered impost is 22 inches wide and the actual capital 20 inches tall. There is a single-cabled necking round the middle of the capital dividing it into two halves, and a cabled double necking below, as one, the cabling here being in opposite directions. The lower, circular, half of the capital has so-called Jews' harp ornament[1] all round it. The upper half has similar decoration converted to double spirals towards the corners to suggest volutes (Fig. 28).

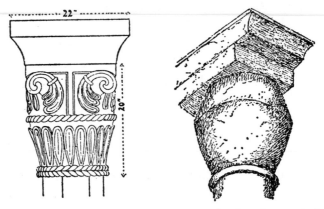

Fig. 28. Lincoln, St. Peter-at-Gowts' Church, Capitals

The tower arch (2) is characteristically late Anglo-Saxon, very high and plain, of one order, with round head of voussoirs, jambs of dressed stones with plain imposts chamfered below on the soffit sides only. Above, *c.* 26 feet above the floor is a large gable headed doorway, chamfered all round, similar in type and position to that at St. Mary-le-Wigford.[2]

MARTON

ST. MARGARET'S CHURCH.[3] The greater part of the tower, nave and chancel are Anglo-Saxon. The tower (3), nave, south wall of the chancel, south aisle and south porch are built of rubble, the greater part of the fabric in herring-bone formation which extends through the walls to the interior. The herring-boning is mainly without spines. The spined appearance of many courses is fictitious; it is due to the

---

[1] See below, pp. 300–2.   [2] Cf. above, p. 286.   [3] G. Baldwin Brown.

(1) *Plate* 117; (2) *Plate* 156; (3) *Plate* 160.

fact that several rows of herring-boning may be separated from other rows by two to five courses of ordinary rubble. When the church was restored in 1904 it was discovered that the tower foundations extended only about 2 feet below ground and consisted of trenches filled with sand and pebbles. It may have been this weakness of foundations that caused the builders to use herring-boning so extensively as a supposed method of strengthening walls.[1] There is very little herring-boning in the belfry stage.

The tall and slender tower tapers somewhat. It was originally plastered but most of the plaster has peeled off. The rather large rough slab quoins are mainly side-alternate, except in the belfry where they are mainly face-alternate. The belfry above the string course is recessed. The low embattled ashlar parapet with its hollow-chamfered string course below is later.

There are no openings in the north and south tower walls below the belfry stage. In the west wall, in the position of a western doorway, is a wide tall plain pointed arch, not original; it is built-up as a recess in brick in which has been inserted a modern round-headed window. Above this arch is an original window opening, very slightly key-holed. It has a double-arched lintel with a semicircular strip-work upper-chamfered hood resting on small corbels above the very massive top jamb stones. The jambs are of five stones each, decreasing in size from the top massive one downwards. It has no separate sill, and has slight single-splay. Above this window is a stone with a human head carved on it. A small square flat slab projects from the wall acting as a kind of protective canopy for the figure, which is very badly weathered.

The belfry openings are of the usual double type with mid-wall shafts but have some late features. The jambs are very rough, of six slabs each mainly face-alternate and not of through-stones. The projecting imposts are chamfered below. The heads are arched lintels with bold mouldings round their outer edges. The mid-wall circular shafts have cubic, not cushion, capitals: the parts below the square abaci are rounded off all round to fit the circular neckings below; the upper parts have crude volutes at the corners. This is a late feature and suggests a post-Conquest date for the church and tower.

On the east wall of the tower are the marks of an earlier high steep gabled roof of the nave; its apex is a little below the string course.

The tower arch has a round head of two rings of voussoirs with rubble filling between the rings. The jambs are of ashlar, three or four stones per course. The thin imposts are chamfered on the soffit and east sides and are returned only a few inches along the wall. The opening is 5 ft. 10 ins. wide and 8 ft. 2 ins. high to the imposts. Above the tower arch and below the apex of the roof marks is a rectangular opening, with a single slab lintel and jambs of slabs. The lower half is visible from the nave,

[1] J. F. Curwen.

the upper half only from the exterior—it is above the nave roof. In view of its position it appears to have been an egress from the tower to an inter-roof space. There are only five other such openings in the county; they are at St. Mary-le-Wigford and St. Peter-at-Gowts' churches in Lincoln, and at Hough-on-the-Hill, Nettleton and Barton-on-Humber.

The nave extends 2 to 3 feet to the north and south of the tower. There are many carved fragments, probably from early standing crosses, built into the west wall of the south aisle; some have interlacement and plaitwork ornament. There are no original south-west or south-east nave quoins; the east and west walls have been integrated into the later walls of the south aisle. The north aisle has been built against the nave with straight joints and the north-east and north-west quoins are plainly visible; they are of irregular slabs similar to those of the tower and mainly side-alternate.

Fig. 29. Marton Church, Capital

The chancel arch is probably Norman. It has recessed angle columns with curious capitals (Fig. 29). They have their faces rather convexly chamfered and their vertical edges slightly chamfered, in principle rather like those at Broughton-by-Brigg, and the roughly rounded faces are covered with incised separate ornaments of spirals, one at each upper corner suggesting volutes, and ellipses pointed below rather like the Jews' harp ornaments at Stow. There is cabled necking below. Baldwin Brown considered that these elaborate capitals imply a post-Conquest date but carrying on of Anglo-Saxon tradition. The approximation to volute capitals is however very crude and suggests rather an Anglo-Saxon mason trying his hand at an unfamiliar design.

NETTLETON

ST. JOHN THE BAPTIST'S CHURCH.[1] Only the lower part of the tower is Anglo-Saxon, dated by Baldwin Brown to the Saxo-Norman Overlap. The upper part,

[1] A. Hamilton Thompson, (c); E. Trollope, (a).

the belfry, was rebuilt in the late fourteenth or early fifteenth century. The body of the church was entirely rebuilt in 1805, and no early quoins or other early features remain in this part.

The lower part of the tower is of early date. It is built of large stones of irregular shape of local ironstone; the surface is much decayed. Large late mediaeval buttresses were built at the north-west and south-west corners and against the middle of the south wall. There is no visible plinth. The tower dimensions are *c*. 13¼ feet wide (north–south) by 12¾ feet long; that is, as at Caistor and unusual with Lincolnshire towers, the width exceeds the length. The ground-floor walls are plastered.

In the west wall at ground level is a round-headed doorway, the jambs of which are of large irregular blocks of stone. The opening narrows slightly upwards to the imposts. The arch head is of thirteen voussoirs in two rings with rubble filling between the rings. Above is a projecting unchamfered strip-work hood mould on the face of which are the remains of roughly carved Jews' harp ornament, similar to that on the tower arch at Stow.[1] The jamb impost blocks are quirked and chamfered and do not extend far enough along the wall to support the hood. The round head encloses a tympanum with modern hatching and a large circular piercing filled with modern coloured glass. Above the doorway is a plain projecting string course and just above this is a tall loop window with arched lintel, aperture *c*. 9 inches wide and splayed internally to 3 feet. The wall here is 3 ft. 3 ins. thick. There is diagonal tooling on the corner stones of the splay. The splay is roofed with flat slabs so that the head is an arched lintel on the exterior and a flat roof on the interior. The exterior head and jambs are badly weathered.

The north wall, like the south but not the west, has an intermediate string course, as at Clee. This is unusual in Lincolnshire towers which normally have single string courses, dividing the belfry from the part below. There are very faint traces of a former window opening at clock chamber level; otherwise the face is plain.

In the south wall, below the intermediate string course and in the upper part of the ground stage, is a slit window with arched lintel and not very wide single internal splay. The jambs on the interior are of three slabs each: the western one with a massive bottom stone, then a tall upright with a small cubical stone above; the eastern jamb has two tall uprights, the lower one being thicker in its other two dimensions, and a small stone above. On the exterior the western jamb is of three large blocks, the eastern of several small ones. The later buttress covers the opening but it has been pierced through from east to west to preserve the purpose for which the opening was made.

The tower arch has a round-head of sixteen voussoirs of uneven size on its eastern face and eighteen very irregular and badly cut on the west; the space between was formerly rubble-filled but is now filled with ashlar through-stones. The eight

[1] See below, pp. 300–2.

voussoirs in the southern half of the east face are plain and the arch head on this side slightly stilted by one course above the impost. The nine voussoirs on the north are moulded with a cavetto and roll, late post-Conquest features. The jambs are faced with ashlar. The imposts are modern renewals, quirked and moulded. The arch is 7 ft. 10½ ins. wide and 10 ft. 10½ ins. high to the imposts; the total height to the crown of the arch is *c.* 14 ft. 6 ins. The jambs are 4 ft. 0½ in. thick; the wall thins upwards to *c.* 3 ft. 3 ins. at the clock chamber.

Above in the tower east wall is a rectangular opening from the tower to a former inter-roof space. Such openings are rare in Lincolnshire; others are at St. Mary-le-Wigford and St. Peter-at-Gowts, Lincoln, Marton, Hough-on-the-Hill and Barton-on-Humber.

ROTHWELL

ST. MARY'S CHURCH.[1] This is a well-preserved typical Lincolnshire tower (1) dated by Baldwin Brown to the Saxo-Norman Overlap. It has a rather tall belfry stage between a lower plain string course and an upper plain parapet. It is built of local ironstone, rather weathered and according to Atkinson strengthened with a later flat buttress. This buttress is in a curious position: against the nave west wall in the angle between nave and tower south wall, a position in which a buttress would seem to be of little or no use (Fig. 30). Baldwin Brown considered it to be not a buttress but the south-west corner of the old nave left *in situ* when the present nave was built a few feet to the east. Its south-west corner has an upright and flat arrangement of stones which no buttress would have. It is not as high as the existing nave, which is not very high by Saxon standards, but it cannot be assumed that the old quoin, if it is an old quoin, is necessarily of its original height. The quoins are of irregular slabs. There is a plinth of two members, both chamfered.

In the west wall is a western doorway with round-headed arch enclosing a plain tympanum, as at nearby Nettleton, and a plain projecting strip-work hood mould above. The head is set back *c.* 3 inches behind the jamb faces. The jambs are of large irregular slabs arranged side-alternately. The imposts are of unequal sizes and are chamfered on wall and soffit faces. The doorway is 2 ft. 9 ins. wide and 6 ft. 11 ins. high to the imposts. Above the western doorway, lighting the ringing chamber, is a small window opening, only 9 inches wide and little more than a foot high, with a very high nearly square arched lintel. It has wide internal splay, the splay, as at Nettleton, being ceiled with flat slabs. Jambs are of one large block each, lying on its side; there is no separate sill.

[1] G. Atkinson, (*b*); G. Baldwin Brown; A. Sutton; A. Hamilton Thompson, (*c*).

(1) *Plate* 161.

In the north wall is a fragment of a chamfered intermediate string course, as at Nettleton, near the east corner. About the centre of the wall is a small window with arched lintel, but no separate sill, similar in size and position to the window in the west wall; the jambs are of two very large stones each.

In the south wall is a small fragment of an intermediate string course (there is no such fragment in the west wall). There are two window openings. The upper one is similar to that on the north in that it has arched lintel and no sill; its eastern jamb is of one very large slab lying on its side, the western one has two smaller stones.

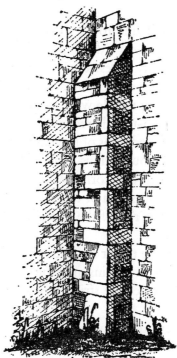

Fig. 30. Rothwell Church, Buttress or Nave Quoin

The lower window, only about 6 feet above the ground, is of similar character but differs in some details from the one above. Its arched lintel is very tall and forms also the upper parts of the jambs; the lower part of each jamb is of one long upright stone. There is no separate sill.

The belfry has the usual four tall double-lights with through-stone central projecting imposts and mid-wall shafts with cubic capitals of advanced design, which suggest a post-Conquest date. The neckings are plain. The bases are semi-bulbous and rest on square slabs. Each double head is of two arched lintels. The jambs are of large blocks not through-stones at the corners with smaller blocks in the soffit faces as filling. All the imposts are chamfered.

The tower arch is plain; the arch head is of voussoirs with ashlar filling. The jambs are plastered and white-washed. The imposts are chamfered on the soffit faces and are returned like string courses along the whole eastern face of the wall on both north and south sides of the arch. The opening is 5 ft. 1 in. wide and 10 ft. 9 ins. high to the imposts. The jambs, i.e. the wall, are 3 ft. 9 ins. thick. There is a two-membered plinth on the east face, 2 ft. 8 ins. high, which is a continuation of the tower plinth.

SCARTHO

ST. GILES' CHURCH.[1] This tall fine tower was dated by Baldwin Brown to the Overlap on account of some late carved details. It has a single string course, below the belfry which is very slightly recessed. The plain, low, ugly parapet may be fifteenth century, the insignificant corner pinnacles may be eighteenth century.

The tower (1) is built of rough rubble with small but regular quoin stones mainly side-alternate. It stands on a two-membered chamfered plinth. Atkinson stated that the south side of the plinth showed signs of fire damage and suggested that the tower may have been built on earlier foundations. The writer could find only one stone in the west and a few in the south-east corner of the nave with such discoloration. In the nave west wall, to north and south of the tower, the original quoins, similar to those of the tower, remain. The rest of the nave is of the thirteenth and fourteenth century.

The internal dimensions of the tower are 9 ft. 9 ins. east–west by 11 ft. 6 ins. wide. On the exterior the west wall is 16 ft. 4 ins. making the wall thickness *c.* 3 ft. 3 ins.

The north wall has no intermediate string course. There are traces of a blocked window.

In the west wall is a western doorway[2] the door of which has been replaced by a modern round-headed window. The plain arch head is of voussoirs of irregular size but equal length and above is a semicircular strip-work hood, chamfered below, projecting to the east faces of the projecting jamb imposts. The imposts are of large blocks of ironstone with slight lower chamfer. The jambs are of rough stones, six on the north and five on the south, arranged in upright and flat manner above the plinth. The opening is 3 ft. 5 ins. wide and 4 ft. 10 ins. high to the top of the imposts. A little above the west doorway is a tall narrow window opening with arched lintel, no separate sill, no imposts, jambs of two big upright slabs each; it has wide inner splay.

[1] G. Atkinson, (*b*); G. Baldwin Brown; A. Sutton; A. Hamilton Thompson, (*c*).
[2] G. Atkinson, (*b*), Pl. facing p. 23. He states the opening extends below present ground-level by 1 ft. 10 ins.; its original height was therefore 6 ft. 8 ins.

(1) *Plate* 162.

In the south wall is a large thirteenth-century doorway, now the main entrance to the church. Above this, about half way to the string course, is a tall and not very narrow window opening with arched lintel, no separate sill and jambs of two upright slabs each. A horizontal sloping weather course cuts across the window near its head. This seems to have been made for the roof of a building extending far above the south doorway, perhaps a two-storeyed porch with a lean-to roof against the tower wall. Far below this and immediately above the thirteenth-century doorway is the blocked upper part of a tall pointed arch, perhaps the original entrance to the church from the porch, now destroyed.

The belfry stage has the usual double-light windows in all four walls, with mid-wall circular shafts and through-stone chamfered projecting imposts. Three of the shafts have capitals elaborately but rather crudely carved with stylized foliage, with plain neckings below (Fig. 31). A double spiral leaf forms a volute at each upper

Fig. 31. Scartho Church, Capital

corner of the capital, while below is an encircling series of what was undoubtedly intended to be stiff stylized leaves turned back slightly outwards at their tips. The eastern capital is plain but is corbelled out on east and west to support the central impost; it is of one piece with the shaft.[1] There are no bases. The heads are arched lintels, two to each double head, jambs are of dressed slabs, not through-stones, and the sills are tall and sloping.

The tower arch (l) is a fine one. As at Clee the arch head has a double band of very regular voussoirs, the lower one being slightly recessed; the voussoirs are also in two rings, an eastern and a western, with rubble filling now plastered between the rings. The jambs are of square-ended slabs. The imposts are short and do not extend

[1] Cf. Bolam, Jarrow and Sompting.

(l) *Plate* 163.

far enough north and south to serve as imposts to the outer order. The opening is 5 ft. 4 ins. wide and 10 ft. 3 ins. high to the imposts.

Above the tower arch is a rectangular opening overlooking the nave, presumably the former access to the tower upper stages. There are openings in similar positions at Thurlby and Winterton.

SPRINGTHORPE

THE CHURCH OF ST. GEORGE AND ST. LAWRENCE.[1] Only the tower (I) is pre-Conquest. It is a fine sturdy tower with a chamfered plinth, much of which is below ground level, but no string courses below the parapet. It is built of greyish stones which look green, probably due to mould growth; similar grey stones have been used for some quoin replacements. The quoins are of rather small side-alternate slabs. Above the plinth are several courses of herring-boning in the south wall and one course in the north wall.

The modern plain parapet, between two hollow-chamfered string courses, projects slightly from the tower. The west wall is 16 ft. 6 ins. wide on the exterior.

In the west wall is an original doorway, now built up. The jambs are of six irregular blocks of limestone each. The projecting imposts are chamfered. It has a flat lintel with a roughly built round head above enclosing a tympanum now filled with three flat slabs. The head is of six stones acting as voussoirs; the north and south bottom 'voussoirs' are roughly shaped massive stones of almost megalithic size. The tympanum has been badly cracked through pressure from above. The blocking is thin; on the interior the former doorway is now a recess 2 ft. 5 ins. wide and 4 ft. 5 ins. high above the plinth. In the blocking a tall narrow rectangular light has been cut; the jambs, lintel and sill are made of circular sectioned shafts or pillars, perhaps from the old belfry openings, now destroyed.

Below the belfry openings there is no opening in the north wall, nor in the west above the doorway. On the south there is one window high up, in the ringing chamber. This window is of peculiar design. It is tall and narrow with no sill. The jambs are of four stones each, two large slabs with a thin one above and below. There is a double-arched lintel cut from a large slab, with a square-edged hood mould part of the single lintel stone: the background of this stone has been cut back to leave the projecting hood. In the lintel stone, above the round opening a large inverted V-shaped depression has been cut which gives the opening a gabled appearance.

Parts of the belfry walls are renewals. The belfry openings are modern. They are of the usual double light type, with heads of three stones each, jambs of ashlar,

[1] E. Trollope, (*b*).

(I) *Plate* 164.

chamfered imposts, scalloped cushion capitals to the circular, not mid-wall, shafts which have tall conical bases, all perhaps in general imitation of earlier openings.

STOW

ST. MARY'S CHURCH.[1] There are many Stows, which is not surprising for the word means 'settlement' or 'resting place'. This Stow is supposed to have got its name as a place where Queen Etheldrede rested on her flight from her husband Ecgfrith of Northumbria in 672. As recorded by Bede, Ecgfrith was a boy when she was married to him; she maintained her virginity for twelve years and then asked to be released from the marriage so that she might found a monastery and become a nun. When he refused she fled from him. When she rested at this place miraculous happenings were reported to occur there which so impressed the credulous people of the age, including Ecgfrith, that the King agreed to release her and helped her to found the monastery at Ely. He also built and endowed a church on the spot, *c.* 678, to commemorate Etheldrede's stay here and the place became known as St. Etheldrede Stow. Later, when the present church of St. Mary was built, the name was changed to St. Mary Stow. It is now usually called simply Stow, Lincs.

Little definite is known about Ecgfrith's church. But a church here was burnt by the Danes in *c.* 870. This church may have been a later one or possibly a later rebuilding of the original church. It was thought by some earlier writers that the lower parts of the existing transepts are remains from this early church, recognizable by the reddish fire marks on the lower exterior walls and on the quoin stones, though there are no marks of fire higher up. There was however another fire in 1198, so little can be learned for dating purposes from the marks. Moreover the very fine large well-dressed chamfered three-membered plinth, and the large well-finished slab quoins are not consistent with so early a date. A large cruciform, genuinely transeptal church (as distinct from a cruciform church with low north and south porticus or 'wings') with a central tower was a rarity in Saxon times. The only others known, Norton in Co. Durham, St. Mary-in-Castro, Dover, Repton (Derby), and perhaps Stanton Lacy (Salop), were built late in the Late Saxon period, towards the end of the eleventh century. Some writers therefore doubt that Ecgfrith could have built such a church in the late seventh century, and it is not certainly known that he did. However, that he could have done so hardly admits of doubt. Although he was hostile to Wilfrid of Ripon, whom he regarded as to some degree responsible for his domestic trouble and whom he sent into exile for eight years,

[1] G. Atkinson, (*a*) and (*b*); G. Baldwin Brown; A. W. Clapham, (*f*); A. Hamilton Thompson, (*c*); E. Trollope, (*b*); V.C.H. *Lincs*, II.

677–85, he would doubtless be familiar with Wilfrid's great transeptal church at Hexham, only recently built. He might well have taken over Wilfrid's masons, perhaps left without employment during Wilfrid's exile, and transferred them to Stow to build a similar church there. The dimensions of the two churches are not very dissimilar. The present length of Stow is 150 feet; some writers think the original church was larger. Hexham was *c.* 165 feet. This is surmise; but at least it seems reasonable surmise, though no more than that.

Nothing is known of any repairs to the church after the burning in 870 until the early part of the eleventh century. It was re-founded as a minster for secular priests by Eadnoth II, bishop of Dorchester, 1006–16, *not* by Eadnoth III, 1034–50, as stated by Atkinson and by Baldwin Brown. The earlier date was established by H. E. Salter and accepted by Clapham and by V.C.H. Eadnoth II, however, was incorrectly called I by these writers; Eadnoth I reigned pre- and post-974, in which year he signed the foundation charter of Ramsey Abbey (Hunts). Later, under Bishop Wulfwig, 1053–7 (not the notorious Bishop Ulf, 1050–2, as stated by some writers), further endowments were given by Earl Leofric of Mercia and his wife Godiva, gifts confirmed by Edward the Confessor. In *c.* 1090, Remigius, first Norman bishop of Lincoln, 1072–92, decided to renovate the church as it was stated to be in a state of decay, and to convert it to a Benedictine abbey.

Atkinson and Trollope agreed that the lower parts of the transepts are pre-870, and the lower part of the tower *c.* 1040. Baldwin Brown was of opinion that all these lower parts were of *c.* 1040. Atkinson thought that the upper parts of the tower and transepts and the whole of the nave were due to Eadnoth. Trollope and Baldwin Brown maintained, more reasonably, that judging from architectural features the nave and upper parts of the transepts were the work of Remigius. Possibly an earlier nave may have been built by Eadnoth which may have been burnt and/or the remains pulled down by Remigius prior to his own renovation. The fine vaulted chancel could not be due to Remigius, as Atkinson thought; the architectural details are too elaborate for his date and are obviously later in type than his known work at Lincoln Cathedral. It must be later. Trollope suggested, though there is no historical record, that it was the work of Bishop Alexander of Lincoln, 1123–47, as perhaps also the nave doorways. The existing chancel vault is a later reconstruction. There were only minor alterations in the thirteenth century. The massive corner piers within the Saxon crossing and which support the pointed crossing arches are fourteenth century. The tower, rising only one stage above the nave roof, with its embattled parapet and pinnacles, is fifteenth century. The whole church was extensively restored by J. L. Pearson in 1850–2.

The existing church (I) is 150 feet long; the nave is 27 feet wide, the chancel

(I) *Plate* 166.

24 feet and the transepts 23 feet wide; the total width across the transepts is, according to Atkinson, 82 feet. The height of the side walls is *c.* 33 feet.

The Tower. Only the lower part as far up as the tops of the magnificent crossing arches is ancient; the upper part above the nave eaves is fifteenth century. It is not known whether there was a Saxon tower. If there was one it may have been a timber superstructure as at Breamore (Hants). The quoins are of large, almost megalithic, well-dressed stones, a late eleventh-century feature though there are early examples at Escomb (Co. Durham); they look later than those at Norton (Co. Durham). They

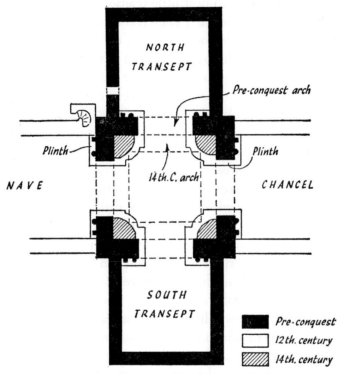

Fig. 32. Stow Church, plan of Crossing

are mainly face-alternate but are not so regular as the transept south-east quoins. The north-east and south-east quoins, like those at Norton, are visible like angular buttresses between the chancel and transepts. The north-west quoin shows above the roof of the low modern vestry. Baldwin Brown considered Stow as perhaps later than Norton on account of the better dressed quoins but in view of Escomb this is perhaps a weak inference.

On the interior (Fig. 32) the four crossing arches (1) are truly magnificent. As at Norton, they do not rest on piers or columns; they are really openings cut through

(1) *Plate* 170.

the walls, not fully Romanesque though showing Romanesque feeling. The round heads rest on very large projecting chamfered imposts. The jambs rest on massive five-membered plinths, the lowest member of which is below the Norman floor level; the upper parts rise 4 ft. 6 ins. above the floor. Down each jamb face are pairs of pilaster strips; the inner strips are half-round like some on Sompting tower (Sussex), an eleventh-century church, and on the tower arches at St. Benet's Cambridge and at Skipwith (Yorkshire, East Riding); the outer ones are square-sectioned. They have large weathered cubical bases which rest rather awkwardly on the plinths below. The plinth in fact seems to bear little relation to the arch above, which with its pilasters might be thought to be a later reconstruction if it were not that the peculiar ornamentation round the hood mould of the western arch head is of identical design with that of the Saxon window head in the south transept.

The jambs are not of through-stones; the soffit faces are lined with ashlar, two or three stones per course, in a Norman manner very common in Lincolnshire tower arches and suggestive of a late eleventh-century date. The jambs are 4 ft. 5 ins. thick. The arches are *c.* 30 feet high to the crowns and 14 ft. 3 ins. wide between the jambs and 11 ft. 2 ins. between the projecting plinths. The Saxon tower above, if there was ever one, has gone and the crossing is now covered by the extended roof of the chancel. To support the later tower the four interior angles of the crossing were filled in the fourteenth century with massive piers carrying pointed crossing arches on the interior of the earlier ones (Fig. 32). These piers are *c.* 5 feet thick east–west and north–south, but the sides facing the crossing have been made pentagonal.

The arch heads are of two rings of voussoirs, an outer and inner, with rubble filling, another common late Lincolnshire feature. Round the face of each arch head are two three-quarter rolls; a half-roll moulding is continued below the imposts as the half-round pilaster strip down the jambs. Outside the rolls is a hollow chamfered hood, the flat upper edge of which above the hollow is decorated with remarkable ornament. The ends of the hood rest on the imposts above the wall space between the two pilaster strips below, i.e. the outer square-edged vertical pilasters are ornamental and appear to support nothing.

The ornament (1) is curious (Fig. 33, (*a*)). It was called by Atkinson Jews' Harp ornament on account of its supposed resemblance to that instrument. Comparison with drawings of Jews' harps given by Elliston Erwood does not reveal any close, or in fact other than a very slender, likeness. Clapham called it palmette, not one of his happiest descriptions for though the motif might conceivably be regarded as derived ultimately from the classical palmette any resemblance to it is surely largely imaginative. Baldwin Brown more reasonably called it a debased floral pattern: the motif does in fact to some degree resemble a floret of such a flower as a daisy,

---

(1) *Plate* 167.

detached from its flower head. Each pattern is a relatively long and narrow raised oval with central depression, bluntly rounded at the top and tapering below to, in some cases, a blunt point. Most however are open below and resemble more than anything else greatly stilted horseshoes. They are arranged closely side by side and symmetrically round the arch head. This resemblance to horse shoes may suggest the origin of the motif. Stilted horseshoes are particularly suited to decorate an annular space, such as that between the central rosette and outer circular border of the carved

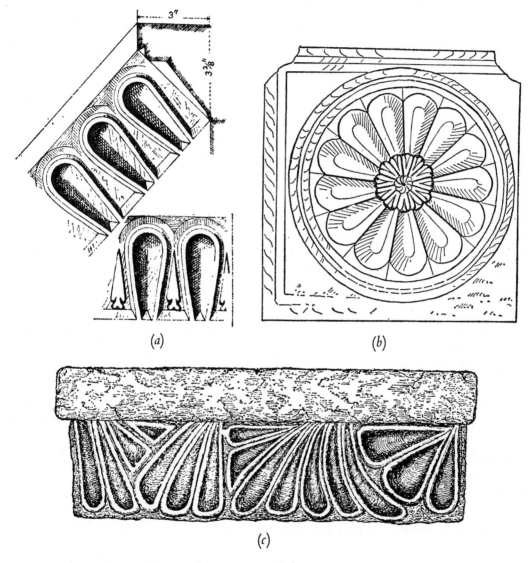

(a) (b)

(c)

Fig. 33. (a) Stow, Jews' Harp Ornament
(b) Hexham, Roman Rosette Stone
(c) Hadstock, Ornament

301

Roman slab found at Hexham (Fig. 33, (*b*)). It is easy, in imagination, to pass from the decoration of an annular to a half-annular space, that is an arch head. Moreover Lincolnshire is rich in Roman remains. It is not unlikely that the experienced crafts-man who carved the Stow ornament—the work is well done and highly finished—was familiar with such Roman patterns. The ornament is purely local, being confined almost entirely to Lindsey. There are examples at Barholme,[1] Barnetby-le-Wold, Coleby, Glentworth, Lincoln (St. Peter-at-Gowts) (Fig. 28), Nettleton, Scartho, and across the county boundary at Carlton-in-Lindrick (Notts); isolated single motifs are also to be seen at Marton (Fig. 29). There is rather similar ornament at Hadstock, Essex (Fig. 33, (*c*)),[2] which a writer in the R.C.H.M.'s volume on Essex described as debased honeysuckle. Baldwin Brown thought it based on the palmette. Like the Stow ornament it might be regarded as palmette—reduced to its very simplest terms, if such an expression is meaningful. The leaves have degenerated into sunk triangles some of which are curved and bent laterally and arranged irregularly, in marked contrast to the strict symmetry of the Stow ornament. He called it *sui generis*, hardly correct in view of its close resemblance to the Stow ornament. Moreover, almost identical ornament is to be seen on a Roman altar at Birrens, in Dumfriesshire, illustrated by Baldwin Brown[3] in another connection; it is curious that he did not apparently notice the similarity.

The Transepts. These are of two dates, as indicated by the signs of fire on the lower courses but not on the upper. The plinths are of three members, each of the two upper ones being $8\frac{1}{2}$ inches high. The lowest member is square-edged; the upper two have 4-inch chamfers on their upper edges. The top member protrudes 7 inches from the wall face and the second 7 inches from the face of the top member. The lowest member projects 3 inches. The south transept original plinth stops short at *c.* 8 or 10 feet from the angle with the chancel. Above the plinth of the south transept are one and a half courses on the west and a single course on the east of fairly large rectangular slabs of limestone, much larger and of more regular shape than the rubble above. There are no buttresses. The quoins are of very large roughly dressed blocks arranged in regular side-alternate manner. They are quite different from the smaller quoin stones of the Norman chancel, which are like clasping stones, and are less well finished and look earlier than those of the lower part of the tower. There are straight joints between transepts and crossing.

The North Transept. In the west wall is a tall narrow doorway (1), hidden on the exterior by a modern vestry into which it now opens. It is 2 ft. $4\frac{3}{4}$ ins. wide at the base tapering slightly to 2 ft. 4 ins. at the top. It is 5 ft. $10\frac{1}{4}$ ins. high to the lower face

---

[1] G. Baldwin Brown, p. 405, fig. 191, A.   [2] See also E. A. Fisher, Pl. 19, A.
[3] G. Baldwin Brown, p. 259, fig. 102.

(1) *Plate* 169.

of the imposts. The imposts are 9 inches thick and chamfered on the soffit sides only. The arch head has ten voussoirs of irregular shape and length. The north jamb has five massive irregular through-stone slabs of upright and flat arrangement. The flats run a considerable distance into the wall and all the flats in both jambs have been cut back to wall level so that through the original plaster they would appear long and short. The arch voussoirs have been cut back in a similar way to show a regular round head through the original plaster. The south jamb has six slabs of very regular upright and flat arrangement, the top flat being immediately below the impost. The jambs are 3 ft. 3 ins. thick. They stand on square-edged projecting plinths. A doorway in this position is most unusual. It may have opened to a porticus or chapel in the angle between transept and nave, rather similar to Britford (Wilts) where an arch opening to the nave still exists. In the west wall, further north, is a tall two-light fourteenth-century window and to the north of this are four stones, two uprights and two flats, of an early blocked window (1). In the north wall is a large circular window (1) chamfered on its inner edge and with a half-round thin raised border on the outer. Immediately below this is a large tall rectangular window each jamb of which is of two long uprights with a flat between. It has no sill; the disturbed condition of the walling below suggests that the window may once have been taller, the lower 'portion being built up later'. The opening is rebated all round on the exterior and has holes where presumably the lighting closures were fitted. In the east wall, very near the chancel wall and opposite to the narrow doorway in the west wall discussed above, was a large round-headed doorway now blocked with rubble; it was *c.* $4\frac{1}{2}$ to 5 feet wide.

The South Transept. It has been stated that there are signs of an early doorway in the west wall; no indications of such a doorway are now apparent. In the south wall is a large circular window (2) similar to the one in the north transept. There is no tall rectangular window below, as in the north transept. Instead there is a large two-light thirteenth-century window a little to the west and below, and to the east is a tall narrow Saxon window (3) with lintel, arched above and below, and a semicircular hollow chamfered hood mould above. The hood is raised out of the lintel block, i.e. hood and lintel are cut from one stone. Below the ends of the hood are two rather long chamfered imposts. Round the chamfer of the hood and imposts is ornament exactly similar to that round the west face of the great western tower arch. The jambs are of four massive slabs each, arranged upright and flat; flats and uprights are cut back to the wall face to show a uniform width through the original plaster. It has no separate sill. This window, like the circular one above, has slight internal splay. On the interior the jambs are similar but there is rubble filling between the exterior and interior jambs, and the head has seven voussoirs instead of an arched lintel; there are no imposts or sill or hood on the interior.

---

(1) *Plate* 168; (2) *Plate* 166; (3) *Plate* 167.

In the west wall of the transept is a tall narrow reputedly twelfth-century window with an arched lintel cut from a rectangular block, on the face of which, above the opening, is raised a short, segmental, imitation hood mould chamfered below. The opening is chamfered all round and has slight internal single-splay. The south jamb is of three large uprights; the north jamb is of four stones, two uprights and two flats; the sill is of one stone. On the ends of the 'hood' are animal or human heads, badly worn. In the east wall, to the north of the thirteenth-century two-light window, is a tall window rather similar to that in the west wall and of the same period. It has an arched lintel, long sill, jambs of three stones each, the central stones being flats. It is chamfered all round and has internal single-splay.

The Nave. The length of the original nave is not known. To judge from traces of foundations of side walls where they joined the transepts, the width must have been about twice that of the present nave, or more than 50 feet. It may therefore have had aisles, as at Hexham. In the north door of the present Norman nave the jambs are of long uprights and short flats though not arranged in strictly regular upright and flat manner. There are tall angle shafts in jamb recesses which are not inserted shafts but are cut out of the jambs themselves; that is, the longs and shorts of the jambs are in one piece with the corresponding drums of the shafts, as at Wittering (Northants) chancel arch. The shafts have square-edged neckings below two-scalloped capitals, the two outer flat faces of which are decorated with the characteristic Saxon step pattern (Fig. 34). The imposts are thin and plain chamfered. The arch head is characteristically Norman with chevron pattern ornament.

The Chancel. All above ground is post-Conquest and later than the nave, probably *c.* 1150. During repairs to foundations *c.* 1850 it was found that the north wall was on the line of, and possibly on, the original foundations. On the south the original plinth of the transept stopped at *c.* 8 or 10 feet from the angle between transept and chancel, and under the base courses of the present Norman south chancel wall were found three pieces of cut stone work at nearly equal distances apart. These looked like the bases of piers belonging to the older structure. Possibly the original chancel had aisles, or a south aisle, or perhaps here was an arched opening to cloisters. The Saxon chancel did not extend as far as the present east wall. The depth of the Norman foundations at the east was *c.* 5 feet, that of the Saxon foundations at the west was at least 6 feet. Between was a narrow strip of natural clay. The width of the foundations of the side walls was not less than 10 feet but the whole area of the Saxon choir seems to have been excavated to a uniform depth and filled up with solid rubble work. This might have been the case with the entire area of the church. No traces of a crypt were found.

The Stair Turret (1). On the north side of the nave and above the modern vestry,

---

(1) *Plate* 168.

which is built round it, and close to the north transept, is a wide rectangular very tall stair turret (Fig. 32), rising to well above the naves eaves, and looking rather like a huge flat buttress. This is twelfth-century work, contemporary with the nave and was formerly within the nave against the west side of the north-west crossing pier. It was removed and rebuilt in its present position during the restoration. The spiral staircase within is lighted by a number of windows most of which have typical

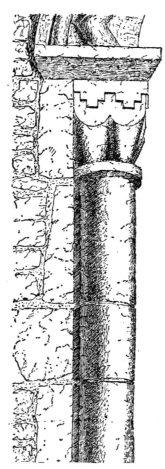

Fig. 34. Stow, Angle Shaft in Nave Norman Doorway

Norman very wide single internal splays. The outer edges of the openings have been filled with thin Saxon window openings re-used from elsewhere. In the north wall near the top is a round-headed single-splayed window with arched lintel, jambs of one large block each, a sill of one stone, and chamfered all round. Below this is a small circular window cut from a single rectangular slab. It is double-splayed. It is moulded on its outer face. The aperture is $9\frac{3}{4}$ inches across and is surrounded by two segmental mouldings, the outer one wider than the inner, and three hollows or grooves. The outermost hollow separates the mouldings from the rectangular block out of which the opening is cut; the innermost groove separates the mouldings from the inner chamfer. The total distance across the mouldings is 22¾ inches. Below this circular window and just above the string course is another round-headed window very similar to the one above; it has no separate sill, the string course acting as such. In the west wall are two windows. The lower one, just above the string, is circular, like the one on the north, but plain. The upper window, in a position corresponding to that of the circular window in the north, is similar to the other round-headed windows. There are also similar windows in the east; these are difficult to see from the exterior owing to the small distance between stair turret and transept.

SWALLOW

HOLY TRINITY CHURCH.[1] This tower is dated by Baldwin Brown to the Saxo-Norman Overlap. It is slightly wider than nearby Cabourn and looks low in proportion as the lower part, below the string course, occupies about two-thirds of the total height, instead of the more usual three-quarters. As at Cabourn the belfry stage with its string course was removed at some time but, unlike Cabourn, it was rebuilt in imitation Norman style with single round-headed openings in the four walls.

The tower is built of rubble with irregular quoins, mostly side-alternate. The north-west and south-west nave quoins are original and similar to those of the tower. The plinth is of two chamfered members. The masonry below the string course, down to about the level of the loop window, is more regularly coursed than that lower down, which is very rough. This is very noticeable and it may be that the upper courses are part of the later rebuilding of the belfry.

There is no original opening in the north or south wall below the belfry; the window in the south wall is modern.

In the west wall is a narrow round-headed doorway. The plain head is of six voussoirs of unequal size, with a modern tympanum not unlike that at Nettleton: it is white with a circular window in the centre. The arch head is flush with the west wall. The long imposts project but not on their soffit sides. They are stated to be quirked and channelled on the outer faces but are too badly weathered for this to be seen; the soffit faces are plain. The arch is recessed *c.* 3 inches behind the jamb soffit faces on the exterior, but not on the interior owing to the internal splay of the jambs; the head is not splayed. The opening is 2 ft. 10½ ins. wide on the interior and 2 ft. 4½ ins. on the exterior. It is 6 feet high to the top of the imposts which are 11 inches thick. The wall here is 3 ft. 6 ins. thick.

[1] G. Baldwin Brown; A. Sutton; A. Hamilton Thompson, (*c*).

Just above the western doorway is a narrow window with wide internal splay, slab jambs and thin sill. Higher up, about half-way to the string course, is a rather short loop window with arched lintel. The jambs are of one very big slab each. It has very wide internal splay with a flat slab ceiling to the head of the splay. The sill is even more deeply splayed to throw the light downwards.

The tower arch (1) is fine. It has a slightly segmental head of fourteen voussoirs of very similar width and length, except the two at the springing which are longer. The arch is in two rings—an eastern and a western—with rubble filling, now plastered, between. The jambs are of large irregular but well-dressed slabs, side-alternate, two or three stones per course. They show diagonal tooling, a Norman feature. The thin imposts are chamfered above and below on the soffit sides only and are not returned along the wall face. The opening is 6 ft. 6½ ins. wide and 7 ft. 8 ins. high to the imposts; to the crown of the arch it is over 11 feet. The jambs are 3 ft. 8 ins. thick.

Syston

St. Mary's Church. Baldwin Brown dated this church to the Saxo-Norman Overlap. It has some very advanced, definitely Norman features; if it is an Overlap church it seems likely to have been built towards the end of the period.

The tower is of three stages separated by two string courses. The lower two stages are of similar heights; the top or belfry stage is shorter. The lower stages are built of rubble with much ashlar repair work round the corners. The belfry and the tall plinth are entirely of ashlar. The lower parts of the nave wall are of similar fabric to the tower.

There is no western doorway. The large three-light western window in the ground stage is of the fourteenth century. The tall narrow opening in the south wall of the second stage has very wide internal splay, though it has an arched lintel cut from one large block, a sill of one slab and jambs of three long slabs each running laterally for some distance into the tower wall. There is no opening in the north wall below the belfry.

The belfry openings are of the usual double-headed type, with arched lintels from two stones to each double head and semi-circular hood moulds, but have very advanced details. The southern opening has a roll moulding round the lower edge of the arched lintel and the hood has a kind of dentate ornament. The central projecting impost is widely chamfered and supported, not by coupled shafts as stated by Baldwin Brown, but by a rectangular slab with attached angle shafts having foliated capitals. There are recessed angle shafts at the jambs, also with round simple

(1) *Plate* 165.

foliated capitals. In the north opening is a genuine mid-wall octagonal shaft with a voluted capital. The arched lintel is chamfered instead of moulded and the hood chamfered above and below. The jambs have no angle shafts and are chamfered. In the west the shaft is mid-wall, the head has some kind of ornamentation instead of a moulding, and the projecting central impost instead of chamfer has an elaborate fillet and roll border; the jambs have no angle shafts.

The tower arch is very fine and apparently late Norman.

The south entrance to the nave has ancient-looking jambs on the interior, three or four stones per course; the head looks renewed. Near the east end of the nave south wall is a tall window with arched lintel with a very wide chamfer above in which is a half-round moulding acting as, or looking like, a hood mould. The jambs are of seven slabs each approximating to upright and flat. The sill is of one slab. The opening is 9 inches wide by *c.* 6 feet high and is rebated all round; it has very wide internal splay.

The chancel arch has soffit rolls. Baldwin Brown regards these as definitely not Norman features; they are rare in Normandy itself. But they occur not infrequently in late Saxon churches, though only very late in the period, and in the Overlap. Other examples are at Langford (Oxon), Wittering (Northants), Clayton, Bosham and Sompting (Sussex). Here, at Syston, the rolls have voluted capitals, a definitely Norman feature not found with the other Saxon examples.

THURLBY

St. Firmin's Church. St. Firmin was born at Pampelona in northern Spain in the third century and was martyred under Diocletian *c.* 303. He Christianized the region which later became Normandy and Picardy where he is still a popular local saint. Dedications to him are rare elsewhere. Thurlby probably owes its dedication to Norman settlers at the time of or possibly before the Conquest. Baldwin Brown considers that the thin nave walls, only 2 ft. 4 ins. thick, the gable-headed opening in the tower east wall, the ancient-looking outer tower arch and other features are 'not positive enough to be pronounced Saxon'; by implication he regarded it as Norman. Certainly the tower is large and massive, almost fortress-like in appearance, differing in this respect from the more customary tall and slender Lincolnshire towers. But there are some unquestionably Saxon features in the building which make it difficult to reject it definitely as Saxon.

The nave arcade is Norman with fifteenth-century clerestory windows. The nave is plastered on the interior. There are no signs of early windows. The chancel was rebuilt in the thirteenth century when the transepts or side chapels were added.

The tower is built of flattish rubble in courses. The quoins are large irregular slabs with some approximation to upright and flat arrangement. The later diagonal corner buttresses hide some of the quoining. The north-west and south-west nave quoins, visible to the north and south of the tower, approximate to face-alternate. The south-east and north-east quoins, visible above the chancel, are of rough square blocks. There is no plinth. The tower has three stages separated by two string courses; the lower string has a slight upper chamfer, the upper one a wide chamfer which gives it a sharp-edged appearance. The stages are of decreasing heights and the upper ones considerably recessed behind those below. It is very wide, 19 ft. 8 ins. along the exterior west wall and about 12 ft. 5 or 6 ins. on the interior; the walls are therefore *c.* 3 ft. 8 ins. thick. There is no western doorway or other original opening in the west, north or south walls below the belfry. The window in the west wall of the ground stage is fourteenth century; it is not known whether this replaced an earlier opening.

The two-light belfry openings are of the early fourteenth century. Above the belfry the frieze decorated with a kind of saltire ornament and the embattled parapet with eight pinnacles are later; the short broach spire is fourteenth century.

The tower arch (1) was originally very fine and wide. It had a head of twenty-one small voussoirs of very even size and jambs of ten slabs each, rather irregularly arranged. Jambs and arch head are flush with the wall. The long thin imposts project and narrow somewhat towards north and south where they are returned some distance along the wall. There is no sign of subsidence of the arch head but it was strengthened by the insertion within it of a fine Norman arch. The earlier arch was 9 ft. 6 ins. wide and *c.* 9 feet high to the imposts. It is plainly visible on both east and west wall faces. The jamb stones show diagonal tooling, a Norman feature, so the original arch if Saxon must be of late date.

Above the tower arch, in the east wall of the second stage, is a large gable-headed opening now blocked, in a position where openings are commonly found in Saxon towers. There are only two others in Lincolnshire, at Scartho and Winterton. The jambs are of five stones each, arranged upright-flat-upright-flat-upright, those on the north being rather irregular. There are no imposts and no sill. The gable stones have not been bevelled at their tops to meet flush against each other at the apex; they touch only at their top lower edges. One jamb stone is carved with a viking's head with a horned helmet and flowing moustache, probably a re-used stone from elsewhere. The opening is *c.* 3 feet wide and *c.* 4 ft. 6 ins. to the base of the gable head.

WAITHE

ST. MARTIN'S CHURCH.[1] This tower (2) differs in some respects from the usual Lincolnshire type and should be regarded as allied rather than as a normal member of

[1] A. Hamilton Thompson, (*c*); the Bishop of Nottingham, (*a*).

(1) *Plate* 171; (2) *Plate* 172.

the group. Originally it appears to have been the eastern part of an aisleless nave, the lower parts of its north and south walls being flush with the exterior of the nave north and south walls; that is, it was an axial tower in a central or eastern position. The ground floor formed a kind of presbytery between nave and chancel. The rest of the present church is modern, 1869, including the shallow transept (shallow like a porch but as high as the roof ridge of the nave) against the south wall of the tower. This transept-porch forms the main entrance to the church, through lateral interior doors; the south wall of the tower remains unbroken within the transept.

The tower is of two stages, a taller one below separated by a square-edged string course from a shorter, though relatively tall, belfry. It is built of irregularly coursed rubble blocks; the top seven courses below the string and the whole of the belfry are of rectangular ashlar blocks. The quoins are of rather small slabs, face-alternate. On the north, where alone it could be seen, there is no projecting plinth. Instead there is a base course of large rectangular blocks. Apart from the east and west arches there are no original openings below the belfry.

The later belfry has the usual double lights with arched lintels, two to each double head. The openings are very tall, about half the height of the rather tall belfry. The central columns are thick, with cushion capitals and neckings, but no bases. The sloping sills (a late feature) rest on the string course. Above is a plain parapet between two string courses.

In the interior the tower has low plain east and west arches leading to the nave and chancel. The jambs and heads are of small slabs, all side-alternate, presumably with rubble filling though only the outer rings are plainly visible through the whitewash. The jambs are 3 ft. 8 ins. thick. The arches are *c.* 8 feet high and 8 ft. 2 ins. wide, and the heads spring direct from the jambs with no intervening imposts. The tower measures internally *c.* 10 ft. 6 ins. each way. It is faced with small ashlar blocks, regularly cut but rather roughly jointed in real Norman manner.

WINTERTON

ALL SAINTS' CHURCH.[1] The tower resembles nearby Alkborough. The lower part of the tower and part of the west wall of the nave are original. Micklethwaite suggested a date of *c.* 1052 or earlier. Fowler thought it may have been built by Hugh Lupus, the first Norman earl of Chester, who died in 1101. Hugh was registered in Domesday Book as the principal landowner in Winterton, and in his old age was a considerable church builder. The church was rebuilt *c.* 1200 when another storey was added to the tower. Possibly this may explain Fowler's Norman dating. Baldwin Brown also considered it to be certainly post-Conquest though he admitted that the lower portion is Saxon in form and detail.

[1] G. Baldwin Brown; J. T. Fowler; J. T. Micklethwaite, (*b*).

The eleventh-century tower is built with straight joints against the earlier nave west wall, which is clearly pre-Conquest for its west face, with original plaster and whitewash still on it, can be seen on the south to run in behind the east extremity of the tower south wall. This is interesting as a rare example of Saxon whitewash still existing. The date of the Saxon nave is not known; Baldwin Brown suggested *c.* 950–1000 for the west wall, but the extent to which the present nave other than the west wall is original is not known. Marks of the very high-pitched chancel former roof are visible on the exterior of the east wall of the nave. The tower west wall is *c.* 3 ft. 9 ins. thick; the east wall or nave west wall is 3 ft. 3 ins.; the nave north and south walls are stated to be 2 ft. 9 ins. thick. The quoins are of small, cubical blocks of limestone, like those at Alkborough. There is a one-membered plinth to the west wall only.

There are three stages separated by two string courses. The ground stage is very tall, occupying about two-thirds of the total height; the second stage, the belfry, is recessed behind the ground stage; the third stage is very short and only slightly recessed, and is of the late twelfth or early thirteenth century. The embattled parapet, above another string course, and pinnacles are modern. In the north wall only of the ground stage is an extra string course, a few feet below the main string.

The west doorway has a segmentally arched lintel. The jambs are of seven slabs each. On the north the slabs are of roughly similar lengths; on the south they are approximately upright and flat, the top long flat serving as an impost to the lintel. In the south wall, visible only from within the aisle, is a narrow window near the top of the ground stage and just below the level of the aisle roof; it has an arched lintel, no sill, and jambs of three slabs each, arranged long-short-long. There is no corresponding window in the north wall.

The second, or belfry, stage has the usual double-light windows. The jambs are of six stones each, rather similar to the tower quoins. The mid-wall shafts, which are renewals, have square slab bases and support central, projecting, chamfered imposts. The heads are arched lintels on the west and north, but of voussoirs on the south. The capitals are of rough cushion type: they appear to be small rectangular under-blocks to the central imposts but with their narrow ends cut to rough cushion shape, rather like those at Alkborough. The south capital has a chequered pattern on it, which is Norman though not exclusively so. The east belfry window is visible only within the nave. Above each belfry window, in the short upper stage only, is a circular opening, or apparent 'sound' hole, cut from a single stone except the one on the west which is cut from two stones, an upper and a lower.

The tower arch has ashlar jambs, two or three stones per course, with plinths chamfered on the soffit faces only. The imposts, which look like renewals, are chamfered all round with a small half-round quirk immediately above the chamfer. The arch head is of nineteen short voussoirs, of very similar sizes, almost square, though the two at the springing are about three times as long as the others, a common Anglo-Saxon feature. The arch is 7 ft. 8 ins. high to the imposts and 8 ft. 6 ins. wide. The jambs are 3 ft. 3 ins. thick.

Above the tower arch, in the tower east wall and below the east belfry window, is a tall rectangular opening with flat lintel, jambs of upright and flat slabs and a sill which may be a renewal. The inner lintel, distinct from the outer one, is made of an ancient grave slab which has on it a cross in plain relief. This may be a later renewal. Such openings occur frequently in the second stages of Saxon towers as at Scartho and Thurlby. Here the opening is in the first, though very tall, stage. Possibly this stage was originally divided internally into two stages, with a floor between the opening and the arch below.

The return walls from the tower arch along the north and south nave walls as far as the beginning of the later arcades, i.e. for *c.* 4 ft. 5 ins. from the tower arch eastern face, and up to the tops of the nave column capitals may be pre-Conquest. The terminal early chamfered imposts at the west end of this early wall are still visible.

Part IV

EAST ANGLIA and ESSEX

EAST ANGLIA

HISTORICAL INTRODUCTION

Although the two counties of Norfolk and Suffolk were originally areas of settlement of two separate groups of Anglian peoples—the North Folk and the South Folk—they soon became united into a single kingdom of the East Angles. This had some natural protection from its truculent and powerful neighbour, Mercia, by intervening fenland. Although there were occasional inroads from Mercia, more perhaps of the nature of raids than of actual invasions, and at one period a vague kind of suzerainty was exercised by Mercia, East Anglia was able to develop as a separate kingdom, politically, culturally and ecclesiastically. Its greatest king, the pagan Rædwald, 616–24 or 625, was named by Bede as the third Bretwalda of England. He was succeeded by his step-son, Sigeberht, who had been exiled by Rædwald and brought up and educated as a Christian in the monastery at Luxeuil in Burgundy. Sigeberht introduced Christianity among his people and c. 630 invited Felix, a Burgundian, to be the first bishop of the East Angles. Felix had his seat at Dunwich, near the south-east coast of what is now Suffolk. Later, in 671, Archbishop Theodore split the diocese into two, leaving the Dunwich see to control Suffolk and founding another at North Elmham,[1] some 17 miles north-west of Norwich, for Norfolk. The great Danish invasions began in East Anglia in 865 and from that time till the early tenth century the area became an independent Danish kingdom, with a Danish king, within the Danelaw. It was reincorporated into Anglo-Saxon England when Edward the Elder, 899–924, reunified the country.

It has always been a rich and prosperous part of the country. In the later Middle Ages it was famous for its wool. The magnificent and beautiful churches of the fifteenth and sixteenth centuries, for which Suffolk in particular is justly famous, were built out of the profits of this industry. In Anglo-Saxon times too it was rich and prosperous and a vast number of churches were built during this period. According to the Victoria County History no less a number than 604 are mentioned in Domesday Book—243 in Norfolk and 361 in Suffolk—larger numbers than in any other county; Lincolnshire comes next with 222. Morley, who made a close study of the Suffolk churches, states that 468 'townships' in the county are mentioned in Domesday Book and that in only 96 of these no churches are referred to. In the other 372 were 450 churches: two had twelve each, one (South Elmham) had eight, two

[1] See below, p. 331.

315

had five each, eight had three and twenty-five had two each; the remaining 334 had one each. These figures do not agree with those of the V.C.H. though both groups are large. This is not really surprising. The difficulties of interpretation of Domesday Book statements are well known[1] and understood; the Book was primarily an economic survey and is interested only in churches in their economic aspect, i.e. their value. Thus 'all the churches [at Beeston, Norfolk] are included in the valuation of the manors'; and at Beeston St. Anne's there was 'half a church worth 12 pence'. The latter entry is interesting as it indicates that some churches were held in moieties, i.e. one church might belong to several owners. The writer has not checked the above figures. Checking seemed unnecessary as their sole significance in the present context is their large size, which shows perhaps better than anything else could the great populousness and prosperity in Anglo-Saxon times of East Anglia and Lincolnshire.

Curiously the churches appear to have been built in clusters, reminiscent of the groups of churches in early Irish monasteries. Thus, South Elmham was not a village but a district containing a number of churches around each of which a village grew up. Even today South Elmham is an area comprising nine parishes: South Elmham St. Cross, South Elmham St. James—St. Margaret—St. Peter—St. Michael—St. Nicholas—and so on. It is this cluster development which may account partially for the large number of churches recorded in Domesday Book, but not entirely so; there must have been a population great enough to need so many and prosperous enough to be able to build them. This cluster development of churches and settlements was doubtless a result of the agrarian and social organization of the area. The manorial system, usual in other parts of the country, developed late in East Anglia though it appears to have been widely established there by the time of Domesday Book. The early organization of the district, continued throughout the Danish occupation, was on a communal, not manorial basis: communities of small settlements interdependent within larger groupings.

The area was colonized, from probably the late fifth century, not by large armies but by many small groups of independent settlers who were later federated into larger groups forming a district of villages. These later still became federated into the two major groups of North Folk and South Folk who under a strong leader eventually became a unified East Anglia.

Perhaps the most striking feature of these early churches, including also those of the Norman period, is the wide distribution of circular western towers. The round tower is above all a characteristic of East Anglian church architecture: there are very few in England outside this area, only four, and the foundations only of four others in Essex, two in Cambridgeshire, one in Northamptonshire, two in Berkshire, one in Surrey and three in Sussex. There are approximately 170 in East Anglia, 129 in Norfolk and 41 (Cautley) or 42 (Morley) in Suffolk.

[1] See W. Page, op. cit.

Three different reasons have been put forward and vigorously supported by different writers for the wide spread of round towers in this area. One of these may be accepted quite definitely as being *a* factor, perhaps a main factor; the absence of building stone in the area. East Anglia—and Essex—have only two geological strata. North and west of a line running north–south through Norwich to near Ipswich and then south-west, the area consists of chalk with abundant flints. (There is a small strip of fenland in the extreme north-west corner of Norfolk around King's Lynn.) To the east and south of this line is low-lying alluvial clay. It was difficult in early days to transport heavy building stone across country, along poor roads or tracks, across marshy fen—perhaps involving some trans-shipment for transport down rivers. In Norman times it was easier and cheaper to bring stone by sea from Normandy; the stone for the Norman cathedral of Norwich came from Caen in Normandy. The East Anglian builders had to use what local material was available, usually flints from the chalk, sometimes pebbles, sometimes pudding stone, a type of conglomerate. No stone was available for quoining. Corners of naves and chancels could be and were made of the same material as the walls but corners of towers, in view of the heavier loads the walls have to carry, need strengthening. The difficulty was overcome by dispensing with corners, by making the towers of circular section. Such towers, especially when they taper upwards as some do, are very strong, as is indicated by the great number which have outlasted the churches to which they were attached.

The flints or other materials used were often laid in courses, though sometimes uncoursed, and with abundant mortar. Occasionally, not often, the flints were broken for use in the surface only in fairly regular courses and with their flat sides outwards. The towers appear to have been built in stages of *c.* 10 or 12 feet at a time and presumably allowed to settle before the next stage was built. Window openings were mostly circular with double-splayed apertures, rarely if ever more than 9 inches in diameter, and without stone dressings. Occasionally both window openings and doorways were gable-headed. Doorways and arches had no stone facings in jambs or arch heads and had only small or no imposts. The towers range in diameter from 10 to 20 feet and in wall thickness between $2\frac{1}{2}$ and 5 feet. They had no staircases; ladders were used for access to the upper stages as they are today. Ladders in use today are heavy and roughly but strongly made. Some may be original, but most perhaps are later replacements of similar type. The outside members are often just the dressed halves of a tree, sometimes roughly moulded. The rungs are often shaped and carried through the side members at intervals and pinned to prevent spreading. They are usually *c.* 20 feet long.

Some towers have two or three string courses corresponding to three or four internal stages; others have no strings. Many have later, thirteenth to fifteenth century, often octagonal, top or belfry stages. Others again have had some or all of their original small window and door openings replaced by later and larger ones with proper stone dressings. For these various reasons—lack of quoining and stone dressings, replaced windows and doorways, general similarity of walling—it is particularly difficult to date more than a few of these towers. Perhaps about thirty show more or less signs of pre-Conquest origin, some quite definitely so. The remainder are considered by most writers to be of the Norman period, except a few—perhaps a dozen—which are reputed to be post-Norman. The evidence however for Norman dating is slender, certainly no stronger than that in favour of pre-Conquest dates for most, as some writers claim to be the case.[1] The truth is that there are few features in these towers to justify a definite attribution of a Norman date for the towers as a whole, as distinct from the individual features themselves. In a few cases a Norman date may be reasonably assumed from the excessive thickness of the wall, as at Syleham (Suffolk) where it is 5 feet.

The question of dating however does not seem to be of much importance, or even interest. These towers are all of a type, belonging to a local group, are all much alike, and yet, as may be seen from the plates, showing considerable differences among themselves; it is indeed surprising how different two or more rather similar flint cylinders can be made to look.

At first no doubt these churches were of timber, for the whole area was well wooded, and probably many or most would belong to the group of 'field churches';[2] they were small as so many of them are today. Later they would be rebuilt in flints or other local material. During the great monastic revival in Edgar's reign, under St. Dunstan and Æthelwold, there was doubtless much activity in church building, rebuilding perhaps of wooden churches in more durable materials, and restorations. Morley considers that there is 'excellent reason for believing that a considerable proportion of Saxon churches, that is generally assigned to the "early Norman period", was executed before the Conquest'.

The origin of round towers is obscure. Early writers such as John Britton attributed them to the Danes. This was denied by Gage on the ground that there are none in Lincolnshire or anywhere else in Danish England north of the Humber, and that there are none in Denmark, Sweden or the valley of the Elbe. More recently Morley has supported, or revived, the Danish theory on the ground that the greatest distribution of round towers in the area corresponds with the greatest distribution of Danish place-names. This is not convincing. The Danes were dominant in East Anglia as, later, the Normans were dominant throughout England; but they had no particular tradition of building in other than timber. If they founded many churches in their settlements it is more than likely that Saxon masons would do or take part in the building.

Cautley was of the opinion that round towers were built originally for defence, as

---

[1] C. Morley; S. E. Rigold, (*b*).   [2] See above, p. 30.

refuges against Danish raiders, and that the churches were built later against the towers. There is some evidence to support this view. Many of the towers originally had no western or eastern doorways, or indeed any openings at all in the ground stage. There was often a doorway of ingress to the second stage in the east wall which could be reached by a ladder from the ground. Most of the other openings were windows of the slit variety. Such towers would be strong refuges against raiders, though they would be of little use against serious invasion as the refuges could be starved out. There is a considerable concentration of round towers between the rivers Yare and Waveney, i.e. between Yarmouth and Lowestoft, an area which was a favourite landing place for raiding parties. It is however certainly true that many round towers were built originally as western towers of existing churches, for the lower eastern faces of some are more or less flat to make attachment to a nave easier. But a western church tower would still be useful as a refuge, although the nave thatch if ignited might be a danger. The builders may well have designed these towers for defence as well as for ecclesiastical purposes.

Another theory put forward by J. J. Raven was that originally these towers were the Saxon lords' bell towers. Under a law of Æthelstan of 937 a bell tower had to be erected on the estate of every thegn; later, churches founded by local thegns would be built against the existing bell towers. This is unlikely to be generally true: the lord's bell tower might (assuming Æthelstan's edict was widely obeyed) have been no more than a bell turret; churches were normally much older than their attached towers; and in some cases the lower flat eastern face of a round tower is an obvious indication that the tower was built for the church and not the church for the tower.

To summarize, there would seem to be little doubt that these towers were built during a period of great building activity, in a rich prosperous and populous area, and were circular in plan owing to lack of local building stone. When were they built? Although the general consensus of opinion is that the great majority are Norman (J. C. Cox), a few perhaps post-Norman and only about twenty or so really pre-Conquest, there seems little evidence to support this view, except for the belfry stages, many of which are without doubt post-Conquest, some being as late as the thirteenth and fifteenth centuries. As regards the body of the towers the only evidence of date is what can be seen in the walling and the openings; the dates may have been too hastily judged by that of the window openings and their dressings. In some cases, as at Little Saxham with its elaborate and beautiful late Norman ornamentation and particularly regular flint walling, the tower may be Norman throughout. At the other end of the scale is Roughton with its rough walling, complete absence of stone dressings and where the double belfry lights with mid-wall shafts are of flint: quite clearly an all-Anglo-Saxon tower. In between these two are all the others, some containing no Norman features, others containing few or many Norman features, but most showing some features which are or may probably or possibly be Anglo-Saxon, or features which, for all the evidence there is, might just as likely be Saxon as Norman, or Norman as Saxon. The main evidence relied on is the presence or absence and type of stone dressings; even so, when the openings have arched lintels, or gabled heads, or jambs of irregular stone slabs they may be Saxon or, if of post-Conquest date, inserted by Saxon masons.

The difficulty of dating round towers may be illustrated by comparing the opinions of three well-known writers on Norfolk churches, J. C. Cox, Baldwin Brown and J. M. Cautley. Cox gave a list of 23 which he considered were certainly, probably, possibly, wholly or in part Saxon. In the body of his book he described five of his 23 as Norman, leaving only 18 as Saxon. Baldwin Brown deleted two from Cox's 23 and added two others, making his list to number 23. Cautley's list contained 37 towers. Sixteen of Cox's 18 were common to all three lists. Great Ryburgh is in all three lists yet A. B. Whittingham wrote of it: 'it appears to me to belong to a group of early Norman work which exists in West Norfolk and probably had its origin in the early Norman work at Castle Acre. The tower arch is recessed in characteristic Norman manner,[1] and there appears to me to be no feature in the tower which can definitely be put down as Saxon.'

Recently S. E. Rigold[2] has defended the view that the great majority of these towers though not necessarily pre-Conquest are essentially Saxon, or, as he prefers to express it more generally, *premier roman* or First Romanesque in style. They are a local East Anglian variety of that First Romanesque style which developed in Lombardy in the early ninth century and spread westwards. They were erected, he thinks, in the century between *c.* 1015 and *c.* 1115 and their style was not affected significantly by the Norman Conquest. They were built as attached western bell towers. They may have been intended secondarily as watch towers, but not as refuges or for defence, being too small for such purposes.

It is difficult to justify any strict separation of these towers into age-groups. They are so alike in general, and often in specific, characteristics that the phrase *sui generis* can be applied appropriately to them. They can be studied properly only as a group, regardless of chronology. To choose a few which are supposed by some to be pre-Conquest, either wholly or in part, often on unconvincing grounds, is to say the least arbitrary, and perhaps not really meaningful. It is to be hoped that some day someone will study the group in detail and produce an authoritative monograph on it.[3] For the purpose of the present book the difficulty has been evaded rather than solved: only five undoubtedly Saxon towers have been selected for study. They are: Bessingham, 3½ miles SW. of Cromer; Colney, 5 miles W. of Norwich; East Lexham, 4 miles E. by N. of Castle Acre; Haddiscoe, 15 miles SE. of Norwich and 9 miles SW. of Yarmouth; and Roughton, 3 miles S. of Cromer.

---

[1] But cf. Colney, below, p. 322. [2] Op. cit., (*b*).
[3] C. J. W. Messant's recent book does not meet the need entirely: see S. E. Rigold, (*b*).

ROUND-TOWERED CHURCHES

BESSINGHAM

ST. MARY'S CHURCH. The tower (I) on the exterior is of three stages built of different materials. The ground stage, occupying about one-fifth of the total height, is of large brownish pudding stone of various sizes laid in much mortar. The second stage is mainly of flints. The third stage (really two as it has two ranges of window openings), occupying more than half the total height, is of pudding stone roughly coursed especially near the top. The top few courses and battlements are later. The tower is of Saxon proportions, tall and slender. The walls are thick, more than 4 feet, about one and a half times the thickness of the nave walls. It has no taper and no slight filling in the angles as there is at Witton and some other churches. The east wall is slightly flattened to fit against the nave.

In the ground stage is no sign of an original western doorway or of any other opening on the exterior. In the second stage in the west wall is a wide, short, round-headed opening, single-splayed internally. It has no sill. The head and jambs are of flattish stones with no imposts. In the lower part of the third stage, rather high up, is what appears to be a blocked circular opening; the thin slabs of the upper half are plainly visible. In the north wall was a narrow window in the second stage and a similar but taller one in the stage above; both are blocked with bricks. In the south wall of the third stage is a similar brick-blocked window; this one had a double-arched lintel, no sill, and jambs of selected walling stones laid flat on one another; it is just possible to see that they were intended as jambs and not merely walling.

The belfry windows are of the usual double-light type but with gabled stone heads. The jambs are of small stones with small slab imposts and bases and no sills. The mid-wall shafts are circular with no capitals or bases and support unchamfered slightly projecting central imposts. The gable-heads have gabled hood moulds of small stones resting on their own separate small imposts. Below the imposts the stones run down the jambs like strip-work and these also rest on their own small imposts. There is a cubical corbel projecting from above each right hand (of the observer) gable head of each pair of openings, but not on the left ones.

Baldwin Brown dated the tower to the Overlap.

The north-west and south-west nave quoins are of slabs of various sizes in roughly face-alternate arrangement. They are much worn. About two-thirds of the north wall appears to be original. It is of similar fabric to the lower part of the tower. Most of the original plaster has peeled off. The early north-east quoins are visible at the

---

(I) *Plate* 173.

straight joint between the early wall and its later eastern extension. The rest of the north wall and the east and south walls are later; they are of split flints with some admixture of stone.

The tower arch (1) is round-headed and of Saxon proportions, very tall and narrow. Later stone dressings were presumably added to the early opening as at Colney. It has small imposts, chamfered on their soffit sides. The opening is *c.* 9 feet high to the imposts and 3 ft. 8 ins. wide. The jambs near the imposts are *c.* 4 ft. 1 in. thick; they are thinner below where the east face of the wall is rather deeply recessed. All details are hidden by plaster.

Above is a large gable-headed opening, in a typically Anglo-Saxon position, presumably an ingress to the second stage of the tower.

COLNEY

ST. ANDREW'S CHURCH. The tower is of uncoursed rather small broken flints. It has no string course. The angles with the nave have very small flint fillings as at Witton nicely finished off to look like flint quoins. The tower has no apparent taper or flattening on the east side; the west end of the nave roof, now slated, is made to fit the round tower wall.

In the south wall about half way up is a square-headed double-splayed window, blocked with flints. There are similar blocked windows in the north and west, but no sign of one in the east. In the west wall the narrow round-headed window about 8 feet up is modern. The belfry windows are single, pointed, wide and look modern, perhaps of the restoration of 1886. The simple plain brick battlements and coping are also modern.

The tower arch is round-headed, tall and rather narrow: *c.* 12 feet high to the imposts and 6 ft. 1 in. wide. Its head is of two rings of voussoirs; any flint filling between the rings is hidden by plaster. The imposts are hollow chamfered with a quirk above the chamfer. This arch is interesting. J. Gunn writing in 1849 described the arch as rough and primitive, of thin flints of a shape selected to best form an arch, the imposts were of several pieces of rough stone. Gunn was describing an earlier, perhaps the original Saxon arch. The present arch dressings, Norman looking, are apparently modern but appear to have misled Baldwin Brown into assuming a late eleventh-century Overlap date for the tower. This is a good illustration of the difficulties and pitfalls in the problem of dating these round towers.

The Nave. The north-west quoin is mainly of flint, with some interspersed flat stone slabs; the south-west quoin is a modern stone renewal.

---

(1) *Plate* 174.

In the south wall, just to the east and on a level with the ridge of the south porch gabled roof, are the remains of a round-headed window turned in Roman bricks: they may be the upper part of a large circular window. About half-way along the south wall there are signs of a similar window: there are no Roman bricks here but the walling is disturbed and the outline of a former circular opening is plain. No signs of these openings are visible on the interior which has been plastered.

The nave and chancel walls are continuous with no apparent break. The north wall of nave and chancel bulge badly above; three buttresses were erected here at some time.

EAST LEXHAM

ST. ANDREW'S CHURCH. Lexham is mentioned in Domesday Book as possessing one church. The existing church is small and has nave, chancel, south porch and sturdy round western tower. The nave and chancel are structurally one, that is of the same width. The nave north-west and south-west quoins are of large blocks approximating to upright and flat.

The tower (1) is certainly Anglo-Saxon and was dated by Baldwin Brown to post-950. It is a wide tower built of roughly coursed flints interspersed with many very much larger broken flints. The top third is very roughly octagonal and is recessed behind the lower stage by means of a ramp of flints of considerable height. There is no original string course. The tower is finished above with some half-dozen courses of brick repair work with a string course in lieu of parapet. In the west wall is a tall window of wide lancet type chamfered all round. It may have replaced an earlier opening for the jambs are of Saxon type: a tall pillar stone below with three shorter ones above. The pointed head is cut from one stone. There is no other opening on the exterior below the belfry.

The belfry openings are curious. There are three only, one facing east, the others facing north-west and south-west. They are placed just above the ramp. All are of double-lights but all are different. The north-west opening is taller than the others. The two heads and jambs are cut from very thin stone with half-round mouldings on the outer edges. The central shaft is a tall slender bulging baluster with a thin square capital or impost and a heavy conical base; rather heavy clumsy single neckings separate the shaft from capital and base. The south-west opening is very primitive (2). The heads are of flints, the jambs of rough shapeless stones. The very fat circular shaft is built up of flints and mortar. The impost above is massive, square, and so widely chamfered below at corners as well as sides that it looks like a much flattened cushion type of flattened capital. The under-hanging part of the double arch head is

---

(1) *Plate* 175; (2) *Plate* 176.

splayed outwards below to meet the impost with a wider base. The whole is recessed slightly behind the main wall face.

The eastern opening has no central shaft; instead, there is an equal-armed cross with straight expanding arms, head and shaft which divides the aperture into four. It may be a later, though early, replacement and may originally have been a transenna or lighting fitment for windows such as are found at Barnack. None of the shafts is mid-wall; all are quite near the outer wall face.

In the interior the ground floor stage has been lined inside and outside within the nave with fine modern ashlar, and has been given a plaster ceiling. A modern pointed doorway has been cut through the tower east wall. There is no indication of an earlier doorway or arch. The tower interior above is untouched and its very rough original walling is plain.

HADDISCOE

ST. MARY'S CHURCH. The round western tower (1) is almost entirely late Anglo-Saxon. It is 58 feet high with an internal diameter of only 8 feet. The walls are 4 feet thick and are of well-coursed flints. There are small angle fillings, not of the usual flints but of very irregular small stone slabs; they extend up as far as the first string course. The tower tapers throughout its entire height. This is unusual in round towers; as a rule the top or belfry stages do not taper even when the lower parts do. There are four external stages separated by three string courses, chamfered below. Above the belfry is a tall embattled parapet of *c.* 1400 with deeply chequered pattern. The heavy string course below the parapet is supported by a ring of many quirked and moulded corbels.

The ground stage is taller than the second and third together, between 20 and 25 feet. It has only one external opening, a tall, relatively narrow, window in the west. It is in better condition than those higher up and looks later; Gage wrote that it was later. But it is structurally identical with the others except that it has a single-arched lintel whereas the other lintels are double-arched (arched above and below). It may be a renewal to the old pattern.

In the second and third stages are three windows in each, on north, west and south. They all rest on the string courses, having no other sills. The jambs are of three large blocks each. All these windows are chamfered.

The belfry stage (2) has gable-headed double lights, relatively very tall and narrow. The gable heads have renewed linings. The mid-wall octagonal shafts have cubical scalloped capitals and bases and plain neckings, and support plain central imposts. The jambs are of slabs with flint fillings between the inner and outer faces. They are

(1) *Plate* 177; (2) *Plate* 178.

recessed and have angle shafts with scalloped cubical capitals and bases. The jambs rest on large slab slightly projecting bases. There is a double row of billet ornament running as a gabled hood mould round each gable head; it rests on its own separate imposts which are rather above the level of the jamb imposts. The ornament is continued down the sides of the jambs and rests below on separate imposts above the level of the jamb bases. There is a carved projecting head at the apex of each gable. The billet ornament is Norman, perhaps the earliest Norman ornament to be introduced into England and used in Anglo-Saxon settings. This Norman embellishment is an early Norman addition to a Saxon structure. It occurs also in this area at nearby Herringfleet and at Dunham Magna.

The tower arch (1) leading to the nave is of characteristic Saxon proportions, tall and narrow. It has a round head of voussoirs, plain, square-cut, with the springing set back a little behind the jambs. The thin imposts are chamfered. The arch is 3 ft. 5 ins. wide and the jambs (wall) 3 ft. 3 ins. thick.

Above the tower arch is a large round-headed opening, presumably an ingress to the tower second stage so common in Saxon towers. The head is of voussoirs and the jambs of seven or eight slabs, mainly side-alternate with flint fillings. There are no imposts.

The nave south-west quoin is of Norman small stone work, side-alternate with fine joints. On the north-west the quoin is similar above the aisle roof; below this there is a straight joint, in so far as flints can be said to form a straight joint, but no quoin stones.

ROUGHTON

ST. MARY'S CHURCH. This round tower (2) is almost certainly Saxon, though some writers say it is only Saxon at the base. It is not mentioned by Baldwin Brown. But it looks very definitely Saxon with its tall and slender proportions and complete absence of stone dressings. It appears to have been built in several stages in different types of material. The lowest three courses are of flint. The next 3 or 4 feet are of pudding stone with no flints but with a few courses of herring-boning, generally considered to be a late feature;[1] this is the only herring-boning in the tower. In the next 2 or 3 feet, to as far as the circular windows, the material is mainly flint with some pudding stone. Then comes a stretch of 3 or 4 feet of small flints. Above this almost as far as the belfry windows is mainly large broken flints with some pudding stone. The belfry is mainly pudding stone with flints. The top few courses and the

---

[1] See above, p. 174.

string course, of short slabs, with battlemented parapet above are later, not Saxon. The fabric is roughly coursed with plenty of mortar. There are segmental angle fillings in the angles between tower and nave.

About 8 or 9 feet above ground are two double-splayed circular windows, one rather to the west of south the other to the west of north. The south opening has its upper half of selected flints arranged in voussoir fashion. The large later window in the west, on a level with these circular openings, may have replaced an earlier circular window. Higher up, on a level with the nave roof and a little to the east of south and north and on the west are three tall round-headed windows, unsplayed, with no imposts; the heads and jambs are of very thin and irregular sized slabs.

The belfry openings are relatively quite unusually tall and narrow. The double gable heads are of very rough slabs. The jambs are of selected pudding stone slabs like many in the walls. The central imposts are built up of pudding stone and mortar. The 'shafts' are not mid-wall or shafts; they are pieces of rough walling extending throughout the wall thickness with roughly half-round ends, so they might be mistaken for shafts when viewed from the ground.

The tower arch leading to the nave is tall and wide: its width is 6 ft. 8 ins., its height nearly that of the nave arcade. The arch head is egg-shaped and dies into the jambs as there are no imposts. Above the tower arch is a tall wide opening, now blocked, with an egg-shaped head. These two openings and the interior ground stage of the tower are now plastered, as is the whole church interior, so the details of the openings are hidden.

The church was restored in 1925 by W. D. Caroë. He was of the opinion that the nave west wall and probably 10 or 12 feet of the chancel north wall east of the chancel arch are original; the differences are visible on the exterior. The original church was largely reconstructed in the early fourteenth century.

SQUARE-TOWERED CHURCHES

Early square towers are less numerous in East Anglia than round towers. Only eight are certainly pre-Conquest and five of these are ruins. They are: Bawsey, *c.* 5 miles S. of Castle Rising and *c.* 2 miles SE. of King's Lynn; Castle Rising Chapel, *c.* 6 miles NE. of King's Lynn; Dunham Magna, *c.* 4 miles E. of Castle Acre and *c.* 7 miles W. by N. of East Dereham; Newton, 1 mile E. of Castle Acre; North Elmham, 7 miles SE. of Fakenham; South Elmham (Suffolk), 4 miles S. by W. of Bungay; Weybourne, 7 miles W. by N. of Cromer; Debenham (Suffolk), 9 miles ENE. of Stowmarket.

The first seven are axial towers, five being centrally placed and two western.

Bawsey and Castle Rising (both ruins) and Debenham (only the ground stage of this tower is pre-Conquest; it has good upright and flat quoins) are excluded from detailed consideration.

DUNHAM MAGNA

ST. ANDREW'S CHURCH.[1] Originally there were two churches here: St. Mary's and St. Andrew's. It is not really known which of the two the existing church is. The other church has disappeared. It was probably nearby on the site of the present rectory garden where various fragments, some Norman, some perhaps pre-Norman, have been dug up from time to time. The fragments suggest that the lost church may have been the finer of the two. It is known that the one originally named St. Mary's was the less important church, a chapel of the other one. In the reign of Henry II both were separate parishes under Castle Acre priory. In the seventeenth century the two parishes were combined and the other church fell into ruin.

The church (I) has nave, chancel, south porch and square axial tower in a central position. The fabric is stated to have some of the oldest work in the county, at least as old as Edward the Confessor's reign. It is built of rough flints interspersed with Roman tiles. Traces of foundations of a Saxon semicircular apse were found below the site of the present altar when the chancel was rebuilt in the fifteenth century. Evidence of pre-Conquest date is abundant in both tower and nave; but there are many Norman details. Baldwin Brown described it as a Saxon church in scheme with many Norman details. He included it among his Saxo-Norman Overlap churches but elsewhere wrote that it may be dated to the mid-eleventh century. The quoins are of very regular upright and flat work. Those of the tower on the east are continued to the ground as the tower is wider than the chancel; on the west the tower quoins cease at nave wall level as the tower and nave walls are continuous. The nave walls are only two feet thick; the tower walls are 3 ft. 9 ins. As the outer north and south tower walls are flush with the nave walls on the exterior the extra thickness required to support the tower is on the interior. The church stands on a single-membered square-edged plinth. The walls were plastered but much of the plaster has peeled off. The only string course is below the low embattled later parapet.

In the ground stage of the tower in the south wall, but not in the north, is a round-headed double-splayed Saxon window. In the second stage are two windows, one in the north and one in the south wall, similar to the one below but more deeply double-splayed and with narrower apertures. All are plastered. In the east and west walls, about on a level with the north and south windows, are two very narrow door-ways, now blocked. The west one below the nave roof was once visible from the nave but is now hidden by plaster except one projecting stone which is to be seen

[1] G. Baldwin Brown; G. A. Carthew; J. C. Cox, (*a*); J. F. Williams.

(I) *Plate* 182.

above the hood mould of the western arch (1); the east one above the chancel roof is stated to have been visible from the exterior. It is no longer visible; it is hidden by signs of repair work to the wall at this spot, roughly mortared over. If they were for ingress to the tower only one would be necessary; it seems likely that they were doorways of egress leading either to eastern and western galleries or roof chambers; or perhaps one was an ingress to the tower and the other an egress.

The belfry windows in all four walls are very tall and wide, of the usual double-light type but with Norman details; the latter may be later insertions. The jambs are of mixed small stone slabs and flints, the heads of small blocks. The mid-wall circular shafts have cushion capitals; and bases of an elaborate Saxo-Norman type: a somewhat squashed Saxon-looking bulbous lower half, above which is a member hollow-chamfered all round between two tiny plain chamfers (Fig. 35). There are

Fig. 35. Dunham Magna Church, Shaft Bare

plain neckings below the capitals and above the bases. Between the capitals and the long central projecting imposts they support are short, almost square, intermediate impost blocks; both sets of imposts are chamfered, the lower ones all round, the upper ones on the outer ends only. The thin jamb imposts are badly worn. Above the belfry double arch heads on the east and west walls, but not on north or south, are two double-splayed circular sound holes.

There is a blocked gable-headed western doorway (2) in the nave, as at Holy Trinity, Colchester. This was the main entrance; the existing rectangular south doorway is a later insertion. The blocking appears to be of red brick cemented over. The opening was 5 ft. 4 ins. high to the beginning of the gable and 3 ft. 6 ins. wide. There are no imposts. The head has a gabled hood mould of square-cut billet orna-ment which rests on thin imposts decorated below with three-step ornament. The billeted hood is carried vertically down below the imposts. It is not known whether there was a western window above the doorway; the present later large three-light window has removed any evidence. The present south and north doorways are later.

In the upper part of the nave north wall near the west end is a small double-splayed round-headed window with an arch head turned in Roman bricks. There were originally four such windows, two in the north and two in the south wall. The other three have been built up but the heads of Roman bricks of the two south

---

windows are plainly visible on the exterior wall. Below these windows on the interior is tall round-headed blank arcading (1), part of the original pre-Conquest design but much altered in the thirteenth century or later. There are eight bays of arcading on the north wall with bays 3 ft. 11 ins. wide, the pilasters or flat shafts are 13 inches wide and the relief is 3 inches deep. On the south wall there are nine bays: the five eastern ones correspond with those on the north wall; numbers six and nine are *c.* 3 ft. 6 ins. wide, and numbers seven and eight less than 3 feet. The two narrowest have been disturbed to some extent by the insertion of the present south doorway. Possibly their narrow width may be connected with an early narrow south doorway, though this is conjecture. The arch heads of the arcading are turned in Roman bricks. They are supported by flint pilasters, six of which have imposts of Barnack stone; the others have no imposts. The imposts have zigzag ornament on three and saltire ornament on the other three between upper and lower quirks, ornament which indicates an Overlap date. The lower corners are stepped in Roman bricks. Originally the flint arcading framed panels of flint walling; now all has been plastered, except the carved imposts, and all details are hidden.

There are of course two tower arches (2) of which the eastern one is the chancel arch. They are *c.* 15 ft. 6 ins. high. The western one is 7 ft. 4 ins. wide with jambs 3 ft. 4 ins. thick; the eastern one is 6 ft. 7 ins. wide and its jambs are 3 ft. 6½ ins. wide. The arch heads appear to be turned in Roman bricks and the jambs were probably formed of carefully set flints, a practice not unusual in East Anglia. Details of structure, except of stone dressings, are hidden by the thick plaster with which the entire interior of the church is covered. In the western arch the large slab imposts were carved with star or saltire ornament like some of the nave arcade imposts. On the west face this ornament was at some time cut off flush with the wall to make room for a rood loft. The ends of the half-round hood mould were also cut off probably for the same purpose. There is no ornament on the east face. The eastern tower arch, or chancel arch, is rather similar to the western. The imposts however are cabled. There is no ornament on the east face. On the west there are two half-round hood moulds. The inner one rests on the ends of the cabled imposts. The outer one rests on its own small separate corbels a little above impost level but extends a short distance below where the ends are sharply cut off. It may be that originally they extended to the ground.

NEWTON-BY-CASTLE ACRE

ALL SAINT'S CHURCH.[1] This consists of nave, low chancel and low square tower. Cox was of opinion that the tower was central with north and south transepts and

[1] G. Baldwin Brown; J. C. Cox, (*a*); J. F. Williams.

---

(1) *Plate* 184; (2) *Plate* 185.

that the transepts fell into ruin and were removed in the eighteenth century. Williams regarded it as an axial tower in a central position as at nearby Dunham Magna but that, unlike most axial towers, its north and south walls are in line with the chancel walls, not with the nave. The chancel walls are in fact continuous with the tower walls with no intervening quoins. There are no signs in the north wall of a blocked opening which may have led to a former porticus nor of any undue roughness on the exterior wall suggestive of attachment to a porticus. On the south however the indications are plain: there are signs of a blocked doorway, within which is a later lancet window, and just above is a horizontal break in the walling on a level with the chancel eaves which might be where a porticus lean-to roof was attached to the tower wall; also at about 4 feet east of the nave wall are very rough breaks in the wall with projecting pieces which look like the attachments of a former north–south wall, probably the west wall of a porticus; the distance from here to the chancel is *c.* 12 ft. 8 ins. It seems clear that the tower is axial, continuous with the chancel and had a south but not a north porticus.

The tower (1) like the rest of the church is built of flints. The quoins are of irregular rather small stone slabs with much repair work, some in brick. There is no plinth. There is a plain string course on the south wall only. Above the string is a double-splayed round-headed window with jambs of rough thin flat slabs. The head of modern brick is not splayed. The upper part of the opening was blocked at some time; the original head visible in the wall above the later brick head is of similar stones to the jambs. There is no opening in the north wall below the belfry. On the west wall are the marks of the steep-gabled earlier and higher roof of the nave; the present roof is of modern red tiles.

The belfry openings are of the usual double-light type, but with gable heads. Those on the west and north are of Saxon type; the heads are of Roman bricks arranged in step pattern, i.e. each brick over-sailing or projecting beyond the one below; some are in such good condition they may be renewals. The central shafts are fat balusters; the western one has a chamfered central impost which does not project beyond the wall face, the northern one has no impost. The south and east openings have Norman-type circular columns with rough cubical capitals and neckings. The jambs are very irregular with much repair work, some with old bricks and flint, but a few original stones remain; the jambs have flint fillings between the inner and outer faces.

The pyramidal red-tiled roof is modern.

There is a faint indication on the exterior of the nave west wall of what may have been a narrow western doorway. It seems possible however that the main entrance to the church was through the south porticus.

---

(1) *Plate* 180.

In the interior are two fine east and west tower arches. The eastern one, the chancel arch, is of Saxon type. Its head is rather deeply segmental. The projecting imposts are chamfered on their soffit and eastern ends. Other details are hidden by plaster. It stands on a 14-inch chamfered plinth. The opening is *c.* 9 feet high to the imposts and 4 ft. 7 ins. wide. The jambs are 4 ft. 3½ ins. thick on the north and 4 ft. 4½ ins. on the south.

The western tower arch is a pointed fourteenth-century renewal. Its jambs are only 3 ft. 7 ins. thick.

On the interior of the tower south wall at ground-floor level, that is on the interior of the blocked doorway which is so plainly visible on the exterior, a rough heavily built plain and curiously skew arch projects inwards from the wall. It stands on a plinth 7 to 11 inches thick and 14 to 16 inches high. The arch is 3 ft. 3 ins. deep and 5 ft. 3 ins. wide. It looks as though it was once a monumental entrance, perhaps the main entrance to the church.

J. C. Cox regarded the tower as early Norman with some Saxon work. Baldwin Brown considered it pre-Conquest, post-950, and earlier than the nave. There appears to be nothing characteristically early Norman about the tower except the south and east belfry shafts and capitals, which may well be later insertions in view of their difference from the Saxon balusters on north and west.

NORTH ELMHAM

THE OLD SAXON CATHEDRAL.[1] North Elmham presents an enigma, in fact two enigmas. When Archbishop Theodore in 673 divided the see of Dunwich he established a new bishopric at Elmham. It is generally considered that this Elmham was North Elmham, Norfolk. Some writers[2] however have argued with vigour and skill, though not convincingly, that Theodore's new see was fixed at South Elmham, Suffolk, where there is also an 'Old Minster'. The problem is outside the scope of this book and must be left to the historians. It is sufficient here to indicate the problem and the relevant writers, and to add that modern opinion is almost entirely in favour of North Elmham as the seat of Theodore's bishopric. South Elmham is not and was never a village; it was an area, a district, comprising nine separate parishes. An important piece of evidence put forward by Howlett was that the earliest literary references to *South* Elmham are of the mid-thirteenth century; all earlier references are to Elmham only, and are plainly indicative of North Elmham.

The other enigma is architectural. The building has some very early and also some late features which make it extremely difficult to estimate its date.

[1] T. Butterick; A. W. Clapham and W. H. Godfrey; R. Howlett; S. E. Rigold, (*a*).
[2] In particular H. Harrod, 1874; J. J. Raven, 1898; F. S. Stevenson, 1926.

The original church was of timber and was not rebuilt in stone until the eleventh century. Floors of the earlier timber building have been discovered below the existing ruins.

The church was built in the south-west corner of a large earthwork which was about 300 feet square. The enclosure was surrounded by a deep ditch the upcast from which was spread over the 'island' to form a nearly level plot raised by 5 feet. After the see was transferred to Thetford in 1075 and from Thetford to Norwich in 1094, Elmham was neglected. In the late fourteenth century the church was made into a manor house by Bishop Hugh Despencer. Hugh surrounded the house with a shallow ditch which destroyed part of the apse. It seems likely that he made the outer ditch too. The house ended at the eastern crossing. It was occupied up to the end of the sixteenth century and was then either demolished or allowed to fall into ruin. Only a few fragments of walling were standing in 1891; the rest had become completely buried. The vicar, A. G. Legge, in 1871 did some excavation work but nothing much was learned from it. T. Butterick in 1903 first recognized the church as Saxon. He later supplied a drawing of the site and remains which was published by R. Howlett in 1913. The ruins were fairly thoroughly, though not completely, excavated in 1925 by A. W. Clapham and W. H. Godfrey. Later excavations were carried out by H.M. Ministry of Works under the direction of Mr. S. E. Rigold and much additional information obtained especially concerning the problem of dating.

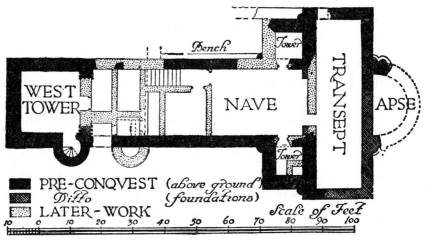

Fig. 36. North Elmham Cathedral, plan

The church consisted (Fig. 36) of aisleless nave, transepts of tau form (i.e. they were at the east end with no presbyterial space between them and the apse), an almost semicircular apse, a western axial tower, and square flanking towers, or stair turrets, in the angles between transepts and nave. There was a small semicircular stair turret projecting from the east end of the tower south wall.

332

The bases of the walls of the transepts and side towers, and the foundations of the apse are of large flint rubble in courses. Above this the material is coursed rubble of fairly large blocks of pudding stone or conglomerate, stained dark brown with iron. The western tower and nave are entirely of pudding stone. The quoins and dressings were also of pudding stone except (*a*) the surviving west jamb of the north transept north doorway, (*b*) the quoins of the western splay of the blocked north doorway of the nave, (*c*) the quoins, where visible, of the western tower, and (*d*) the bases of the responds of the tower arch to nave; all these are of oolitic limestone. In a few places the masons attempted to use pudding stone as ashlar for facings.

The nave is 72 feet by 20 feet on the interior;[1] the apse is 18 feet wide by *c*. 11 feet deep, the flanking towers 8 ft. 6 ins. square. The western tower is *c*. 18 ft. 6 ins. square inside, i.e. about 18 inches narrower than the nave interior; its exterior width is *c*. 27 feet, the same as the nave. The nave and transept walls are *c*. $3\frac{1}{2}$ feet thick, those of the three towers *c*. 9 inches thicker; the north wall of nave and tower appears to be a little thinner than the south wall. The overall exterior length of the building is 132 feet, and the exterior width across the transepts is 58 feet. On the interior the transepts are approximately 52 feet by 14 feet across.

The apse is now only at ground level, except the sleeper wall across the chord of the apse and the beginning of the curved wall at both north and south ends. On the south the base of a quarter-circular angle pilaster remains. On the north rather more wall survives with the bases of two pilasters: the quarter-circular angle pilaster and an adjacent semicircular one. They all have off-sets at the base projecting *c*. 7 inches. The semicircular pilaster is *c*. 1 ft. 10 ins. in diameter. Only a bit of the shaft survives but its shape is established by the remains of an adjoining piece of curved mortar-facing containing the mortar-face of the bit of wall between the pilasters, *c*. 9 inches. It is not known whether the pilasters went all round the apse wall at 9-inch intervals—if so there would have been fifteen—or whether they were spaced in groups to allow of windows wider than the 9-inch intervals.

The east and west walls of the transepts are at ground level, the north and most of the west are above ground. The west wall formed the east wall of Bishop Hugh's house. The north door in the north-west corner is cut straight through the wall; it has no rebate, a definite late Saxon feature. The base of the western jamb remains. The eastern jamb has been partly cut back and a rough rebate made, probably when the house was built.

There are quarter-circular pilasters in the re-entrant angles between transepts and flanking towers. The south one is plainly visible on the whole existing height of the exterior wall; the north pilaster is buried in the later, fourteenth century, thickening of the wall. This thickening runs along and beyond the north wall of the north tower; its object is unknown. These quadrant pilaster-buttresses are similar to some

[1] Clapham and Godfrey; Rigold gives 65 feet.

at Roughton and elsewhere in Norfolk in the angles between round tower and nave. Perhaps they are a local peculiarity, an East Anglian contribution to building technique.

Underlying the flint courses of the west wall of the south arm is a curious dip in the wall with a rather abrupt termination; this may possibly indicate a difference in date from the pudding stone walling above. Of the arch between transept and nave only the footings of the two responds remain; these appear on the plan to the west of the later walling.

The south wall of the nave is largely intact up to *c.* 8 feet. The north wall is much patched and altered. Towards its west end is the internal west jamb of a doorway; there is no indication of it on the exterior wall. There is also a flint bench along the north wall, *c.* 18 inches deep, of probably late fourteenth-century date: it was built against the earlier wall probably as a footing of a timber superstructure, perhaps Bishop Despencer's kitchen. There are quarter-circular pilasters in the re-entrant angles between turrets and nave, the northern one destroyed almost to ground level.

The flanking towers have no special features. The two doors opening to the nave were reconstructed in the late fourteenth century. The narrow doorways opening to the transepts are blocked but visible. The north tower had a small doorway also from the west, with no rebate. This doorway and that in the north of the north transept may suggest that the clergy entered from that side. That these towers are flanking towers, and not merely stair turrets, is indicated by the greater thickness of the walls compared with those of the nave and transepts. They may also have served as porticus. The north turret has been much altered, its western face having been almost entirely rebuilt, perhaps in the fourteenth century.

The west face of the western tower is still buried in masses of earth. There was a wide arch between tower and nave of which the whole base of the north respond and one stone of the south respond remain; the base is rectangular with a plain-chamfered plinth. This arch succeeded an earlier and narrower arch the base of which is visible beneath the existing one. About 18 inches to the east of the line of the arch in the north wall is a line of ashlar quoins of a former doorway; there are moulded bases of engaged columns with a sill of four flat stones between and a straight joint on the west. There was a similar doorway on the south, remains of which are hidden by Bishop Despencer's half-round turret. They are probably of the same date, probably post-Conquest, as the widened tower eastern arch. At the same time the tall slightly splayed western doorway in the tower was blocked.

The interpretation which Clapham and Godfrey drew from the somewhat unpromising observational material cannot now be accepted without qualification in view of Rigold's recent work. It is however worth reviewing in detail, not only on account of its relevance to this particular building but as a fine example of archaeological reasoning at its best. The church plan employed at Elmham is a very ancient one: an east end of the tau form with an apse projecting direct from the transept. The form belongs to the earliest church-building period after the Peace of the Church of A.D. 313. It occurs in the more important Constantinian churches in Rome: at old St. Peter's, at St. John Lateran and at the second church of St. Paul without the Walls; and at the small Romano-British church at Silchester, near Reading. It was employed at the early seventh-century abbey church of St. Denis, near Paris, and supposedly also in Wilfrid's great church at Hexham,[1] also seventh century. North of the Alps the plan died out well before the late eighth- and early ninth-century Carolingian Revival, though it continued to be used in Italy. Rigold pointed out that the plan was revived again in northern Europe in the eleventh century, mainly in large aisled churches. At Elmham the transept is attached to an aisleless nave. The Carolingian builders modified the general plan by introducing a presbyterial space between apse and transepts. The very early plan for the east end of Elmham therefore suggests an early date, say *c.* 673 when Theodore founded the diocese. Moreover Theodore would be familiar with the plan, having come direct from Italy to Canterbury. On the other hand the plan was not adopted in any other church built under Theodore's influence or in his time. Butterick however was of the opinion that the first church at Peterborough,[2] dated *c.* 654 and therefore earlier than Theodore, may have had this tau form. Against such an early date for Elmham is the general structure which indicates unmistakably a much later date. The western tower for example must be post-Danish, i.e. post-*c.* 870, for such towers were not introduced into England till after the Danish invasions. But the tower cannot be much later in date than the rest of the building as indicated by the general similarity in walling; it has, unlike the rest of the church, ashlar quoins and so may be later, but not much later. (These quoins however may be later insertions.) The flanking towers are certainly contemporary with the transepts. It is not known whether they were stair turrets as well as flanking towers for it is not known whether they had staircases, wooden or other. But they belong to the type, an early type which however is found in some early eleventh-century churches such as St. Germain des Prés in Paris. The normal type in Carolingian times was circular. Moreover such towers normally flanked the western front or the eastern presbytery; at Elmham there was no eastern presbytery and the square turrets were on the west of the transepts.

Flat pilaster strips were used widely by the Anglo-Saxons often as purely decorative features. Semicircular pilasters were uncommon, but were employed occasionally either alone or with flat ones. They occur at Stow (Lincs), Sompting (Sussex) and Skipwith (Yorks); all three are eleventh-century churches. At Elmham they are more numerous than elsewhere. They belong to a different category from the semicircular *buttresses* of some eleventh- and twelfth-century Romanesque churches; pilasters, it must be emphasized, are often purely decorative. They may be derived

[1] See above, pp. 68, 70 (Fig 3).   [2] See above, p. 222.

ultimately from Lombard bands, well known in Italian Romanesque and in the Rhineland. These consisted of arcaded corbel tables below the eaves supported at intervals by shafts or pilasters carried down the walls every third or fourth arch, the intervening arch heads resting on corbels. Occasionally alternate supports were carried down as pilasters but examples of every one being carried down as, apparently, round Elmham apse are rare if not unique.

Clapham and Godfrey concluded that the church must be a later rebuilding of an earlier one and that either the early plan of the east end was retained, and the church perhaps built on the early foundations, or that the builders deliberately archaicized. They suggested as a probable date the second half of the tenth century (suggested earlier by Baldwin Brown on no very clear grounds) or the first half of the eleventh century 'with a possible interval between the building of the main structure and the western tower and a balance of probability in favour of the later date'. The church is mentioned in Domesday Book as endowed with sixty acres and worth five shillings and four pence per annum.

The later excavations of Rigold definitely indicated three building periods. The apse, transept and corner turrets were built probably early in the eleventh century, perhaps *c.* 1020, to replace the earlier timber square east end and chancel. Rather later, perhaps *c.* 1050, the timber nave was rebuilt in stone and the western tower with its narrow western doorway and eastern arch erected. The third stage, which 'may be shortly after the Conquest' or perhaps as late as 1080, comprised the blocking of the western doorway, the insertion of the north and south doorways at the west end of the nave and the widening and reconstruction of the tower arch. The ashlar quoins of the tower may have been inserted at this time.

SOUTH ELMHAM

THE OLD MINSTER.[1] This ruined church stands in a quadrangular enclosure of over four acres which has been known for centuries as the Minster Yard. The enclosure is surrounded by a bank and ditch, possibly of Roman origin. G. E. Fox stated that though Roman in type the evidence for Roman occupation or use is conflicting and has not been established. There is no definite Roman material in the walls of the building.

The church consisted of nave, apse and square western annexe or perhaps tower (Fig. 37). The total exterior dimensions of the building are 101 ft. 5 ins. by 35 feet. It is built of flint rubble and exceedingly hard mortar, the latter a very characteristic Saxon feature. On both interior and exterior it was faced to a depth of *c.* 6 inches

[1] G. Baldwin Brown; A. W. Clapham, (*a*); R. Howlett; J. T. Micklethwaite, (*d*); C. R. Peers, (*a*); B. B. Woodward.

with flints and pebbles brought to a fairly even finish with mortar. This facing and all salient angles have been extensively stripped off and used as building material elsewhere. It remains chiefly on the upper part of the south wall and western annexe and at all re-entrant angles. The whole outer facings of the north and lower west walls have been removed.

A queer feature is the put-log holes. All are triangular, tapering slightly inwards, and *c.* 8 inches wide at the base. Most of the lower ones point upwards, and the upper ones downwards. They are unusually close together vertically, there being four ranges in a height of *c.* 14 feet. All have a coating of mortar but none have been filled in. Howlett thought this indicated that the building was never completed, that building

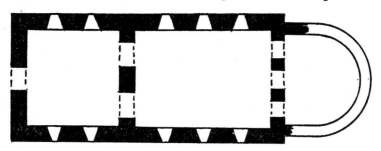

Fig. 37. South Elmham, 'Old Minster', plan

was interrupted by the pre-870 Danish raids and was not resumed owing to the Danish occupation of East Anglia. Had the interference been due to the early eleventh-century raids and invasions by Sweyn the building might well have been completed as the subsequent Danish occupation under Canute was a Christian one.

The apse is now foundations only except a short piece at the west end of the south wall where it is 3 feet thick. The apse is stilted; its inner dimensions are 24 ft. 5 ins. wide by 21 ft. 3 ins. deep.

The nave is 38 feet by 27 feet on the interior; its north, south and east walls were 3 ft. 10 ins. thick. The north wall is almost entirely gone, except a piece of about 6 feet at the west end, which remains to a considerable height, and the west jamb of its western window. More of the south wall remains including portions of three window openings. The eastern window remains almost to its full height including part of its head. The south-east corner is in better condition than the rest of the church; about three inches of its salient angle have gone and it is overgrown with ivy, but otherwise it is in good order. Some original plaster, of similar hard quality to the mortar, remains. The mortar is so good that it has not weathered since exposure through the removal of facings; it still shows marks of the bonding ends of the flint facings. There is no indication here of special quoining—only flints and pebbles.

The opening to the apse is 20 ft. 9 ins. wide. It has square responds of nave wall thickness, 3 ft. 10 ins. A foundation across the full width of the opening is at a higher level than the presumed and probable floor level of the nave. The opening is too wide for a single arch to be likely. The foundation suggests a triple arcade as at St. Pancras and other early Kentish churches; it would in fact be difficult to explain on any other hypothesis.

The western chamber is square, 26 feet each way on the interior, with walls 4 ft. 6 ins. thick, including the east wall. This thickening suggests that the walls were intended to carry a tower; on the exterior the walls are flush with the nave walls, the thickening being on the interior, which indicates a western axial tower as at North Elmham. The tower is inferential as nothing remains above *c.* 14 or 15 feet. In its eastern wall is a central pier, or rather a length of walling some 7 or 8 feet wide, on either side of which was an opening with square jambs slightly narrower than the central pier, each opening being 6 ft. 8½ ins. wide. There are two window openings in each north and south wall. The east one on the north and the west one on the south remain to their full height, except for a little masonry gone at the crowns. Heads, jambs and sills are single-splayed, the sill splays being flatter than the others. The sills retain at their joints with the jambs some of the plaster with which the whole surface of the openings was covered. There is no indication of stone dressings in the arch heads or jambs; what remains is of flint rubble. The west window in the south wall is in a part of the wall where the surface facings are perfect to within a few inches of the opening; so little of the exterior angle of the jamb is missing that it is difficult to believe there were original stone dressings. On the other hand very thin stone quoins and jambs are not uncommon in the district and Peers reported that the appearance of the jambs of the north-west window might suggest earlier thin stone dressings there; but the indications are faint and inconclusive. The window openings were 5 feet high to the springings of the round heads, and 1 ft. 7 ins. wide. The sight line of the sills is *c.* 7 feet above present ground level.

The west wall above *c.* 5 feet is less despoiled than that below; the upper part overhangs the lower considerably and is held up by the strength of the mortar. Part of the jambs and springing of a large arched central opening are plainly visible in the west wall; it was 6 feet wide and *c.* 10 feet high to the springing. The opening is not splayed; it was evidently the western portal.

The dating of the church presents difficulties; like North Elmham it is an enigma. The very hard mortar suggests an early Saxon date. Micklethwaite thought it Saxon; so also did Howlett and B. B. Woodward. The windows are taller and wider than is usual with late Saxon or early Norman windows. This, with the absence of specific Saxon details, might suggest a date of *c.* 1140, though the hard mortar is hardly consistent with a late Norman date. The window splaying too is hardly wide enough to be Norman. Wide western portals with no rebates or splays were not usual in the twelfth century but were common in early, even in very early, Saxon buildings.

There are or were such portals at St. Pancras, Canterbury, where it was 7 ft. 9 ins. wide, altered during building to 6 ft. 6 ins.; at St. Martin's, Canterbury, where it has been destroyed but appears to have been *c.* 7 feet wide; and at Bradwell juxta Mare, Essex, where it was *c.* 5 feet. These three churches are early to middle seventh century. The proportions of the nave are similar to the early Kentish churches. Thus we have: South Elmham, 38 feet by 27 feet; St. Martin, Canterbury, 40 feet by 25 feet; St. Pancras, Canterbury, 42 feet by 26 feet; and Rochester, 42 feet by 30 feet. The rather narrow single-splaying of windows occurs at Jarrow and Monkwearmouth and other early Saxon churches. Unrebated jambs of doorways occur throughout the entire Saxon period, but are more characteristic of the Late than of the Early Saxon period. The large western portal suggests an entrance to a porch, towers being unknown in early Saxon buildings; there were such porches and portals at St. Pancras, Brixworth, Corbridge, Monkwearmouth, and elsewhere. The nave walls are unusually thick for early Saxon work, but so are those at Brixworth. It is evident that many features at South Elmham while not characteristically Saxon are characteristically early, and strongly reminiscent of the early Kentish churches, which themselves, though early, are not characteristically Saxon: they were foreign churches built by foreign masons on English soil.[1] Peers was of opinion that the church is early Saxon and might be dated to *c.* 670. Against this is the western annexe: surely such thick walls, some 8 or 9 inches thicker than those of the nave, were intended to support something heavier than a porch; early porches were not given thickened walls. The annexe is of the same date as the nave: if it were later it would have been built against the thinner west wall of the nave; but the west wall of the nave here is the east wall of the annexe and is of the same thickness as the other annexe walls. Such unporch-like western annexes were uncommon in Saxon times. There was a similar one at Daglingworth (Glos): it was 16 feet square on the exterior and of the same exterior width as the nave; its walls were 3 ft. 9 ins. thick compared with the nave's 2 ft. 8 ins. and the chancel's 2 ft. 4 ins. Only the south wall now remains; the rest was incorporated into the church when the present tower was built in the fifteenth century. There is no record of an early tower at Daglingworth. There was also one at Boarhunt (Hants), a late Saxon church; here however there was no thickening of the walls. There were north and south nave doorways at Boarhunt, only a south doorway at Daglingworth, and no nave doorway at all at South Elmham.

Baldwin Brown, who was familiar with Peers's work, maintained his own conviction that Elmham was Norman. Clapham wrote 'it stands equally isolated whether it be placed [after the Conquest], in the tenth century, or in the seventh'; which states the problem concisely but does not help towards a solution. The enigma remains.

[1] See A. W. Clapham, (*a*); E. A. Fisher.

WEYBOURNE

ALL SAINTS' CHURCH.[1] The manor of Weybourne was held in the reign of Edward the Confessor by Haakon or Haco, son of Sweyn the eldest son of Earl Godwin. Haakon was slain at Hastings in the last rally round the standard with his uncles Gyrth and Leofwine. After the Conquest the manor, with many other estates, passed to Hugh of Avranches, Hugh Lupus, Earl of Chester, a nephew of the Conqueror. A sub-feudatory under him was Ranulph de Mesnilgarin, lord of Mesnilgarin near Contances, Normandy. He is named as holding the manor, though a church is not mentioned, in Domesday Book. His was a prolific family, which is reputed to have thrown out at least thirteen different branches and three bastard ones. It has been stated that heirs male still existed in the nineteenth century under the name of Mainwaring. By the late twelfth century the name had become Meyngarin and a Sir Ralph of that name granted the manor and church and graveyard to the Augustinian or Black Canons, and made it subordinate to the priory of West Acre. This Order of Canons lived according to a Rule derived from that drawn up by St. Augustine of Hippo (d. 430) for the clergy of his episcopal household. It was an Order which filled the gap between the monk and the secular priest. The Canons lived in a community subject to monastic rule but were free to serve churches in the district as parish priests, usually churches belonging to their Order and from which they received some income in the form of tithes. The first Augustinian or Austin House in England was St. Botolph's priory, Colchester, founded in 1095. During the twelfth century the number of houses increased greatly especially in East Anglia, the great House at West Acre, Norfolk, being founded soon after 1100 and its subsidiary at Weybourne soon after 1200. The date of the transfer of Weybourne to West Acre is doubtful but was probably in the reign of John (1200–16). At this time the church was at least a century old. It consisted of nave, central axial tower and presumably a small chancel. Baldwin Brown stated that the ground floor of the tower was used as a chancel. No traces of an early chancel have been found; the presence of graves to the east of the old tower has prevented extensive excavation here. Possibly there may have been a south porticus off the tower. Jessop suggested that the Saxon church was monastic. This is doubtful. It is not mentioned in any extant list of Saxon monasteries. Fairweather wrote that the Austin Canons' 'provisions for parochial arrangements from the first distinctly suggest that parochial rights existed and were in working order'.

The Canons early began altering and enlarging the church, alterations which were continued over several centuries.[2] Early in the thirteenth century they built a larger

[1] G. Baldwin Brown; F. H. Fairweather, (*a*); A. Jessop; C. R. Manning.
[2] See plan in F. H. Fairweather, (*a*).

chancel. In the late thirteenth they destroyed the south wall of the nave and replaced it with an arcade of three bays leading into a new church (part of the present one); so the old nave became a north aisle. Early in the fourteenth century north and south transepts were built east of the tower and the new chancel extended further east. At the same time a great arch, still existing, was cut through the east wall of the tower and the ground floor of the tower was vaulted. The new church to the south was also extended on the east (and also to the west) by the addition of a new chancel, the present one, built against the south wall of the old tower. Late in the fourteenth century alterations were made to the west wall of the tower and the east bay of the early thirteenth-century nave arcade walled up. After the Dissolution the old Saxon nave, which for over three centuries had been the north aisle of the later church, was allowed to fall into ruin. It was rebuilt, as a north aisle, in 1866 on the original Saxon foundations.

The church was built of flints with some dark red ferrugineous sandstone obtainable in some parts of Norfolk. The tower quoins are mainly of large, uncut, flattish pebbles or flints with some interspersed flat rather long pieces of sandstone. The axial tower is of pre-Conquest type and technique. Like those at Bawsey and Newton the nave walls projected laterally from the tower by about their own thickness. The length of the entire church, assuming a small square chancel, was *c.* 80 feet. In the tower south wall is a rough round head of an early blocked opening, centrally placed, which may have led to a south porticus in the position now occupied by the present fourteenth-century chancel. A large recess in the north wall of this chancel marks the position of the former opening. Excavation has revealed no similar adjunct on the north. Bawsey and Newton also had early openings in their tower south walls but none in the north.

Apart from the ruin of the tower nothing remains of the old church except the foundations of the old nave on which the later walls of the north aisle of the existing church have been built.

The south half of the tower remains to its full height, including enough of the east and west walls to show the south jambs of the east and west belfry openings. The north wall has disappeared except its eastern tear-away from the east wall and the north east angle, leaving the entire interior elevation of the south wall exposed to view. The lower part of the south wall forms the north wall of the present chancel; the upper part stands well above the rather high chancel roof (1).

There is a thin string course about half way up the exposed upper half of the tower. On the interior are the marks of three early blocked openings, vertically disposed and all above the ground stage blocked opening leading to the supposed porticus. The details of the top opening are obscured by being cut through by the bonding of the fourteenth-century vaulting. The two lower openings appear to have been round-headed. In the south-west angle the remains are visible of a small doorway which led to the early fourteenth-century chancel; and in the south-east corner is a triangular niche of brick, probably a later lamp niche, for this corner must always have been dark. In the west wall is visible the south springing of a round-headed arch, blocked at an early date, which was formerly the opening to the Saxon nave. In the early blocking at its north end is the base of a jamb of the narrow doorway which was inserted when the arch was blocked. On the exterior of the west wall, i.e. on the remaining upper south portion of it, is the weathering of the early nave roof; it was just above a large inserted late window of which only a jamb remains. On the exterior of the east wall the north-east and south-east original quoins remain; the later work is built against them with straight joints. The width of the tower at this point is *c.* 18 ft. 6 ins. On the interior it is 11 ft. 9 ins. square, making the walls *c.* 3 ft. 4 ins. thick.

The blocked belfry openings are visible above the string course on the south wall. They were of the usual double-light type but no mid-wall work remains. The high-pitched heads are pointed or gabled. There is lower segmentally headed blind arcading on each side of the belfry openings, two bays to each. All are of flint. The jambs are flat and pilaster-like and rest on the string course. There are no imposts. According to Fairweather the openings are not really gabled but are lancets; the sides of the apparent gables are curved and he thought they were a thirteenth-century remodelling with the old materials of the early lights. This conclusion is not entirely convincing. The work is rough, the heads very irregular. In the south wall the heads of the eastern arcading are flatter and lower than those of the western. The east half-gable is definitely curved; also it extends to a lower level than the middle and western ones. The other three half-gables are straight. The lateral arcading is continued round the east and west walls as far as the central couplet of belfry openings, of which only the southern jambs and half-gables remain; these half-gables are curved like those on the south. The arcading, if not the belfry openings, may be original; there seems to be no reason for doubting this. The openings may be original too; the curvature of some half-gables may not have been intentional, but merely the result of poor craftsmanship. Above and on either side of the belfry openings except in the west wall is a circular sound hole. They are blocked on the interior but the blocking is thin enough to allow the double-splaying to be seen.

The date of the church is uncertain. The double-splayed circular openings are a Saxon feature. Fairweather's doubts about the age of the belfry openings and the absence of mid-wall work in the openings afford no help in dating the remains. If post-Conquest they could not be much later in view of the Saxon technique and absence of stone dressings. Baldwin Brown considered the church as definitely pre-Conquest but did not suggest a date. In an area where positive evidence is scanty there are no buildings, apart possibly from the two Elmhams, showing features of definite pre-Canute (1016–35) date. Weybourne may perhaps be regarded reasonably as of mid-eleventh century, plus or minus twenty years or so.

According to Fairweather's plan the church is orientated in a direction approximately 30° S. of E. This is unusual, indeed quite exceptional. Cave[1] found that of the English churches of all periods studied by him 48 per cent were orientated between E. and E. +20° N., and 27 per cent between E. and E. +20° S. Only 1·7 per cent were orientated further south than E. +20°, i.e. only 11 out of 642.

[1] See above, p. 49.

ESSEX

HISTORICAL INTRODUCTION

The origin of Essex—the kingdom of the East Saxons—is obscure. The area was colonized by Saxons perhaps from Kent possibly about the mid-sixth century and its later associations were with Kent, not—as might have been expected—with its near neighbour to the north, East Anglia. An illustration of this may be the rarity of round towers in Essex compared with the very large number of such towers in East Anglia. The kingdom expanded westwards, absorbing the Middle Saxons of what is now Middlesex and part of Hertfordshire and from the early seventh century London was its most important town. The first attempt to Christianize the area was made by King Æthelberht of Kent who persuaded his nephew Saberht of Essex to be baptized. Æthelberht built a church in London, supposedly on the site of the present St. Paul's. Mellitus, one of Augustine's monks, was appointed bishop in 604. The attempt was hardly more than a gesture. On the death of Saberht *c.* 616 Mellitus was driven from the area and did not return. A more successful attempt to introduce Christianity was made some forty years later when King Oswiu of Northumbria persuaded the East Saxon king, Sigeberht, to accept Christianity and to receive Cedd, a brother of the better known Chad, as bishop of the area in *c.* 655. Cedd was a real missionary bishop with no fixed seat; he travelled about the area making converts. Shortly before he returned home to Northumbria in 664 to die, he built the church of St. Peter-on-the-Wall at Bradwell juxta Mare, the Saxon Ythancaestir, near the Roman fort of Othona. A great part of this church is standing today. Being towerless it does not concern us here. It may be said however that architecturally it is a member of the Kentish group of early churches, with apse, north and south porticus and western porch; unlike the Kentish churches it had the Northumbrian features, due doubtless to Cedd, of relatively long and high nave.[1]

Essex, though one of the seven kingdoms of the Saxon Heptarchy, was never one of the big three, nor did it ever produce a bretwalda. It lost its independence rather soon after reaching its maximum expansion. It became subordinate to Wulfhere of Mercia *c.* 665 and under the great Offa was hardly more than a mere province of Mercia. It submitted to Egbert of Wessex in 825, became a part of the Danelaw after Alfred's peace with the Danish Guthrun in 886, and was finally reconquered by Edward the Elder in 911–17; after which it became merely a part of Anglo-Saxon

[1] See however above, p. 87, *n.* 2.

England under an Ealderman. Its history is undistinguished; it produced, so far as is known, no great men. Two nunneries, at Barking and St. Osyth, and a foundation at West Tilbury, were founded in the mid-seventh century, and a monastery at Waltham Cross by Earl Harold, later King Harold, in 1060. No traces of these now exist. There are twenty-two churches which are pre-Conquest or contain pre-Conquest fragments. Six have towers, all of the late eleventh century. These are: Holy Trinity, Colchester; Little Bardfield, 6 miles NE. of Great Dunmow; Corringham, 6 miles NE. of Tilbury; Steeple Bumpstead, 9 miles E. of Saffron Walden; West Mersea, 8 miles S. of Colchester; and Tollesbury, 7 miles ENE. of Maldon. Corringham, Steeple Bumpstead and West Mersea are not dealt with below.

COLCHESTER

HOLY TRINITY CHURCH.[1] Only the tower and the west wall of the nave are pre-Conquest; this is the only Saxon monument in Colchester. The tower (I) is built largely of flints with a considerable profusion of Roman bricks. The quoins are entirely of Roman bricks. It is of three stages, separated by two string courses each of which consists of two courses of projecting Roman bricks. The stages are not recessed. The ground stage occupies more than half the total height; it is about three times the height of the second stage and considerably taller than the third stage. At the top are a few courses of eighteenth-century bricks, a projecting cornice and a low pyramidal roof. The tower is of Saxon proportions, tall and slender, 11 ft. 6 ins. square on the interior. It is of late Saxon date and is built with a straight joint against the earlier west wall of the nave. The walls are *c.* $3\frac{1}{2}$ feet thick.

In the ground stage at about half way up is a large wide round-headed window in the north and south wall. Like all the other openings the heads and jambs are in Roman bricks. The sills are walling. In the west wall there is a western doorway (2), gable-headed, made entirely of Roman bricks. The gable sides are of Roman bricks sloping at an angle of about 45° and are finished clumsily at the apex. The imposts are of three over-sailing double courses of bricks, i.e. arranged in characteristic Saxon three-stepped pattern. There is a gable-headed hood mould of three courses of bricks which has its own imposts of three courses projecting from the wall but not over-sailing. It is carried below the imposts to the ground as pilasters composed of horizontally laid bricks.

In the second stage in the north and south walls there is a shallow round-headed recess (I) resting on the string course and centrally placed. The heads and jambs are of

[1] R.C.H.M., *Essex*, III.

(I) *Plates* 190, 191; (2) *Plates* 190, 192.

walling with a few Roman bricks here and there. In the west wall are two double-splayed windows, now blocked thinly, also of walling and Roman bricks and resting on the string course. Between these but placed lower is a taller round-headed window with head and jambs and sill largely of Roman bricks; the string course forms the imposts, so most of the window is below the string.

The third stage is the belfry. It has two ranges of openings. The lower range is of one tall round-headed window in each wall, resting on the string courses which act as sills. Like the other windows they are outlined in mixed flint and Roman bricks. The south window (1) (but not those on the other walls) is built in the central bay of five bays of round-headed blind wall arcading. The arcading occupies the entire wall width between the quoins and is composed wholly of Roman bricks. The upper range of windows consists of couplets: double round-headed windows outlined in Roman bricks and separated by a rectangular pier of Roman bricks—really just a piece of walling. Between the two ranges of windows are slight traces of low round-headed wall arcading marked out by small fragments of bricks, most of which have probably fallen out. On the east wall the arches are continued down as strips of upright bricks; but the work is much weathered and very indistinct.

The nave west wall is 18 ft. 6 ins. wide. The original wall is *c.* 28 feet high to the gable base, the line of which is indicated inside the tower by a raking break in the upper bonding on the tower east wall. Below the gable in the second stage of the tower are traces of a blocked opening.

The tower arch (2) is later than the wall; it is a late pre-Conquest insertion probably of the same age as the tower. It is entirely of Roman bricks. It is round-headed, of one square-cut order. The jambs have bases of plain three-stepped off-sets and the large imposts are of three over-sailing double courses. The opening has on both faces a strip-work hood mould of Roman bricks resting on the imposts, but continued below as vertical brick pilaster work to about half way to the ground: possibly originally it extended to the ground.

LITTLE BARDFIELD

ST. KATHARINE'S CHURCH.[1] The nave and the western tower are pre-Conquest, probably eleventh century (Fig. 38); Baldwin Brown suggested post-1040. The walls are of flint and pebble rubble with dressings of clunch; some tiles in the older parts of the walls may be Roman. The nave roof is of modern tiling. The chancel is later, possibly fourteenth century. The embattled tower parapet and spire are modern.

[1] R.C.H.M., *Essex*, I.

(1) *Plate* 191; (2) *Plate* 189.

The nave is 33 ft. 6 ins. long by 20 feet on the interior. At the east end of the north wall is a blocked round-headed window, probably pre-Conquest. In the south wall, above the west jamb of the south doorway, is a blocked double-splayed round-headed Saxon window. The other three openings, two in the north and one in the south wall, are fourteenth and fifteenth century.

Unlike that at Colchester the tower (I) is not of typical Saxon proportions; its width makes it look rather squat, rather like a Norman tower. However, it shows

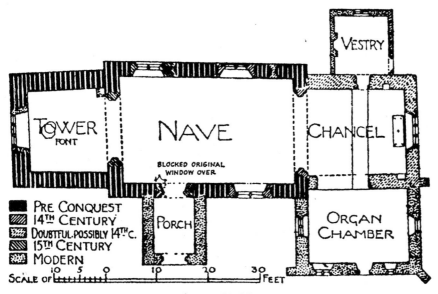

Fig. 38. Little Bardfield Church, plan

the bad setting-out often found in Saxon churches: there is not a strict right angle in the tower and the nave west wall is not at strict right angles to the north and south walls (Fig. 38). The tower is $21\frac{1}{2}$ feet wide at the west on the exterior and *c.* 18 inches wider at the east end. The walls are *c.* 6 inches thicker than the nave walls which are slightly less than 3 feet.

There is a little rough herring-boning on the top stage, but none below. This may suggest Norman repair work.

The tower has five recessed stages separated by string courses of the same rubble material as the walls. The ground stage is considerably taller than the others; the other four do not differ m uch though the fourth is appreciably shorter than the others. The large ground-floor west window is modern. Below this are traces of an early blocked western doorway. The second stage on the interior is included in the first —there is no separating floor; it has no openings.

(I) *Plate* 187.

In the third stage are two tall, not very narrow round-headed windows in the north, south and west walls. In the fourth stage are two tall very narrow round-headed windows centrally placed but close together in each of the four walls; the heads are rather near the fourth string course. In the fifth stage are windows similar to those in the fourth but they are widely separated and rest on the string. Those on the north and east are blocked. None of these windows has any dressings. The jambs and sills are indistinguishable from walling; the heads are just distinct from walling, being composed of selected stones. The heads too are wider than the distance between the jambs, having an almost keyhole appearance. The openings are not splayed.

In the north wall of the top stage is a modern window in addition to the early ones.

TOLLESBURY

ST. MARY THE VIRGIN'S CHURCH.[1] When this church was restored in 1875 many Roman tiles, including some flue tiles, were found built into the nave, tower and

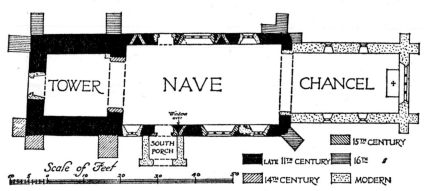

Fig. 39. Tollesbury Church, plan

south doorway. These may indicate the former existence of a Roman house on or near the site.

The nave and tower are late eleventh century. Both show the bad setting out frequent in Saxon buildings; there is not a strict right angle in nave or tower plan (Fig. 39). The chancel is modern; the corner buttresses to nave and tower are sixteenth century. The walls are of boulder clay except the upper two stages of the tower which are of red brick, probably of the sixteenth or early seventeenth century. The dressings are of clunch and Roman bricks.

The nave is 41 ft. 9 ins. long by 21 ft. 6 ins. on the interior, the walls *c.* 3 feet thick. In the north wall are three original blocked windows, double-splayed but with very

[1] R.C.H.M., *Essex*, III.

shallow outer splay. They are high up and visible only on the exterior. The jambs and rough round heads are of boulder clay. One of the windows has been opened out. In the south wall is one early window similar to those on the north though rather better built. It is above the east jamb of the south doorway opposite the middle north window. The south porch is modern; the south doorway is fifteenth-century and is thin and built flush with the exterior wall. It is built within the tall original eleventh-century doorway (1) of Roman bricks, round-headed and with no imposts; it is a striking feature of the interior.

The tower is of three stages, only the ground stage being Saxon. It has the same exterior width, 27 feet, as the nave and is therefore a western axial tower. Its walls are massive, over 5 feet thick, obviously intended to support a tower and indicate that the upper stages are brick replacements of earlier stages. The internal dimensions are *c.* 16 feet north–south by *c.* 17 feet east–west.

The wide tower arch is probably fourteenth century. Above is a relieving arch, roughly built partly in Roman bricks, perhaps the old material from the original tower arch. The western doorway and window above are modern.

---

(1) *Plate* 188.

Part V

ENGLAND SOUTH OF THE THAMES

KENT

HISTORICAL INTRODUCTION

This was one of the three Saxon kingdoms which developed in England south of the Thames; the other two were Sussex and Wessex. The story of the foundation of Kent is too well known to need more than the briefest mention here. It was the earliest of the Anglo-Saxon kingdoms to be established. The traditional date of its beginning is 449, nearly a hundred years before the establishment of Bernicia in the north. Kent, on account of its nearness to Gaul, had always had close trading and cultural relations with the Continent. It became the most advanced, both materially and culturally, of all the Anglo-Saxon kingdoms. In its early days it was also the most powerful of them. Its greatest king, and its first to become really known in history, was Æthelberht, c. 560–616. He was third in Bede's list of bretwaldas and he appears to have exercised some kind of suzerainty over all England south of the Humber. He was also the first Anglo-Saxon king to commit to writing the laws and customs of his people, another indication of the relatively high degree of culture in this part of England. His marriage to the Christian Bertha, daughter of King Charibert of Paris, gave him some knowledge of and perhaps sympathy with the Christian religion and in 597 he received the mission of St. Augustine and his forty monks with tolerance and friendliness. He later became a Christian and no doubt played his part as royal patron in the building of the well-known group of churches of Augustine's time. These churches, of which only ruins or foundations survive, are usually considered the earliest of the Saxon churches. They were certainly the earliest churches to be built in Saxon England, but they were not really Saxon churches; they were foreign churches built by foreign masons in a foreign style. They are interesting and important on account of their great influence on the style of architecture which developed in England in the Early Saxon period, i.e. up to the first great Danish invasion of 865–86. Augustine built three churches in Canterbury: his cathedral church of Christ Church, within the city, and his monastic church of SS. Peter and Paul, and St. Pancras close to it, just outside the city wall. Others of the same group put up in the half-century after Augustine's death were: St. Andrew's at Rochester and St. Paul's in London (nothing of this one remains) built by Æthelberht in 604; St. Mary's at Canterbury, a few yards east of St. Pancras, built c. 620 by King Eadbald, Æthelberht's son and successor, after his tardy conversion to Christianity; St. Mary's at Lyminge, the church of a nunnery founded *c.* 633 by Æthelberga, daughter of Æthelberht and widow of Edwin of Northumbria; and St. Mary's, Reculver, *c.* 669. They were of course towerless. They have been described and discussed in much detail by several writers.[1] Eadbald, the pagan son of Æthelberht and Bertha, succeeded Æthelberht in 616 and reigned until 640. In the early, pagan, years of his reign the Church in Kent was almost extinguished. Eadbald accepted Christianity *c.* 620 but his earlier enthusiasm later became dulled. The Church just lingered on until it was revived, revitalized and reorganized by the great Archbishop Theodore, 668–90. Under him Christian culture and influence spread throughout the entire country and his Church became a national church. He also established a scriptorium at Canterbury, ruled over for two years by Benedict Biscop and then for forty by Theodore's friend and close companion, Hadrian. The Canterbury scriptorium was of great cultural importance and influence throughout the entire Saxon period. It influenced, as a source of inspiration through Biscop, the scriptoria which Biscop established at Jarrow and Monkwearmouth; through them it influenced Bede, and through Bede the later scriptorium at York. Apart from such indirect influence it was for centuries a direct channel for interchange of cultural and artistic ideas between south-east England and the great western-continental centres of art and learning.

Theodore must have built churches in his own diocese of Kent, though nothing is known of them; as discussed above,[2] he may well have been responsible for the great church at Brixworth (Northants). The era of Theodore may be regarded as the high-water mark of the influence of independent Saxon Kent. Politically it never exceeded, or even again reached, the power of Æthelberht, and after his time it became progressively less important as the power of first Northumbria and then Mercia steadily grew. It became a mere province of Mercia under Offa *c.* 762 and remained subordinate to that kingdom until both Mercia and Kent were conquered by Egbert of Wessex in 825. After that it was no more than merely a part of England, though it remained culturally important and influential for centuries. In Edgar's reign, for example, one should note the importance of Kentish influence in the great monastic revival for which that remarkable trio, St. Dunstan of Canterbury, St. Æthelwold of Winchester and St. Oswald of Worcester and York, were responsible.

It is perhaps surprising that there are so few pre-Conquest churches in Kent.[3] This may be due in part to the importance of Kent in the Middle Ages as in earlier ages as an alley-way of culture and trade between England and France, to growing population resulting from increasing prosperity, and its nearness to London. As population increased more and larger churches would be needed; the earlier Saxon ones would be added to, altered, transformed, pulled down and rebuilt throughout

---

[1] G. Baldwin Brown; A. W. Clapham, (*a*); W. H. St. J. Hope; Canon R. C. Jenkins; Canon G. M. Livett; C. R. Peers, (*a*) and (*c*); C. R. Peers and A. W. Clapham; Canon C. F. Routledge, (*e*).

[2] p. 201.   [3] See below, p. 419.

the centuries. Today there is only one towered church of the Saxon period, that of St. Mary-in-Castro, Dover. The other church considered here, St. Martin's at Canterbury, had so far as is known no Saxon tower. It is included here on account of its great intrinsic interest and as an example of the early Kentish group of churches which in many respects it resembles but to which it does not really belong.

CANTERBURY

ST. MARTIN'S CHURCH.[1] This church stands about half a mile to the east of the city wall, just off the Roman road from Rutupiae (Richborough) to Durovernum (Canterbury). The site rises considerably from west to east.

The church has some claim to be the oldest church in England, or at least that some part of its fabric still standing is part of the earliest church building now standing in England. Clapham agreed that St. Martin's 'represents' the church related by Bede to have been 'built of old while the Romans still occupied Britain' and given by

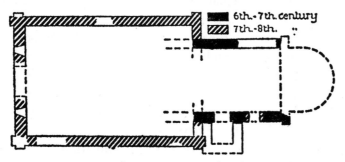

Fig. 40. Canterbury, St. Martin's Church, plan

King Æthelberht of Kent to his Queen Bertha and her Gaulish chaplain Liudhard. Here she is supposed to have worshipped throughout her long married life. Augustine and his forty monks are stated to have begun their ministration here in 597.

The Chancel. The earliest parts of the existing church are the north and south walls of the western part of the chancel (1) and remains of a small porticus on the south side (Fig. 40). The chancel is 14 feet wide and the earliest part extends c. 18 feet east of the chancel arch wall. The walls are 2 ft. 2 ins. thick and are built of Roman bricks laid evenly on one another, four or five bricks per foot including the wide mortar joints, which are about as wide as the bricks are thick. The workmanship of the south

[1] E. P. L. Brock; G. Baldwin Brown; A. W. Clapham, (a), (b) and (c); Hardcastle; J. T. Micklethwaite, (b); C. R. Peers, (a); Canon C. F. Routledge, (a), (b), (c) and (d).

(1) *Plate* 194.

wall is good though rather rough; it is possibly Roman and almost certainly pre-Augustinian. The north wall was almost destroyed to make way for a vestry in 1844; it shows no feature of special interest.

In the south wall are two blocked early doorways (1); one near the west end is square-headed, the other further east is round-headed. They are both cut straight through the walls. The square-headed opening (2) is original with the wall and was the entrance to the south porticus. It has jambs of Roman bricks and lintel and sill of massive blocks of green sandstone. It is 5 ft. 5 ins. high by 3 ft. 4 ins. wide. The round-headed doorway (3) is only 4 ft. 2 ins. to the east of the other. It is slightly taller and narrower. It is 5 ft. 10 ins. high to the imposts; the jambs incline upwards, rather more on the west than east, and are 2 ft. 3½ ins. apart at the base and 2 ft. 1 in. at the arch springing. The head is of converging blocks of Kentish rag, about 1 inch apart but rather closer near the crown. It is set back about an inch behind the jambs. The imposts are of two Roman bricks each, the upper one overhanging the lower and the lower one overhanging the jamb soffit faces; they are flush with the wall face. It is reputed to be the doorway used by Queen Bertha. She may have used a doorway in this position, but not this particular doorway for it appears to be a later insertion, though its inclined jambs show it to be of the Saxon period. That it is an insertion is indicated by a break all round in the masonry, plainly visible on both wall faces. The jambs on the interior are of Roman bricks with occasional pieces of Kentish rag. The exterior jambs are almost entirely of Roman bricks. Under the western impost, 3 ft. 8 ins. above the sill, is an inserted, re-used piece of freestone, *c.* 3½ inches high. (The white stone in Pl. 193.) On this are some letters, parts of an inscription suggested to be of the ninth or tenth century: HONORE . . . STÆ . . . ET OMNIV̄ SCORV̄. . . . It has been translated as 'To the honour of Saint . . . and All Saints'. It may have been part of the dedication stone of a church or of an altar. One Saxon archbishop issued an order that a stone should be placed at the corner of each altar specifying the name of the saint or saints to whom it was dedicated.

The early chancel wall extends *c.* 6 ft. 9 ins. to the east of the round-headed doorway. Here a break in the fabric is observable especially on the exterior; it is a rough straight joint running right through the wall, indicating presumably the position of the east end of the original chancel. The break (1) occurs just east of a modern flat buttress which is however the successor of an early buttress of similar pilaster form. The next 2 feet are rather irregular, perhaps marking the beginning of a Roman apse. A rough brick inner face to the wall on the line of this buttress and foundations projecting *c.* 2 feet north from this face under the chancel floor suggest there was a return here, possibly to an apse, though this is conjectural. The wall immediately to the east of this for *c.* 8 ft. 3 ins. is of different workmanship, though still of Roman

---

(1) *Plate* 194; (2) *Plate* 196; (3) *Plates* 193, 195.

bricks; it has six bricks per foot and is probably a late twelfth-century extension. The extreme 12 feet of the east end are later still, perhaps thirteenth century; it is of mixed Roman bricks and flints. On the interior south wall and overlapping the two late extensions to the chancel is a very wide round-headed recess built entirely of Roman bricks; it is probably thirteenth-century sedilia.

Near the western square-headed south doorway excavation revealed the foundations of two exterior walls at right angles to the chancel wall; these were the east and west walls of the porticus (Fig. 40). The foundations of the south wall have been destroyed, presumably through repeated grave-digging. The east and west walls were 4 ft. 9 ins. apart and 2 ft. 2 ins. thick and entirely of Roman bricks. Between the two foundation walls near the sill of the doorway a portion still exists of the original flooring of *opus signinum*, a kind of cement mixed with powdered brick. These foundation walls are of similar workmanship to the early chancel wall and are constructively bonded into it. They rest on footing courses one brick deep which form the top of shallow foundations of flints and stones. The brick footing is continued along the chancel wall under the sill of the doorway; it is of irregular projection. There is some evidence on the chancel wall, on each side of the doorway up to the lintel height, that the porticus walls were bonded into the chancel wall. The only fragment of the porticus remaining above ground is a strip of brickwork of *c.* 5 inches projection in the re-entrant angle between the south wall of the chancel and the east wall of the nave. It seems to have been left when the rest of the porticus was destroyed. It formed the western half of the thickness of the west wall at this point, the eastern half being cut away, as is indicated by the rough ends of the broken bricks. In the north wall of the chancel, just east of the present chancel arch and below the floor level, are several projecting courses which suggest that there may have been a cross wall here.

The Nave. The nave is of later date than the chancel, perhaps of the seventh century (Fig. 40). Its walls are of different character. The west wall (1) is of rough-hewn Kentish ragstone with very many occasional blocks of white chalk bonded together with Roman bricks which are arranged sometimes in single courses, sometimes in double or triple courses, but not continuously throughout the length of the wall and often not running horizontally. Between the Roman bonding courses the ragstone is arranged in single and here and there in five or six courses. The mortar joints are uneven and in places up to 4 inches wide. The original mortar appears to have been rather white and full of small pebbles as at St. Pancras. The nave walls had buttresses like St. Pancras, Reculver and some other Augustinian Kentish churches. There are pairs of small angle buttresses at the north-west and south-east (2) corners and a single one a little to the east of the centre of the south wall, and of a width equal to the wall thickness. All are bonded into the walls; i.e. they are genuine thickenings of the walls at those points. The buttresses are tall and shallow, projecting *c.* 10 inches from the wall face. There were probably similar pairs of buttresses at all four corners. They have courses of chalk in their lower portions and sloping heads of Roman bricks. The one on the south wall is different: it is much shorter and in plan is a flattened segment of a circle. Originally it may have been similar to the others; it shows signs of having been cut back to its present shape, and above are the remains of a patch of brickwork, at the level of the head of the south-east buttress, which looks like the bonding of a similar head. The walls are much patched and repaired especially in the south-west corner which has been rebuilt without buttresses, and in the middle of the north wall where a doorway, now blocked, was inserted at some time. This doorway was 4 ft. 2 ins. wide and has jambs of dressed Caen stone; it is probably Norman.

The nave quoins, in so far as they are not hidden by the buttresses, appear to be mainly of stone slabs in face-alternate arrangement below, and Roman bricks above with some rebuilding.

The nave is irregularly set out. It is 24 ft. 9 ins. wide at the east end and 24 ft. 5 ins. at the west; the north wall is $4\frac{1}{2}$ inches shorter than the south. The west wall is 2 ft. $4\frac{1}{2}$ ins. thick, the other three 1 ft. 10 ins. The length of the nave is 38 feet.

In the west wall (I) are the remains of three early openings. In the centre is a blocked archway, filled in flush with the wall with Roman bricks and rubble of flints and chalk. It is *c.* 17 ft. 6 ins. high and *c.* 7 ft. 2 ins. wide; a few inches of the crown were cut away when the upper part of the western gable was rebuilt. It has no dressed jambs and no real arch head. It has either lost its dressings or was finished with thick plaster to hide irregularities in head and jamb soffits. Its lower part is disguised by the mediaeval western doorway. Clapham thought it probable that the original arrangement was the same as that at Brixworth, namely two arches, one above the other, opening into the two storeys of a two-storeyed porch later replaced entirely by the existing fourteenth-century tower.

There are two window openings *c.* 2 feet respectively to the north and south of the central blocked opening. The upper 18 inches or so of each are extensions made in later Saxon or Norman times. Peers suggested that the extensions were perhaps intended to light an added western gallery in the nave entered from a room over the porch, i.e. from the upper storey of the presumed porch; or the porch may at that time have been replaced by a tower. In the latter event the tall central opening may have replaced a western doorway to the porch with a window above it, as at Brixworth and Bradwell juxta Mare (Essex); more like Brixworth perhaps, as Bradwell window is far above the doorway. The lower parts of these windows are original.

(I) *Plate* 198.

They have jambs of chalk blocks and some Roman bricks with white mortar joints. The arch heads were turned originally in Roman bricks, a few of which are still visible. The later upper parts are of rough voussoirs, really just blocks, of Kentish ragstone with some Roman bricks. The openings are 2 ft. 8 ins. wide and were originally 4 feet high to the crown of the arch heads. The jambs appear to be single-splayed towards the nave. The south window is blocked flush with the wall face. The north one has only thin blocking so the splaying is visible; if it was single-splayed throughout the actual light opening in the outer wall face would be *c.* 12 inches wide. The sills are 9 ft. 9 ins. on the south and 10 feet on the north above floor level. The lower portion of the south window is filled with very thin, much thinner than Roman, mediaeval tiles. The upper extensions were undoubtedly made when the tower was built. Near the south window are some remains of pink plaster still adhering. There is also some pink plaster or mortar among the Roman bricks of the original arch head, just above the springing, of the south window; there is none in the later extension above. Probably the whole interior was covered with it. Routledge stated that pieces of original pink plaster remained in other parts of the nave interior; this is not so now—the other nave walls are covered with modern plaster. The old pink plaster was remarkably hard. It is stated to have been made from imperfectly burned calcium carbonate, siliceous sand and powdered Roman bricks in about equal proportions. Probably the exterior was plastered too. There are bits of dark pink plaster on the exterior south wall of the nave, one group of four pieces close together about half-way between the west end and the rounded buttress.

There are no traces of early windows in the north and south walls; the existing large fourteenth-century windows may hide any earlier ones. In the south-east of the nave, in the east wall, visible only on the exterior (as the interior is plastered) is a blocked square-headed doorway (I); the north jamb is of brick, the south jamb of very rough stone slabs and some bricks. The lintel is of several courses of Roman bricks. The opening was 5 ft. 5 ins. high and 3 feet wide. It would have opened to the side of the south porticus but cannot have been connected with the porticus as the angle buttress, pointing east, adjoining, which must have been part of the original nave, could not have been built if the porticus had been standing at the time.[1] Nothing is known of the use of this doorway; it is in a curious position.

The nave had no north or south doorway. In all the early Kentish churches the entrance was at the west end, usually from a western porch, which however was sometimes a slightly later adjunct. There are two blocked doorways, one in the middle of the north wall the other near the west end of the south wall; both are

[1] See pp. 357, 355 (Fig. 40).

(I) *Plates* 194, 196.

thirteenth century. The north one replaced a Norman doorway. The sole access to the church today is through the west door of the tower.

In the west wall on the exterior immediately north of the tower is a small window (1) with a quadrant head. It has no dressings, only plaster. It is *c.* 18 inches high and 13 inches wide. It leads into a larger square opening in the interior face of the wall and a little to the south of it. This too has no stone dressings, only walling for head and jambs. Neither is Saxon; they are probably a leper window of Norman date.

In the south wall near the east angle buttress is a blocked opening. The round head is of large stones and flints, the sill is of flat bricks and stones, the jambs of stone; jambs and heads are splayed. It is *c.* 3 ft. 9 ins. high and 3 ft. 6 ins. wide. The sill is *c.* 9 to 10 inches above the present ground level. Nothing seems to be known about this opening; it does not appear to be mentioned in the literature.

During the excavations of the late nineteenth century the foundations of a wall were uncovered *c.* 3 feet to the north of the nave south wall and parallel with it (Fig. 40). They were fragmentary, *c.* 18 inches wide and 15 inches deep and largely of flints. They are on a line with the chancel south wall and probably represent the original chancel wall which must have extended further west than it does now. Owing to the presence of graves these foundations could not be followed sufficiently far west to determine the position and nature of the west end of the original chancel. This west end was probably destroyed when the nave was built. There were good reasons for putting the nave so far to the east involving destruction of this part of the chancel: the slope of the ground is so considerable that to have put the nave further west would have required a great deal of levelling up and extra walling.

The dating of the church is problematical. There are three theories: both chancel and nave are of Roman date; the chancel is Roman, the nave Saxon; both chancel and nave are Saxon. All writers are agreed that the chancel is earlier than the nave.

Micklethwaite noticed the structural similarity with St. Pancras, dated to *c.* 600, and he rejected a Roman attribution. He thought it was built specially for Queen Bertha and that it consisted of a nave (the present chancel, part of which is under the later nave) perhaps *c.* 30 feet long with an apse at the east end.

Canon Routledge, under whom as vicar extensive examination, excavation and restoration were carried out in the 1890's, argued at length and with great vigour for a Roman date for both chancel and nave. Bede wrote that at about the time of the coming of Augustine in 597 there was 'on the east side of the city a church dedicated in honour of St. Martin, built of old while the Romans still occupied Britain'. This is strong evidence in view of Bede's reputation as a great and reliable historian. His source of information for his work on the history of Christianity in Kent was Albinus, Abbot of St. Augustine's, himself a pupil of Theodore. Bede states, in

---

(1) *Plate* 197.

accordance with his practice of quoting his authorities, that Albinus referred to his Abbey's records and sent Nothelm, a priest of London, to Rome to search the archives there. It seems impossible to doubt that a Roman-built church was here at the time of St. Augustine. Are the oldest parts of the present St. Martin's parts of this Roman church? There is some architectural evidence in favour of an affirmative answer. The pink plaster found in various places in the church was proved through analysis by some architects, including J. T. Irvine, to be indistinguishable from similar plaster found elsewhere in the area in admittedly Roman buildings. It is stated to be distinguishable from the rather similar later Anglo-Saxon plaster by its greater hardness and lower proportion of sand. Further, the adjacent white and pink plasters or mortars of the western windows have their counterparts in the Roman Pharos at Dover.

The lowest and oldest parts of the nave walls are similar in construction to some known Roman buildings in the county: they are of flint, or rubble elsewhere, bonded at intervals with regular courses of large Roman bricks of irregular size and thickness, varying between 24 and 15 inches in length and $3\frac{3}{4}$ inches in thickness. Differently from the nave, the chancel is entirely of Roman bricks, which again is one of the ordinary methods of Roman building, as seen elsewhere in the area. But some of the Augustinian churches of Kent were also entirely of Roman bricks. Canon G. M. Livett, quoted by Routledge, from his examination agreed with a Roman dating for both nave and chancel and that the chancel was the earlier.

C. R. Peers, while admitting that the masonry of the windows in the west wall was very similar to those in the Roman Pharos at Dover, rejected a Roman dating on account of some similarities between St. Martin's and St. Pancras. He thought both churches, like the other Augustinian churches, were quite unlike any Roman building—though they were built by foreign, presumably Italian, masons. He thought the workmanship at St. Martin's was too rough to be Roman and that it looked like what a non-Roman imitator might build. But the little church at Caerwent (Monmouthshire) 'was of rough construction, and belonged to the very latest phase of the Roman period, if, indeed, it was not a work of the immediately succeeding age'.[1] Bradwell had similar buttresses with brick heads; and the dimensions and proportions of the nave at St. Martin, St. Pancras, Rochester and South Elmham are similar, viz: St. Martin, 38 feet by 24 feet; St. Pancras, 42 feet by 26 feet; Rochester, 42 feet by 28 feet; South Elmham, 38 feet by 27 feet. But, the comparison here is faulty: the other churches should be compared with St. Martin's chancel (which was of unknown length, possibly 30 feet, and only 14 feet wide) not with its nave. Reculver, dated to *c*. 669, had a floor of *opus signinum* and lacing courses of Roman bricks, as at St. Martin's. The only known Romano-British churches remaining, and as excavated foundations only, are Silchester, very different in plan from

[1] A. W. Clapham, (*a*), p. 14.

St. Martin's, and smaller, and Caerwent, not so very different and of comparable size. Peers included St. Martin's in Augustine's group of churches and thought it and St. Pancras were the earliest of the group, built perhaps before 600. His evidence is not strong, and is far from convincing. It might be more reasonable to say that St. Pancras resembles St. Martin's than that St. Martin's resembles St. Pancras; a subtle distinction perhaps but one with possible significant implications. It seems not un-likely that St. Martin's, still in use as a Christian church and one of only two in the city, may have influenced the design and the building style of the churches, of which St. Pancras is the earliest, put up by Augustine's foreign masons. Incidentally this would also explain why Augustine's churches were, like St. Martin's, according to Peers so un-Roman in plan.

Clapham, like Peers, rejected a Roman date. He wrote[1] that the church 'represents' Bede's church but that the 'existing structure incorporates the remains of two early periods': the chancel of the Age of Augustine and the later nave 'perhaps towards the end of the seventh century', that is contemporary with Brixworth with which it shows some slight similarity. Later he wrote:[2] 'there are now no traces of Roman work at St. Martin's.' He did however go so far as to say[3] that in its proportions 'the earlier part of St. Martin's church, Canterbury, approaches more nearly to the Northumbrian model than the Kentish, which may indicate that it was rebuilt by Bertha and her Gaulish chaplain in their native manner before the advent of St. Augustine'. It would be difficult to justify a positive attitude towards the date of this church: the evidence for a Roman date is considerable but far from convincing; the positive evidence against a Roman date appears slender. Perhaps the truth may be found in the tail end of Clapham's remarks: St. Martin's may be a Romano-British church rebuilt by Bertha in a Gaulish manner.

DOVER

THE CHURCH OF ST. MARY IN CASTRO.[4] This church is one of perhaps seven transeptal Anglo-Saxon churches. The others are, or were, Hexham, Norton, Repton, Stow (Lincs) and perhaps Stanton Lacy and Wootton Wawen. Dover is not strictly transeptal. The transepts are narrower than the chancel, which is narrower than the nave. They are also lower than the nave; they are really wings (Fig. 41). But the central tower is fine. The whole design is that of a cruciform, non-transeptal but very advanced wing type (l); the later development to the fully transeptal, though still not fully Romanesque, is found at Norton and Stow.

[1] Op. cit., (c).   [2] Op. cit., (a), p. 14.   [3] Op. cit., (a), p. 42.
[4] G. Baldwin Brown; A. W. Clapham, (a); J. T. Irvine, (g); J. Puckle; G. G. Scott.

(l) *Plate* 199.

It was dated by Baldwin Brown to the second half of the tenth century. Clapham dated it to the late tenth or early eleventh century. Irvine thought the walls were possibly of two dates, one not earlier than *c.* 990, the other perhaps *c.* 1050.

On the exterior the aisleless nave was *c.* 62 feet long by 34 feet wide, the chancel *c.* 27 feet by 25 feet and each transept *c.* 22 feet by 20 feet. The tower is 35 feet east–west by 33 ft. 6 ins. The nave walls were *c.* 32 feet high to the eaves. The tower at the time of the restoration[1] was *c.* 70 feet high; the original height was probably greater.

For long the church had been a ruin; it was disused and roofless in the early eighteenth century. It was used as a coal depot for the Castle and a large arch had

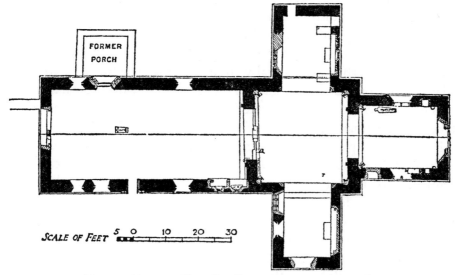

FORMER PORCH

SCALE OF FEET

Fig. 41. Dover, Church of St. Mary-in-Castro, plan

been cut through the north wall of the north transept, near its west end, to allow of the passage of coal carts. There was a great accumulation of earth and rubbish both within and without the church, in places many feet deep. In spite of this the walls were largely intact and sound, and much ancient work remained though large parts of the wall surfaces had been stripped or had decayed and fallen off. The height had become less.

It was thoroughly restored by Sir Gilbert Scott in 1861. In addition to much repair work, the upper part of the tower including the belfry windows and the roofs of nave, chancel and transepts belong to this restoration. Excavation revealed three floor levels, two Saxon and one of the late thirteenth century. That portion of the Saxon floor under the tower was paved with squared chalk slabs about 6 inches thick bedded in hard Saxon mortar. Beds similarly prepared

[1] A. W. Clapham, (*a*), Pl. 36.

were found in other parts of the church. The thirteenth century floor was retained as the floor of the restored church. The foundations were mostly of large flints, with flat pieces of very hard green sandstone at the set-offs and plinth lines. The whole superstructure rested on a very uniform bottom of stiff clay with a large proportion of mixed flints. The strata dip towards the east and in consequence the chancel walls were carried down to a greater depth below floor level than the other base courses.

There were four kinds of stone used in the building: Caen stone in the tower arch imposts; much Kentish rag in some of the quoins; a peculiar kind of coarse oolite similar to that used in the south-east and south-west quoins at St. Mildred's church, Canterbury; and some tufa. The oolite was peculiar in that it is not native to Kent and is rarely found in Saxon churches of the area. It was however used extensively in Roman buildings in the district and has been found in Roman villas at Hartlip and Bignor in Sussex, at Lyminge and at Richborough castle in Kent. The well-known columns formerly in the late seventh-century church at Reculver and later re-erected in the crypt of Canterbury Cathedral were made of it. The St. Mildred quoins are re-used materials from elsewhere: some of the stones have workings on them and one has lewis holes. Such non-Kentish stone in Kentish Saxon churches was very probably taken from Roman ruins, of which there were many in the area and which in fact, as in many other parts of the country, were used for centuries as readily available and easily worked quarries. Dean Buckland, a well-known geologist of the early nineteenth century, thought this non-Kentish oolite in Kent may have been quarried in the Weymouth district.

The walls of the church are mainly of flints. Jambs and arches of windows and parts of quoins are of Roman bricks, some of which are rounded at the edges and others had Roman mortar adhering. The walls are 3 feet thick everywhere; there is no thickening of the walls below the tower. The foundations were good and Puckle reported in 1860 before the rebuilding that the 'lofty arches of both nave and chancel are as firm and true now as when they first rose from their springing'. The tower upper quoins (1) are of Roman bricks with some modern replacements in white stone. Below nave roof level the north-east and south-east tower quoins are mainly of large stones, the lowest ones being massive and arranged in roughly upright and flat manner. There are no tower quoins on the north-west and south-west below nave roof level; the tower and nave walls are continuous, like those of an axial tower and in this respect unlike Breamore (Hants) where the tower is also central and has quoins all the way to the ground. The nave quoins (1) are also mainly of Roman bricks above, with some modern replacements in stone, and of massive stone slabs at the base (2) in some approximation to face-alternate arrangement. The plinth is of flints with a top layer of thin, flat, roughly square stones. Above the plinth in the

---

(1) *Plate* 199; (2) *Plate* 200.

wall are a few courses of stones of various shapes and sizes, below the main fabric of flints; these rubble courses are continued round the nave and along the west walls of the transepts.

The three exterior doorways (nave south and west doorways and the north transept north door) were cut straight through the walls with flat jamb soffit faces, i.e. with no rebates, the doors being hung from hooks and shutting flat against the interior faces. The tower openings were cut similarly straight through. Most windows were round-headed and rather roughly double-splayed, including the sills, equally on both faces. They were centrally grooved all round for the insertion of lighting slabs. Heads and jambs were of Roman bricks, without imposts, sills of flints like the walls; all were plastered. Some windows were not round-headed but originally had double-splayed flat oak lintels. The lintels had perished but the marks of their ends were stated to be plainly visible in the mortar, so clearly as to almost show the grain of the wood.

The main, blocked, south doorway (I), in about the middle of the nave south wall, was left intact by Scott as a fine specimen of the Saxon type of work. It was round-headed, with heads turned in two rings, an upper and a lower, of thin Roman bricks *c.* 12 inches square with wide mortar joints. The head is similar to those at Brixworth but had no intermediate course of bricks laid flat separating the two rings. The western jamb is of upright and flat work, three uprights and three flats, the top flat projecting westwards to act as an impost. The eastern jamb had largely disappeared; enough remains to indicate that it was similar to the western one. Each jamb has its own flat chamfered plinth, which is thinner and below the level of the surrounding nave plinth. The opening was *c.* 10 feet high to the imposts and *c.* 3 ft. 7 ins. wide.

Scott remade the north doorway of the north transept, the one which had been widened to admit coal carts. Originally it was similar to the nave south doorway. The lower part of the western jamb remained showing upright and flat work, and there were indications that the original width was *c.* 2 ft. 8 ins. Scott made a new doorway, the details being based on those found in other fragmentary remains elsewhere in the church. It was thus, as Scott emphasized, not a restoration but an intentional model of a typical Saxon doorway of the period. It is not in fact a very good model: the upright and flat work of the jambs is rather irregular and only one stone is a through-stone. The head is of one ring of Roman bricks and each impost is of two larger Roman bricks projecting in step pattern from the jamb soffit faces. On the interior face of the old jamb fragment was the stump of an ancient hanging hook, run into the jamb with lead, on which the door was suspended.

In the west wall of the north transept, visible on the exterior only, are the remains

---

(I) *Plates* 199, 201.

of the stone jambs of two former openings, now blocked, a smaller one within a larger. The jambs show a slight chamfer.

In the nave south wall, symmetrically placed above and to the east and west of the old blocked central doorway are two large round-headed windows (1) with heads and jambs of Roman bricks, flint sills and no imposts. There are similar windows on the north.

Near the west end with their lintels below the sills of the nave large upper windows are two double-splayed square windows, one in the north and one in the south wall. Their sills are of flints, their jambs of mixed Roman bricks and white stone slabs. On their exteriors they have oak lintels, Scott's renewals; on the interiors their heads are segmental renewals in bricks.

In the nave west wall are five openings: three windows and two doorways. High up in the gable, and above the roof springing, are two round-headed windows with stone jambs and heads renewed in brick. Below, on a level with the nave north and south windows, is a tall large opening. It has a flint sill, stone jambs with stone imposts projecting in step pattern from the jamb soffit faces, and a head of thirteen roughly dressed voussoirs. It is not splayed and was originally probably a doorway, communicating perhaps with the Roman Pharos tower only a few feet distant.

Below is the original western doorway (2) to the nave, very large and crude. It was round-headed with no stone dressings, if it ever had any, remaining; head and jambs are of flint walling. Its present dimensions are *c.* 10 ft. 6 ins. wide and of about the same height. Apparently the inner face has been thinly blocked with flints and a later, pointed, doorway cut through it which has stone dressings, no imposts or capitals and a chamfered head. To the north of this later doorway and also within the old arch, *c.* 5 feet above ground level, is a short, rather wide, double-splayed pointed window, with stone dressings, apparently contemporary with the pointed doorway.

In the transepts there is a large rectangular double-splayed window (1) in each west wall, with flint sills, brick jambs and oak lintels, restored to their original form by Scott. The original transept north and south windows have been replaced by large double lancets widely splayed on the interior.

The tower, on the exterior, has two ranges of window openings (1). The lower range, a little below the apex level of the transept roofs, is of circular openings, three on the north, two on the south, two on the east, none on the west. They are brick faced and double-splayed. The upper range is in the belfry, practically the whole of which including the openings is new work. There are two separate round-headed windows in each wall. Heads and jambs are of bricks, with some replacements in stone; they have no imposts. The lower portions of the north and east windows appear to be original.

---

(1) *Plate* 199; (2) *Plate* 202.

The interior has been spoiled through being lined with Victorian glazed and variegated tiles (1), which present an incongruous appearance against the mellow red brick of the many openings. The church had been restored in the late twelfth century, the work including some ribbed vaulting. In the restoration of 1860 it was found that some of the vaulting ribs had been made from Saxon bulging baluster shafts one side of which, the back side hidden in the vaulting, had been left quite perfect with their original shapes and ornament of rings and flutings. These shafts were *c.* 2 feet long, were of Caen stone and had been carefully turned in a lathe, 'the marks of the turning tool being almost as fresh as if new.' This implied that they could not have been used externally, as in belfry openings; possibly they had formed parts of a screen within the church. In the west arch of the tower the remains of a low wall were found, in the centre of which was a small doorway. This wall had probably been the base of a screen of which the baluster shafts may have been part. Some similar pieces were found near the south-west angle of the tower, probably parts of the same screen. All are now in the Dover Museum.[1]

At the west end of the nave, in the walls above the two square north and south windows, were holes apparently for the reception of the timbers of a floor which was on the lower level of the doorway referred to above. There must have been a gallery here, across the west end of the nave, approached from the outside, perhaps from the Pharos through this doorway.

The interiors of the four clerestory windows (2), immediately above the modern tiling, are very effective: deep and of Roman bricks with no imposts to break the continuity of jambs and arch heads.

Of the four original crossing arches only two remain in their original forms—the western and eastern. The original north and south openings into the transepts, probably narrow as at Breamore, were replaced in the twelfth century by tall wide pointed arches. They are now as wide as the interiors of the transepts, which are narrower than the crossing and not quite centrally placed: the arches are 5 feet from the east and 8 feet from the west tower arches. The eastern and western arches (3), largely original, are very fine. The jambs of the western arch for about a third of their height are of stones, three or four stones per course, some renewed, lying on their faces; the upper two-thirds are of Roman bricks except for about five courses of stones just below the imposts. The eastern arch is almost entirely of Roman bricks. The imposts are of moulded stones (4): a square-cut member above with hollow chamfer on the lower edge and two half-round mouldings between; the return ends are treated similarly. They may be re-used Roman stones. There is flat, square-cut pilaster work *c.* 9 inches wide and with a projection of *c.* 5 inches round the arch

[1] See G. Baldwin Brown, p. 266, fig. 111; A. W. Clapham, (*a*), Pl. 50 (*b*).

---

(1) *Plate* 204; (2) *Plate* 203; (3) *Plates* 204, 205; (4) *Plate* 206.

heads and passing outside the imposts down the jambs, on the western faces only. It is of bricks, one brick per course, round the head, and of stones down the jambs where the jambs are stones. The arches are *c.* 20 feet high to the imposts.

In the wall above the western arch head is a very large, wide though comparatively short, round-headed opening (1). It may have led to an inter-roof space or chamber above the nave but it is too high up to be reached by a ladder. It is not known what kind of access there may have been prior to the vaulting of the crossing. It is not known whether similar openings occurred at Stow as nothing Saxon survives above the crossing. At Norton there are openings in similar positions in all four walls, two in each.

There are no original openings in the chancel. In the north wall near the tower are the remains of two jambs of a former opening, three stones in the west and six in the east jamb arranged in no particular manner.

---

(1) *Plate* 204.

SUSSEX

HISTORICAL INTRODUCTION

Sussex was the most backward and primitive of the kingdoms of the Heptarchy, and was the last to accept Christianity. The area was isolated on the landward side by heavy clay soils and thick forests which made communication difficult. The conquering Saxons from Kent and the evangelizing Wilfrid reached Sussex by sea. A band of Kentish Saxons under a leader Ælle landed near Selsey in 477 and had conquered the coastal part of the area as far east as Pevensey by 491. According to Bede Ælle was the first Bretwalda, but the title at that date could have had little or no territorial significance. It is difficult to believe that Ælle, who had taken fourteen years to conquer a part of Sussex and then faded more or less from history, could have been overlord of Southern England. It is more likely that he gained the title as a valiant soldier who had acquired a great reputation for his military skill and successes. As F. M. Stenton wrote: 'Bretwalda [at least at this early date] is not a formal style accurately expressing the position of its bearer. . . . It belongs to the sphere of encomiastic poetry, and its origin should be sought in the hall of some early king, like Ælle or Ceawlin, whose victories entitled him, in that uncritical atmosphere, to be regarded as lord of Britain.' Nothing more is known of Sussex for nearly 200 years. Æthelwalh, a Sussex prince in exile, married, *c.* 675, Ebba, the daughter of Eanfrith, sub-king of the Hwicce, and accepted baptism, Wulfhere of Mercia acting as godfather.[1] Æthelwalh, with the help of Wulfhere, returned as king to Sussex and attempted, though apparently with little success, to evangelize his people. As recorded by Bede, Dicul, a Scot or more probably an Irish monk, settled with five or six companions at Bosanham (Bosham) about this time. Their teaching appears to have made little impression on the inhabitants. Success followed the efforts of the energetic Wilfrid of Ripon who spent five years, 681–6, of his second exile from Northumbria helping Æthelwalh to convert the South Saxons. He established a monastery at Selsey and, in the words of Bede, 'performed all the duties of a bishop in these parts.' Sussex was conquered and Æthelwalh killed by Cædwalla of Wessex, also a Christian, *c.* 685 and Wilfrid continued his activities for another year, after which he returned to Northumbria. Sussex regained its independence from Wessex *c.* 725 but was conquered by and became a mere province of Mercia under Offa *c.* 771. Later, in 825, after Egbert of Wessex had beaten Mercia in

---

[1] See also above, p. 171.

the decisive battle of Ellandun, Sussex, Kent and Essex submitted to Egbert and as separate kingdoms passed out of history. The subsequent history of Sussex is a part of the history of England.

Wilfrid's work in Sussex was thorough. When he left the district Christianity was firmly established. He is reported to have built some churches in the Meon valley in east Hampshire, an area added with the Isle of Wight to Æthelwalh's dominions by Wulfhere. A Saxon sundial at Warnford Church (Hants) is considered by some writers to be a fragment from Wilfrid's original church.[1] He must have built churches also in Sussex but there are no remains there definitely known to be of his period. Many churches were built in later times of which more than forty remain today either entire or in part or as fragments remaining in the walls of later rebuildings. Five have towers of the Late Saxon period: those at Bosham, Jevington, Singleton, Sompting and, perhaps, South Bersted. South Bersted is not described below; it has little of interest.

BOSHAM

HOLY TRINITY CHURCH.[2] The original dedication is not known. According to an Episcopal Visitation of 1281 it had no dedication. The first mention of a dedication was in a Patent Roll of 1330. But the church had several altars each dedicated to a different saint.

The village is situated on Bosham Channel or Creek in the area known officially as Chichester Harbour. It is an ancient place, of some importance in Roman days. There were Roman settlements at Bosham and round about. Roman pottery and sculptures have been dug up in the district, one large head from the churchyard. But the suggestion of some early writers that there was a Romano-British basilican church on the site of the present church is mere conjecture. The place was a port of considerable importance in Saxon times. It was from here that Earl Harold, later King Harold, sailed on his unfortunate trip to Normandy. His departure and Bosham church are depicted in the Bayeux tapestry. Bosham was a royal manor belonging to Edward the Confessor and may have been a royal manor of Canute's. There is a centuries-old tradition that a small grave at the east end of the nave, near the chancel steps, is that of a young daughter of Canute. The grave was opened in 1865 and found to contain the skeleton of a young girl of about eight years of age, but there was nothing in the coffin, not even grave clothes, to serve as means of identification. There may be some truth in the tradition. It would carry the origin of the church back at least to the period of Canute, a likely date and consistent with the architectural details. Baldwin Brown dated it to the reign of Edward the Confessor

---

[1] See also above, p. 190.
[2] G. Baldwin Brown; A. W. Clapham, (a) and (e); K. H. Macdermott; H. Mitchell.

(1042–66). It was certainly in existence in Edward's time for he granted it to his kinsman, Osbern, later second Bishop of Exeter (1072–1103), a gift confirmed by William the Conqueror. It was a particularly rich church. In Domesday Book it is recorded that in Edward's time it was worth £300 and owned 112 hides of land. The precise size of a hide of land is not known; it certainly varied widely in different parts of the country. Stenton thought it approximated to 40 acres in Wilts and Dorset (it was 120 acres in Cambridgeshire). The commonest church endowment recorded in Domesday Book is about one hide. With 112 hides, equal to perhaps 4,500 acres or more, Bosham's endowment must have been one of the richest in Saxon England. Surely such a large estate must have developed over a considerable period of time by accretion of numerous gifts. Either the church is earlier than Edward the Confessor or even than Canute, or the existing church must have replaced an earlier one of which we know nothing.

The tower, much of the nave and the western third of the chancel are pre-Conquest (Fig. 42). The timber spire shingled with oak is later. The church is badly

Fig. 42. Bosham Church, plan

set out, in true Saxon manner: none of the corners is a right angle, no two walls are parallel or of equal length and the (lengthened) chancel diverges to the south from the axis of the nave by 3 ft. 4½ ins. All walls are thin and of the same thickness everywhere: 2 ft. 6 ins. They are built of fairly large rubble with wide joints. The tower quoins (1) are of rather irregular-sized upright and flat slabs. One upright in the south-west quoin is more than 3 feet tall and has rough tooling, probably by axe, not chisel. Some flats run far into the wall, at least one for *c.* 3 feet and another for 5 ft. 9 ins. There is no plinth. The tower (2) has four stages with string courses between the lower three stages. The west wall is 20 ft. 4½ ins. wide; the interior width is *c.* 15 ft. 4 ins. at the west and *c.* 16 feet at the east. It is *c.* 3 feet longer east–west than north–south. This and the thin walls might suggest a porch tower, but there is no evidence for this; the tower is in fact not a porch tower. Though unusual, there are

(1) *Plate* 210; (2) *Plates* 208, 209.

some Saxon non-porch towers with their longer axes east–west, as at Ledsham, Middleton-by-Pickering and Wharram-le-Street.

In the ground stage there is a round-headed double-splayed window in the north and south walls; each head is of seven voussoirs, the jambs of three slabs each—flat, upright, flat, the top flat serving as impost. There is no western doorway or other opening in the west wall of this stage. In the second stage are single round-headed windows in the north, west and south walls, similar to but taller and narrower than those below in the north and south. In the third stage in the west wall is a single tall blocked round-headed window, badly worn. On the south and north were originally double round-headed openings of the usual Saxon belfry type. The heads were of ten real voussoirs each, with the centre voussoir common to both heads. Each jamb is of three flats and two very tall uprights, the top flats serving as imposts. They were the original belfry openings; they are now blocked and modern neo-Gothic double windows inserted in the blockings. In the fourth stage in the west is an original double opening of belfry type. It has a round head of four voussoirs to each half, central straight shaft with a capital brought to roughly circular form below by means of chamfered edges, and plain necking below the capital. The central and jamb imposts are thin square slabs. The base to the shaft is like the capital reversed and stands on a thin square stone like the impost above. The jambs are of roughly square slabs in no particular arrangement. The openings in the north, south and east walls are of modern neo-Gothic.

The tower arch (I) is fine but dwarfed by the truly magnificent chancel arch. Its head is of voussoirs in two rings with rubble filling between the rings. The lowest three arch stones on each side are not voussoirs but flat stones running further into the walls than the very even voussoirs above, and cut to appropriate shape on their soffit ends. The sloping of the joints to a common centre only begins at the fourth stone above the imposts. The head is slightly horse-shoed and set back slightly behind the jamb soffit faces. The jambs are of six upright and very long flat slabs each, the top flat being immediately below the impost. The uprights are through-stones, the flats are three per course. The imposts are hollow chamfered on their soffit ends only and are not returned along the walls. The arch is 6 ft. 11 ins. wide and 8 ft. 8 ins. to the lower side of the imposts.

Above the tower arch *c.* 18 feet above floor level, is a large gable-headed opening (I) cut straight through the wall, i.e. with no splay. It now contains glass but was originally a doorway opening from the second stage of the tower to a gallery across the west end of the nave, as a similar opening did at Deerhurst. This gallery was removed in the mid-nineteenth century. Whether this was the original reason for the doorway is not known; but it is likely that it was intended as a means of ingress to

---

(I) *Plate* 213.

the second stage of the tower, perhaps by ladder from the nave, as was the case in many other Saxon churches. To the south of this doorway is a small rectangular opening made of four stones: a massive lintel and sill and two thinner upright stones as jambs. Above and slightly to the north of the gable-headed doorway is a fairly large round-headed opening with no dressings (1). Its sill is 29 feet above floor level and on a level with the top of the nave walls. It was probably an ingress to an inter-roof space or chamber above the nave.

The nave is 56 feet long and *c.* 23 feet wide. It is high, 29 feet to the eaves. The quoins (1) are rather different from those of the tower; they are of large square slabs in no particular arrangement. There are three circular single-splayed original windows high up in the north wall.

The chancel is nearly as high as the nave and *c.* 18 feet wide. It is not built centrally against the nave but *c.* 3 feet to the south of centre. Only the western third, *c.* 15 feet, is of Saxon date; the next third or slightly more is Norman and the eastern third is late twelfth century. The Saxon and Norman parts are stated to have ended apsidally. The three parts are plainly evident on the interior through slight differences in the walling (2). The Norman middle section also differs from the Saxon part in having some herring-boning in its walls. In the north wall of the Saxon part are the remains of an original single-splayed window, blocked and cut into by a later twelfth-century window. It had a round head of selected stones, not voussoirs, jambs also of selected rubble and no imposts.

The chancel arch (3) is magnificent, one of the finest in the country. It is centrally placed in the chancel west wall and therefore a little to the south of centre viewed from the nave. It is taller and wider than the tower arch. It is of very late Saxon design, and not necessarily of the same date as the main fabric. It has soffit rolls and normal angle shafts running up the jambs and round the head. The complicated bases and capitals are alike though the members of the capitals are thinner than those of the bases. The jambs stand on two huge slabs or plinths; the lower one, square-cut, measures 4 feet east–west and rather less north–south and is 8 inches thick; the upper one is a circular disc 3 ft. 6 ins. in diameter and 8 inches high with a half-round edge. They have been stated to be re-used Roman stones but there is no evidence for a Roman origin and Baldwin Brown considered them to be characteristically Saxon. Massive stones in quoins and bases are indeed characteristic Saxon features. On these two stones stand the actual bases of the columns, a tall circular chamfered base 8 inches high with two quirks, and above that a flat faced band (a kind of complex wide necking) 6 inches high, chamfered above and below between two quirks. The capitals are similar to the bases, though of course reversed, with a similar round-edged disc and square-cut abacus above. There is a half-round, or rather segmental,

---

(1) *Plate* 213; (2) *Plate* 212; (3) *Plates* 211, 212.

strip-work hood mould round the arch head on both east and west faces. Unlike many other chancel and tower arches, both faces are similar.

The distance between the two massive plinths is 9 ft. 5 ins. The plinths protrude from the walls *c.* 2½ feet so the width of the opening behind the dressings would be *c.* 14 ft. 5 ins. It is *c.* 20 feet high to the square abaci.

JEVINGTON

ST. ANDREW'S CHURCH. This church is in a fine position in the South Downs, 2 miles SSW. of Polegate and 4 miles NW. of Eastbourne. The nave and western tower are at least in part Saxon but were so drastically over-restored in 1873 that many original features have been destroyed or obscured. Baldwin Brown dated it to the Overlap. The whole church is built of uncoursed flint except the nave south wall which is of roughly dressed square stones below with some flints above. In the tower south wall are many large and small stones among the rubble, and there are some courses of large stones just above the Saxon blocked window in the north wall. There is also some flint herring-boning high up in the tower especially below the north belfry opening. Herring-boning is supposed to have been used for strengthening purposes and is usually found in the lower parts of buildings, sometimes as at Breamore in Norman repair work. Here, at Jevington, it is high up where no extra strengthening is needed. The north-east quoin is of rather large slabs in irregular upright and flat arrangement. The north-west and south-west quoins do not appear to be original; the south-east quoin is largely hidden by a buttress; the upper part appears to be modern. There is no plinth, only a modern dressing of cement round the north wall of the tower and north aisle. The tower is capped with a low pyramidal roof.

The tower looks massive and low, though it has thin walls. It is 18 feet square on the interior and *c.* 23 feet on the exterior; the walls are *c.* 2 ft. 6 ins. thick. It is of two stages, the upper one recessed above a string course. In the north and south walls are two round-headed modern windows, one in each wall, about 10 feet from the ground. Above these are the remains of the heads of two earlier windows turned in Roman bricks; they are not strictly gable-headed but, as W. H. Legge put it, are 'not round-headed, but inclined to be obtusely angular'. In Grimm's drawing of the south face of the tower as it was in 1784[1] the window now blocked is shown as open and no belfry opening is shown. The present belfry openings in the north and south walls are of the 1873 restoration and are in neo-Norman style. They are double round-headed openings with plain jambs and each is enclosed under a wide pointed arch with its own jambs outside those of the double opening. The mid-wall shafts

[1] Reproduced by W. H. Legge.

are original and re-used; they are banded and lathe-turned like those at St. Albans Abbey and some formerly in St. Mary-in-Castro, Dover. Above each double opening and within the enclosing arch head is a circular sound hole; there are two others above each pointed enclosing arch. They are modern or modern renewals.

The western doorway is in modern neo-Norman style. The tower arch was much altered in 1873. The jambs appear to be original; they are of upright and flat slabs, some of which are through-stones. The imposts are plain with slight hollow chamfer and are returned along the walls as string courses; they are undoubtedly renewals. The arch head is recessed on both faces, though not deeply, but is not really of two orders. There is no separate outer order built on an inner order; each voussoir is common to both rings, being cut to appropriate shape. The head has two rings of voussoirs, an eastern and a western, with ashlar soffit. It is a renewal. The two smaller arched openings, one to the north and one to the south of the main arch, are also of the 1873 restoration. There is strip-work round the head and down the sides of the jambs. The opening is 5 ft. 8 ins. wide and the jambs 2 ft. 1 in. thick.

The fine carving of Christ now attached to the nave interior north wall near the west end was discovered in the tower in 1785. It is no part of the architecture of the church and cannot be discussed here. It has been dealt with by T. D. Kendrick and by D. Talbot Rice who consider it to be one of the very few remaining pieces of Saxon sculpture in the country showing the Scandinavian Urnes type of ornament. The two grotesque animals at the feet of Christ consist almost entirely of complicated Urnes interlacements. Talbot Rice thinks it probably very late pre-Conquest *c.* 1050; Kendrick that it must be post-Conquest, probably *c.* 1100.

SINGLETON

ST. JOHN THE EVANGELIST'S CHURCH. Singleton is situated *c.* 5 miles S. by W. of Midhurst and 6 miles N. by E. of Chichester. The village and church are mentioned in Domesday Book as Silletone. The place was of some importance for the church is stated to have owned three hides and one rod of land, a considerable possession. The tower is dated to *c.* 950 or 1000; the aisled nave and chancel are mid-thirteenth century.

The tower (I) is built of flint with some later ashlar above as repair work. The quoins are of well-dressed big stone work arranged side-alternately. The tower is of three stages with later plain battlemented parapet. The lower stage is plastered; the upper stages, which are not recessed, are rough-cast. There is a small chamfered plinth.

(I) *Plate* 207.

The tower is *c.* 14 feet wide (north–south) on the interior and 21 ft. 11 ins. on the exterior, which makes the walls *c.* 4 feet thick, rather thick for a tower of this date; Baldwin Brown gave a thickness of 2 ft. 8 ins. The interior length (east–west) is 17 feet. Though longer east–west than north–south it is not a porch tower and there is no indication of a western doorway.

In the ground stage there is a round-headed double-splayed window in the north, south and west wall. The heads are of voussoirs, jambs of three slabs each and they have no imposts. The south window is hidden by a later buttress; the west one is at a higher level than the others. In the second stage on the north are two single-splayed round-headed windows close together; the heads are of voussoirs, jambs of slabs and no imposts. There are no openings in this stage on the west or south. In the east wall, above the tower arch, is a larger tall opening, unsplayed and therefore probably a doorway. It has a gabled head, unusual in so large an opening, and the jambs slope inwards at their lower corners, making the sill appear three-sided.

In the third or belfry stage in the north wall is a single round-headed window with head of voussoirs, slab jambs and chamfered all round. There is no opening in the south or west. In the east, on a level with the north opening, is a large later opening with perhaps original jambs. The head is a flat lintel narrower than the opening, so the jambs are curved inwards to meet it.

The tower arch is pointed though the jambs have some through-stones; it was probably reconstructed in the thirteenth century. It is *c.* 9 ft. 10 ins. wide and 7 ft. 6 ins. to the imposts. The jambs are 2 ft. 8 ins. thick.

SOMPTING

ST. MARY'S CHURCH.[1] Sompting is 2 miles ENE. of Worthing. The church is of complex plan developed through various additions in the twelfth to the fourteenth centuries. The tower and part of the nave are Saxon. The village and the church are mentioned in Domesday Book under the name of Sultinges. The original dedication is not known; the earliest mention of it is in a grant of land made in 1442 to 'the church of St. Mary of Sultinge'. Baldwin Brown dated the tower to the Overlap, Clapham to the early eleventh century; it is almost certainly pre-Conquest.

The tower (I) is built of uncoursed flints with some Roman bricks here and there in the north and west tower walls. It was formerly plastered, but much of the plaster has peeled off. It is of two stages on the exterior, separated by a curiously decorated

---

[1] M. B. Adam; J. L. André, (*b*); G. Baldwin Brown; A. W. Clapham, (*a*) and (*d*); E. G. M. Fletcher and F. D. C. Jackson; C. R. Peers, (*b*); T. Rickman, (*b*).

(I) *Plates* 214, 215, 216.

string course. The string is square-cut with a series of curved hollowed-out depressions, half-ellipses, cut round the lower edges. It has been described as a kind of billet ornament but is really quite different. The ground stage occupies little more than a quarter of the total height. On the west (1) there are no openings above the ground stage and below the belfry, which is not separated on the exterior from the stages below. On the south (2) there is one small window above the string course suggestive of a second internal stage; and on the north (3) there are two ranges of window openings between string and belfry indicating four internal stages including ground stage and belfry.

The south-east quoin is of genuine long and short work, though rather irregular above the string course. The south-west quoin below the string is of big stone work arranged mainly on end in rough long and short arrangement; above the string this quoin is, like the south-east one, of rather irregular long and short work. The north-west quoin and north-east quoin above the string course are similar; they are of small square or short slabs on end throughout the entire height. On both sides of the south-west quoin, i.e. in the south and west walls, and extending to the string course, are real long and short thin buttresses (4). There is evidence that there may have been similar small buttresses at the north-west quoin, replaced by the later larger buttresses. Fletcher and Jackson maintain that the apparent south-east quoin (2) below the string is not a real quoin for the nave and tower are of the same width and the nave north and south walls are continuous with the tower north and south walls. The apparent south-east quoin below the string is a projecting long and short pilaster-buttress at the junction of nave and tower walls. Similarly there is no north-east tower quoin below the string course but faint indications remain of a projecting pilaster-buttress, as on the south-east.

There are also, placed centrally in the north, south and west walls, genuine long and short pilaster strips; they are square-cut below the string and of half-round plan above. The square-cut lower portion is intact on the south wall where it stands on a projecting base; some parts remain on the west but only faint indications on the north. The half-round strips above the string are complete on all three walls. They extend upwards into the apices of the helm-shaped roof where they end below projecting square corbels; according to Rickman's drawing (Fig. 43) the corbels were hollow chamfered round the lower half. Below the belfry openings these pilaster strips are interrupted by capitals, which are presumably decorative for they could serve no useful purpose where they are (Fig. 43). Two of them are floriated, closely similar to those on the soffit roll capitals of the tower arch. The capital on the west is too badly worn to be recognized but according to Rickman's drawing it was decorated with a human face. Fletcher and Jackson consider that the pilaster strips

---

(1) *Plate* 215; (2) *Plate* 214; (3) *Plate* 216; (4) *Plates* 214, 215.

below the string course are all genuine structural buttresses, but that the strip-work above is decorative; this arrangement is similar to that at Barnack. It should be noted that the north-west and south-west quoins below the string are, rather abnormally, flush with the wall face and were originally plastered like the walls; the quoins above the string project in the usual manner and were not plastered. The south-east apparent quoin below the string projects like the pilaster buttresses; which is further evidence that this is really a buttress and not a quoin.

Fig. 43. Sompting Tower, two Windows and Pilaster Strip Work

There is neither a window nor a doorway in the south wall of the ground stage. In the west (1) there is a tall narrow blocked round-headed opening to the north of the central pilaster. It has slab jambs, no imposts, thin sill and a half-round head cut from a single stone. It is rebated all round, including the sill, possibly for the fixing of lighting slabs; it is too far above ground level to be a doorway. The other two openings on the west—one a window, the other a doorway—with their north jambs cutting into the central pilaster, are later. In the north wall (2) to the east of the central pilaster is a tall simple round-headed window, splayed all round.

Above the string course, in the south wall of the second stage, is a small gable-headed window (3) to the east of the central pilaster. The gable is of two thin slabs: each jamb has a tall massive centre slab with a smaller slab above and below. The sill is one slab between the jambs.

---

(1) *Plate* 215; (2) *Plate* 216; (3) *Plate* 214.

378

In the north wall are two ranges of windows (1) above the string and below the belfry. The lower pair is of small gable-headed openings, one of the pair being on each side of the central pilaster. The central common jamb is a single massive circular pillar stone. The outer jambs are of single stones with half-round outer faces. The sill is too badly worn to be recognizable as a sill. According to Rickman's drawing (Fig. 44) it was massive with some queer incised carvings on the face; it may possibly have been a cross fragment re-used. Higher up are two separate single windows,

Fig. 44. Sompting Tower, double gable-headed Window

close together and one on each side of the central pilaster. They are larger than those below. They are round-headed and both heads and jambs have half-round outer faces (Fig. 43). Both heads are below and are enclosed by a larger round head in the wall turned in Roman bricks not shown in Rickman's drawing. Both have massive sills apparently formerly decorated, like the gable-headed pair below (Fig. 44).

The north and south belfry openings are similar; those on the west and east are alike but differ from those on north and south. The east and west windows (2) are pairs of single gable-headed openings; the gable sides have half-round edges. The eastern pair have stone jambs; the western openings have jambs of Roman bricks. The north and south openings are interesting (3) and unusual (Fig. 45). They are tall double openings of the usual Saxon belfry type, two pairs in each wall, one on each

Fig. 45. Sompting Tower, Belfry Opening with corbelled-out Capital

(1) *Plate* 216; (2) *Plate* 215; (3) *Plates* 214, 216.

379

side of the central pilaster. The round heads are not cut from single stones and heads and jambs are half-round on their outer edges. The sills are square-cut and sloping. The central mid-wall shafts are plain and straight, not bulging balusters, and do not support mid-wall projecting imposts. Instead their upper ends are corbelled out to north and south to support the double heads above. Such corbelled-cut capitals occur also at Jarrow and Bolam; all three are of late eleventh-century date. Baldwin Brown thought this form originated in Italy; that it passed from there to the Rhineland, where it became popular, and then to England in the late eleventh century. There is a very similar capital at Trier Cathedral in the Rhineland of the same date.[1]

The tower roof is of the Rhenish helm type, a form developed in the Rhineland where it became popular. There are fine, though later, examples at the Abbey Church at Laach,[2] at Andernach[2] and Coblentz Cathedrals and at the Apostles' Church at Cologne. It consists of a four-sided gabled roof with the apices of the gables placed centrally in the tower walls and the lower corners of the gables above the tower quoins; the roof faces are trapezoidal. It is the only Saxon tower which is known to have retained its original roof form. There was a similar one at Flixton, Suffolk, until it was pulled down and rebuilt last century. There may have been one at St. Benet's, Cambridge.

The tower arch is (1) fine and of unusual interest. Its round head is of voussoirs. The jambs are of slabs, face-alternate and approximating to upright and flat in that some of the stones are thinner than others and run further into the walls. They stand on very thin square-cut plinths. There are soffit rolls, a late Saxon feature, round the head and down the jambs and which stand on chamfered half-round bases. There are thin, square-cut abaci below the arch head cut to appropriate shapes, and below the abaci are capitals with unusual decoration. The capitals of the soffit rolls are foliated and similar to those on the exterior half-round pilaster strips. Clapham describes the ornament as 'imitated more or less remotely from classical examples'. Each has three layers of rather crudely stylized leaves, with turned back tips, similar to those at Scartho (Fig. 31).[3] Clapham thought them derived from the palmette which was easier to reproduce than the acanthus and which is found occasionally in Saxon work down to the end of the Saxon period. This may be so; but it could be equally well explained as an attempt to reproduce a type of Norman foliated capital not yet very familiar in Saxon England. Moreover, the acanthus is found elsewhere in the church. The capitals above the jambs on either side of the soffit roll capitals are quite different. They are voluted capitals of original design. The corner volutes are boldly carved, reminiscent of those at Glentworth (Fig. 24)[4] but simpler. They might be described as trumpet spirals with clusters of grapes at their centres.

[1] See G. Baldwin Brown, p. 247, fig. 97.   [2] See T. G. Jackson, Vol. 2, Pls. 90 and 93.   [3] p. 295.   [4] p. 276

(1) *Plate* 217.

In the chancel, south of the altar, is a gable-headed piscina (1) with rather primitive but highly finished interlacing acanthus ornament. Identical carving occurs on the flat lintel of a rectangular recess to the north of the altar, and on three strips of frieze behind the altar incorporated in a later reredos. All are probably re-used portions from an earlier larger design.

In the south chapel is a carving of a bishop (2), or apostle, for he is nimbed. It is very primitively Anglo-Saxon in execution: the body is in a frontal attitude, the head in profile; one enormous eye is in the top side of the forehead; the hands are very large; the pastoral staff stands apparently unaided on its point. It is interesting as it has simple palmette ornament rather similar to that on the tower arch soffit roll capitals, and a stiff leaf ornament on the capitals which might almost be the originals of the Jews' harp ornament at Stow and elsewhere.

---

(1) *Plate* 219; (2) *Plate* 218.

WESSEX

HISTORICAL INTRODUCTION

Although Wessex is so closely associated with the extreme south-central part of southern England it did not originate there. The earliest settlements of the West Saxons were in the valley of the upper Thames, in south Oxfordshire and Berkshire. The story in the early Anglo-Saxon Chronicle that the West Saxons landed under their leaders Cerdic and his grandson Cynric in 495 at the head of Southampton Water and that they fought their way northwards and established their kingdom in Hampshire and Wiltshire is no longer accepted. The archaeological evidence indicates that the settlers worked their way up the Thames valley, and some perhaps along the Icknield Way from the Wash, to settle in the Berkshire area, round about the year 500. Cerdic's men were probably small groups of adventurers, great fighters but too few to form permanent settlements. They lived off the land they had invaded and fought their way northwards until under Cynric's son Ceawlin, 560–91, they reached the permanent West Saxon settlements in Berkshire which had been established more than half a century earlier. Ceawlin, a great warrior, named by Bede the second Bretwalda of England, was accepted as their king by the established West Saxons and became the first real King of Wessex of the House of Cerdic. Under Ceawlin the expansion of Wessex began. About 577 he penetrated into the south part of the land of Hwicce and occupied the area round Gloucester and Cirencester. Expansion then continued southwards, in the direction from which Cerdic and Cynric had come, into Wiltshire and Hampshire. Under his immediate successors Wessex was unable to withstand the growing power of Mercia. All Wessex north of the Thames, including Dorchester, its ecclesiastical centre and at that period its only bishopric, passed permanently to Mercia and the rest of Wessex became for a period more or less subordinate to Mercia. Under two strong kings, Cædwalla 685–8 and Ine 688–726, the strength of Wessex revived and a fresh period of consolidation and expansion developed. Cædwalla conquered Sussex and the Isle of Wight. Under Ine the West Saxons penetrated the Forest of Selwood, hitherto their western boundary, and occupied parts of Somerset and Devon. A Saxon monastery was founded at Exeter before 700. Ine was the greatest of the early Wessex kings. He strengthened and consolidated his kingdom and re-organized the Church in Wessex. He drew up a famous code of West Saxon law which was later incorporated in the even more famous code of Alfred the Great. He was an intensely religious man and his religion proved a tragedy for his country. He resigned his kingship in 726 in order to die in a monastery in Rome. After him Wessex fell again into internal disorder and became subject to Mercia, at this time more powerful than ever under the two successive kings Æthelbald and Offa.

Nearly a century later the third great king of Wessex arose, Egbert, 802–39, a descendent of Ine's brother. He had been expelled from Kent, where his father was sub-king, by Offa in 789. He spent some years in the France of Charlemagne and after Offa's death returned and was accepted as king by the West Saxons. For twenty years Egbert quietly consolidated and strengthened his country. Then the great trial of strength occurred between him and the Mercian king, no longer an Offa, at Ellandun in 825. The power of Mercia was destroyed and Mercia, East Anglia, Essex, Kent and Sussex submitted to Egbert; the unification of England had begun.

Christianity had been introduced into Wessex by Birinus, an independent missionary, *c.* 635. The king, Cynegils (611–43) accepted it and made Birinus the first bishop of the West Saxons with his seat at Dorchester. After a few years Birinus left Wessex and disappeared from history as suddenly as he had entered it. It is doubtful whether he had converted many of the people, but he had made an impression which was permanent. Christianity continued to expand its influence, due partly no doubt, as had been the case earlier in Northumbria, to the devoutly religious character of some of the West Saxon kings, including the greatest. Moreover Celtic Christianity had for long been dominant in the south-west, beyond Selwood; Glastonbury Abbey in Somerset and Malmesbury in Wilts were originally Celtic foundations. The Celtic Church was only loosely organized. Its influence was spread mainly through isolated monasteries and individual small groups of hermits, such as Dicul of Bosham. But the Christian influence was there which made it easier for the later West Saxon kings, all of whom were of the Roman persuasion, to establish a properly organized Church.

For some years after the departure of Birinus Wessex had no bishop. Then Bishop Agilbert, a Frank, arrived *c.* 650 to continue the work. King Cenwalh (643–72) son of Cynegils, made him second bishop of Dorchester. Later *c.* 660 the king established a second bishopric at Winchester to which he appointed Wine, a Saxon, as bishop. Agilbert soon after left Wessex, the Dorchester area passed to Mercia and Winchester was the only diocese of Wessex for nearly half a century. Cenwalh's son and successor Centwine, 676–*c.* 685, was recorded by Aldhelm, the famous Abbot of Malmesbury, as the founder of many churches. It was the great Ine who first organized the Church in Wessex. He created a separate bishopric at Sherborne in 705 to look after the needs of 'Wessex beyond Selwood' and appointed Aldhelm as the first bishop (705–9). These two were the only sees in Wessex for more than two centuries. Under Edward the Elder, as part of his reorganization of England after his conquest of the Danelaw, a see of Ramsbury was split off from Winchester to serve

Berkshire and Wiltshire, and the two sees of Wells and Crediton were divided off from Sherborne to serve respectively Somerset, and Devon and Cornwall. Later a separate see of St. Germans was created for Cornwall. These sees proved too small to be self-supporting and under Edward the Confessor Ramsbury was reunited to Sherborne, St. Germans was abolished and Cornwall and Devon were included in a new bishopric of Exeter, transferred from Crediton.

Winchester remained throughout the centuries the 'mother' diocese of Wessex and its greatest centre of religious and cultural life. Its scriptorium rivalled that of Canterbury and from the mid-tenth century exceeded Canterbury in fame; for it was at Winchester at about this period that the famous 'Winchester School' of book illumination developed and spread throughout the southern part of England: Winchester illumination was produced at monasteries as far apart as Exeter, Glastonbury, Canterbury, Abingdon and Ramsey (Hunts). Perhaps its most famous product, produced probably at Winchester, was the Benedictional of St. Æthelwold, formerly at Chatsworth and now in the British Museum. The School was tersely and aptly described by T. D. Kendrick as the best thing in English art, English born, the first really English thing in English art; and its influence outlived the Saxon period.

From the above slight and entirely inadequate sketch of Wessex history it may be inferred that there are many pre-Conquest churches in the area. There are at least 16 in Hampshire, and about 20 altogether in Berkshire, Wilts and Dorset, the four counties which comprise the real Wessex. Some are of very early date; those with towers are later. The porch below the post-Conquest tower of Titchfield, Hants, is of very early date. A doorway at Somerford Keynes, Wilts, is of similar date, perhaps early eighth century, and shows probably Celtic influence. Celtic influence too was evident in the two stair turrets, no longer existing, at Teignmouth and Bishopsteignton, Devon. The famous little church at Bradford-on-Avon, Wilts, was originally part of the monastery founded there by Aldhelm in the early eighth century. There are however only four towered churches, or seven if one includes Surrey in the area, all of the eleventh century. They are Wickham (Berks), Netheravon (Wilts), Breamore and Warblington (Hants) and Compton, St. Mary's, Guildford, and Wotton (Surrey).

BERKSHIRE

WICKHAM

ST. SWITHIN'S CHURCH.[1] This church is situated on the Roman road from Speen (the Roman Spinae) near Newbury to the north-west. On the exterior the tower (I) is of two stages, a tall lower stage occupying about two-thirds of the total height and a rather disproportionately tall upper belfry stage above the only string course. Only the lower stage is Saxon. Baldwin Brown dated it to 950–1040, V.C.H. to probably eleventh century and certainly pre-Conquest. There are no fragmentary remains of other parts of the early church. The aisled nave, chancel, south porch and belfry stage with its string course are modern.

When the small old nave and chancel were demolished in 1845 it was found that the nave, containing much early work, had been built against the tower with a straight joint. From this it was inferred that the tower was older than the nave and originally may have been separate, and built for defence only: it had no western entrance, the only entrances discovered when the rough-cast was stripped from the walls being a blocked round-headed doorway in the south wall about eight feet above ground level; the jambs of the doorway were not original.

The tower is built of flints set diagonally. The stone slab quoins are of fairly good upright and flat work, though rather irregular above. It is *c.* 10 ft. 6 ins. square on the interior, but a little wider at the east than at the west. On the exterior the west wall is 17 feet wide, which makes the north and south walls *c.* 3 ft. 3 ins. thick. There is a chamfered plinth of one member.

On the interior the Saxon tower was of three stages, indicated on the exterior by the three ranges of openings. The lower two stages are open on the interior with no floor between them; a floor separates the second and third stages. In the west wall, about half way up, lighting what would have been the second stage, is a small round-headed double-splayed window; it has been restored on the exterior with cement. Had there been a floor between the two lower stages the ground stage, with only a doorway, would have been dark, which suggests that the first stage was probably a double one. Opposite this window, in the east wall above the tower arch, is a much larger taller round-headed opening cut straight through the wall. It is visible from

[1] G. Baldwin Brown; C. E. Keysor, (*c*); V.C.H., *Berks*, IV.

(I) *Plate* 220.

the west, i.e. from inside the tower; on the nave side it has been given a modern pointed head and over-elaborate neo-Gothic dressings and fillings. It may have been a door of ingress to an inter-roof space above the small nave.

The third stage, the original belfry, has the usual double-light round-headed openings in the north and south walls. The south one is partly a renewal. The north one is badly worn and looks entirely original. The heads are of voussoirs, the square jambs are of upright and flat stones going about half way through the walls; i.e. they are not complete through-stones. The bottom stone of the east jamb of the north opening is a large square thin slab on end; those above are smaller. The mid-wall straight shafts are 3 ft. 3 ins. tall including capitals and bases. The capitals and bases are similar; they are rather elaborately moulded with three hollow chamfer-like mouldings. Baldwin Brown thought they were re-used Roman features. There is a small half-round ring or band round each shaft a few inches below the capital. There are square abaci between capitals and central unchamfered imposts; there are similar square slabs between the bases and the stone sills. In the west wall of the Saxon belfry is a single wide double-splayed opening similar to that in the stage below. There may have been one in the east wall where it is now built up with brickwork.

The modern fourth stage, the present belfry, with plain embattled parapet above, has in each wall two round-headed two-light windows of modern Norman design.

When the church was rebuilt in 1845 the tower had a tiled pyramidal roof above the Saxon stage. When this was removed, for the erection of the new belfry, openings were discovered of the beam holes of an earlier flat roof. There had also been a coping. The tower arch to nave is large and of over-elaborate modern neo-Gothic.

The south aisle overlaps the tower by *c.* 3½ feet, the north aisle by *c.* 13½ feet. The exterior tower north wall, now within the aisle, has been faced with ashlar; on the interior, opposite the blocked south doorway, are the marks of a similar but wider round-headed opening. Nothing is known of this former opening. It may not be Saxon: if the tower were built for defence there would not be two doorways in the ground floor.

386

DEVONSHIRE

EAST TEIGNMOUTH AND BISHOPSTEIGNTON.[1]

These two churches, only two miles apart, no longer exist. They were so closely similar they may be considered together. The church of St. Michael the Archangel at East Teignmouth is in an almost unique position; it is possibly nearer the open sea than any other church in England. During heavy south-westerly gales the seas crash on the roadway and the spray lashes the fabric of the church. The present church, consecrated in 1823, replaced an ancient church, undoubtedly at least in part a Saxon one, which was destroyed in 1811 as it was too small to meet the needs of an increased congregation. St. Michael's had the oldest dated dedication in the diocese of Exeter. In 1044 Edward the Confessor gave to his chaplain, Leofric, afterwards first bishop of Exeter, the manor of Dawlish, including St. Michael's church which is mentioned by name in the Charter: the land was described as bounded on one side 'by the Street on the West of St. Michael's Church'. The Charter is still in Exeter Cathedral Library. Apparently therefore the church—or a church—here was built prior to 1044. Churches at East Teignmouth and at Exminster are also mentioned, the only two Devon churches to be so mentioned, in the Exeter Domesday Book of 1086. A rather impressionistic sketch of the church (I) indicates its general appearance: a fortress-like tower with a short high chancel and lower small nave and south porch. Cornelius stated that both nave and chancel were narrower than the tower, and that the church may have been turriform. The plain tower parapet was supported on corbels of human and animal heads, which suggest a Norman origin for the parapet. The building in the sketch to the north of the chancel is not mentioned in the literature, which is scanty, and is quite inexplicable.

The most interesting part of the church was the tall, slender, circular stair turret attached to the south-west corner of the tower and extending well above the tower roof. There was a rectangular doorway at the base, and one curious round-headed slit window is shown near the top. The turret had a low conical, or mushroom-shaped, cap. Its resemblance in proportions and conical cap to Irish round towers is striking.

The church at Bishopsteignton was closely similar, as revealed by a contemporary

[1] C. F. Cornelius.

(I) *Plate* 221.

sketch when the church was demolished in the early nineteenth century. The conical capped circular stair turret was attached to the south-east corner of the tower. These two Irish-looking round towers may possibly indicate the influence of Celtic Christianity in this part of Devonshire in early Saxon times, emanating perhaps from Glastonbury.

HAMPSHIRE

Breamore

St. Mary's Church.[1] This church was recognized as Saxon by the vicar, A. du Boulay Hill, during its restoration in 1897. Baldwin Brown dated it to the second half of the tenth century, Clapham to the mid-tenth century. From the nature of the inscription over the arch to the south porticus the last decade of the tenth or the first decade of the eleventh century would seem a likely date.

The church (1) consists (Fig. 46) of an exceptionally long aisleless nave, 51 feet by 21 feet, a chancel, 20 feet by 14 feet, a central tower, 20 feet by 20 ft. 6 ins., and a

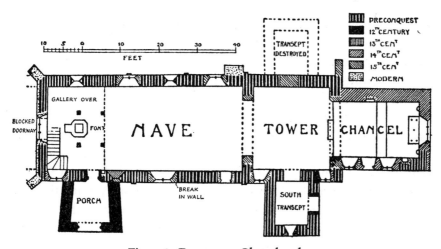

Fig. 46. Breamore Church, plan

south porticus, 11 feet by 8 feet. The walls are 3 feet thick everywhere, including the tower, giving a total exterior length for the whole church of 103 feet. The church appears to have been planned more carefully than was usual in the Saxon period. Its exterior dimensions are in multiples of 27 feet. The exterior length of the chancel is 27 feet, the same as that of the tower; the exterior width across the porticus from north to south is 54 feet, the same as the distance from the exterior face of the nave

---

[1] G. Baldwin Brown; A. W. Clapham, (a); A. R. and P. M. Green; A. du Boulay Hill; V.C.H., *Hants*, IV.

(1) *Plate 222.*

west wall to the tower. Also the interior width of the tower equals the interior length of the chancel. The north porticus has disappeared though the marks of its gable are plain on the exterior of the north wall. The nave western wall was largely rebuilt in modern times and diagonal corner buttresses added to it. There was originally a western adjunct as wide as the nave of which traces remain of the north wall and, below ground, of the western doorway opening from it to the nave. Such wide western adjuncts are a rare, and Saxon, feature. There were similar chambers at Boarhunt (Hants), Daglingworth (Glos) and South Elmham (Suff).[1] The church is cruciform or winged, not truly transeptal. The wings are narrow porticus communicating with the main church by narrow arches. They are also in a very unusual position, projecting north and south from a central tower: porticus normally flanked a nave or overlapped nave and chancel. At Breamore their association with a central tower might be regarded as an advanced step in the development of the truly transeptal church from the non-transeptal but cruciform winged church with no central tower, as at Worth (Sussex). The porticus at Breamore are the only ones in Hampshire.

The walls are of whole flints, coursed in the lower parts and uncoursed above, with flat tile-shaped stones, some Roman bricks, interspersed at infrequent intervals. There are also some scattered pieces of green sandstone and ironstone here and there. Many individual flints and flat stones are laid obliquely, but are too individual to be called herring-boning. The statement in the Victoria County History that 'its walls [are] built of whole flints set herring bone fashion' is not correct. It is doubtful if there is any early herring-boning anywhere in the walls. There are two patches only, both in the south porticus. One is on a level with and to the east of the small thirteenth-century lancet window inserted in the earlier partially blocked Saxon window in the south wall. It is probably repair work contemporary with the lancet. The other piece is of dark grey tile-shaped stones laid obliquely in the footings of the porticus south wall, in one place of two courses not arranged in chevron fashion, i.e. not true herring-boning. This also is probably later repair work.

The upper south-west and south-east nave quoins are visible above the modern buttress; they are slab work in face-alternate arrangement and may be in part renewals. The tower quoins are original and interesting (1). Although the tower north and south walls are flush with the nave walls, as with axial towers, the western tower quoins continue to the ground; the tower is genuinely central and not axial. The tower and porticus quoins are similar: they are of large roughly dressed slabs showing an irregular approximation to upright and flat arrangement. The porticus south-east quoin (2) is more regular than the others: the stones are better dressed,

---

[1] See above, pp. 336–8.

---

(1) *Plates* 222, 223; (2) *Plate* 224.

more even in size and arranged in mixed face- and side-alternate manner. The two bottom quoin stones of the two south-east quoins have their corners cut off, whether intentionally or not is not known.

There are four flat pilaster strips on the nave exterior walls, two on the north and two on the south (1). The upper part of the western one on the north was destroyed when the fifteenth-century window was inserted. Those on the south correspond in position to those on the north. They are 11 inches wide, rather wider than Saxon pilasters usually were (6 to 8 inches), and of only 1½ inches projection, less than usual. They are cut back to the wall surface so that through the original plaster they appeared as genuine long and short work.

There are two Saxon windows high up in the nave north wall, one near the west end, the other rather east of central (Fig. 46). A similar blocked one is in the south wall, partly hidden by the eastern wall of the twelfth-century south porch. These windows are large, round-headed, double-splayed and with openings narrowing slightly upwards. There is a similar window (2) in the east wall of the porticus: it is plain, round-headed, double-splayed, with aperture narrowing slightly upwards, has no imposts and is plastered so that no details of its structure are visible. Below this is a twelfth-century round-headed doorway. There is no indication that this replaced an earlier Saxon one; this is indeed unlikely for lateral porticus normally had no external openings. There was a rather similar window (3) in the south wall. This was blocked and a small lancet inserted in the thirteenth century. The blocking is plainly visible below the lancet.

The tower originally was of two stages on the interior separated by a floor *c.* 15 feet above the ground, later removed. The upper floor was originally the ringing chamber; it was reached by ladder from the south porticus through a narrow square-headed doorway. The upper floor was lighted by four windows, two in the south wall, one on either side of the porticus. The south-east one has been destroyed. The others were round-headed, double-splayed and plastered, like the other Saxon windows in the church. They now have rectangular stone frames set in their outer splays (3). The masonry tower (4) did not rise above the very high nave roof ridge. The present chancel is much lower than the nave but was originally of the same height, as is indicated by the roof marks on the tower east wall. Nave and chancel therefore acted as east and west abutments to the tower. On north and south the unusually tall porticus were also useful abutments. The present superstructure is of timber which probably replaced an earlier timber structure which was the belfry. Breamore may be regarded as a good attempt to build a stable central tower without any thickening of the walls (as was usual with axial towers). Stability was obtained by (*a*) low height of 54 feet, (*b*) small light timber superstructure, (*c*) quoins to the

---

(1) *Plate* 225; (2) *Plate* 224; (3) *Plate* 223; (4) *Plate* 222.

ground, (*d*) nave and chancel as high as the tower, (*e*) unusually high north and south porticus.

The chancel is of the same plan as the Saxon chancel and is built probably on the original foundations. Certainly the lower part of the south wall is original. The rest was rebuilt to a lower height in the fourteenth century. The new part is of knapped flints with old flintwork here and there. The quoins may be the original stones re-used. There are no original openings and no Saxon features visible on the interior.

In the interior of the church the tower east and west arches were replaced by wider arches in the fifteenth century. No traces of the original western arch remain but du Boulay Hill uncovered the foundations of the eastern arch, which was 6 ft. 8 ins. wide. The opening to the north porticus was blocked in the fifteenth century. The jambs and ends of the gabled roof remain in the wall and show that the opening was of the same width as the southern one. The arch to the south porticus (I) is original. It is characteristically tall and narrow: 10 ft. 8 ins. high by 4 ft. 11 ins. wide. The jambs are of green sandstone, but not through-stones. The head is of through-stones, but not of real voussoirs; it consists of six stones of different lengths cut to shape. The imposts are massive, square-cut but with cable moulding along the upper and lower edges and ends of the impost soffit faces. The cabling may have continued along the north and south ends but, if so, it has been cut away.

An inscription cut round the arch head was discovered in 1897. The letters are six inches tall and filled with red coloured lime. It reads HER SWUTELAD SEO GECWYD-RÆDNES DE. . . . It was translated by W. J. Andrews as 'Here is manifested the Word (or Covenant) to thee . . .', an Anglo-Saxon version of Titus, 1.3. Professor Napier[1] suggested that the last word meant 'which' and not 'to thee', and that the inscription may have been continued elsewhere, perhaps over the eastern arch and round the one leading to the north porticus. In fact, above the existing eastern arch are three letters DES, slightly smaller than and of rather different type from the main inscription, but perhaps contemporary and part of the suggested longer inscription.

Andrews, who was an authority on numismatics, pointed out[2] that early Anglo-Saxon letters, such as those on St. Cuthbert's coffin (*c.* 698), are angular: s was a reversed z; w resembled our P but had a straight-sided triangle instead of a loop. At Breamore s occurs three times, twice as a modern s and once as a reversed z; the w is triangular, not looped. Apparently this inscription was made at a date when the s was in its transitional stage from the reversed z to s and the early w was used.

---

[1] *Trans. Philological Soc.*, 1903–6, p. 293.   [2] Quoted by A. R. and P. M. Green.

(I) *Plate 226.*

These conditions only occurred together towards the end of the reign of Ethelred II (978–1016). Coins of Ethelred at Winchester show all three forms of these two letters, as at Breamore. In coins of Canute (1016–35) also at Winchester the s form and the looped w were used. This dates the inscription rather closely, and presumably the church too.

On the exterior wall above the twelfth-century south doorway and protected by the fifteenth-century porch is a large rood, more than 7 feet high, with a carved crucifixion. It is badly mutilated, having been cut back almost to the wall surface. It is further obscured by later plaster all round, and covering much of it, on which are paintings of other scenes. Its consideration is beyond the scope of this book. It and other similar sculptures have been discussed by other writers, notably by T. D. Kendrick,[1] D. Talbot Rice,[2] and—the Breamore one in particular—by du Boulay Hill and by A. R. and P. M. Green. A few general observations must suffice here. Crucifixions of a rood-like type were not uncommon in Saxon churches. Besides Breamore there are five others in Hampshire: one at Headbourne Worthy, two at Romsey,[3] two very small ones at New Alresford; there are two at Langford (I) (Oxon), two rather small ones at Daglingworth[3] and at Wormington (Glos), possibly one at Barton-on-Humber (2) (Lincs) and almost certainly one at Bradford-on-Avon[3] (Wilts). Those at Breamore, Headbourne Worthy, Langford and one at Romsey are on the outer walls and Kendrick is of opinion that the first two at least were intended to adorn the exterior walls. It is difficult to believe that such highly finished carvings were intended for exterior positions; their large rood-like size and character seem almost to presuppose a prominent internal site, such as above a chancel arch facing a nave. All that remains of the Bradford-on-Avon rood is in that position. In some cases there are plain indications that the roods have been moved from elsewhere. The smaller one at Langford has certainly been moved and has been wrongly reconstructed: the Virgin and St. John have been put back on the wrong sides of the Cross and in consequence have their backs to it. Green makes out a strong case, though not entirely convincing, for the Breamore Rood having been moved. There is evidence that the arms may have been reversed during reconstruction, i.e. replaced on the wrong side and upside down. This would also explain the excessive distortion of the body. Earlier, du Boulay Hill was of the opinion that the rood is in its original position—over an original Saxon doorway which was replaced by the present doorway and a low porch in the twelfth century. The roof of the porch was probably below the central figure of the rood. In the fifteenth century the porch was raised into a second storey, the upper stage being used as a chapel; it was plastered and the existing frescoes added.

[1] See his Pl. XL.   [2] See his Pl. 16a.   [3] See E. A. Fisher, Pls. 41, 43a, 44.

(I) *Plate* 114; (2) *Plate* 135.

WARBLINGTON

THE CHURCH OF ST. THOMAS OF CANTERBURY.[1] The original dedication is not known; it was obviously not the present one. The church is a large one which has grown up in rather piece-meal fashion round and in place of an earlier Saxon one. The first church probably consisted of nave, chancel and western two- or three-staged porch; if the porch was of three stages it would really be a tower. A larger nave was built in the early thirteenth century to the west of the west tower, the earlier nave being made the chancel. The ground stage of the tower was removed to give free access between the new nave and the old nave, or new chancel. In the late thirteenth century north and south aisles were added and the chancel (old nave) made longer. The north and south walls of the nave were at the same time extended as far as the east wall of the tower (I) and the nave new east wall returned to meet the east face of the tower. The third stage, if not already there as part of the Saxon tower, was added at the same time. The lancet windows in the north and south walls of the third stage are of this period. The only Saxon part remaining is the second stage, and possibly the fabric of the third stage, of the tower. It is wedged, as it were, with no supporting ground floor, between nave and chancel. It is visible on the exterior only from the north and south. The tower is very small, only 9 feet square; the walls are 2 ft. 3 ins. thick so the interior is only 4 ft. 6 ins. square. There are openings—doorways—in the north, south and west walls, but not one in the east. They may have opened to lateral buildings of some kind. There are blocks of masonry abutting the arches under the tower which may perhaps be or contain parts of the walling of such adjuncts; the east responds of the thirteenth-century arcades may have been built against these supposed earlier blocks for the eastern limits of the aisles are in line with these masses. Such openings leading to lateral adjuncts were common in Saxon towers; the arrangements at Netheravon (Wilts) are similar, and probably originally at Christ Church, Canterbury. The north and south doorways (2) are similar and very primitive. The jambs are of rough selected flattish pieces of stone rubble laid on one another. The round-heads are of similar construction, of stones selected for their shape, thicker at one end, and arranged to form a rough arch. There are no imposts; the jambs are carried down to floor level and are cut straight through the walls: they are doorways, not windows.

The western opening (3) is visible only from the nave. It was given stone dressings in the thirteenth century: jambs of excellent upright and flat work, a very thin sill

---

[1] A. R. and P. M. Green; C. R. Peers in V.C.H., *Hants*, III.

(I) *Plate 227*; (2) *Plates 227, 228*; (3) *Plate 229*.

and head of real voussoirs. In the wall face above this opening is the gable end of a former roof and the western quoins of the third stage of the present tower. The gable end must be earlier than the quoins above, but it is uncertain whether it represents a saddle back roof of the Saxon tower or the gable end of a former rather tall western adjunct.

The third stage of the tower (1) appears to be of similar fabric to the second. It may possibly be Saxon, though perhaps later than the second stage, in which thirteenth-century lancets have been cut. The wall around the lancet looks disturbed as though there was a larger earlier opening here. The top stage is of different fabric. It was built *c.* 1830 to replace a wooden bell turret.

---

(1) *Plate* 227.

SURREY

COMPTON

ST. NICHOLAS' CHURCH.[1] This is an attractive church *c.* 2 miles west by south of Guildford; it is really beautiful. It has been well and carefully restored and very evidently is well cared for. The first modern restoration was in 1843; further work was done in 1869, 1906 and 1953. The nave and aisles are contained under a single-gabled roof, which has slightly different slopes over nave and aisles. Clerestory lighting is by attractive nineteenth-century three-light dormer windows in the south roof. The church has a two-storeyed chancel, each storey with its own separate altar, a feature unique in Britain; some writers say unique in Europe.

The tower, all four nave quoins, portions of the nave walls, and the lower portion of the chancel north wall containing a low square window are pre- or early post-Conquest. Baldwin Brown does not mention the church. P. Johnston, in the Victoria County History of Surrey, dates the tower to *c.* 1075. It is difficult to accept so late a date for so primitive-looking a structure (I) with such primitive openings. It looks much earlier. It is built of ragstone rubble of widely varying sizes showing little or no attempt at coursing. There are no buttresses, no string course, no staircase, no dressed stone quoins or window surrounds. The windows are merely round-headed slit openings in the rubble fabric. The incongruous large window in the tower west wall is modern. The tower quoins are of thin selected uncut ragstone slabs laid flat on one another; the nave quoins are similar. There is no plinth.

There are tall narrow round-headed windows high up with heads and jambs of selected rubble slabs, one window in each wall; the one on the east is at a higher level to avoid the apex of the nave gable.

Other similar, but narrower, windows are in the south and north walls nearly half way up. There may have been one in the west wall: the walling above and around the head of the modern window has been remade with rectangular rubble blocks, evidently different and later than the rest of the walling.

The tower is *c.* 10 feet square on the interior; the west wall is 16 ft. 5 ins. wide on the exterior. The walls are therefore *c.* 3 ft. 3 ins. thick.

The nave is 47 ft. 6 ins. long by 18 feet wide at the west end and 16 ft. 6 ins. wide at the east.

[1] J. L. André, (a); V.C.H., *Surrey*, III.

(I) *Plate* 230.

The original chancel is dated to *c.* 1080. In the lower part of the north wall is a small rectangular window with a very wide single-splay towards the exterior. The splay is not straight-sided but deeply concave. It is supposed to have lighted an anchorite's cell close to or perhaps attached to the chancel. This would certainly explain the external splaying of the opening. At a later date, *c.* 1180, the chancel walls were heightened to accommodate an upper storey, an additional low chancel arch to the east of the main chancel arch being built to support it. The lower, original, chancel walls were thickened by the addition of an internal skin *c.* 1 foot thick. It is stated that the original plaster remains between this skin and the earlier walls.

The tower arch and main, western chancel arch are dated to *c.* 1165. The tower arch is very slightly pointed; it replaced an earlier and smaller opening of which nothing else is known.

GUILDFORD

ST. MARY'S CHURCH.[1] This church was the original parish church of the earliest Guildford, a little place which grew up between the Castle and the High Street. The church is of complicated plan as it grew up in a rather piece-meal manner round the old tower in the late eleventh, twelfth and thirteenth centuries. The chancel north wall is in line with the tower north wall; the chancel south wall is a little to the south of the tower; the nave diverges slightly to the north. The ground rises considerably towards the east; in consequence there are many steps from west to east within the church and the nave floor also slopes upwards. Only the tower is Saxon. Baldwin Brown dated it to post-950; *c.* 1030, towards the end of Canute's reign, seems likely. The tower is now central but originally was either axial between nave and chancel, or western and possibly turriform as no trace of an early nave has been found. It is built of flints, as can be seen above the roofs on all four sides; the lower part within the church is plastered. There are no separate quoins. A few bricks of Roman type occur here and there in the quoins and walls. The string course and embattled parapet are later. There are wide shallow pilaster strips of flint on all four walls, two on the west and four on each of the other walls, originally running to the ground. These are genuine buttresses, not merely decorative pilasters; they are local thickenings, structurally parts of the walls, like the very early buttresses at St. Martin's, Canterbury, and the long and short stone ones at Sompting. On the north and south walls they are within the church, showing that the transepts are later additions. Those on the south wall within the church measure 20 inches wide by six inches projection, including the plaster of unknown thickness. The embattled parapet is modern, and the top 5 feet of walling below the parapet are not original.

There are six large belfry windows probably of the thirteenth and fourteenth

[1] G. Baldwin Brown; P. M. Johnston in V.C.H., *Surrey*, II and III; J. H. Parker.

centuries: two trefoiled lights at different levels on the north and one on the east; two on the south, one trefoiled light and one tall lancet; and one lancet on the west. The tall lancet on the south has an older rear arch belonging to an earlier and wider arch.

The second stage was lighted by two double-splayed windows, not opposite each other, in the north and south walls. The one on the south has jambs of dressed stones and Roman bricks and an arched lintel. The north one is blocked. In the ground stage, on north and south and now within the church, are two double-splayed windows, one in each wall between two pilaster strips and *c.* 12 feet above floor level. They were not opposite each other; the north one is almost centrally placed, the south one to the east of centre. Their western jambs have been cut into by two centrally placed Norman arches erected when the transepts were built in the early twelfth century.

The large rectangular doorway near the north end of the tower west wall over-looking the nave is fifteenth century; it opened to a rood loft.

WOTTON

ST. JOHN THE EVANGELIST'S CHURCH.[1] Wotton is eight miles east by south of Guildford and three miles west by south of Dorking. The place, but not the church, is mentioned in Domesday Book. The architectural details suggest a church of *c.* mid-eleventh century. Both tower and nave are largely pre-Conquest. The tower is built of hard yellow Bargate stone rubble. Some of the original plaster remains. There is no plinth. The quoins are of rather small slabs of mixed face- and side-alternate arrangement. The tower is 14 ft. 2 ins. wide, north–south, by 11 feet on the interior. The east and west walls are 2 ft. 4 ins. thick; the north and south walls are 3 feet thick up to a height of *c.* 8 feet, at which height there is a set-back on the interior of *c.* 4 ins. in each wall making the wall thickness above this *c.* 2 ft. 8 ins., the same as that of the other walls. The nave is 33 feet long by 18 feet and the chancel 19 feet by 15 feet. The nave is lofty, *c.* 18 feet to the eaves. The large stones of the nave north-west quoin, mainly on end, and of the tower arch and jambs, and the tooling by pick, not axe or chisel, all suggest an early date, of perhaps *c.* 1050.

There was an arch now built up in the west wall of the tower. It is sited a few inches north of centre. The jambs and imposts are similar to those of the tower arch, but the head is obtusely pointed. This may be due to the crown being re-set when it was blocked in the thirteenth century and a window inserted in it. The V.C.H. regards the arch as a puzzle: into what did it open? Was there a porticus or western adjunct? But why should it have opened into anything, except the tower? Many

[1] F. R. Fairbank; V.C.H., *Surrey*, III.

Saxon towers have western and eastern, more or less monumental, openings. The later south porch, built on earlier foundations of unknown date, projects from the tower. Within this porch in the tower south wall is a curious doorway dated probably *c.* 1200. To the west of this doorway and high up is an early small blocked window, narrow and splayed, though not widely. Higher still, just below the roof, are four windows—two in the north wall, one each in the west and south, but not one in the east. Those on the south and west are small and rectangular, of four stones each, chamfered. Those on the north, vertically placed, have jambs of two stones each.

The tower arch is roughly built of large stones, square-cut head and jambs. The head is stilted and set back *c.* 6 ins. behind the jamb faces; it is of through-stones. The jambs have only one through-stone, they are otherwise of two and three stones per course. The imposts are rudely chamfered on their soffit faces and ends, which are not returned. The plinths are chamfered and are 2 feet high and 2 ft. 5 ins. deep (east-west). The opening is 8 ft. 2 ins. wide between the plinths, and 8 ft. 8 ins. between jambs. It is very high, almost up to the springing of the nave roof, *c.* 18 feet.

The belfry is a narrow, short timber superstructure, much narrower than the tower. The pyramidal belfry roof and the tower roof below the belfry are of Horsham stone slabs.

The nave north wall is pre-Conquest. It is blind for more than half its length though there might be remains of original openings behind the ivy; the whole interior is plastered. The south wall is also pre-Conquest but shows no traces of any original openings.

Of the original chancel arch, destroyed in 1858 during rebuilding, little appears to be known. It was probably narrow, square-edged and not more than 6 feet wide.

WILTSHIRE

NETHERAVON

ALL SAINTS' CHURCH.[1] This church presents problems. It is still disputed whether the tower, now western, was originally western or central. Its date also is in doubt. Micklethwaite, apparently on the basis only of examination of Ponting's drawings, suggested the ninth century, an almost impossible date for a tower; and that the western portal was altered and the eastern tower arch renewed at a late date. Ponting thought it early Norman, built perhaps with the help of Saxon masons. Baldwin Brown included it in his Overlap series and regarded the tower as 'probably of post-Conquest workmanship'. Brakspear thought it not much later than 1050–75 and perhaps pre-Conquest.

The tower is 21 feet square on the exterior at the base and 68 feet high to the top of the parapet. It is built of flint rubble with very regular rather small slab quoins. The quoin slabs are of similar heights and arranged in upright and flat manner. Much apparently original plaster remains on the exterior, flush with the quoins. The tower has two exterior stages, the lower one about twice the height of the upper. The upper stage is recessed *c.* 3 inches behind the lower but has no string course. There is no batter on the interior; on the exterior there is slight batter to the lower stage and perhaps above the off-set. The ground stage is divided internally into two stages by a perhaps later floor. The walls are *c.* 4 feet thick.

There is a wide, tall western portal, 7 ft. 10 ins. wide and 15 feet to the crown of the arch, and a similar but rather taller eastern tower arch.[2] The floor line of the eastern arch is a foot below that of the western arch and 1 ft. 8 ins. above that of the nave, following the slope of the ground towards the river. The western arch is stilted and is of one order with a bold half-round roll round each edge. The jambs have recessed half-columns at each edge with voluted capitals below imposts. One impost has billet ornament on it; the other is plain but looks unfinished. Between the imposts is incised animal ornament: a lion type on one and possibly an ape on the other. The tower eastern arch is similar but in addition to angle shafts has half-round soffit rolls round the head and down the jambs, rather like those at Clayton and Bosham (Sussex) and at Longford only 35 miles to the north in Oxfordshire. The soffit rolls are a late Saxon and Saxo-Norman Overlap feature, but, according to

[1] H. Brakspear, (*b*); G. Baldwin Brown; J. T. Micklethwaite, (*b*); C. E. Ponting.
[2] Drawings of details of both arches are given by Ponting.

Baldwin Brown, are 'really not a Norman feature'. The voluted capitals and the billet ornament of the western arch are Norman features; the dressings of this arch may be later replacements.

To the north and south of the western portal are two short buttresses which originally were projecting pieces of walling, remnants of walls running west which have long since disappeared, later converted to buttresses.

In the north and south walls are two small doorways at ground level. They have flat lintels with round heads above, and jambs of slabs similar to the tower quoins. Both were built up at some time but the south one was opened out in the restoration of 1888. They are not quite centrally placed, being slightly to the west of centre. To the west of these doorways and close to the tower quoins are projecting fragments of former walls running north–south. The aisle west walls overlap the tower by about 5 feet. The internal ends of these walls where they join the tower differ from the rest of the wall and resemble the projecting fragmentary walling at the west. Earlier walls evidently preceded the aisle west walls similar to those on the west. They were only 2 feet thick and 9 ft. 5 ins. apart, probably the walls of small north and south porticus into which the north and south doorways opened. There was similar walling, prior to the buttresses, on the west wall belonging to a western adjunct. On this evidence L. Brock[1] suggested that the tower was originally central with a small chancel or perhaps apse to the east and nave to the west. Ponting disputed this on reasonable grounds. He pointed out that the western adjunct could not have been more than 10 ft. 8 ins. wide and 17 feet high, and with walls only 2 feet thick: singularly modest dimensions for a nave attached to so large a tower. Further, the east wall of the present nave is nearly 4 feet thick, similar to that of the tower walls, 'and there can be little doubt that it is of the same early work as the tower.' Moreover the present mainly thirteenth-century nave is not quite centrally placed with regard to the tower. The north arcade is in line with the north wall of the tower; the south arcade is about one foot to the south of the tower south wall. Between the south arcade and the tower south-east quoin is a bit of old work projecting a foot or so to the east and south of the tower quoins[2] and in line with the nave south arcade. The implications seem clear, if not convincing. The original nave was to the east of the tower on the site of the present nave and of similar dimensions to the present one; the present nave east wall is the original east wall; the present north arcade was either cut through the old wall or it was built on the line of the old wall; the old south wall was pulled down and rebuilt about a foot further south. Ponting thought the western adjunct may have been a porch or a baptistry or possibly even a western apse. Brakspear, who knew of Ponting's work and views, accepted the older idea of a central tower with nave to the west and small chancel to the east; but he gave no reasons for his contrary opinion.

[1] Quoted by Ponting.   [2] Shown in Ponting's plan, and in Baldwin Brown, p. 338, fig. 152.

Above the tower arch and just above the floor line of the upper storey of the ground stage is a doorway of ingress either to the upper storey from the nave, or into an inter-roof chamber above the nave: the opening is below the marks of the old gable on the tower wall. There is a similar doorway at a rather lower level, *c.* 17 feet above ground level, in the north wall, opening originally perhaps to an upper floor of the northern adjunct or into an inter-roof space. The sill of this doorway is corbelled out as though for a ladder to be reared against it, which would seem to suggest that it was an ingress to this stage of the tower from the porticus. The opening is only 4 ft. 9 ins. high. This stage is lighted by two round-headed, wide, single-splayed windows in the north and south walls.

The top stage of the tower appears to be of the same age as the lower. It has in the west face only a small round-headed opening just above the off-set. There may have been similar openings in the other three faces. If so, they were replaced in the thirteenth century by two-light lancets, each pair sharing a single central jamb. The corbel table above was added at the same time (when the nave was remodelled). The parapet and corner pinnacles are dated 1626.

ADDENDUM

LIST OF ANGLO-SAXON CHURCHES

Below are given the names of those Anglo-Saxon churches which the writer has been able to locate. In compiling the list a wide definition of such churches has been accepted. There are relatively few entire churches of the Saxon period. There are many more towers—about one hundred and twenty—which are mainly or partly Saxon. A majority of the churches however are so-called because, though they are largely rebuildings of later dates, they have retained in their fabric features, details, fragments, bits and pieces which are recognizably of Saxon character and which certainly or probably belonged to Saxon churches formerly on the sites. Such features may be: arches, windows, doorways—open or blocked—parts of heads or jambs of openings, quoining, pilasters, or pieces of walling very thin or very high. In some buildings the retained details, though ancient, may not be sufficiently recognisable to be considered as positively or probably Saxon, but only possibly or doubtfully or even very doubtfully of the Saxon period.[1] Some of the less unlikely of these are given and are indicated in the maps by crosses.

Post-Conquest churches of the Saxo-Norman Overlap which have Saxon characters are included. The round towers of East Anglia are, for reasons discussed in the text, not included except the five described above as examples of the group, and a very few others which are attached to definitely Saxon naves.

The maps are not drawn on any particular scale though Nos. 1, 2, 4 and 5 are on the same scale. No. 3, of Lincolnshire, is on a larger scale to accommodate the great number of churches in that county. A separate map of Sussex (No. 6) has been given for the same reason.

Too much should not be read into the relative concentrations of churches in the different areas. Many churches must have been destroyed, often to be replaced by larger ones, throughout the centuries due to the needs of increasing population resulting from industrialization. It is probably true however that the present great concentrations in Lincolnshire and East Anglia (in the latter area due mainly to its 170 round towers) are reflections of the great prosperity and populousness of those areas in Saxon times; Domesday Book references to churches in these two areas are very much more numerous than those for any other district.

[1] Caution is necessary in inferring an earlier Saxon church on a site from a single remaining feature such as a circular window or a gable-headed opening. Such a detail might have been inserted by a Saxon mason assisting Norman masters in the building of a post-Conquest church.

Addendum

The high concentration in Sussex is surprising. This area was the most isolated and, both politically and culturally, the most backward of all the Anglo-Saxon kingdoms; and it was the last to accept Christianity.

The churches are arranged in alphabetical and numerical order under counties. The serial numbers correspond to those on the maps and will enable readers to identify the sites. The briefest possible notes are given about each church except those described in detail in the text, which are printed in capitals.

I. ENGLAND NORTH OF THE HUMBER

NORTHUMBERLAND

1. Alnmouth: unexcavated foundations only.
2. Alnham: nave NE. and SE. quoins; very doubtful.
3. BOLAM.
4. Brandon: foundations only, presumed Saxon.
5. BYWELL: (a) ST. ANDREW.
     (b) ST. PETER.
6. CORBRIDGE.
7. Edlingham: nave W. wall, and W. doorway with two windows above; probable.
8. Eglingham: old chancel arch rebuilt in 1837 possibly Saxon; very long nave.
9. Heddon-on-the-Wall: nave walls in part, and SE. quoin.
10. HEXHAM: (a) ST. ANDREW.
      (b) ST. MARY.
11. INGRAM.
12. Long Houghton: possibly lower part of nave N. wall, NE. quoin, and E. wall and chancel arch.
13. OVINGHAM.
14. WARDEN.
15. WHITTINGHAM.

CO. DURHAM

1. Aycliffe: nave in part.
2. BILLINGHAM.
3. Escomb: entire church, nave and chancel.
4. Hart: nave N., E. and W. walls and quoins, and part of chancel arch with gable-headed window above.
5. JARROW.

6. MONKWEARMOUTH.
7. NORTON.
8. Pittington: nave walls in part, and windows.
9. Seaham: nave in part, windows, herring-boning.
10. Staindrop: nave N. and S. walls, and window.

YORKSHIRE: NORTH RIDING

1. APPLETON-LE-STREET.
2. Gilling: nave N. and S. walls in part; probably eleventh century.
3. Hackness: nave E. wall and chancel arch.
4. Hornby: tower only Saxon, *c.* 1080.
5. HOVINGHAM.
6. Kirby Hill, or Kirkby-on-the-Moor: parts of nave probably late tenth century.
7. Kirkdale: nave and dated inscription.
8. Masham: nave and W. quoins probably *c.* 1100.
9. MIDDLETON-BY-PICKERING.
10. Terrington: W. half of nave S. wall.

YORKSHIRE: EAST RIDING

1. SKIPWITH.
2. WEAVERTHORPE.
3. WHARRAM-LE-STREET.

YORKSHIRE: WEST RIDING

1. BARDSEY.
2. BURGHWALLIS.
3. Collingham: quoining, nave and chancel walls in part, possibly.
4. High Melton: chancel arch possible but doubtful.
5. KIRK HAMMERTON.
6. Laughton-en-le-Morthen: N. doorway.
7. LEDSHAM.
8. Little Ouseburn: tower arch possible but doubtful.
9. MONK FRYSTON.
10. Ripon: cathedral crypt, late seventh century.
11. Ryther: chancel arch probable.
12. Stainton: chancel arch, doubtful.

Addendum

York City

1. St. Mary the Younger, in Bishop Hill Junior.

Cumberland

1. Cleator: 3 ft. of base of the Norman chancel N. wall is of round cobbles, possibly Saxon.
2. Edenhall: tiny Saxon window high up in nave N. wall; possibly priest's door in chancel.
3. Over Denton: fabric probably Saxon though some think it Norman.

Westmorland

1. Beetham: probably lower part of tower.
2. Crosby Garrett: remains of narrow, eleventh century but early post-Conquest, chancel arch.
3. Long Marton: nave and W. half of chancel *c.* 1100; of two tympana one looks Norman, the other Saxon.
4. Morland.
5. Ormside: nave N. and S. walls, NE. quoin, W. half of chancel N. wall; late eleventh century.

Lancashire

1. Heysham: (*a*) St. Patrick's Chapel: ruins of E. wall and parts of N. and S. wall; and S. doorway; possibly eighth century.
   (*b*) Parish Church: nave in part, W. and part of E. walls; blocked W. doorway re-erected in churchyard.
2. Lancaster: possibly N. half of nave W. wall.

II. ENGLAND BETWEEN HUMBER AND THAMES: THE MIDLAND COUNTIES

Bedfordshire

1. Bedford: St. Peter de Merton.
2. Clapham.
3. Kensworth: nave and part of chancel probably *c.* 1100.

406

4. Stevington: lower part of tower; probably nave walls (very thin).
5. Turvey: part of nave.

BUCKINGHAMSHIRE

1. Bradenham: nave possible but doubtful.
2. Hardwick: nave and double splayed window, probable.
3. Iver: quoins and other details.
4. LAVENDON.
5. Lillingstone Dayrell: nave E. and W. walls and W. and chancel arches.
6. Little Missenden: possibly nave.
7. Newton Blossomville: parts of nave walls and one window are 11th century.
8. Wing: nave, N. aisle, apse, crypt.

CAMBRIDGESHIRE

1. Bartlow: Saxon round tower.
2. CAMBRIDGE: (*a*) ST. BENET.
      (*b*) St. Giles: details, perhaps chancel arch.
3. Ickleton: probably nave.

CHESHIRE

1. Bebington: there was a Saxon church here; possibly a few stones remain in nave S. wall.
2. Chester: St. John the Baptist: pieces of stonework in crypt discovered in 1937.

DERBYSHIRE

1. Ault Hucknell: possibly the very small chancel arch which is the E. arch of the central tower; the tower W. arch is massive Norman.
2. Marston Montgomery: possibly the very small chancel arch.
3. REPTON.
4. Stanton-by-Bridge: nave in part, SE. quoin.

GLOUCESTERSHIRE

1. Ampney Crucis: possibly parts of nave.
2. Ampney St. Peter: nave in part.

3. Ashleworth: probable, fragments in nave walls, crude N. doorway.
4. Bagendon: possibly base of tower.
5. Bibury: parts of nave walls, circular window, chancel arch in part.
6. Bitton: nave, details in chancel walls.
7. Churchdown: doubtful, fragments in nave N. wall.
8. Coln Rogers: nave and chancel, pilasters, quoins.
9. Daglingworth: most of nave and part of chancel.
10. DEERHURST: (*a*) ST. MARY.
    (*b*) Duke Odda's Chapel: nave and chancel.
11. Duntisbourne Rous: possible; blocked N. and S. doorways, herring-boning.
12. Edgeworth: some upright and flat work, possibly N. doorway.
13. Farmcote: nave walls, two small windows, probably blocked chancel arch.
14. Hawkesbury: parts of inner N. doorway and of nave very high N. and W. walls.
15. Lassington: very doubtful; tower base supposed to be Saxon.
16. Lemington: probably tiny chancel arch.
17. Leonard Stanley: excavated foundations of old church probably Saxon.
18. Mickleton: fragments in nave walls.
19. Miserdon: nave N. and S. doorways.
20. Rodmartin: fragments in nave N. and S. walls.
21. Saintbury: probable; blocked N. doorway, Saxon sundial.
22. Somerford Keynes: very early Saxon doorway.
23. Winstone: blocked N. doorway.

HEREFORDSHIRE

1. Edvin Loach: ruined nave; tower later.
2. Hereford: Bishop's palace chapel.
3. Kilpeck: some megalithic quoining.
4. Peterstow: base of nave N. wall.
5. Tedstone Delamere: possibly part of nave walls.

HERTFORDSHIRE

1. Great Amwall: probably nave and chancel.
2. Little Munden: probably parts of nave and chancel walls.
3. Northchurch: part of W. and all of S. wall of nave; indications at W. end of a former square chamber of Saxon period.
4. Reed: nave.
5. St. Albans, St. Michael: fragments in nave and chancel walls possible but doubtful.

6. Tewin: nave probably late eleventh or possibly early twelfth century; also very small window in nave N. wall and remains of window on interior of S. wall.
7. Walkern: nave walls probably eleventh century.
8. Westmill: part of nave SE. quoin.

Huntingdonshire

1. Haddon: probably nave E. wall but not chancel arch.
2. Great Paxton: nave and piers of crossing.
3. Upwood: chancel arch and part of nave N. wall *c.* 1100.
4. Woodston: part of wall and small window in lower part of modern tower W. wall.

Leicestershire

1. Birstall: window in chancel.
2. Leicester, St. Nicholas: fragments in nave W. wall; two small windows with round heads of double rows of Roman bricks; probably Saxon.

Middlesex

1. Kingsbury: possible, perhaps probable.

Northamptonshire

1. Barnack.
2. Brigstock.
3. Brixworth.
4. Earls Barton.
5. Gayton: gable-headed W. doorway, probable.
6. Geddington: nave, blocked early window, gable-headed blind arcading.
7. Greens Norton: nave, gable-headed opening above chancel arch.
8. Helpston: nave in part.
9. Nassington: nave in part; SW. quoin; blocked opening in W. wall.
10. Pattishall: nave, quoins, blocked N. doorway; fine chancel arch probably post-Conquest but with Saxon features.
11. Peakirk: much of nave thin walls, NE. and SE. quoins.
12. Peterborough.
13. Stowe-Nine-Churches.
14. Twywell: possibly fragments in nave N. wall.

15. Wansford: nave W. and part of S. walls; W. doorway and early Saxon opening above.
16. Wittering: nave and chancel and very fine chancel arch; nave SE. and SW. and chancel E. quoins.

NOTTINGHAMSHIRE

1. CARLTON-IN-LINDRICK.
2. East Bridgeford: remains below present church.
3. Everton: tympanum of S. doorway looks Saxon.
4. Plumtree: tower is Norman but traces of Saxon foundations were discovered during rebuilding of tower in 1906.
5. Sutton-on-Trent: traces of Saxon foundations with herring-boning above were discovered during rebuilding of tower in 1902–3.
6. Thoroton: double splayed narrow window (22 inches by $4\frac{1}{2}$ inches) built into vestry wall.

OXFORDSHIRE

1. CAVERSFIELD.
2. LANGFORD.
3. NORTH LEIGH.
4. OXFORD: (*a*) ST. MICHAEL.
             (*b*) Cathedral, a few stones in E. wall only.
5. Swalcliffe: nave.

RUTLAND

1. MARKET OVERTON.

SHROPSHIRE

1. Barrow: probably chancel N., S. and W. walls and chancel arch.
2. Delbury, or Diddlebury: nave, and probably the lower part of W. tower.
3. Much Wenlock: excavated early fragments possibly Saxon.
4. Shrewsbury, St. Mary: parts of early foundations are below present church.
5. STANTON LACY.
6. Stottesdon: nave W. wall; but tympanum of W. doorway more likely Norman.
7. Wroxeter: nave W. wall in part; W. doorway and tympanum are post-Conquest, late eleventh century.

Addendum

STAFFORDSHIRE

1. Houghton: some interior masonry of nave N. and W. walls possibly Saxon; also part of blocked opening in N. end of nave W. wall.

WARWICKSHIRE

1. Kingsbury: one window in chancel.
2. Quinton: probably nave walling in part.
3. Ryton-on-Dunsmore: N. and S. walls of nave and chancel.
4. Whitchurch: W. half of nave N. and S. walls, not W. wall.
5. WOOTTON WAWEN.

WORCESTERSHIRE

1. Elmley Castle: parts of nave and chancel walls.
2. Teddington: fragments in walls; perhaps chancel arch.
3. Tredington: nave in part, windows, indications of former W. gallery.

III. LINCOLNSHIRE

1. ALKBOROUGH.
2. Barholme: nave in part.
3. Barnetby-le-Wold: tower and nave walls in part.
4. BARTON-ON-HUMBER.
5. BRACEBRIDGE.
6. BRANSTON.
7. BROUGHTON-BY-BRIGG.
8. CABOURN.
9. CAISTOR.
10. CLEE, or OLD CLEE.
11. Coleby: tower, nave NW. and SW. quoins.
12. Colsterworth: details; two arches of nave N. arcade set in herring-boning may be Saxon.
13. Corringham: tower, part of nave SW. quoin.
14. Cranwell: nave NE. quoin and other details.
15. Cuxwold: tower in part, some nave quoins.
16. Digby: nave SE. quoin.
17. GLENTWORTH.
18. GREAT HALE.

19. Hagworthingham: some rough work in tower, very doubtful, no positive evidence.
20. Hainton: tower in part.
21. Harmston: tower.
22. Harpswell: tower.
23. Heapham: tower.
24. Holton-le-Clay: lower half of tower and part of nave.
25. HOUGH-ON-THE-HILL.
26. Irby-upon-Humber: probably tower in part.
27. Laceby: tower doubtful; S. doorway perhaps.
28. LINCOLN: (*a*) ST. BENEDICT.
            (*b*) ST. MARY-LE-WIGFORD.
            (*c*) ST. PETER-AT-GOWTS.
29. Little Bytham: parts of tower and of nave; quoins.
30. Lusby: nave and chancel in part.
31. MARTON.
32. NETTLETON.
33. North Reston: chancel arch and window.
34. Ropsley: nave.
35. ROTHWELL.
36. SCARTHO.
37. Scotter: S. door has square lintel and rude tympanum which 'appears to be certainly pre-Conquest'; the rest is Norman.
38. Skillington: nave SE. quoin.
39. SPRINGTHORPE.
40. Stewton: original chancel arch was Saxon; other fragments discovered in 1903 restoration.
41. STOW.
42. Stragglethorpe: nave.
43. SWALLOW.
44. SYSTON.
45. Tallington: possible; fragments of long and short work at E. end of N. aisle, and apparently Saxon stones in N. wall.
46. THURLBY.
47. WAITHE.
48. Willoughby: two stones in interior tower S. wall have Saxon zig-zag tooling; no other remains.
49. Wilsford: possible; nave exterior SE. and interior NE. quoins appear to be Saxon.
50. WINTERTON.
51. Worlaby: very fine tower arch left in rebuilt church.

IV. EAST ANGLIA AND ESSEX

Norfolk

1. Bawsey: mainly ruins; nave W. wall, N. and S. walls of E. axial tower, apse foundations.
2. BESSINGHAM.
3. Castle Rising Chapel: ruins only; nave, E. axial tower, apse; probably Overlap period.
4. COLNEY.
5. Coltishall: part of nave, two circular double-splayed windows in N. wall, fragments in chancel walls; possibly part of W. square tower.
6. Cringleford: circular double-splayed windows in nave and chancel.
7. DUNHAM MAGNA.
8. EAST LEXHAM.
9. Framingham Earl: double-splayed circular window in chancel; round W. tower.
10. Gateley: blocked doorway with head and jambs of Roman bricks; probably Saxon.
11. Gressenhall: traces brought to light in 1901 restoration.
12. HADDISCOE.
13. Houghton-on-the-Hill: quoins and double-splayed circular windows.
14. NEWTON-BY-CASTLE ACRE.
15. NORTH ELMHAM.
16. Norwich: St. Mary at Coslany: tower.
17. Rockland, All Saints: nave in part, W. quoins, herring-boning.
18. ROUGHTON.
19. Scole: probably some quoining.
20. South Lopham; circular windows.
21. Thetford: foundations of early eleventh-century church recently excavated.
22. West Barsham: two double-splayed circular windows.
23. WEYBOURNE.
24. Witton-by-Walsham: W. half of tower walls, NW., NE., and SW. quoins, circular windows, W. round tower.

Suffolk

1. Barsham: quoining, and lower part of tower.
2. Blundeston: circular window in nave N. wall, not double-splayed but cut from single block; blocked arch head in Roman bricks.

3. Bungay, Holy Trinity: nave N. wall in part; round tower partly Saxon.
4. Claydon: nave NW. and SW. quoins.
5. Darsham: possibly nave walls, with Roman bricks, in part.
6. Debenham: lower part of square W. tower.
7. Gosbeck: nave NE. and SE. quoins, one window; possibly N. doorway.
8. Hasketon: a window.
9. Hemingstone: nave SW. quoin.
10. SOUTH ELMHAM, THE OLD MINSTER.
11. Syleham: nave NW. quoin, and possibly tower base.
12. Thornham Parva: one small circular window.
13. Ufford: part of nave N. wall.
14. Walpole: nave SE. quoin; exterior pilasters on chancel N. and S. walls.

ESSEX

1. Bradwell juxta Mare, St. Peter on the Wall: nave, mid-seventh century.
2. Broomfield: probably nave S. and E. walls and part of chancel S. wall. Round tower probably twelfth century.
3. Chickney: nave and part of chancel.
4. Chipping Ongar: nave and chancel probably late eleventh century.
5. COLCHESTER, HOLY TRINITY.
6. Corringham: tower and parts of nave and chancel probably late eleventh century.
7. Fobbing: probably part of nave N. wall.
8. Great Stambridge: nave W. wall, NE., NW. and SW. quoins, bit of chancel N. wall at W.
9. Greensted-juxta-Ongar: timber nave, eleventh century.
10. Hadstock: nave and part of N. transept.
11. Inworth: nave and part of chancel.
12. Langford: S. doorway *c.* 1100; has a W. apse and formerly had an E. one of late eleventh or early twelfth century.
13. LITTLE BARDFIELD.
14. Stamborne: probably part of tower.
15. Steeple Bumpstead: lower half of tower, late eleventh century.
16. Strethall: nave.
17. Sturmer: part of nave.
18. TOLLESBURY.
19. Waltham Abbey: probably a bit of walling in base of nave S. wall.
20. Wendens Ambo: nave and part of tower probably late eleventh century.
21. West Mersea: tower, Roman bricks in nave fabric.
22. Weathersfield: probably NW. corner of nave.

Addendum

V. ENGLAND SOUTH OF THE THAMES

KENT

1. CANTERBURY: (*a*) ST. MARTIN.
   (*b*) St. Mildred: megalithic quoins.
   (*c*) St. Mary: excavated foundations, early seventh century.
   (*d*) St. Pancras: foundations and some walling, early seventh century.
   (*e*) SS. Peter and Paul: excavated foundations, early seventh century.
   (*f*) Abbot Wulfric's Rotunda: base only, mid-eleventh century.
2. Cheriton: details.
3. DOVER, ST. MARY-IN-CASTRO.
4. Leeds: nave.
5. Lower Halstow: part of chancel.
6. Lydd: fragments.
7. Lyminge: excavated foundations, seventh century.
8. Reculver, St. Mary: excavated remains, seventh century.
9. Rochester, St. Andrew: excavated foundations, seventh century.
10. Shorne: nave.
11. Stone-by-Faversham: fragments, some say Romano-British.
12. Swanscombe: double-splayed window in Roman bricks, much masonry in Roman bricks.
13. Whitfield: nave; chancel in part.

SUSSEX

1. Aldingbourne: possibly part of nave walls.
2. Arlington: nave quoins and much of nave walls, one window.
3. Bexhill, St. Peter: possibly; very thin nave walls at W. (23 inches) and great height (20 feet).
4. Bignor: possibly; massive plain chancel arch, no other evidence.
5. Bishopstone: S. porch and most of nave walls.
6. Bolney: S. doorway, and two chancel windows *c.* 1100.
7. BOSHAM.
8. Buncton Chapel: possibly chancel arch; also Roman bricks in flint and rubble walls, some herring-boning.
9. Burpham: small blocked window, and blocked doorway with chamfered lintel and jambs; possibly Saxo-Norman Overlap.

10. Chichester, St. Olave: possibly blocked nave S. doorway and undercroft.
11. Chithurst: probably Overlap period; thin walls (26 inches), horse-shoe chancel arch of Saxon type, some herring-boning.
12. Clayton: nave and chancel and chancel arch.
13. Eastergate: possible; tiny window with arched lintel; herring-boning in chancel in Roman bricks.
14. Elsted: part of ruined nave N. wall of herring-boning, over 20 feet high; chancel arch of Saxon type.
15. Ferring: possible; blocked window in nave S. wall similar to that at Burpham.
16. Ford: parts of nave N. and S. walls and two windows.
17. Friston: part of nave walls; head of blocked window, and part head and jamb of blocked doorway in S. wall.
18. Hardham: two narrow (6 inches) tapering windows, single-splayed, and with exterior arched lintels; rude blocked S. doorway.
19. Horsted Keynes: re-erected doorway in N. aisle.
20. Itchingfield: possible; very high nave walls.
21. JEVINGTON.
22. Lewes, St. John-sub-Castro: blocked S. doorway, chancel arch.
23. Lurgashall: possible; tall narrow doorway and herring-boning the only evidence.
24. Lyminster: probable; part of chancel arch and head of blocked S. doorway.
25. Old Shoreham: nave NW. quoin and W. part of nave N. wall, probably.
26. Ovingdean: doubtful; chancel arch similar to Rumboldswyke and Westhampnett; thin chancel walls ($2\frac{1}{2}$ feet).
27. Poling: parts of nave, one window.
28. Rottingdean: very doubtful; fragments including broken baluster shafts (perhaps from earlier church) built into the walls.
29. Rumboldswyke: probably nave and chancel.
30. Selham: probable; narrow ($4\frac{1}{2}$ feet) chancel arch with soffit rolls (cf. Botolphs and Clayton), much altered: voluted capitals *below* massive imposts with Saxon ornamentation (including foliage and animals).
31. SINGLETON.
32. Slaugham: doubtful; blocked doorway similar to Bolney.
33. SOMPTING.
34. South Bersted: details in tower very doubtful.
35. Botolphs: nave S. wall, plain chancel arch with rough imposts and soffit rolls.
36. Stopham: details.
37. Stoughton: nave in part, double-splayed window, probably chancel arch.
38. Upmardon: fragments of earlier chancel arch in existing one which is a clumsy enlargement of the earlier narrower and lower arch; very doutful.
39. Walberton: nothing left of earlier church except a gable cross now lost.

40. Westdean: window and blocked doorway in nave N. wall.
41. West Dean: blocked doorway in N. wall.
42. Westhampnett: probable; chancel S. wall thin ($2\frac{1}{2}$ feet) with an apparently Saxon window; Saxon chancel arch destroyed 1867; herring-boning in Roman bricks.
43. Wivelsfield: doubtful; doorway similar to Bolney built into modern N. aisle.
44. Woolbeding: probable; nave NW. and NE. quoins, pilasters.
45. Worth: entire church, nave, apse, N. and S. porticus.

BERKSHIRE

1. Aston Upthorpe: probable; window in nave N. wall, blocked S. doorway, and perhaps rear arch of N. doorway.
2. Bucklebury: E. parts of nave N. and S. walls, and SE. quoin.
3. Cholsey: originally probably cruciform with central tower; base of tower remains to height of nave roof ridge.
4. South Moreton: probable; nave W. and part of S. wall, and probably blocked W. doorway.
5. Wallingford, St. Lawrence' Church: nave and chancel walls.
6. Waltham St. Lawrence: probable; very thin nave N. and S. walls.
7. WICKHAM.

DEVONSHIRE

1. BISHOPSTEIGNTON.
2. EAST TEIGNMOUTH.
3. Sidbury: crypt.

DORSET

1. Shaftesbury Abbey: one strip of walling only.
2. Sherborne Abbey: two door jambs and other fragments in W. front exterior.
3. Wareham, St. Martin's Church: nave and chancel.
4. Worth Matravers: pilaster strips and part of nave walls.

HAMPSHIRE

1. Arreton, Isle of Wight: part of nave.
2. Boarhunt: pilasters on nave and chancel walls; W. chamber; windows.
3. BREAMORE.

4. Corhampton: chancel arch and part of chancel; most of nave including W. and in part S. doorways; pilasters; quoins; sundial.
5. Fareham; nave NW. quoin.
6. Hambledon: parts of nave and chancel.
7. Hannington: megalithic NE. quoins.
8. Headbourne Worthy: nave and chancel; pilasters; quoins; rood.
9. Hinton Ampner: N. doorway, pilaster strips, NE. quoin.
10. Laverstoke: parts of nave N. and S. walls, NE. and SE. quoins, blocked S. doorway.
11. Little Somborne: part of nave, pilasters, quoins.
12. Quarley: details; probably of Overlap period.
13. Romsey Abbey: apse found by excavation below present church; two roods.
14. Soberton: possible; fragments in walls.
15. Tichborne: part of chancel; very wide (13 to 24 inches) and projecting (3 inches) pilaster strips; but thick walls—probably Overlap in date.
16. Titchfield: W. porch, nave W. and S. walls, SW. and SE. megalithic quoins.
17. Upton Grey: fragments in walls and in chancel arch.
18. WARBLINGTON.

SOMERSET

1. Glastonbury Abbey: some excavated foundations of chancel, N. and S. porticus, and crypt.
2. Milborne Port: possibly fragments in walls.

SURREY

1. Albury, Old Church: nave, at latest pre-1086.
2. Chaldon: nave W. and E. walls, 11th century.
3. COMPTON.
4. East Clandon: nave, very late 11th century.
5. Fetcham: nave and chancel walls in part; tapering window.
6. Godalming: nave E. wall with two circular eye-holes in gable.
7. GUILDFORD, ST. MARY.
8. Shere: probably part of nave N. wall.
9. Stoke D'Abernon: much of chancel and nave walls; blocked doorway.
10. Thursley: much of chancel and nave walls, three windows.
11. West Horsley: possibly parts of nave.
12. Witley: nave walls and one window.

13. Wonersh: possibly nave N. wall.
14. WOTTON.

WILTSHIRE

1. Avebury: nave; window; details.
2. Bradford-on-Avon: nave, chancel, N. porticus; tall and narrow characteristically early Saxon chancel arch.
3. Bremhill: nave.
4. Britford: nave and details.
5. Burcombe: some quoining.
6. Knook: small church, and tympanum.
7. Limpley Stoke: details.
8. Manningford Bruce: most of church, with apse; possibly tenth century.
9. NETHERAVON.

MAPS SHOWING THE DISTRIBUTION OF ANGLO-SAXON CHURCHES

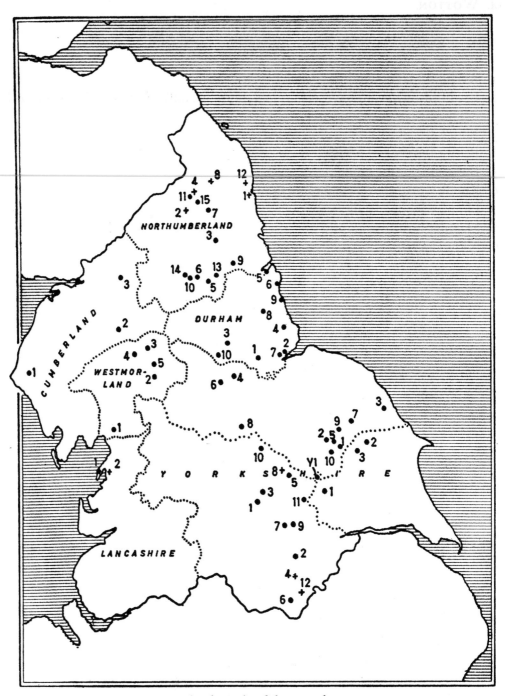

England north of the Humber

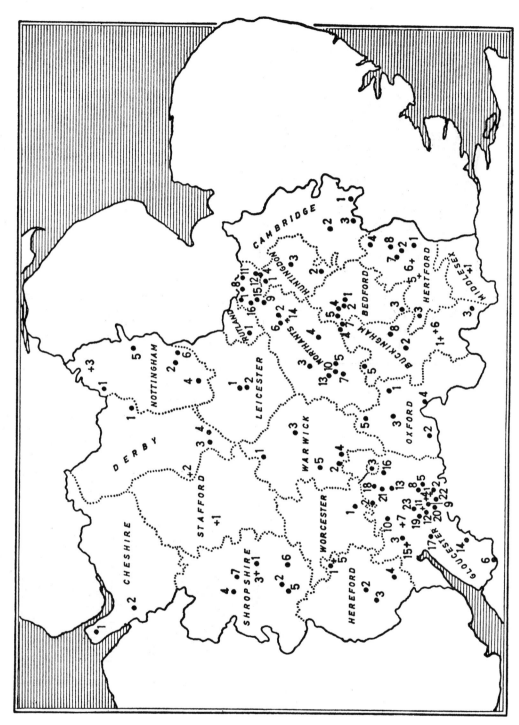

England between Humber and Thames

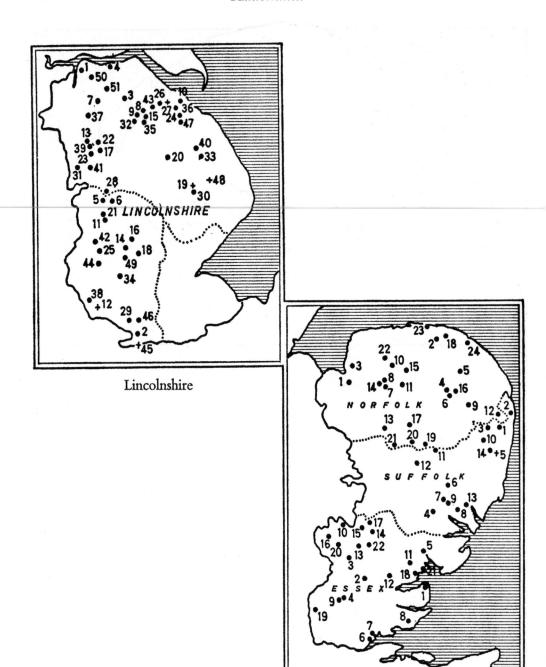

Lincolnshire

East Anglia and Essex

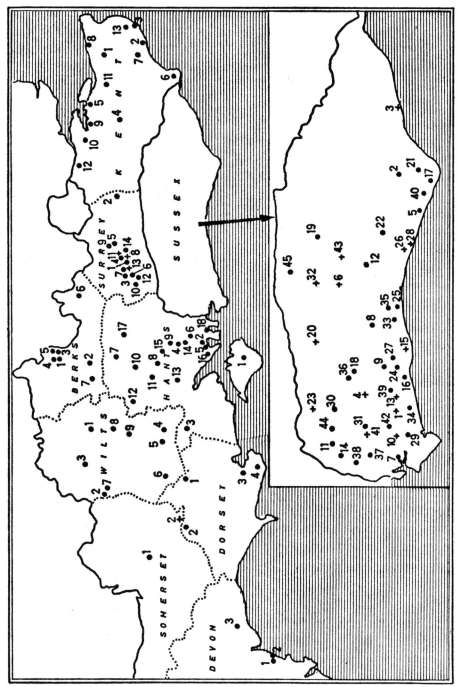

England south of the Thames

BIBLIOGRAPHY

ABBREVIATIONS USED

Anglia	*Anglia: Zeitschrift für Englische Philologie.*
Ant. J.	*Society of Antiquaries Journal.*
Arch.	*Archaeologia.*
Arch. J.	*Archaeological Journal.*
Arch. Ael.	*Archaeologia Aeliana.*
Arch. Cant.	*Archaeologia Cantiana.*
Ass. Arch. Socs.	*Associated Architectural Societies' Reports and Papers.*
Bris. & Glos. Arch. Soc.	*Transactions of the Bristol and Gloucester Archaeological Society.*
Bucks, Berks & Oxon Arch. J.	*Bucks, Berks and Oxon Archaeological Journal.*
Cumb. & West. Arch. Soc.	*Transactions of the Cumberland & Westmorland Archaeological Society.*
Derbys. Arch. Soc.	*Journal of the Derbyshire Archaeological and Natural History Society.*
Devon Ass. Trans.	*Reports and Transactions of the Devonshire Association for the Advancement of Science, Literature and Art.*
Durham & North. Arch. Soc.	*Transactions of the Archaeological and Architectural Society of Durham and Northumberland.*
Hants Field Club	*Hampshire Field Club and Archaeological Society.*
J. Br. Arch. Ass.	*Journal of the British Archaeological Association.*
Norf. Arch.	*Norfolk Archaeology, or Transactions of the Norfolk and Norwich Archaeological Society.*
Northants Arch. Soc.	*Northamptonshire Architectural and Archaeological Society.*
Proc. Soc. Ant. Scot.	*Proceedings of the Society of Antiquaries of Scotland.*
Proc. Soc. Ant. Newcastle-on-Tyne	*Proceedings of the Society of Antiquaries of Newcastle-on-Tyne.*
Proc. Suff. Arch. Inst.	*Proceedings of the Suffolk Institute of Archaeology and National History.*
R.C.H.M.	*Royal Commission on Historical Monuments (England).*

Bibliography

Sund. Ant. Soc.	*Antiquities of Sunderland: Papers Printed by Sunderland Antiquarian Society.*
Surrey Arch. Coll.	*Surrey Archaeological Collections.*
Sussex Arch. Coll.	*Sussex Archaeological Collections.*
V.C.H.	*Victoria County Histories.*
Wilts Mag.	*Wiltshire Archaeological and Natural History Magazine.*

Adam, M. B., 'Sompting Church,' *Building News*, Jan. 26th, 1872.

Aelred of Rievaulx, *The Saints of Hexham*, see under Raine, J.

Airey, W., 'Festival Orientation,' *Ass. Arch. Socs.*, iii, 1856, pp. 19–27.

Allcroft, G. Hadrian, 'The Circle and the Cross,' Chaps. xxii–xxiv, *Arch. J.*, 2nd Ser., xxxi, 1924, pp. 189–307.

Allen, J. Romilly, 'Early Christian Sculptures in Northamptonshire,' *Ass. Arch. Socs.*, xix, 1888, pp. 398–423.

André, J. L., (*a*) 'Compton Church,' *Surrey Arch. Coll.*, xii, 1894, pp. 1–19.

   (*b*) 'Sompting Church,' *Sussex Arch Coll.*, xli, 1898, pp. 7–24.

Anon., *The Church of St. Wystan, Repton* (illustrated by Elizabeth J. Lysens), Derby, 1950.

Anon., J. L. P., 'Stanton Lacy Church, near Ludlow, Shropshire,' *Arch. J.*, iii, 1846, pp. 297–8.

Ashpitel, A., 'Repton Church and Priory', *J. Br. Arch. Ass.*, vii, 1852, pp. 263–283.

Atkinson, George, (*a*) 'On the Restoration in Progress at Stow Church, Lincolnshire,' *Ass. Arch. Socs.*, i, 1850–1, pp. 315–26.

   (*b*) 'On Saxon Architecture, and the Early Churches in the neighbourhood of Grimsby,' *Ass. Arch. Socs.*, v, pt. 1, 1859, pp. 23–33.

Bayly, James, *Four Churches in the Deanery of Buckrose*, 1894.

Bazeley, Canon, 'Deerhurst Church and Saxon Chapel,' *J. Br. Arch. Ass.*, N.S., xix, 1913, pp. 66–70.

Bede, (*a*) *Baedae Opera Historica*; with English translation by J. E. King, 2 vols. (Loeb Classical Library), 1930. (Includes *A History of the English Church and People; The Lives of the Abbots of Wearmouth and Jarrow;* and *The Anonymous Life of Ceolfrid.*)

   (*b*) *A History of the English Church and People*, translated by L. Sherley-Price, London, 1955.

Benson, H., 'Church Orientation and Patronal Festivals,' *Ant. J.* xxxvi, 1956, pp. 205–13.

Bilson, John, (*a*) 'Weaverthorpe Church and its Builder,' *Arch.*, lxxii, N.S., xxii, 1921–2, pp. 51–70.

(*b*) 'Wharram-le-Street Church, Yorkshire, and St. Rule's Church, St. Andrews,' *Arch.*, N.S., xxiii, 1922–3, pp. 55–72.

Boyle, J. R., (*a*) *The County of Durham: Its Castles, Churches and Manor Houses*, London, 1892.

(*b*) 'On the Monastery and Church of St. Paul, Jarrow,' *Arch. Ael.* 2nd Ser., x, 1885, pp. 195–216.

(*c*) 'On the Windows in the South Wall of the Chancel of St. Paul's Church, Jarrow,' *Arch. Ael.*, 2nd Ser., x, 1885, pp. 217–19.

(*d*) 'On the Monastery and Church of St. Peter, Monkwearmouth', *Arch. Ael.*, 2nd Ser., xi, 1886, pp. 33–51.

Brakspear, H., (*a*) 'Repton Church,' *Arch. J.*, lxxi, 1914, pp. 387–93.

(*b*) 'Netheravon Church,' *Wilts Mag.*, xlvii, 1935–7, pp. 606–7.

Brereton, R. P., (*a*) 'Notes on some Unrecorded Saxon Work in or near Northamptonshire,' *Ass. Arch. Socs.*, xxvii, 1904, pp. 397–400.

(*b*) 'Some Unrecorded Saxon Churches,' *The Reliquary*, 4th Ser., xi, 1905 pp. 111–26.

Britton, John, *Architectural Antiquities,* Vol. v, London, 1826.

Brock, E. P. L., 'Christianity in Britain in Roman Times with reference to Recent Discoveries at Canterbury,' *Arch. Cant.*, xv, 1883, pp. 38–55.

Brøndsted, J., *Early English Ornament*, London, 1924.

Brown, G. Baldwin, *The Arts in Early England,* Vol. ii, *Anglo-Saxon Architecture*, London, 1925.

Brown, Robert, *Notes on the Early History of Barton-on-Humber*, 2 vols., 1906.

Bruce-Mitford, R. L. S., (*a*) *The Sutton Hoo Ship Burial*, London (The British Museum), 1926.

(*b*) 'The Sutton Hoo Ship Burial,' *Proc. Suff. Arch. Inst.*, xxv, 1952, pp. 1–78.

Bryant, T. Hugh, *County Churches Series: Suffolk*, 2 vols., 1912.

Buckler, J. C., 'Notes on Saxon Architecture, with a Description of Deerhurst Priory, Gloucestershire,' *Bris. & Glos. Arch. Soc.*, xi, 1886–7, pp. 6–81.

Butterick, T., 'Ruins of a pre-Conquest Church at North Elmham in Norfolk,' *The Builder*, lxxxiv, March 14th, 1903, pp. 267–70.

Butterworth, George, (*a*) *Deerhurst*, London, 1887.

(*b*) 'The Ancient Apse at Deerhurst Church,' *Bris. & Glos. Arch. Soc.*, xiv, 1889–90, pp. 48–9.

(*c*) 'Deerhurst', *Bris. & Glos. Arch. Soc.*, xxv, 1902, pp. 68–76.

Camden, William, *Britain*, seventeenth century; also revised edition by Edmund Gibson, 1722.

Candidus, Hugh, see Mellows, W. T.

Bibliography

Carpenter, R. H., 'St. Andrew's Church, Brigstock,' *Ass. Arch. Socs.*, xiii, 1876, pp. 237–48.

Carthew, G. A., 'Notices of the Saxon or Early Norman Church at Great Dunham,' *Norf. Arch.*, i, 1847, pp. 91–9.

Cautley, H. M., (a) *Suffolk Churches and their Treasures*, London, 1937.
　(b) *Norfolk Churches*, London, 1949.

Cave, C. J. P., 'The Orientation of Churches,' *Ant. J.*, xxx, 1950, pp. 47–51.

Clapham, A. W., (a) *English Romanesque Architecture before the Conquest*, Oxford, 1930.
　(b) *English Romanesque Architecture after the Conquest*, Oxford, 1934.
　(c) 'Note on St. Martin's Church, Canterbury,' *Arch. J.*, lxxxvi, 1929, pp. 280–1.
　(d) 'Sompting Church,' *Arch. J.*, xcii, 1935, pp. 405–9.
　(e) 'Bosham Church,' *Arch. J.*, xcii, 1935, p. 411.
　(f) 'Stow Church, Lincolnshire,' *Arch. J.*, ciii, 1946, pp. 168–70.
　(g) 'Barton-on-Humber Church,' *Arch. J.*, ciii, 1946, pp. 179–81.
　(h) 'Two Carved Stones at Monkwearmouth,' *Arch. Ael.*, 4th Ser., xxviii, 1950, pp. 1–6.

Clapham, A. W. and Godfrey, W. H., 'The Saxon Cathedral at Elmham,' *Ant. J.*, vi, 1926, pp. 402–9.

Clemoës, Peter (editor), *The Anglo-Saxons*, London, 1959. (Contains chapter on *Some Little Known Aspects of Pre-Conquest Churches*, by H. M. Taylor.)

Cobbet, L., 'The Windows Inserted in the Tower of St. Benet's Church, Cambridge, in 1586.' *Proc. Camb. Ant. Soc.*, xxviii, 1927, pp. 83–90.

Colgrave, B., 'Saint Peter's Church, Monkwearmouth,' *Durham & North. Arch. Soc.*, x, Pt. ii, 1948, pp. 179–94.

Colgrave, B. and Romans, T., *A Guide to St. Paul's Church, Jarrow, and its Monastic Buildings*, Gloucester, 1954.

Collingwood, R. G., 'The Bewcastle Cross,' *Cumb. & West. Arch. Soc.*, N.S., xxxv, 1935, pp. 1–29.

Collingwood, W. G., *Northumbrian Crosses of the pre-Norman Age*, London, 1927.

Conant, K. J., *Carolingian and Romanesque Architecture, 800–1200*, London, 1959.

Cornelius, C. F., 'Ancient Devon Parish Churches within a Ten Mile Radius of Newton Abbot,' *Devon Ass. Trans.*, lxxviii, 1946, pp. 123–56.

Cox, J. C., (a) *County Church Series: Norfolk*, 2 vols., London, 1911.
　(b) 'A Note on the Restoration of Repton Church,' *Derbys. Arch. Soc.*, viii, 1886, pp. 231–6.
　(c) 'A Note on the Discoveries at Repton Priory and Church,' *Derbys. Arch. Soc.*, xxxiv, 1912, pp. 75–8.

Curwen, J. F., 'Herring-Bone Work as seen at Egremont Castle,' *Cumb. & West. Arch. Soc.*, N.S., xxviii, 1928, pp. 142–8.

de Paor, M. and L., *Early Christian Ireland*, London, 1958.

Dickens, Bruce, 'Note on the Dedication Stone of St. Mary-le-Wigford,' *Arch. J.*, ciii, 1946, pp. 163–5.

Dryden, Sir Henry, (*a*) 'On the Chancel of Brixworth Church,' *Ass. Arch. Socs.*, xx, 1890, pp. 343–52.

    (*b*) 'On Two Sculptures in Brixworth Church, Northamptonshire,' *Ass. Arch. Socs.*, xxiii, 1893, pp. 77–82.

Dugdale, William, *Monasticon Anglicanum*, ed. by J. Caley, H. Ellis and B. Bandinel, 6 vols., 1817–30.

Eddius Stephanus, *The Life of Bishop Wilfrid*, text, translation and notes by B. Colgrave, Cambridge, 1927.

Eeles, F. C., 'The Orientation of Scottish Churches,' *Proc. Soc. Ant. Scot.*, 4th Ser., xii, 1914, p. 169.

Elliston-Erwood, F. C., 'Notes on Bronze Objects from Shooter's Hill, Kent, and Elsewhere and on the Antique Forms of "Jew's Harps",' *Arch. Cant.*, lvi, 1943, pp. 34–40.

Fairbank, F. R., 'Wotton Church', *Surrey Arch. Coll.*, xvii, 1902, pp. 1–10.

Fairweather, F. H., (*a*) 'Weybourne Priory', *Norf. Arch.*, xxiv, 1932, pp. 201–28.

    (*b*) *Aisleless Apsidal Churches of Great Britain*, Colchester, 1933.

Fisher, E. A., *An Introduction to Anglo-Saxon Architecture and Sculpture*, London, 1959.

Fletcher, E. G. M. and Jackson, E. D. C., ' "Long and Short" Quoins and Pilaster Strips in Saxon Churches,' *J. Br. Arch. Ass.*, 3rd Ser., ix, 1944, pp. 12–29. (See also under Jackson and Fletcher.)

Fowler, C. Hodgson, 'Glentworth Church,' *Ass. Arch. Socs.*, xiv, Pt. i, 1877, pp. 57–60.

Fowler, J. T., 'Notes on All Saints' Church, Winterton', *Ass. Arch. Socs.*, xix, 1887, pp. 363–75.

Freeman, E. A., *English Towns and Districts*, London, 1883.

Gage, John, 'Observations on the Ecclesiastical Round Towers of Norfolk and Suffolk,' *Arch.*, xxiii, 1831, pp. 10–17.

Gibson, John, 'The Parish Church of Warden, Northumberland,' *Durham & North. Arch. Soc.*, vii, Pt. ii, 1936, pp. 216–22.

Gilbert, E. C., (*a*) 'New Views on Warden, Bywell and Heddon-on-the-Wall Churches,' *Arch. Ael.*, 4th Ser., xxiv, 1946, pp. 157–76.

    (*b*) 'Anglian Remains at St. Peter's, Monkwearmouth,' *Arch. Ael.*, 4th Ser., xxv, 1947, pp. 140–78.

    (*c*) 'Anglo-Saxon Work at Billingham Church,' *Proc. Soc. Ant. Newcastle-on-Tyne*, 4th Ser., xi, 1946–50, pp. 195–204.

    (*d*) 'The Anglian Remains at Jarrow Church,' *Proc. Soc. Ant. Newcastle-on-Tyne*, 5th Ser., i, 1955, pp. 311–33.

(*e*) 'Deerhurst Priory Church,' *Bris. & Glos. Arch. Soc.,* lxi, 1939, pp. 294–307.

(*f*) 'Deerhurst Priory Church Revisited,' *Bris. & Glos. Arch. Soc.,* lxxiii, 1954, pp. 73–114.

(*g*) *A Guide to the Priory Church and Saxon Chapel, Deerhurst, Gloucestershire,* Tewkesbury, 1958.

Green, A. R., 'Anglo-Saxon Sundials,' *Ant. J.,* viii, 1928, pp. 489–516.

Green, A. R. and P. M., *Saxon Architecture and Sculpture in Hampshire,* Winchester, 1951.

Greenwell, Canon W., Report of the Greenwell Committee: I. St. Peter's Monkwearmouth, pp. 141–4; II. Appendix, Church Reports No. iii, St. Peter's, Monkwearmouth, pp. 1–8; both in *Durham & North. Arch. Soc.,* i, 1864–8.

Gunn, R. J., 'Notices of Remains of Ecclesiastical Architecture in Norfolk, supposed to be of the Saxon Period,' *Arch. J.,* vi, 1849, pp. 359–63.

Haigh, D. H., 'Deerhurst Church, Gloucestershire,' *J. Br. Arch. Ass.,* i, 1846, pp. 9–19.

Hall, John, 'The Date of the Monastic Remains at St. Peter's Church, Monkwearmouth,' *Sund. Ant. Soc.,* viii, 1918–25, pp. 36–62; Appendix on work of repairing tower and west wall, by W. and T. R. Milburn, pp. 63–74.

Hall, J. W. F., *Mediaeval Lincoln,* Cambridge, 1948.

Hardcastle, 'St. Martin's Church, Canterbury,' *Arch. J.,* lxxxiv, 1927, p. 464.

Harrison, Frederic, *Notes on Sussex Churches,* 4th Ed., Hove, 1920.

Harrod, H., 'On the Site of the Bishopric of Elmham,' *Proc. Suff. Arch. Inst.,* iv, 1874, pp. 7–13.

Hartshorne, A., 'Six Plates of Brixworth Church from Drawings in Perspective by E. Roberts,' *Spring Gardens Sketch Book,* 3, 1868–9 (pls. 13–18).

Hill, A. de Boulay, 'A Saxon Church at Breamore, Hants,' *Arch. J.,* 2nd Ser. v, 1898, pp. 84–7.

Hipkins, F. C., (*a*) *Repton: Village, Abbey, Church, Priory and School,* Derby, 1894.

(*b*) *Repton and Its Neighbourhood,* 2nd Ed., 1899.

(*c*) *Repton: Its Abbey, Church, Priory and School,* in *Memorials of Old Derbyshire,* ed. by J. C. Cox, 1907, pp. 114–32.

(*d*) 'A Note on the most recent Discoveries in Repton Church Crypt,' *Derbys. Arch. Soc.,* xxiii, 1901, pp. 105–7.

Hodges, C. C., (*a*) 'The Pre-Conquest Churches of Northumbria,' *The Reliquary,* 3rd Ser., vii, 1893, pp. 1–18, 65–85, 140–56; viii, 1894, pp. 2–12, 65–83, 193–205.

(*b*) 'Ovingham Church,' *Proc. Soc. Ant. Newcastle-on-Tyne,* i, 1925, pp. 279–282.

(*c*) 'The Church of St. Bartholomew, Whittingham, Northumberland,' *Arch. Ael.,* 4th Ser., v, 1928, pp. 81–7.

Hodges, C. C. and Gibson, J., (*a*) *An Historical Guide to Hexham and Its Abbey*, Newcastle, 1889.

(*b*) *Hexham and Its Abbey*, Hexham and London, 1919.

Hodgkin, R. H., *A History of the Anglo-Saxons*, 3rd Ed., 2 vols., Oxford, 1952.

Hodgson, J. F., 'St. Paul's Church, Jarrow,' *Durham & North. Arch. Soc.*, vi, 1906–11, pp. 31 *et seq.*

Honeyman, H. L., 'Some Early Masonry in north Northumberland,' *Arch. Ael.*, 4th Ser., xii, 1935, pp. 158–87.

Hope, W. H. St. J., (*a*) 'Repton Priory, Derbyshire,' *Arch. J.*, xli, 1884, pp. 349–63.

(*b*) 'On the Augustan Priory of the Holy Trinity at Repton, Derbyshire,' *Derbys. Arch. Soc.*, vi, 1884, pp. 75–96, vii, 1885, pp. 154–61.

(*c*) The Architectural History of the Cathedral Church and Monastery of St. Andrew at Rochester, *Arch. Cant.*, xxiii, 1898, pp. 194–328.

(*d*) Excavations at St. Austin's Abbey, Canterbury, *Arch. Cant.*, xxv, 1902, pp. 222–43. (1. The Chapel of St. Pancras, pp. 223–37; 2. The Chapel of SS. Peter and Paul, pp. 238–43.)

(*e*) Recent Discoveries in the Abbey Church of St. Austin at Canterbury, *Arch.*, lxvi, 1915, pp. 377–400.

Howlett, R., 'The Ancient See of Elmham,' *Norf. Arch.*, xviii, Pt. 11, 1913, pp. 105–28.

Howorth, Sir Henry H., 'The Codex Amiatinus: Its History and Importance,' *Arch. J.*, 2nd Ser., xxii, 1915, pp. 49–68.

Hunter Blair, P., *An Introduction to Anglo-Saxon England*, Cambridge, 1956.

Hutchinson, William, *The History and Antiquities of the County Palatine of Durham*, 3 vols., London, 1823.

Irvine, J. T., (*a*) 'On the Crypt beneath the Chancel of Repton Church, Derbyshire,' *Derbys. Arch. Soc.*, v, 1883, 162–72.

(*b*) 'Notes on the Discoveries made in the Nave and Aisle of Repton Church during the late Restoration,' *Derbys. Arch. Soc.*, xiv, 1892, pp. 158–60.

(*c*) 'Discussion on Repton Church,' *J. Br. Arch. Ass.*, L, 1894, pp. 179, 248–50.

(*d*) 'Account of the pre-Norman Remains discovered at Peterborough in 1884,' *Ass. Arch. Socs.*, xvii, 1884, pp. 277–83.

(*e*) 'Account of the Discovery of part of the Saxon Abbey Church at Peterborough,' *J. Br. Arch. Ass.*, L, 1894, pp. 45–54.

(*f*) 'Could Archbishop Wilfrid have built the Saxon Tower of Barnack Church?' *J. Br. Arch. Ass.*, N.S., v, 1899, pp. 24–8.

(*g*) 'Dover Castle Church,' *J. Br. Arch Ass.*, XLI, 1885, pp. 284–8.

Jackson, E. D. C. and Fletcher, E. G. M., (*a*) 'Further Notes on "Long and Short" Quoins in Saxon Churches,' *J. Br. Arch. Ass.*, 3rd Ser., xii, 1949, pp. 1–18.

(*b*) 'Constructional Characteristics in Anglo-Saxon Churches,' *J. Br. Arch. Ass.*, 3rd Ser., xiv, 1951, pp. 11–26.

Bibliography

(c) 'Porch and Porticus in Saxon Churches,' *J. Br. Arch. Ass.*, 3rd Ser., xix, 1956, pp. 1–13.

(d) 'Excavations at Brixworth,' 1958, *J. Br. Arch. Ass.,* 3rd Ser., xxiv, 1961, pp.1–15.

(See also under Fletcher and Jackson.)

Jackson, Sir T. G., *Byzantine and Romanesque Architecture*, 2 vols., 2nd Ed., Cambridge, 1920.

Jenkins, Canon R. C., 'Remarks on the Early Churches and Basilicas in Connection with the Recent Discoveries at Lyminge,' *Arch. Cant.*, x, 1876, pp. ci–ciii.

Jessep, H. L., (a) *Anglo Saxon Church Architecture in Sussex*, London, n.d.

(b) *Notes on pre-Conquest Church Architecture in Hampshire and Surrey*, Winchester, 1913.

Jessop, A., 'Weybourn Priory,' *Norf. Arch.*, x, 1888, pp. 271–6.

Kendrick, T. D., *Late Saxon and Viking Art*, London, 1949.

Keysor, C. E., (a) 'A Day's Excursion among the Churches of South-East Norfolk,' *Arch. J.*, 2nd Ser., xiv, 1907, pp. 91–109.

(b) 'Notes on the Architecture of the Churches of Brigstock and Stanion, Northamptonshire,' *J. Br. Arch. Ass.*, xxvi, 1920, pp. 1–21.

(c) 'Notes on the Churches of the Lambourn Valley,' *Berks, Bucks & Oxon Arch. J.*, xxvii, 1922, pp. 114–36.

Knowles, W. H., 'Deerhurst Priory Church: including the Results of Excavations conducted during 1926,' *Arch.*, 2nd Ser., xxvii, 1928, pp. 141–64.

Legge, W. Heneage, 'The Villages and Churches in the Hundred of Willingdon,' *The Reliquary*, 3rd Ser., vii, 1901, pp. 1–10, 145–57.

Livett, Canon G. M., 'Foundations of the Saxon Cathedral at Rochester,' *Arch. Cant.*, xviii, 1889, pp. 261–78.

Longstaffe, W. H. D., (a) 'Hexham Church: Saxon Hexham,' *Arch. Ael.*, 1st Ser., v, 1861, pp. 150–4.

(b) 'Norton,' *Arch. Ael.*, 2nd Ser., xv, 1892, pp. 1–13.

Macdermott, K. H., *Bosham Church: Its History and Antiquities*, 3rd Ed., Chichester, 1926.

Manning, C. R., 'Weybourne Church and Priory,' *Norf. Arch.*, x, 1888, pp. 262–70.

Martin, R. R., '*The Church of St. Michael at the North Gate, Oxford*, 5th Ed., 1957.

Mellows, W. T. (editor), *The Chronicle of Hugh Candidus, A Monk of Peterborough*, Oxford, 1949.

Messant, C. J. W., *The Round Towers of English Parish Churches*, Norwich, 1958.

Micklethwaite, J. T., (a) 'On the Crypts at Hexham and Ripon,' *Arch. J.*, xxxix, 1882, pp. 347–54.

(b) 'Something About Saxon Church Building,' *Arch. J.*, liii, 1896, pp. 293–351.

(c) 'Some Further Notes on Saxon Churches,' *Arch. J.*, lv, 1898, pp. 340–9.

(d) 'The Old Minster at South Elmham,' *Proc. Suff. Arch. Inst.*, xvi, Pt. i, 1916, pp. 29–35.

Mitchell, H., 'On the Early Traditions of Bosham, and the Discovery of the Stone Coffin containing the Remains of a Daughter of King Canute in the Nave of Bosham Church,' *Sussex Arch. Coll.*, xviii, 1866, pp. 1–9.

Morley, C., (a) 'On Traces of Saxon Architecture yet Remaining in the County of Suffolk,' *Proc. Suff. Arch. Inst.*, xviii, Pt. i, 1922, pp. 1–28.

(b) 'Circular Towers,' *Proc. Suff. Arch. Inst.*, xviii, Pt. ii, 1923, pp. 144–55.

Northumberland, The History of, (a) Vol. iii, 1896; (b) Vol. vi, 1902; (c) Vol. x, 1914; (d) Vol. xii, 1926.

Nottingham, The Bishop of, (a) 'The Churches of Great Grimsby and Other Parishes,' *Ass. Arch. Socs.*, xiv, Pt. ii, 1878, pp. 151–66.

(b) 'Notes on the Churches of Barton-on-Humber,' *Ass. Arch. Socs.*, xix, Pt. ii, 1888, pp. 313–18.

Oakeshott, Walter, *The Sequence of English Mediaeval Art*, London, 1950.

Page, R. I., 'Language and Dating in O.E. Inscriptions,' *Anglia*, 77, 1959, pp. 385–406.

Page, W., 'Some Remarks on the Churches of the Domesday Survey,' *Arch.*, lxvi, 2nd Ser., xvi, 1914–15, pp. 61–102.

Paintin, H., *Three Oxfordshire Churches, Kencott, Broadwell and Langford*, Oxford, 1911.

Parker, J. H., 'The Church of St. Mary, Guildford,' *Arch. J.*, xxix, 1872, pp. 170–80.

Pavey, A. K., 'Some Notes on the Parochial History of Brixworth,' *Ass. Arch. Socs.*, xxvi, 1902, pp. 441–8.

Peers, C. R., (a) 'On Saxon Churches of the St. Pancras Type,' *Arch. J.*, lviii, 2nd Ser., viii, 1901, pp. 401–34.

(b) 'Review of Baldwin Brown's Anglo-Saxon Architecture,' *Ant. J.*, VI, 1926, pp. 209–12.

(c) 'Reculver: the Saxon Church and Cross,' *Arch.*, 2nd Ser., xxvii, 1928, pp. 241–56.

Peers, C. R. and Clapham, A. W., 'St. Augustine's Abbey, Canterbury, before the Norman Conquest,' *Arch.*, lxxvii, 2nd Ser., xxvii, 1928, pp. 201–18.

Pevsner, N., *The Buildings of England*, London (Penguin Books): (a) Cambridgeshire, 1954; (b) Derbyshire, 1953; (c) County Durham, 1953; (d) Essex, 1954; (e) Northumberland, 1957; (f) Nottinghamshire, 1951; (g) Shropshire, 1958; (h) Yorkshire, West Riding, 1959.

Pollock, L. A., 'Wootton Wawen Church,' *Arch. J.*, lxxxiii, 1926, pp. 308–9.

Ponting, C. E., 'The Churches of Sherston, Corston and Netheravon,' *Wilts Mag.*, xxxi, 1900–1, pp. 343–57.

Bibliography

Poole, G. A., (*a*) 'On the Saxon Church of All Saints, Brixworth,' *Ass. Arch. Socs.*, I, 1850, pp. 122–33.

    (*b*) 'On the Abbey Church of Peterborough,' *Ass. Arch. Socs.*, III, 1855, pp. 187–99.

Puckle, J., *The Church and Fortress of Dover Castle*, Oxford, 1864.

Radford, C. A. R., (*a*) 'The Saxon Church,' *Northants Arch. Soc.*, lix, 1953, pp. 17–28.

    (*b*) 'Earls Barton Church,' *Arch. J.*, cx, 1953, pp. 196–7.

    (*c*) 'Brixworth Church,' *Arch. J.*, cx, 1953, pp. 202–5.

    (*d*) 'St. Paul's Church, Jarrow,' *Arch. J.*, cxi, 1954, pp. 203–9.

    (*e*) 'St. Peter's Church, Monkwearmouth,' *Arch. J.*, cxi, 1954, pp. 209–11.

Raine, James, *Priory of Hexham*, Vol. I, pub. by the Surtees Society, Durham, 1864. Includes:

    (*a*) Richard of Hexham: Ricardus, prior Hagustaldensis—*Historia de antiqua et moderno statu ecclesiae Hagustaldensis*;

    (*b*) Aelred of Rievaulx, *The Saints of Hexham*.

Raven, J. J., 'The "Old Minster", South Elmham,' *Proc. Suff. Arch. Inst.*, x, Pt. i, 1898, pp. 1–6.

Richard of Hexham: see under Raine, J.

Rickman, Thomas, (*a*) 'Further Observations on the Ecclesiastical Architecture of France and England,' *Arch.*, xxvi, 1836, pp. 26–46.

    (*b*) *An Attempt to Discriminate the Styles of Architecture in England*, 5th Ed., London, 1848.

Rigold, S. E., (*a*) *North Elmham Cathedral*, Ministry of Works Bulletin, H.M. Stationery Office, 1960.

    (*b*) 'Review of C. J. W. Messant's "The Round Towers of English Parish Churches",' *Arch. J.*, cxv, 1958, pub. 1960, pp. 264–5.

Roberts, E., 'On Brixworth Church, Northamptonshire,' *J. Br. Arch. Ass.*, xix, 1863, pp. 285–305.

Routledge, Canon C. F., (*a*) *The Church of St. Martin, Canterbury*, London, 1898.

    (*b*) 'St. Martin's Church, Canterbury,' *Arch. Cant.*, xiv, 1882, pp. 108–12.

    (*c*) 'Notes on Discoveries at St. Martin's Church, Canterbury,' *Arch. Cant.*, xv, 1883, pp. 56–8.

    (*d*) 'St. Martin's Church, Canterbury,' *Arch. Cant.*, xxii, 1897, pp. 1–28.

    (*e*) 'The Church of St. Peter and St. Paul, Canterbury,' *Arch. Cant.*, xxv, 1902, pp. 238–43.

Royal Commission on Historical Monuments (England): Vols. on

    (*a*) *Buckinghamshire*, Vol. ii, 1913;

    (*b*) *City of Cambridge*, Pt. ii, 1959;

    (*c*) *Essex*, Vol. i, 1916; Vol. iii, 1922;

(*d*) *City of Oxford*, 1939;

(*e*) *Westmorland*, 1936.

Salter, H. E., *The Eynsham Cartulary*, Oxford, 1907, I, esp. p. x.

Savage, Rev. E. S. and Hodges, C. C., *A Record of All Works connected with Hexham Abbey since January, 1899, and now in Progress*, Hexham, 1907.

Savage, Canon H. E., 'Jarrow Church and Monastery,' *Arch. Ael.*, 2nd Ser., xxii, 1900, pp. 30–60.

Sayles, G. O., *The Mediaeval Foundations of England*, London, 1948.

Scott, G. Gilbert, 'The Church on the Castle Hill, Dover,' *Arch. Cant.*, V, 1863, pp. 1–18.

Shore, T. W., 'The Orientation of Churches in Hampshire,' *Hants Field Club*, Shore Memorial Vol., p. 95.

Simeon of Durham, (*a*) *The Historical Works of Simeon of Durham*, trans. by J. Stevenson in *The Church Historians of England*, Vol. III, Pt. II, London, 1855.

(*b*) *Symeonis Monachi Opera Omnia*, Vol. I, *Historia Ecclesiae Dunelmensis* London, 1882; Vol. II, *Historia Regum*, London, 1885 (ed. by Thomas Arnold).

Stacye, J., 'On Certain Early Remains in the Church of Carlton-in-Lindrick, Notts.,' *Ass. Arch. Socs.*, x, Pt. i, 1869, pp. 165–9.

Stenton, F. M., (*a*) *Anglo-Saxon England*, 2nd Ed., Oxford, 1947.

(*b*) 'The Lincolnshire Domesday Book and the Lindsey Survey,' *Lincolnshire Record Soc. Trans.*, xix, 1921, Introduction, p. xxxiii.

Stevenson, F. S., 'The Present State of the Elmham Controversy,' *Norf. Arch.*, xix, Pt. ii, 1926, pp. 110–16.

Street, G. E., *Bosham Church*, Chichester, 1934.

Strzgowski, J., (*a*) *Origins of Christian Church Art*, Oxford, 1923.

(*b*) *Early Church Art in Northern Europe*, London, 1928.

Surtees, J. R., *The History and Antiquities of the County Palatine of Durham*, Vols. 1–4 (1816, 1820, 1823, 1840).

Sutton, Arthur, 'A Description of Churches (in Lincolnshire) visited in June, 1907,' *Ass. Arch. Socs.*, xxix, Pt. i, 1907, pp. 71–90.

Syers, H. S., (*a*) 'The Building of Barnack Church,' *Ass. Arch. Socs.*, xxiii, 1895, pp. 143–51.

(*b*) 'Barnack Church,' *J. Br. Arch. Ass.*, N.S., V, 1899, pp. 13–24.

Sympson, E. M., 'Where was Sidnacester?' *Ass. Arch. Socs.*, xxviii, Pt. i, 1905, pp. 87–94.

Talbot Rice, D., *English Art, 871–1100*, Oxford, 1952.

Taylor, H. M.: see under Clemoës, Peter.

Taylor, W. T., *Hexham Abbey, 674–1958*, 2nd Ed., Hexham, 1958.

Thompson, A. Hamilton, (*a*) *The Ground Plan of the English Parish Church*, Cambridge, 1911.

(*b*) *The Village Churches of Yorkshire*, in *Memorials of Old Yorkshire*, ed. by T. M. Fallows, London, 1909.

(*c*) 'Pre-Conquest Church Towers in North Lincolnshire,' *Ass. Arch. Socs.*, xxix, Pt. i, 1907, pp. 43–70.

(*d*) 'Brixworth Church,' *Arch. J.*, lxix, N.S., xviii, 1912, pp. 504–10.

(*e*) 'Some Characteristics of the Parish Churches of Northumberland,' *Arch. Ael.*, 3rd Ser., xviii, 1921, pp. 19–28.

(*f*) 'Deerhurst Church and Odda's Chapel,' *Arch. J.*, lxxviii, N.S., xxviii, 1921, pp. 434–6.

(*g*) 'Recent Excavations at Repton Priory,' *Derbys. Arch. Soc.*, xlv, 1923, pp. 14–23.

(*h*) 'The Churches of St. Mary-le-Wigford, St. Benedict, and St. Peter-at-Gowts, Lincoln,' *Arch. J.*, CIII, 1946, pp. 162–6.

Trollope, E., (*a*) 'Notes on Market Rasen, and other Places in its Vicinity,' *Ass. Arch. Socs.*, vi, Pt. i, 1861, pp. 139–75.

(*b*) 'Notes on Grimsby and other Places in its Vicinity,' *Ass. Arch. Socs.*, viii, Pt. ii, 1866, pp. 213–54.

(*c*) 'Notes on Churches visited in June, 1867,' *Ass. Arch. Socs.*, ix, Pt. i, 1867, pp. 1–37.

Varah, W. E., *The Notable Churches of Barton-on-Humber*, Barton-on-Humber, 1929.

Victoria County Histories: (*a*) *Bedfordshire*, iii, 1912; (*b*) *Berkshire*, iv, 1924; (*c*) *Buckinghamshire*, iv, 1927; (*d*) *Cumberland*, ii, 1905; (*e*) *Durham*, iii, 1928; (*f*) *Hampshire*, iii (1908), iv (1911); (*g*) *Lincolnshire*, ii, 1906; (*h*) *Norfolk*, ii, 1906; (*j*) *Northamptonshire*, i (1902), ii (1906), iii (1930), iv (1937); (*k*) *Rutland*, ii (1935); (*l*) *Surrey*, ii (1905), iii (1911); (*m*) *Warwickshire*, iii (1945); (*n*) *Yorkshire, North Riding*, i (1914), ii (1923).

Walbran, J. R., 'On St. Wilfrid, and the Saxon Church of Ripon,' *Ass. Arch. Socs.*, v, Pt. i, 1859, pp. 63–96.

Watkins, C. F., *The Basilica, and the Basilican Church at Brixworth*, 1867.

Whittingham, A., 'Great Ryburgh Church,' *Norf. Arch.*, xxvi, 1938, p. xxxiv.

Wilkinson, Sir Gardner, 'Long and Short Work,' *Ass. Arch. Socs.*, vii, 1863, pp. 41–52.

William of Malmesbury, *de Gestis Pontificum Anglorum*, ed. by N. E. S. A. Hamilton, Rolls Series, lii, 1870.

Williams, J. F., 'Great Dunham Church,' *J. Br. Arch. Ass.*, N.S., xxxi, 1925, pp. 114–18.

Willis, R. and Clark, J. W., *The Ancient History of the University of Cambridge*, 1886, (Vol. i, The Church of St. Benedict, pp. 271–88).

Wilson, F. R., *An Architectural Survey of the Churches in the Archdeaconry of Lindisfarne* Newcastle-on-Tyne, 1870.

Bibliography

Woodward, B. B., 'The Old Minster, South Elmham,' *Proc. Suff. Arch. Inst.,* iv, 1874, pp. 1–7.

Woodward, S., 'Observations on the Round Church Towers of Norfolk,' *Arch.,* xxiii, 1831, pp. 7–9.

Woolley, C. L., 'Corstopitum,' *Arch. Ael.,* 3rd Ser., iii, 1907, pp. 161–86.

Wordsworth, J., 'Anglo-Saxon Dedicatory Inscription in the Tower of St. Mary-le-Wigford Church in Lincoln,' *Ass. Arch. Socs.,* xv, Pt. i, 1879, pp. 16–17.

Zarnecki, George, (*a*) *English Romanesque Sculpture, 1066–1140,* London, 1951.

    (*b*) *Later English Romanesque Sculpture, 1140–1210,* London, 1953.

INDEX OF PERSONS

INDEX OF PLACES AND SITES[1]

References to plates are in heavier type

[1] See also list of churches in the Addendum, pp. 404–19.

GENERAL AND ARCHITECTURAL INDEX[1]

References to plates are in heavier type

[1] Not all the very many architectural details mentioned in the text are indexed. One arched lintel, one gabled head is very like another; only those which show interesting deviations from normal design are listed. Most examples of the less common forms of quoining—megalithic, pillar, long-and-short, upright-and-flat—are given, but not the great number of side- or face-alternate slab quoins, the predominant type in the late Saxon period. Major features—towers, openings, church plans, ornamentation, etc.—are classified and are indexed under their headings and sub-headings, not under specified locations. Details of post-Norman date, mentioned in the text only incidentally, are omitted as they are not relevant to the proper subject of the book.

ings, keyhole) 103, 249, 274, 293; double arched lintel, 51, 82, 160, of peculiar design, 296, triangular, 56, of two rings, inner and outer, 62, 218

Lisenen, 33, 216

Lombard bands, 217, 336

Loop windows, see under Windows

Matrix ecclesia, see under Churches

Mercia, origin, history, 147ff.; supremacy of, under Wulfhere, later under Æthelbald and Offa, greatness of Offa, first papal legatine mission to England, 148; decline of Mercia, 149; development of Christianity in, 148; two great ecclesiastical centres, Lichfield and Repton, 149, 163; Mercian art, 149; E. Midland or Fenland School, 149, SW. Mercian standing crosses, 149; Mercian architecture, 150

Merovingian (Frankish) influence, see under Gallic

Middle Anglia, origin, 147; incorporated in Mercia, 147, 245; see of Leicester, 147; art, 149

Minsters, see Churches

Mortar, see under Walling

MSS, illuminated, 49, 58, 149, 99–100; *Codex Amiatinus*, 43, 78; Book of Durrow, 99–100; Book of Cerne, 149; Lindisfarne Gospels, 43, 78, 100; St. Chad's Gospels, 100; Winchester School, Benedictional of St. Æthelwold, 384

Narthex, 58, 59, 75, 81, 82, 86, 93, 202, 256; see also under Churches, adjuncts to

Naves, great length of, 46, 52, 58, 87, 175; great height of, see under Walling; two-storeyed naves, 88, 175

North Elmham, see of, site of, 331

Northumbria, development from Bernicia and Deira, supremacy of N., Paulinus' ministry, 41; rapid spread of Christianity in, 42, 46, under royal and ecclesiastical patronage, 42, 46, 47; greatness of K. Aldfrith, 42; North. art, 42, 43, 78; Celtic influence, 44, 100; early North. churches, type, 31; churches of Biscop and Wilfrid, characteristics and differences, 46; North. influence on Bradwell-juxta-Mare ch. (Essex), 47, 87n.

Openings, circular, 31, 135, 256, 278, 281, 303, 305–6, 317, 321, 323, 326, 342, 366, 408, 413, 418, **130**, **131**, **166**, **168**; chamfered, peculiar, 138; curious op. to N. and S. of chancel arch, 262–3; gable-headed, 32, 82, 102, 249, 258, 281, 309, 317, 322, 324, **23**, **83**, **84**, **132**; of R. bricks, 330, **180**, see also under Doorways; double op., gabled, decorated, unique, 185–7, **72**, **73**, see also under Belfry openings; heads, bad setting of, 117, 120, 157, 158, 208, 227, 234, 394, **96**, **110**, **228**, parabolic, 137, 326, **56**, **102**, segmental, 152, 241, 311, 331; keyhole op., see under Windows; keystone, unusual, 120, 198, 240, **91**; lintels, see under Lintels; loop op., see under Windows; narrowing upwards, 53, 106, 127, 128, 129, 133, 139, 184, 185, 198, 249, 391, 418, **91**, see also under Doorways; quintuple op., 211, 220, **99**, **101**; rectangular or square, 52, 63, 88, 89, 94, 96, 110, 116, 356; squints, 96, 185; stilted, 63, 127, 128, 249, 263, 400, see also under Lintels; triangular op., 169, 176, **71**, **72**; triple op., 203, 211, **96**; op. w. no dressings, 317; round headed, one order, rubble, 62, 89, 234, of large slabs, 32, 81, 176; of two rings, inner and outer, rubble filling, 107, 152, **27**; of R. bricks, 203, 204, 205, 208, 209, 211, 323, 328, 329, 345–6, 349, 359, 365, 366, 367, 374, 379, 409, 413, 415, **93**, **95**, **96**, **188**, **189**, **203**, **204**, **205**, **206**; R. arches re-used, 61, 62–3, 88, **10**; of voussoirs, 32, 80, 88, 309, 311, massive, 198, 299, of through-stones, 89, 92, 93, 133, 139, 160, 195, 198, 224, 236, 240, 250, 256, **64**, **65**, **86**, **105**, not of through-stones, 134, 230, 237, 261, 271, 400, of long curved vous., 90, 101, 192, 263; of two rings, inner and outer, no filling, 110, ashlar filling, 291, 293, rubble filling, 101, 117, 124, 137, 155, 250, 262, 269, 272, 277, 286, 289, 291, 295, 300, 307, 310, 372; upper and lower rings, flush, 75, 250, of R. bricks, 203, 208, 365, **93**, **97**, slightly recessed, 250, 272, 295, apparent, not really recessed, 92, **18**; three or more vous. per course, 250, 278; w. relieving arches above, see under Arches, relieving; two orders, vous., 101, 116, 127, 130, 136, 138, 144, 266, **60**, on one face only, 125, 128, 129, 130, 230, 267, of elaborate and unique design, 267, **142**; one or two orders, w. springers long and cut to curved shape, 110, 138, 240, 269, 312, 372, **59**;

1. Canterbury, St. Mildred's Church: Megalithic Quoins

2. Billingham, Tower, S. face

4. Bolam, Tower, NW. Quoin

3. Bolam, Tower, S. face

6. Bolam, Tower, N. Belfry Opening

5. Bolam, Tower, S. Belfry Opening

7. Bywell, St. Andrew's Tower, upper part from SW.

8. Corbridge, Tower from SE.

9. Corbridge, Tower
W. Doorway

10. Corbridge,
Tower Arch from SE.

11. Jarrow, Chancel
S. Wall, exterior.

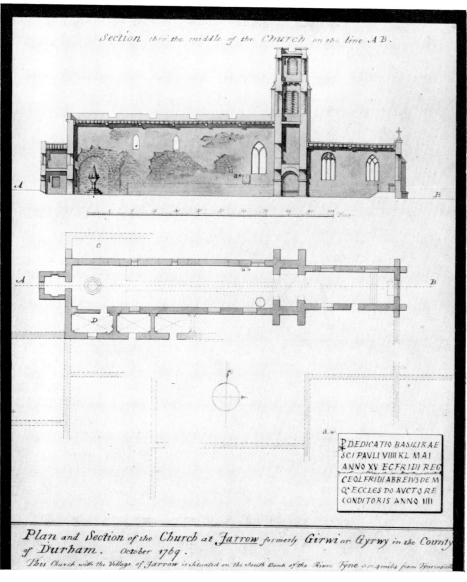

Section thro' the middle of the Church on the line A B.

A   B

A   B

P DEDICATIO BASILIKAE
SCI PAVLI VIIII KL MAI
ANNO XV ECFRIDI REC
CEOLFRIDI ABB EIVSDE M
Q' ECCLES DO AVCTORE
CONDITORIS ANNO IIII

Plan and Section of the Church at Jarrow formerly Girwi or Gyrwy in the County of Durham. October 1769.
This Church with the Village of Jarrow is situated on the South Bank of the River Tyne 3 or 4 miles from Tynemouth

12. Jarrow, plan and section of Church as in 1769

13. Jarrow, Tower and Chancel from SE.

14. Jarrow, Tower Arch from Nave

15. Jarrow, Gable-headed doorway in monastic remains

16. Jarrow, Dedication Stone

17. Monkwearmouth, Tower, upper part from SW.

18. Monkwearmouth, Tower, lower part from SW.

19. Monkwearmouth, Nave W. Wall, from E.

20. Norton, Tower and S. Transept from SE.

22. Norton, Arch to S. Transept

21. Monkwearmouth, Balusters and
Animal Ornament in W. Porch

24. Ovingham, Tower from SW.

23. Norton, Window in S. Wall of Tower
from the Crossing

26. Warden, Tower, detail of S. face

25. Warden, Tower from SW.

28. Morland, Tower from SW.

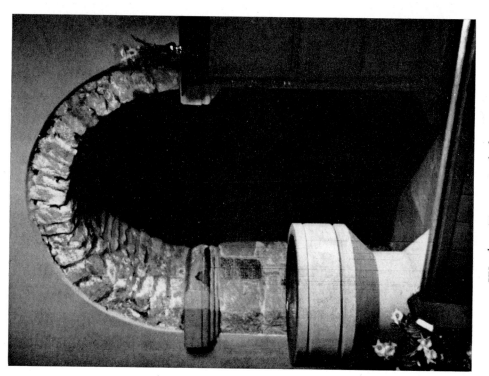

27. Warden, Tower Arch from Nave

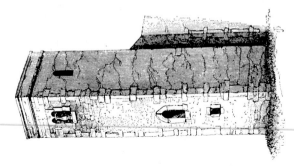

30. Whittingham, Tower before the 1840 restoration

29. Whittingham, Tower from NW.

32. Appleton-le-Street, Tower from SW.

31. Whittingham, SW. Quoins of Tower and Nave

34. Hovingham, Tower Arch from Nave

33. Hovingham, Tower from SW.

36. Middleton-by-Pickering, lower W. face of Tower

35. Middleton-by-Pickering, S. view of Tower

37. Skipwith, Tower from SW.

38. Skipwith, Tower Arch from Nave

39. Weaverthorpe,
Church from SW.

40. Weaverthorpe,
Tower Arch from Nave

41. Weaverthorpe,
Chancel Arch from W.

42. Weaverthorpe,
head of Nave
S. Doorway

43. Wharram-le-Street,
Tower from W.

44. Wharram-le-Street,
original W. Doorway
of Tower

45. Wharram-le-Street,
Tower Arch from Nave

46. Wharram-le-Street, Chancel Arch, N. Capital

47. Wharram-le-Street, Chancel Arch, S. Capital

49. Bardsey, Tower, upper part of S. face

48. Bardsey, Tower from SW.

51. Burghwallis, Tower and part of Nave from SE.

50. Bardsey, Nave W. Wall from E.

52. Ledsham, Tower, S. Doorway and SW. Quoins

53. Kirk Hammerton, Church from SE.

54. Monk Fryston,
Tower from S.

55. York,
St. Mary Bishop Hill Junior,
Tower from SW.

57. Kirk Hammerton, Nave S. Doorway

56. Kirk Hammerton, Tower W. Doorway.

59. Kirk Hammerton, Chancel Arch from W.

58. Kirk Hammerton, Tower Arch from E.

61. Clapham, Tower from SE.

60. York, St. Mary Bishop Hill Junior, Tower Arch from E.

63. Cambridge, St. Benet, Tower from NW.

62. Lavendon, Tower from N.

65. Cambridge, St. Benet, Tower Arch detail

64. Cambridge, St. Benet, Tower Arch from Nave

67. Repton, Crypt

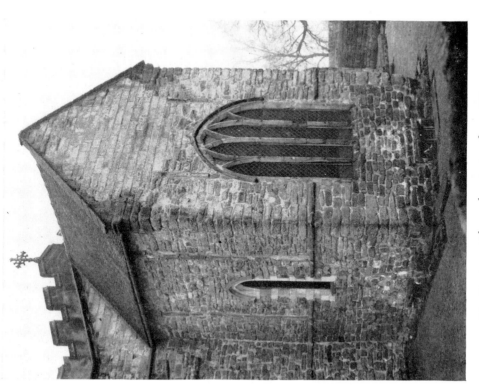

66. Repton, Chancel exterior from SE.

68. Repton, Column and Capital
from N. Transept Arch

69. Repton, Columns in Crypt

70. Deerhurst, Tower, lower part of W. face

72. Deerhurst, upper part of Nave W. Wall

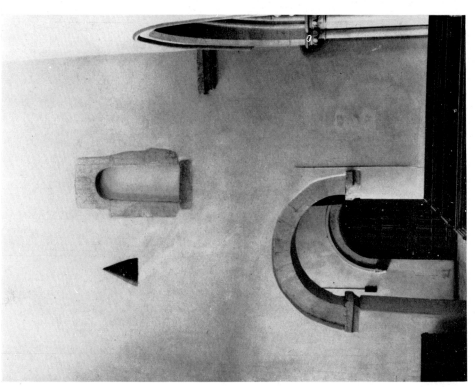

71. Deerhurst, lower part of Nave W. Wall

74. Deerhurst, upper W. Wall of former SW. Porticus from S. Aisle

73. Deerhurst, gable-headed double opening in Tower E. Wall

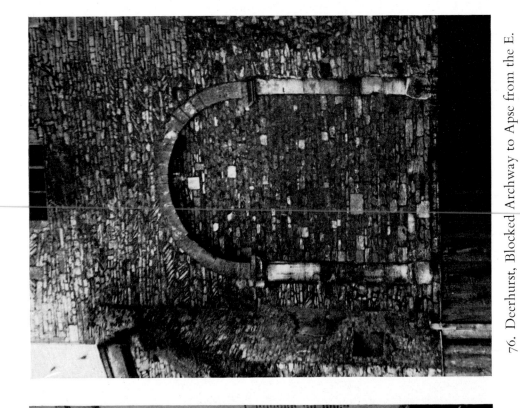

76. Deerhurst, Blocked Archway to Apse from the E.

75. Deerhurst, openings to former N. Porticus and Blocked Arch to Apse from SW.

78. Deerhurst,
Capital in Blocked Arch to Apse

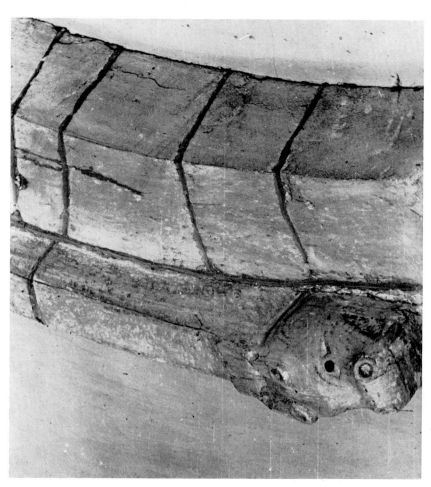

77. Deerhurst, Animal Head Label Stop in Blocked Arch to Apse
(Detail of Pl. 75)

80. Deerhurst, Animal Head above Tower
Middle Arch

79. Deerhurst, Animal Head above Tower W. Doorway

82. Deerhurst, Defaced Virgin and Child over Tower Middle Arch

81. Deerhurst, Angel on Apse Exterior

83. Barnack, Tower from SW.

84. Barnack, upper part of Tower
S. Wall

85. Barnack, Tower S. Doorway

86. Barnack,
Tower Arch from E.

87. Brigstock,
general view from SW.

88. Brigstock, Tower and Stair Turret from SW.

90. Brigstock, Tower N. Arch and Window,
and Tower Arch N. Jamb, from Nave

89. Brigstock, Tower Arch, N. part, from Nave

92. Brigstock, gable-headed Doorway to Stair Turret, from Tower

91. Brigstock, Tower S. Window, and Nave SW. Quoin, from S. Aisle

93. Brixworth,
general view from S.

94. Brixworth,
ambulatory and original
N. Buttress of Apse

95. Brixworth, Stair Turret and Tower from S.

96. Brixworth,
Nave W. Wall
from E.

97. Brixworth,
E. end of Nave
N. Wall, interior

98. Earls Barton, Tower
W. Doorway

99. Earls Barton, Tower from SW.

101. Earls Barton, top two stages of Tower from S.

100. Earls Barton, Tower from NW.

103. Wing, Apse from SE.

102. Earls Barton, middle section of Tower S. Wall

105. Stowe–Nine–Churches, Tower Arch from Nave

104. Stowe–Nine–Churches, Tower from SW.

107. Carlton-in-Lindrick, Tower Arch from Nave

106. Carlton-in-Lindrick, Tower from W.

108. Geddington,
Arcading on Nave
S. Wall

109. Caversfield, Tower from N.

110. Caversfield, Tower N. Window

111. North Leigh,
Tower from NW.

112. Langford, Tower from S.

113. Langford, Windows, Pilasters and Decorated Sundial
in Tower S. Wall exterior

114. Langford, S. Porch and Roods

115. Langford,
Chancel Arch from W.

116. Langford, Chancel Arch and Tower
W. Arch, from E.

117. Langford, Chancel Arch Capitals

118. Langford, Chancel Arch Bases

119. Market Overton,
Balusters, now part of
stile in churchyard

120. Market Overton, Carved Stones lying against Tower W. Wall

121. Stanton Lacy, Nave W. Wall, exterior

122. Stanton Lacy, Nave N. Doorway

123. Oxford, St. Michael's Tower from NW.

124. Wootton Wawen, general view from S.

125. Wootton Wawen, Tower
N. Arch from interior

126. Wootton Wawen,
Tower S. Arch from S.

128. Wootton Wawen, Tower E. Arch from W.

127. Wootton Wawen, Tower W. Arch from W.

130. Barton-on-Humber, general view from SW.

129. Alkborough, Tower from SW.

131. Barton-on-Humber,
Western Annexe from NW.

132. Barton-on-Humber,
Tower N. Doorway

133. Barton-on-Humber, lower part of Tower S. face

135. Barton-on-Humber, Tower W. and E. Arches from W.

134. Barton-on-Humber, Tower W. Arch from E.

137. Bracebridge, Tower from SW.

136. Barton-on-Humber, Tower E. Wall from Nave

138. Bracebridge, Chancel and
Tower Arches from Altar Steps

139. Branston,
Norman Arcading
on Tower W. Wall

140. Branston, Tower from SW.

142. Broughton-by-Brigg, Tower Arch from W.

141. Broughton-by-Brigg, Tower from S.

144. Cabourn, Tower W. Doorway

143. Cabourn, Tower from NW.

145. Cabourn, Tower Arch from Nave

146. Caistor, Tower Arch from Nave

148. Old Clee, Tower Arch from Nave

147. Old Clee, Tower,
W. Doorway and NW. Quoins

150. Glentworth, Tower Arch from Chancel

149. Glentworth, Tower from SW.

152. Lincoln, St. Benedict, Tower from W.

151. Hough-on-the-Hill,
Tower and Stair Turret from NW.

154. Lincoln, St. Mary-le-Wigford, Tower, upper part from SW.

153. Lincoln, St. Mary-le-Wigford, Tower, lower part from SW.

156. Lincoln, St. Peter-at-Gowts,
Tower Arch from Nave

155. Lincoln, St. Mary-le-Wigford,
Tower Arch from Nave

157. Lincoln, St. Peter-at-Gowts, Tower from NW.

158. Lincoln, St. Peter-at-Gowts, Tower, lower part from NW.

159. Lincoln, St. Peter-at-Gowts, Tower, upper part from SW.

161. Rothwell, Tower from SW.

160. Marton, Tower from SW.

163. Scartho, Tower Arch from Nave

162. Scartho, Tower from SW.

164. Springthorpe, Tower from SW.

165. Swallow, Tower Arch from Nave

166. Stow, general view from SE.

167. Stow, Saxon Window in S. Transept S. Wall

168. Stow,
N. Transept from NW.

169. Stow, N. Transept
W. Doorway from interior

170. Stow, Tower, W. Arch from Nave

171. Thurlby, Tower Arch from Nave

172. Waithe, general view from SW.

173. Bessingham, Tower from SW.

174. Bessingham, Tower Arch
and Upper Doorway, from Nave

176. East Lexham, Tower from SW.

175. East Lexham, Tower from NW.

178. Haddiscoe, Belfry Window

177. Haddiscoe, Tower from NW.

179. Haddiscoe, Tower Arch
and Upper Doorway, from Nave

180. Newton-by-Castle Acre,
Tower from SW.

181. Roughton, Tower from N.

183. Dunham Magna, W. Doorway

182. Dunham Magna, Tower from SW.

185. Dunham Magna, Tower, W. and E. Arches from Nave

184. Dunham Magna, Nave Arcading

187. Little Bardfield, Tower from SW.

186. Weybourne, Saxon Tower from S.

189. Colchester, Holy Trinity, Tower Arch from Nave

188. Tollesbury, Nave S. Doorway from interior

191. Colchester, Holy Trinity, Tower from S.

190. Colchester, Holy Trinity, Tower from NW.

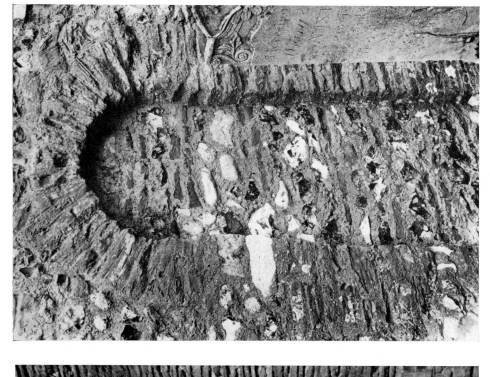

193. Canterbury, St. Martin,
Blocked Saxon Doorway in Chancel S. Wall, exterior

192. Colchester, Holy Trinity, Tower, W. Doorway

194. Canterbury, St. Martin, general view from SE.

195. Canterbury, St. Martin, Blocked Saxon Doorway in Chancel
S. Wall, interior

196. Canterbury, St. Martin,
two Blocked Doorways and Buttress
at SE. of Chancel and SE. of Nave

197. Canterbury, St. Martin,
Buttress at NW. corner of Nave

198. Canterbury, St. Martin, Nave W. Wall from Nave

199. Dover, St. Mary-in-Castro, general view from SW.

200. Dover, St. Mary-in-Castro,
Nave SW. Quoin

201. Dover, St. Mary-in-Castro,
Blocked Saxon Doorway in Nave
S. Wall, exterior

203. Dover, St. Mary-in-Castro, S. Clerestory Window

202. Dover, St. Mary-in-Castro, Nave W. Doorway

205. Dover, St. Mary-in-Castro,
Tower E. Arch (Chancel Arch) from W.

204. Dover, St. Mary-in-Castro,
Tower W. Arch from Nave

207. Singleton, Tower from NW.

206. Dover, St. Mary-in-Castro,
Tower W. Arch, detail

209. Bosham, Tower from N.

208. Bosham, Tower from W.

210. Bosham, Tower, SW. corner, detail

211. Bosham, Chancel Arch, Base of S. Shaft

212. Bosham, Chancel, N. Side, interior

213. Bosham, Nave W. Wall, from E.

214. Sompting, Tower from S.

215. Sompting, Tower from W.

216. Sompting, Tower from N.

217. Sompting, Tower Arch,
N. Capital and Jamb

218. Sompting, carving of a bishop

219. Sompting, Saxon Carved Piscina

220. Wickham, Tower from SW.

221. Teignmouth, Sketch of Old St. Michael's Church

222. Breamore, general view from SW.

223. Breamore, S. Porticus from SW.

224. Breamore, S. Porticus from E.

225. Breamore, Pilaster Strip Work on Nave N. Wall

226. Breamore, Arch to S. Porticus

227. Warblington, Tower from S.

228. Warblington, Tower S. Doorway

229. Warblington,
W. face of Tower from Nave

230. Compton, Tower from SW.